9-5   Disney Limits the Sales of *Fantasia* to 50

9-6   Will a Merger of Two Hospitals Decrease

10-1   Trouble in the Orange Cartel

10-2   More Suppliers of Fine Caviar

10-3   Encouraging Competition among Suppliers

10-4   Retail Tire Prices

10-5   Auction Markets

10-6   Detecting the Effects of Facilitating Practices

10-7   Which Brands Enter Late and Which Enter Early?

10-8   Credible Commitment for *Independence Day*

11-1   The Effect of a Change in Management on Operations

11-2   Cummins Engine Company

12-1   Universities Are Learning More about Differences in the Price Elasticity of Demand of their Students

12-2   Should a Firm Expand into the European Market?

12-3   Pricing a Renault in Belgium and in England

12-4   Why Did IBM and Xerox Lease Rather Than Sell Their Machines?

13-1   IBM Sues a Former Employee

13-2   Testing New Toys at Small Toy Stores

13-3   Toys "R" Us Wants Toy Manufacturers to Sell to It Exclusively

13-4   Ben and Jerry versus Goliath

14-1   The Free Agency Market in Professional Baseball

14-2   The Used Pickup Truck Market

14-3   The Price Premium at McDonald's

14-4   A Price Premium in Labor Markets

15-1   Markdowns by Merchandise Group

16-1   Mustering Out of the Military

16-2   Personal Bankruptcy

16-3   Freeing Prices in Russia

16-4   The Historical Trend in Crude Oil Prices

17-1   Substitution and Scale Effects in the Airline Industry

17-2   A General Assistance Program and the Work-Leisure Choice

17-3   Has the Wage Premium for a College Education Peaked?

17-4   Turnover and Tenure in the United States and in Japan

17-5   Problems with the Use of Incentive Pay

18-1   Minimizing Information Requirements in Experimental Competitive Markets

18-2   Impediments to Trading Water Rights in California

18-3   Reducing the Price of Capital by Subsidizing Small Businesses

19-1   Internalizing an Externality in a Shopping Mall

19-2   Allowing the Coase Theorem to Work

19-3   Neighborhoods for Sale

19-4   View Wars and Defining Property Rights

19-5   Saving the African Elephant

PRICE
THEORY
AND
APPLICATIONS

PRICE
THEORY
AND
APPLICATIONS

Second Edition

B. Peter Pashigian
Graduate School of Business
University of Chicago

Boston, Massachusetts   Burr Ridge, Illinois   Dubuque, Iowa
Madison, Wisconsin   New York, New York   San Francisco, California   St. Louis, Missouri

Irwin/McGraw-Hill

A Division of The **McGraw·Hill** *Companies*

PRICE THEORY AND APPLICATIONS

Copyright © 1998 by The McGraw-Hill Companies, Inc. All rights reserved. Previous edition © 1995 by The McGraw-Hill Companies, Inc. Printed in the United States of America. Except as permitted under the United States Copyright Act of 1976, no part of this publication may be reproduced or distributed in any form or by any means, or stored in a data base or retrieval system, without the prior written permission of the publisher.

This book is printed on acid-free paper.

2 3 4 5 6 7 8 9 0   DOC/DOC   9 0 9 8   (U.S. edition)
1*2 3 4 5 6 7 8 9 0   DOC/DOC   9 0 9 8 7   (International edition)

ISBN 0-07-048778-2

Vice president and editorial director: *Michael W. Junior*
Sponsoring editor: *Lucille Sutton*
Senior project manager: *Beth Cigler*
Designer: *Michael Warrell*
Compositor: *Ruttle, Shaw & Wetherill*
Typeface: *10/12 Century Schoolbook*
Printer: *R. R. Donnelley & Sons Company*

Library of Congress Cataloging-in-Publication Data

Pashigian, B. Peter (Bedros Peter)
    Price theory and applications / B. Peter Pashigian. —2nd ed.
       p.   cm.
    Includes index.
    ISBN 0-07-048778-2 (alk. paper)
      1. Microeconomics.   2. Prices.   I. Title.
HB172.P26   1997
   338.5'2—dc21   97-1282

INTERNATIONAL EDITION
Copyright © 1998. Exclusive rights by The McGraw-Hill Companies, Inc., for manufacture and export.
This book cannot be re-exported from the country to which it is consigned by McGraw-Hill.
The International Edition is not available in North America.

When ordering this title, use ISBN 0-07-115462-0.

http://www.mhcollege.com

PREFACE

The second edition of *Price Theory and Applications* continues the objectives and expectations of the first edition by clearly presenting the essentials of microeconomic theory and, equally important, applying the theory to consumer and firm behavior.

As the book's title suggests, my underlying conviction is that microeconomics can best be taught through an artful blend of theory and application. One without the other represents a failing. It is an unfortunate fact of life that many students who take intermediate microeconomics courses will never take another economics course. Only a minority of students take upper-level courses where they have an opportunity to apply the theory. In most business schools microeconomics is a required course but students seldom go on to apply the theory in advanced work. Given this fleeting rendezvous with microeconomics, I believe the study of microeconomics can be made worthwhile and even exciting by showing how the theory can be applied.

Each chapter in the second edition of *Price Theory and Applications* includes interesting and serious real-world applications, not only hypothetical examples. Former students have praised the applications and I believe readers of the second edition will too. Numerous reviewers of the second edition have been struck by the successful integration of the theory with unique and relevant applications. As one reviewer wrote, "Pashigian's greatest strengths are the breadth and relevance of his applications." This is a source of personal satisfaction since my objective was to write a rigorous book that showed how theory can be applied. I wrote this textbook because I thought the existing books could be improved upon. Some were books in logic that left students wondering why they had learned the theory. Others skimped on theory and presented applications that at times were either contrived or only distantly related to the theory. I have made a conscientious effort to motivate students' interest in theory by using incisive real-world applications in every chapter that lend an empirical dimension to the book.

The central premise of the book is that much behavior can be explained as a rational response to economic incentives. Because the theory has general applicability, the analyses in *Price Theory and Applications* deal with issues that are not specific to one economy but are universal to all modern economies. For instance, incentives matter even for a staple like water, which is essential for life. Even for water, when its price rises, consumers use less of it by modifying their behavior in numerous little ways, such as watering their lawns less frequently, taking shorter showers, and using mulch to preserve moisture for their plants. When the price of cotton rises because of a disease that has diminished the Asian cotton crop, producers throughout the world respond to the higher prices by shifting into cotton production and out of production of other crops. Obvious or subtle responses like these to changing economic incentives occur daily in local economies and throughout the world economy. Understanding the role of incentives is the most important lesson that students can gain from their study of microeconomics.

Distinctive Features of the Book

To find fresh and interesting applications, I look more to private sector behavior and less to government behavior, which is the more conventional practice in many microeconomics textbooks. I believe the favorable response to the book is due in part because I did not use the cut-and-dried applications involving the government. Other applications prepare students for the end-of-chapter Review Questions and Exercises, which are another especially valuable feature of the book that test the students' understanding of the theory by asking them to apply the theory in new and different situations. Applying microeconomic theory to new situations is exactly what many students will be doing the rest of their working lives.

Core Chapters 1, 2, part of 3, and 5 through 10 cover consumer behavior, the theory of the firm, and price formation under different structures. A differentiating feature of this book is its systematic examination of several topics that are either not treated or treated superficially elsewhere. Numerous reviewers have mentioned that a strength of the book is Part V, dealing with pricing practices and policies. Chapters 12 through 15 in Part V develop several models that help explain firms' price policies. Chapter 12, "Price Discrimination," presents an in-depth examination of the different forms of price discrimination. Unlike most books where the free rider problem is discussed but only in the context of the provision of public goods, Chapter 13, "The Free Rider Problem and Pricing," shows how frequently private markets face free rider problems and how firms use prices and other methods to circumvent these problems. Students find this topic fascinating and consistently rank the chapter among the most interesting, and I urge instructors to include part or all of the chapter in their course outlines. Chapter 14, "Market Behavior with Asymmetric Information," discusses how firms acquire a reputation for honesty and how private markets adapt to situations where asymmetric information exists. Chapter 15, "Pricing under Uncertainty," introduces the topic of uncertainty by showing how the theory of pricing under uncertainty explains seasonal variation in pricing and the growing frequency of sales.

Other chapters also treat significant subjects that are often ignored. The cost of time receives comprehensive treatment in Chapter 4, "The Cost of Time and the Theory of Consumer Behavior." With more women in the work force and with women's earnings rising faster than men's, time plays a more and more influential role in explaining consumer behavior and should receive greater recognition in microeconomics texts. Another important but ignored topic is the governance of the firm. After the decade of the 80s when many hostile takeovers and mergers occurred, can a modern textbook ignore the topic of firm governance and the role of product and capital markets in monitoring the policies of management? Much has been learned about the role of the capital market in monitoring management performance in the last 15 years and this topic receives full treatment in Chapter 11, "Monitoring the Corporation: Corporate Governance."

Changes for the Second Edition

Changes have been made to virtually all chapters. Care has been taken to rewrite theory sections and Applications when students' or reviewers' comments have asked for greater clarity. We have also clarified and simplified the Figures so they can be more easily understood. In many chapters fresh and up-to-date Applications replace older ones. New Review Questions and Exercises have been added in the second edition, and in response to suggestions by adopters, some easier exercises have been added. More difficult exercises are now marked with asterisks (*).

In response to suggestions by users, the second edition of *Price Theory and Applications* presents an intuitive explanation of consumer surplus in the body of Chapter 3 and presents the "correct" formal derivation of consumer surplus using indifference curves at the end of Chapter 3 in the Appendix. Chapter 8 includes an interesting new application of when a firm should introduce a new cost-reducing innovation and retire an older technology by looking at the retirement of the Boeing 707 after the price of jet fuel increased. In Chapter 8, for instructors who like to use consumer and producer surplus in a partial equilibrium welfare analysis, I have included a section on the effect of taxes, trade limitations, and market restrictions on total surplus. The gains from trade are also illustrated in Chapter 8 in a new Application entitled "Banana Wars: Total Surplus and the Gains from Trade," which examines the impact on consumer and producer surplus in the United States and in Europe after the European Union's imposed quotas on banana imports from Latin America. Partial equilibrium welfare analysis reappears in Chapter 9 in a new Application where readers consider the consequences of a merger between two hospitals that may reduce the cost of supplying health care but may also create a monopoly.

The concept of strategic interaction is introduced at the beginning of Chapter 10, "Oligopoly and Monopolistic Competition." In response to adopters' requests, the second edition gives a more extended analysis of repeated games, sequential games, and the theory of monopolistic competition. I have filled out the discussion of price discrimination in Chapter 12 by including a section on when bundling is profitable. Besides considering a specific version of the lemons problem, a more general model of the lemons problem is presented in Chapter 14, which now includes an extended discussion of the moral hazard problem and an analysis of when a monopolist will acquire a reputation for reliability and honesty. Among the new additions to Chapter 17, "Wage Determination in Labor Markets," is a section on the effects of the minimum wage and Applications that deal with substitution and scale effects in the airline industry and the topic of whether the wage premium for a college education has peaked.

These and other changes will make the second edition of *Price Theory and Applications* even more interesting and educational for instructors and students alike and will contribute to an increased understanding of how the price system functions.

Alternative Course Designs

Deciding which topics to include in a course is always a challenge, so some guidance may be helpful. The modular form of the book gives instructors considerable flexibility with regard to both content and level of difficulty. For a quarter course offered in an economics department an instructor may include Chapters 1–3, 5–10, and parts of Chapters 17–19. For a quarter course offered in a business school an instructor may include Chapters 1–2, the section of Chapter 3 on consumer surplus, and Chapters 4 and 6–10, and then select sections from Chapters 11–15. Instructors in business schools often do not include production theory and they can confidently skip to Chapter 6 where the development of the cost functions of the firm is independently derived. For a semester course offered by a department an instructor may include Chapters 1–10, all or part of 12, and 17–19, and then select among Chapters 4, 11, and 13–16. For a semester course a business school instructor may include Chapters 1–4, and 6–13 and supplement these chapters with parts of Chapters 14–15, 17, and 19.

Alternative Levels of Rigor

Price Theory and Applications was written and organized to give the instructor considerable flexibility in deciding whether to include or exclude, as appropriate, the sections denoted by asterisks (*), which cover more difficult material. There is also flexibility in the use of mathematics with most of the calculus placed in footnotes or in appendixes. Special care was taken to keep the exposition clear without sacrificing rigor. The second edition of *Price Theory and Applications* is appropriate for students with diverse backgrounds and interests.

The Teaching and Learning Package

Study Guide   Professor Thomas Carroll of the University of Nevada at Las Vegas has prepared a detailed and user-friendly Study Guide that summarizes the major points in each chapter and gives the student ample opportunity to work multiple-choice and short answer problems.

Test Bank   I was especially pleased when Charles Upton, now at Kent State University, agreed to do the Test Bank, since we saw eye-to-eye as to how a microeconomics course should be taught when Charles was a colleague at the University of Chicago. The Test Bank includes a variety of new short answer and story problems that test a student's understanding of each chapter's fundamentals.

Instructor's Resource Manual   The Instructor's Resource Manual is once again prepared by Richard Peck. It follows the lead of the textbook in the application of economic concepts to real-world problems. Shane Greenstein at the University of Illinois contributed questions, some of which are included in the text and others in the Instructor's Resource Manual.

The Test Bank is available in a computerized format and an electronic version of the Instructor's Resource Manual is available to adopters by special request to your local Irwin-McGraw-Hill sales representative.

Acknowledgments

The second edition has benefited from the contributions of many. First, many thanks to those adopters of the first edition who suggested changes for the second edition. I have used this book in two different courses that I teach in the Graduate School of Business at the University of Chicago and extend my thanks to my former students who completed questionnaires, offered their opinions, and identified sections requiring greater clarity. The second edition is better because of their efforts. I want to particularly praise Jeanne Mey Sun who diligently read each chapter, correcting errors and suggesting rephrasing. I want to single out Lucille Sutton, Economics Editor at McGraw-Hill, who supervised the second edition while managing it from one stage to another. Accolades go to Stephanie Cappiello, Assistant Editor, who performed admirably while finding reviewers and tending to seemingly endless details. A word of appreciation is extended to Beth Cigler, Senior Project Manager, who guided the book through the production process.

Many economists across the country offered suggestions for the second edition after reading chapters in the first edition. Others read revised chapters for the second edition and made further suggestions. I am indebted to them for sharing their suggestions, praise, and criticism. They include **Jack Adams,** University of Arkansas at Little Rock; **James D. Adams,** University of Florida; **Michael Balch,** The University of Iowa; **David S. Ball,** North Carolina State University; **Howard Beales,** George Washington University; **Gautam Bhattacharya,** University of Kansas; **Michael R. Butler,** Texas Christian University; **David A. Butz,** University of Michigan; **Richard R. Cornwall,** Middlebury College; **Carl E. Enomoto,** New Mexico State University; **Paul G. Farnham,** Georgia State University; **Raymond J. Farrow,** Seattle University; **Robert G. Hansen,** Dartmouth College; **Donald B. Hausch,** University of Wisconsin–Madison; **Joseph W. Hunt,** Shippensburg University; **Thomas R. Ireland,** University of Missouri–St. Louis; **David R. Kamerschen,** University of Georgia; **Daniel Leonard,** Flinders University of South Australia; **Karen Lombard,** University of Miami; **Richard Manning,** Brigham Young University; **Thomas E. Merz,** Michigan Technlogical University; **Paul F. Okello,** The University of Texas at Arlington; **Sol Shallt,** University of Wisconsin–Milwaukee; **Paula Tkac,** University of Notre Dame; **Charles W. Upton,** Kent State University; **Juuso Valimaki,** Northwestern University; and **Chiou-nan Yeh,** Alabama State University.

Finally, a special word of gratitude to my wife Rose, who exhibited such patience once again while sharing her husband with the second edition of *Price Theory and Applications.*

B. Peter Pashigian

ABOUT THE AUTHOR

B. Peter Pashigian is Professor of Economics in the Graduate School of Business at the University of Chicago. He received his Ph.D. from the Department of Economics at the Massachusetts Institute of Technology. He has published articles in the *American Economic Review*, the *Journal of Political Economy*, *The Journal of Law and Economics*, *The Quarterly Journal of Economics*, and other leading journals on diverse topics such as why firms have sales; farmer opposition to futures markets; political support and opposition to environmental regulation; the demand and supply of lawyers; and other topics. He has served as coeditor of the *Journal of Business* and is a member of the executive committee of the George J. Stigler Center for the Study of the State and the Economy.

CONTENTS IN BRIEF

PART I
Introduction: Supply and Demand   1
CHAPTER 1   Pricing and the Demand and Supply Model   3

PART II
Consumer Behavior   45
CHAPTER 2   Consumer Behavior and Market Demand   47
CHAPTER 3   Extending the Theory of Consumer Behavior   93
CHAPTER 4   The Cost of Time and the Theory of Consumer Behavior   142

PART III
The Firm: Its Technology and Costs   169
CHAPTER 5   The Production Function and Costs of the Firm   171
CHAPTER 6   The Cost Functions of the Firm   217

PART IV
Firm and Market Behavior   253
CHAPTER 7   The Supply Functions of a Competitive Firm   255
CHAPTER 8   Price Determination in a Competitive Industry   277
CHAPTER 9   Monopoly   327
CHAPTER 10   Oligopoly and Monopolistic Competition   367
CHAPTER 11   Monitoring the Corporation: Corporate Governance   416

PART V
Pricing: Practices and Policies   443
CHAPTER 12   Price Discrimination   445
CHAPTER 13   The Free Rider Problem and Pricing   487
CHAPTER 14   Market Behavior with Asymmetric Information   517
CHAPTER 15   Pricing under Uncertainty   556

PART VI
Intertemporal Equilibrium and Factor Markets   581
CHAPTER 16   Consumer and Supplier Behavior over Time   583
CHAPTER 17   Wage Determination in Labor Markets   624

PART VII
Markets and Economic Efficiency   665
CHAPTER 18   Economic Efficiency and General Equilibrium   667
CHAPTER 19   Externalities and Public Goods   699

Suggested Answers to Selected Exercises and Problem Sets   724
Index   751

CONTENTS

PART I INTRODUCTION: SUPPLY AND DEMAND   *1*

CHAPTER 1
Pricing and the Demand and Supply Model   *3*

1-1   The Meaning of Demand and Supply   *5*

1-2   The Market Demand Function   *5*
Movement along a Demand Function • Application 1-1: The Rising Price of Wood and the Demand for Wood • Shifts in the Demand Function

1-3   The Market Supply Function   *10*
Movements along the Supply Function • Shifts in the Supply Function

1-4   Market Equilibrium   *13*
The Everyday Meaning of Demand and Supply • Problems with the Analysis

1-5   Changes in Equilibrium: Shifts in Market Demand and Market Supply Functions   *17*
Shifts in Demand • Application 1-2: Demand and Supply on Valentine's Day • An Explanation of Shortages and Surpluses • Application 1-3: Cotton Is King Again, but How Long the Reign? • Application 1-4: Should Your Company Support a Lobbying Effort to Reduce the Price of an Input?

1-6   The Price Elasticity of Demand and Supply   *27*
Price Elasticity of Demand • Point Price Elasticity of Demand • Arc Price Elasticity of Demand • Application 1-5: The Price Elasticity of Demand for First Class Mail • Determinants of the Price Elasticity of Demand • Price Elasticity of Supply

Summary   *38*
Key Terms   *38*
Review Questions   *39*
Exercises   *40*
Problem Set: Estimating the Price Elasticity of Demand   *42*

PART II CONSUMER BEHAVIOR   *45*

CHAPTER 2
Consumer Behavior and Market Demand   *47*

2-1   Building the Consumer Behavior Model   *48*
Assumptions about Consumer Behavior

2-2   Describing Consumer Preferences   *49*
Indifference Curves • The Marginal Rate of Substitution • The Indifference Map of a Consumer • Assigning Numbers to Indifference Curves

2-3   Properties of Indifference Curves   *57*

2-4   Budget Constraint   *58*
Affordable Market Baskets • Shifts in the Budget Constraint

2-5   The Consumer's Consumption Decision   *64*
Finding the Market Basket That Maximizes Utility and Satisfies the Budget Constraint • Specialization of Consumption • Application 2-1: Pricing to Break into an Established Market

6-6   The Number of Firms and the Long-Run Cost Function   *242*
Diseconomies of Scale and Industries with Many Firms • Economies of Scale
and Industries with Few Firms • Application 6-5: The Emergence of the Standard
Oil Company • Application 6-6: Size of Firm and Technological Change in the
Steel Industry

Summary   *248*
Key Terms   *248*
Review Questions   *248*
Exercises   *249*

PART IV   FIRM AND MARKET BEHAVIOR   *253*

CHAPTER 7
The Supply Functions of a Competitive Firm

The Supply Functions of a Competitive Firm   *255*
7-1   The Competitive Firm   *255*
The Price-Taking Assumption • The Price Elasticity of Demand of a Competitive
Firm • Application 7-1: The Price Elasticity of Demand of Firms in Eastern
Europe and Russia

7-2   The Short-Run Supply Function of a Competitive Firm   *261*
Finding an Output That Maximizes Total Short-Run Profits • The Short-Run
Supply Function of a Competitive Firm • Application 7-2: Short-Run Costs,
Break-Even Analysis, and Profit-Maximizing Behavior • Application 7-3: When to
Lay Up an Oil Tanker

7-3   The Long-Run Supply Function of a Competitive Firm   *269*
Finding an Output That Maximizes Long-Run Profits • The Long-Run Supply
Function of a Competitive Firm

Summary   *273*
Key Terms   *273*
Review Questions   *273*
Exercises   *274*
Problem Set: Should Your Company Honor a Contract?   *275*

CHAPTER 8
Price Determination in a Competitive Industry

Price Determination in a Competitive Industry   *277*
8-1   Requirements for Long- and Short-Run Industry Equilibria   *278*
Long-Run Industry Equilibrium • Short-Run Industry Equilibrium •
Typical Competitive Industries

8-2   Price Determination in a Constant-Cost Industry   *279*
Two Assumptions of a Constant-Cost Industry • The Long-Run Industry Supply
Function in a Constant-Cost Industry • Long-Run Industry Equilibrium in a
Constant-Cost Industry

8-3   Moving from One Long-Run Equilibrium to Another   *283*
The Short-Run Industry Supply Function and Equilibrium Price • High Prices
Cure High Prices • The Role of Profits • Application 8-1: Helping the Victims of
Hurricane Andrew

8-4   Price Determination in an Increasing-Cost Industry   *291*
A Rising Factor Price When Industry Output Expands • Economic Rent or
Producer Surplus • Differences in Firm Costs Due to Differences in Managerial
Ability • Long-Run Industry Equilibrium When Managerial Ability Differs

*8-5   Adoption of a Cost-Reducing Innovation   *299*
Application 8-2: Higher Jet Fuel Price Downs the Boeing 707 • Application 8-3:
Regularities in the Evolution of Industries

8-6   Raising the Costs for New Entrants   *307*
          How Licensing Changes the Shape of the Long-Run Industry Supply Function •
          Application 8-4: The Value of a License
8-7   The Effect of Taxes, Trade Limitations, and Market Restrictions on Total
          Surplus   *310*
          Imposing a Per Unit Tax on a Competitive Firm • Long-Run Effects of a Per Unit
          Tax • Banana Wars: Total Surplus and the Gains from Trade • The Effect of a
          Per Unit Tax on Consumer and Producer Surplus
          Summary   *321*
          Key Terms   *322*
          Review Questions   *322*
          Exercises   *323*

CHAPTER 9
Monopoly   *327*
9-1   Assumptions of the Pure Monopoly Model   *328*
9-2   The Monopolist as a Price Maker   *329*
          The Demand Function of a Monopolist • The Total and Marginal Revenue
          Functions • Measuring the Change in Revenue by the Area under the Marginal
          Revenue Function
9-3   The Theory of Monopoly Pricing   *337*
          Application 9-1: Are Firms in the Cigarette and Oil Industries Monopolists? •
          Application 9-2: Privatizing a Near Monopoly in the Czech Republic •
          *Application 9-3: Using a Quota to Create a Partial Monopolist
9-4   Adjusting from One Long-Run Equilibrium to Another   *347*
*9-5 Adoption of a Cost-Reducing Innovation   *347*
9-6   Competing to Be a Monopolist   *351*
          Application 9-4: Alternative Methods of Selling a Monopoly
9-7   The Tyranny of Durability   *352*
          Actions the Monopolist Can Take to Reassure Buyers • Application 9-5: Disney
          Limits the Sales of *Fantasia* to 50 Days
9-8   Taxing a Monopolist   *358*
9-9   The Social Objection to Monopoly   *360*
          Application 9-6: Will a Merger of Two Hospitals Decrease Total Surplus?
          Summary   *362*
          Key Terms   *363*
          Review Questions   *364*
          Exercises   *364*

CHAPTER 10
Oligopoly and Monopolistic Competition   *367*
10-1 Cooperation among Price-Taking Firms: Cartel Behavior   *368*
          Application 10-1: Trouble in the Orange Cartel
10-2 Price and Output with Oligopoly   *371*
          Cooperative Behavior and the Incentive to Cheat
10-3 Models of Noncooperative Behavior   *376*
          The Cournot Model • The Reaction or Best Response Function of Each
          Cournot Rival • The Nash Equilibrium • Application 10-2: More Suppliers of
          Fine Caviar • The Cournot Model with n Competitors • The Bertrand
          Model • Application 10-3: Encouraging Competition among Suppliers
10-4 The Effect of the Number of Rivals on Price   *388*
          Application 10-4: Retail Tire Prices • Application 10-5: Auction Markets

10-5 Facilitating and Preventing Collusion   *391*
          Meeting Competition • Application 10-6: Detecting the Effects of Facilitating
          Practices • Preventing Collusion

10-6 A Case Study: The Electrical Manufacturers' Conspiracy   *394*
          Collusion and Cheating • Product and Industry Characteristics and
          Successful Collusion • The Cost of Detecting Price Chiseling

10-7 Game Theory and Noncooperative Strategies   *398*
          Dominant Strategies • A Dominant Strategy for Only One Firm •
          Application 10-7: Which Brands Enter Late and Which Enter Early? •
          Nash Equilibria • Repeated Games • Sequential Games • Application 10-8:
          Credible Commitment for *Independence Day*

10-8 Monopolistic Competition   *409*
Summary   *411*
Key Terms   *411*
Review Questions   *412*
Exercises   *412*
Appendix: How the Number of Rivals Affects Firm Output and
          Price in the Cournot Model   *414*

CHAPTER 11
Monitoring the Corporation: Corporate Governance   *416*

11-1 External Monitors: Product and Capital Markets   *417*
          Application 11-1: The Effect of a Change in Management on Operations

11-2 The Free Rider Problem and the Tender Offer   *419*
11-3 Internal Monitors of Management   *422*
          Expense Preference • Ex Post Settling Up
11-4 The Principal-Agent Relationship and Ownership Structure   *425*
11-5 Expense Preference under a Profit Constraint   *429*
          The Profit Constraint • Deregulation and Import Competition
11-6 The Unregulated Firm and Expense Preference   *434*
          Application 11-2: Cummins Engine Company
11-7 How the Market for Corporate Control Functions   *435*
          The Effectiveness of Internal Monitors • The Effectiveness of External
          Monitors • Evidence about Takeovers • The Effect of Takeovers on
          the Stock Performance of Targets and Acquirers
Summary   *441*
Key Terms   *441*
Review Questions   *441*
Exercises   *442*

PART V PRICING: PRACTICES AND POLICIES   *443*

CHAPTER 12
Price Discrimination   *445*

12-1 Revenue Enhancement: The Goal of Price Discrimination   *446*
12-2 First-Degree (Perfect) Price Discrimination   *448*
12-3 Second-Degree Price Discrimination   *449*
12-4 Third-Degree Price Discrimination   *452*
          Methods of Grouping Consumers: Examples • Finding the Optimal Pricing
          Policy for a Given Total Quantity • Price Elasticity and Pricing Strategy •
          Application 12-1: Universities Are Learning More about Differences in the Price
          Elasticity of Demand of their Students • Reconsideration of the Examples •

Finding the Optimum Output to Produce and Prices to Charge • Application 12-2: Should a Firm Expand into the European Market? • Preventing Arbitrage • Application 12-3: Pricing a Renault in Belgium and in England • The Difference between Second- and Third-Degree Price Discrimination

12-5   Bundling   *471*

12-6   Two-Part Tariffs   *474*
Setting the Fixed Fee and Per Unit Price for Identical Consumers • Setting the Fixed Fee and Per Unit Price for Different Types of Consumers • Using Two-Part Tariffs to Price Consumer Capital Goods • Application 12-4: Why Did IBM and Xerox Lease Rather Than Sell Their Machines?

Summary   *480*
Key Terms   *481*
Review Questions   *481*
Exercises   *481*

CHAPTER 13
The Free Rider Problem and Pricing

   487

13-1   Free Rider Problems in Different Markets   *488*
Application 13-1: IBM Sues a Former Employee

13-2   Why Are Manufacturers Interested in the Retail Price?   *492*
Case 1: GM's Restriction on Dealer Sales • Case 2: IBM and Apple Restrictions on Dealers • Case 3: Discounting Prince Tennis Rackets

13-3   Benefiting from Retail Price Competition   *494*
Allowing Free Entry of Retailers • Deriving the Inverse Wholesale Demand Function • Maximizing the Profits of the Manufacturer

13-4   The Special Service Theory and the Free Rider Problem in Retailing   *499*
The Special Service Theory • Resale Price Maintenance and the Special Service Theory • Applying the Theory to Explain Behavior • The Role of Each Assumption • Why Does Free-Riding Appear in Retailing? • Dealing with the Free Rider Problem without Using a Minimum Suggested Retail Price • The Objection to RPM: Facilitating a Cartel

13-5   Free-Riding with Quality Certification   *507*
Application 13-2: Testing New Toys at Small Toy Stores • Application 13-3. Toys "R" Us Wants Toy Manufacturers to Sell to It Exclusively

13-6   Free Rider Problems between Manufacturers   *510*
Application 13-4: Ben and Jerry versus Goliath

Summary   *512*
Key Terms   *512*
Review Questions   *513*
Exercises   *513*
Problem Set: A Young Designer and the Free Rider Problem   *515*

CHAPTER 14
Market Behavior with Asymmetric Information

   517

14-1   Consequences of Asymmetric Information   *518*
Example: Health Insurance • Example: Automobile Insurance • Example: Borrowing in the Credit Market

14-2   Asymmetric Information and Adverse Selection   *520*
A Lemons Model • Equilibrium Prices and Quantities with Complete Information • Equilibrium Price and Quantity with Asymmetric Information • *A More General Treatment of the Lemons Problem • Overcoming Asymmetric Information • Identifying Markets for Lemons • Application 14-1: The Free Agency Market in Professional Baseball • Application 14-2: The Used Pickup Truck Market

14-3   Moral Hazard   *532*
14-4   Asymmetric Information and Potential Cheating   *534*
            An Honest Monopolist? • Modeling Competitive Behavior under Asymmetric
            Information • Promising and Delivering a High- or a Minimum-Quality
            Product • Promising High Quality but Delivering Low Quality • Actual Quality
            Produced in Competitive Markets
14-5   How Does a Competitive Industry Supply a High-Quality Product?   *540*
            Delivering a High-Quality Product with a Price Premium • The Incentive to
            Cheat • Cheating versus Honesty • Application 14-3: The Price Premium at
            McDonald's • Application 14-4: A Price Premium in Labor Markets •
            Nonsalvageable Investments • When the Required Price Premium
            Is Unknown • Conclusions about the Klein-Leffler Model
Summary   *549*
Key Terms   *549*
Review Questions   *549*
Exercises   *550*
Problem Set: Integration and Opportunistic Behavior   *552*
Appendix: Present-Value Calculations   *553*

CHAPTER 15
Pricing under Uncertainty   *556*
15-1   Seasonal Variation in Men's and Women's Apparel Prices   *557*
15-2   The Growth in Markdowns over Time   *558*
15-3   Uncertainty about Consumer Tastes   *559*
            Pricing Fashion Apparel: A Numerical Example • A Model with More Colors
15-4   Selecting a Price Policy   *565*
            A Single-Price Policy • A Two-Price Policy • Selecting the Initial and
            Markdown Prices to Maximize Expected Revenue • Changing the Probability
            Distribution of Prices
15-5   Using the Theory to Understand Markdown Pricing Practices   *573*
            Application 15-1: Markdowns by Merchandise Group • Differences in Market
            Equilibrium Prices under Certainty and Uncertainty • When to
            Apply the Uncertainty Theory
Summary   *577*
Key Terms   *577*
Review Questions   *577*
Exercises   *577*

PART VI **INTERTEMPORAL EQUILIBRIUM**
AND FACTOR MARKETS   *581*

CHAPTER 16
Consumer and Supplier Behavior over Time   *583*
16-1   Telescoping the Future into the Present   *584*
            Application 16-1: Mustering Out of the Military
16-2   Consumption Spending over Time   *588*
            The Intertemporal Budget Constraint • Intertemporal Preferences •
            Intertemporal Utility Maximization of the Consumer • The Importance of
            Present Value of Income • The Effect on Saving of an Increase in Current
            or Future Income • Application 16-2: Personal Bankruptcy • Saving,
            Borrowing, and the Interest Rate • The Equilibrium Interest Rate

16-3   Depletion of a Natural Resource   *608*
When to Sell a Nonrenewable Resource • Application 16-3: Freeing Prices
in Russia • Market Equilibrium Prices • The Effect of the Interest Rate on
Equilibrium Prices • Application 16-4: The Historical Trend in Crude Oil
Prices • A Renewable Resource

Summary   *620*
Key Terms   *621*
Review Questions   *621*
Exercises   *622*

CHAPTER 17
Wage Determination in Labor Markets   *624*
17-1   The Derived Demand Function for Labor   *625*
A Competitive Firm's Short-Run Demand Function for Labor • A Competitive
Firm's Long-Run Demand Function for Labor • Application 17-1: Substitution
and Scale Effects in the Airline Industry • The Short- and Long-Run Market
Demand Functions for Labor
17-2   The Supply Function of Labor   *636*
The Work-Leisure Choice • The Income and Substitution Effects of
a Wage Change • Application 17-2: A General Assistance Program and
the Work-Leisure Choice • The Aggregate Supply Function of Labor
and the Equilibrium Wage • The Effect of a Minimum Wage on the
Employment of Workers
17-3   Demand for Labor by a Price-Making Firm   *645*
17-4   Investment in Human Capital   *646*
The Present Value of Earnings • The Equilibrium Earnings of a College
Graduate • Application 17-3: Has the Wage Premium for a College Education
Peaked?
17-5   Training Employees   *652*
General Training • Firm-Specific Training • Application 17-4: Turnover and
Tenure in the United States and in Japan
17-6   Compensation Based on Input or Output   *657*
Application 17-5: Problems with the Use of Incentive Pay
17-7   Using Wage Policy as an Incentive Mechanism   *659*
Incentive Compensation and Mandatory Retirement

Summary   *662*
Key Terms   *662*
Review Questions   *662*
Exercises   *663*

PART VII   **MARKETS AND ECONOMIC EFFICIENCY**   *665*

CHAPTER 18
Economic Efficiency and General Equilibrium   *667*
18-1   General Equilibrium Analysis   *668*
18-2   Command and Control Policies of the Wizard   *669*
18-3   Economic Efficiency   *671*
Pareto Efficiency in Exchange • The Contract Curve • A Competitive Product
Market and Pareto Efficiency in Exchange • Application 18-1: Minimizing
Information Requirements in Experimental Competitive Markets • Impediments
to Pareto Efficiency • Application 18-2: Impediments to Trading Water Rights in
California • Pareto Efficiency in Production • Competitive Factor Markets
and Pareto Efficiency • Application 18-3: Reducing the Price of Capital

by Subsidizing Small Businesses • Pareto Efficiency in Product Mix •
Competitive Markets and Product Mix Efficiency

18-4   Departures from Pareto Efficiency Caused by Monopoly   *693*
Summary   *696*
Key Terms   *696*
Review Questions   *697*
Exercises   *697*

CHAPTER 19
Externalities and Public Goods   *699*

19-1   External Effects and Pareto Efficiency   *700*
Internalizing the Externality • Application 19-1: Internalizing an Externality in a
Shopping Mall • Maximizing Social Surplus with a Per Unit Tax •
The Coase Theorem • Application 19-2: Allowing the Coase Theorem to
Work • Transaction Costs • Application 19-3: Neighborhoods for
Sale • Application 19-4: View Wars and Defining Property Rights • Application
19-5: Saving the African Elephant • Taxation and Pareto Efficiency

19-2   Public Goods and Pareto Efficiency   *716*
The Optimal Quantity of a Public Good • Financing a Public Good

Summary   *721*
Key Terms   *721*
Review Questions   *722*
Exercises   *722*

Suggested Answers to Selected Exercises and Problem Sets   *724*
Index   *751*

INTRODUCTION: SUPPLY AND DEMAND

■ **Chapter 1**
Pricing and
the Demand and Supply Model

C H A P T E R 1

PRICING AND THE DEMAND AND SUPPLY MODEL

■ **1-1 The Meaning of Demand and Supply**

■ **1-2 The Market Demand Function**

Movement along a Demand Function

Application 1-1: The Rising Price of Wood and the Demand for Wood

Shifts in the Demand Function

■ **1-3 The Market Supply Function**

Movements along the Supply Function

Shifts in the Supply Function

■ **1-4 Market Equilibrium**

The Everyday Meaning of Demand and Supply

Problems with the Analysis

■ **1-5 Changes in Equilibrium: Shifts in Market Demand and Market Supply Functions**

Shifts in Demand

Application 1-2: Demand and Supply on Valentine's Day

An Explanation of Shortages and Surpluses

Application 1-3: Cotton Is King Again, but How Long the Reign?

Application 1-4: Should Your Company Support a Lobbying Effort to Reduce the Price of an Input?

■ **1-6 The Price Elasticity of Demand and Supply**

Price Elasticity of Demand

Point Price Elasticity of Demand

Arc Price Elasticity of Demand

Application 1-5: The Price Elasticity of Demand for First Class Mail

Determinants of the Price Elasticity of Demand

Price Elasticity of Supply

■ **Summary**

■ **Key Terms**

■ **Review Questions**

■ **Exercises**

■ **Problem Set: Estimating the Price Elasticity of Demand**

Among the decisions you make before purchasing a good is whether the price is too high and, if it is not too high, how many units to purchase. Just as price influences consumers, so too does it influence the behavior of firms. The price determines whether a firm will produce a product and, if so, the number of units it will supply. Clearly, price influences the behavior of buyers and suppliers. We would like to go beyond this, however, and ask how prices are determined and what causes them to change. The answers to these questions are the subject of this book, and in finding these answers, we will see how prices help allocate the scarce resources used to produce goods and services.

Modern industrial economies produce an incredible array of products and services, and how this all comes about is truly miraculous. How do producers know that consumers want more VCRs and fewer radios, more fashionable and less basic clothing, more fish and less beef, and more prepared foods and fewer home-cooked meals? Prices play a vital role in signaling suppliers that consumers want more of some products and fewer of others. Similarly, prices convey information from suppliers to demanders that the cost of a good is higher or lower than before. After reading this book, you will have a better understanding and a greater appreciation of the way prices transmit messages between consumers and producers.

Throughout this book we will use *models* to explain behavior. Economists use **demand and supply models**—simplifications of reality—to describe the behavior of demanders and suppliers. In developing a model, a model builder starts with certain assumptions and then proceeds to develop the implications of those assumptions. Model builders try to economize on the number of assumptions while developing theories that are general enough to explain a broad range of behavior. For example, to explain the price of in-line skates, one model builder might start by assuming consumers will buy fewer skates if the skate price is high. Another model builder might start by assuming consumers will buy *more* skates if the skate price is high. This second model builder might argue that consumers believe skate quality and price are related so more skates are demanded at a higher price.

How do we ever know whether one model is better than another? We could probably spend many hours debating which assumption is superior but not come to a final resolution. A more promising approach would be to derive the testable predictions of a model and determine if they are confirmed by the evidence. Our two models predict different responses for price and quality when the cost of producing skates changes. Exercise 8 at the end of this chapter asks you to derive the price and quantity predictions of the two models when the cost of producing skates changes. Then, by examining actual price and quantity changes in the skate market after the cost of production changes, you can determine which model better explains the data. By confronting the theory with evidence, we expose the strengths and limitations of each model, and this helps us choose among models. By testing models in this way, economists expand their knowledge and understanding of markets and the economy.

This chapter introduces the fundamental building blocks of demand and supply that economists use in their models and begins to explain how prices are determined. The demand and supply model is applied repeatedly throughout the book and serves as a powerful tool for demonstrating how markets work. After presenting the concepts of demand and supply and building the basic model, we use the model to predict how market behavior and prices change when conditions change. As you work through the chapter, try to develop a facility in solving problems with the model. The true test of your understanding of demand and supply concepts is whether you can apply them in different situations.

1-1 THE MEANING OF DEMAND AND SUPPLY

Economists use "demand" and "supply" in a very precise way, and this chapter begins by explaining what these terms mean to an economist. Later in the chapter the economist's usage is contrasted with everyday usage of the terms.

The economist's view of demanders and suppliers rests on one fundamental premise: demanders and suppliers respond to incentives. For example, consumers react to a lower price by demanding more units of a good, and a higher price induces producers to supply more units of a good.

If you are comfortable with the notion that consumers modify demands and producers change supplies in response to price changes, you are already thinking like an economist. If you want to know something about the demand or supply for crude oil, you would not ask, "What is the demand for crude oil?" or "What is the supply of crude oil?" Because the demand and supply of crude oil depend on its price, no one can answer these questions without specifying a price. An economist would phrase the question differently: "What will be the quantity demanded or the quantity supplied of crude oil if the price is $20 per barrel?"

1-2 THE MARKET DEMAND FUNCTION

Let's consider how you might respond as the price per can of your favorite fruit drink declines. Table 1-1 shows how the number of cans of fruit drink per week that you demand changes as the price per can changes.

Table 1-1 RELATIONSHIP BETWEEN THE NUMBER OF CANS OF FRUIT DRINK DEMANDED PER WEEK AND THE PRICE PER CAN FOR ONE CONSUMER

PRICE PER CAN ($)	CANS DEMANDED PER WEEK
3.00	2
2.00	4
1.00	5
0.50	7

If the price per can is $3, you might drink only a few cans a week given that it is so expensive. On the other hand, if the price is only 50 cents a can, you might drink a can a day. As the price decreases, the quantity you demand increases. The relationship between the quantity of cans you demand per week and the price per can is your individual demand function.

Other consumers have individual demand functions for the same fruit drink, and adding up the individual quantities demanded by all individuals at each price results in what economists call the market demand function.[1]

> The **market demand function** expresses the relationship between the total quantity demanded and the price of the product per unit of time, holding other factors constant.

The relationship between the price and the aggregate quantity demanded can be expressed as

$$Q_d = D(P) \qquad \text{(Market Demand Function)} \qquad \text{(1-1)}$$

where Q_d is the quantity demanded, P is the price per unit, and D is the notation for a function. Equation 1-1 shows the total quantity demanded at each price, and Figure 1-1 illustrates the market demand function. The prices along the demand function are commonly called demand prices and represent maximum amounts buyers will pay.

Throughout the book we follow the convention of placing price on the vertical axis and quantity demanded on the horizontal axis. Uppercase letters designate market demand, the aggregate quantity demanded by all consumers, and lowercase letters indicate the quantity demanded by a single consumer.

Movement along a Demand Function

The total quantity demanded increases when the price of the product drops. If the price is P_1, the quantity demanded is Q_1 units per period. If the price decreases to P_2, the quantity demanded increases from Q_1 to Q_2 units. This is seen on the graph as a movement *along* the demand function *DD*. A movement along a demand function always involves a change in the *price* of the product in question and a change in the *total quantity demanded* of that product.

The inverse relationship between the price and the quantity demanded is called the *law of demand*. The increase in the quantity demanded in response to a price decline is due to two effects. First, consumers who are already buying the product increase the quantity demanded when the price falls. Second, new consumers who have never purchased the product before decide to buy it because of the lower price. The behavior of both groups causes the quantity demanded to increase when the price decreases.

---

[1] Individual demand functions are summed horizontally to derive the market demand function.

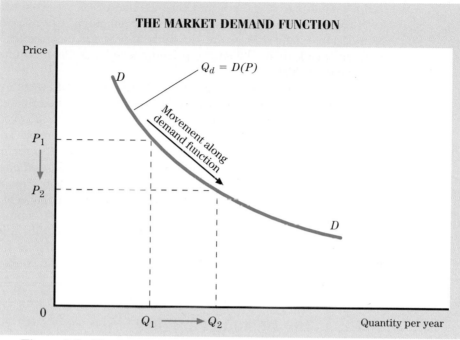

Figure 1-1   The quantity demanded Q_d increases when the price P decreases. At a price of P_1 the quantity demanded is Q_1. When the price is reduced to P_2, the quantity demanded increases to Q_2. This relationship is called the law of demand.

The **law of demand** describes the inverse relationship between the quantity demanded and the price of the product.

APPLICATION **1-1**

The Rising Price of Wood and the Demand for Wood

Economist Nathan Rosenberg describes an interesting episode from American economic history that illustrates the law of demand.[2] He notes that the United States possesses vast forest resources in contrast to England's limited timber resources. The price of wood was relatively low in the United States compared with England during the first half of the nineteenth century. Since the price of wood was relatively low compared to the price of labor, Americans were generous in the use of wood in comparison with the English. In the United States fireplaces were deliberately built large to accommodate large logs. This saved on labor by

[2] Nathan Rosenberg, "Innovative Responses to Materials Shortages," *American Economic Review* LXIII, no. 2 (May 1973), pp. 111–18.

reducing cutting but did not maximize BTUs. Americans used timber for all sorts of purposes undreamed of in England. It was employed extensively in the construction of houses and bridges, for the framing of steam engines, for canal locks, and even for plank roads. When the price of wood was low, the quantity demanded was relatively high.

The price of timber increased rapidly in the United States during the second half of the nineteenth century and the quantity demanded decreased. Before the Civil War, wood was used to power railroad engines, but 20 years later coal had virtually displaced it because the price of timber had increased relative to that of coal, iron, and other fuels. Iron and steel were substituted for wood in the construction of ships, machinery, and bridges. The price of wood continued to rise in the early 1900s and increased fourfold from 1870 to 1950. This resulted in other minerals being substituted for wood. The per capita consumption of mineral products increased 10 times over this period, whereas the per capita consumption of wood peaked at the turn of the century. By 1950 per capita wood consumption was only half of what it had been in 1900. Clearly, the rise in the price of wood reduced the quantity demanded.

Shifts in the Demand Function

So far, we have focused on what happens to the quantity demanded of a product when the price of the item changes. However, the price is only one of several determinants of the total quantity demanded. Changes in the other variables, unlike a change in the price of the product, *shifts* the position of the demand function. The position of the demand function will shift because of a change in (1) the income of consumers, (2) the prices of other goods, or (3) the tastes of consumers. Let's consider how each of these changes shifts the demand function.

For many goods and services, a rise in the income of buyers causes the total quantity demanded to increase at each price. As income increases, the demand functions for luxury automobiles like Mercedes-Benz, BMW, Lexus, and Cadillac shift to the right. The demand function shifts outward as shown in Figure 1-2. If the price is P_1, the quantity demanded is Q_1 on the original demand function, DD. After household income increases, the demand function shifts to the right and becomes $D'D'$. The aggregate quantity demanded at the price of P_1 increases from Q_1 to Q_1' because income increases. For a few products, however, the demand function can shift in the direction *opposite* the income change. For example, during a recession, when income falls, the demand for second-hand clothing increases.

The demand function can shift also if the price of another good changes and consumers consider this good a *substitute* for the other. For example, a rise in the price of riding public transportation shifts the demand for automobiles outward. A rise in the price of steel shifts the demand function for aluminum to the right because steel and aluminum are considered substitutes; automobile companies substitute aluminum for steel in producing cars. Likewise, an increase in the price of polyester may shift the demand function for cotton apparel outward.

It should not be assumed that a change in the price of a related product always

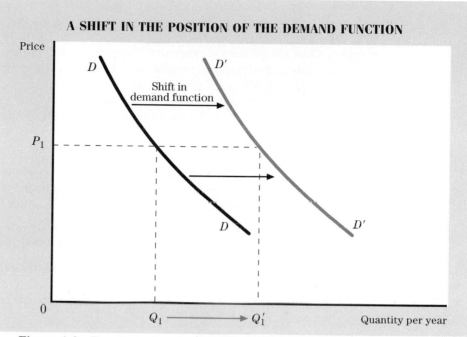

Figure 1-2 The demand curve shifts from DD to $D'D'$ because household income increases, the price of a substitute rises, or tastes change so that consumers prefer the good more than before. At each price the quantity demanded increases. For example, at the price of P_1, the quantity demanded increases from Q_1 to Q_1'.

shifts the demand function of the product in question in the same direction. When the price of a product changes and the demand function of a related product shifts in the opposite direction, the two goods are called *complements*. Consider the following illustration: In May 1992 American Airlines and other airlines cut passenger fares by 50 percent, and the quantity demanded increased. How did the reduction in air fares affect the demand function for rental cars, hotels, and travel agents? Draw a graph showing how the demand for rental cars shifts when the air fare declines. One determinant of the demand for rental cars is the number of airline passengers. A decrease in air fares increases the number of passengers and therefore increases the demand for rental cars. Your graph should relate the daily rate for a rental car to the quantity of rental cars demanded before and after the air fare decreases. It should also show the demand function for rental cars shifting outward after the reduction in fares. Therefore, passenger trips and rental car use are complements.

Finally, the demand function shifts to the right if tastes change and consumers prefer the product more than before. If income and all prices are constant and the quantity demanded changes, this indicates that a change in tastes has caused the shift in the demand function.

In summary, two different types of changes have been considered, and it is important to distinguish between them when applying the demand and supply model. In the first instance the change involved movement along the demand function when the product's own price changed. In the second instance, the demand function shifted position because of a change in the income of consumers, in the price of a related good, or in tastes.

To test your understanding of the distinction between movement along a demand function and a shift in the position of the demand function, try interpreting the following statements:

1. "The quantity of automobiles demanded in the United States may not reach 15 million units next year because the prices for new cars will be substantially higher than current prices." This statement is an example of a movement along a demand curve.

2. "I'd buy a Mercedes if they didn't cost so much." This statement says one consumer's quantity demanded vanishes because the price is too high.

3. "A fall in the price of personal computers (PCs) increases the demand for software programs." This statement says that the demand for software programs depends on the price of PCs and shifts outward when the PC price decreases.

4. "The demand for new MBAs will increase by 5 percent next year." This statement is so vague that the cause of the increase is unclear. It could describe a rightward shift in the demand function for MBAs, or it could imply that the quantity demanded will increase by 5 percent if the salary of MBAs decreases.

1-3 THE MARKET SUPPLY FUNCTION

The market supply function indicates the total quantity supplied at each price by all sellers. The quantity supplied is not a fixed amount determined by the physical capabilities of each firm; rather, a higher price induces producers to supply larger quantities.

> The **supply function** expresses the relationship between the total quantity supplied and the price received by all suppliers per unit of time, holding other factors constant.

The market supply function can be expressed symbolically as

$$Q_s = S(P) \qquad \text{(Market Supply Function)} \qquad \text{(1-2)}$$

where P is the price that producers receive and Q_s is the total quantity supplied by all producers. Just as the market demand function shows how consumers respond to price changes, the market supply function reflects how producers respond to price changes.

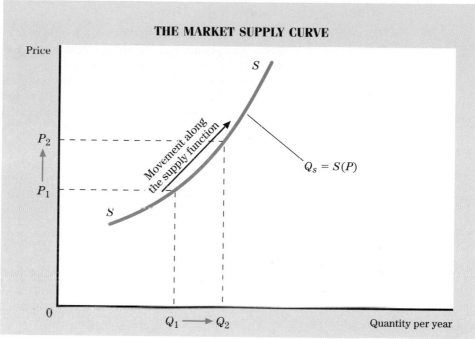

Figure 1-3   Quantity supplied increases from Q_1 to Q_2 when the price that suppliers receive increases from P_1 to P_2.

Movements along the Supply Function

Figure 1-3 shows a representative market supply function. The price of the product is on the vertical axis, and the quantity supplied is on the horizontal axis. The supply function SS shows that suppliers offer Q_1 units of a good if the price they receive is P_1, and a larger total quantity of Q_2 units if the price they receive is P_2. The changes in the price and the quantity supplied result in a movement *along* the supply function. The prices along the supply function are commonly called supply prices, indicating minimum amounts sellers must receive.

When the slope is positive, the total quantity supplied increases at higher prices because (1) existing producers supply a larger quantity at the higher price and (2) some firms that are not particularly efficient at producing this item stay out of the industry when the price is low and enter the market when the price is higher. Both effects increase the quantity supplied at higher prices. The crude oil industry is a good example of an industry with a positively sloped supply function. Many oil wells in the United States and throughout the world are inactive or remain undiscovered when the price of crude oil is only $14 per barrel, but producers pump crude oil or seek new wells when they receive $50 per barrel. This happened in 1974 after crude oil prices shot up, and the number of wells drilled around the world increased.

Shifts in the Supply Function

The supply function shows the relationship between the price of a product and the total quantity supplied. The position of the supply function shifts due to a change in production costs. These costs change when input prices or the state of technology change. If the hourly wage rate or the price of a raw material rises, the supply function shifts inward (to the left) because the cost of producing the product increases. Figure 1-4 shows that producers supplied Q_1 units at a price of P_1 before a rise in wage rates or in raw material prices. At the same price P_1, they are willing to supply only Q_2 units when the costs of production increase. The supply function therefore shifts to the left.

> The supply function shifts when the price of an input changes or the state of technology changes.

When a technological breakthrough allows firms to economize on the use of some inputs, the cost of producing the product declines and the supply function shifts outward (to the right). Producers are willing to offer a larger quantity at each price because the technological breakthrough allows them to provide the product at a lower cost than before. The Japanese have cut costs by adopting just-in-time inventory practices. Parts arrive just when they are ready to be used in the final

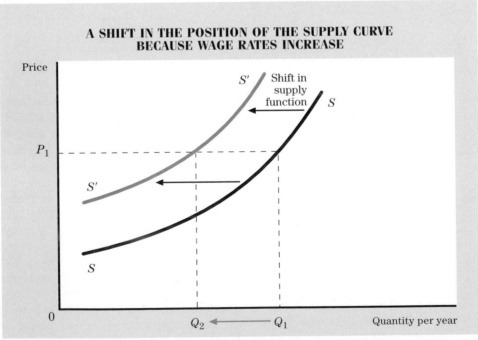

**A SHIFT IN THE POSITION OF THE SUPPLY CURVE
BECAUSE WAGE RATES INCREASE**

Figure 1-4   The supply curve shifts to the left from *SS* to *S'S'* because the cost of producing the product increases.

assembly of a product, thereby eliminating the cost of stockpiling inventory. As a result, Japanese manufacturers of automobiles have reduced their production costs and shifted their supply functions to the right. Similarly, Wal-Mart and other major discount retailers have developed intricate conveyor systems that reduce inventory costs by shortening the time that merchandise remains in their warehouses. These changes in operational methods cause the supply function to shift outward.

Supply functions also shift because of changes in government regulations. As an example, some regulated public utilities in Ohio, Indiana, and Illinois use high-sulfur, dirty coal to produce electricity. When burned, high-sulfur coal emits pollutants that degrade air quality not only in these states but in other areas as well. Proposed changes in federal environmental legislation require the utilities to lower emissions by installing scrubbers, purchasing more expensive low-sulfur coal, etc., thereby increasing the cost of producing electricity for utilities using high-sulfur coal. As a result the supply function for electricity will shift to the left.

In summary, the quantity supplied is not a constant determined by some measure of physical productive capacity. Rather, producers increase the quantity supplied when they receive a higher price, and decrease the quantity supplied when the price decreases. The supply function shifts with changes in the cost of producing a product or when the knowledge of production methods expands.

The demand function indicates the quantity demanded if the price is P, and the supply function indicates the quantity supplied if the price is P. The next step, which combines the behavior of consumers and producers, will determine the price in the marketplace.

1-4   MARKET EQUILIBRIUM

To determine the market price, we must make some assumptions about the behavior of participants in the market. This chapter deals with competitive markets. While more will be said about the meaning of a competitive market later, for now we simply assume there are many demanders and suppliers in the market resulting in no single demander or supplier being able to influence the market price.

To find the market price for a given good, we superimpose the demand and supply functions for a particular product on the same graph (see Figure 1-5). Although there are many prices that could exist in this market, there is only one at which the quantity demanded is equal to the quantity supplied, and only one that is expected to persist in the marketplace. Before identifying that price, the concept of an equilibrium must be introduced.

> A **market equilibrium** exists when the quantity demanded equals the quantity supplied.

This definition of equilibrium emphasizes a balance between the quantity demanded and the quantity supplied. Among the prices on the vertical axis in Figure 1-5, P_e receives special attention because it is the only price where the total quantity demanded equals the total quantity supplied. If the price is P_e, then the quantity demanded *and* supplied is equal to Q_e. P_e is the **equilibrium price,** and Q_e is the

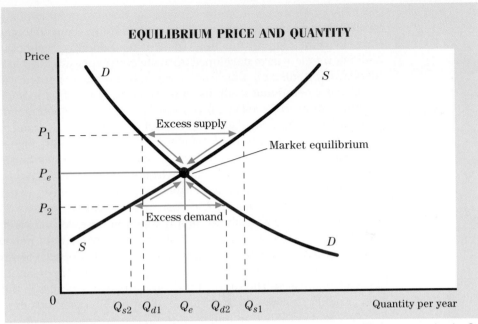

Figure 1-5   The market equilibrium price is P_e, and the equilibrium quantity is Q_e. When the price equals P_e, the quantity demanded and the quantity supplied are the same and are equal to Q_e. When the price equals P_1, the quantity supplied Q_{s1} exceeds the quantity demanded Q_{d1}. When the price equals P_2, the quantity demanded Q_{d2} exceeds the quantity supplied Q_{s2}.

equilibrium quantity. Economists single out P_e because they believe it has a higher probability of being the market price than any other price. Because the total quantity demanded equals the total quantity supplied at this price, P_e is not likely to change once it occurs. Of all the prices on the vertical axis, only P_e satisfies this condition.

At any other price there is a discrepancy between the quantity demanded and the quantity supplied. At the price of P_1 the quantity supplied Q_{s1} exceeds the quantity demanded Q_{d1}. The difference between the quantity supplied and the quantity demanded is the **excess supply.** When there is an excess supply, a surplus appears as suppliers find that they cannot sell all that they have produced at P_1. To reduce the growing inventories, they begin to haggle, offer discounts, and lower prices. As prices fall, two changes occur: The quantity demanded increases, and the quantity supplied decreases. Excess supply shrinks as the difference between the quantity supplied and the quantity demanded diminishes. *Both* sides of the market adjust to eliminate the excess supply. Therefore any price above P_e is unlikely to persist because the excess supply causes the price to decrease.

What happens if the price is below P_e? At a price of P_2 the quantity demanded Q_{d2} exceeds the quantity supplied Q_{s2}. There is an **excess demand.** Too many potential buyers cannot find goods to purchase, and stores that have goods have long lines of waiting customers. This is what happens when prices are too low. In many developing countries the government deliberately keeps bread prices low, and waiting lines are an everyday occurrence. For example, the price of a loaf of bread in the former Soviet Union had not increased from the end of World War II until the early 1990s, and shopping was just one long wait in line.

If the price is below the equilibrium price, what do buyers do to obtain the product? They begin to offer higher prices to purchase the limited supply, and a price like P_2 cannot persist in the marketplace. As the price increases, the quantity demanded decreases, the quantity supplied increases, and the excess demand decreases. Whether the price is above or below the equilibrium price, it moves in the direction of P_e, and any excess demand or excess supply ultimately disappears.

When the price is equal to P_e, there is no reason for it to change unless the position of either the demand or the supply function shifts. Given the demand and supply functions in Figure 1-5, we say the equilibrium price is P_e and that price is more likely to persist in the marketplace than any other price. If the price is not equal to P_e, its movement will be in the direction of P_e.

The equilibrium price and quantity are determined simultaneously. The equilibrium quantity is the one at which the quantity demanded equals the quantity supplied:

$$Q_e = Q_d = Q_s \qquad \text{(Equilibrium Quantity)} \tag{1-3}$$

The equilibrium price is the one at which the quantity demanded equals the quantity supplied. We substitute the expressions for the quantity demanded Q_d and the quantity supplied Q_s to determine the equilibrium price:

$$D(P_e) = S(P_e) \qquad \text{(Determination of the Equilibrium Price)} \tag{1-4}$$

The equilibrium price can be found by solving equation 1-4 for the equilibrium price. The left-hand side is the quantity demanded, and the right-hand side is the quantity supplied. As Figure 1-5 shows, P_e is the only price where the market is in equilibrium—where Q_d equals Q_s. Given P_e, we can find Q_e by substituting P_e into either the demand function (equation 1-1) or the supply function (equation 1-2).

The Everyday Meaning of Demand and Supply

The economist's usage of the terms "demand" and "supply" is quite different from layman's everyday usage. An important contemporary issue, the impending energy crisis, illustrates the difference. You may have read, perhaps with some trepidation, about the energy crisis some geologists believe to be around the corner. Since the oil embargo in 1974, when the price of crude oil jumped dramatically, the public has begun to heed the warnings of geologists and environmentalists who predict a depletion of petroleum supplies. The dismal prognosis is that world demand for crude oil will continue to grow in the future but that the supply of crude oil is finite or at best only marginally expandable. Although no one can pinpoint the exact year, public policy experts, environmentalists, and others say the United

States and the world will face another energy crisis as global oil reserves are depleted. There will come a time, they say, when demand will catch up with, and surpass, supply. With this will come all the inevitable consequences of a shortage—long waits at gasoline stations and irksome allocations placed on industry and consumers to restrict use of the limited supply of crude oil.

This unpleasant scenario is an entirely convincing one to the average person. More often than not, he or she thinks of demand as the number of barrels needed to heat houses and factories or to operate automobiles and trucks, and supply as the physical amount of crude oil that can be produced. A graph will illustrate this ordinary interpretation of demand and supply. In Figure 1-6 the predicted demand and supply of barrels of crude oil are on the vertical axis, and *time* is on the horizontal axis.

Figure 1-6 shows that the demand grows faster than the supply over time. There will be a surplus of crude oil during the second half of the 1990s when supply exceeds demand. If the predictions are accurate, however, this surplus will steadily dwindle and the shortage will begin to hit sometime in the first decade of the 21st century.

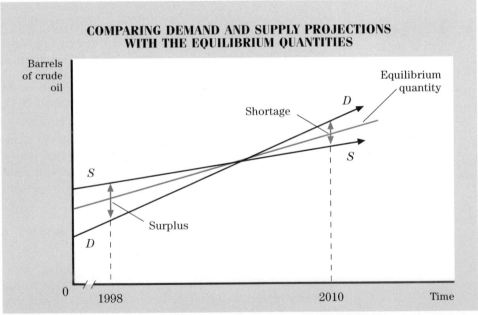

Figure 1-6   Based on the everyday usage of the terms "demand" and "supply," *DD* represents needs and *SS* represents production capability. During the first half of the 1990s supply is projected to exceed demand and there is a surplus. During the first decade of the 21st century demand is projected to exceed supply. In the economist's model price adjusts to equate the quantity demanded with the quantity supplied so that the equilibrium quantity is produced each year. The solid line without the arrow shows how the equilibrium quantity changes over time.

Problems with the Analysis

Relying on a demand and supply model allows you to identify two problems with this way of looking at how the crude oil market operates. First, the two lines for demand and supply show that demand virtually *never* equals supply. Most of the time there is either a shortage or a surplus because needs and production capabilities are different. This might sound plausible to the average person, but is it true? Would firms continue to produce a product for which there is less demand? Why should you expect to see a lengthy pattern of surpluses or shortages?

If "demand" means need and "supply" means production capacity, a shortage or a surplus is inevitable because price plays no role in the analysis. Because the average person fails to understand how price adjusts to equate the quantity demanded with the quantity supplied, he or she believes management is essential to bring a balance to the market and control shortages and surpluses. Balance requires greater reliance on control policies such as rationing, conservation, and other demand-reducing policies or on joint government and industry programs that increase supply by developing new technologies.

This assumed behavior can be contrasted with the behavior of demanders and suppliers in the economist's model where price plays the critical role in equating differences between the quantity demanded and the quantity supplied. Price is constantly changing to bring the market into equilibrium. Thus, long waits at gasoline stations are less likely to persist because higher gasoline prices will increase the quantity supplied and reduce the quantity demanded. The economist's model has only one line, rather than two, with each point on the line representing the equilibrium quantity where the quantity demanded equals the quantity supplied. In Figure 1-6 the line without an arrow shows the equilibrium quantity over time, where the price changes each year and the quantity demanded equals the quantity supplied. The projected excess supply during the second half of the 1990s disappears because the price decreases until the quantity demanded is equal to the quantity supplied. The projected shortage disappears because the price increases during the first decade of the 21st century.

1-5   CHANGES IN EQUILIBRIUM: SHIFTS IN MARKET DEMAND AND MARKET SUPPLY FUNCTIONS

The demand and supply model can be used to predict how the equilibrium price and quantity will change when either the demand or the supply function shifts or when both shift.

Shifts in Demand

Figure 1-7 shows what happens to the equilibrium price and quantity when the market demand for the product increases from DD to $D'D'$. The increase in market demand causes the equilibrium price to increase from P_1 to P_2, and the equilibrium quantity to increase from Q_1 to Q_2. The equilibrium price and quantity increase when the market demand increases because the supply function slopes upward.

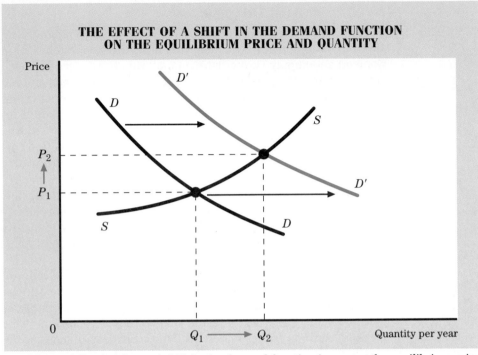

Figure 1-7   A rightward shift in the demand function increases the equilibrium price and equilibrium quantity when the supply function has a positive slope. The shift in the market demand curve causes existing suppliers to produce more, and more suppliers to enter the industry, increasing the quantity supplied from Q_1 to Q_2.

This is an appropriate time to revisit the crude oil example. Figure 1-6 shows separate lines for demand and supply based on everyday usage of the terms "demand" and "supply." The line without an arrow in Figure 1-6 shows the equilibrium quantity for each year when the price adjusts to equate the quantity demanded with the quantity supplied. In Figure 1-7 suppose DD is the market demand function for crude oil in 1998, $D'D'$ is the market demand function in 2010, and SS is the market supply function of crude oil, which does not shift. What does the market equilibrium analysis imply about the difference between the quantity demanded and the quantity supplied in the two years? By using the theory of markets—the demand and supply model—you should conclude that the quantity demanded and the quantity supplied are equal to Q_1 in 1998 and, although both increase over time, are equal to Q_2 in 2010.

Q_1 is the equilibrium quantity in 1998 when the market demand function is DD because the price is P_1. The market is in equilibrium, and the equilibrium quantity is equal to the quantity demanded *and* the quantity supplied. In 2010 the market demand function shifts, the equilibrium quantity becomes Q_2, and the equilibrium price increases to P_2. Each year the price adjusts so that the quantity demanded equals the quantity supplied. The lines for the quantity demanded and the quantity supplied are not separate because the price changes to equate the quantity demanded to the quantity supplied. The separate solid lines for demand and supply in Figure 1-6 are a result of faulty economic thinking because they assume that price has no effect on the behavior of demanders or suppliers.

APPLICATION **1-2**

Demand and Supply on Valentine's Day

Valentine's Day is not only the most romantic day of the year but also a big business day in some industries. Fifty percent of cut roses sold in February are sold on Valentine's Day. On Valentine's Day in a recent year, the price of a dozen roses jumped from $8.00 to $19.99 at one local store in Chicago. Another bestseller on Valentine's Day is candy. About 13 percent of the annual sales of candy take place on Valentine's Day. Yet the price of a box of chocolates increases modestly if at all on this holiday. Why does the price of roses increase on Valentine's Day but not the price of a box of chocolates?

The behavior of prices tells us about the different shapes of the supply functions for roses and candy. We can use the demand and supply model to explain why the price behavior is different for these two products. In Figure 1-8*a* the demand function for cut roses on an ordinary day is *DD*, and on Valentine's Day it is *D'D'*. To explain the price behavior, the supply function for roses must have a relatively steep slope like *SS*. The quantity of roses supplied on any day increases only if the price rises substantially. The price rise on Valentine's Day reflects the fact that increasing the supply of cut roses for Valentine's Day would require more land devoted to producing roses and less to producing other flowers. Also, it is not possible to produce more cut roses before Valentine's Day and store them until the holiday arrives.

In contrast, *DD* in Figure 1-8*b* is the demand for a box of chocolates on an ordinary day, and *D'D'* is the demand on Valentine's Day. The supply function for a box of chocolates is relatively flat because retailers build up stocks beforehand to meet the expected increase in demand. This means that producers of chocolates are able to increase production before the holiday without increasing the unit production cost substantially. Therefore, the price of chocolates increases only modestly on Valentine's Day.

A difference in the *shape* of the supply functions explains why the price of roses increases more than the price of chocolates on Valentine's Day.

An Explanation of Shortages and Surpluses

If the market price in each year is the equilibrium price, there is neither an excess demand nor an excess supply and the market moves from one equilibrium position to another when the demand function shifts. It appears, however, that the demand and supply model cannot explain shortages or surpluses. The model can tell you when and why you might expect a shortage or a surplus, and it tells you that the market will correct itself and return to equilibrium. Still, this most basic demand

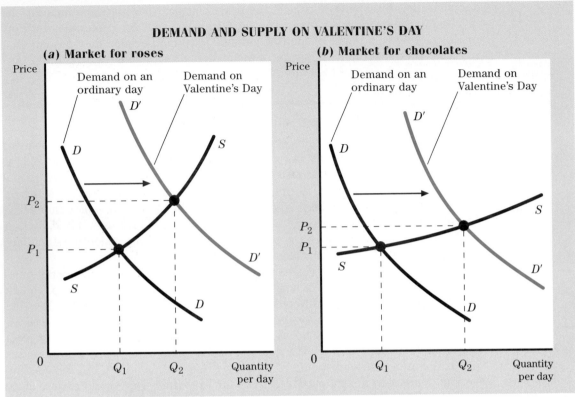

Figure 1-8 (*a*) An increase in demand for roses on Valentine's Day increases the price from P_1 to P_2. (*b*) The price of chocolates changes by less on Valentine's Day because the supply function is flatter.

and supply model cannot explain some persistent shortages that last for long periods of time.

To begin, consider the argument that shortages occur whenever the demand function shifts to the right at a faster rate than the supply function. In the growth phase of a new industry the demand function might shift to the right by 25 percent per year while the supply function shifts to the right by only 10 percent. Then, you might predict that a shortage will appear because demand is growing more rapidly than supply. Although the argument sounds plausible, it does not stand up to analysis. Differential growth rates for demand and supply functions are not the reason for a shortage or a surplus. If the demand function shifts to the right more rapidly than the supply function, the correct prediction of the model is not that a shortage will appear but that the price will increase. The price increase is what prevents a potential shortage from becoming an actual shortage by reducing the quantity demanded and increasing the quantity supplied so that any excess demand evaporates.

Figure 1-9 shows the demand function shifting to the right more rapidly than

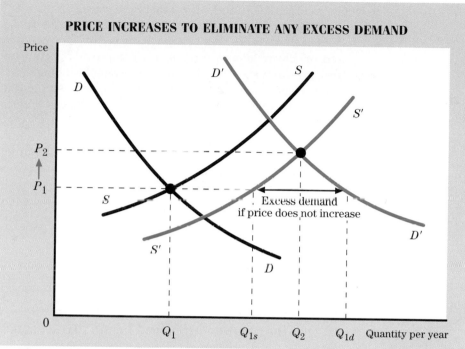

Figure 1-9   The demand function shifts to the right at a faster rate than the supply function. The demand curve shifts from DD to $D'D'$, and the supply curve shifts from SS to $S'S'$. If the price remains at P_1, a shortage will appear because the quantity demanded equals Q_{1d} and is greater than the quantity supplied Q_{1s}. The shortage does not appear because the price rises from P_1 to P_2. Differential rates of growth of the demand and supply functions do not explain why shortages and surpluses exist.

the supply function. The initial demand function is DD, the original supply function is SS, and the equilibrium price is P_1. The demand and supply functions shift to the right and become $D'D'$ and $S'S'$, respectively. The equilibrium price increases from P_1 to P_2, and the equilibrium quantity increases from Q_1 to Q_2. If the price does not change but remains at P_1, a shortage will appear as excess demand because the quantity demanded will be Q_{1d} and the quantity supplied will be Q_{1s}. The price increase eliminates a potential shortage of $Q_{1d} - Q_{1s}$ by reducing the quantity demanded to Q_2 and increasing the quantity supplied to Q_2. So it is not true that shortages occur just because the demand and supply functions do not increase or decrease at the same rate.

However, this example indicates when a shortage or a surplus will appear. If the price cannot change because of regulations or if the price adjusts sluggishly to shifts in demand and supply, then a shortage can occur. Thus one reason for a shortage is that the price cannot perform the role of increasing the quantity supplied and decreasing the quantity demanded. Price controls are legal maximums that are binding whenever the control price is below the equilibrium price. For example, New York City and a few other cities have placed rent controls on some apartments for decades and created a perpetual excess demand for rental housing since controlled rents are well below what equilibrium rents would be.

Fixed or slowly adjusting prices do not provide a complete explanation of shortages and surpluses. There are notable examples of persistent excess demand in private markets such as those for sporting events and entertainment that the model does not explain satisfactorily. In these instances there is no government interference in the operation of the market. Well-known rock groups like Metallica perform periodic outdoor concerts. Their concerts sell out in advance in virtually every city on the tour, and holders of tickets can resell them for considerably more than the initial ticket price. Another classic, if dated, example, was the 1950s hit musical *My Fair Lady*, which played for years on Broadway and was sold out night after night for long stretches of time. Likewise, the Montreal Canadiens have been a very successful hockey team for many decades. Home games sell out consistently, and tickets are difficult to find.[3] Why doesn't management raise prices and eliminate the excess demand? This remains an unanswered question that is beginning to attract the attention of economists.[4]

APPLICATION **1-3**

Cotton Is King Again, but How Long the Reign?[5]

In May 1995 the price of cotton cracked the $1.00-a-pound level for the first time since the Civil War. In June 1995 the cotton price hit the $1.11-per-pound level. World cotton prices have been rising since the early 90s. What explains the price surge? Did price increase because market demand for cotton increased? Experts say there is little reason to believe the demand function for cotton has increased appreciably. Turning to the supply side, American cotton farmers throughout the South and elsewhere, some of whom stopped planting cotton long ago, are now planting more cotton, and rising U.S. production of cotton attests to their success. The rising price is not due to reduced supply in the United States. Any explanation for the rising cotton price must be found abroad, specifically in Asia. In fact, a deadly insect has caused major cotton crop failures in China, a major cotton supplier, and in other Asian countries.

The demand and supply model can be adapted to analyze this situation. We can simplify our analysis by considering just two supply sources: Asia and the rest of the world. Panels (a) and (b) of Figure 1-10 show the Asian supply function of cotton (S_a) and the rest of the world's supply function (S_r), respectively. To find

[3] Season ticket holders often will their tickets to family members.
[4] A Nobel prize winner has suggested that consumers' demand function shifts outward as market demand grows larger. Consumers infer the quality of a restaurant is high if many consumers try to patronize the restaurant. If so, a firm has an incentive to keep prices lower. A curious reader should wait until completing Chapter 9 and then read Gary S. Becker, "A Note on Restaurant Pricing and Other Examples of Social Influences on Price," *Journal of Political Economy* 99, (October 1991), pp. 1109–16.
[5] For further details see Andrea Gerlin and Scott McCarthy, "King Cotton Reigns Once Again in South as Production Surges," *The Wall Street Journal*, May 2, 1995.

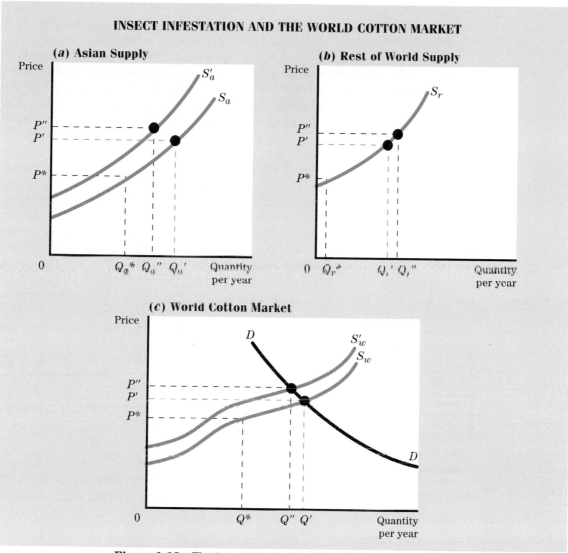

Figure 1-10 The insect infestation shifts the Asian supply function inward (panel a) and the world supply function shifts inward and becomes S'_w (panel c). The equilibrium price rises from P' to P''. Because they receive a higher price, suppliers in the rest of the world expand output from Q'_r to Q''_r (panel b).

the total world supply at each price, we sum horizontal the quantity supplied by Asian suppliers and by suppliers from the rest of the world at each price. For example, if the price is P^*, Asian suppliers supply $Q_a{}^*$ lbs, and the rest of the world supplies $Q_r{}^*$ lbs. So, the total quantity supplied at price P^* is $Q_a{}^* + Q_r{}^* = Q^*$ lbs, shown in panel (c). By repeating this procedure for different prices, a world supply function S_w is derived in panel (c) and is a horizontal summation of the two supply functions. DD in panel (c) is the world demand function. Given the world demand and supply functions, the equilibrium price is P', and the equilibrium quantity is Q', with Q_a' lbs supplied by Asia and Q_r' supplied by the rest of the world.

The insect infestation causes the Asian supply function to shift inwards to S_a' because the infestation causes a smaller quantity to be supplied at each price. Since the insect infestation has not affected other countries, the supply function of the rest of the world is unaffected. Because less is supplied at each price, the *world* supply function becomes S'_w. The infestation causes the equilibrium cotton price to increase to P'' and the equilibrium quantity to decrease to Q''. In panel (a) the quantity supplied by Asian producers falls to Q_a''. However, the quantity supplied by the rest of the world increases to Q_r'' because the cotton price increases.

The misfortune of some producers becomes the forture of others. Non-Asian sellers not only receive a higher price than before but the higher price induces these suppliers to produce more. At over $1.00 per pound, producing cotton has become a very profitable undertaking. This sequence of events has been played out many times in many markets and over many years. When a drought hit Texas and Oklahoma in the spring of 1996 and wiped out the winter wheat crop, farmers planting in other states with normal rainfall benefited from higher wheat prices caused by the arid conditions facing the farmers in the Southwest.

How long will the higher cotton price last? Apparently, not for long since the cotton price is already beginning to fall and had dropped to 85 cents per pound by June 1996, still relatively high. As the Asian supply function begins to shift outward with an unchangeable demand function, the cotton price will decline and the process reverses itself. Cotton's reign may not last long.

APPLICATION 1-4

Should Your Company Support a Lobbying Effort to Reduce the Price of an Input?

Your company uses a raw material, A, to produce product X. Over the last five years the price of A has grown rapidly and so has the cost of producing X. The CEOs of several leading companies in industry X want to end the upward cost spiral. They argue that the cost of producing X will decline if they can obtain congressional approval to lower the price of A. If the cost of producing X declines, the producers of X expect a temporary benefit because the price of X will not decrease immediately by the full amount of the cost reduction. You are invited to join the campaign and support the lobbying effort.

The idea sounds good, so you ask your staff to study the possible effects of a price ceiling. The majority of your staff members support the idea. They think that any policy that reduces the cost of X will benefit the company, basing this conclusions on the following reasoning. Before a price ceiling is imposed, the demand and supply functions for A are D_A and S_A in Figure 1-11a, and the equilibrium price

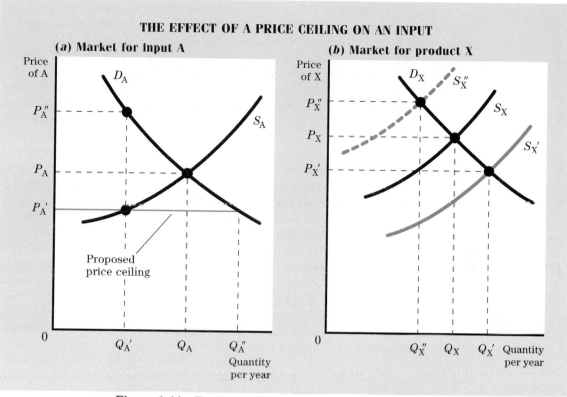

THE EFFECT OF A PRICE CEILING ON AN INPUT

(a) Market for input A   **(b) Market for product X**

Figure 1-11   The effect of a price ceiling on an input causes the price of the final good to rise, not fall. A price ceiling of P_A' is placed on an input, and the quantity supplied of A decreases to Q_A'. Demanders then incur added costs to acquire the limited supply of Q_A'. The difference between P_A'' and P_A' represents the added cost incurred by firms to acquire Q_A', which increases the cost of producing X. The supply curve of X shifts upward and to the left, and the price of X increases because of the price ceiling.

of A is P_A. The demand and supply functions for X are D_X and S_X in Figure 1-11*b*, and the equilibrium price of X is P_X. By imposing a price ceiling of P_A', the price of A, and the cost of producing X, decreases. The majority argue that this will cause the supply function of X to shift to the right from S_X to S_X'. They claim that the equilibrium price of X will decline to P_X' and that the equilibrium quantity will increase to Q_X'. Consequently, they recommend that the firm support the lobbying effort.

There is one dissenter, however. She believes that the argument of the majority has a fundamental weakness. (Try to guess what it is before reading on.) She thinks that producers of A will react to the price ceiling by supplying only Q_A' (movement along the supply function for A in Figure 1-11*a*). Given the excess demand, our company will fare poorly unless it's better than other input buyers in getting the limited quantities. What puzzles her is that the argument of the majority implies that more of X is produced (the quantity of X will go from Q_X to Q_X') although the production of A declines. She does not believe this will happen and thinks the argument of the majority is illogical. She maintains that the firm should not sign on to the lobbying campaign, her basic point being that any policy that reduces the output of an important input will only harm the company.

Would you side with the majority, or are the points raised by the dissenter valid? What will happen when a price ceiling is introduced? At first the price ceiling creates an excess demand of $Q_A'' - Q_A'$. Then market forces begin to eliminate the excess demand. Let us assume that the government enforces a price ceiling. This means a supplier of A cannot obtain a price higher than P_A'. Clearly, there is a potential for waiting lines to develop. At the ceiling price producers supply only Q_A' units of A. The demand function says that demanders of A are willing to pay up to P_A'' for Q_A' units of A and will adopt all kinds of tactics to increase their chances of getting their hands on Q_A'. They will have their buyers on the telephone, courting the suppliers of A as they try to obtain the limited quantities of A. The entertainment budgets of demanders will soar, and they might even offer bribes.

Of course, these tactics are not cost-free, and they raise the real price of A. Not only do demanders have to pay P_A' to suppliers who have access to the limited supply of A, but they must also incur the added cost of courting suppliers. These practices raise the price of A to demanders of A. The intense competition for the limited supply of A could raise the "effective" price of A to P_A'' and in this way ration Q_A' among potential buyers. Under this scenario, the introduction of a price ceiling, far from lowering the price of A, will cause the effective price to increase. If so, the supply function of X shifts to the left to S_X'' and the quantity of X produced declines from Q_X to Q_X''. Under this scenario a price ceiling on an input, which at first looks so advantageous to the firm, turns out to be harmful.

This situation can occur where there are regulated prices. An interesting example is rent control for apartment buildings. Lucky renters find with time that they live in valuable apartments: the regulated rent is well below the market clearing rent. Because of rent control, builders may construct fewer apartments, and the stock of rental housing may decline or grow less rapidly. Current renters may receive attractive offers to sublease their apartments—these offers are sometimes called "key money." Since the current renter cannot sublease the apartment at a higher rent, the market clears by setting an artificially high price for the apartment key. Of course, landlords oppose rent control since the original renters benefit and not the landlords, who continue to receive the regulated rent.

Another example of a price ceiling is federal regulation of natural gas prices in interstate commerce. These regulations created a serious excess demand problem when manufacturers of goods found that they could not obtain supplies of natural gas. Gas producers supplied less natural gas to interstate pipeline companies, and in turn, these companies supplied less natural gas to manufacturers with contracts that permitted the pipeline company to interrupt service. Curtailment of natural gas deliveries increased substantially from 1,031 billion cubic feet in 1972–1973 to 3,770 in 1976–1977. Manufacturers not only had more difficulty finding natural gas, but were forced to substitute more expensive energy such as oil or electricity.

1-6   THE PRICE ELASTICITY OF DEMAND AND SUPPLY

To this point, we have used the demand and supply model to predict changes in the behavior of demanders and suppliers when either the demand or supply function shifts or when a market is out of equilibrium. Now we revisit the demand and supply functions and introduce measures that conveniently summarize the sensitivity of the quantity demanded or supplied to a change in the price.

The sensitivity of the quantity demanded to a price change differs enormously from product to product as the following two examples show. If American Airlines increases the air fare from Chicago to Los Angeles while other airlines do not, the number of passengers on American's flights will fall precipitously because many passengers will switch to lower-priced airlines. A small percentage price increase causes a relatively large drop in the quantity demanded. On the other hand, if a publisher raises the price of a textbook, many instructors will continue to assign the book and often be unaware of the price increase or learn about it only later. Although a few instructors will select substitute books, the overall effect will be a small percentage decline in the quantity demanded relative to the percentage price increase. The different quantitative responses to a price change reflect the different shapes of the demand functions.

Why is it important to know how sensitive the quantity demanded is to a change in price? Because this sensitivity signals how much the firm's total revenue will increase or decrease in response to a price change. If a cereal manufacturer cuts prices by 10 percent but the quantity demanded increases by only 2 percent, the cereal firm's total revenue will be lower at the lower price. Whether total revenue increases or decreases depends on how large the percentage change in the quantity demanded is relative to the percentage change in price. The price elasticity of demand is a simple and useful way of determining whether revenue will rise or fall.

Price Elasticity of Demand

The *price elasticity of demand* measures the percentage change in quantity relative to the percentage change in price. If the percentage change in the quantity demanded is larger than the percentage change in price, then total revenue will change in the opposite direction to the price change. Returning to the cereal example from before, if a cereal manufacturer cuts price by 10 percent and the quantity demanded increases by 12 percent, the cereal firm will earn more total revenue than before.

> The **price elasticity of demand** measures the percentage change in the quantity demanded relative to the percentage change in price.

To see this, consider Figure 1-12. Let the demand function for a product that the firm sells be *DD*. If the price is P_1, the quantity demanded is Q_1. The total revenue R the firm receives equals the price per unit times the quantity demanded:

$$R = PQ \qquad \text{(Total Revenue)} \tag{1-5}$$

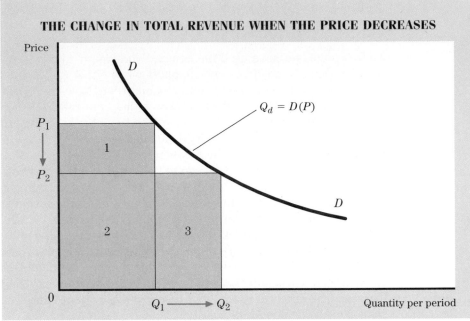

Figure 1-12   When the price is reduced from P_1 to P_2, the quantity demanded increases from Q_1 to Q_2. Total revenue may be higher, lower, or the same after the price is reduced. Area 1 represents the loss in revenue because demanders who would have paid P_1 purchase the product at the lower price of P_2. Area 3 represents the increase in revenue because the lower price increases the total quantity demanded from Q_1 to Q_2.

If the price is P_1, $R = P_1Q_1$, the sum of areas 1 and 2. When the price falls to P_2, the quantity demanded increases to Q_2. Total revenue is now $R = P_2Q_2$ or the sum of areas 2 and 3. The change in total revenue received by the firm is the net effect of two opposing changes. At the higher price of P_1 the quantity demanded is only Q_1 units. At the lower price of P_2, demanders who would purchase Q_1 units at the higher price can purchase them at the lower price of P_2. This effect reduces total revenue, and the size of the loss is equal to area 1. At the lower price of P_2 the firm can now sell more units because the quantity demanded increases from Q_1 to Q_2. This effect increases total revenue, and the size of the increase is equal to area 3. Whether a price change increases or decreases total revenue depends on the relative sizes of these two opposing effects, area 1 compared to area 3.

Using this analysis, we can describe the response of revenue to a change in price as follows:

1. If the total revenue changes in the direction opposite the price change (e.g., total revenue decreases when price increases), the demand is **price-elastic.**

2. If the total revenue does not change when the price changes, the demand has **unitary elasticity.**

3. If the total revenue changes in the same direction that the price changes (e.g., total revenue increases when price increases), the demand is **price-inelastic.**

To calculate the numerical value of the price elasticity, economists use different measures depending on whether the price change is tiny or large. For tiny price changes, economists use the point price elasticity of demand; for large price changes, they use the arc price elasticity.

Point Price Elasticity of Demand

The **point price elasticity of demand** measures the sensitivity of the quantity demanded relative to a tiny price change starting at *a point* on the demand function. For a tiny change in price of ΔP, consider the resulting percentage change in the quantity demanded, $\Delta Q/Q$, relative to the percentage change in price, $\Delta P/P$. The expression for the point price elasticity of demand, E_P, is

$$E_P = \frac{\dfrac{\Delta Q}{Q}}{\dfrac{\Delta P}{P}} \qquad \text{(Point Elasticity of Demand)} \qquad \textbf{(1-6)}$$

One immediate point to notice is that the sign of the point price elasticity of demand is negative: recall from the law of demand that a price decrease increases the quantity demanded so that ΔP and ΔQ are of opposite signs. Suppose price decreases from \$10 to \$9.90 so the percentage price decrease is $-.10/\$10 = -.01$, or 1 percent, and the quantity demanded increases from 20 units to 22 units so the percentage change in the quantity demand is $2/20 = .10$, or 10 percent. Using the formula, the point price elasticity of demand equals -10, meaning that a 1 percent price decrease causes a 10 percent increase in the quantity demanded. In this example, the quantity demanded is relatively sensitive to a tiny percentage price change.

Although the numerical value of the price elasticity is negative, readers should be aware that economists sometimes use the terms high and low price elasticity to refer to price *elastic* and *inelastic* demand respectively. Thus a good with $E_P < -1$ has a relatively high elasticity of demand (price-elastic), while a good with $0 > E_p > -1$ has a relatively low elasticity of demand (price-inelastic). An easy way to resolve this apparent contradiction is to define price-elastic as the absolute value of the price elasticity $|E_P| > 1$ and price-inelastic demand as $|E_P| < 1$. So a price elasticity of -10 would be referred to as a high price elasticity. A price elasticity of $-.8$ for gasoline would be referred to as a low price elasticity. When we say the price elasticity is high or low, we are referring to the absolute value of the price elasticity.

By reworking the formula for the point price elasticity, we can emphasize a second point—the point price elasticity is not equal to the slope of the demand function. The formula for the point price elasticity can be rewritten as

$$E_P = \frac{\Delta Q}{\Delta P} \frac{P}{Q} \qquad \qquad \textbf{(1-6}a\textbf{)}$$

This expression shows that the point price elasticity equals $\Delta Q/\Delta P$, which is the slope of the demand function $Q_d = D(P)$,[6] *times* the ratio of price to the quantity demanded.[7] You want to exercise care and avoid a common mistake when calculating the price elasticity. Since price is plotted on the vertical axis in the figures, the slope of the demand curves in the figures is $\Delta P/\Delta Q$. The slope that is required to calculate the price elasticity in equation 1-6a is however $\Delta Q/\Delta P$ which is equal to $1/\Delta P/\Delta Q$. For example, suppose the demand function is expressed as $P = 1,000 - 4Q$. The slope $\Delta P/\Delta Q$ of this linear equation is -4. The required slope to calculate the price elasticity is $\Delta Q/\Delta P$, which equals $-1/4$.

Even if the slope of the demand function is constant, P/Q will change as the price increases or decreases (movement along the demand function). Except for some special cases, the numerical value of the price elasticity is different at different points on the demand function since $\Delta Q/\Delta P$ and/or P/Q change. At the risk of belaboring this point, we remind you that the point price elasticity does not equal the slope of the demand function but equals the demand function's slope *times* P/Q.

Arc Price Elasticity of Demand

The **arc price elasticity of demand** also measures the percentage change in quantity relative to the percentage change in price but the method of calculating the percentage changes is slightly different. Economists use the arc price elasticity concept when *the price change is large.* For example, a university would use the arc price elasticity to determine if total tuition income will rise or fall after student tuition is raised from \$8,000 to \$9,000 per year, or by more than 12 percent. The formula for the arc price elasticity is

$$E_P = \frac{\dfrac{\Delta Q}{(Q_1 + Q_2)/2}}{\dfrac{\Delta P}{(P_1 + P_2)/2}} \qquad \text{(Arc Price Elasticity of Demand)} \qquad \textbf{(1-7)}$$

---

[6] Or the reciprocal of the slope of the *inverse demand function* $P = D(Q_d)$, which by convention is illustrated in all figures throughout this book.

[7] As ΔP becomes smaller and smaller, the expression for the point price elasticity becomes $E_P = dQ/dP \, P/Q$ where dQ/dP is the slope of demand function at a point on the demand function where price is P and the quantity demanded is Q.

The arc price elasticity is the ratio of two magnitudes that resemble but are not exactly equal to percentage changes. The numerator in the formula is the change in the quantity demanded (ΔQ) divided by the average of the two quantities demanded at the two prices, $(Q_1 + Q_2)/2$, and the denominator is the change in the price (ΔP) divided by the average of the two prices, $(P_1 + P_2)/2$. The numerator is the average percentage change in the quantity demanded, while the denominator is the average percentage change in price.

> The **arc price elasticity** equals the change in quantity relative to the average quantity demanded divided by the change in price relative to the average price.

The fraction in the formula for the arc price elasticity can be simplified for easier calculation.

$$E_P = \frac{\dfrac{\Delta Q}{(Q_1 + Q_2)/2}}{\dfrac{\Delta P}{(P_1 + P_2)/2}} = \frac{\dfrac{2\,\Delta Q}{Q_1 + Q_2}}{\dfrac{2\,\Delta P}{P_1 + P_2}} \qquad (1\text{-}7a)$$

Multiplying the numerator and the denominator by $\frac{1}{2}$ yields

$$E_P = \frac{\Delta Q/(Q_1 + Q_2)}{\Delta P/(P_1 + P_2)} = \frac{\Delta Q}{\Delta P}\frac{P_1 + P_2}{Q_1 + Q_2} \qquad (1\text{-}7b)$$

Two points should be noted about the last expression in equation 1-7b. First, the numerical value of the arc elasticity is always negative because $\Delta Q/\Delta P$ is negative; the quantity demanded changes in the direction opposite the price change. Second, the arc price elasticity is the slope of the demand function between the two points ($\Delta Q/\Delta P$) times a factor equal to the sum of the two prices divided by the sum of the two quantities. Therefore, the arc price elasticity is *not* equal to the slope of the demand function. A straight-line demand function has a constant slope, but the value of the arc price elasticity changes because $(P_1 + P_2)/(Q_1 + Q_2)$ changes when moving along a straight-line demand function.[8]

The numerical value of the arc price elasticity will determine which way total revenue changs when price changes. There are three possible outcomes to keep in mind:

---

[8] A straight-line (linear) demand function can be expressed as

$$Q = a - bP$$

where a and b are constants. The slope of the demand function is

$$\frac{\Delta Q}{\Delta P} = -b$$

Therefore, the slope of a linear demand function is constant and independent of price. The arc price elasticity for a linear demand function is

$$E_P = -b\,\frac{P_1 + P_2}{Q_1 + Q_2}$$

Table 1-2   REVENUE CHANGES DUE TO A PRICE CHANGE FOR DIFFERENT VALUES OF ARC PRICE ELASTICITY

PRICE ELASTICITY, E_P	PRICE CHANGE, ΔP	REVENUE CHANGE, ΔR
Price-elastic, $E_P < -1$	$\Delta P > 0$	$\Delta R < 0$
	$\Delta P < 0$	$\Delta R > 0$
Unitary, $E_P = -1$	$\Delta P > 0$	$\Delta R = 0$
	$\Delta P < 0$	$\Delta R = 0$
Price-inelastic, $0 > E_P > -1$	$\Delta P > 0$	$\Delta R > 0$
	$\Delta P < 0$	$\Delta R < 0$

1. If the value of the arc price elasticity is *less than* -1, the demand is *price-elastic* and the total revenue changes in the direction opposite the price change.[9] A decrease in price increases total revenue.

2. If the value of the arc price elasticity is *equal to* -1, the demand has *unitary elasticity*. A price change does not change total revenue.

3. If the value of the arc price elasticity is *between* -1 *and 0*, the demand is *price-inelastic*. This means that total revenue changes in the same direction as the price change. A decrease in price decreases total revenue.

Table 1-2 summarizes how total revenue changes for increases and decreases in price when the demand is price-elastic, has unitary elasticity, or is price-inelastic.

Footnote 9 proves that total revenue increases when price decreases if the arc price elasticity is less than -1. By using similar reasoning, it can be shown that

---

[9] For example, we want to show that total revenue increases when price decreases if $E_P < -1$. If E_P is less than -1, then

$$E_P = \frac{(Q_2 - Q_1)(P_1 + P_2)}{(P_2 - P_1)(Q_1 + Q_2)} < -1$$

where $\Delta Q = Q_2 - Q_1$ and $\Delta P = P_2 - P_1$. Because $P_2 - P_1$ is negative, multiplying both sides of the inequality by $(P_2 - P_1)(Q_1 + Q_2)$, a negative number, reverses the inequality and yields

$$(Q_2 - Q_1)(P_1 + P_2) > -(P_2 - P_1)(Q_1 + Q_2)$$

Expanding both sides of the inequality results in

$$P_1 Q_2 - P_1 Q_1 + P_2 Q_2 - P_2 Q_1 > -P_2 Q_1 + P_1 Q_1 - P_2 Q_2 + P_1 Q_2$$

Adding $P_2 Q_1$ and subtracting $P_1 Q_2$ on both sides of the inequality, and dividing both sides by 2, yields

$$P_2 Q_2 > P_1 Q_1$$

If $E_P < -1$, $P_2 Q_2 > P_1 Q_1$, and so the total revenue increases when the price falls from P_1 to P_2. Demand is price-elastic. Similar derivations would show that $P_2 Q_2 = P_1 Q_1$ when $E_P = -1$, and $P_2 Q_2 < P_1 Q_1$ when $E_P > -1$.

total revenue remains constant if the arc price elasticity equals -1 and total revenue increases when price increases if the arc price elasticity is greater than -1. For example, recent statistical studies estimate that the price elasticity for cigarettes is around $-.7$ or $-.8$. A general price increase will therefore increase the total revenue of cigarette companies.

Let's apply the formula for arc price elasticity by working through an example. A manufacturer of in-line skates wants to know whether demand is price-elastic or price-inelastic. Consumers were asked in a survey to report how many skates they would demand at different prices. The responses are shown in Table 1-3.

Is the demand for skates price-elastic or price-inelastic? This question does not have a simple yes or no answer because it depends on which two prices are being compared.

If the price drops from $200 to $150, the quantity demanded increases from 14,000 to 38,000 skates. When the price is $200, total revenue is $200 \times 14,000 = $2.8 million. If the price is $150, the total revenue is $150 \times 38,000 = $5.7 million. A price cut increases total revenue, and so demand is price-elastic between $200 and $150.

We can use the formula for the arc price elasticity in equation 1-7b to calculate the numerical value:

$$E_P = \frac{\Delta Q}{\Delta P} \frac{P_1 + P_2}{Q_1 + Q_2}$$

$\Delta Q = 38,000 - 14,000 = 24,000$ skates, and $\Delta P = \$150 - \$200 = -\$50$. So, $\Delta Q/\Delta P = 24,000/-\$50. P_1 + P_2 - \$350$, and $(Q_1 + Q_2) = 52,000$ units. Therefore, the value of the arc price elasticity is

$$E_P = \frac{24}{-\$50} \times \frac{\$350}{52} = \frac{6}{-\$1} \times \frac{\$7}{13}$$

$$= \frac{\$42}{-\$13} = -3.23$$

Since the estimated arc elasticity of -3.23 is less than -1, demand is price-elastic between $150 and $200. Just because demand is price-elastic between $200 and $150 does not mean that it is price-elastic for all pairs of prices. The price

Table 1-3   THE DEMAND FOR IN-LINE SKATES

PRICE OF IN-LINE SKATES ($)	QUANTITY OF IN-LINE SKATES DEMANDED (THOUSANDS)
200	14
150	38
100	56
50	66

elasticity usually changes in moving along a given demand function. To check this, calculate the arc price elasticity when the price decreases from $100 to $50. You should find the estimate of the price elasticity is -0.25. Demand is price-inelastic so total revenue decreases when the price decreases from $100 to $50.

When estimating the price elasticity for a product by using observed prices and quantities, you must take care to use only observations from two different points on the *same* demand function. You must be reasonably certain that the price-quantity pairs used to calculate the price elasticity come from the same demand function. If you derive an estimate of the price elasticity from price-quantity pairs on two different demand functions, your estimate of the price elasticity will be inaccurate. You are erroneously attributing all the increase in the quantity demanded to the price reduction. For example, suppose the demand function for vacations shifts because the incomes of consumers increase just when the price decreases because of lower travel costs. Part of the increase in the quantity demanded is due to the lower price, a movement along the demand curve, but part of the increase is due to the increase in income that *shifts* the demand function to the right. Your estimate of the price elasticity will be wrong because it reflects both changes, whereas the arc price elasticity measures only the effect of the price change on the quantity demanded on a given demand function. You might infer demand is price-elastic and lower the price to increase total revenue when demand is actually price-inelastic. By relying on the incorrect estimate you could easily make a pricing mistake.

APPLICATION **1-5**

The Price Elasticity of Demand for First Class Mail

Economist Frank Wolak has estimated the household sector's price elasticity of demand for first class postal service and found that the price elasticity is becoming more elastic over time.[10] Table 1-4 shows the price elasticity estimates from 1986 to 1994. According to Wolak's elasticity estimates, demand was price-inelastic in

[10] Frank Wolak, "Changes in the Household-Level Demand for Postal Delivery Services from 1986 to 1994," Center for Economic Policy Research Publication, Number 464, Stanford Univeristy, May 1996, unpublished paper.

Table 1-4   **PRICE ELASTICITY FOR FIRST CLASS MAIL, 1986–94**

YEAR	PRICE ELASTICITY	YEAR	PRICE ELASTICITY
1986	$-.857$	1992	-1.06
1988	$-.925$	1994	-1.13
1990	$-.992$		

1986 so the postal service could have raised the price of a first class stamp and expected total revenue to increase. However, the price elasticity changed so that by 1990 it was near -1 so revenue would not change much if the postal service increased price. By 1994 demand had become price-elastic so the postal service can no longer find more revenue from the household sector by raising the price of a first class stamp. It appears that feasible pricing options of the postal service are becoming more limited over time.

Determinants of the Price Elasticity of Demand

Several factors affect the size of the price elasticity.

1. If each demander spends a small percent of his or her total income on the product, then the demand for the product will be price-inelastic. A consumer may spend much time and effort getting the best price for a $20,000 automobile but later pay virtually the quoted price to have rear mud flaps installed on the new car.

2. Another important determinant of the price elasticity is the number of equivalent products available. If there are many substitute products, demand will be more price-elastic. A small rise in price will cause massive substitution by consumers toward nearly equivalent products. Low-cost airlines make the demand for established carriers more elastic.

3. Goods for which consumers spend an increasing proportion of their income as their income increases also have more elastic demand functions, holding other factors constant.

4. The price elasticity of demand can change over time as consumers obtain more information about substitute products. Often the demand function becomes more price-elastic over time. An unexpected price increase may not cause the quantity demanded to fall by much immediately. Users of the product will not know of alternative products or suppliers and therefore will not reduce the quantity demanded by much in the short run. Given more time, buyers will search out and find alternative products. So in the long run, the quantity demanded decreases by more because of the initial price increase. A price increase that looks very successful to a firm in the short run may prove to be a mistake in the long run.

Figure 1-13 shows how the demand function rotates around the original equilibrium point over time because price increases from P_1 to P_2. Initially the demand function is DD and the price is P_1, and so the quantity demanded is Q_1. Now suppose the price increases from P_1 to P_2. Because of the increase, consumers reduce the quantity demanded modestly to Q_2 at first. If the price increase catches them unprepared, they bear it in the short run. As demanders investigate and find alternatives for this product, the demand function becomes more price-elastic. It changes position and becomes the long-run demand function labeled $D'D'$. The long-run demand function has become price-elastic between the prices of P_1 and P_2. In the long run the price increase causes the quantity demanded to decrease to Q_3.

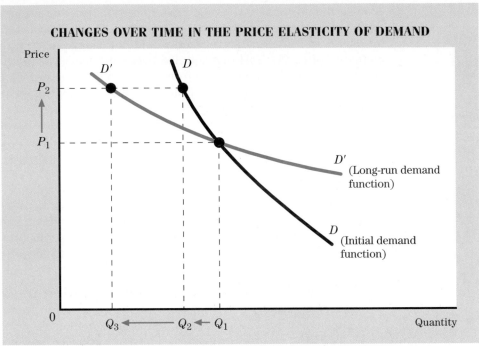

Figure 1-13   The initial demand curve is *DD*. A price increase from P_1 to P_2 causes
the quantity demanded to decrease from Q_1 to Q_2. The long-run demand curve is $D'D'$
and is more elastic than *DD*. Given sufficient time for demanders to find equivalent
products, the demand curve becomes more elastic in the long run and the quantity
demanded decreases from Q_2 to Q_3.

The events following the quadrupling of oil prices in 1974 demonstrate the
difference between immediate and longer-term effects of a price increase. At first,
the quantity demanded of gasoline declined modestly. Up until then, statistical
models had estimated the demand for gasoline to be price-inelastic, with small
price elasticities of about -0.2 to -0.4. Oil company executives and economists
thought that Americans would never alter their driving habits and many predicted
that the quantity demanded would fall only modestly when gasoline prices increased. However, the rise in the price of gasoline resulted in a number of long-
run substitutions. The size of cars decreased and mileage per gallon increased.
Consumers began to use their automobiles more efficiently by planning fewer
shopping trips, economizing on the use of gasoline, and taking shorter vacation
trips. Over time, the quantity demanded decreased by a larger percentage, and the
size of the decrease surprised even some experts in the oil industry.

Price Elasticity of Supply

The quantity supplied changes when the price changes. For some products the
change in the quantity supplied is modest when the price increases, but for others
it is larger. The price elasticity of supply measures the sensitivity of the quantity

supplied to a price change. You will recall that the price of cut roses increased more than the price of chocolates on Valentine's Day because the supply function of roses is less sensitive to price (less elastic) than the supply function of chocolates.

> The **price elasticity of supply** measures the percentage change in the quantity supplied relative to the percentage change in price.

Just as there are two measures for the price elasticity of demand, economists use point and arc price elasticities on the supply side depending on whether the price changes are tiny or large. The **price elasticity of supply** measures the percentage change in the quantity supplied due to the percentage change in price. Since the quantity supplied usually increases at a higher price, the price elasticity of supply is usually positive unlike the price elasticity of demand, which is negative.

The **point price elasticity of supply** measures the sensitivity of the quantity supplied to a price change at a point on the supply function. For a tiny price change of ΔP and the resulting change of ΔQ, the expression for the point price elasticity of supply, N_P, is

$$N_P = \frac{\frac{\Delta Q}{Q}}{\frac{\Delta P}{P}} = \frac{\Delta Q}{\Delta P}\frac{P}{Q} \qquad \text{(Point Price Elasticity of Supply)} \qquad \textbf{(1-8)}$$

The formula for the arc price elasticity of supply (N_P) describes the relative responsiveness of the quantity supplied to a price change between two points on the supply function. The same formula is used for the arc price elasticity of supply as for the arc price elasticity of demand:

$$N_P = \frac{\frac{\Delta Q}{(Q_1 + Q_2)/2}}{\frac{\Delta P}{(P_1 + P_2)/2}} \qquad \text{(Arc Price Elasticity of Supply)} \qquad \textbf{(1-9)}$$

$$= \frac{\Delta Q}{\Delta P}\frac{P_1 + P_2}{Q_1 + Q_2}$$

Although the formulas for the price elasticities are identical, their application sets the price elasticity of supply apart from the price elasticity of demand. The observations for price and quantity come from two points on the supply function, not on the demand function.

The arc price elasticity of supply equals the change in quantity relative to the quantity supplied divided by the change in price relative to the average price. As long as the supply function has a positive slope, the numerical value of the price elasticity of supply is positive. If the quantity supplied barely changes when the price changes, the price elasticity of supply is close to zero. In this case the supply function is steeper—more like the supply function for cut roses in Figure 1-8. As the quantity supplied becomes more sensitive to a price change, the price elasticity of supply becomes a larger positive number—more like the supply function for chocolates in Figure 1-8.[11]

SUMMARY

■ The quantity demanded and the quantity supplied depend on the price of the product.

■ The demand function shows how the quantity demanded varies with the price of the product. The law of demand states that the quantity demanded is inversely related to the price of the product.

■ A change in the income of households, in the price of substitutes or complements, or in the tastes of consumers shifts the position of the demand function.

■ The market supply function shows how the quantity supplied changes as the price changes. The supply function shifts if the price of an input changes or if there is a technological innovation.

■ Market equilibrium exists when the market price equates the quantity demanded with the quantity supplied. At other prices there is either an excess supply or an excess demand and the price changes in the direction of reducing the excess.

■ Shortages or surpluses can exist if prices do not or cannot adjust to excess demand or excess supply.

■ The numerical value of the price elasticity of demand determines whether total revenue increases, decreases, or stays the same when the price of a product changes. If the price elasticity is less than -1, demand is price-elastic and total revenue changes in the direction opposite the change in price. If the price elasticity is -1, demand has unitary elasticity and total revenue does not change when the price changes. If the price elasticity is greater than -1, demand is price-inelastic and total revenue changes in the same direction as the change in price.

■ The price elasticity of supply shows the sensitivity of the quantity supplied to a price change. As long as the supply function has a positive slope, the price elasticity of supply is positive.

KEY TERMS

demand and supply model
quantity demanded and movement along a
    demand function
law of demand
market equilibrium
quantity supplied and movement along a
    supply function
equilibrium price and quantity
point and arc price elasticity of demand or
    supply

demand function
shift in the demand function
supply function
shift in the supply function
excess demand and supply
price-elastic, unitary, and price-inelastic
    demand

---

[11] In other words, the price elasticity is low when $0 < N_P < 1$, it is of unitary elasticity when $N_P = 1$, and it is high when $N_P > 1$.

REVIEW QUESTIONS

1. Describe what the demand and supply functions represent.
2. What is the meaning of an equilibrium price and quantity?
3. Movement along the demand function involves a change in the price of a product, whereas a shift in the position of the demand function involves a change in the price of another good. Explain why you agree or disagree with this statement.
4. If price does not change, the market equilibrium has not changed. Explain why you agree or disagree.
5. What causes shifts in the demand function? in the supply function?
6. Because a fall in consumer income shifts the demand function inward, consumers may nevertheless demand the same quantity of a good if the price of the good falls. Explain why you agree or disagree with this statement.
7. More turkeys are eaten on Thanksgiving Day than on any other day of the year. Yet, the price per pound of turkey barely changes around Thanksgiving; for this to happen, the supply function of turkeys must shift outward. Explain why you agree or disagree with this statement.
8. Explain which of the following events represent movement along a demand function or a shift in the demand function for a box of tissues.
   a. A technological change reduces the cost of paper.
   b. The ski season begins when the temperature falls below freezing.
   c. The prices of cold remedies increase.
   d. A restriction is placed on the number of trees that can be cut.
9. The demand function for electrical engineers has increased relative to the demand function for civil engineers. If the salary of electrical engineers has not increased relative to the salary of civil engineers, what

does this say about the shapes of the supply functions of electrical engineers? Can you give some reasons why the supply function has this shape?

10. If favorable weather shifts the supply function for wheat outward by 10 percent at each price, then favorable weather will increase the equilibrium quantity of wheat by less than 10 percent. What shape must the supply function have for this statement to be true? Provide an economic explanation of why the supply function shifts by more than the equilibrium quantity.
11. If the price of a product increases by 20 percent and the quantity demanded decreases by 20 percent, demand is unit elastic. Use the formula for the arc price elasticity of demand to calculate the price elasticity and explain why you agree or disagree with this statement.
12. Price falls from $200 to $180. What is the required percentage increase in quantity so that total revenue is constant?
13. If a surplus appears when the supply function decreases less than the demand function at the price paid in the recent past, then a surplus reveals itself by a fall in price and a rise in the quantity consumed. Do you agree or disagree with this statement?
14. Comment critically on this statement: A decline in coffee imports and increased retail demand for coffee because of lower retail coffee prices explain why consumers are drinking less coffee.
15. It is legal to give permission to *donate* parts of your body to others after death. It is illegal for individuals to *sell* parts of their bodies to others. Use the demand and supply model to predict the consequences of this ban.
16. Toronto, Canada, has a rent ceiling on apartments. Individuals hoping to sublease a rent-controlled apartment adver-

tise or distribute leaflets in a building that they like, offering a cash reward—called key money—for anyone willing to sublease their apartment. Use the demand and supply model to explain this practice. What determines the amount of the key money?

17. In the figure below two supply functions have the same slope. Which supply function has the smaller point price elasticity of supply at the price of P? Explain your answer.

18. The point price elasticity or demand for first class postal service declined from $-.857$ in 1986 to -1.13 in 1994. What reasons would you give to explain why postal demand is becoming more price-elastic?

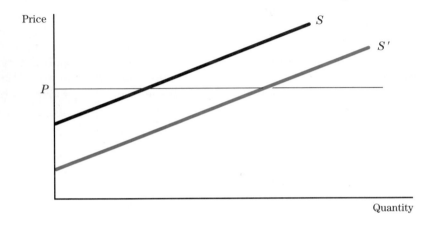

EXERCISES

1. The figure below shows two demand functions, DD and $D'D'$. At each price the quantity demanded is greater on $D'D'$ than on DD. Given these demand functions, can you say that a shortage is more likely if the demand function is $D'D'$ and that a surplus is more likely if the demand function is DD? Explain why or why not.

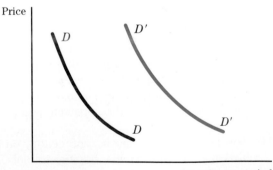

2. The demand function for a product is a straight line and is $Q = 1,000 - 4P$. Calculate the point price elasticity when the price is $25, and when it is $200. (For those students whose calculus is rusty, the slope of the linear demand function is constant and equals -4.) Is total revenue higher or lower at the lower price?

3. A mass transit district is facing a financial crisis. Because no further subsidies are available from either the city or the state, it has increased fares by 75 percent. After the first year of the fare increase, the district reports a revenue increase of 52 percent.
   a. Using these figures, estimate the percentage drop in riders because of the fare increase.
   b. Give an estimate of the arc price elasticity of demand.

4. If the government places a per unit tax on the production of a good, the price of the product will increase and the quantity supplied by producers will increase because the producer will receive a higher price. Explain why you agree or disagree with this statement. (*Hint:* Show what happens to the supply function when the government levies a per unit tax on suppliers. Before the tax, suppliers offer Q at each P. What price must they receive after the government imposes the tax if they are still willing to offer the same Q?)

5. In Application 1-3 the rise in the price of cotton is caused by the inward shift in the Asian supply curve of cotton and not an increase in the demand for cotton. What evidence presented in Application 1-3 is inconsistent with the demand shift hypothesis?

*6. In March 1994 the United Steelworkers union went on strike at Wheeling-Pittsburgh, the nation's 10th-largest steel manufacturer. Industry analysts did not think that the other domestic steel makers could benefit from the strike because they were already operating at or near full capacity. As one analyst noted, "Everybody is out of flat rolled steel so imports will have to fill the void." If the other domestic steel producers do not benefit from the strike, what are the analysts assuming about the shape of the import supply function? Draw the supply function of steel.

*7. In the spring of 1996 U.S. gasoline prices increased sharply owing to increased demand and an unusually cold spring that delayed U.S. refiners' shifting from production of heating oil to production of gasoline. The higher prices caused daily gasoline imports from Europe to increase. Upon learning of the rise in gasoline imports, several observers of the gasoline market predicted that the rise in imports will cause U.S. gasoline prices to fall.

   a. According to the information above, what is the shape of the supply function for gasoline imports?

   b. Explain why the rise in imports will or will not cause U.S. gasoline prices to fall.

   c. What would happen to U.S. gasoline prices and the quantity of gasoline imports if the transportation cost of shipping gasoline from Europe to the U.S. falls? Use a graph to show the effect of a fall in transport costs on the equilibrium price and quantity.

8. Suppose an agnostic disputed the law of demand—that the market demand function slopes down—and claimed that the market demand function for in-line skates slopes upward. How would you convince him or her otherwise? One way to convince the agnostic is to develop predictions of a model with an upward sloping demand function and see if they are supported by evidence. On a graph draw a market demand function that is upward sloping. Draw a supply function that intersects the demand function so that there is an excess supply at prices above the equilibrium price. What does this model predict will happen to the equilibrium price and quantity if the cost of production of in-line skates falls and the supply function shifts to the right? Now compare these predictions with those from a model where the market demand function slopes downward. Can you bring some evidence to bear on the issue? Can you think of any industries where the supply function has shifted to the right? What has happened to price and quantity? Does the evidence support the model with a downward sloping demand function or the agnostic's model?

PROBLEM SET

Estimating the Price Elasticity of Demand

You have been appointed manager of a division that sells replacement parts for air conditioners to wholesalers. The division has been losing money during the last two years, and your mandate is to turn the situation around quickly.

You decide to examine all aspects of the division's performance. You appoint five members to a pricing committee and ask them to recommend a procedure for reviewing the pricing decisions for major parts sold by the division. The committee is to report back in two weeks so that a comprehensive review of the pricing of all parts can begin.

The pricing committee submits the report as requested, but because of the limited amount of time it restricts the review to a few parts whose prices have changed during the last four years. The committee members propose the following procedure to determine whether the firm should raise or lower the price of individual parts.

Recommended Methodology

The committee uses part 1006 to illustrate the recommended procedure.

- *Step 1.* Review the past pricing history to determine when the price changed. The price history of part 1006 reveals the price was $20 per unit until April 1, 1993, when it increased by 50 percent to $30.
- *Step 2.* Assemble monthly sales data (in 1,000 units) to determine how the quantity sold responded to the price change. The sales history of part 1006 from 1992 to 1995 is shown in the accompanying table.
- *Step 3.* Calculate a price elasticity of demand.

MONTH	1992	1993	1994	1995
January	12	14	12	7
February	13	13	15	8
March	18	20	16	11
April	25	23	18	14
May	29	27	20	19
June	32	30	23	24
July	42	33	26	26
August	48	31	29	31
September	38	28	24	26
October	38	25	18	23
November	20	14	12	14
December	10	9	5	7

The committee cannot agree on how to implement the procedure. They disagree about which quantity data should be used to calculate the price elasticity. Two different proposals are being considered.

- *Proposal 1.* Three members suggest that the price elasticity should be calculated by comparing cumulative sales during the six months before the price increase with cumulative sales during the first six months after the price increase. They argue that the figures for less than six months may contain too many random effects that will distort the price elasticity estimates. If data for more than six months are used to calculate the elasticity, they fear that the assumption that other variables are constant would be violated.
- *Proposal 2.* Two members recommend that cumulative sales for the 12 months before the price increase be compared with cumulative sales for the 12 months after the price increase.

Questions

1. Calculate the price elasticities using the two recommended procedures.
2. Why do the two estimates differ? With the use of demand functions explain what factors determine the estimate obtained by using the first procedure.
3. Which of the two procedures would you favor? Explain why.
4. Did the 1993 price change increase or decrease total revenue? If you were a member of the pricing committee, would you be satisfied with either proposal or would you suggest still another one?
5. What other information, besides that presented in the table, would you like to have to improve your estimate of the price elasticity or, at the very least, to determine any bias in the estimates?

P A R T II

CONSUMER BEHAVIOR

- **Chapter 2**
  Consumer Behavior and
  Market Demand
- **Chapter 3**
  Extending the Theory of
  Consumer Behavior
- **Chapter 4**
  The Cost of Time and
  the Theory of Consumer Behavior

CHAPTER 2

CONSUMER BEHAVIOR AND MARKET DEMAND

■ **2-1 Building the Consumer Behavior Model**
Assumptions about Consumer Behavior

■ **2-2 Describing Consumer Preferences**
Indifference Curves
The Marginal Rate of Substitution
The Indifference Map of a Consumer
Assigning Numbers to Indifference Curves

■ **2-3 Properties of Indifference Curves**

■ **2-4 Budget Constraint**
Affordable Market Baskets
Shifts in the Budget Constraint

■ **2-5 The Consumer's Consumption Decision**
Finding the Market Basket That Maximizes Utility and Satisfies the Budget Constraint
Specialization of Consumption
Application 2-1: Pricing to Break into an Established Market

■ **2-6 Introducing a Composite Good into the Consumer Behavior Model**

■ **2-7 The Market Demand Function**
The Consumer's Demand Function
Application 2-2: Measuring Brand Loyalty by Relative Frequency of Purchase
Market Demand: Adding Up the Individual Demand Functions
Application 2-3: Why Are Americans Eating More Poultry and Less Red Meat?

■ **2-8 Substitutes and Complements**

■ **2-9 Applying the Consumer Behavior Model**
Application 2-4: Earmarked versus General-Purpose Grants

■ **Summary**

■ **Key Terms**

■ **Review Questions**

■ **Exercises**

■ **Problem Set: Will a Challenge Grant Increase Alumni Contributions?**

Chapter 1 showed that the intersection of the market demand and supply functions determines the equilibrium price and quantity. This chapter goes behind the market demand function for a good and shows just where this function comes from. The centerpiece of the analysis is the consumer, and so we build a model that focuses on the behavior of an individual. In short, a consumer picks a basket of goods that makes him or her as well off as possible given the consumer's tastes, the prices of goods, and the income of the consumer. Working within the confines of this model, you will learn how to derive the consumer's demand function for a good and what causes shifts in its position. Even more important, you will find that the theory of consumer behavior is a useful tool for analyzing an amazing variety of important questions. A hint of this variety is illustrated by the following questions. If most consumers repurchase a brand, what does this strong brand loyalty imply about the price elasticity of demand? How will the well-being of a needy consumer differ if the government gives an earmarked versus a general-purpose grant to the consumer? If a well-heeled alumnus gives a challenge grant to your university promising to augment the donation of each alumnus or alumna, will each alum increase his or her annual giving? Once you master the theory of consumer behavior, you will find some surprising answers to these and other interesting questions.

2-1 BUILDING THE CONSUMER BEHAVIOR MODEL

Consumers purchase a diverse set of goods ranging from housing to food to movies to fitness equipment, and each individual selects a different market basket of goods. A market basket is a collection of quantities of different goods. Table 2-1 lists possible market baskets having just two goods, chicken and beef.

Each row represents a market basket with a certain number of pounds of chicken and a certain number of pounds of beef.

> A **market basket** specifies the quantities of different goods consumed per unit of time.

Before we can develop a theory of consumer behavior, some assumptions must be made about the way a consumer behaves. These assumptions are the foundation of our theory of consumer behavior.

Assumptions about Consumer Behavior

In selecting among market baskets, it is assumed that consumers can distinguish between the benefits of consuming one market basket or another. More specifically, it is assumed that they (1) can rank market baskets by the benefits obtained, (2) are consistent in their choices, (3) satisfy a transitivity condition, and (4) prefer more of a good to less of it. These assumptions are described as follows:

1. *Completeness.* At the most basic level a consumer must be capable of making decisions. When comparing market baskets 1 and 2 in Table 2-1, he or she can express a preference for market basket 1 (10 pounds of chicken and 4 pounds of beef) over market basket 2 (9 pounds of chicken and 6

Table 2-1   EXAMPLES OF MARKET BASKETS

MARKET BASKET	POUNDS OF CHICKEN	POUNDS OF BEEF
1	10	4
2	9	6
3	0	12
4	8	8

pounds of beef), an indifference between the two market baskets, or a preference for market basket 2 over market basket 1. Therefore, an individual must be able to *rank* market baskets. We could, but do not, require the consumer to specify how much better off he or she will be by consuming one market basket rather than another. All that is needed is an ability to *rank* market baskets solely on the basis of the person's own well-being.

2. *Consistency.* Our consumer demonstrates a consistent preference ordering. If market basket 1 is preferred to market basket 2, then he or she demonstrates consistency by maintaining the preference ranking. Throughout this chapter we assume that tastes are stable.

3. *Transitivity.* The requirement of **transitivity** eliminates contradictions in the consumer's preference ordering. An example will illustrate the meaning of "transitivity." If a consumer prefers market basket 1 to market basket 2 in Table 2-1 and prefers market basket 2 to market basket 3, then these preferences satisfy the transitivity assumption if market basket 1 is preferred to market basket 3.

4. *More is preferred to less (nonsatiation).* Our consumer prefers more of any good that increases his or her well-being, choosing a market basket that contains more units of at least one good over another with the same number of units of the other goods.

These are the minimal requirements placed on each consumer in developing the consumer behavior model. They are not demanding requirements, and so economists proceed as if most individuals can satisfy these conditions.

2-2   DESCRIBING CONSUMER PREFERENCES

Economists have a very precise concept in mind when referring to consumer *preferences* or *tastes*. This section introduces the concept of the indifference curve and illustrates how a consumer's preferences can be described with a set of indifference curves.

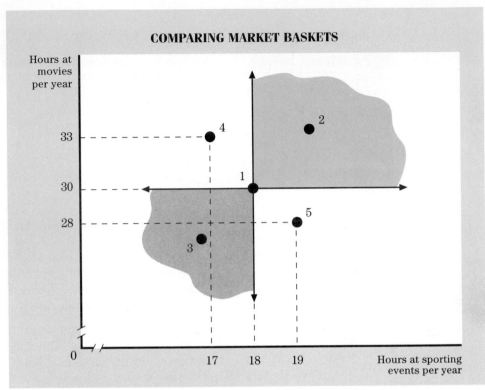

Figure 2-1   The consumer prefers all market baskets in the shaded area to the northeast of market basket 1. Market basket 2 is preferred because more of both goods are included than in market basket 1. All market baskets in the gray area to the southwest of market basket 1 are inferior to market basket 1. The consumer prefers market basket 1 to market basket 3 because market basket 3 has fewer of both goods than market basket 1. The consumer may or may not be better off by consuming market baskets 4 and 5 than by consuming market basket 1.

Indifference Curves

An indifference curve represents a set of market baskets where the well-being of the consumer is the same no matter which basket is consumed. Let's determine which market baskets are in the set. To begin, consider a market basket of just two goods. Let hours at the movies per year be one good and hours at sporting events per year be the other. In Figure 2-1 hours attending movies are on the y or vertical axis, and hours at sporting events on the x or horizontal axis. Each point on the diagram represents a market basket—different quantities of the two goods. For example, market basket 1 includes 30 hours at the movies a year and 18 hours attending sporting events a year.

From the graph, you can make some observations about the well-being of the consumer. Market basket 2 has more of both goods than market basket 1, and so you can conclude that the consumer's well-being or utility is higher with market basket 2. ("Well-being" and "utility" are used interchangeably throughout this chapter to describe the level of satisfaction of the purchaser.) The consumer prefers any market basket to the northeast of market basket 1, such as market basket 2. The opposite is true for market basket 3, which includes fewer hours at the movies and at sporting events than market basket 1. Therefore market basket 1 is preferred to market basket 3 and to any market basket southwest of market basket 1. We can sum up by saying that the consumer prefers market basket 2 to market basket 1, and market basket 1 to market basket 3. Clearly, neither market basket 2 nor market basket 3 is on the same indifference curve as market basket 1 because the consumer is not indifferent between these two market baskets.

Market baskets 4 and 5 are another story. Market basket 4 includes more movies but fewer sporting events, and market basket 5 includes fewer movies and more sporting events. Suppose our consumer expresses an indifference between market baskets 1 and 4 and 1 and 5. By transitivity, the consumer is also indifferent between market baskets 4 and 5 so the consumer's utility is the same whether market basket 1, 4, or 5 is purchased because they are all on the same indifference curve. The consumer expresses indifference among attending (1) 33 hours of movies and 17 hours of sporting events (market basket 4), (2) 30 hours of movies and 18 hours of sporting events (market basket 1), and (3) 28 hours of movies and 19 hours of sporting events (market basket 5).

> An **indifference curve** represents a set of market baskets where the well-being of the consumer is the same.

These are just three of many market baskets among which the consumer professes indifference. In Figure 2-2 these as well as many other market baskets are connected by a curve called an indifference curve. The consumer is indifferent among all market baskets on the curve labeled U_1 because all market baskets on a given indifference curve produce the same level of utility. The basic idea underlying the notion of an indifference curve is the concept of substitutability, which tells us how willing a consumer is to substitute one good for another and still remain indifferent. For example, an individual does not have to attend 18 hours of sporting events per year to reach a certain level of well-being. Even the most avid sports fan receives some enjoyment from seeing the classic film *Gone With the Wind*. Although the shapes of indifference curves differ from one consumer to another, each person is generally willing to substitute hours at sporting events for hours at the movies at some rate where he or she is indifferent.

Two extreme cases of indifference curves are worth noting. In one case the indifference curve is a straight line, and in the second case it has an L shape. When the indifference curve is a straight line, the consumer substitutes one good for another at a constant rate no matter how many units of each good are purchased, that is, irrespective of the consumer's current market basket. When this occurs, we call the two goods **perfect substitutes.** In Figure 2-3a the indifference curve between Y and X is a straight line. For example, your indifference curve between $5 bills and $1 bills always has a slope of $-\frac{1}{5}$ because you are always willing to give up one $5 bill for five $1 bills. If brand names mean little to you, you are

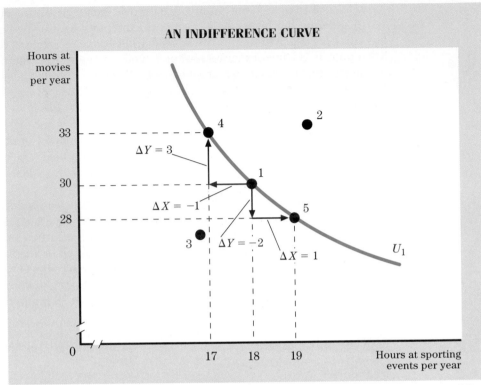

Figure 2-2 The consumer is indifferent between all market baskets on the indifference curve labeled U_1 and is as well off consuming market basket 1, 4, or 5. Market basket 3 is inferior to any market basket on the indifference curve U_1, and market basket 2 is preferred to any market basket on the indifference curve U_1.

willing to substitute one can of Del Monte corn for one can of a generic brand of corn no matter how many cans of Del Monte corn you consume.

The second special case occurs when two goods are used together in some fixed proportion. Then the indifference curve has an L shape (Figure 2-3*b*), and we call the two goods **perfect complements.** If you have one right and one left shoe, for example, another left shoe does not increase your utility. If you always add two teaspoons of sugar to every cup of coffee and think a third teaspoon adds nothing to the taste, you use coffee and sugar in fixed proportions and the two goods are perfect complements.

Between these two extreme presentations of the shape of indifference curves is the more common indifference curve like the one in Figure 2-2.

The Marginal Rate of Substitution

The slope of the indifference curve at any point measures the consumer's *personal* tradeoff between two goods that keeps the consumer's utility constant. The slope of the indifference curve at any point is called the *marginal rate of substitution* (MRS).

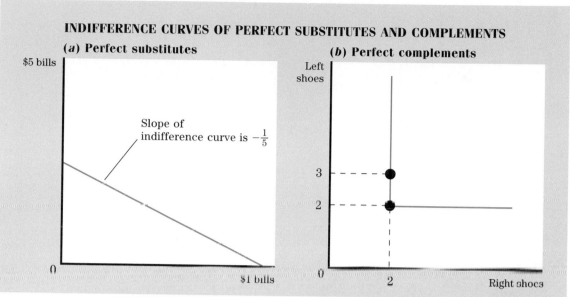

Figure 2-3 (*a*) The consumer is willing to substitute units of Y ($5 bills) for units of X ($1 bills) at a constant rate and still remain indifferent. The two goods are perfect substitutes. (*b*) Right and left shoes are perfect complements. The indifference curve has an L shape because Y (left shoes) and X (right shoes) are used in a fixed proportion.

The **marginal rate of substitution** is the slope of the indifference curve. It is negative and measures the tradeoff between two goods that keeps the consumer's utility constant.

The marginal rate of substitution can be expressed as

$$\text{MRS}_{YX} = \left.\frac{\Delta Y}{\Delta X}\right|_{U=\text{constant}} \qquad \text{(Marginal Rate of Substitution)} \qquad \textbf{(2-1)}$$

It indicates how much of one good the consumer is willing to give up for a given increase in another good and is equal to the slope of the indifference curve, $\Delta Y/\Delta X$. The notation $|_{U=\text{constant}}$ means that the utility of the consumer is constant, and so the slope is being measured along a given indifference curve.

Assuming an increase in hours at the movies or at sporting events increases the consumer's utility, the slope of an indifference curve must be negative if utility is to remain constant. For example, an individual can remain indifferent between market baskets 1 and 5 in Figure 2-2 only if he or she reduces hours at the movies when spending another hour at a sporting event. This is why the MRS is negative.

In the more typical case, the slope of the indifference curve changes as the consumer moves along the curve. Figure 2-4 is another version of Figure 2-2. Starting with a market basket of 33 hours per year at the movies and 17 hours per year at sporting events (market basket 4), this individual is willing to give up 3

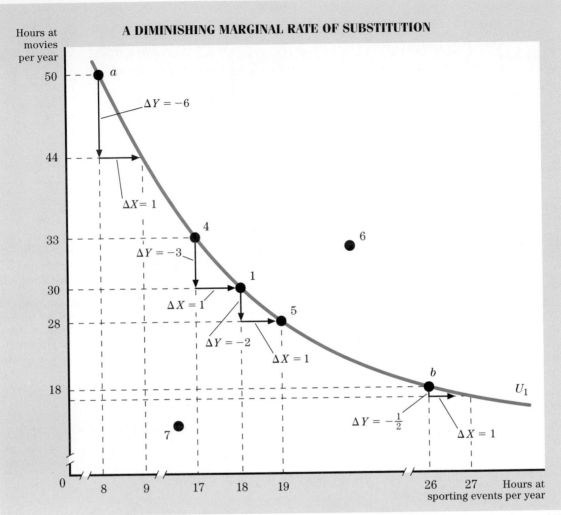

Figure 2-4 A diminishing marginal rate of substitution means that the slope of the indifference curve becomes flatter as the consumer spends more time at sporting events. Starting with market basket a, the consumer is willing to spend 6 fewer hours at the movies for 1 more hour at sporting events and remain indifferent. The marginal rate of substitution is -6. With market basket b the consumer spends 26 hours at sporting events and is willing to forgo only $\frac{1}{2}$ hour for 1 more hour at the movies. The marginal rate of substitution is $-\frac{1}{2}$.

hours at the movies for 1 more hour at sporting events. Because more time is being spent at sporting events and less time at the movies than before, the consumer is now willing to give up only 2 hours at the movies to spend 1 more hour at sporting events. There is an even larger difference between the slopes along the indifference curve when comparing market baskets a and b. With market basket a the consumer spends 50 hours at the movies and just 8 hours at sporting events per year but is willing to give up 6 hours at the movies for 1 hour at sporting events and remain indifferent. The slope of the indifference curve is $\Delta Y/\Delta X = -\frac{6}{1}$. With market basket b only 18 hours are spent at the movies and 26 hours at sporting events. The consumer will sacrifice only a half hour of time at the movies for 1 more hour at sporting events and still remain indifferent. The slope of the indifference curve is $\Delta Y/\Delta X = -\frac{1}{2}/1 = -\frac{1}{2}$. When moving down along the indifference curve, the slope of the curve becomes flatter as it increases numerically from -6 for market basket a to $-\frac{1}{2}$ for market basket b.[1] Therefore, indifference curves typically exhibit a *diminishing rate of substitution.*

> A **diminishing marginal rate of substitution** means the slope of the indifference curve becomes flatter as the quantity of X increases.

The consumer is willing to give up fewer and fewer hours of movies for one more hour at sporting events as more time is spent at sporting events. If you attended a professional sporting event on 51 weekends of the year and saw only one movie on the remaining weekend, you might be willing to substitute two fewer sporting events to see one more movie, given that you are seeing so many sporting events per year. However, if you went to the movies 50 weekends of the year and saw only two sporting events a year, you might be willing to give up fewer than two sporting events to see one more movie given that you rarely see a sporting event.

The Indifference Map of a Consumer

An **indifference map** includes all of the indifference curves of a consumer, and every market basket is on one of these indifference curves. The indifference curve U_1 in Figure 2-4 is just one of several and demonstrates that the same utility is obtained with market basket 4, 1, or 5. Any market basket above U_1, such as market basket 6, is on a different indifference curve and provides more utility than market basket 4, 1, or 5. And any market basket below U_1, such as market basket 7, is on another indifference curve and provides less utility. The curves lying above U_1 represent higher levels of utility, and those lying below U_1 represent lower levels.

For example, Figure 2-5 shows only three of the many indifference curves of a consumer. Market baskets b and c are on U_3, and so the consumer is indifferent between them. On the other hand, market basket b on indifference curve U_3 is preferred to market basket a on indifference curve U_2 because it includes more of each good. The transitivity requirement says that market basket c is also preferred to market basket a since market basket b is preferred to market basket a. To summarize, any market basket on an indifference curve to the northeast of another indifference curve is preferred to any market basket on the original indifference curve.

---

[1] The use of the adjective "diminishing" can be explained by the fact that the *absolute value* of the slope of the indifference curve *decreases* as the consumer moves along the indifference curve from left to right.

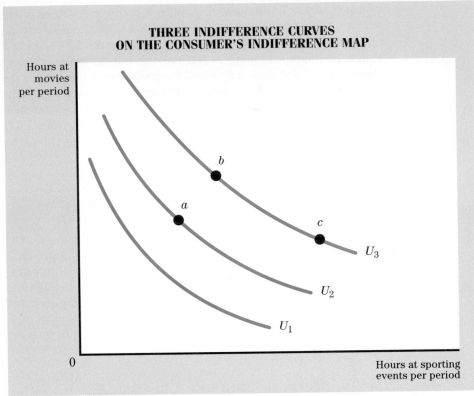

**THREE INDIFFERENCE CURVES
ON THE CONSUMER'S INDIFFERENCE MAP**

Figure 2-5 An indifference map includes all the indifference curves of a consumer. Here three sample indifference curves are shown. The consumer is better off selecting market baskets on higher indifference curves and prefers market baskets *b* and *c* to market basket *a*.

Assigning Numbers to Indifference Curves

Our consumer does not have to know how much better off he or she will be by purchasing one market basket rather than another but must just rank the market baskets to create an indifference map. Suppose that an individual assigns numbers called utility numbers to indifference curves. All market baskets on the same indifference curve would then have the same utility number, and larger numbers would be assigned to market baskets on higher indifference curves. In this way the consumer could attach a number to each market basket. A function that relates the quantity consumed of each good to a utility number summarizes the preferences of the consumer.

The consumer's **utility function** is

$$U = U(X,Y) \qquad \text{(Utility Function)} \qquad \textbf{(2-2)}$$

Equation 2-2 says that the consumer's utility (as represented by the assigned number) depends on the quantities of *X* and *Y* consumed. Utility is measured in subjective units called *utils*.[2] Because the numbers assigned to indifference curves by the consumer are arbitrary, they can be replaced by another number system as long as the consumer's ranking of the indifference curves is preserved. The theory of consumer behavior does not depend on any particular assignment of numbers to the indifference curves but only on the ranking of these curves.

To summarize, each consumer has a utility function that expresses his or her well-being or utility as a function of the quantity consumed of each good.

2-3 PROPERTIES OF INDIFFERENCE CURVES

The indifference map for a consumer describes the individual's tastes or preferences. Although personal tastes may differ, the indifference curves of each purchaser must satisfy the following conditions:

1. *The slope of an indifference curve must be negative.*[3] You have already learned why indifference curves must have a negative slope if the consumption of more of each good increases the well-being of the consumer.

2. *Indifference curves must not touch.* The transitivity assumption prevents indifference curves from touching or intersecting one another. Two indifference curves of a consumer intersect in Figure 2-6. This individual prefers market basket b to market basket a because market basket b has more of each good. However, market baskets a and c are equivalent since they are on U_1. Therefore, market basket b should be preferred to market basket c if the transitivity condition is to be satisfied. However, market baskets b and c are on U_0, and so the consumer is indifferent between them and therefore between market baskets a and b. This cannot be because market basket b contains more goods. Therefore, indifference curves cannot intersect.

---

[2] Given the utility function, marginal utility is the increase in utils for a tiny increase in X or Y. For tiny changes in X, marginal utility is defined as $\partial U/\partial X$, or the increase in utility from an infinitesimal change in X holding Y constant. The same interpretation can be given to $\partial U/\partial Y$. It turns out that a consumer's marginal rate of substitution equals the negative of the ratio of marginal utilities. To demonstrate this, consider only those changes in Y, dY, and X, dX, such that utility is constant (a movement along an indifference curve): since $U = U(X,Y)$, and letting $dU = 0$, we have

$$dU = 0 = \frac{\partial U}{\partial Y}dY + \frac{\partial U}{\partial X}dX$$

or, upon rearranging,

$$\text{MRS}_{YX} = \frac{dY}{dX} = -\frac{\frac{\partial U}{\partial X}}{\frac{\partial U}{\partial Y}}$$

Therefore, the marginal rate of substitution, which itself must be negative because both marginal utilities are positive, is equal to the negative of the ratio of marginal utilities.

[3] The slope of the indifference curve $\frac{dY}{dX}$ is negative. Diminishing marginal rate of substitution requires

$$\frac{d\left(\frac{dY}{dX}\right)}{dX} > 0.$$

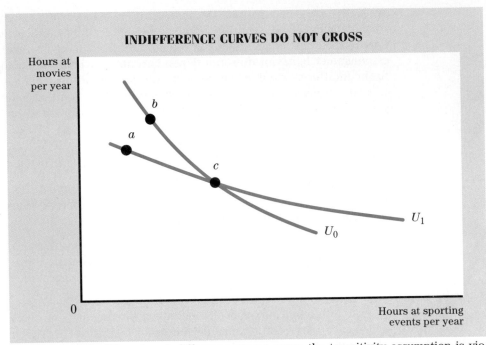

Figure 2-6 When two indifference curves cross, the transitivity assumption is violated. A consumer professes an indifference between market baskets *a* and *c* and also expresses a preference for market basket *b* over market basket *a*. Therefore, the consumer should prefer market basket *b* over market basket *c*. However, the consumer expresses an indifference between market baskets *b* and *c*.

This completes our examination of consumer preferences as expressed by the consumer's indifference map. Now we bring the consumer back to reality by identifying which market baskets are affordable.

2-4 BUDGET CONSTRAINT

A consumer's income and the price of each good limit the choice of market baskets. Consumers can afford only a subset of all possible market baskets because each one faces a **budget constraint** that limits the number of affordable market baskets. Such limitations are familiar to everyone: You might like to drive an expensive Mercedes-Benz or have a house in the south of France, but your budget constraint forces you to make more modest selections. In our model of consumer behavior, choice of a market basket depends on willingness and ability to purchase goods.

Affordable Market Baskets

This chapter considers a single-period model of consumption in which the consumer has no reason to save. (Later, Chapter 16 describes the consumption decision where the consumer may decide to borrow or save in the present in order to consume less or more in the future.) In this chapter a person's total expenditure on goods and services is equal to income. To demonstrate how income and market prices determine what market baskets the consumer can afford, let's continue to assume that the individual purchases just two goods, X and Y. Income is I, the price of a unit of X is P_X, and the price of each unit of Y is P_Y. It is also assumed that the buyer can purchase each unit of either good at their respective market prices.

The budget constraint is expressed as

$$P_X X + P_Y Y = I \qquad \text{(Budget Constraint)} \qquad \text{(2-3)}$$

where $P_X X$ is total expenditure on X, and $P_Y Y$ is total expenditure on Y. Equation 2-3 says that total expenditure on goods is equal to income. Initially, we will assume that the prices are constant and do not vary with the quantity purchased. The consumer selects from the market baskets of X and Y that satisfy his or her budget constraint (equation 2-3).

> The **budget constraint** shows which market baskets the consumer can afford.

By rearranging the budget constraint equation, we can tell just how many units of Y can be consumed for any given quantity of X. Equation 2-3 can be rearranged to show this by subtracting $P_X X$ from both sides and then dividing both sides by P_Y to obtain

$$Y = \frac{I}{P_Y} - \frac{P_X}{P_Y} X \qquad \text{(Tradeoff between Y and X)} \qquad \text{(2-4)}$$

Equation 2-4 is an equation of a straight line. Figure 2-7 is the graph of equation 2-4, where Y is hours at the movies per year and X is hours at sporting events per year. The quantity of Y and the quantity of X are the two variables, I/P_Y is the y intercept of the straight line, and $-P_X/P_Y$ is the slope of the straight line. If the consumer does not purchase any units of X ($X = 0$), he spends all income on Y and is able to purchase I/P_Y units of Y. Dividing income by the price of Y yields the maximum number of units of Y that can be purchased, Consequently, one affordable market basket is zero units of X and I/P_Y units of Y. Now suppose the consumer purchases only X ($Y = 0$). How many units of X can he purchase? If you set $Y = 0$ in equation 2-4 and solve for X, you will find that $X = I/P_X$. Dividing income by the price of X gives the maximum quantity of X that the individual can consume. So another affordable market basket is I/P_X units of X and no units of Y. These are the ends or the intercepts of the budget line. An example will make the calculation of these end points clearer. Suppose the monthly income of the consumer is $2,000. The price of X is $50, and the price of Y is $10. Then, the budget constraint becomes

$$Y = 200 - 5X$$

The consumer can buy $2000/$10 = 200 units of Y by spending all income on Y, and $2000/$50 = 40 units of X by spending all income on X.

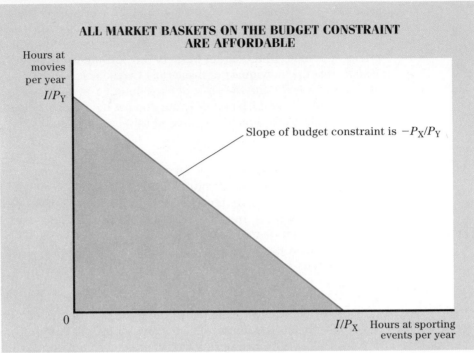

**ALL MARKET BASKETS ON THE BUDGET CONSTRAINT
ARE AFFORDABLE**

Hours at
movies
per year
I/P_Y

Slope of budget constraint is $-P_X/P_Y$

0 I/P_X Hours at sporting
                                                              events per year

Figure 2-7   Given the income of the consumer and the prices of X and Y, the consumer can purchase any market basket on or below the budget constraint in the shaded area. Each point on the budget line represents an affordable market basket of a certain number of units of Y and a certain number of units of X. If all income is spent on Y, the consumer purchases I/P_Y units of Y. If all income is spent on X, the consumer purchases I/P_X units of X. The slope of the budget constraint is $-P_X/P_Y$ and shows the reduction in the number of units of Y purchased for each unit increase in X.

The slope of equation 2-4 is $-P_X/P_Y$, the negative of the price of X divided by the price of Y. The slope of the budget constraint is negative because more units of Y can be purchased only if fewer units of X are bought. It measures the rate at which the consumption of Y must be reduced for each unit increase in X given the price ratio P_X/P_Y. In our numerical example $-P_X/P_Y = -\$50/\$10 = -5$. By purchasing one less unit of X (reducing the expenditure for X by $50), the buyer can purchase five more units of Y (increasing the expenditure for Y by $50). To distinguish between the slope of the budget constraint and the slope of the indifference curve it is useful to think of the slope of the budget constraint as the *market's* marginal rate of substitution and the slope of the indifference curve as the consumer's *personal* marginal rate of substitution.

We have assumed that the consumer pays the same price regardless of the number of units purchased. What happens to the shape of the budget line if the price depends on the quantity purchased? Sometimes, firms offer quantity discounts. A store advertisement that says "Buy one dress at the regular price and

**50 PERCENT OFF THE SECOND OR EVERY SECOND PURCHASE
CHANGES THE BUDGET CONSTRAINT**

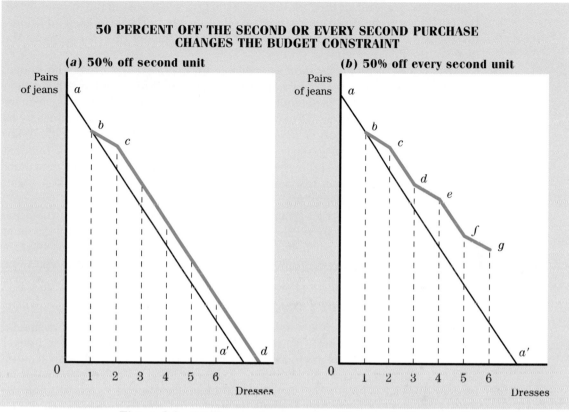

Figure 2-8 (*a*) The consumer receives 50 percent off on only the second unit purchased. When the price of a dress is $100, the budget constraint is the line *aa'*. A pricing promotion that reduces the price for only the second dress by 50 percent changes the budget constraint to *abcd*. The slope of the segment *bc* is half the slope of *ab* because of the 50 percent discount. The price is $100 for subsequent dresses. (*b*) The consumer receives a 50 percent discount on every second purchase. The price of the first, third, and fifth dresses is $100. The price of the second, fourth, sixth, and so on, is $50. The budget contraint becomes *abcdefg*.

get 50 percent off the second dress" is offering a quantity discount on every second dress purchased. Let's see how the shape of the budget constraint changes under two different discount policies. Suppose in the first case the firm offers a 50 percent discount on only the *second* unit purchased. In the second case the firm offers a discount of 50 percent on *every second* item purchased.

Using our example of dresses, let's assume that the consumer chooses among market baskets composed of dresses and jeans, and that the consumer gets 50 percent off for every second dress if the consumer pays full price for the first dress. In Figure 2-8*a* and *b* the price of a dress is $100 and the line *aa'* is the budget constraint when no discount is available. When a 50 percent discount becomes available on only the second dress, the budget constraint becomes *abcd* in

Figure 2-8*a*. The cost of the first dress is $100 and when buying the second dress, the consumer pays $50. If more than two dresses are purchased, each additional dress costs $100. This is why the slope of the line segment *cd* is the same as the slope of the line segment *ab*.

When a 50 percent discount is available on *every second* dress, the budget constraint becomes a series of connected segments with every other segment having the same slope. The second dress can be purchased at $50 if the consumer pays $100 for the first dress. Because the price of the second dress declines by 50 percent, the slope of the segment *bc* is one-half of the slope of the segment *ab*. For the third dress, the buyer pays the full price of $100 and so the slope of segment *cd* equals the slope of *ab* and is therefore steeper than segment *bc*. The consumer qualifies for the 50 percent discount on the fourth dress so the slope of segment *de* is the same as the slope of *bc*.

There are many different types of quantity discounts, but for all of them the price depends in some way on the quantity purchased. With a quantity discount the budget line is no longer a straight line. Quantity discounts offer the buyer a larger set of affordable opportunities by shifting some portion of the budget line outward.

Shifts in the Budget Constraint

Let's return to our original example of movies and sporting events and assume a constant price for each unit. We now determine how the position of the budget constraint shifts when the income of the consumer or the price of X or Y changes. Observe what happens when income increases from I to I^*. The y intercept increases from I/P_Y to I^*/P_Y and the x intercept increases from I/P_X to I^*/P_X, but the slope of the budget constraint, $-P_X/P_Y$, is unaffected. Each intercept increases by the same proportion. Therefore, an increase in income causes a parallel shift outward of the budget constraint in Figure 2-9. The shaded area shows the expanded set of affordable market baskets. Before the increase in income, the consumer could spend Y_0 hours at the movies and X_0 hours at sporting events. After an increase in income, the consumer can spend Y^* hours at the movies while still spending X_0 hours at sporting events.

A decrease in the price of either good allows the buyer to purchase some market baskets that were not affordable before. A fall in the price of X from P_X to P_X^* does not change the amount of Y the consumer could buy if he or she spent all income on Y (the intercept I/P_Y),but it makes the budget constraint flatter. The new slope is $-P_X^*/P_Y$, increasing in value from some initial negative number to a smaller negative number. When the price of X is $50 and the price of Y is $10, the consumer must purchase five fewer units of Y to consume one more unit of X. When the price of X drops to $20, the consumer sacrifices only two units of Y to consume another unit of X. Therefore, as the price of X falls, the budget constraint becomes flatter, and in this particular example the slope increases from -5 to -2. Figure 2-10*a* shows the budget line rotating outward around I/P_Y. The buyer can still only spend I/P_Y hours at the movies after the price of an hour of sporting events decreases if all income is spent on movies. On the other hand, the consumer

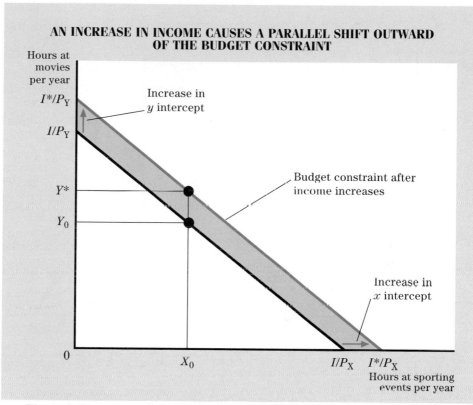

**AN INCREASE IN INCOME CAUSES A PARALLEL SHIFT OUTWARD
OF THE BUDGET CONSTRAINT**

Figure 2-9   An increase in income from I to I^* causes a parallel outward shift in the budget constraint. The slope of the budget constraint is $-P_X/P_Y$ and is unaffected when income increases. After income increases to I^*, the consumer has more affordable opportunities. If the individual consumes X_0 units, he or she can now consume Y^* units rather than Y_0 units.

can now spend I/P_X^* hours at sporting events if all income is spent on X. The shaded area shows the expanded set of opportunities when the price of X decreases.

A fall in the price of Y also allows the purchaser to select from a larger set of affordable market baskets. Equation 2-4 shows that the y intercept increases and the slope decreases. If the price of Y decreases from P_Y to P_Y^*, the y intercept increases to I/P_Y^* and makes the budget line steeper. The slope of the budget constraint becomes $-P_X/P_Y^*$, which is smaller than $-P_X/P_Y$. In our example, the budget constraint becomes steeper as the slope of the budget constraint decreases from -5 to -10 when the price of Y decreases from \$10 to \$5. Now the consumer can buy 10 more units of Y by choosing 1 less unit of X. Figure 2-10b shows the budget line rotating around the x intercept as the price of Y decreases: a decrease in the price of Y does not change total hours spent at sporting events if all income

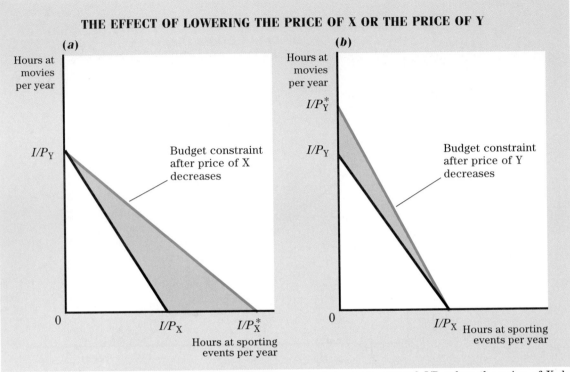

Figure 2-10   (*a*) The budget constraint rotates around I/P_Y when the price of X decreases. (*b*) The budget constraint rotates around I/P_X when the price of Y decreases. A reduction in the price of X or of Y increases the affordable opportunities available to the consumer.

is spent on sporting events. Here again, the shaded area shows the expanded set of market baskets that can be purchased when the price of Y decreases.

If all prices and income change by a common percentage, then equation 2-4 indicates that the budget constraint is unaffected and does not change position. If inflation increases all prices and consumer income by 10 percent a year, affordable opportunities do not change and the budget constraint stays put. The percentage increase in income offsets the equivalent percentage increase in all prices. The consumer is not any richer if income increases by 10 percent and prices also increase by 10 percent.

2-5   THE CONSUMER'S CONSUMPTION DECISION

Tastes and the consumer's budget constraint—the two essential components of the consumer behavior model—have been introduced. The indifference map of the consumer describes the person's preferences and comparative likes. The budget constraint brings a sense of reality to the consumer by defining which market baskets are affordable. Now we bring the two components together and explain how the consumer determines which one of the many affordable market baskets to purchase.

Finding the Market Basket That Maximizes Utility and Satisfies the Budget Constraint

The goal of the consumer is to gain **maximal utility** while satisfying the budget constraint. Although all market baskets on the budget constraint are affordable, the buyer wants to select the one that places her on her highest indifference curve.

> The goal of the consumer is to maximize utility while satisfying the budget constraint.

What market basket allows the consumer to achieve this goal? In Figure 2-11 the budget constraint is superimposed on the indifference map, but only three of

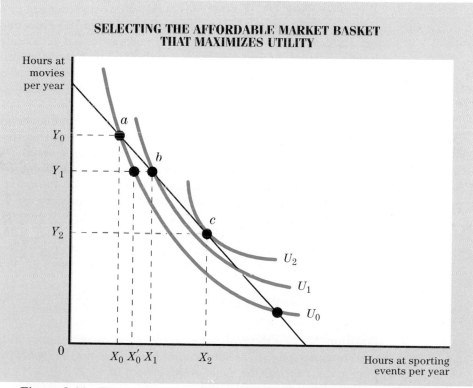

Figure 2-11 The consumer maximizes utility and reaches indifference curve U_2 by selecting market basket c where the marginal rate of substitution equals the slope of the budget constraint. By purchasing the market basket of X_2 and Y_2 units, the consumer not only satisfies the budget constraint but reaches the highest affordable indifference curve.

the many indifference curves are shown. Because the consumer must satisfy the budget constraint, she can purchase any market basket on the budget line. Market basket a with Y_0 hours at the movies and X_0 hours at sporting events is affordable because it is on the budget constraint and this market basket places the consumer on indifference curve U_0.

Is this the best the consumer can do? Suppose she decides to spend fewer hours at the movies and more hours at sporting events while remaining on the budget constraint by spending X_1 hours at the movies and Y_1 hours at sporting events. By moving along the budget constraint from market basket a to market basket b, the consumer moves from U_0 to a higher indifference curve, U_1. With the same income as before, the consumer's utility is higher so market basket b is a better buy than market basket a. Why does utility rise? To remain indifferent when moving away from a, the consumer's *personal* marginal rate of substitution requires an increse of $X_1 - X_0'$ sporting event hours for $Y_0 - Y_1$ fewer hours at the movies. The *market's* marginal rate of substitution is determined by the slope of the budget line $-P_X/P_Y$ and offers better terms. For the same $Y_0 - Y_1$ fewer hours at the movies, the consumer can buy $X_1 - X_0$ more hours at sporting events. Because $X_1 - X_0$ exceeds $X_0' - X_0$, the consumer's utility increases by consuming more X and less Y. This is why market basket b is a better buy than market basket a. In this case, utility increases when fewer hours are spent at the movies and more at sporting events. An important point to note is that the slope of the indifference curve is different from the slope of the budget constraint when the consumer purchases market basket a, b, or d. When this is true, the buyer prefers a different affordable market basket.

What market basket allows the buyer to reach the highest indifference curve while satisyfing the budget constraint? With market basket c, the highest possible indifference curve, U_2, can be reached by purchasing a market basket of X_2 units of X and Y_2 units of Y while satisfying the budget constraint. Market basket c is the best buy. The distinguishing feature of this market basket is that the slope of the budget line and the slope of the indifference curve U_2 are equal. In contrast, the indifference curve is steeper than the budget line with market basket a or b and flatter than the budget line with market basket d. Only with market basket c is the budget line tangent to an indifference curve. A necessary condition for the consumer to maximize utility subject to the budget constraint is

$$\mathrm{MRS}_{YX} = -\frac{P_X}{P_Y} \qquad \begin{array}{l} \text{(Condition for Maximizing Utility} \\ \text{Subject to Budget Constraint)} \end{array} \qquad \textbf{(2-5)}$$

Equation 2-5 says the consumer divides total income between the two goods so that the marginal rate of substitution between Y and X equals the negative of the price ratio, which is the slope of the budget line.[4]

---

[4] Mathematically, the consumer maximizes $U = U(X,Y)$ subject to the budget constraint $Y = I/P_Y - P_X/P_Y X$. One way to solve this problem is to substitute the constraint into the utility function so that the utility function becomes $U = U(X, I/P_Y - P_X/P_Y X)$, which depends only on X. A necessary condition for maximizing utility is $\partial U/\partial X - \partial U/\partial Y\, P_X/P_Y = 0$, which can be written as $\mathrm{MRS}_{YX} = -\partial U/\partial X/\partial U/\partial Y = -P_X/P_Y$. The consumer selects a market basket where the slope of the indifference curve equals the slope of the budget constraint.

When selecting a market basket containing both goods, a consumer maximizes utility by equating his or her marginal rate of substitution with the market's marginal rate of substitution.

Notice that the consumer purchases a market basket consisting of units of *both* X and Y—not just of X or of Y but a portfolio of goods. This is surely the more common case since most studies of consumer behavior show that people purchase a variety of goods, not just one. Still, consumers do not purchase all possible goods in the marketplace. The diet of most millionaires includes caviar but not turnips, and few middle-class families have $50,000 automobiles parked in their garages.

Specialization of Consumption

The consumer behavior model can explain why buyers do not purchase certain goods. To do so, we return to the two-good model. Figure 2-12*a* and *b* shows the

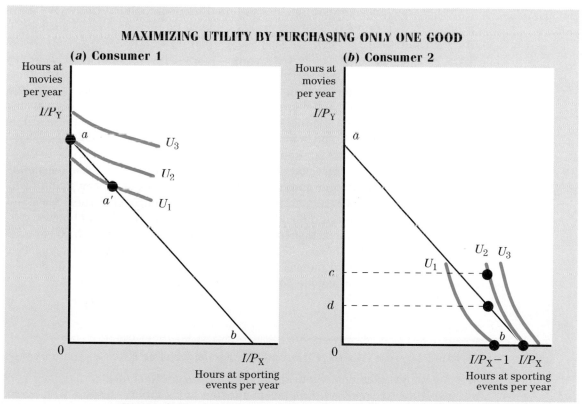

Figure 2-12   (*a*) Consumer 1 maximizes utility by specializing and going only to the movies. She purchases market basket *a*. The slope of her indifference curve at point *a* is flatter than the slope of the budget constraint. (*b*) Consumer 2 maximizes utility by attending only sporting events. He purchases market basket *b*. The slope of his indifference curve at point *b* is steeper than the slope of the budget constraint.

indifference curves of two consumers. Consumer 1 in Figure 2-12a has indifference curves labeled U_1 to U_3, and consumer 2 in Figure 2-12b has different indifference curves labeled U_1 to U_3. Consumer 1 has a penchant for movies and will remain indifferent by requiring a larger increase in hours at sporting events in place of one less hour at the movies. Her indifference curves are relatively flat, and the marginal rate of substitution is large. Consumer 2 is just the opposite. To be indifferent, he requires many more hours at the movies in place of one less hour at a sporting event.

Let's suppose the budget constraint is the same for the two consumers. In Figure 2-12 the budget line is superimposed on the indifference curves of the two consumers. Consumer 1 maximizes utility and reaches her indifference curve U_2 by selecting market basket a and consuming only movies. In contrast, consumer 2 maximizes his utility and reaches U_2 by selecting market basket b and attending only sporting events. The different *tastes* of the two consumers explain the different market baskets they select. These solutions are called *corner solutions* because both consumers are at one boundary or the other of the budget constraint.

Both market baskets show **specialization of consumption.** Consumer 1 does not purchase any hours of sporting events because the marginal rate of substitution is greater than the slope of the budget line, $\mathrm{MRS_{YX}} > -P_X/P_Y$, when she selects market basket a. If she purchases a market basket that includes some hours at sporting events like a', her utility declines. For consumer 2, his marginal rate of substitution is smaller than the slope of the budget line, $\mathrm{MRS_{YX}} < -P_X/P_Y$, when he selects market basket b. If he spends one less hour at a sporting event, $I/P_X - 1$ in Figure 2-12b, the market allows him to purchase fewer hours at the movies than he requires to be indifferent (compare quantities c and d). This is why he specializes and attends only sporting events.

Consumer 1 can truthfully say she never goes to sporting events, and consumer 2 can truthfully say he never goes to the movies. This does not mean that he will never go to the movies or that she will never go to sporting events. Their decisions are not etched in stone but depend on the budget constraint. If the budget constraint shifts because of a change in the price of either good, then both consumers will change their behavior and begin purchasing a market basket that includes both goods. If the price of movies falls or the price of sporting events increases, his market basket might include both movies and sporting events.

APPLICATION 2-1

Pricing to Break into an Established Market

Your company is planning to introduce a new frozen gourmet meal into the market. An outside market research firm has conducted focus group sessions with many consumers to see how well the new product stands up against brand A, the market leader, and has developed consumer preference maps for brand A and for your product. The market research firm summarizes the indifference map for a typical respondent in Figure 2-13.

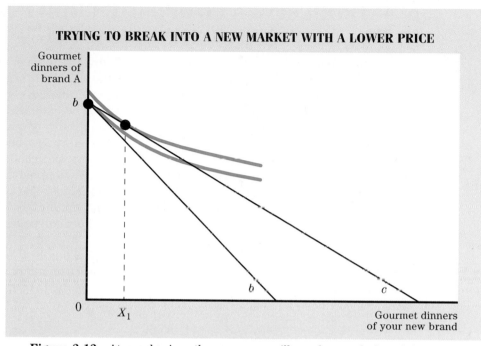

Figure 2-13   At equal prices the consumer will purchase only brand A rather than your new gourmet dinner. If your price is 15 percent lower, the consumer will purchase X_1 dinners per year of your new product. The success of the new product depends on whether the cost of producing it is lower than the costs faced by the seller of Brand A.

The number of gourmet meals per year of brand A is on the y axis, and the number of gourmet meals per year of the new product is on the x axis. The indifference curves are fairly flat and show that a representative consumer remains indifferent only when *several* of your gourmet dinners are substituted for one brand A gourmet meal. These are discouraging findings. Your new product is clearly not a perfect substitute for brand A since consumers are not willing to trade one of your dinners for brand A meals on a one-to-one basis. Let's assume that a consumer spends a certain amount on gourmet meals during the year, and so the budget line of the consumer is *bb* if you match brand A's price. The budget line has a slope of -1. If the market research firm has accurately reported the preferences of consumers, your new product will fail if you introduce it at this price because consumers will buy brand A rather than your product if the prices are equal. They will maximize utility by purchasing only brand A because $\text{MRS}_{YX} > -P_X/P_Y$.

What are your alternatives? You can introduce the new product at a lower price if you still hope to break into the market. The budget line *bc* assumes you introduce your product at a 15 percent discount. At this price the estimated quantity demanded is X_1 units per year per consumer. So, a 15 percent price discount will allow you to enter the market.

2-6   INTRODUCING A COMPOSITE GOOD INTO THE CONSUMER BEHAVIOR MODEL

A typical consumer purchases many goods and services, not just two. As you can imagine, it would be next to impossible to show the quantity of n goods purchased on a two-dimensional graph. This raises the question of whether consumer behavior theory applies only to two goods or whether it can be extended to cover more. Fortunately, we can reduce the more complicated problem of many goods to one of just two goods and apply the two-good model of consumer behavior. This can be done by introducing a pseudo-good called a composite good. Let's assume a market basket consists of n goods, one of which is X. A **composite good** is defined as the number of dollars spent on the other $n - 1$ goods. The two goods in the consumer's utility function become units of X and units of S, where S is total spending on all goods other than X. You can think of the composite good as having a price of $1.

Let's apply the composite good concept in explaining how frequently a consumer eats out at a restaurant. In Figure 2-14 total spending on all goods other than dinners eaten at a restaurant is on the y axis, and the frequency of dining out

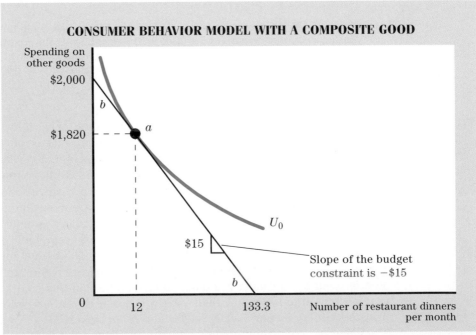

Figure 2-14   The slope of the budget constraint is $-\$15$ because each dinner costs $15. Market basket a maximizes the consumer's utility and satisfies the budget constraint. The marginal rate of substitution between the composite good and the frequency of eating out is $-\$15$. The consumer purchases 12 meals out, spending $180 per month on restaurant meals and $1,820 on other goods.

each month is on the x axis. If the consumer's monthly income is $2,000, the y intercept of the budget constraint is at $2,000 ($P_Y = \$1$, and the Y intercept is I/P_Y). The y intercept shows the total amount spent on other goods when the individual spends nothing on restaurant dinners. Suppose the price of a dinner at the consumer's favorite restaurant is $15. Then the slope of the budget constraint is -15. Each dinner reduces the amount that can be spent on other goods by $15.

The indifference curve U_0 shows the consumer's tradeoff between spending on other goods and eating out. The budget constraint is bb in Figure 2-14. The consumer maximizes utility subject to the budget constraint by selecting a market basket where the marginal rate of substitution of the indifference curve is 15, the slope of the budget constraint. Assume that utility is maximized by eating out 12 evenings per month and spending $180 on restaurant dinners and therefore $1,820 on other goods. The distance between $2,000 and the amount spent on other goods on the y axis measures the amount spent on restaurant meals per month— $180.

By using a composite good, we can allow for the purchase of n goods and still retain the simplicity of the two-good model.

2-7 THE MARKET DEMAND FUNCTION

One goal of this chapter is to derive the market demand function for a good—the relationship between the price and the quantity demanded by all consumers. To derive the market demand function, we must know how to determine each consumer's demand function, and for this we rely on the utility maximization model of consumer behavior. After this function is obtained, you will see how easy it is to derive the market demand function. Then, we will have a theory of market demand that is firmly anchored to the utility-maximizing behavior of each consumer.

The Consumer's Demand Function

Let's start with a given budget line for a consumer. We take as given the person's income I, the initial price of Y, P_Y^1, and the price of X, P_X^1. In Figure 2-15a the budget line is aa, and market basket A maximizes the consumer's utility. Market basket A includes X_1 units of X and Y_1 units of Y. Therefore, this consumer will demand X_1 units of X if the price of X is P_X^1, given that income is I and the price of Y is P_Y^1.

Holding the consumer's income and the price of Y constant, we can determine which market basket will be selected if the price of X decreases to P_X^2. The budget constraint rotates around point a on the y-axis and becomes budget line ab. The consumer maximizes utility by selecting market basket B, which has X_2 units of X and Y_2 units of Y. This consumer demands X_2 units of X when the price of X is P_X^2, given an income of I and a price of P_Y^1. We find the quantity demanded at P_X^1 and at P_X^2 by determining which market basket maximizes utility at each price of X. Figure 2-15a shows three points of tangency of the budget line to the corre-

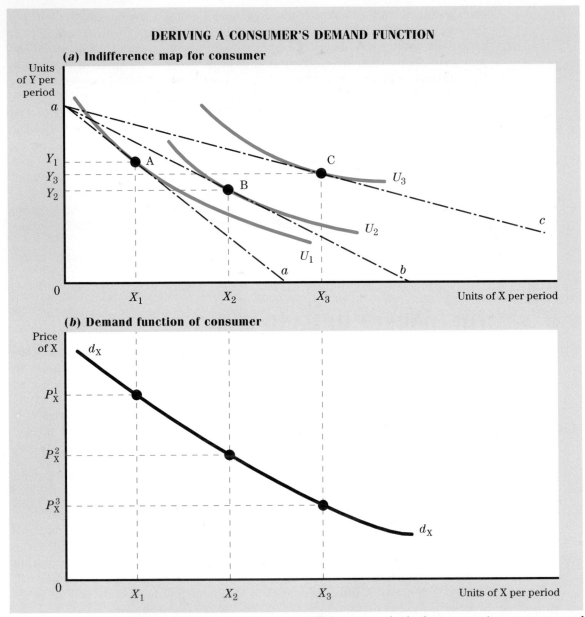

DERIVING A CONSUMER'S DEMAND FUNCTION

Figure 2-15 (*a*) As the price of X decreases, the budget constraint rotates around point *a* and the consumer selects different market baskets. (*b*) The consumer's demand function for X relates the price to the quantity demanded of X.

sponding indifference curves. Each point determines the optimum market basket for the consumer and has a different price of X associated with it. These points of tangency identify market baskets A, B, and C. As the price of X decreases, and with the price of Y, the indifference map, and income held constant, the consumer changes the optimum market basket and therefore the quantities demanded of X and Y.

We have all the information needed to derive the consumer's demand function for X, $d_X d_X$, in Figure 2-15*b*, which differs from Figure 2-15*a* in that the price of X rather than the number of units of Y is on the vertical axis. The buyer demands X_1 units if the price is P_X^1. The quantity demanded is X_2 if the price is P_X^2, and X_3 units if the price is P_X^3. You should have a clear understanding about what is constant and what changes as we move along $d_X d_X$. Consumer income and the price of Y are constant, and the price of X and the quantities of X and of Y change as the individual selects different market baskets that maximize his or her utility at each price of X.

APPLICATION **2-2**

Measuring Brand Loyalty by Relative Frequency of Purchase

Market researchers often measure brand loyalty by the relative frequency with which a consumer purchases a particular brand.[5] Over a year, one person may buy a given brand more than 90 percent of the time, whereas another may buy it only 10 percent of the time. For some products consumers buy only one brand to the exclusion of all others. They drink either Coke or Pepsi, but not both, or purchase only one brand of coffee. A popular measure of brand loyalty is *relative frequency of purchase*.

Table 2-2 shows the distribution of customers of Cool-It, a branded ice tea, by the relative frequency of purchase of Cool-It over a year. Ninety-two percent of Cool-It customers bought Cool-It at least 95 percent of the time over the past year.

Table 2-2   RELATIVE FREQUENCY OF COOL-IT ICE TEA

Percentage Relative Frequency of Purchase of Cool-It	Percent of Cool-It Customers
95% or higher	92%
90–94.9	3
0–5	5

[5] This example is motivated by the discussion in a more technical paper by Greg M. Allensby and Peter E. Rossi, "Quality Perceptions and Asymmetric Switching Between Brands," *Marketing Science* 10, no. 3 (Summer 1991), pp. 185–204.

Another 3 percent of customers purchased the brand more than 90 but less than 95 percent of the time. At the other extreme are the other 5 percent of customers who buy the brand at most only 5 percent of the time. Cool-It has an impressive repeat-purchase probability record. Because so many of the customers repurchase Cool-It, it is hard to resist the notion that most customers are closely attached to the brand. It appears that most customers value Cool-It's taste so much that they consider Cool-It only when they make a purchase. With this level of brand loyalty shouldn't the company be thinking of raising Cool-It's price?

The fundamental question is what inference a firm can draw about the price elasticity of demand from a high repeat-purchase probability. The theory of consumer behavior can help provide some answers. We will assume that Cool-It faces a competitor's brand, Brand B.

In Figure 2-16a units of Cool-It are on the y axis and units of brand B are on the x axis. Consumer 1's indifference curves, labeled $_1U_0$ and $_1U_1$, are steeper than those of consumer 2 in Figure 2-16b. Consumer 1 must receive more units of Cool-It for one less unit of brand B to remain indifferent than does consumer 2.

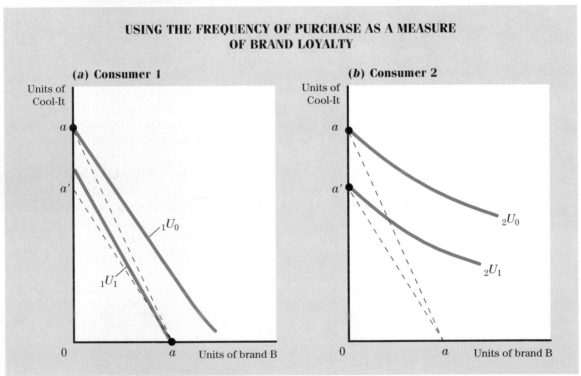

USING THE FREQUENCY OF PURCHASE AS A MEASURE OF BRAND LOYALTY

Figure 2-16   When the budget line is aa, both consumer 1 and consumer 2 maximize utility by always buying Cool-It. However, they respond differently if the price of Cool-It increases. An increase in the price of Cool-It shifts the budget line to $a'a$. Consumer 1 switches to Brand B but consumer 2 continues to purchase Cool-It. Although both consumers have a history of purchasing Cool-It, they exhibit different consumption responses to an increase in the price.

The initial budget line is aa for both consumers, and maximal utility is obtained by selecting market basket a and purchasing only Cool-It. Both consumers will have a history of purchasing only Cool-It and will exhibit brand loyalty to Cool-It like those customers in the first row of Table 2-2.

By looking at the purchasing behavior of these two customers, a marketing manager might easily conclude that they are so loyal to Cool-It that it is the only brand they consider when shopping and therefore that they will continue to buy it even if its price increases. When the price of Cool-It increases, the budget line becomes $a'a$. Consumer 1 switches to brand B, whereas consumer 2 continues to purchase Cool-It. Although both consumers have identical histories of brand loyalty, their responses to a price cut are different. Therefore, a history of making repeat purchases does not mean that brand selection by all such consumers is independent of price. Rather, it is important to know whether the repeat-purchase probability is high because relative brand prices are stable or is high even when relative brand prices change.

Market Demand: Adding Up the Individual Demand Functions

The market demand function shows the total quantity demanded of a product by all consumers at each price. It is derived by summing the demand curve of each consumer horizontally. For each price, the quantity demanded by each consumer is added to derive the total quantity demanded in the market. Individual demand functions differ because income and tastes differ across consumers. Figure 2-17 shows the individual demand curves of X for just three of a large number of consumers. The market demand function is DD and is a horizontal summation of the individual demand curves of all consumers in the market. Consumer 1 has a positive demand for X only if the price is less than P_1. The quantity demanded by consumers 2 and 3 becomes positive at prices less than P_2 and P_3, respectively.

> The **market demand function** is a horizontal summation of all individual consumer demand functions.

We refer to prices P_1, P_2, and P_3 as reservation prices for each of the consumers. A *reservation price* is the lowest price at which the consumer's quantity demanded is zero. Because the demand functions of consumers differ, they have different reservation prices.

APPLICATION 2-3

Why Are Americans Eating More Poultry and Less Red Meat?

American eating habits have been changing over the years. One noteworthy change is the greater consumption of chicken and turkey and lesser consumption of red

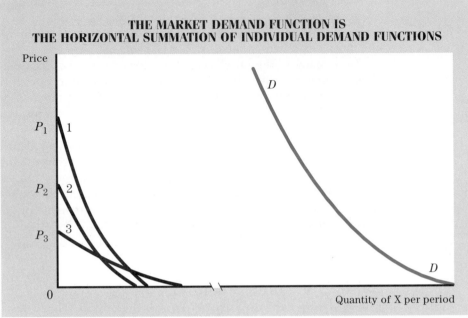

**THE MARKET DEMAND FUNCTION IS
THE HORIZONTAL SUMMATION OF INDIVIDUAL DEMAND FUNCTIONS**

Figure 2-17   The market demand function is obtained by summing horizontally the demand curves of all consumers. The demand functions of only three among many consumers are shown. The quantity demanded by consumer 1 is positive only if the price of X is less than P_1. The quantity demanded by consumer 2 is positive if the price is less than P_2. Consumer 3 will not demand any units of X unless the price is less than P_3.

meats such as beef, lamb, and pork. A popular explanation for this dietary change is the greater awareness of the relation between diet and health. Americans have become much more informed in recent years about the connection between red meat consumption and heart and other diseases. If the change in consumption patterns is due to greater information, then we can treat it as a change in tastes caused by new information that causes the individual and the market demand functions to shift outward for poultry and inward for red meats. Let's see if the empirical evidence confirms this health information hypothesis by looking for shifts in the market demand function for chicken.

Table 2-3 shows estimates of the per capita consumption of poultry (chicken and turkey) and of red meat (beef, pork, veal, and lamb) from 1970 to 1990. These are only estimates because the U.S. Department of Agriculture (USDA) takes the total production of poultry, converts it to the equivalent of boneless, trimmed meat, and divides by the total population. Per capita poultry consumption has increased, while red meat consumption has declined. Are health concerns the primary cause of the change, or can it be explained as a response to price changes?

Researchers at the USDA studied this question and came up with some interesting and surprising answers. Their findings suggest that price not health plays

Table 2-3   ESTIMATED PER CAPITA CONSUMPTION OF POULTRY AND RED MEAT

YEAR	PER CAPITA CONSUMPTION OF POULTRY (LB)	PER CAPITA CONSUMPTION OF RED MEAT (LB)
1970	33.8	132.3
1975	32.9	126.2
1980	40.6	126.4
1985	45.2	124.9
1990	55.4	112.4

Source: Judith Jones Putnam and Jane E. Allshouse, *Food Consumption, Prices, and Expenditures, 1970–1990* (SB-840, Economic Research Service, USDA, August 1992).

the dominant role. Figure 2-18 is a diagram of the inflation-adjusted retail price per pound of chicken and per capita pounds of chicken consumed from 1950 to 1990. Each point on the figure represents a yearly observation. From the figure you can see that the inflation-adjusted price of poultry declined dramatically over this period—by about 75 percent. Because the price of chicken has declined absolutely and relatively to the prices of red meat, the per capita quantity demanded has increased.

It appears that the yearly observations made between 1950 and 1983 are the consequence of a stable per capita demand function and a supply function that has shifted downward over time. Figure 2-19 illustrates this process with a hypothetical supply function that shifts downward over time and a hypothetical stable demand function. The observations of price and per capita quantity consumed trace out the demand function of a representative consumer. This is one way of explaining the decline in the price of chicken and the increase in the quantities consumed over time. Because the price declines started in the 1950s, well before concerns about diet and health surfaced, it appears that changes in relative prices are primarily responsible for the changes in the type of meat Americans eat.

There is a hint that the demand function may have shifted to the right since 1983 because the inflation-adjusted price has not changed appreciably although per capita consumption has increased. However, the USDA researchers suggest that this is an artifact of the data. Per capita human consumption is not really growing as rapidly as Figure 2-18 indicates because of the growing use of chicken in pet foods.

It appears that changes in the selection of meat by American consumers are largely explained by changes in the relative prices of the different types of meat and that health concerns play a secondary role in causing these changes.

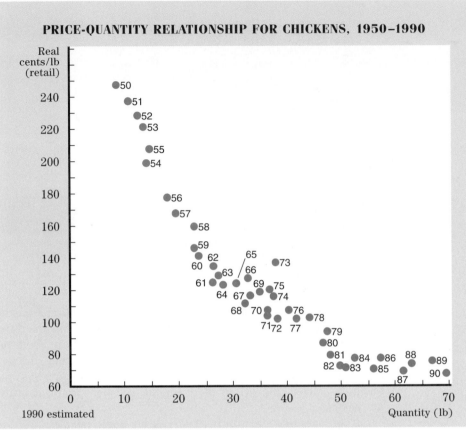

Figure 2-18   Annual observations of real retail chicken price and the number of gross pounds consumed appear to trace out the consumer's demand function. [Mark R. Weimar and Richard P. Stillman, "Market Trends Driving Broiler Consumption," *Livestock and Poultry Situation and Outlook Report*, (LPS-44, Economic Research Service, USDA, November 1990).]

2-8   SUBSTITUTES AND COMPLEMENTS

Chapter 1 described how the demand function for a good shifts when the price of another good changes. When air fares decrease, the market demand function for rental cars shifts outward. On the other hand, the market demand function for 100 percent cotton shirts shifts inward when the price of polyester shirts decreases. The demand function for a good can shift when the price of another good changes. The theory of consumer behavior can explain these different reactions.

Let's see how the quantity demanded of X by a utility-maximizing consumer changes when the price of Y, another good, changes. Suppose the price of X is P_X^1, consumer income is I, and both are constant. If the price of Y *decreases*, the

A SHIFTING SUPPLY FUNCTION AND A STABLE DEMAND FUNCTION

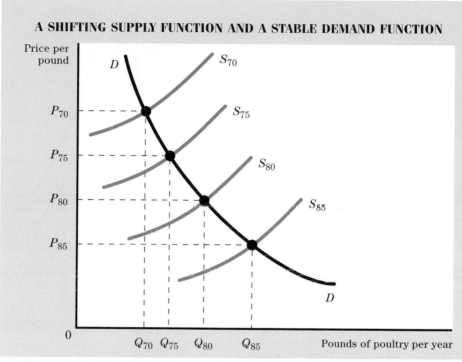

Figure 2-19   The demand function for poultry is stable, but the supply function shifts to the right because it becomes cheaper to produce poultry over time. The equilibrium prices and quantities trace out the demand function.

consumer's budget constraint rotates around the x intercept and the individual selects a new market basket. Figure 2-20a shows that market basket A is purchased initially and that market basket B is bought after the price of Y decreases. Market basket B includes more units of X. Given income and the price of X, a decrease in the price of Y *increases* the quantity demanded of X from X_1 to X_2. This is what happens to the demand function for rental cars when air fares fall, or to the demand function for software programs when prices of personal computers fall. Figure 2-20b shows that the demand function for rental cars shifts outward from D to D' when air fares fall. At a price of P_X^1, the quantity demanded of rental cars increases from X_1 to X_2 when air fares decrease. When the demand function for X shifts outward because the price of Y decreases, X and Y are called complements.

When the price of Y changes and the quantity demanded of X changes in the opposite direction, with the price of X held constant, X and Y are called **complements**.

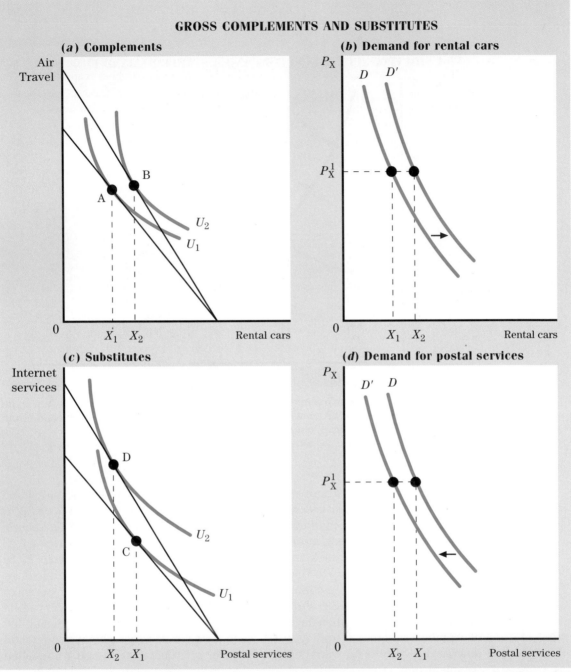

GROSS COMPLEMENTS AND SUBSTITUTES

(*a*) Complements

Air Travel

A

B

U_2

U_1

0   X_1 X_2 Rental cars

(*b*) Demand for rental cars

P_X

D D'

P_X^1

0   X_1 X_2 Rental cars

(*c*) Substitutes

Internet services

D

C

U_2

U_1

0   X_2 X_1 Postal services

(*d*) Demand for postal services

P_X

D' D

P_X^1

0   X_2 X_1 Postal services

Figure 2-20   When the price of Y decreases, the demand function for X can shift outward (*b*) or shift inward (*d*). When a change in the price of Y changes the quantity demanded of X in the opposite direction, X and Y are called complements. (*b*) A decrease in air fares increases the quantity demanded of rental cars at the price of P_X^1. When a change in the price of Y changes the quantity demanded of X in the same direction at a given price of X, X and Y are called substitutes. (*d*) A decrease in the price of using the Internet decreases the quantity demanded of postal services at the price of P_X^1.

In Figure 2-20c the price of Y decreases, the price of X remains at P_X^1, and income is I. Before the price of Y changes, the consumer purchases market basket C. The budget constraint rotates around the intercept on the horizontal axis when the price of Y decreases, and the consumer purchases market basket D. The quantity demanded of X decreases from X_1 to X_2 when the price of Y decreases. This is what happens for example when the price of using the Internet falls and the demand for postal services shifts inward. Figure 2-20d shows that the demand function for postal services shifts inward from D to D' when the price of using the Internet falls. Instead of using letters to communicate, consumers use the Internet. The quantity demanded of postal services decreases from X_1 to X_2 when the price of X is P_X^1. If a decrease in the price of Y causes the demand function of X to shift inward and the quantity demanded of X to decrease, X and Y are called substitutes.

> When the price of Y changes and the quantity demanded of X changes in the same direction, with the price of X held constant, X and Y are called **substitutes.**

We can determine whether two goods are substitutes or complements by the sign of the arc cross-price elasticity of demand. The **arc cross-price elasticity of demand** measures the average percentage change in the quantity of one good relative to the average percentage change in the price of another. If the two goods are X and Y, the arc cross-price elasticity of demand is

$$E_{YP_X} = \frac{\Delta Y}{\Delta P_X} \frac{P_X^1 + P_X^2}{Y_1 + Y_2} \qquad \text{(Arc Cross-Price Elasticity of Demand)} \qquad \textbf{(2-6)}$$

This expression is similar to the equation for the arc price elasticity of demand. The only difference is that the change in the quantity of X has been replaced by the change in the quantity of Y, and the sum of the units of X by the sum of the units of Y. Equation 2-6 measures the response of Y to a change in the price of X. If X and Y are gross complements, then $\Delta Y/\Delta P_X$ is negative and the arc cross price elasticity of demand is negative as in the rental car example. If they are gross substitutes, then $\Delta Y/\Delta P_X$ is positive and the arc cross-price elasticity of demand is positive as in the Internet example.

2-9   APPLYING THE CONSUMER BEHAVIOR MODEL

This section applies the theory of consumer behavior by comparing the responses of consumers when they must spend a subsidy on a particular good or when the subsidy is unrestricted. This public policy question is treated in some detail to give you some practice in applying the consumer behavior model. It is hoped you will then be able to apply the theory successfully to other problems. In the problem set at the end of this chapter you can use the theory of consumer behavior to investigate the incentive effects of a challenge grant with which a major donor hopes to increase other donations to a university by agreeing to augment any contributions from the alumni.

APPLICATION 2-4

Earmarked versus General-Purpose Grants

Governments provide grants to needy citizens, and the often stated purpose of a grant program is to increase the well-being of the recipients. Frequently, grants are tied to expenditure on a specific good. For example, recipients of food stamps must spend them on food. What are the consequences of giving earmarked grants rather than unrestricted money grants?

Let's analyze a public program for providing decent housing to low-income families. Suppose the government issues a voucher of H dollars per month that must be spent on housing. The public expects the recipient to spend the earmarked grant on housing so that total spending on housing increases by the amount of the grant.

We can use the model of consumer behavior to analyze the consequences of providing an earmarked rather than a general-purpose grant of the same amount. Let's begin by showing the market basket the consumer selects before any grant is available. In Figure 2-21a and b total spending on all goods other than housing is on the vertical axis, and square footage of an apartment is on the horizontal axis. Without a grant program, consumers 1 and 2 each have an income of I^* and a budget constraint of BB', where the slope of the budget line is equal to the price per square foot of living space. Let R_1 be the rent per square foot of living space, assuming that an apartment with 400 square feet rents for half the amount of an apartment with 800 square feet. Let's consider consumer 2 first. Her indifference curves are $_2U_0$ and $_2U_1$ in Figure 2-21b. She maximizes utility by selecting market basket a, which includes an apartment with $_2f_0$ square feet, spending S_2 on other goods, and spending $I^* - S_2$ on housing.

When an earmarked grant is made available, the government gives the recipient a voucher for H dollars per month and the landlord deposits the voucher and receives payment from the government. What we must do is determine how the budget constraint shifts when an earmarked grant is provided. By dividing H by R_1, we find out how many more square feet the recipient can rent with the earmarked subsidy. If the voucher is worth \$400 a month and R_1 equals \$2 per square foot, the consumer can afford to rent an apartment that is larger by 200 square feet. For example, if she continues to spend S_2 on other goods, a larger apartment with $_2f_0 + 200$ square feet can be rented for a monthly rent of $I^* - S_2 + H$. With the earmarked grant, market basket a' becomes an affordable market basket. If the consumer was homeless before the grant became available and spent nothing on housing and I^* on other goods (the market basket at point B), she can continue to spend I^* on other goods but now can rent an apartment of 200 square feet. Therefore, she can purchase market basket e on the solid line CC'. With the earmarked grant, apartment size can be increased by H/R_1 for every market basket on BB'. A grant that earmarks spending on housing shifts BB' horizontally, and so the consumer's new budget line becomes the line CC'. Not surprisingly, an earmarked grant expands the affordable opportunities for the recipient, but only in a

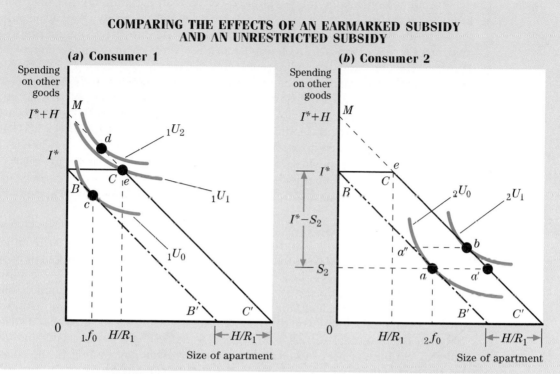

**COMPARING THE EFFECTS OF AN EARMARKED SUBSIDY
AND AN UNRESTRICTED SUBSIDY**

Figure 2-21 An earmarked subsidy offers the recipient fewer opportunities than a money subsidy with no strings attached. With an earmarked subsidy the budget constraint shifts horizontally from BB' to CC', and with a money subsidy it shifts outward from BB' to MCC'. (*a*) With a money subsidy consumer 1 can spend less than H dollars on additional rent if he so desires. Without a subsidy consumer 1 purchases market basket c. With a money subsidy he can reach the indifference curve $_1U_2$ by purchasing market basket d. With an earmarked subsidy consumer 1 reaches only indifference curve $_1U_1$ by purchasing market basket e. (*b*) Without a subsidy consumer 2 purchases market basket a. She purchases market basket b under either form of subsidy.

particular way. Segment Me is not available since we assume (1) it is illegal to resell the voucher and (2) our consumer does not violate the law.

However, an unrestricted grant of H dollars opens up still more opportunities for the recipient. If she receives an unrestricted money grant of H dollars, BB' shifts outward and becomes the new budget line MCC'. The consumer is free to spend *all* the money grant on other goods. Therefore, she has the option of spending $I^* + H$ on other goods and spending nothing on housing. An unrestricted grant is similar to an increase in income, and the budget constraint shifts out in a parallel fashion. The difference between the budget line with a money grant and with an earmarked grant is the segment MC. All other things being equal, the recipient prefers a money grant to an earmarked grant because she can afford more market baskets with an unrestricted money grant.

For some consumers utility will be lower with an earmarked grant than with a money grant, and for others there will be no effect on utility. We can use the model to illustrate the two cases: If the recipient of an unrestricted grant rents an apartment smaller than H/R_1 feet, utility can be lower with an earmarked grant. In Figure 2-21a consumer 1's indifference curves are $_1U_0$, $_1U_1$, and $_1U_2$. Without a grant, he purchases market basket c where the indifference curve $_1U_0$ is tangent to the budget line BB'. This individual rents a very small apartment of size $_1f_0$ and spends little on housing. When a money grant becomes available, he purchases market basket d where the indifference curve $_1U_2$ is tangent to MCC'. With an earmarked grant he maximizes utility by purchasing market basket e where the indifference curve $_1U_2$ touches the edge of the budget line CC' and rents a larger apartment of size H/R_1 than with a money grant. However, he reaches only $_1U_1$ with an earmarked grant and so is worse off with an earmarked than with an unrestricted grant.

On the other hand, in Figure 2-21b consumer 2 starts with market basket a and purchases market basket b with either an earmarked or a money grant. With either type of grant consumer 2 does not simply take the grant and increase spending on housing. Rather, what she does is spend more on other goods and set aside a smaller amount of I^* to be spent on housing. To make up for this reduction, she uses the grant. By spending more on other goods and less on housing with her private income of I^*, she would ordinarily end up with market basket a''. Then, she takes the grant and spends it on housing to select the now affordable market basket b. So both types of grant have a partial crowding-out effect in the sense that the recipient cuts back partially on the private amount set aside for housing. Therefore, subsidies of this kind will not increase spending on housing by the full amount of the grant. The intuition behind this result goes something like this. If your monthly income increased by $500 a month, would you spend all the increase on housing? Chances are you would spend some of it on housing, some on food, some on clothing, and so on. The grant is like an increase in income, and you will maximize utility by spending the higher income on all goods, not just on housing.

If the goal of a grant program is to maximize the utility of the recipient, then an earmarked grant program does not achieve that goal for the consumer in Figure 2-21a. To explain the nature of these subsidy programs, we have to assume that the well-being of the givers is also important. They appear to be saying that *their* utility is higher if they know or think they know that the subsidy is being spent in particular ways and on particular goods. The givers believe that recipients must spend the grant on housing or food and not on other goods that the givers consider less essential. Moreover, an earmarked program cannot be justified as a means to prevent recipients from consuming more of other goods. In fact, recipients end up consuming more housing and more of other goods under both programs.

SUMMARY

■ A consumer ranks all market baskets while satisfying the consistency and transitivity conditions.

■ An indifference curve represents a set of market baskets such that the well-being of the consumer is the same.

- The marginal rate of substitution is the slope of an indifference curve. It is negative and measures a particular consumer's tradeoff between two goods such that the consumer remains indifferent.
- Indifference curves have negative slopes if more of each good increases well-being and the curves do not touch.
- The budget constraint of a consumer determines what market baskets the individual can afford.
- The goal of a consumer is to reach the highest indifference curve while satisfying the budget constraint.
- A consumer who purchases two goods maximizes utility by making the marginal rate of substitution equal to the slope of the budget line. The consumer's marginal

- rate of substitution is equal to the market's.
- The consumer's demand function for a good is derived by determining the quantity demanded at each price of the good, holding other prices and consumer income constant.
- The market demand function is the horizontal sum of the individual demand functions.
- When the price of a related product changes and the quantity demanded of this product changes in the opposite direction, the two products are complements.
- When the price of a related product changes and the quantity demanded of this product changes in the same direction, the two products are substitutes.

KEY TERMS

market basket
indifference curve
diminishing marginal rate of substitution
indifference map
affordable market baskets
specialization of consumption
consumer demand function
substitutes and complements
arc cross-price elasticity of demand

marginal rate of substitution
utility function
perfect substitutes and perfect
   complements
budget constraint
maximal utility
composite good
market demand function
earmarked and unrestricted subsidies

REVIEW QUESTIONS

1. What is the marginal rate of substitution? What is the marginal rate of substitution between nickels and dimes?
2. What happens to the budget constraint if the price of X and Y both increase by K percent? Draw a graph of the budget constraint.
3. What do a consumer's indifference curves look like if X and Y are perfect substitutes?
4. What do a consumer's indifference curves look like if X and Y are perfect complements?

5. A consumer is indifferent between a 5 percent decrease in income or a 5 percent increase in all prices. Explain why you agree or disagree.
6. If the price of Y is $8, the price of X is $4, and the marginal rate of substitution with my current market basket is -2, will my utility increase if I purchase more X and less Y? Draw a graph of the consumer's situation.
7. If I maximize utility by purchasing X and Y, what must be the relationship between

my marginal rate of substitution and the slope of the budget constraint?

8. A consumer spends all of his income on other goods and does not buy any cups of gourmet coffee when the price per cup is $2.00. Is the consumer maximizing utility if the consumer's marginal rate of substitution equals -3 when the consumer does not consume any coffee? Explain your answer.

9. When the price of X is $10 and the price of Y is $30, a consumer purchases 100 units of X and 50 units of Y. Because 100 units of X and 50 units of Y are purchased, the consumer must be willing to substitute 2 units of X for 1 unit of Y to remain indifferent. Given the prices, 3 units of X can be substituted for each unit of Y along the budget constraint. Therefore, the consumer is not maximizing utility. Explain why you agree or disagree with this statement.

10. If the price of X falls and I purchase more units of X while spending more on all other goods, my demand function for X can be either price-elastic or price-inelastic. Explain why you agree or disagree with this statement.

11. Every consumer will prefer a price policy that gives 50 percent off the price on every second unit purchased to one that gives 25 percent off on every unit purchased. Explain why you agree or disagree.

12. According to the terms of a buying club, a consumer with income I who joins will save 5 percent on the price of every good purchased. Using a graph, show the largest membership fee M the buying club can charge and still convince the consumer to join.

13. To estimate the price elasticity of demand for bathing suits, you should compare the price and quantity sold from June to August with the price and quantity sold during any other three month period to derive an estimate. Explain why you agree or disagree with the statement.

14. To estimate the price elasticity of supply for turkeys, you should compare the price and quantity sold in November with the price and quantity sold in a normal month. Explain why you agree or disagree with the statement.

15. The growth of greeting cards has been sluggish in recent years. What arguments would you present to explain why the market for greeting cards has not been expanding?

EXERCISES

1. Suppose you buy two goods, beef and fish. As the price of beef falls relative to the price of fish, you buy slightly more beef than formerly. Show this behavior with indifference curves and locate your approximate position.

2. The data in the table on page 87 show the prices of X and Y, the annual income of the consumer, and the quantities of X consumed during the last 6 years.
   a. What pair of years would you use to calculate the price elasticity of the demand for X? Explain why you selected this pair. What is the arc price elasticity of demand for X?
   b. The calculation of the price elasticity of the demand for X is biased because of a change in preference for X and Y if you use which two years to calculate the price elasticity?
   c. Given your answer to question b, what two years would you use to determine if X and Y are complements or substitutes?
   d. What pair of years would you use to calculate the price elasticity of the de-

YEAR	PRICE OF X ($)	QUANTITY OF X	PRICE OF Y ($)	ANNUAL INCOME ($)
1987	100	80	50	20,000
1988	110	90	40	18,000
1989	90	100	40	18,000
1990	100	100	50	20,000
1991	100	90	40	20,000
1992	100	110	40	25,000

mand for Y? Explain why you selected this pair of years.

3. What does the consumer's demand function for X look like if X and Y are perfect substitutes?

4. What is the consumer's demand function for X if X and Y are perfect complements?

5. A consumer has run out of laundry detergent and has to decide how much detergent to purchase at the supermarket. Use indifference curves to analyze a consumer's purchase decision when the consumer purchases two goods: (1) spending on other goods and (2) containers of laundry detergent. Then show the consumer's budget constraint when the per container price is $5.00. Show a situation where the consumer maximizes utility by buying 3 containers of laundry detergent. What is the consumer's marginal rate of substitution?

6. Suppose a grocery store charges a per container price of $5.00 if the consumer purchases 3 or fewer containers but $2.50 per container for *all* containers if the consumer purchases more than 3 containers.

   a. Show the budget constraint of the consumer.

   b. This price promotion will not affect those consumers who would buy 3 or fewer containers if the price of every container was $5.00 but will encourage buyers who would buy more than 3 containers when the per container price is $5.00 to buy even more. Explain why you agree or disagree with this statement.

*7. By accumulating miles on business trips, an employee can convert mileage into "free" leisure trips for personal use. Consider a consumer whose utility depends on (a) spending on other goods and (b) T airplane trips for leisure travel. In the absence of a frequent flyer program the consumer has an income of I and the price of a trip is P_a.

   a. On a graph find the market basket that maximizes the utility of the consumer. Suppose the employee maximizes utility by taking T_1 leisure trips.

   b. Show how the frequent flyer program shifts the budget line of the consumer. Assume that the employee flies enough miles to qualify for T^* additional leisure trips.

   c. Will the total number of leisure trips the employee takes increase from T_1 to $T_1 + T^*$? Explain why or why not.

   d. Assume that the employer requires all reservations for business trips be made by the company, so that the employee does not receive any leisure trips from frequent flyer programs, but increases the compensation of the employee by $P_a T^*$. If the employee pays 28 percent of income in taxes, what will the individual's budget constraint look like? Explain why taxes on income cause the employee to prefer benefits from the frequent flyer program over an increase in income.

*8. Absenteeism is a costly problem for many firms. It disrupts production and reduces labor productivity. Suppose a firm plans to reward attendance. Currently, the firm pays workers a wage of D dollars per day.

Assume that the "two" goods in the utility function of a worker are spending on other goods and days of leisure (L). The worker will consume more of both "goods" if the budget constraint shifts outward in a parallel fashion. Let days of leisure of a worker be $L = 365 - W$, where W is the number of days worked. The income earned by a worker is spent on goods.

A review of the attendance records of all workers employed by the firm reveals the average number of days worked per year was 210. Some worked as many as 250 days per year, whereas others showed up for work as few as 180 days. Dissatisfied with this performance, management would like to raise the average to 220 days per year. To reduce absenteeism, it is considering this proposal: Offer a flat annual bonus of B dollars to each production worker who works at least 220 days a year.

a. Write out an expression for the income of the worker. Draw the budget constraint for a typical production worker.

b. With the aid of a graph show how the employer's proposal changes the budget constraint of the worker.

c. Show the effect of the proposal on the total days worked by employees who were initially (1) working less than 220 days per year; (2) working 220 or more days per year.

d. Will the proposal raise the average days worked to 220? Explain why or why not.

9. Suppose computer prices continue to fall. Will the demand function for paper shift outward or inward as more consumers own computers? What arguments would you make that computers and paper are complements or substitutes?

10. When a firm charges a price P' for each unit of its product, some consumers do not purchase it. To induce those consumers who did not buy to buy, the firm offers a discount of 25 percent on just the second unit. Even with a discount on just the second unit (*a*) some consumers still do not try the product, (*b*) others purchase one unit, and (*c*) still others purchase two units. Are all three responses to the quantity discount consistent with utility maximization? Use indifference curves to explain your answer.

*11. To encourage more spending on education by local school districts, the state government plans to offer aid. Suppose that within each district all families are alike but that districts differ because of differences in income and spend different amounts on education. A particular district is currently spending $500 per student, and the state would like to raise this amount to $550 per student. The utility function of each family in the district includes two goods, spending on other goods and spending on education. The state is considering two proposals:

- *Lump sum grant 1.* The state will pay $50 per child toward educational expenditures if the district spends more than $100 per child.
- *Lump sum grant 2.* The state will pay $50 per child toward educational expenditures if the district spends more than $550 per child.

a. Show the indifference curves of a representative family in the district that spends $500 per child. Show how each proposal would alter the budget constraint of the family.

b. With the aid of graphs, indicate whether the families in a district are more likely to increase per pupil expenditure (i.e., total per pupil expenditure less per pupil state aid) under proposal 1 or under proposal 2.

c. Is it possible to determine if total spending on education per pupil (i.e., local plus state spending) will be higher under proposal 1 or under proposal 2? Explain your answer.

*12. Eric J. Gleacher, an alumnus of the Graduate School of Business at the University of Chicago, presented the GSB with a $15 million Challenge Grant. For the five most recent graduating classes, Gleacher will give $4 to the GSB for every dollar donated by a recent grad. For all other alumni,

Gleacher will give $2 for each additional dollar donated over and above the graduate's most recent annual donation.

a. Consider a 1996 graduate whose income is spent on other goods and on a donation to the GSB. Show how the graduate's budget constraint is changed by the Gleacher Challenge Grant.

b. Consider a graduate of the class of 1988 and show how the graduate's budget constraint is changed by the Gleacher Challenge Grant.

c. Will each graduate increase the amount donated compared to what would have been donated without the Challenge Grant? Will any graduate decrease the amount donated? Explain your answer.

PROBLEM SET

Will a Challenge Grant Increase Alumni Contributions?

The year is 2021. You received your undergraduate degree in the mid-1990s and have had a successful and financially rewarding career. Over the years you have made annual contributions to your university and are aware of its progress and its problems. Because you hold a warm spot in your heart for your alma mater, you decide to do something special by giving it a major donation.

During a recent conversation, the president of the university expressed a desire to expand the science building, to find a new home for the social sciences faculty, and to improve the facilities for intramural athletics. High on the president's wish list is a major donation and an increase in the percentage of contributors donating at least $100 per year from the current 35 percent to 50 percent (column 2 in Table 2-4 indicates 65 percent of donors give less than $100). She reports that most

alumni increase their contributions as their income increases.

You decide that the time is right to make a large donation to the university, but you want to create an incentive mechanism that will raise alumni contributions. A challenge grant seems to be the perfect solution. You will donate $100 to the university for any alumni gift between $100 and $299. You hope the challenge grant will stimulate those giving less than $100 to increase their contribution to $100, and some of those giving between $100 and $299 to increase their contribution also.

You ask the alumni office to estimate how the challenge grant will change the distribution of contributions. The predicted distribution in column 3 of Table 2-4 shows that the percentage giving $100 or more will increase to 50 percent. The alumni office also predicts that the percentage giving between $100 and $299 will increase and that those who give more than $299 will give with or without a challenge grant.

Table 2-4   ACTUAL AND PREDICTED DISTRIBUTION OF CONTRIBUTORS BY AMOUNT CONTRIBUTED

AMOUNT CONTRIBUTED BY EACH INDIVIDUAL IN 2020 ($) (1)	PERCENT OF THOSE GIVING IN 2020 (2)	PREDICTED PERCENT OF THOSE GIVING IN 2021 BECAUSE OF CHALLENGE GRANT (3)
$0–$49	40	35
$50–$99	25	15
$100–$149	13	27
$150–$199	10	10
$200–$299	7	8
$300–	5	5

You hire an economist to evaluate the predictions made by the alumni office. In particular, you ask about the effect of the challenge grant on (1) those currently contributing less than $100, (2) those contributing between $100 and $299, and (3) those contributing more than $300.

To analyze the effects of the challenge grant, the economist builds a simple model of the behavior of an individual donor. Suppose the two goods in the utility function of an individual donor are (1) a composite good that represents spending on other goods and (2) the total donation to the university that arises from the individual's contribution. This assumes that each contributor receives utility from the sum of his or her contribution and the contribution from the challenge grant that is triggered by the individual's contribution. If the utility of the donor depends *only* on the individual's direct contribution, the challenge grant will have no incentive effect.

The economist first considers the effect of the challenge grant on donors currently contributing less than $100. The donor in Figure 2-22a is unaffected by the challenge grant. Total spending on other goods is on the vertical axis,

and the total contribution that results from the individual's donation is on the horizontal axis. The income of this donor is I^*, and the budget constraint is the line I^*f. Without a challenge grant every dollar contributed to the university by this individual reduces the amount spent on other goods by a corresponding dollar. Therefore the slope of the budget constraint equals -1. Market basket a maximizes the donor's utility because it makes the marginal rate of substitution equal to the slope of the budget constraint. The individual in Figure 2-22a has a modest income and contributes just $25 per year.

How does the challenge grant change the budget constraint of this consumer? If the individual contributes less than $100, the budget constraint remains the same. If the individual contributes between $100 and $299, the contribution triggers another $100. Hypothetically, you could think of the donor as receiving a check for $100 from the challenge grant, forwarded to the university with a solemn promise to contribute any amount from $100 to $299. Therefore, for gifts between $100 and $299, the budget constraint shifts horizontally to the right by $100. For example, the donor's contri-

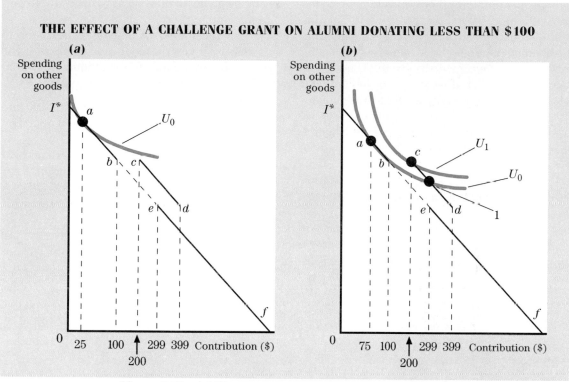

THE EFFECT OF A CHALLENGE GRANT ON ALUMNI DONATING LESS THAN $100

Figure 2-22   (*a*) The consumer is unaffected by the challenge grant and continues to donate $25 to the university. (*b*) The consumer purchases market basket *c* and increases his or her donation from $75 to $100 because of the challenge grant.

bution of $100 is augmented by $100 from the challenge grant, so that the total contribution is $200. If any amount between $100 and $299 is contributed, the donation triggers another $100 contribution. Any gift of more than $299 does not qualify for a challenge grant. With the challenge grant the new budget constraint of the donor becomes the line segments I^* to b, c to d, and e to f. There is a discontinuity between points b and c and between points d and e. Because the indifference curve U_0 in Figure 2-22a does not intersect the new budget line, the consumer maximizes utility by continuing to donate $25 to the university. The challenge grant has no effect on the consumer's decision.

The consumer in Figure 2-22b has a different preference map but the same income. With-

out the challenge grant the indifference curve U_0 is tangent to the budget constraint with market basket a where the individual donates $75 to the university. With the challenge grant this donor's contribution increases from $75 to $100 and the donor reaches U_1 by contributing $100 per year. This case differs from the previous one because U_0 cuts through the new budget constraint at point 1. The utility of this individual is increased by the purchase of market basket c. He or she contributes $100 and thereby triggers a $100 challenge contribution. The challenge grant induces this individual to contribute $25 more and increases the total amount donated by $125, that is, $25 from the individual and $100 from the challenge grant. Without the challenge grant the donor must reduce spending on other goods by $25 to donate $25 more. With the challenge grant the cost of giving declines because a $25 reduction in spending on other goods increases total contributions to the university by $125, not by a mere $25. For this donor, the challenge grant has reduced the price of giving to the university.

Donors who contributed amounts slightly less than $100 are more likely to respond to the challenge grant than those giving substantially less than $100, although some of these latter alumni could also be affected. The predictions of the alumni office look reasonable. Of those giving less than $50 a smaller fraction respond to the challenge grant (the percentage drops by only five percentage points) than in the group giving between $50 and $99 (the per-

centage giving in this category drops by 10 percentage points).

Use the model of consumer behavior to explain why you do or do not agree with the remaining predictions of the alumni office concerning the effect of the challenge grant.

1. Will donors who give between $100 and $299 increase their individual contributions?
2. Are donors who give more than $299 unaffected by the challenge grant?
3. Comment on the incentive effects of a challenge grant in view of your answers to questions 1 and 2.
4. Will the challenge grant increase total private contributions? Explain why or why not.

CHAPTER 3

EXTENDING THE THEORY OF CONSUMER BEHAVIOR

■ **3-1   The Shape of the Consumer's Demand Function**
Measuring the Income Effect
Income Elasticity of Demand
Measuring the Substitution Effect
Combining the Two Effects
The Effect of a Price Change on the
    Quantity Demanded
Application 3-1: Subsidizing Day Care
Application 3-2: How Different Is
    Water?
The Slope of the Demand Function
The Size of Each Effect
Observing the Effect of Each
    Determinant
■ **3-2   Consumer Surplus**
Marginal Value
Using the Consumer Surplus Concept

* ■ **3-3   Uncertainty and Consumer Decision Making**
The Expected Income Hypothesis
The Expected Utility Hypothesis
Risk Aversion and Risk Taking
Buying Insurance
Application 3-3: Why Is Earthquake
    Insurance a Slow Seller in
    California?
■ **Summary**
■ **Key Terms**
■ **Review Questions**
■ **Exercises**
■ *Appendix: Deriving Marginal Values**

* More difficult material.

In this chapter we use the theory of consumer behavior to explain why consumers respond differently to incentives. In the first part of the chapter we explain why some consumers have more elastic demand curves than do others. What factors make one consumer's quantity demanded increase by more than another consumer's when price decreases? To get a better handle on why consumers respond differently to a price cut, economists have found it useful to decompose the change in a consumer's quantity demanded into two parts. One part of the increase occurs because a price cut releases income that can be used to purchase more of the product. This effect is called the income effect. The other part of the increase occurs because the good whose price has fallen is now cheaper relative to other goods and the consumer substitutes toward the lower-priced good and demands more units. This effect is called the substitution effect. By working with the income and substitution effects, we can say when a price change will cause a larger or smaller change in the quantity demanded.

Every time a consumer buys a good or a service, the consumer is better off—barring fraud and misrepresentation. Voluntary trade benefits both parties. In technical terms a trade—a good for money or for another good—permits the consumer to move to a higher indifference curve. So the consumer enjoys a surplus by trading. Quite naturally, this surplus is called *consumer surplus* by economists. Since a consumer is better off by trading, can we measure this improvement in some objective way by using dollars? Consumer surplus is a monetary measure of how much more a consumer would be willing to pay for the product above what the consumer actually pays. Knowing the value of consumer surplus is of interest to firms and public officials alike. Firms want to know the value of consumer surplus because they see it as a potential source of additional revenue. In a similar vein public officials want to know how consumer surplus changes in order to evaluate the desirability of policies such as a tax or a tariff on a product or the construction of a highway in a remote region of the country.

The final section of the chapter shifts gears by placing the consumer in an uncertain environment where each decision does not lead to a known outcome but to multiple possible outcomes. Of interest is how decisions are made in such an uncertain environment. Why do some individuals go out of their way to avoid risky situations, whereas others take risks and flourish in risky environments? Some choose to go into industries where there is considerable uncertainty about what they will earn, whereas others choose a more secure existence by selecting employment where their income is more predictable. We will explain why some people are willing to pay an insurance premium that lowers their wealth to convert a risky situation into a more certain one.

3-1   THE SHAPE OF THE CONSUMER'S DEMAND FUNCTION

Since consumers respond differently to a given price cut, they must have different demand functions. A price reduction can cause a large increase in the quantity demanded by one consumer and a more modest one by another. Figure 3-1*a* and

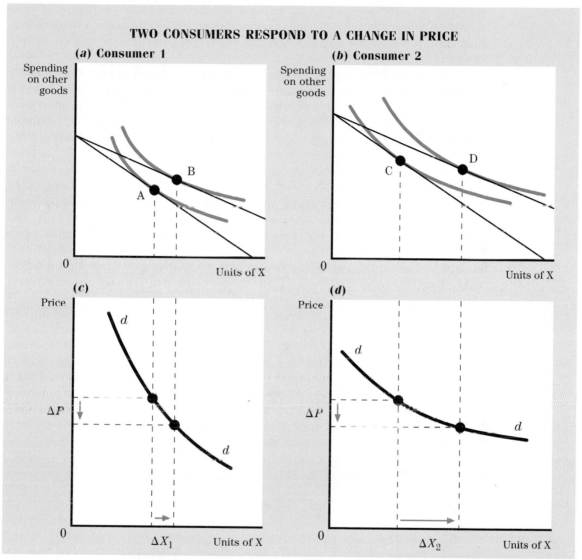

Figure 3-1   When the price changes by ΔP, the quantity demanded by consumer 1 increases by only ΔX_1. It increases by ΔX_2, a larger amount, for consumer 2.

b shows the indifference curves for two consumers. Spending on other goods is on the vertical axis, and units of X are on the horizontal axis. Although both consumers purchase goods at the same prices, they have different tastes (indifference maps) and incomes. Initially, consumer 1 maximizes utility by selecting market basket A, while consumer 2 purchases market basket C. When the price of X decreases, the budget line rotates around the intercept on the y axis and consumer 1 purchases market basket B while consumer 2 selects market basket D. The different demand functions dd of the two consumers are shown in Figure 3-1c and d. When the price falls by ΔP, the quantity demanded by consumer 1 increases by only ΔX_1, whereas the quantity demanded by consumer 2 increases by ΔX_2, a larger amount.

Just why do these two consumers respond differently to a price cut? To identify the factors affecting the response, consider someone who purchases X and a composite good. How does a change in the price of X affect the consumer's behavior? From the buyer's perspective, a price reduction of X immediately releases income that was formerly spent on X. You can use these funds by purchasing more units of X or by spending more on the composite good, or both. So, a price reduction creates an increase in disposable funds that the consumer can use to purchase more of some or all goods. If the price decreases by ΔP and X equals the number of units initially consumed, the individual now has $-(\Delta P)X$ more income to spend on X and the composite good. For example, you are richer by \$10 if you consume 10 units of X and the price of X falls by \$1. Because a price cut releases income, it resembles an increase in income and shifts outward the budget constraint. Consequently, the consumer can select a new market basket on a higher indifference curve.

> The change in quantity demanded of X due to the change in money income is the **income effect.**

However, a price cut does more than simply release income to be spent on X and on other goods. To see why, let's ask how you would respond if that extra income due to the price cut was taken away from you so that you could not move to a higher indifference curve. You still would not buy the original market basket. Why not? Because the price of X is now cheaper relative to other goods than before, you will demand more units of the now cheaper X and fewer of other goods.

> The **substitution effect** measures the change in the quantity demanded due to a change in the relative price of X holding utility constant, that is, while remaining on the same indifference curve.

Hypothetically, we view the consumer as separating the total change in the quantity demanded of X caused by a price change into a change due to the income effect and the change due to the substitution effect. This introduction to these two effects is altogether too brief. We need to discuss each effect in greater detail and show how to measure each one. Then, we will join the two effects and describe situations where the consumer's response to a price change will be large or small.

Measuring the Income Effect

Let's take up the *income effect* first. Figure 3-2a shows two of the consumer's indifference curves, U_0 and U_1. Total spending S on other goods is on the vertical axis, and units of X are on the horizontal axis. Consider a situation where the income of the consumer is I_0 and the price of X is P_X. The initial budget constraint

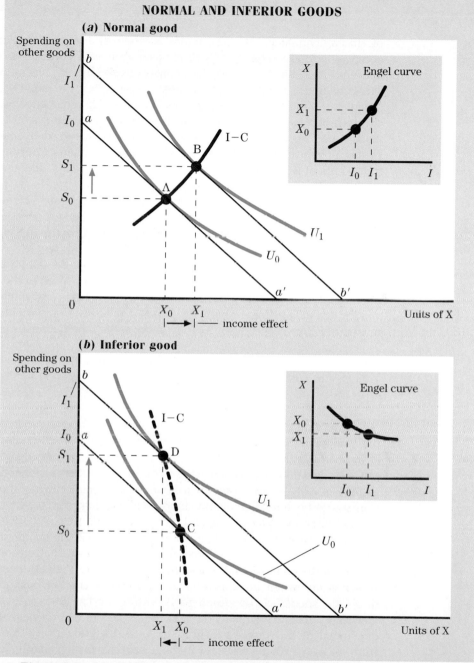

NORMAL AND INFERIOR GOODS

(a) Normal good

(b) Inferior good

Figure 3-2 (*a*) An increase in income shifts the budget constraint from *aa′* to *bb′*. The consumer increases the consumption of X from X_0 to X_1 units. The income-consumption curve connects all points of tangency between the budget constraint and the indifference curve as income increases. When an increase in income increases the number of units consumed, the good is a normal good. The Engel curve shows the relationship between the income of the consumer and the quantity demanded and has a positive slope when the good is a normal good. The utility function in (*b*) is different from the utility function in (*a*). (*b*) An increase in income reduces the number of units consumed from X_0 to X_1. When an increase in income reduces the number of units consumed, the good is an inferior good and the Engel curve has a negative slope.

of this individual is aa', and it has a slope of $-P_X$ because spending on the composite good declines by $-P_X$ for each unit of X consumed. The buyer maximizes utility subject to the budget constraint aa' by purchasing market basket A. The consumer's marginal rate of substitution equals the slope of the budget constraint when the consumer purchases X_0 units of X and spends S_0 dollars on other goods. If income increases to I_1, the budget constraint shifts outward in a parallel fashion and becomes bb'. The consumer purchases market basket B, which includes X_1 units of X, and spends S_1 dollars on other goods. This consumer demands more units of X and spends more on other goods because income increases while prices remain constant. Only two points of tangency between the budget constraint and an indifference curve are shown, but there is one for every level of income. All points of tangency between successive budget constraints and the appropriate indifference curves can be connected to form the **income-consumption curve,** I-C.

An **Engel curve** shows the relationship between the quantity demanded of X and the income of the consumer with prices held constant. In the smaller graph in Figure 3-2*a* consumer income is on the horizontal axis and units of X are on the vertical axis. The Engel curve for X has a positive slope when the quantity demanded of X increases from X_0 to X_1 units as income increases from I_0 to I_1.

> When the quantity demanded of a good changes in the same direction as the change in income, we call the good a **normal good** and the Engel curve has a positive slope.

Some examples of normal goods are housing, durable goods, treadmills, eating out, and vacations. Chances are that your first house will be a starter house with limited square footage, but that you will move to larger quarters with greater privacy when your income increases. Durable goods are often normal goods. When income is low, families opt for a lower-priced economy car that provides basic transportation, but when income increases, they may purchase a larger automobile with a better and quieter ride and more safety features.

An increase in income does not always increase the quantity consumed, however. In Figure 3-2*b* the indifference curves are such that an increase in income *decreases* the quantity of X consumed. Initially, the budget constraint of the consumer is aa' when income is I_0. She purchases market basket C with X_0 units of X and spends S_0 on other goods. After income increases to I_1, the budget constraint becomes bb' and the consumer prefers market basket D. The quantity demanded of X decreases from X_0 to X_1 and spending on other goods increases from S_0 to S_1. An increase in income decreases the quantity demanded. When the quantity demanded changes in the direction *opposite* the income change, the good is called an inferior good. The smaller graph in Figure 3-2*b* shows that the Engel curve has a negative slope when the good is an inferior good because the quantity demanded decreases when income increases holding prices constant. As an aside, we should note that inferior goods are not inferior in the everyday use of the word.

When the quantity demanded of a good changes in the direction opposite the change in income, the good is an **inferior good** and the Engel curve has a negative slope.

An example of an inferior good might be hamburger meat, polyester clothing, or shopping at second-hand clothing stores. Although it is common to classify a product as either a normal or an inferior good, this does not mean that everyone treats the product in the same way at all income levels. A consumer might consider a good a normal good for some changes in income and an inferior good for other changes in income. Another point to keep in mind is the heterogeneity among consumers. Some consumers may treat a product as an inferior good, whereas others treat it as a normal good. Peanut butter may be an inferior good for you but a normal good for your younger sister or brother.

Income Elasticity of Demand

Income elasticity of demand is a measure that economists use to compare the percentage change in the quantity demanded due to a percentage change in income.[1] The expression for the arc income elasticity of demand is

$$E_I = \frac{\dfrac{\Delta X}{(X_0 + X_1)/2}}{\dfrac{\Delta I}{(I_0 + I_1)/2}} = \frac{\Delta X}{\Delta I}\frac{I_0 + I_1}{X_0 + X_1} \qquad \text{(Arc Income Elasticity of Demand)} \qquad \textbf{(3-1)}$$

$$= \frac{X_1 - X_0}{I_1 - I_0}\frac{I_0 + I_1}{X_0 + X_1}$$

Equation 3-1 shows the arc income elasticity of demand as the ratio of the change in the quantity demanded to the average quantity demanded at the two income levels, divided by the change in income relative to the average income holding prices constant. E_I is positive for a normal good because the quantity demanded increases when income increases, and is negative for an inferior good because the quantity demanded decreases when income increases.

The **arc income elasticity of demand** measures the ratio of the change in the quantity demanded relative to the average quantity divided by the change in income relative to the average income.

Even if a good is a normal good, that does not necessarily mean that a consumer will spend an increasing share of income on it as income increases. This

---

[1] For infinitesimal changes in income, you would use the following formula for the *point income elasticity of demand:*

$$E_I = \frac{dX}{dI}\frac{I}{X}$$

occurs only if E_I is greater than 1. Then the percentage increase in the quantity demanded exceeds the percentage increase in income, and so the share of income spent on X increases when income increases because prices are constant. If $0 < E_I < 1$, a good is a normal good but the consumer spends a decreasing share of income on it as income rises because prices are constant. After you receive your degree, your income will increase and you will consume more units per year of most food items, although the share of income spent on food will probably go down. On the other hand, the share of income spent on leisure time activities will probably increase.

Table 3-1 shows how expenditures per household on selected athletic footwear and equipment increase with higher household income. While the figures in Table 3-1 resemble Engle curves, they are not strictly so since they are expenditures and not quantities. If we assume as a first approximation, however, that prices are the same for all households, then we can say that increases in expenditure reflect increases in quantities. We see that in every category household expenditure increases with household income but the rate of increase differs substantially between products. The smallest percentage increase between the lowest and the highest income classes is for gym shoes and the largest is for golf club sets. These data suggest that the income elasticity is highest for golf club sets. For gym shoes, household expenditure does not even double as household income increases by more than 5 times. In contrast, household expenditure on golf club sets is very sensitive to household income, increasing by just under 17 times as income in-

Table 3-1   AVERAGE HOUSEHOLD EXPENDITURE ON SELECTED ATHLETIC FOOTWEAR AND EQUIPMENT

Household Income ($ thousands)	Gym Shoes/ Sneakers	Jogging and Running Shoes	Treadmills	In-Line Wheel Skates	Golf Club Sets
Less than $15	$ 6.55	$ 2.45	$ 2.50	$ .83	$ 1.00
$15–$25	12.08	4.71	4.40	1.62	3.32
$25–$35	15.61	6.89	8.29	3.60	6.02
$35–$50	21.77	8.75	13.06	5.29	5.96
$50–$75	21.06	10.74	14.94	8.26	11.66
More than $75	17.67	13.65	20.80	7.89	17.92
Percent increase for households with less than $15 to more than $75	170%	457%	732%	851%	1692%

Source: National Sporting Goods Association, *The Sporting Goods Market in 1995*, 1995.

creases fivefold. Golf is clearly a rich person's sport. As U.S. household real income increases, we would predict an increasing share of household expenditure will go to sellers of treadmills, in-line skates, golfing equipment, and so on.

Measuring the Substitution Effect

The *substitution effect* focuses on how a consumer responds when the relative price of X changes in such a way that his or her utility remains constant.

How can we measure the substitution effect? In Chapter 2 you learned that the budget constraint rotates around the intercept on the vertical axis when the price of X changes while income and other prices remain constant. If the price of X falls and the budget constraint rotates outward, the consumer purchases a different market basket on a higher indifference curve, and so the consumer's utility increases. However, the substitution effect measures the change in the quantity demanded when relative prices change with *utility held constant.* To keep the consumer on the original indifference curve so that utility is unchanged, we change money income as the price changes by just enough so that the consumer finds a new market basket on the original indifference curve where the slope of the new budget constraint equals the slope of the indifference curve.

Figure 3-3 shows how the substitution effect can be found when the initial price of X is P_X. The consumer starts with market basket A on indifference curve U_0 and purchases X_0 units of X while spending S_0 dollars on other goods on budget line *aa*. When the price of X falls to P_X', the budget line *aa* in Figure 3-3 will rotate outward around point *a* and become the dashed budget line *ab*. If nothing else changes, the consumer will reach a higher indifference curve. To prevent utility from increasing, we *decrease* income by enough to shift the budget line *ab* back to U_0 until it becomes *cc* where it is tangent to indifference curve U_0 at market basket B. In this way we see that the reduction in the relative price of X causes the consumer to substitute market basket B for market basket A and therefore to increase the quantity demanded from X_0 to X_1. *The relative price of X is lower, and so cc is flatter than aa.* The consumer responds to a fall in the relative price of X by purchasing more units of X and spending less on other goods. Therefore, the sign of the substitution effect is negative because a change in the relative price of X changes the quantity demanded in the opposite direction.[2]

Combining the Two Effects

Let's combine the income and substitution effects and show how a change in price changes the quantity demanded. The resulting change in the quantity demanded is the sum of the two effects. We can express this as

Change in quantity demanded	=	Change in quantity demanded due to substitution effect	+	Change in quantity demanded due to income effect

[2] The substitution effect is zero in the special case when X is a perfect complement with spending on other goods and the indifference curve is L-shaped.

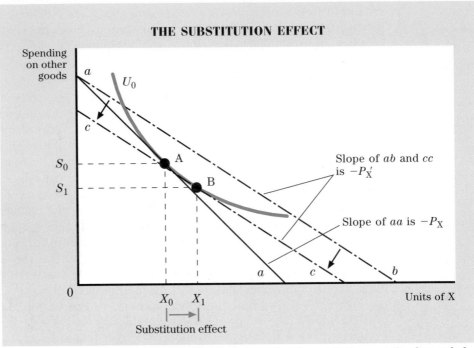

Figure 3-3   The substitution effect measures the change in the quantity demanded of X when the relative price of X changes and utility is constant. A decrease in the price of X offset by a decrease in income keeps the consumer on the same indifference curve. The consumer moves from the original market basket A to market basket B. The quantity demanded increases from X_0 to X_1 because of a fall in the relative price of X. The substitution effect is negative. A change in the relative price of X changes the quantity demanded in the opposite direction.

Figure 3-4 combines both effects to show how the quantity demanded changes. The initial budget constraint is aa when income is I_0 and the price of X is P_X. The consumer maximizes utility by selecting market basket A, purchasing X_0 units, and spending S_0 dollars on other goods. When the price of X decreases to P'_X, the budget line becomes ab. The slope of ab equals the slope of the indifference curve U_1 when the consumer selects market basket B, purchases X_2 units of X, and spends S_2 dollars on other goods. The total quantity demanded increases from X_0 to X_2 when the price falls, and so the demand function in Figure 3-4b has a negative slope.

The increase in the quantity demanded of X, $X_2 - X_0$, is partly due to the substitution effect and partly due to the income effect. Recall that the substitution effect measures the change in the quantity demanded when the relative price of X changes with utility held constant. To find this quantity, we shift the budget constraint to cc by decreasing the relative price of X and changing income so that utility is unchanged. The consumer would select market basket C where the slope of cc equals the slope of indifference curve U_0. The substitution effect

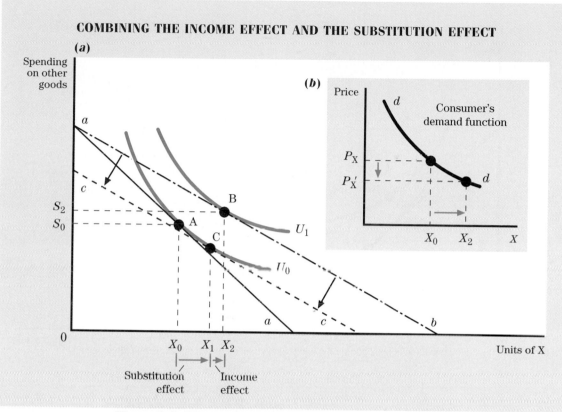

Figure 3-4   The price of X is decreased and the quantity demanded by the consumer increases from X_0 to X_2. The total change can be separated into the sum of the substitution effect and the income effect. The change in the quantity demanded because of the substitution effect is $X_1 - X_0$. The change in the quantity demanded because of the income effect is $X_2 - X_1$. Because the good is a normal good, the income effect is positive. (*b*) The demand function of this consumer has a negative slope.

is the increase in the quantity demanded from X_0 to X_1 units. The income effect shifts the budget line outward in a parallel fashion from *cc* to *ab* because the price reduction makes additional income available to spend on X and on the composite good. The consumer moves from market basket C to market basket B, and the income effect increases the quantity demanded by $X_2 - X_1$. Combining the two effects, we find the quantity demanded increases from X_0 to X_2.

When the good is a normal good, the income effect reinforces the substitution effect, and so the quantity demanded must increase when the price falls; and the demand function has a negative slope.

> If the good is a normal good, a consumer demands more units at a lower price and so the demand function of the consumer has a negative slope.

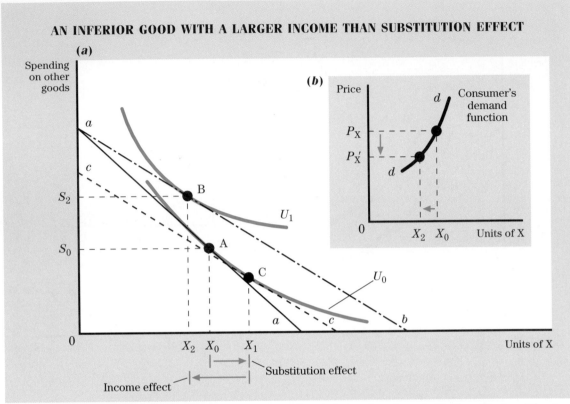

Figure 3-5   When the income effect is larger than the substitution effect and the good is an inferior good, the demand function has a positive slope. When the price decreases to P'_X, the quantity demanded by the consumer decreases from X_0 to X_2. (*b*) The demand function has a positive slope. The substitution effect is $X_1 - X_0$, and the income effect is $X_2 - X_1$. The income effect is negative and overwhelms the substitution effect.

What predictions can we make when the good is an inferior good? Figure 3-5 shows a case where the good is an inferior good *and* the income effect is larger than the substitution effect. In this case a decrease in the price of X *decreases* the quantity demanded. The initial budget constraint is *aa*. The consumer purchases X_0 units of X with market basket A in Figure 3-5*a*. When the price falls from P_X to P'_X, the budget constraint becomes *ab*, the consumer selects market basket B, and the total quantity demanded decreases from X_0 to X_2. Figure 3-5*b* shows that the demand curve has a positive slope. The quantity demanded decreases when the price falls from P_X to P'_X. A utility-maximizing consumer can have a positively sloped demand function.

Again, we separate the total change in the quantity demanded from X_0 to X_2 into a change caused by the substitution effect and a change caused by the income effect. The substitution effect is $X_1 - X_0$. As always, the quantity demanded changes in the direction opposite the price change. What makes this case different from the previous one is the sign and the size of the income effect. An increase in income shifts the budget constraint from cc to ab. Since X is an inferior good, the quantity demanded decreases from X_1 to X_2 when income increases. The net effect of the two opposing changes is $X_2 - X_0$. The income effect not only decreases the quantity demanded but overwhelms the substitution effect so the net effect is a fall in the quantity demanded due to a fall in price. The consumer's demand function in Figure 3-5b has a *positive* slope. When this occurs, economists refer to the good as a **Giffen good.**

Sometimes students mistakenly conclude that the demand curve has a positive slope if the good is an inferior good. Try to avoid this mistake. Although a good is an inferior good, the demand function will have a negative slope if the substitution effect is larger than the income effect. In Figure 3-6 the substitution effect, $X_1 - X_0$, is larger than the income effect, $X_2 - X_1$, and so the demand function has a negative slope although the good is an inferior good. To summarize, the slope of the demand function can be either positive or negative if the good is an inferior good.

> If a good is an inferior good, the consumer may demand more or fewer units when the price decreases. The slope of the demand function can be negative or positive.

The Effect of a Price Change on the Quantity Demanded

The change in the quantity demanded due to a price change is:

> Total Effect   =   Substitution Effect   +   Income Effect

Table 3-2 summarizes the different cases and shows the effects of a price increase or decrease on the quantity demanded for a normal good and for an inferior good.

The substitution and income effects reinforce each other when the good is a normal good. For example, column 1 of Table 3-2 shows that a price increase causes the quantity demanded to decrease $(-)$ because of the substitution effect. The income effect also decreases the quantity demanded $(-)$. Therefore, the quantity demanded decreases when the price increases. Column 2 summarizes the effects of a price decrease on the quantity demanded. If the good is an inferior good, the slope of the demand function can be either positive or negative. Column 3 shows that the substitution effect decreases the quantity demanded $(-)$ when the price increases. On the other hand, the income effect is positive $(+)$. Whether the quantity demanded increases or decreases depends on whether the substitution effect is larger or smaller than the income effect. The net effect on the quantity demanded cannot be predicted when the good is an inferior good. Consequently, the slope of the consumer's demand curve can be either positive or negative.

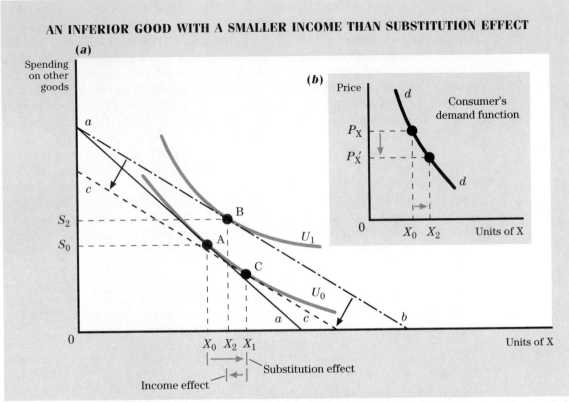

Figure 3-6   When the income effect is smaller than the substitution effect and the good is an inferior good, the demand function has a negative slope. When the price decreases to P_X', the quantity demanded by the consumer increases from X_0 to X_2. (*b*) The demand function has a negative slope. The substitution effect is $X_1 - X_0$ and the income effect is $X_2 - X_1$. The income effect is negative but is smaller than the substitution effect so the net effect of a price decrease is to increase the quantity demanded of X.

You must also be careful not to infer that the *market* demand function has a positive slope just because a few consumer demand functions have a positive slope. In Chapter 2 the negatively sloped market demand function was derived by summing the individual demand functions horizontally. Although some consumers may have a positively sloped demand function over the same range of prices, it is improbable that all of them will have demand functions that slope upward over the same range of prices. If a few consumers have a positively sloped demand function while most have the more common negatively sloped demand functions, the market demand function will have a negative slope. Therefore, economists do not expect to observe and have not observed positively sloped market demand functions.

Table 3-2   CHANGE IN QUANTITY DEMANDED FOR NORMAL AND INFERIOR GOODS

	Normal Good		Inferior Good	
	PRICE INCREASE (1)	PRICE DECREASE (2)	PRICE INCREASE (3)	PRICE DECREASE (4)
Change in quantity demanded due to substitution effect (holding utility constant)	(−)	(+)	(−)	(+)
Change in quantity demanded due to income effect (holding prices constant)	(−)	(+)	(+)	(−)
Total change in quantity demanded	(−)	(+)	(+) or (−)	(+) or (−)
Slope of demand function	(−)	(−)	(+) or (−)	(+) or (−)

APPLICATION 3-1

Subsidizing Day Care

We can apply the analysis of income and substitution effects to study how the demand for day care is affected by a price subsidy as compared to a lump sum subsidy. Day care is an important issue for many families. Legislators are aware of the increasing demand by working parents of young children to do something about day care. Assume they are evaluating two subsidy programs.

- *Program 1.* A family receives a subsidy of *s dollars per day* for each day a child attends an authorized day care facility.
- *Program 2.* Each family with a child registered in an authorized day care facility receives a *lump sum* subsidy.

A trade association of day care providers and groups representing day care users both favor a subsidy but cannot agree on which program to support. The trade association actively lobbies for the per day subsidy, whereas users of child care favor the lump sum program. The opposition of the trade association to program 2 exasperates several members of Congress. They have repeatedly assured the trade association that government spending on day care will be the same no matter which program is adopted. Therefore, they cannot understand why the trade association is being so obstinate.

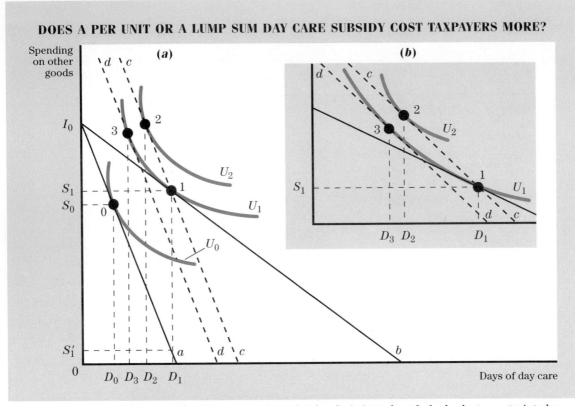

DOES A PER UNIT OR A LUMP SUM DAY CARE SUBSIDY COST TAXPAYERS MORE?

Figure 3-7   When a per day subsidy of s is introduced, the budget constraint changes from $I_0 a$ to $I_0 b$. The family increases the number of days of child care from D_0 to D_1. The subsidy received by the family is $S_1 - S_1'$, the difference between $I_0 b$ and $I_0 a$ when the family uses D_1 days. A lump sum subsidy shifts the budget constraint from $I_0 a$ to cc. The budget line cc intersects U_1 at market basket 1. Under a lump sum subsidy the family selects market basket 2 on the indifference curve U_2. A smaller lump sum subsidy is necessary if the family is permitted to reach only indifference curve U_1. The budget constraint dd is tangent to U_1 with market basket 3. The move from market basket 3 to market basket 1 is the substitution effect. The family prefers a lump sum subsidy because it reaches a higher indifference curve. The day care industry prefers a per unit subsidy because the quantity demanded will be higher.

Is the disagreement between the providers and the users much ado about nothing? Let's see how the two programs affect a representative family. In Figure 3-7 a composite good is on the vertical axis, and the number of days of care is on the horizontal axis. Suppose a family with an income of I_0 currently purchases day care services for a child at a price of P_0 per day. $I_0 a$ is the initial budget constraint of the family and has a slope of $-P_0$. The family maximizes utility by selecting market basket 0 on U_0, purchasing D_0 days of day care, and spending S_0 dollars on other goods. Under program 1 the family receives a daily subsidy of s dollars, and so the daily price of day care falls from P_0 to $P_0 - s$. The price reduction rotates the budget constraint to I_0b. The family selects market basket 1 on U_1, where the slope of U_1 equals the slope of I_0b. The family purchases D_1 days of care and spends S_1 on the composite good. The subsidy lowers the effective price of child care, and the family purchases more.

Now let's calculate the total subsidy received by the family. For any given number of days of child care, the vertical distance between the budget constraint I_0b and the budget constraint I_0a is the total amount of the subsidy received by the family. When the family purchases D_1 days, the total dollar subsidy is equal to the distance $S_1 - S_1'$ between I_0b and I_0a. Remember that S denotes total spending on the composite good and s is the daily subsidy. If the family had purchased D_1 days of child care without the subsidy, it could spend only S_1' dollars on the composite good. With a per day subsidy, the family spends S_1 dollars on the composite good while still using D_1 days of child care. The family can spend more on the composite good because it is given a per day subsidy. It receives a total subsidy of sD_1 that equals the increase in spending on other goods from S_1' to S_1. To review, $S_1 - S_1'$ is the total dollar subsidy received by the family when it purchases D_1 days of child care with a per day subsidy of s.

Will the family respond differently to a lump sum subsidy? The lump sum subsidy is determined so that the per family cost to taxpayers for the two programs is the same. We already know that the total subsidy received by the family is $S_1 - S_1'$ under the per day subsidy. The lump sum subsidy program must cost taxpayers the same amount. To make the total cost the same, the family's lump sum subsidy must be large enough so that the new budget line cc allows the family to purchase market basket 1. The distance between the two budget lines cc and I_0a is $S_1 - S_1'$ no matter how many days of day care the family selects under a lump sum subsidy (I_0a and cc are parallel to each other). Therefore, a lump sum subsidy of $S_1 - S_1'$ makes the total cost of the two programs the same.

You can begin to see why the trade association and the users of child care have different points of view. When the two subsidy programs cost the same, the family prefers a lump sum subsidy. The family will move along cc to market basket 2 and reach a higher indifference curve U_2 by contracting for only D_2 days of child care under a lump sum subsidy. Although the parents could select D_1 days under a lump sum subsidy, they prefer not to because the relative price of day care has not changed. The slope of cc equals $-P_0$, which is larger in absolute value than $-(P_0 - s)$, the slope of I_0b. In other words the relative price of day care is higher under the lump sum subsidy than under the per day subsidy, and so parents will demand relatively fewer days under that plan. The lump sum subsidy does not affect relative prices, whereas the per day subsidy does. Since the slope of I_0b equals the slope of the indifference curve U_1 with market basket 1, the slope of the budget constraint cc cannot equal the slope of the indifference curve U_1 with market basket 1. By reducing the number of child care days and increasing spending on other goods, the utility of the family increases. Under a lump sum subsidy the family is better off by purchasing less day care because the relative price is unaffected.

The change from D_1 to D_2 approximates but does not equal the substitution effect by changing from a per day subsidy to a lump sum subsidy. Although the relative price of day care increases with this change, the family moves to a higher indifference curve by decreasing day care from D_1 to D_2 days.

How much would the lump sum subsidy program cost if the lump sum subsidy just allowed the family to reach indifference curve U_1 with market basket 3? The budget line dd in the inset is just tangent to U_1. Because dd lies below cc, this lump sum subsidy costs taxpayers less. The difference between cc and dd at any D represents the lower cost of this lump sum program. Starting from market basket 1, the price of day care can be raised by eliminating the per day subsidy and then offering a lump sum subsidy (moving from market basket 1 to market basket 3) so that the family is on indifference curve U_1. The change from D_1 to D_3 is the true substitution effect arising from a decision to adopt a lump sum rather than a per day subsidy. Therefore, offering a lump sum payment for child care that makes the family as well off as a daily subsidy would cost taxpayers less.

In summary, the welfare of the family improves more if it receives a lump sum subsidy that costs the same as a per day subsidy. The day care trade association probably opposes the lump sum subsidy program because the days of child care demanded by the family would be lower under the lump sum proposal than under the per day subsidy program. The different positions taken by the trade association and by the users of day care are not due to faulty reasoning on the part of either party. Both sides know which side their bread is buttered on.

APPLICATION 3-2

How Different Is Water?

No doubt you have heard the expression, "Water is the essence of life." If, as is commonly believed, water is a necessity, then the demand for water should be independent of its price.[3] But is water really that different from other goods? What many people forget is that water is used for many functions: drinking, bathing, washing clothing, watering plants. Depending on incentives, consumers can use water carefully or use it lavishly. If water is very expensive, a consumer will make sure little water is spilled when filling up a glass and take fewer and shorter showers. Water is cheap in Chicago. A resident's water bill is independent of usage. Chicagoans do not pay more for water if they leave their sprinklers on all night or if they do not fix a leaking faucet or if they plant trees and other plants that need to be watered continuously.

We can use our analysis of income and substitution effects to analyze a consumer's demand for water. Let's begin by considering a consumer with income of I_0 whose utility depends on spending on other goods and consumption of gallons of water per year. When a consumer literally faces a zero price for water, the slope of the consumer's budget constraint aa is zero. In Figure 3-8 the consumer's marginal rate of substitution is negative along indifference curve U_0 if the consumer

---

[3] In the limit, this would imply that the price elasticity of demand for water is zero, i.e., demand is perfectly inelastic.

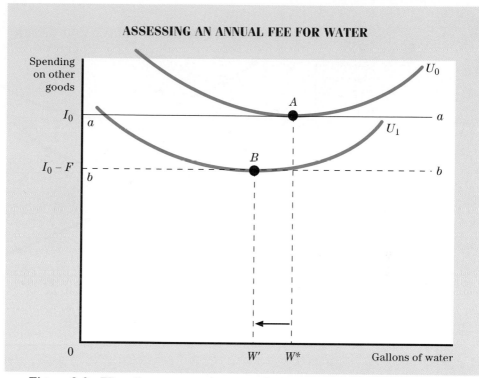

Figure 3-8   When the consumer is assessed a fixed annual water bill, the consumer cuts back on water consumption from W^* to W' gallons per year assuming water is a normal good. The change in water consumption measures the income effect.

uses less than W^* gallons of water but becomes positive if the consumer uses more than W^*. Water becomes a "bad" rather than a "good" for this consumer when used beyond W^*.[4] For example, a consumer's utility decreases if she waters her plants so excessively that her plants die. For a consumer to remain indifferent when water use increases beyond W^*, the consumer must receive more of other goods. Consequently, the consumer's marginal rate of substitution becomes positive when a good becomes a "bad."

The budget constraint aa in Figure 3-8 is tangent to U_0 at point A where the consumer uses W^* gallons per year. Since the price of water is zero, the consumer spends all of I_0 on other goods. The consumer increases water consumption until the marginal rate of substitution is zero. Now let's consider what happens to water consumption if each resident is assessed a fixed fee to use city water. Suppose the annual water assessment is F. This fixed amount must be paid by a resident to use any water. The consumer budget constraint shifts down to $I_0 - F$ and becomes

---

[4] Whereas a negative MRS means that consuming more water requires less spending on other goods if utility is to remain constant, a positive MRS indicates that a higher consumption of water requires more spending on other goods if utility is to remain constant.

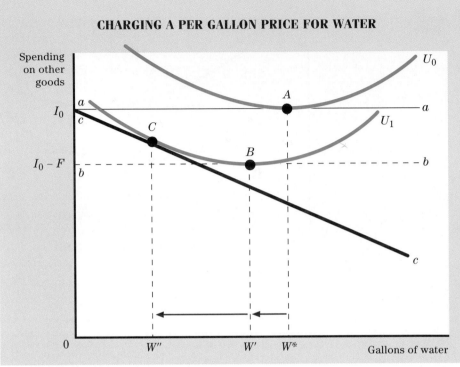

Figure 3-9   When the city charges a per gallon price for water but eliminates the fixed annual water bill, the consumer's budget constraint shifts from *bb* to *cc*. Water consumption decreases from W' to W'' gallons per year. The substitution effect is the change from W' to W''.

bb. With this new budget constraint the consumer maximizes utility at point B on indifference curve U_1 by using W' gallons of water where the consumer's marginal rate of substitution is zero. With both prices constant there is no substitution effect. However, net income has decreased as a result of the water assessment, and this consumer decreases water consumption. Therefore, water is a normal good. The difference $W^* - W'$ measures the income effect and, in this case, also the total change in the quantity of water demanded.

While the resident cuts back on water consumption when an annual fee is charged, the reduction is not likely to be large because the annual water bill in Chicago is only around $200. We can ask whether the city could adopt a different pricing policy that would conserve more water and still not reduce the consumer's utility. Suppose the city increases the per gallon water price and simultaneously eliminates the annual assessment. In Figure 3-9 the budget constraint becomes *cc* when the city eliminates the annual assessment but raises the per gallon price so that the consumer can remain on indifference curve U_1. At point C, where the new budget constraint *cc* is tangent to indifference curve U_1, the consumer uses W''

gallons of water. The difference $W'' - W'$ measures the substitution effect. The reduction in water use from W' to W'' occurs because the per gallon price is increased, which by itself would reduce utility, but the annual assessment is eliminated to keep the consumer on U_1. Therefore, by pricing water, the city encourages more water conservation without reducing the consumer's utility. To summarize, the change in water consumption from W^* to W' is the income effect and the change from W' to W'' is the substitution effect.

What evidence do we have that consumers treat water like other goods? In a study of an interesting pricing experiment in Boulder, Colorado, where the pricing of water changed from a fixed assessment to a metered price, Steve Hanke reported that water usage dropped substantially when the metered pricing was introduced.[5] Water use for sprinkling yards and lawns and even for in-house use dropped substantially. Surprisingly, in-house use dropped by 36 percent as consumers repaired leaks in plumbing systems and learned to use dishpans instead of allowing the water to flow constantly when washing dishes. Hanke's study indicates water is not different. Higher water prices will reduce water usage.

The Slope of the Demand Function

In the introduction to this chapter we asked why the quantity demanded increases more for some consumers than for others. The income and substitution effects can be used to explain when and why the responses of consumers differ. We can draw up a convenient checklist that tells us when either the substitution or the income effect is large so that the change in the quantity demanded caused by a price change is large. Although the analysis focuses on the slope of the demand curve, much of what we say applies to the consumer's price elasticity of demand as well.

The consumer's demand function expresses the quantity demanded as a function of the price of the product with income and other prices held constant. The demand function is expressed as

$$X - d(P) \qquad \text{(Consumer's Demand Function)} \qquad \textbf{(3-2)}$$

where the symbol d denotes the consumer's demand function. The slope of the demand function is $\Delta X/\Delta P$ and depends on the magnitude of the substitution and income effects. So, we want to know when the size of the income or substitution effect is large to determine when a price change causes a large change in the quantity demanded.

The substitution effect measures the change in the quantity demanded due to a price change holding utility constant. The expression $(\Delta X/\Delta P)|_{U=c}$ represents the substitution effect. The expresson $|_{U=c}$ means "utility is constant." So, we can determine $\Delta X/\Delta P$ by measuring how the quantity demanded changes along a given indifference curve as the relative price of X changes. We know that the sign of $(\Delta X/\Delta P)|_{U=c}$ is always negative because the consumer demands more units of X when the price falls.

---

[5] Steve H. Hanke, "Demand for Water under Dynamic Conditions," *Water Resources Research* 6, no. 5, pp. 1253–60.

However, the slope of the demand curve depends not only on the substitution effect but also on the income effect. We already know that the income effect is positive for a normal good. Now we want to investigate when the income effect will be large.

The explanation of the size of the income effect is a little more involved. This effect depends on two factors: (1) how much income becomes available when the price of X decreases, and (2) how many more units of X the consumer demands because income has increased. The income that becomes available per dollar change in price depends on the number of units the individual is currently consuming. A price decrease releases income to be spent on goods equal to $\Delta I = -(\Delta P)X$ (the negative sign is required because a decrease in the price of X releases more income to purchase more of all goods). For a price decrease of ΔP, more funds become available to the consumer the larger the number of units of X the individual consumes. The change in income per dollar decrease in price $(\Delta I/\Delta P)$ is equal to $-X$, and $\Delta X/\Delta I$ represents the increase in the quantity demanded of X per dollar increase in income. Therefore, the change in the quantity demanded because of the income effect is $-X(\Delta X/\Delta I)$.

A numerical example will clarify how to calculate the income effect. If you rent a movie for home viewing on your VCR 30 times a year and the rental price decreases by \$1, you will have \$30 more to spend each year on movies and other goods. In this case $\Delta I/\Delta P = -X = -30$. So, $-X$ represents the additional dollars released when the price decreases by \$1. Furthermore, assume that you demand one more movie per \$10 increase in income, and so $\Delta X/\Delta I = 0.1$ unit per dollar increase in income. Then, the change in the quantity demanded because of the income effect is $30 \times 0.1 = 3$ more movies per year per dollar decrease in price.

Our graphical analysis of the income and substitution effects showed that the change in the quantity demanded due to a price change is the sum of the changes caused by the substitution and income effects. Therefore, we can express the slope of the consumer's demand function as

$$\frac{\Delta X}{\Delta P} = \frac{\Delta X}{\Delta P}\bigg|_{U=c} - X\left(\frac{\Delta X}{\Delta I}\right) \qquad \text{(Slope of Consumer's Demand Function)} \qquad \textbf{(3-3)}$$

Equation 3-3 is called the **Slutsky equation** and is named after the economist who first derived it. The Slutsky equation simply says that the slope of the demand function equals the sum of the contributions of the substitution and income effects.[6] The sign of the substitution effect is always negative. When the income effect is zero, the slope of the demand function is negative because the substitution effect is always negative. If the good is a normal good, the income effect is also negative

---

[6] Strictly speaking, equation 3-3 holds exactly for infinitesimal changes in price; that is,

$$\frac{\partial X}{\partial P} = \frac{\partial X}{\partial P}\bigg|_{U=c} - X\frac{\partial X}{\partial I}$$

where $\partial X/\partial P$ represents an infinitesimal change in X with respect to an infinitesimal change in the price of X with all other prices held constant and $\partial X/\partial I$ is the infinitesimal change in the quantity demanded with respect to an infinitesimal change in I.

because $-X(\Delta X/\Delta I)$ is negative since $\Delta X/\Delta I$ is positive, and therefore the demand function must have a negative slope. If the good is an inferior good, then the income effect is $-X(\Delta X/\Delta I)$ and is positive. Therefore, the slope of the demand curve can be either positive or negative.

The Size of Each Effect

Equation 3-3 shows how the slope of the demand function depends on the substitution and income effects. By carefully considering each effect separately, we can discover situations when the substitution of income effect will be large or small.[7]

The Size of the Substitution Effect   The substitution effect is larger if the consumer considers X a close rather than a distant substitute for other goods. If X is a close substitute for other goods, the quantity demanded will increase by a larger amount when the price falls, holding the consumer's utility constant. In Figure 3-10a units of Y, another good, are on the y axis, and units of X are on the x axis. You may remember from Chapter 2 that the indifference curve is a straight line when two goods are perfect substitutes. The indifference curve of the consumer in Figure 3-10 resembles but is not quite a straight line. The shape of the indifference curve between Y and X indicates that the consumer is just about willing to give up the same number of units of Y for each unit of X no matter how many units of X he or she consumes.

If two goods are close to being perfect complements, each indifference curve looks more like an L. In Chapter 2 it was noted that one right shoe and one left shoe are perfect complements. The indifference curve in Figure 3-10b resembles but is not quite a right angle. For a given increase in X, the consumer is willing to give up smaller and smaller amounts of Y at lower levels of Y to remain indifferent.

Figure 3-10 shows how the size of the substitution effect depends on whether the two goods are close substitutes or close complements. In Figure 3-10a, for a

---

[7] The equation in footnote 6 can be converted into an expression for the point price elasticity of demand.

$$\frac{\partial X}{\partial P} = \frac{\partial X}{\partial P}\bigg|_{U=c} - X\frac{\partial X}{\partial I}$$

Multiplying both sides of the equation by the ratio of P/X results in

$$\frac{P}{X}\frac{\partial X}{\partial P} = \frac{P}{X}\frac{\partial X}{\partial P}\bigg|_{U=c} - \frac{P}{X}X\frac{\partial X}{\partial I}$$

Multiplying the numerator and the denominator of the last term by I yields

$$\frac{P}{X}\frac{\partial X}{\partial P} = \frac{P}{X}\frac{\partial X}{\partial P}\bigg|_{U=c} - \frac{PX}{I}\left(\frac{I}{X}\frac{\partial X}{\partial I}\right)$$

$$E_p = E_p^c - (s)(E_I)$$

The left-hand side is the point price elasticity of demand E_p. The point price elasticity equals the percentage change in the quantity demanded for an infinitesimal percentage change in price. The first term on the right-hand side is called the *compensated price elasticity of demand* E_p^c and measures the price elasticity of demand with utility held constant. The second term on the right-hand side is the product of the share of income spent on the good, $s = PX/I$, and the point income elasticity of demand, $E_I = (I/X)(\partial X/\partial I)$. The point income elasticity of demand can be interpreted as the percentage change in the quantity demanded due to an infinitesimal percentage change in income.

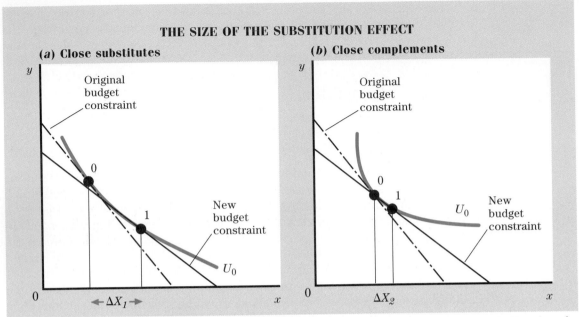

Figure 3-10   The indifference curve in (*a*) appears more like a straight line than the indifference curve in (*b*), which appears more like a right angle. In each case the consumer starts with market basket 0 and selects market basket 1 because of the substitution effect. The substitution effect is ΔX_1 in (*a*) and ΔX_2 in (*b*). The substitution effect is larger in (*a*), when the two goods are close substitutes, than in (*b*), when the two goods are close complements.

given price decrease from P_X to P_X', the substitution effect ΔX_1 is larger when the two goods are close substitutes. This is more like the case where the consumer considers Green Giant peas a close substitute for Del Monte peas and so will purchase Green Giant if the price decreases. The substitution effect, ΔX_2, in Figure 3-10*b* is smaller when the two goods are close complements.

The Size of the Income Effect   When the price of X falls, the consumer finds $-(\Delta P)X$ dollars available to spend on X and other goods. For a given change in price, more funds become available the larger X is. If I buy just a few units of X and spend only a small percentage of my income on X, only a few dollars become available for me to spend on X and other goods when the price of X falls. A fall in the price of mangoes is not likely to cause a large income effect for most individuals because most consumers eat only a few, if any, mangoes per year. If I consume many units of X and spend a large percentage of my income on a good, for example, housing, a price reduction on a house will release a considerable sum that I might use to purchase a still larger house, an automobile, clothing, or more vacations. The income effect is larger because the budget line shifts outward in a parallel fashion by a larger amount when the price of X decreases.

The second component of the income effect is the responsiveness of the quantity demanded to a change in income ($\Delta X/\Delta I$). The consumer's demand for different goods responds differently when income increases. For example, a 10 percent increase in consumer income may increase an individual's demand for vacation days by 20 percent because the income elasticity of demand for vacations exceeds 1. On the other hand, a 10 percent increase in income may increase his or her demand for soft drinks by only 1 percent.

Observing the Effect of Each Determinant

To sum up, $\Delta X/\Delta P$, the slope of the demand function, depends on (1) whether X is a close or an imperfect substitute for some other good, (2) whether a large or a small percentage of income is spent on X, and (3) how much the consumer's demand for X increases when income increases. These three items jointly determine the slope of the demand function and the consumer's price elasticity of demand.

Keep this checklist of determinants in mind as you consider the following analysis. Some business decisions depend on an estimate of the price elasticity of demand. Often, speed is essential and decisions are made with limited information. Suppose you need to estimate the price elasticity of demand for a product you are selling. You do not have the luxury of hiring a high-priced consultant to complete an elaborate statistical study. More often than not, business managers have to make decisions with very little hard information available. In these situations you will have to guess about the likely size of the price elasticity of demand. Let's illustrate how our checklist might help organize your thinking.

Would you expect that the demand function for a given brand in a product category is more price elastic than the demand for all brands within a product category? For example, we may want to estimate the price elasticity of demand for Christian Dior shirts or for all expensive shirts. Would you expect the price elasticity of demand for Christian Dior dress shirts to be more elastic or less elastic than the price elasticity of demand for all brands in the same price class? You might use the following argument. There are probably more close substitutes for a single brand within a product category than there are close substitutes between product categories. If so, you could plausibly argue that the demand for an individual brand would be more elastic than the demand for the whole category. If the price of Christian Dior shirts is increased, how will consumers react? Some consumers will purchase a Giorgio Armani shirt or a Perry Ellis shirt, which they consider a close substitute.

On the other hand, suppose the prices of all expensive dress shirts increase. Many consumers may find the shirts in middle- and low-price classes more distant substitutes for shirts in the higher-price class. You can make a plausible argument that shirts within a price class are closer substitutes than shirts in different price classes. The size of the substitution effect between brands within a price class will be larger than between shirts in different price classes. Therefore, if you are considering an independent price increase for your higher-priced brand name dress shirt, you should expect a larger decrease in the quantity demanded because there are many available close substitutes. Your demand function will be more price-elastic than the demand for all higher-priced shirts. The theory of consumer behavior suggests that the substitution effect between goods that are closer substitutes will be larger. The demand function for Christian Dior dress shirts will be more elastic than the demand function for all expensive dress shirts.

In this example the comparative assessment of price elasticities depends on the comparative size of the substitution effects. Income effects are ignored because the share of total income spent on dress shirts is trivial and the fraction of income spent on shirts of a particular brand is still smaller.

Consider another example. Although the market is changing rapidly, there currently are fewer substitute automobiles in the luxury price class (Lincoln, Cadillac, Acura, Lexus, etc.) than in the middle- and lower-price classes (Taurus, Accord, Maxima, Camry, Lumina, etc.). The product space appears more densely filled in the middle- and lower-price classes than in the luxury field. If so, the theory of consumer behavior predicts that the demand function for a specific make in the luxury price class will be less elastic than the demand function for a specific make in the middle-price class. Here again, income effects are ignored.

Finally, the income effect and therefore the slope of the consumer's demand function depend on the quantity purchased and on $\Delta X/\Delta I$. Suppose consumers could be classified into two groups. Members of one group purchase a few units per year, whereas each member of the other group purchases a large volume each year. If you are planning to reduce the price to members in one of the two groups, which group will increase the quantity demanded by a larger amount? Would you offer the price cut to the group with members who individually purchase a small quantity or to the group with members who individually purchase a large quantity? When other factors are held constant, a consumer who purchases a large quantity will have a more elastic demand function because the income effect is larger. A price reduction will cause a larger increase in the quantity demanded if the price cut is offered to members of this group holding other factors constant. The analysis says that when all other factors are held constant, the demand function will be more elastic the larger the percentage of income spent on the good.

3-2   CONSUMER SURPLUS

If we ignore fraud and misrepresentation, a consumer is willing to buy a product because he or she is better off consuming the product than doing without it. Every purchase, whether it is a soft drink, in-line skates, medical care, golf clubs, or listening to a rock concert, leaves the buyer better off, given the price of the good or the service. We can make an even stronger statement and say that the consumer expects every purchase to be a bargain whether the consumer pays a low competitive price or has to pay a higher monopoly price. This claim may sound a little outrageous, but it is true. How can a purchase be a bargain if the consumer has no alternative sources of supply and has to pay a higher price? Even when a consumer pays the higher price, he or she makes the purchase because utility is higher after consuming the good than it would have been without the good. The consumer obtains a surplus by buying the good and therefore would be willing to pay even more than go without the good. In this sense the consumer receives a bargain even though the price paid might have been higher than a competitive price. Indeed, the definition of consumer surplus emphasizes the difference between the most that a consumer would pay and the amount actually paid. In this section we show how consumer surplus can be derived from the consumer's demand function.

> **Consumer surplus** is the difference between the maximum amount the purchaser would pay to consume a given quantity and the actual amount paid.

Marginal Value

Figure 3-11 shows a consumer's demand function for renting videos. The consumer is willing to pay as much as $12 for the first video. This is the consumer's **marginal value**—sometimes called the consumer's *marginal willingness to pay*—for the first video. Suppose the video store rents each video at $3. Since the consumer is willing to pay as much as $12 for the first video but only has to pay $3, the consumer receives a surplus of $9. This difference is the consumer's surplus for renting the first video. The consumer's marginal value for the second video is only $8, less than the marginal value for the first video. So the consumer is willing to pay at most $20 to see two videos per month. If the consumer had to pay more than $20 to see two videos per month, the consumer would refuse to rent any videos but spend all income on other goods. Since all videos rent for $3, the consumer receives a surplus of $5 by renting the second unit. Altogether, the consumer's total surplus equals $9 + $5 = $14 by renting two videos per month. By repeating this argument for successive videos, Figure 3-11 shows that the marginal value exceeds the rental price up to and including the fifth video and is less than the rental price for the sixth video. So the consumer rents five videos per month. Consumer surplus for successive units decreases until it is just $.25 for the fifth video. A consumer that maximizes consumer surplus will determine the quantity to buy such that marginal value equals price. Given the steps in marginal values in Figure 3-11, the consumer will rent five videos because the marginal value exceeds the rental price up to and including the fifth video.

> Marginal value is the most that a consumer is willing to pay for each additional unit of a good.

Altogether, the consumer is willing to pay a maximum of $33.50 for five videos per month but only has to pay $15. Consumer surplus is maximized if the consumer rents five videos equaling $9 + $5 + $3 + $1.25 + $.25 = $18.50. If the consumer rents either fewer or more than five videos, the consumer's surplus will decline. An interested reader is urged to read the appendix to this chapter to learn how a

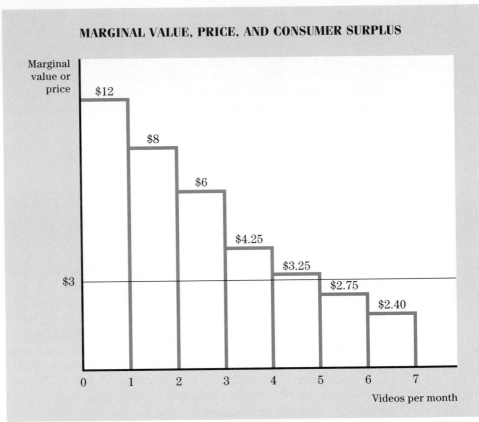

Figure 3-11   The marginal value of successive videos declines. When the price per video is $3, the consumer rents five videos per month. Consumer surplus is $9 for the first video, $5 for the second, etc., and equals $18.50 for five videos. When the price falls to $2.50, the consumer rents six videos per month. Consumer surplus increases by 5 × $.50 + $.25 or by $2.75.

consumer's marginal values are derived and to learn when the consumer's demand function traces out the consumer's marginal values.

Using the Consumer Surplus Concept

We can use the concept of consumer surplus to show how a firm can introduce a price policy that will increase its revenue. Suppose a bar is located near campus and is the only bar within 40 miles. The bar owner charges $2 for a bottle of beer. Figure 3-12 shows the demand function of a typical student. The student's marginal value is $5 for the first unit, $3.50 for the second, and so on. When the bar owner charges $2 per bottle, the student demands four bottles per month so the owner collects $8 per student per month, or area R in Figure 3-12. While the owner collects

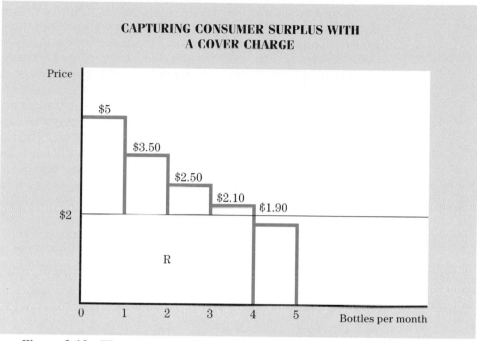

**CAPTURING CONSUMER SURPLUS WITH
A COVER CHARGE**

Figure 3-12   When the per bottle price is $2, the consumer drinks four bottles per month and consumer surplus equals $5.10. A monthly cover charge equal to the consumer surplus increases the bar's total revenue from $8 to $13.10 per student.

$8 per student per month, the student walks away with a surplus of $5.10. Could a more ingenious pricing policy increase revenue by still more? Suppose the owner doesn't change the $2 bottle price but decides to add a monthly cover charge. The monthly charge allows the student to buy bottles of beer at the $2 price. How should the owner determine the cover charge? The student's consumer surplus is $5.10 when the student drinks four bottles per month and this puts an upper limit on the cover charge. If the owner charges more than $5.10, the student will walk away and not patronize the bar. The student's utility is higher by not buying any beer than by paying more than $5.10 for the cover charge. On the other hand, if the cover charge is less than $5.10, the bar owner is leaving money on the table because the student's surplus is still positive; the student is still willing to pay more for the cover charge rather than not patronize the bar. If the owner charges $5.10 for the cover and $2 per bottle, the owner extracts all of the student's consumer surplus and increases total revenue from $8 to $13.10 per student per month, a 64 percent increase. Thus, given the per bottle price, the owner wants to set the cover charge equal to the demander's consumer surplus. In Chapter 12 we will return to this topic and show how the owner can pick the per bottle price and the cover charge to increase revenue by still more.

Many government policies are designed to protect consumers, for instance, clean air and water policies, but some policies protect producers and harm consumers. We can use the concept of consumer surplus to evaluate the effect of these policies on consumer surplus. For example, the United States has a sugar quota that prevents foreign suppliers from selling as much sugar as they would like to in the United States. The quota increases the U.S. price of a pound of sugar by shifting the supply function of domestic and imported sugar inward and reduces consumer surplus. In Figure 3-13 the market demand curve for sugar is DD. Without the quota the U.S. price of a pound of sugar would be P_0 and consumers would purchase Q_0 pounds of sugar. With the quota the price of sugar increases to P_1 and the quantity of sugar consumed falls to only Q_1 pounds. Without a quota, consumer surplus is equal to the sum of areas 1, 2, and 3. With a quota, it falls by the sum of areas 1 and 2 and becomes area 3. The price received by suppliers increases by $P_1 - P_0$, and Q_1 pounds are sold at the higher price. Area 1 represents a transfer from consumers to producers as the incomes of domestic suppliers of sugar increase because of the quota. What about area 2? It represents part of the loss in consumer surplus. No other group receives an offsetting benefit from this loss,

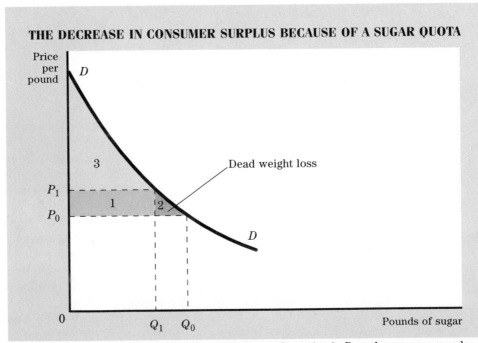

Figure 3-13   Without the sugar quota the market price is P_0 and consumer surplus is the sum of areas 1, 2, and 3. The sugar quota increases the price per pound to P_1. Consumer surplus decreases by the sum of areas 1 and 2 and now equals area 3. Area 1 is transferred from consumers to suppliers. Area 2 represents a loss to consumers with no offsetting gain to any other group and is referred to as a dead weight loss.

which occurs because the industry contracts in size when the price of sugar increases. This loss is called a dead weight loss.

> A **dead weight loss** represents the decrease in consumer surplus that is not transferred to some other group.

Many farm programs require acreage reductions before the farmer qualifies for government subsidies. The objective is to raise farmers' income by reducing supply and raising prices. Economists have estimated the cost to consumers of agricultural income support programs. Table 3-3 presents some estimates of the loss in consumer surplus from the government programs that restrict supply or directly raise prices. The milk and sugar price support programs cause the largest reductions in consumer surplus.

*3-3   UNCERTAINTY AND CONSUMER DECISION MAKING

In the first two sections of this chapter we assumed that the consumer makes decisions under certainty. If a consumer purchases a house, he or she knows the benefits of ownership. However, there are situations where the consequences of a decision are not known with certainty. An individual who has just received an MBA and has entered an industry still faces considerable uncertainty concerning how much she will earn. Will her talents be a good or a poor match for the requirements of the position? Individuals make some important decisions whose outcomes are uncertain. This section considers decision making under uncertainty.

Table 3-3   LOSS IN CONSUMER SURPLUS FROM GOVERNMENT INCOME SUPPORT PROGRAMS, 1987

Commodity	Loss in Consumer Surplus ($ billions per year)
Corn	$ .5–1.1
Sugar	1.1–2.5
Milk	1.6–3.1
Wheat	.1–.3
Rice	.02–.06
Peanuts	.2–.4
Tobacco	.4–.7

Source: Council of Economic Advisors, *Economic Report of the President, 1987*, U.S. Government Printing Office.

When uncertainty exists, a decision does not lead to a single outcome but to several possible outcomes with different probabilities. If you decide to purchase a house in Los Angeles, you are not certain of enjoying all its benefits. You are taking a gamble. One remote but distinct outcome is that your dream home will be leveled or damaged extensively by an earthquake. Or, if you have invested in a college education and look forward to a prosperous career, you may not receive the benefits of the education you have worked for so diligently. There is a small probability that you will be killed in an automobile accident. Each of these dismal events has only a small probability of occurring, but if it does it is devastating. In each example an individual makes a decision where multiple outcomes are possible.

Since more than single outcomes are associated with decisions, it makes little sense to say that the individual maximizes utility, because multiple possible outcomes have multiple possible utilities. To analyze decision making under uncertainty, we must replace utility maximization with some other goal. This section considers two competing models of what an individual maximizes: the expected income and the expected utility hypotheses.

The Expected Income Hypothesis

The expected income hypothesis states that an individual selects from among possible uncertain situations to maximize expected income. The following example illustrates some implications of the expected income hypothesis. Let's assume that you plan to start your own business and have narrowed your choice to industry A or industry B. Assume you know that you can earn $75,000 a year in industry A. Given your talents, industry A is the safe industry for you to enter. Many newcomers are unsuccessful in industry B. In industry B the probability is .75 that you will not do well and will earn only $25,000 a year. On the other hand, the probability is .25 that you will be a success and earn $225,000. Which industry would you enter?

The complication occurs because there are two possible outcomes in industry B. If you knew you would be a success in industry B and earn $225,000, you would definitely enter industry B. If you knew you would be a colossal failure in industry B, you would enter industry A. The problem is you do not know whether you are going to be successful or unsuccessful.

The expected income hypothesis states that an individual enters the industry with the highest expected income. Expected income weights the income of each outcome by its probability of occurrence and sums this product over all possible outcomes or states of nature.

Expected income is a probability-weighted average of income over all outcomes.

The expression for expected income is

$$EI = \Sigma \, p_i I_i \qquad \text{(Expected Income)} \tag{3-4}$$

where p_i is the **probability** that the ith outcome or state of nature will occur (earthquake or no earthquake) and I_i is the resulting income under that outcome. The symbol Σ means that we add up all products of the probability and income for all states of nature or outcomes.

Let's calculate the expected income of the two choices and see whether industry A or industry B has the higher expected income. Expected income in industry A is $EI_A = 1(\$75,000) = \$75,000$ because the probability of earning $75,000 is 1. On the other hand, if you enter industry B, there are two possible outcomes. Your expected income is

$$EI_B = 0.75(\$25,000) + 0.25(\$225,000) = \$75,000$$

One way of interpreting expected income in industry B is to think of a large number of individuals with similar backgrounds entering industry B. We can expect that about 75 percent will be failures and earn only $25,000 a year and that 25 percent will earn $225,000 a year. Averaging the income of all entrants, we find the average income is $75,000.

So, it turns out that expected income in the two industries is the same. If you base your entry decision solely on maximizing expected income, you should be indifferent between industries A and B and be willing to flip a coin to decide.

The Expected Utility Hypothesis

Chances are, however, that most individuals would not express an indifference between entering the two industries. Although the expected income of the two choices is the same, many would prefer to enter industry A and only a minority would select industry B. Those favoring industry A would express concern over the different possible outcomes in industry B and view the diversity of outcomes as something to avoid. To them, industry B is a risky business where you might struggle by with only $25,000 annually or receive a handsome yearly income of $225,000. Whether you react favorably or unfavorably to these extreme outcomes depends on how much more utility you receive from $225,000 and how much less utility you receive from $25,000. Somehow, the analysis of decision making under uncertainty must take account of the *utility* that the consumer derives from higher- and lower-income outcomes.

Assuming this approach has some merit, we need to consider the utility of income. We must know how much better off or worse off the individual will be if income is higher or lower. To do this, we introduce the consumer's **utility of income function:**

$$U = U(I) \qquad \text{(Utility of Income Function)} \qquad \text{(3-5)}$$

where U is the individual's utility (in personal units called utils) and I is income. Figure 3-14a to c shows the utility of the consumer as a function of income. In all three cases utility increases with increases in income, and so $\Delta U/\Delta I > 0$. The slope of the utility function is **marginal utility.** What differentiates the three cases

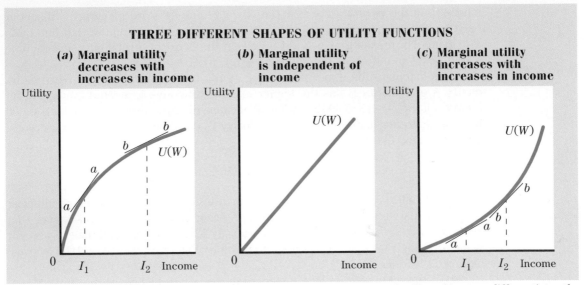

THREE DIFFERENT SHAPES OF UTILITY FUNCTIONS

Figure 3-14   The effect of income on the marginal utility of income differentiates the three utility-of-income functions. (*a*) Marginal utility decreases with increases in income. (*b*) Marginal utility is independent of income. (*c*) Finally, marginal utility increases with increases in income.

is how marginal utility changes with changes in income. In Figure 3-14*a* marginal utility *decreases* with increases in income. Each dollar increase in income causes successively smaller increases in marginal utility. The slope of the utility function in Figure 3-14*a* decreases with increases in I. Notice that the slope of the tangent *aa* when $I = I_1$ is steeper than the slope of the tangent *bb* when $I = I_2$. Mathematically, this means the second derivative of the utility function is negative because the slope of the utility function decreases with increases in income. In Figure 3-14*b* the marginal utility of incomes does not change with changes in income. Marginal utility, the slope of the utility function, is *constant* and independent of I. In Figure 3-14*c* the slope of the utility function increases with I. The slope of the tangent *aa* is less than the slope of the tangent *bb*. Marginal utility *increases* with increases in the income of the consumer. We distinguish between the different shapes of the utility function because it has much to do with the degree of risk an individual is comfortable with.

Now that the utility of income function has been introduced, we can consider the expected utility hypothesis. Some economists have proposed that consumers select from among uncertain situations so that expected utility is maximized. Expected utility weights the *utility of income* by the *probability* of that outcome or state of nature and sums the product over all possible outcomes.

$$EU = \Sigma p_i U(I_i) \qquad \text{(Expected Utility)} \qquad \text{(3-6)}$$

Table 3-4   EXPECTED INCOME AND EXPECTED UTILITY OF ENTERING INDUSTRY A OR B

INCOME ($) (1)	PROBABILITY OF OUTCOME IN INDUSTRY A, (p_i) (2)	PROBABILITY OF OUTCOME IN INDUSTRY B, (p_i) (3)	UTILITY OF INCOME, $U(I_i)$ (4)	CONTRIBUTION TO EXPECTED UTILITY FOR INDUSTRY A, $(p_i U(I_i))$ (5)	CONTRIBUTION TO EXPECTED UTILITY FOR INDUSTRY B, $(p_i U(I_i))$ (6)
25,000		.75	4 utils		3 utils
75,000	1		10	10 utils	
225,000		.25	16		4 utils
Expected income	$75,000	$75,000			
Expected utility				10 utils	7 utils

Expected utility is a probability-weighted average of the utilities of the consumer over all outcomes.

Let's compare the predictions of the expected income and the expected utility hypotheses in our example involving industries A and B. Table 3-4 shows the outcomes (income) in column 1, and the probability of each outcome in columns 2 and 3. Column 4 lists the utility of income for each outcome and shows a utility function that corresponds to the utility function in Figure 3-14a. Finally, columns 5 and 6 indicate the expected utility of each outcome. Row 4 shows the expected income of each decision, and row 5 the expected utility of each decision. In Table 3-4 the expected income of the two choices is the same and is equal to $75,000, but the expected utilities of the two industries are different. Column 5 shows the individual contributions to expected utility of each outcome if you enter industry A and earn $75,000: the contribution to expected utility is $pU(\$75,000) = 1(10) = 10$ utils. On the other hand, if you enter industry B, the expected utility is only 7 utils. If you are maximizing expected utility, you will enter industry A.

The shape of your utility function determines your choice of employment. From column 4 note that utility increases, but at a decreasing rate, as income increases. A tripling of income from $25,000 to $75,000 does not triple utility. An increase from $25,000 to $75,000 increases utility from 4 to 10 utils or only $2\frac{1}{2}$ times. An increase in income from $75,000 to $225,000, a threefold increase, increases utility by less than twofold. So, a relatively high income does not add that much more utility, and a relatively low income causes a comparatively large decrease in utility compared to the certain outcome in industry A. This is the reason many individuals would be reluctant to enter industry B.

Risk Aversion and Risk Taking

Let's show how an individual's decision depends on the shape of the utility function. Some people are **risk-averse** and avoid risky situations, whereas others are **risk takers** and flourish in uncertain environments. Still others may be said to be **risk-neutral.** The expected utility hypothesis explains this difference in behavior by the different shapes of the individuals' utility functions. We consider two individuals with different utility functions. The first has the utility function $U_1(I_i)$ in Figure 3-15a, and the second has the utility function $U_2(I_i)$ in Figure 3-15b. Utility is measured in utils on the vertical axis, and income on the horizontal axis. The marginal utility of $U_1(I_i)$ decreases and the marginal utility of $U_2(I_i)$ increases with increases in income. How do these two individuals decide which industry to enter?

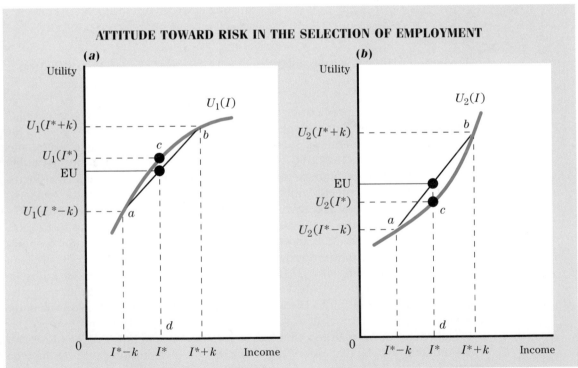

ATTITUDE TOWARD RISK IN THE SELECTION OF EMPLOYMENT

Figure 3-15   (a) The individual with the utility function $U_1(I)$ prefers industry A with the certain earnings of I^* and $U_1(I^*)$ rather than the EU in industry B. (b) The individual with $U_2(I)$ is a risk taker and prefers industry B with its uncertain prospects because EU is greater than $U_2(I^*)$.

In industry A each receives a certain income of I^*, while in industry B each receives $I^* - k$ with probability p and $I^* + k$ with probability $1 - p$. If the individual enters industry B, expected income EI_B is

$$EI_B = p(I^* - k) + (1 - p)(I^* + k)$$

Collecting terms, we have

$$EI_B = [p + (1 - p)]I^* + [-p + (1 - p)]k$$

$$= I^* + (1 - 2p)k$$

If $p = \frac{1}{2}$, $EI_B = I^*$. Then, the expected income in the two industries is the same. Although the expected income is the same, this does not mean that the expected utility is the same. Now let's compare the expected utility of the two industries. For the first individual the expected utility from entering industry A is simply $U_1(I^*)$, and for the second individual it is $U_2(I^*)$. For the first individual the expected utility of entering industry B is

$$EU_B = .5U_1(I^* - k) + .5U_1(I^* + k) = \frac{U_1(I^* - k) + U_1(I^* + k)}{2}$$

or the average of the two utilities. The same is true for the second individual because the expected utility is

$$EU_B = .5U_2(I^* - k) + .5U_2(I^* + k) = \frac{U_2(I^* - k) + U_2(I^* + k)}{2}$$

Expected utility is the average of the two utilities of each individual when $p = \frac{1}{2}$.

Figure 3-15 shows that the expected utility in industry A is $U_1(I^*)$ for the first individual and $U_2(I^*)$ for the second individual because each individual is certain of earning I^*. Because expected utility in industry B is the average of utilities for both individuals, expected utility is the midpoint between $U_1(I^* - k)$ and $U_1(I^* + k)$ for the first individual (Figure 3-15a), and the midpoint between $U_2(I^* - k)$ and $U_2(I^* + k)$ for the second individual (Figure 3-15b).

Now it becomes clearer why individual 1 prefers industry A to industry B, because the utility from the certain income of I^* in industry A (point c) is greater than the expected utility of entering industry B; that is, $U_1(I^*) > .5U_1(I^* - k) + .5U_1(I^* + k)$. On the other hand, individual 2 prefers industry B because expected utility is higher than the utility of the certain income of I^* in industry A (point c); that is, $.5U_2(I^* - k) + .5U_2(I^* + k) > U_2(I^*)$. The different choices are due to the different shapes of the utility functions. Marginal utility of income decreases with increases in income for individual 1. Individual 1 receives a relatively small increase in utility when income increases by k and loses relatively more utility when income decreases by k. Just the opposite is true for individual 2. Individual 2 receives relatively large increases in utility when income increases by k and suffers a relatively small decrease in utility when income decreases by k. We can say that individual 1 is risk-averse because he tends to avoid uncertain situations, while individual 2 is a risk taker because she tends to prefer the uncertain situation. The basic point of the analysis is that the shape of the utility function determines whether an individual is a risk taker or a risk avoider.

Everyday behavior indicates that people differ in their attitudes toward risk. If you always fasten your seat belt when you enter your automobile, your behavior reflects risk aversion. Fastening your seat belt each time you enter your car is a nuisance for most people, although in some states driving without a seat belt is a violation of the law. For other drivers, it is a small cost to incur each time they enter an automobile because of the smaller loss if an accident does happen. They incur this cost to purchase more certainty. A person who does not use a seat belt avoids this cost but faces greater uncertainty. The seat belt user's utility function resembles $U_1(I)$.

We have shown that expected utility is the average of the two utilities when $p = \frac{1}{2}$. However, a graphic measure of expected utility can be obtained for any value of p, not only for $p = \frac{1}{2}$, by following three steps.

1. Construct a chord from $U(I^* - k)$ to $U(I^* + k)$. In Figure 3-15 the chord is the line ab.

2. Calculate expected income in the uncertain activity from the expression $EI = p(I^* - k) + (1 - p)(I^* + k)$. As p increases from 0 to 1, EI decreases from $I^* + k$ to $I^* - k$.

3. Determine expected utility by working directly up to the chord ab at an income of EI. In Figure 3-15 expected income is I^* because $p = \frac{1}{2}$, and expected utility of an uncertain event is a point on the chord ab at the value of expected income on the horizontal axis. When p is closer to 0, expected utility is on ab but closer to point b. When p is closer to 1, expected utility is closer to point a on the chord ab.

Table 3-5 reviews the decisions made by a risk avoider, a risk-neutral individual, and a risk taker when comparing a certain situation with an uncertain one with the *same expected income*. The risk avoider has a utility function where $\Delta^2 U/\Delta I^2 < 0$ and prefers certainty. The risk-neutral individual has a linear utility function where $\Delta^2 U/\Delta I^2 = 0$ and so is indifferent. The risk taker has a utility function where $\Delta^2 U/\Delta I^2 > 0$ and prefers to gamble.

Buying Insurance

Many individuals will go out of their way to avoid risky situations. They seek ways of insuring against a loss. Let's assume that you own a house in Los Angeles with a market value of V dollars. The probability of an earthquake is p, and the loss is L if an earthquake occurs. Your expected wealth is

$$EW = p(V - L) + (1 - p)V = V - pL$$

Suppose you decide to purchase earthquake insurance. The insurance company agrees to restore the value of the house if there is an earthquake, and charges you a premium of P. The premium is made up of two components. The first component equals the expected loss of the insurance company, or pL. From the company's point of view there is a probability p of an earthquake that causes a

Table 3-5   RESPONSE OF RISK-AVERSE, RISK-NEUTRAL, AND RISK-TAKING INDIVIDUALS TO AN UNCERTAIN SITUATION WITH THE SAME EXPECTED INCOME

TYPE OF INDIVIDUAL	SECOND DERIVATIVE OF UTILITY FUNCTION		CHOICE
Risk avoider	$\dfrac{\Delta^2 U}{\Delta I^2} < 0$	Marginal utility of income decreases with income.	Prefers certainty
Risk-neutral	$\dfrac{\Delta^2 U}{\Delta I^2} = 0$	Marginal utility of income is constant.	Indifferent
Risk taker	$\dfrac{\Delta^2 U}{\Delta I^2} > 0$	Marginal utility of income increases with income.	Prefers uncertainty

loss of L. Therefore, the expected loss is pL. For example, if the probability of an earthquake is .01 and a house suffers a $1 million loss, then the expected loss is $10,000. The second component of the premium is called the **load factor** or O. It represents the cost of running the insurance company and any profit earned by the company.

The **premium** charged by the insurance company for coverage equal to L is

$$P = pL + O \qquad \text{(Premium of Insurance Company)} \qquad (3\text{-}7)$$

If you purchase insurance and an earthquake occurs, your wealth is equal to $V - L + L - P = V - P$. Your loss L is covered by the insurance company's payment of L, and so your wealth decreases by the amount of the premium. If no earthquake occurs, your wealth is also equal to $V - P$ because you pay a premium of P. Purchasing an insurance policy shows that you are willing to pay a premium of P in exchange for a certain outcome of $V - P$ and a certain utility of $U(V - P)$. If you purchase insurance, your expected wealth, EW, is

$$EW = p(V - P) + (1 - p)(V - P) = V - P = V - pL - O$$

We know that your expected wealth is $V - pL$ if you do not purchase insurance. Purchasing insurance shows that you are willing to settle for lower expected wealth (by the amount O) in exchange for a certain utility.

Let's determine when a risk-averse consumer will purchase insurance. Figure 3-16 shows the utility function of such an individual. Without insurance wealth is either V, if no loss occurs, or $V - L$, if a loss occurs. The chord connecting $U(V - L)$ and $U(V)$ is ab, and expected wealth is $EW = p(V - L) + (1 - p)V = V - pL$. With insurance, the expected utility of the individual is $U(V - P)$. The consumer prefers insurance if the utility of the certain outcome, $U(V - P)$, is greater than the expected utility, EU, which is equal to cd if insurance is not purchased. With an insurance policy the expected wealth of the individual is $V - P = V - pL - O$. If the loading factor is not too large, a risk-averse individual

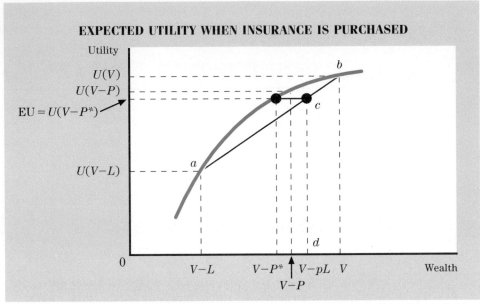

Figure 3-16   If an individual purchases insurance, the expected utility of the individual is $U(V - P)$, where P is the premium. As long as the premium is not too large, so that $P < P^*$, the expected utility from purchasing insurance is greater than the expected utility of not purchasing insurance.

will purchase insurance because $U(V - P)$ is greater than the expected utility without an insurance policy.

As the loading charge increases, the consumer will at some point decide not to purchase insurance. We can determine what premium makes a risk-averse individual indifferent between buying and not buying insurance. The premium P^* must be large enough so that $U(V - P^*) = $ EU in Figure 3-16. Then, the individual is indifferent between the utility of a certain wealth of $V - P^*$ and the expected utility of owning a home without insurance. If the premium exceeds P^*, even a risk-averse individual will not purchase insurance.

In summary, a risk-averse individual will pay a premium that exceeds the expected loss in order to get some peace of mind. This is an acceptable tradeoff for a risk-averse individual who maximizes expected utility. However, even a risk-averse individual will not purchase insurance if the premium is too large and exceeds P^*.

APPLICATION 3-3

Why Is Earthquake Insurance a Slow Seller in California?

On October 17, 1989, at 5:04 PM a major earthquake registering 6.9 on the Richter scale struck the San Francisco Bay Area. The tremor set off many fires and caused extensive damage to houses and apartments throughout the Bay Area. Highway pillars collapsed, crushing cars on lower-level ramps, and a section of the Bay Bridge connecting San Francisco and Oakland collapsed.

Periodic warnings have been and continue to be issued to Californians that the "big one" is yet to come. Yet only 20 percent of the houses in California have earthquake insurance. On the other hand, most Californians insure their automobiles for comprehensive damage. This raises the interesting question of why they don't heed the warnings of experts and insure their homes for damage caused by earthquakes.

By working with the expected utility hypothesis we can come up with two explanations for why many Californians refuse to purchase earthquake insurance. The first reason is that it is too expensive. If the loading charge is sufficiently large on earthquake insurance, a risk-averse individual will not buy it. In 1989, earthquake insurance for a brick home cost about $6,000 a year for $500,000 coverage. For a frame house, the cost was $630 a year for similar coverage because a frame house is more flexible and can better withstand the stresses caused by an earthquake.[8] These cost estimates do not indicate if the loading charge is sufficiently high to discourage purchase of earthquake insurance, but the expense probably does deter some individuals from becoming insured.

A second reason is that homeowners without insurance expect to receive aid from the rest of the country through federal government disaster programs when the "big one" hits. The government provides insurance at bargain rates. California is a large state with considerable political influence, and it is likely that federal disaster aid will be forthcoming if a major earthquake occurs. After all, Alaska received disaster aid after a major earthquake, and owners of oceanfront properties along the path of hurricanes have received assistance.

Let's see how the expectation of aid alters the decision to purchase insurance. Figure 3-17 shows that an individual will purchase earthquake insurance and pay a premium of P if no aid is expected. The expected utility of this homeowner is $U(V - P)$ at point a, where P is the premium and the expected wealth of the individual is $V - P = V - pL - O$, whereas the expected utility is lower if the individual does not purchase insurance (point e). Suppose the individual expects the government to supply aid in the form of a grant G, where $G \leq L$, to cover some fraction of the earthquake loss if the residence is *not* covered by insurance. If an earthquake occurs, the wealth of this homeowner without insurance is $V - L + G$. Therefore, the expected utility is

$$EU = pU(V - L + G) + (1 - p)U(V)$$

when the individual qualifies for aid because he does not have insurance. The expected wealth of the individual is $EW = p(V - L + G) + (1 - p)V = V - pL + pG$ and is higher if the homeowner does not purchase insurance. Expected utility may be higher depending on the value of G. If $G = L$, the expected

[8] Robert J. Cole, "Who Pays? Insurers Tallying, but Policies on Houses Are Few," *New York Times*, October 19, 1989.

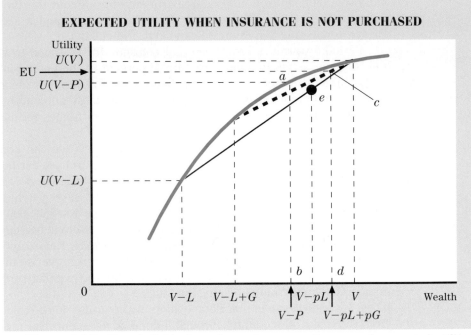

EXPECTED UTILITY WHEN INSURANCE IS NOT PURCHASED

Figure 3-17   If an individual purchases insurance, the person's expected utility is $U(V - P)$, where P is the premium. If the government grants aid equal to G to all those without insurance, the expected utility of not buying insurance is EU, which is greater than $U(V - P)$, expected utility with insurance.

utility of not purchasing insurance is $U(V)$, which is greater than the expected utility of buying insurance, $U(V - P)$. The government provides full insurance and does not charge a premium. If $G = 0$, we already know that the individual prefers to purchase insurance. Therefore, there are some values of G between 0 and L where the homeowner will decide not to purchase insurance. Figure 3-17 shows a case where G is large enough so that the individual does not purchase earthquake insurance. Expected utility is cd when the homeowner does not purchase insurance but receives aid, and ab when he purchases insurance and does not qualify for aid.

By providing disaster aid the government discourages the purchase of insurance and encourages individuals to take risks. On the Atlantic and Gulf coasts many people build summer homes along the oceanfront directly in the path of hurricanes and vulnerable to damage. Periodically, hurricanes cause extensive damage to oceanfront properties. The homes are rebuilt along the same oceanfront with federal disaster aid, and so by providing disaster aid the government subsidizes this type of risk-taking behavior.

In summary, the expected utility hypothesis offers two possible explanations for the reluctance of Californians to purchase earthquake insurance.

SUMMARY

- The income effect measures the change in the quantity demanded caused by a change in income when prices are held constant.
- The quantity demanded changes in the same direction as the change in income for a normal good and in the opposite direction for an inferior good.
- The substitution effect measures the change in the quantity demanded caused by a relative price change with the utility of the consumer held constant.
- The demand function of a consumer has a negative slope if the good is a normal good.
- The slope of the demand function can be either positive or negative if the good is an inferior good.
- The combined effect of the substitution and income effects determines the slope of the demand function.
- The demand function will be more elastic if (*a*) the product is a close substitute for another product, (*b*) the consumer spends a higher percentage of income on the good, and (*c*) the income elasticity of demand is large.
- Marginal value shows the maximum amount a consumer will pay for successive units of a good.
- Consumer surplus is the difference between the maximum amount the consumer would be willing to pay and the actual amount paid
- Expected income is a probability-weighted average of incomes for all possible outcomes.
- Expected utility is a probability-weighted average of utility for all possible outcomes.
- A risk-averse individual prefers to purchase insurance if the premium is not too high.
- A risk taker prefers an uncertain situation and will not purchase insurance.

KEY TERMS

income and substitution effects
Engel curve
Arc income elasticity of demand
Giffen good
slope of the demand function
Marginal value
probability
utility of income function
expected utility
insurance
load factor

normal and inferior goods
income-consumption curve
Slutsky equation
consumer surplus
dead weight loss
expected income
marginal utility
risk-taking, risk-neutral, and risk-averse
   individuals
premium

REVIEW QUESTIONS

1. If a good is a normal good, the consumer spends an increasing fraction of total income on it as income increases. Explain why you agree or disagree with this statement.

2. If a consumer increases but then de-

creases his demand for a good with successive increases in income, an economist would say the good is a normal good if the increase in the quantity demanded exceeds the decrease in the quantity demanded. Do you agree or disagree with this statement?

3. Explain why you agree or disagree with the following statements:
   a. If a good is a normal good, the demand function has a negative slope.
   b. If a demand curve has a negative slope, the good is a normal good.
   c. If a good is an inferior good, the demand curve has a positive slope.
   d. If a demand curve has a positive slope in the relevant price range, the good is a normal good.
   e. If a demand function has a positive slope in the relevant price range, the good is an inferior good.
   f. If an increase in income does not change the demand for a good, the demand function can have either a positive or a negative slope.

4. An economist would classify a new automobile that does not start in cold weather as an inferior good. Explain why you agree or disagree.

5. If two goods are perfect complements, the substitution effect is zero. Explain why you agree or disagree with this statement.

6. If two goods are perfect substitutes, the substitution effect is zero. Explain why you agree or disagree with this statement.

7. If two goods are perfect complements, the income effect is positive. Explain why you agree or disagree with this statement.

8. When price increases, would you need to raise or lower the consumer's income to measure the substitution effect? Explain.

9. When the price of a pint of strawberries is $2.80, I buy six pints per month. When the price falls to $2, I buy eight pints per month.
   a. Given this information, can you tell whether strawberries are a *normal* good for me?
   b. If I buy one more pint of strawberries when my monthly income increases by $6, can you determine the size of my income effect? my substitution effect? Explain.

10. More and more domestic and foreign auto manufacturers are introducing sports utility vehicles into the U.S. market. How will this affect a consumer's price elasticity of demand for sports utility vehicles?

11. A consumer does not subscribe to cable television service. Draw the indifference curve and the budget constraint of this individual. What is his or her consumer surplus?

12. After cable service was deregulated, cable companies raised the rates for basic service. Draw a graph and show how the consumer surplus of demanders changed. Can you measure the loss in consumer surplus by multiplying the increase in the basic rate by the number of subscribers to basic service after rates were increased? Explain why or why not.

13. You can shop at either of two supermarkets. You base your decision solely on the price of a market basket of goods. If you find one supermarket charges a penny more for the market basket, you will shop at the other store. What is your consumer surplus from shopping at either store?

14. A risk-averse individual always prefers to be insured rather than uninsured. Explain why you agree or disagree with this statement.

15. A risk-neutral individual never purchases insurance that includes a loading charge. Explain why you agree or disagree with this statement.

EXERCISES

1. What is an income-consumption line? Would you expect the slope of an income-consumption line to be greater for golf clubs than for softballs? Explain.
2. When your annual income was $22,000, you went to the movies 48 times per year and saw 2 professional basketball games per year. After you received an $8,000 raise, you went to the movies 40 times and saw 6 professional basketball games per year. What must you assume is constant to estimate your income elasticity of demand for movies and basketball games accurately? Calculate your income elasticity of demand for movies and for professional basketball games.
3. A consumer participates in an experiment. First, the price of Y is $5 and the price of X is $10. Then, the income of the consumer changes, and a record is made of the units of X and Y that he or she purchases (see the following table).

INCOME ($)	UNITS OF X	UNITS OF Y
200	11	18
220	12	20
240	13	22
260	14	24

The same consumer participates in a second experiment. This time income is held constant at $220 and the price of Y is $5. The price of X is changed, and the number of units of X consumed is recorded. The results of the second experiment are shown in the right-hand table above.

The experimenter notices that the consumer buys fewer units of X when the price declines from $P_X = \$10$ to $P_X = \$5$ and claims the consumer is not acting ir-

PRICE OF X ($)	UNITS OF X
20	4
15	6
10	12
5	10

rationally. Do you agree or disagree? Explain your answer.

4. The income-consumption line of a consumer is derived with prices held constant. After the price of X falls, a second income-consumption line is derived. Explain why the two income-consumption lines cannot cross.
5. If price is increased and the consumer's demand for steaks decreases, the substitution effect is greater than the income effect. Explain why you agree or disagree.
6. The slope of the demand function is -1.2 for a consumer currently purchasing three units of a good. A $1 increase in income increases the quantity demanded by five units. Is the behavior of the consumer consistent with rational behavior? Explain why or why not.
7. What does the opposition of the day care industry to a lump sum subsidy (see Application 3-1) tell you about the sign of the income effect?
8. Explain why a wealthy individual's demand function for a good is or is not more elastic than the demand function of a less wealthy consumer.
9. A jazz club charges $5 per drink and has a weekday audience of 40 patrons and a weekend audience of 80 patrons. The club introduces a cover charge of $15 on weekends but not during weekdays. What does

this pricing policy indicate about differences in the consumer surplus of weekday and weekend patrons?

10. Suppose you are operating an amusement park that offers different rides. Assume the typical patron has a downward sloping demand function for rides.

    a. With a graph show what is the maximum amount you can charge a consumer to enter the park if the rides are free.

    b. What is the maximum amount you can charge a consumer to enter the park if the price per ride is $4?

11. You submit a new book about the Internet to a publisher. The publisher agrees to publish the book and offers you two payment alternatives: (1) you will receive a fixed fee of $180,000 independent of how well the book does or (2) you will receive $400,000 if the book sells 10,000 or more copies and nothing if fewer than 10,000 copies are sold in its first three years on the market. If the probability of selling 10,000 copies or more is .5 and you accept the second alternative, does this demonstrate that you are a risk taker? Explain.

12. Think of a decision you had to make where there was some uncertainty about the outcome. Did your decision suggest you are a risk-averse or a risk-taking person?

*13. An individual's utility U depends on the individual's wealth W according to the utility function $U = 100(W)^{.5}$. This individual is planning to enter one of two occupations:

    ▪ In occupation 1 wealth will be either $133,300 with probability $p = .6$ or $50,000 with probability $(1 - p) = .4$.
    ▪ In occupation 2 wealth will be either $180,000 with probability $p = .5$ or $20,000 with probability $(1 - p) = .5$.

    a. If the individual maximizes expected wealth, which occupation would the individual enter?

    b. Calculate the expected utility in each occupation.

    c. If the individual enters occupation 1, what can you infer about the shape of his or her utility function? (*Hint:* What decision would the individual make if the individual's utility function was $U = 100 (W)^{1.5}$?)

*14. You are in the market for a new house and see a house with a market value of $220,000. Because you are not an expert on housing construction, you worry that there may be an expensive hidden defect. Suppose the probability of a major foundation defect that would cost $40,000 to repair is .05. Before you commit to purchasing the house, you decide to use the services of a highly recommended inspection service. The inspection service charges $2,500 to inspect the house and to identify major defects that the existing owner will have to correct before you will purchase the house. Assume the inspection service has a probability of 1 of finding the defect if it exists.

    a. If you do not use the inspection services, what is the expected value of the house?

    b. If you purchase the inspection services and then the house, what does this say about the shape of your utility function?

    c. Use a graph to show your expected utility if you purchase the inspection service and the house.

    d. With the use of a graph show the maximum amount that the inspection service could charge before you would not purchase the inspection service.

*15. A risk taker hopes to rebuild a house on a Gulf Coast beach after it has been destroyed by a hurricane. The government hopes to discourage rebuilding on the beach. How much would the government have to pay the homeowner to prevent the individual from rebuilding?

■ CHAPTER 3 APPENDIX

*Deriving Marginal Values

The consumer's demand function in Figure 3-11 shows the marginal values that a consumer places on successive videos. How does a consumer determine his or her marginal value of successive videos? In this appendix we use indifference curves to derive the consumer's marginal values and specify the conditions under which a consumer's demand function accurately measures the consumer's marginal values.

In Figure 3-18 spending on a composite good is on the vertical axis and number of videos per month is on the horizontal axis. The consumer's income is I_0. If the consumer does not rent any videos and spends all income on other goods, the consumer's utility is U_0. To determine the marginal value for the first video, ask what is the maximum amount the consumer would pay for the first video so that the consumer remains on indifference curve U_0. From Figure 3-11 the marginal value (MV) for the first video equals $12. The consumer would be willing to reduce spending on other goods by $12 and no more than $12 to rent the first video. If the consumer paid more than $12, the consumer would slip to a lower indifference curve and would be worse off. It would be better not to rent any videos than to pay more than $12 for the video.

If the consumer pays $12 for the first video, what is the marginal value of the second video? The consumer is willing to pay $8 for the second video because the consumer will still remain on U_0. If the consmer pays $12 for the first and $8 for the second video, the consumer rents two videos per month and could still remain on U_0. Proceeding in this manner until we come to the fifth video, we find that the marginal value of the fifth video is $3.25. To summarize, we find the marginal value for successive videos by moving down along the indifference curve U_0. Marginal value for the good on the x axis equals the marginal rate of substitution along the indifference curve U_0. For example, the marginal rate of substitution is -12 for the first video. As the consumer moves down along U_0, marginal value decreases because the consumer is willing to give up less and less spending on other goods as the number of videos increases. We can think of the consumer moving down U_0 in response to successive decreases in the relative price of videos holding utility constant and tracing out a series of marginal values. Because the consumer is moving along a given indifference curve, the consumer's marginal values for successive videos measure successive substitution effects.

The marginal values in Figure 3-18 correspond to the successive points on the consumer's demand function in Figure 3-11. When the price of each video is $3, aa is the consumer's budget constraint in Figure 3-18 and has a slope of -3. The slope of aa is tangent to the indifference curve U_1 when the consumer rents five videos per month. It is no accident that the consumer's marginal rate of substitution equals the market's marginal rate of substitution when the consumer rents five videos. We have deliberately drawn U_1 so that it is a vertical displacement of U_0. Consequently, the slope of U_1 equals the slope of U_0 for any given number of videos. With this special configuration of indifference curves, there are no income effects. Holding prices constant, the consumer does not demand more videos as income increases. When a video rents for $3, the consumer rents five videos because the marginal value of the fifth video is slightly more than $3 while the marginal value of the sixth video is slightly less than $3. When there are no income effects, the points on the demand function trace out a consumer's marginal values exactly. Therefore, the area under the demand function and above the price line accurately measures consumer surplus.

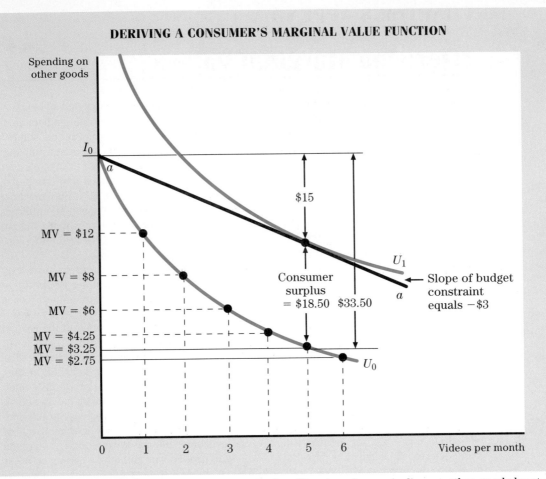

DERIVING A CONSUMER'S MARGINAL VALUE FUNCTION

Figure 3-18   The consumer is willing to reduce spending on other goods by at most $12 to rent the first video, $8 for the second, etc. Marginal values (MV) are shown on the vertical axis. Altogether the consumer will pay at most $33.50 to rent five videos per month. At a rental price of $3 per video, the consumer pays only $15 for five videos. Hence, the consumer surplus equals $18.50 for renting five videos per month.

If there was a positive income effect, then the consumer would demand more than five videos if the price was $3, say six videos. The indifference curve U_1 would not be a vertical displacement of U_0, as it is in Figure 3-18, but would be positioned differently. The budget constraint aa would be tangent to an indifference curve when the consumer rents six videos. The consumer's demand function would now reflect the substitution effect and a positive income effect and show the consumer demanding six videos when the price is $3. However, Figure 3-18 shows that the consumer's marginal value on U_0 is only $2.75 for the sixth video. Yet the consumer's demand function shows the consumer would be willing to pay $3 for the sixth video. With income effects, the demand function does not exactly measure the consumer's marginal value for successive videos.

When economists calculate measures of consumer surplus, they usually assume that the observations on the demand function measure marginal values and are implicitly assuming that income effects are small. For most goods, this is a good approximation. The substitution effect is likely to be of much larger magnitude than the income effect. Footnote 7 in Chapter 3 shows that the size of the income effect depends directly on the share of income spent on the good. For many goods, the share of a consumer's income spent on a good is negligible so the income effect is small, and the approximation is a reasonable one. This approximation is probably less defensible for something like housing, however, which accounts for a significant proportion of the income of most consumers.

CHAPTER 4

THE COST OF TIME AND THE THEORY OF CONSUMER BEHAVIOR

■ **4-1 Affordable Market Baskets**

The Limits of Time

The Budget Constraint

Deriving the Full Price Budget Constraint

Full Prices

Application 4-1: Walgreens Offers Convenience

Using the Full Price Budget Constraint to Find Affordable Market Baskets

Shifts in the Full Price Budget Constraint

■ **4-2 The Revised Consumer Behavior Model**

Choosing a Market Basket

The Effects of a Change in Nonwage Income and the Wage Rate

Application 4-2: Which Consumers Purchase Gasoline at Below the Market Price?

■ **4-3 Finding the Lowest Full Price**

Dependence of the Full Price on the Market Price

Application 4-3: How Much More Will Some Consumers Pay to Save Time?

■ **4-4 The Rising Cost of Women's Time**

The Increasing Number of Working Women

Differences in the Cost of Time for Females and Males

The Increase in Female Earnings Relative to Male Earnings

■ **Summary**

■ **Key Terms**

■ **Review Questions**

■ **Exercises**

In Chapters 2 and 3 we assumed that the the price paid by the consumer is the only cost of consuming a good. For some goods, this is an accurate estimate of the cost of consumption. For others, the market price is only a small fraction of the total cost of consuming the product. What would you say is the cost of reading the novel *War and Peace?* It certainly is not the price of the book. A dedicated reader will set aside many hours for reading, hours that he or she might have otherwise applied to earning income. On the other hand, what would you say is the price of consuming a hamburger at a fast-food outlet? Here the market price of the product comes closer to the total cost of consumption. It takes just a few minutes to order and eat a hamburger. These two extreme examples illustrate that for some products consumption is more time-intensive than for others. Therefore, the "price" of some goods is not the market price but must include the time required for consumption.

Not only does consumption take more time for some goods than for others, but the value of time differs from one person to another. Two individuals with the same tastes make different decisions about how many units of a good to consume although they can purchase the good at the same market price. Suppose the earnings of one person depend on hours of work and his hourly wage, while another more fortunate person sits back and receives the same income from dividends and interest. The cost of consuming is different for the two individuals. For the individual whose earnings depend on hours of work, time devoted to consuming is lost income. The higher the wage rate, the greater the income loss. For the individual who receives dividend and interest income, time spent on consumption has little effect on income. She receives dividend checks regardless of how she spends her time, and so she can use time in any way without losing income. While one individual may be well-read and a great conversationalist, the other has barely enough time to read the daily newspaper. The value of time also affects the types of goods that a consumer purchases.

This chapter modifies the theory of consumer behavior presented in Chapter 2 by introducing a more comprehensive measure of the price of a good. Here, we expand the theory to include time as a scarce resource that a consumer allocates to consumption and work activities. Nobel Prize winner Gary Becker is the foremost proponent of incorporating time explicitly into the theory.[1] He suggests that a deeper understanding of consumer behavior can be gained by recognizing that consumers not only allocate income between different products but also allocate time between earning and consuming activities.

4-1   AFFORDABLE MARKET BASKETS

Time is another constraint in addition to income that determines what market baskets the consumer can afford. For example, it takes time to sleep, to shop, to watch TV, to eat, or to daydream. The familiar lament "Where did all the time go?" expresses the **time constraint.** A consumer allocates time to an array of activities,

---

[1] Gary S. Becker, "A Theory of the Allocation of Time," *Economic Journal* 75 (September 1965), pp. 493–517.

just as he or she spends income on a range of goods. To observe the impact of time on the consumption decision, we look at the effects of limited time on the choice of goods. Again, the useful two-good model simplifies the situation confronting the consumer and still allows us to identify the effect of a scarce resource on the consumer's behavior.

The Limits of Time

To include time in the analysis, we introduce the total time constraint. In the model, total time available to the consumer is T hours per period, where a period can be a day, a week, or a month. T is a constant and outside the control of the individual. In our simplified model the consumer spends time either *working* or *consuming X and Y*, the two goods in the model. The individual decides how much time to allocate to work and to consuming each unit of X or Y. This interpretation of "consuming" includes the time spent shopping for and preparing the good for consumption, as well as the time used to consume it. For example, consuming a steak includes the time required to shop at a supermarket, to prepare and cook the steak, and to eat the steak and clean up afterward. Reading a book includes the total time required to purchase, read, and think about the book.

Because the consumption of goods requires time, it is necessary to specify how much time is used to consume each unit of X and Y. Initially, it is assumed that the consumer uses t_X hours to consume each unit of X and t_Y hours to consume each unit of Y, where both t_X and t_Y are constants outside the individual's control. Work is the other activity that requires time in this simplified model where T_w is the hours of work per period. In the model the individual manages time by determining how much time to allocate for the consumption of each good and for work.

The consumer satisfies the time constraint

$$\frac{\text{Time spent}}{\text{consuming X}} + \frac{\text{Time spent}}{\text{consuming Y}} + \frac{\text{Time}}{\text{working}} = \frac{\text{Total}}{\text{time}}$$

$$t_X X + t_Y Y + T_w = T \qquad \text{(Total Time Constraint)} \qquad \textbf{(4-1)}$$

Equation 4-1 says that time spent consuming goods X and Y and working equals the total time available. The time used to consume X units of X is $t_X X$ because it takes t_X hours to consume each unit of X. Similarly, the time needed to consume Y units of Y is $t_Y Y$. For example, if each movie you see lasts 2 hours and you see 30 movies a year, then the time involved is 60 hours.

In the model an individual picks the number of hours to work per period. This may strike you as somewhat unrealistic. In how many industries can a worker decide how many hours to work? Not many. However, this is too narrow a view of the job selection process. By selecting among industries and firms within industries, each individual can work the number of hours best suited for the individual. Anyone working for an investment banking or consulting firm knows that he or she will put in many hours per year. On the other hand, if you work for a manufacturing firm, your work hours will be less. If you are self-employed, you decide how many hours to work. Part-time work and multiple jobs are alternatives for those individuals who desire to work less or more. There is a gradation in expected work hours among industries and types of employment. Within this broader perspective an individual has control over hours of work.

The Budget Constraint

The budget constraint of the consumer is slightly more complicated when time is included in the consumer behavior model. Earned income is equal to hours worked per period times the hourly wage w. In addition the consumer may receive nonwage income V, which includes pensions, dividends, social security payments, and so on.[2] So, total income is the sum of wage and nonwage income or $wT_w + V$. Consequently, income is no longer a constant but depends on how many hours are spent at work. As before, the market price is P_X for each unit of X and P_Y for each unit of Y. Total expenditures on X and Y are $P_X X$ and $P_Y Y$, respectively.

The budget constraint requires that total spending on X and Y equal total income. The revised budget constraint is written as

$$\text{Total spending} = \text{Total income}$$

$$P_X X + P_Y Y = wT_w + V \qquad \text{(Revised Budget Constraint)} \qquad \textbf{(4-2)}$$

Deriving the Full Price Budget Constraint

Let's determine which market baskets satisfy the time and the budget constraints of the consumer. Given hours worked, the consumer earns income of $wT_w + V$ and spends it on X and Y such that the time constraint (equation 4-1) and the budget constraint (equation 4-2) are satisfied. Only one market basket of X and Y will satisfy both constraints. By repeating this procedure for each T_w, different market baskets of X and Y that satisfy the time and budget constraints can be determined.

How many units of Y the consumer can purchase for each quantity of X can be determined by combining the time and income constraints. First, solve equation 4-2 for T_w by subtracting V from both sides of the equation and then dividing both sides by w to get

$$T_w = \frac{P_X X + P_Y Y - V}{w}$$

Then substitute the expression for T_w into equation 4-1 to obtain the *full price budget constraint*.[3]

$$(P_X + wt_X)X + (P_Y + wt_Y)Y = wT + V \qquad \text{(Full Price Budget Constraint)} \qquad \textbf{(4-3)}$$

Full income F_I is on the right-hand side and is defined as $wT + V$.

---

[2] It is assumed that the consumer does not spend time collecting nonwage income.

[3] This expression is derived by substituting the expression for T_w into equation 4-1 to obtain

$$t_X X + t_Y Y + \frac{P_X X + P_Y Y - V}{w} = T$$

To simplify the fraction, multiply both sides of the equation by w and add V to both sides to get

$$wt_X X + wt_Y Y + P_X X + P_Y Y = wT + V$$

After collecting terms, we have equation 4-3.

Full income is the consumer's income if all available time is spent working.

Full Prices

A useful interpretation of the "price" of consuming a unit of X or Y can be obtained by examining the expressions in parentheses on the left-hand side of equation 4-3. These terms are the full price of consuming a unit of either good. The full price of X or Y is defined as

$$\text{Full price} = \text{Market price} + \text{Opportunity cost of time}$$

$$F_X = P_X + wt_X \qquad \text{(Full Price of X)} \tag{4-4}$$

$$F_Y = P_Y + wt_Y \qquad \text{(Full Price of Y)} \tag{4-5}$$

where F_X and F_Y are the symbols for the full prices of X and Y. The full price of either good is the market price plus the opportunity cost of consuming a good. By opportunity cost we mean the income forgone because of time used in consumption. Because you use t_X hours to consume each unit of X, your forgone income is wt_X, and so wt_X is the **opportunity cost of time.**

The **full price** of a good is equal to the market price of the good plus the consumer's opportunity cost of time required to consume the good.

As mentioned in the introduction to this chapter, the full price depends on the time required to consume a good and the consumer's own wage rate. The full price of a good reflects the expression "time is money." With this interpretation of full prices, the full price budget constraint can be reinterpreted as saying total money expenditure plus forgone income of consuming goods X and Y must equal full income.

In setting prices and understanding consumer behavior, firms must realize that the consumer uses full prices and not simply market prices to determine how many units of each good to purchase. One firm may set a very low market price but provide very little service, or it may be located a long distance from the consumer. A buyer could decide to purchase the product from another seller who charges a higher market price but offers quicker service and a lower full price. You might very well purchase a higher-priced graphics or drawing software program that has few bugs in it and a complete, elaborate, well-written manual rather than a lower-priced graphics or drawing program with an incomplete or confusing manual because of the extra time you would have to spend trying to decipher the manual or to recover data lost as a result of program glitches.

Because the full price has two components, a firm can reduce the price to consumers in either of two ways. Firms can compete with each other by lowering the market price or by reducing the consumption time of the consumer, both of which decrease the full price. Although businesspeople do not use the term "full price," they are constantly thinking about full prices when they design pricing and marketing strategies. They often talk about offering more convenience to the consumer. What they are thinking about is ways to reduce consumption time. For example, firms offer convenience by locating items where consumers can easily find them, by eliminating stock shortages, providing checkout and sales staff, reducing shipping time, and providing one-stop shopping.

APPLICATION 4-1

Walgreens Offers Convenience[4]

Walgreens is one of the fastest-growing major drugstore chains, with outlets primarily in the Midwest. The firm relies on a nationwide computer system for ordering and stocking merchandise and for filling prescriptions and is dedicated to customer convenience. Walgreens firmly believes that consumers value convenience as much as good price when shopping for prescriptions and other drugstore merchandise. Management feels that providing convenience is critical to the success of the company, and Walgreens stores are laid out so that the consumer can enter, purchase, and leave quickly. The average Walgreens customer buys two items in less than 10 minutes. The company has adopted a policy of establishing most stores as isolated units, rather than as parts of shopping centers. In this way, the managers believe, consumers are better able to save time by parking near each Walgreens outlet, which is not always possible if units are located in shopping centers.

The prices charged by the company are not the lowest in the industry. Deep discount drug outlets and some supermarkets charge lower prices, but Walgreens has successfully competed with these low-price competitors by offering convenience. Ease of access and quick, reliable service are what the firm strives for. The president of Walgreens aptly summarized the company's philosophy at the 1990 annual meeting: "We believe the retailer who wastes consumers' time in the 90s is committing competitive suicide."

Using the Full Price Budget Constraint to Find Affordable Market Baskets

Equation 4-3 combined the separate time and budget constraints into a single **full price budget constraint.** To find those market baskets of X and Y that the consumer can afford, equation 4-3 can be rearranged to show how many units of Y can be consumed for any quantity of X. It is solved for Y by subtracting $(P_X + wt_X)X$ from both sides and dividing both sides by $P_Y + wt_Y$:

$$Y = \frac{wT + V}{P_Y + wt_Y} - \left(\frac{P_X + wt_X}{P_Y + wt_Y}\right)X$$

$$= \frac{\text{Full income}}{\text{Full price of Y}} - \left(\frac{\text{Full price of X}}{\text{Full price of Y}}\right)X \qquad \begin{array}{l}\text{(Full Price Budget} \\ \text{Constraint Rearranged)}\end{array} \qquad \textbf{(4-6)}$$

[4] Based on Eben Shapiro, "A Drugstore Industry Leader Raises the Level of Its Game," *New York Times,* August 26, 1990, p. F16. See also Nancy Ryan, "Simplicity Is Walgreens' Cure for the '90's," *Chicago Tribune,* January 21, 1991, Section 4, p. 1.

Table 4-1   THE FULL PRICE BUDGET CONSTRAINT

1. Hours to consume a unit of X	$t_X = 0.5$ or 30 minutes
2. Hours to consume a unit of Y	$t_Y = 1$ hour
3. Total time	$T = 60$ hours
4. Price of X	$P_X = \$20$ per unit
5. Price of Y	$P_Y = \$15$ per unit
6. Hourly wage rate	$w = \$10$ per hour
7. Nonwage income	$V = 0$
8. Full price of X	$F_X = P_X + w_X t_X = \$20 + \$10(0.5) = \$25$
9. Full price of Y	$F_Y = P_Y + w t_Y = \$15 + \$10(1) = \$25$
10. Full income	$F_I = \$10(60) = \$600$

Equation 4-6 is the equation of a straight line between Y and X. The y intercept is $(wT + V)/(P_Y + wt_Y)$, and the absolute value of the slope is $(P_X + wt_X)/(P_Y + wt_Y)$. Before graphing equation 4-6, let's provide an interpretation of the intercept and the slope of this linear equation in Y and X. If the consumer does not purchase any X, equation 4-6 says the number of units of Y that she can purchase is equal to full income divided by the full price of Y, or $(wT + V)/(P_Y + wt_Y)$. To be more specific, let's consider a numerical example and show how the full price budget constraint can be derived. In rows 1 to 7 of Table 4-1 numerical values are assigned for each of the constants.

Figure 4-1 shows the full price budget constraint. The y intercept is equal to full income divided by the full price of Y. Row 10 of Table 4-1 shows that full income is $600, and row 9 shows that the full price of Y is $25, and so the individual can consume $600/$25 = 24 units of Y if nothing is spent on X. If 24 units of Y are consumed, money income is equal to $wT - wt_Y Y$, or $600 - $240 = $360. Since the price of Y is $15, total spending on Y is $15(24) = $360. So, expenditures match income. Since the individual consumes 24 units of Y and each takes 1 hour, he or she spends 24 hours consuming Y and works $60 - 24 = 36$ hours.

Shifts in the Full Price Budget Constraint

In the numerical example we assumed that nonwage income is zero. If the consumer has nonwage income and receives an increase in dividend income, nonwage income increases from V to V'. The intercept on the vertical axis increases from $(wT + V)/(P_Y + wt_Y)$ to $(wT + V')/(P_Y + wt_Y)$, but $-F_X/F_Y$, the slope of the full price budget constraint, does not change when V changes. Figure 4-2 shows a

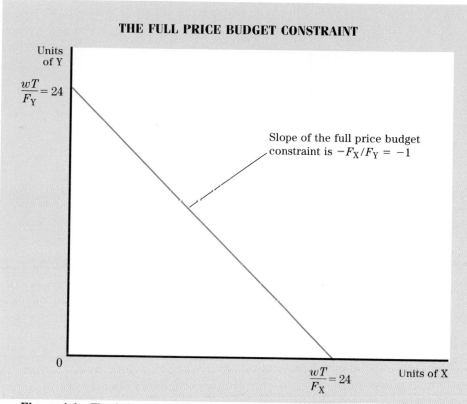

Figure 4-1   The full price budget constraint shows how many units of Y the individual can consume for a given number of units of X while satisfying the time and the budget constraints. In the numerical example the consumer can purchase 24 units of either Y or X if he or she purchases only Y or only X. Although the market price of X is greater than the market price of Y, the full price of X equals the full price of Y and the slope of the full price budget constraint equals −1.

parallel outward shift in the full price budget just as an increase in income caused a parallel shift in the budget line in Chapter 2.

The easiest way to observe the effect of changes in the wage rate is to assume that the consumer has no nonwage income ($V = 0$) and to look at how an increase in w shifts the full price budget constraint. The full price budget constraint can be expressed as

$$Y = \frac{T}{(P_Y/w) + t_Y} - \left[\frac{(P_X/w) + t_X}{(P_Y/w) + t_Y}\right] X \qquad \textbf{(4-7)}$$

Equation 4-7 shows that the intercept increases when w increases because P_Y/w decreases. A consumer who just buys Y can purchase more units of Y when the wage increases. Returning to our numerical example, if the wage rate increases from \$10 to \$15 an hour, the consumer's full income increases from \$600 to \$900

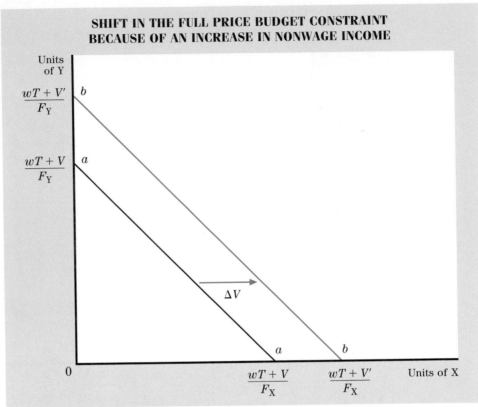

**SHIFT IN THE FULL PRICE BUDGET CONSTRAINT
BECAUSE OF AN INCREASE IN NONWAGE INCOME**

Figure 4-2   The full price budget constraint shifts outward when nonwage income increases. Because the full prices of the goods are unaffected, the slope of the full price budget constraint does not change.

and the full price of Y increases from \$25 to \$30 and so the consumer can now purchase \$900/\$30 = 30 units of Y.

To determine when the percentage change in the full price of X increases by less than the full price of Y, it is insightful to rewrite the expression for the **ratio of full prices** to better understand how the ratio of full prices changes when w changes.

$$\left(\frac{(P_X/w) + t_X}{(P_Y/w) + t_Y}\right) = \frac{P_X}{P_Y}\left(\frac{1 + w(t_X/P_X)}{1 + w(t_Y/P_Y)}\right) \qquad (4\text{-}8)$$

Since the price of Y and of X are constants, an increase in w will increase the full price of X by less than the full price of Y if

$$\frac{t_X}{P_X} < \frac{t_Y}{P_Y} \qquad \text{(Time per Dollar of Expenditure Inequality)} \qquad (4\text{-}9)$$

An increase in the wage rate will lower the full price of X relative to the full price of Y if the t/P ratio of X is less than the t/P ratio of Y.

The ratio on the left-hand side of equation 4-9 is the number of hours (in minutes) used to consume X per dollar spent on a unit of X. It measures the time intensity of X per dollar spent on X. Similarly, the ratio on the right-hand side is the time intensity of Y per dollar spent on Y. In our numerical example, t_X/P_X is 30 minutes divided by \$20, or $1\frac{1}{2}$ minutes per dollar. Every dollar expenditure for X requires a time commitment of $1\frac{1}{2}$ minutes. For Y, t_Y/P_Y equals 60 minutes divided by \$15, or 4 minutes per dollar. Every dollar expenditure for Y requires a 4-minute time commitment. X is less time-intensive per dollar of expenditure than Y. Because Y uses more time per dollar than X, a rise in the wage rate increases the full price of Y proportionately more than that of X. When the wage rate increases, the full price of X increases by a smaller percentage than the full price of Y. In our new terminology the full price of X falls relative to the full price of Y. As the wage rate increases, the consumer finds that X is becoming cheaper relative to Y although the market prices of X and Y are *constant*.

It may seem counterintuitive that the magnitudes of t/P for the two goods and not simply the magnitudes of t for the two goods determine whether the full price of X increases by more or less than the full price of Y when the w rate increases. To convince yourself, consider this example. Suppose $t_X = 2$ hours and $t_Y = 1$ hour so $t_X > t_Y$. The consumer uses more time to consume X than Y. But suppose that $P_X = \$100$ and $P_Y = \$2$ so $t_X/P_X < t_Y/P_Y$. At a wage rate of \$10, the full price of X is \$120 while the full price of Y is \$12. However, a rise in the wage to \$20 increases the full price of X by only 16.6 percent to \$140 and the full price of Y by 83.3 percent to \$22 so the ratio of full prices decreases. This occurs because P_X is large relative to the time to consume X while P_Y is small relative to the time to consume Y.

Figure 4-3 shows how the full price budget constraint shifts outward and becomes flatter when w increases. The full price budget constraint is the line aa when the wage rate is \$10 per hour and becomes bb when the wage rate increases to \$15 per hour. The increase in the wage rate shifts the full price budget constraint outward to the northeast *and* changes its slope. In our numerical example, the y intercept increases to 30 units when the wage rate increases from \$10 to \$15 an hour. The slope of the full price budget constraint increases from -1 to $-\$27.5/\$30 = -0.917$, and the full price budget constraint becomes flatter.[5]

To summarize, a rise in nonwage income has no effect on the slope of the full price budget constraint because relative full prices are unaffected. On the other hand, a rise in the wage rate will affect relative full prices if the t/P ratios differ among goods. If the t/P ratios differ, the purchaser will substitute toward goods that are less time-intensive per dollar of expenditure. Therefore, a consumer's

[5] Recall that $F_X = P_X + wt_X = \$20 + \$15(.5) = \$27.50$, $F_Y = P_Y + wt_Y = \$15 + \$15(1) = \$30$, and the slope of the full price budget constraint $= -F_X/F_Y$.

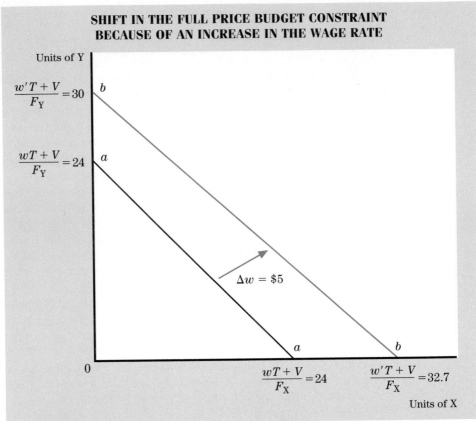

SHIFT IN THE FULL PRICE BUDGET CONSTRAINT
BECAUSE OF AN INCREASE IN THE WAGE RATE

Units of Y

$\dfrac{w'T + V}{F_Y} = 30$ b

$\dfrac{wT + V}{F_Y} = 24$ a

$\Delta w = \$5$

0   a   b

$\dfrac{wT + V}{F_X} = 24$ $\dfrac{w'T + V}{F_X} = 32.7$

Units of X

Figure 4-3   When the wage rate increases from \$10 to \$15 per hour, the full price budget constraint shifts from *aa* to *bb*. It becomes flatter when the wage rate increases if X is less time-intensive per dollar expenditure than Y. Because the full price of X increases by less than the full price of Y, the full price budget constraint becomes flatter. X becomes cheaper relative to Y when *w* increases.

response to an increase in income is different depending on the source of the increased income.

4-2   THE REVISED CONSUMER BEHAVIOR MODEL

In Chapter 2, the goal of the consumer was to select a market basket that maximized utility subject to the constraint that expenditures match income. Now, the full price budget constraint has been included and takes account of the time and the income constraints. As before, the consumer's indifference map is defined over all market baskets of X and Y. The goal of the consumer is to find one that maximizes utility subject to the full price budget constraint.

Choosing a Market Basket

Figure 4-4 shows one indifference curve of a consumer and the full price budget constraint. The marginal rate of substitution between Y and X is the slope of the indifference curve at each point on the curve. The consumer selects a market basket on the full price budget constraint where the marginal rate of substitution between Y and X is equal to the slope of the full price budget constraint:

$$\text{MRS}_{YX} = -\frac{F_X}{F_Y} \qquad \text{(Condition for Maximizing Utility Subject to the Full Price Budget Constraint)} \qquad \textbf{(4-10)}$$

where MRS_{YX} denotes the marginal rate of substitution between Y and X. The consumer satisfies this condition by selecting a market basket containing X_0 units of X and Y_0 units of Y.

> If the consumer purchases both goods, he or she selects a market basket where the marginal rate of substitution is equal to the slope of the full price budget constraint.

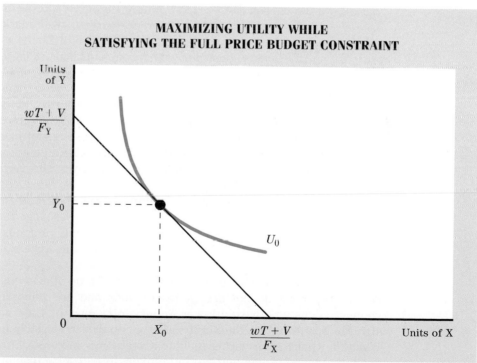

MAXIMIZING UTILITY WHILE SATISFYING THE FULL PRICE BUDGET CONSTRAINT

Figure 4-4   The consumer maximizes utility by selecting a market basket of X_0 and Y_0 where the marginal rate of substitution is equal to the slope of the full price budget constraint.

The Effects of a Change in Nonwage Income and the Wage Rate

We can determine how this revised model of consumer behavior differs from the simpler but more limited model presented in Chapter 2. First, let's consider how consumer behavior changes when income changes. In the simpler model there was only one income source so it was clear what an increase in income meant. But in this revised model the type of income change must be specified, for it makes a difference. An increase in nonwage income shifts the full price budget constraint outward without changing its slope. On the other hand, a rise in the wage rate shifts the full price budget constraint outward and changes its slope as well. So, we need to keep track of the source of the increased income to predict how the consumer reacts.

Figure 4-5 shows how an increase in nonwage income shifts the full price budget constraint outward in a parallel fashion from aa to bb so that the consumer can reach indifference curve U_1. When nonwage income increases, the consumer moves from market basket A to market basket B and increases purchases of X from X_0 to X_1 and of Y from Y_0 to Y_1.

Beginning again with market basket A, consider an increase in the wage rate that allows the consumer to reach indifference curve U_1. The budget constraint becomes cc and is tangent to the indifference curve U_1 with market basket C. If X is less time-intensive per dollar than Y, the full price of X falls relative to the full price of Y and the budget constraint cc shifts out and becomes flatter. The consumer selects market basket C and purchases X_2 units of X and Y_2 units of Y because of this increase in the wage rate. The increase in the wage rate encourages the consumer to substitute toward X and away from Y because X has a lower t/P ratio. When the wage rate increases, the consumer buys relatively fewer units of goods with higher t/P ratios and may even stop consuming some of these goods.

When the wage rate increases, the consumer substitutes toward good X because X is less time-intensive per dollar of expenditure. This version of consumer behavior theory tells us that a person with a lower wage rate faces a different ratio of full prices than a person with a higher wage rate. When other factors are held constant, the types of goods that individuals with lower wage rates purchase are more time-intensive per dollar of expenditure. The mix of goods bought shifts in the direction of goods with lower t/P ratios when the wage rate increases over time.

Here are some examples of how the cost of time affects consumer behavior: Some restaurants do not accept reservations and are generally frequented by younger adults who have a lower **opportunity cost of time** and are willing to stand in line for up to 2 hours to eat at a popular, moderately priced restaurant. When they reach their thirties and their wage rates and cost of time increase, they decline to stand in line and are more likely to patronize restaurants that accept reservations. This difference in behavior is due in part to changes in the cost of time.

The cost of time affects when individuals shop. For working men and women,

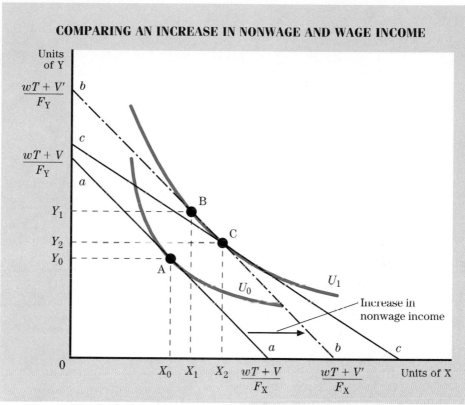

COMPARING AN INCREASE IN NONWAGE AND WAGE INCOME

Figure 4-5 An increase in nonwage income does not change the slope of the full price budget constraint and therefore shifts the full price budget constraint from *aa* to *bb*. With market basket B the consumer purchases X_1 and Y_1 units. An increase in the wage rate makes the full price budget constraint flatter if X is less time intensive per dollar than Y. The consumer substitutes toward X and purchases market basket C. The market basket purchased depends on the source of the increased income.

the relative cost of time is higher during the work week than during the weekend, and they respond by shopping less during weekdays after work and concentrate more on weekend shopping. In contrast the relative cost of time of shopping for nonworking men and women is lower during the week than on the weekend. Another advantage of shopping during the weekday is that there are fewer people in the stores and the sales staff can offer more help than on the weekend. Figure 4-6 shows that more full-time workers than nonworking individuals shop for groceries on the weekend.

College students often debate and argue among themselves, an activity with a high t/P ratio. Bull sessions in dorms are commonplace on most campuses. The propensity to argue and the length of debates diminish with age in part because the opportunity cost of time increases with age.

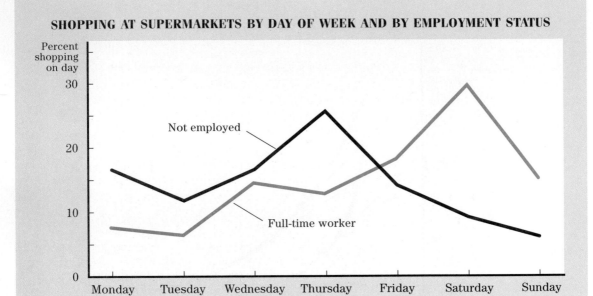

SHOPPING AT SUPERMARKETS BY DAY OF WEEK AND BY EMPLOYMENT STATUS

Figure 4-6   Relatively more working individuals shop for groceries on weekends, whereas relatively more nonworking people shop during the week. [*Progressive Grocer*, April 1989.]

APPLICATION 4-2

Which Consumers Purchase Gasoline at Below the Market Price?[6]

In 1980 company-owned Chevron stations in California were mandated to reduce the price of gasoline by 16 to 21 cents per gallon below the current market price because of a past violation of ceiling price regulations. Other independently owned stations selling Chevron gasoline were unaffected and continued to sell Chevron at the market price. Economists Robert Deacon and Jon Sonstelie surveyed the customers who purchased gasoline at the lower-priced company-owned stations as well as those who purchased gasoline at the higher-priced independently owned stations.

The lower-priced stations attracted so many more customers that waiting lines formed. Deacon and Sonstelie found that customers at Chevron-owned stations waited on average an extra 14.6 minutes to purchase gasoline at an average discount of 18.5 cents per gallon. Since the average purchase was 10.5 gallons, the economists estimated that anyone with a wage rate of less than $7.98 per hour would prefer to buy gasoline at the lower-priced station. Economists derive this

[6] Based on Robert T. Deacon and Jon Sonstelie, "Rationing by Waiting and the Value of Time: Results from a Natural Experiment," *Journal of Political Economy* 93, no. 4 (1985), pp. 627–47.

estimated wage rate by noting that a customer would be indifferent between stations if

$$(P_i - P_c)g = w(t_c - t_i)$$

where P_c and P_i are the prices at the company-owned and independently owned stations, respectively, t_c and t_i are the waiting times at the company-owned and independently owned stations, respectively, g is the number of gallons purchased, and w is the individual's wage rate. Since the average difference in price was 18.5 cents per gallon, the average difference in waiting time was 14.6 minutes and the average number of gallons bought at all stations was 10.5 gallons, the authors calculated that a wage of $7.98 per hour just made the consumer indifferent between the two types of stations. A consumer with a wage rate of less than $7.98 would be more likely to wait in line to purchase gasoline at a company-owned station.

Although Deacon and Sonstelie didn't confirm the estimated wage rate, their predictions were supported by the behavior of gas station patrons. The lower-priced stations attracted more automobiles with larger tank capacities and sold more gallons per transaction. The cars waiting in line at company-owned stations had fewer adult passengers in them. The total opportunity cost of time of all the passengers in a car was lower at company-owned stations. It was also discovered that a higher percentage of unemployed workers and a lower percentage of full-time employed workers were in line at company-owned stations.

This imaginative study shows how the opportunity cost of time of consumers affects the choice of gas station.

4-3 FINDING THE LOWEST FULL PRICE

Up to now, it has been assumed that a consumer uses a fixed amount of time to consume each unit of a good. In the model, the consumer uses t_X hours to consume each unit of X. Often the amount of time used to consume a unit of a good is not a constant but is under the control of the consumer. There are many everyday illustrations where the individual determines the amount of time used to consume a unit of a good.

1. You can select a dentist who charges a high hourly rate but takes patients on time, or you can go to another dentist who charges a low hourly rate but keeps you waiting for your appointment. If you are willing to pay a higher fee, you can save time.

2. You can fly on the Concorde from New York to London at a cost of $7,877 round trip, or you can fly first class on a Boeing 747 that takes 3 hours longer for a round trip fare of $7,004. Some consumers and firms are willing to pay the $873 to save 3 hours of flying time.

3. You can live in the suburbs and spend more time commuting, or you can live in the central city and pay a higher rent but save on commuting time. If you are willing to pay more for housing, you can save time.

4. You can shop at a higher-priced store that employs knowledgeable sales-people and is seldom out of stock. Or, you can run from one low-priced store to another, each of which has fewer salespeople and frequent shortages of merchandise.

5. If you do a load of laundry at home, it will cost you about $2.10 per load for soap, bleach, and so on (assuming you already have a washer and dryer) and will take 3/4 of an hour of your time, or you could take your laundry to a laundromat and have it done for you. The laundromat will charge you $8 per load but it will only take 1/6 of an hour of your time.

These illustrations show that individuals have a choice between paying a higher price and saving time or paying a lower price and using more time. The consumer has some control over t_X and t_Y, and so these values are really not constant. To see how the consumer balances the tradeoff between the price paid and the time saved, the theory must be modified.

Dependence of the Full Price on the Market Price

This section examines the price-time tradeoff to see how the consumer determines the full price of a product. Let us concentrate on good X. We assume that the consumer can shop for X at different stores. Some stores offer more service and charge higher prices, and a consumer who decides to shop at these stores pays a higher price but spends less time shopping. Other stores offer less service and charge lower prices, and an individual who shops at these stores pays a lower price but spends more time shopping.

By paying a higher price P_X, the consumer reduces consumption time t_X. So there is an inverse relationship between the price paid and t_X. It is assumed that the consumer can choose from a continuous array of price-time combinations. Let the function

$$t_X = g(P_X) \qquad \text{(Price-Time Tradeoff)} \tag{4-11}$$

describe the price-time choices in the marketplace. The consumer can select a high P_X–low t_X store or a low P_X–high t_X store. In other words, the slope of the price-time function is negative.

$$\frac{\Delta t_X}{\Delta P_X} = \frac{\Delta[g(P_X)]}{\Delta P_X} < 0$$

In Figure 4-7 the price at one store is P_X^1, but the consumer has to shop for only t_X^1 hours. The price at another store is only P_X^2, but shopping time is t_X^2 hours. Substituting the expression for t_X in equation 4-11 into the expression for the full price of X yields

$$F_X = P_X + wt_X = P_X + wg(P_X) \tag{4-12}$$

Equation 4-12 says that the full price of X paid by the consumer depends on the market price, which in turn depends on the type of store the consumer patronizes.

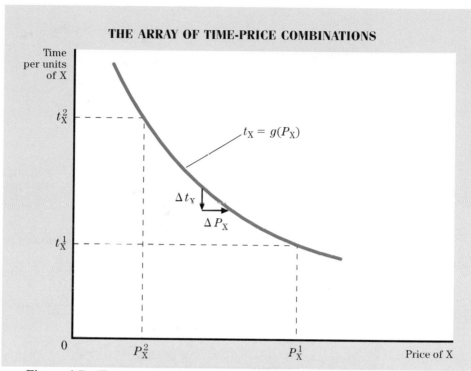

THE ARRAY OF TIME-PRICE COMBINATIONS

$t_X = g(P_X)$

Δt_X

ΔP_X

Time per units of X

t_X^2

t_X^1

0

P_X^2

P_X^1

Price of X

Figure 4-7   The consumer faces an array of price-time tradeoffs. If he or she shops at a higher-price store and pays P_X^1, the individual saves on time and only uses t_X^1 hours per unit of X. If the consumer pays a lower price of P_X^2, he or she uses t_X^2 hours per unit of X.

Before the consumer selects a market basket, he or she has to know the full prices of X and Y. However, there is not a single full price of X, but many. We assume that each individual selects the type of store that minimizes the full price. To achieve this minimum full price, he or she balances increases in the price paid for the good against the decrease in the opportunity cost of time.

Figure 4-8 shows the optimal solution for a consumer. Dollars per unit of X are on the vertical axis, and the price of X is on the horizontal axis. The full price of X is $P_X + wt_X = P_X + wg(P_X)$ and can be derived as a function of P_X by adding the two components vertically. The 45-degree line labeled *aa* represents the first component, P_X, the market price paid by the consumer. The 45-degree line merely transposes the price the consumer pays from the x axis to the y axis. The second component of the full price is $wg(P_X)$, which in Figure 4-8 is the curve *bb*. Curve *bb* slopes downward because shopping time decreases when the consumer pays a higher price; $\Delta t_X/\Delta P_X < 0$. The full price curve *cc* is formed by summing the *aa* and *bb* functions vertically. An important point to realize is that the full price of X decreases and then increases as P_X increases. At first, as P_X increases, the full price

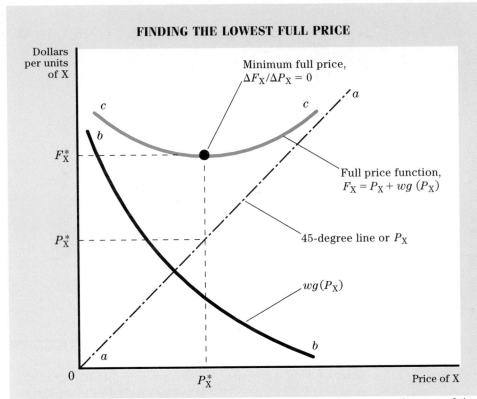

Figure 4-8   The full price equals the market price plus the opportunity cost of time. The function aa is a 45-degree line and shows the price paid by the consumer. The function bb shows the opportunity cost of time $wg(P_X)$ decreases if the consumer pays a higher price. The full price function is cc and is the vertical sum of the aa and bb functions. The minimum full price for this individual occurs when the consumer shops at a store that charges a price of P_X^*.

decreases because the decrease in the opportunity cost of time is greater than the increase in the market price paid for the product.

In Figure 4-8 the minimum full price of X is F_X^* and occurs when $P_X = P_X^*$. The consumer **minimizes the full price** when a dollar increase in the market price of X equals the savings in time.[7]

$$1 = -w \frac{\Delta t_X}{\Delta P_X} \qquad \text{(Condition for the Minimum Full Price)} \qquad \textbf{(4-13)}$$

[7] The full price, $F_X = P_X + wt_X$, is minimized when the slope of the full price function is zero. Using calculus, this condition requires

$$\frac{dF_X}{dP_X} = 1 + w \frac{dt_X}{dP_X} = 0$$

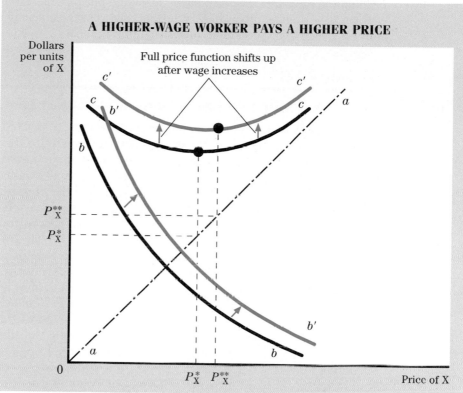

Figure 4-9 An increase in the wage rate increases the value of the savings in time. The *bb* function shifts up and becomes *b'b'*. The distance between the *b'b'* function and the *bb* function is smaller when P_X is larger. The full price function shifts up and becomes the function labeled *c'c'*. The price that minimizes the full price increases from P_X^* to P_X^{**}.

The left-hand side of equation 4-13 represents a dollar increase in the price of X. The dollar savings obtained from the reduced time spent shopping is on the right-hand side of the equation and is $-w\,\Delta t_X/\Delta P_X$.

We can use this model showing how a consumer minimizes the full price to determine how an increase in w changes the market price an individual is willing to pay. Equation 4-13 indicates that the opportunity cost of time increases when w increases. The curve *bb* in Figure 4-9 shifts up and becomes *b'b'* when the wage increases. The distance between *b'b'* and *bb* diminishes as P_X increases.[8] Because *bb* shifts upward, the full price curve shifts upward and becomes *c'c'*. The minimum of the new full price curve occurs at P_X^{**}, a higher price. What this means is that an increase in w causes the consumer to shop at a more expensive store where he or she can save the now more valuable time. Higher-wage consumers are more

[8] When $\Delta t_X/\Delta P_X$ is close to zero, a rise in w increases the value of the time savings by less than when $\Delta t_X/\Delta P_X$ is far different from zero.

willing to pay higher prices to save more time per purchase than are lower-wage consumers. Holding other things constant, higher-wage consumers will pay higher prices to economize still more on consumption time.

APPLICATION 4-3

How Much More Will Some Consumers Pay to Save Time?

There is plenty of evidence that consumers are willing to pay more to save time in the kitchen. The food industry has been very responsive to the changing cost of time of consumers. A Bureau of Labor Statistics study reported that the number of two-earner families increased from 29 percent of all families in the 1972–74 period to 36 percent in 1990 and thereby increased the opportunity cost of time spent preparing foods.[9] Consequentially, consumers have changed their food spending patterns over this period. Miscellaneous prepared foods include items bought in the grocery and other food stores that are fresh, frozen, canned, and packaged, and that are precooked and ready-to-serve cold or after heating. Miscellaneous prepared foods' share of in-home food expenditures increased from 8 percent in the 1972–74 period to 15 percent in 1992. There may also be a long-term trend toward eating more food away from home. Away-from-home food expenditure was 27 percent of total food expenditures from 1972 to 1974 and increased to 37 percent in 1990 before dipping to 33 percent during the 1992 recession year. The report mentions the possibility that consumers are using prepared foods as a substitute for eating out in recession years, but separating the effects of the recession from the effects of increased substitutability is difficult. We will have to wait for new figures to determine if this dip is only temporary.

[9] Bureau of Labor Statistics, "Consumer Expenditure Survey: Quarterly Data from Interview Survey," Report 875, First Quarter 1993.

Table 4-2   THE PRICE OF CONVENIENCE

ITEM PURCHASED	TIME-CONSUMING METHOD	COST PER POUND ($)	TIME-SAVING METHOD	COST PER POUND ($)
Chicken	Perdue whole fryer	1.19	Swanson fried chicken entree with whipped potatoes and corn	3.35
			Stouffer's fried chicken	3.78
			Tyson BBQ chicken meal	2.95
Potatoes	5 lbs of potatoes	0.44	Ore-Ida golden fries	0.97
			Frozen Stouffer's potatoes au gratin	2.33
			Ore-Ida golden crinkles	1.30

Table 4-2 compares the 1996 price of prepared items to the price of the basic ingredient required to make a comparable meal. For chicken, the per pound price of the prepared item averages 182 percent higher than the per pound price of the time-consuming method, while for potatoes, the prepared item is priced 248 percent more than the per pound price for potatoes. While buyers of prepared foods are paying considerably more for prepared foods, they are willing to pay the extra price for the value of the time saved.

4-4   THE RISING COST OF WOMEN'S TIME

The revised model of consumer behavior can help us understand some of the behavior of working women and the marketing policies of firms as they adjust to the changing role of females. With the outbreak of World War II women began to enter the labor force in increasing numbers, and since the mid-1970s their earnings have increased relative to those of men although today they still earn less than men. Both trends have placed increasing demands on their use of time and increased the demand for time-saving products. This section illustrates some of the changes that have occurred because of an increase in the cost of time.

The Increasing Number of Working Women

As women have entered the work force, increasing their cost of time, demand has increased for such time-saving innovations as microwave ovens, frozen foods, videocassette recorders (as a substitute for going to the movies), dishwashers, automatic washers and dryers, and blenders.

Manufacturers and retailers are well aware of these changes and have altered their marketing practices in response to the growth of the female labor force. One such change is the increase in the hours that stores stay open. The business hours of all types of stores have increased over time because the cost of shopping during the workday has increased. Figure 4-10 shows a dramatic increase in the percentage of supermarkets that are open on Sunday. When World War II ended in 1945, few stores opened on Sunday, which was considered a day of rest. Now Sunday openings are the norm. Much of this change is due to the growth of the female work force. Working women increase the demand for longer store hours per day and for openings on more days per week.

Differences in the Cost of Time for Females and Males

Historically, women's wages have been lower than men's wages. This means that the opportunity cost of time is lower for women than for men. Because of these differences, the shopping behavior of the average female is different from that of the average male. For example, women are willing to search more intensively before they decide what to purchase and to spend more time finding bargains. Men take less time to shop, are more likely to purchase at the first opportunity, and are less likely to look for sales or to time their purchases to take advantage of sales.

The different behavior toward shopping shows up in the data. Both males and females buy men's dress shirts, with women purchasing about 60 percent of these

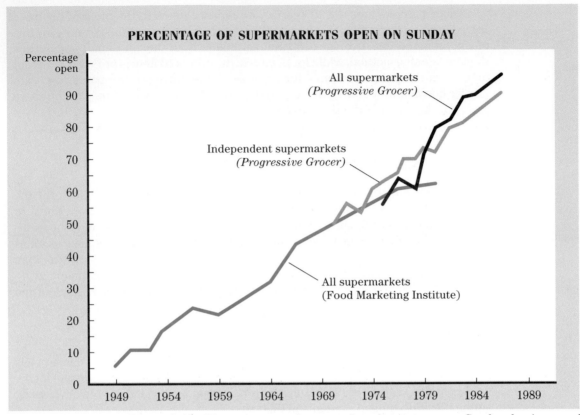

PERCENTAGE OF SUPERMARKETS OPEN ON SUNDAY

Figure 4-10   The percentage of supermarkets that stay open on Sundays has increased since World War II. [Food Marketing Institute and *Progressive Grocer*, various years.]

shirts in husband-and-wife households in 1986. Table 4-3 shows the percentage of shirts bought on sale and the percentage markdown of shirts bought on sale by sex of the buyer. For each category of dress shirt, women purchase a larger percentage on sale and receive a higher percentage markdown off the original price. The sex of the buyer is an important determinant of the probability that the buyer will purchase a dress shirt on sale.

The economics explanation for the observed shopping behavior can be contrasted with the stereotypical view that women are somehow "shoppers" and men are not. The model explains why women are better shoppers than men (for some goods) but not because of some genetic or even cultural reason but because of economic incentives. The economics explanation predicts that differences in shopping behavior will fade if women's earnings continue to rise relative to men's.

The Increase in Female Earnings Relative to Male Earnings

Over approximately the last 20 years women's earnings have risen relative to men's earnings. Table 4-4 shows trends from 1960 to 1988 in the ratio of female-to-male

Table 4-3   NONWHITE DRESS SHIRTS BOUGHT ON SALE AND MARKDOWN OF DRESS SHIRTS BOUGHT ON SALE, BY SEX OF BUYER (Two-Member Households)

TYPE OF SHIRT	Percentage Bought on Sale		Percentage Markdown	
	FEMALE BUYER	MALE BUYER	FEMALE BUYER	MALE BUYER
Domestically produced	63.7	60.9	25.3	24.8
Imported	72.5	66.0	30.1	26.7

Source: Based on data supplied by Market Research Corporation of America.

earnings of full-time workers by age of worker. The ratios declined from 1960 to 1970 and have increased in virtually all age groups since 1970. In 1960 the earnings of women between the years of 25 and 34 were 65 percent of men's earnings. In 1988 the ratio was 76 percent. The cost of time is lower for women than for men but is rising faster for women than for men.

The rise in the cost of women's time means that women will increasingly look for ways to reduce time-intensive activities. If this trend continues, the roles played by males and females in household activities will continue to change. We can expect greater use of the marketplace by women to purchase services that save time. The growth of day care and purchasing food away from home reflects the increasing cost of time of women. In addition we can expect the allocation of responsibilities for shopping, household duties, and so on among the members of a household to change as women's wages rise relative to men's.

The rise in the cost of time of females has far-reaching effects on the way goods are marketed. A person with a higher cost of time is less likely to spend

Table 4-4   FEMALE EARNINGS AS A PERCENTAGE OF MALE EARNINGS

AGE (YR)	1960	1970	1980	1988
20–24	80.6	74.0	77.7	88.5
25–34	65.1	64.9	68.6	76.1
35–44	57.6	53.9	56.2	64.8
45–54	58.0	56.3	54.3	61.7
55–64	64.5	60.3	56.7	58.0

Source: June O'Neil, "Women and Wages," *The American Enterprise,* November/December 1990, pp. 25–31.

time searching for goods with unknown brand names. To economize on time, consumers having a higher cost of time are more likely to rely on well-known brand names. The female shopper will favor brand name goods for herself and for other members of the family. As women's cost of time increases, the demand for brand name merchandise will continue to grow. This is reflected in the rapid increase in trademarks.

Another industry that has grown rapidly is the catalog industry. Much of the growth is related to the increasing cost of time of consumers. The development of new inventory systems and decreases in the cost of shipping have also reduced the cost of meeting the increased demand for goods ordered by telephone. The full price of ordering over the telephone has decreased relative to the full price of personal shopping. Consumers are more willing to place telephone orders when purchasing well-known brand name merchandise than when buying unknown names. So, the increase in the cost of time has not only increased the demand for brand names but has also helped the catalog industry to expand by merchandising branded goods.

This section has touched on only some of the changes in the merchandising of goods that have occurred because of the increasing cost of time of workers. Nevertheless, they appear to be important and permanent. The change in the economic position of females in the work force is a long-run change and is likely to continue into the future unless there is an unforeseen change in economic conditions. This means that the cost of time will continue to rise, and that we can expect to see continued significant changes in the marketing of goods as firms respond.

SUMMARY

- For some products the price paid by an individual represents only a fraction of the cost of the good because consuming a good takes time.
- A consumer must manage not only the budget constraint but also the total time constraint.
- The full price budget constraint shows the number of units of Y a consumer can purchase for a given quantity of X, given the consumer's time and budget constraints.
- Full income is the consumer's maximum income if all time is spent working.
- The full price of a good equals the market price plus the opportunity cost of time.
- An increase in nonwage income shifts the full price budget constraint outward but does not change its slope.

- An increase in the wage rate shifts the full budget constraint outward and lowers the full price of X relative to the full price of Y if the time intensity per dollar spent on X is less than the time intensity per dollar spent on Y.
- Consumers with higher wage rates will substitute more toward goods with lower time-price ratios than consumers with lower wage rates.
- All other things being equal, consumers with higher wage rates will pay higher prices to economize more on their time than will consumers with lower wage rates.

KEY TERMS

time constraint
full price budget constraint
ratio of full prices
minimizing full price
effects of a change in wage rate

full price
full income
opportunity cost of time
effects of a change in nonwage income

REVIEW QUESTIONS

1. What is the "full price" of a product?
2. Present an expression for the consumer's full price budget constraint and explain what "full income" means.
3. When the price of X increases by 10 percent and the price of Y increases by 15 percent, the full price budget constraint becomes flatter; that is, the slope of the full-price budget line increases in value. Explain why you agree or disagree with this statement.
4. When the price of X, the price of Y, and w each increase by 10 percent, the slope of the full price budget constraint does not change. Do you agree or disagree with this statement?
5. What factors cause the full price budget constraint to shift in a parallel fashion?

6. What factors cause the full price budget constraint to shift and change its slope?
7. How do the types of goods and services purchased change for a person who takes early retirement?
8. Describe how the goods that you purchase depend on whether your income is mostly nonwage income or wage income.
9. During a recession many workers are temporarily unemployed. They spend more time painting and fixing up their houses when unemployed than when employed. Can you use the modified theory of consumer behavior to explain this type of behavior?

EXERCISES

1. If the wage rate of an individual increases by 15 percent and a consumer purchases just goods X and Y, the consumer will substitute toward Y if it takes fewer minutes to consume Y than X. Explain why you agree or disagree with this statement.
2. If you hire someone to paint a one-story, 2,500-square-foot house with wood siding, 12 windows, and two doors, it will cost about $2,900 for two coats of paint. If you do it yourself, it will take about 92 hours including preparation time. The estimated cost of materials is about $550. How high must the wage rate be before a do-it-yourselfer hires a professional?

3. Suppose Y is hours of leisure. Let P_Y equal zero and t_Y equal 1. How does the full price of X change relative to the full price of Y if the wage rate increases? Will the consumer consume more or less leisure?
4. Suppose it takes a consumer a fixed amount of time C_X to travel to a store, as well as t_X to consume each unit of X. The total time needed to consume X units is $C_X + t_X X$. For Y, the time required to consume a unit of Y is t_Y. How does this change the full price budget constraint?
5. It takes 10 hours to read a novel. Assuming that hardback books are more durable and more appealing than paperbacks, can you

explain why a higher-wage reader prefers a hardback book and a lower-wage reader prefers a paperback?

6. The table below shows the price and time requirement for (1) doing your own laundry at home, (2) dropping off your laundry at a laundromat, and (3) do-it-yourself at a laundromat.

Type of Service	Price of a Load	Time
Laundry at home	$2.10	3/4 hour
Drop-off at laundromat	$8.00	1/6 hour
Do-it-yourself at the laundromat	$2.75	1.1 hours

   a. If the value of time is $17.00 per hour, what is the optimal choice?
   b. If the consumer's wage rate increases, which type of service will have the smallest percentage increase in the full price? Explain why.

7. Can you explain why some restaurants guarantee to deliver lunches within a specified amount of time or why more companies are guaranteeing that they can change your oil in a certain number of minutes?

8. Some communities have many convenience stores located nearby, while others do not. Suppose you are asked to study the characteristics of communities with and without convenience stores. Use your understanding of the theory of consumer behavior to answer the following questions.
   a. In what way would you expect consumers in communities with convenience stores to differ from consumers in communities without convenience stores?
   b. How would the average price paid for convenience products differ in the two types of communities?

9. Specialist firms have emerged that will take your grocery order, do your shopping, and deliver the groceries. In what kinds of markets would you expect these specialist firms to prosper?

10. If the cost of time is increasing, would you expect the quality of retail services to improve? Do you think it has? If so, give examples. If not, why not? Can you speculate why discount stores have become so popular?

PART III

THE FIRM: ITS TECHNOLOGY AND COSTS

- **Chapter 5**
  The Production Function
  and Costs of the Firm
- **Chapter 6**
  The Cost Functions of the Firm

CHAPTER 5

THE PRODUCTION FUNCTION AND COSTS OF THE FIRM

■ **5-1   The Production Function**

■ **5-2   Changing Factors of Production in the Short and Long Runs**

■ **5-3   The Short-Run Production Function**

The Total, Average, and Marginal Product of Labor

Application 5-1: Distinguishing between Marginal and Average Productivity

■ **5-4   The Long-Run Production Function**

Substitution among Factors

The Marginal Rate of Technical Substitution

Returns to Scale

Returns to Scale and the Cobb-Douglas Production Function

Application 5-2: Substitution and Returns to Scale for a Pipeline Production Function

The Marginal Rate of Technical Substitution and the Marginal Product of Both Factors

■ **5-5   The Isocost Function**

■ **5-6   Minimizing the Total Cost of Producing a Given Quantity**

■ **5-7   The Long- and Short-Run Total Cost Functions**

The Long-Run Total Cost Function

Returns to Scale and the Shape of the Long Run Average Cost Function

Application 5-3: The Long-Run Average Cost Function of a Pipeline

The Short-Run Total Cost Function

■ **5-8   Shifts in the Long-Run Total Cost Function**

A Change in the Price of a Factor

Technological Change

Application 5-4: Substituting Aluminum for Steel in Autos

■ **5-9   The Production Function and Learning-by-Doing**

Application 5-5: Learning-by-Doing in the Semiconductor Industry

Application 5-6: Learning-by-Doing at the Indianapolis 500

■ **Summary**

■ **Key Terms**

■ **Review Questions**

■ **Exercises**

In Chapters 2 through 4 we showed how the individual and market demand functions are derived from utility maximization by the consumer. Now we turn to the supply side of the market and examine how firm and industry supply curves are derived from cost minimization decisions of firms. Not only does a firm decide how many units to produce but it must decide how to produce those units efficiently. As used here, efficiency means that a firm organizes production so that it minimizes the cost of producing any rate of output. Our analysis will show what principle the firm follows in combining workers, machines, and raw materials to produce a given rate of output at the lowest cost. How does the cost of labor, machines, and raw materials affect which combination of factors to use? If a U.S. firm expands abroad, should it use the same production methods as it does in the United States or different ones? When Mercedes Benz decided to produce a new sports utility car in the United States rather than in Germany, did it use the same mix of capital, labor, and raw materials as it uses in Germany or a different mix? Another key issue is how rapidly costs increase when firm size increases. Are large or small firms more efficient? How does the behavior of costs place limits on firm size? These are some of the questions that we deal with in this chapter and that firms around the world answer daily.

5-1   THE PRODUCTION FUNCTION

A firm uses **factors of production** such as labor, capital, and raw materials to produce output. The relationship between inputs and outputs, called the **production function,** describes how a firm organizes the factors of production to produce goods or services.

The quantity that a firm can produce with its factors of production depends on the state of technology. The **state of technology** encompasses existing knowledge about methods of production. For example, it includes knowledge of the heat-resistant properties of metals, chemical reactions among carbon atoms, methods of networking personal computers, sequencing tasks, and store layouts. Therefore, when economists express the production function of a firm, they are assuming a given state of technology for each firm in an industry. When new advances change the state of technology, the production function changes as well.

> A production function describes the *maximum* quantity of output that can be produced with each combination of factors of production given the state of technology.

The production function can be represented as

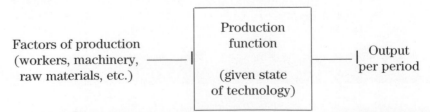

For a given state of technology, the production function describes the physical relationship between the quantities of different inputs and the resulting quantity of output. The management of the firm organizes and combines the factors within the box to produce units of output per period. For example, the production function for wheat describes the number of bushels of wheat a farmer grows per period as the number of acres of land, days of labor, gallons of water, tons of fertilizer, and pounds of seed are varied.

This schematic diagram of the production process sidesteps some important questions, however. It assumes that the tasks performed within the firm are given, although in reality firms decide what tasks to perform. For example, an automobile manufacturer can produce cars by building the bodies, transmissions, suspension systems, and air bags at its own plants, or it can purchase them from other firms and be just a final assembler. For many years the General Motors Corporation manufactured its own automobile bodies, whereas the Chrysler Corporation purchased bodies from an outside supplier. Firms within an industry undertake different decisions regarding whether to purchase or to manufacture components. Yet, the decisions do not appear to be random. It cannot be an accident that all auto manufacturers purchase air bags. Sometimes, firms produce a fraction of total part or service requirements and buy the remainder in the marketplace. McDonald's owns and operates some of its retail outlets and franchises others. Just why some firms vertically integrate either backward into component production or forward into retailing operations raises an important, but difficult, question that economists are beginning to address.

Nobel Prize winner Ronald Coase studied the options that firms have in producing a good.[1] He contrasted the decisions of some firms to produce components themselves with other firms' decisions to use the marketplace and purchase ready-made components. Each alternative has different costs, which Coase identified. Each firm must compare these costs when it decides whether to manufacture everything itself or to rely on suppliers for some or all of the components. For example, the costs of purchasing components in the marketplace include finding reliable and flexible suppliers, determining the market price for each quality of product, and negotiating contracts. Acquiring reliable and accurate information about supplier reputation and market prices is costly. On the other hand, the costs of manufacturing all parts internally include monitoring the efforts of workers and managers and rewarding desirable performance. It is costly to measure worker and manager performance and to control shirking by employees. Using the marketplace is not free, but neither is circumventing the marketplace. More advanced courses discuss how companies make these decisions.[2] Here the tasks performed by a firm are considered to be given.

Our introduction to the production function is similar to the two-good model used to illustrate how the consumer selects a particular market basket (see Chapter 2). In this analysis a similar convention is followed. The quantity produced per

---

[1] R. H. Coase, "The Nature of the Firm," *Economic Journal* IV (1937), pp. 386–405.
[2] For a discussion of these make-or-buy questions, see Paul Milgrom and John Roberts, *Economics, Organization and Management* (Englewood Cliffs, N.J.: Prentice-Hall, 1992), especially chaps. 1, 2, and 16.

Table 5-1   UNITS OF OUTPUT FROM DIFFERENT COMBINATIONS OF FACTORS OF PRODUCTION

NUMBER OF MACHINES, K	Number of Workers, L					
	10	20	30	40	50	60
1	220	390	470	540	600	620
2	320	470	560	605	635	660
3	400	530	600	635	665	685
4	460	550	630	670	690	700
5	490	600	655	685	705	710
6	510	630	665	690	710	712

period is q, and the two factors of production are labor and capital. L can represent the number of workers or aggregate hours of work of a given quality, and K can be the number of machines or machine hours, the area of a plant, or the number of plants. Throughout most of the chapter L is the number of workers and K is the number of machines; however, it should be understood that this is for illustrative purposes only.

We can write the production function symbolically as

$$q = f(L, K) \qquad \text{(Production Function of the Firm)} \qquad \textbf{(5-1)}$$

The function f describes how the inputs L and K are combined to produce units of output per period. For each combination of workers and machines, there is a corresponding quantity of output per period.

Table 5-1 shows the hypothetical quantity produced with different combinations of the two factors of production. Each entry represents the quantity produced when the firm uses a particular combination of workers and machines. For example, three machines and 30 workers produce 600 units per period.

5-2   CHANGING FACTORS OF PRODUCTION IN THE SHORT AND LONG RUNS

Table 5-1 shows what quantity the firm produces when it can vary both L and K. However, sometimes one factor is *fixed*, and so the firm can change output only by changing the other *variable* factor.

When air fares were lowered during the summer of 1992 and the quantity demanded for flights increased, airlines were overwhelmed by the increase in calls from potential travelers seeking low-priced tickets. They could not instantly increase the number of telephone lines or their computer processing capabilities, and so people who called were forced to wait impatiently for an operator. The airlines had only so many telephone lines and operators in the short run, and they had to make do with the existing equipment although they could have put more operators on overtime to meet the overload partially. If the higher quantity demanded had persisted, they would have increased the number of lines and their computer processing capabilities over a longer period of time. Firms cannot change one or several factors of production in the short run but can do so with the passage of time.

A distinction is made between the short and long runs in this chapter and throughout this book. In the **short run,** a company can change some factors of production but has at least one fixed factor. In the **long run,** it can change all factors of production. In our model with just two factors of production—labor and capital—we assume that the firm can adjust only labor in the short run.

5-3   THE SHORT-RUN PRODUCTION FUNCTION

In the short run the firm cannot change the number of machines quickly without incurring an unacceptably high cost, and so it treats the number of machines as fixed. With one fixed factor the short-run production function of the company shows how total output changes as the variable factor—the number of workers—changes. Suppose the firm must work with four machines until it orders and receives more. In the meantime it can increase output only by increasing the number of workers. The accompanying table reproduces the portion of Table 5-1 where the firm has four machines and shows output and output per worker at different employment levels. Total output of the firm increases by 80 units from 550 to 630 units if the company increases employment from 20 to 30 workers. However, the firm can increase total output by only an additional 40 units, to 670 units, as the number of workers increases from 30 to 40. In addition the table shows that output per worker decreases from 46 units to 27.5 units when the number of workers increases from 10 to 20. Each addition of 10 workers produces smaller and smaller increases in output, and so output per worker falls as more workers are employed.

Number of workers	10	20	30	40	50	60
Output	460	550	630	670	690	700
Output per worker	46	27.5	21	16.75	13.8	11.7

Let's examine in a more general way this property of diminishing increases in output as one factor increases while the other factor remains fixed. To do this we return to the general specification of the production function given in equation 5-1 and define different production relationships to be used later when the firm employs each factor in the short and long runs.

The Total, Average, and Marginal Product of Labor

To express the relationship between the variable factor and the total output in a more general way, economists use a function called the total product function. In our model, the **total product function** of labor, TP_L, merely shows the output

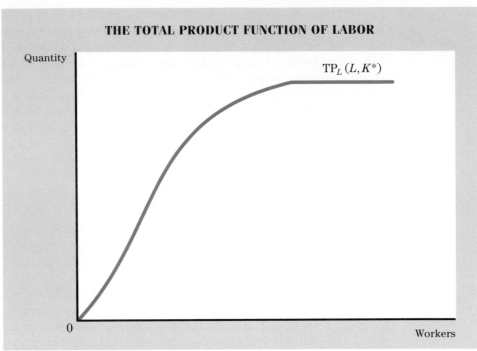

Figure 5-1   The total product function of labor shows the relationship between the quantity produced and the quantity of the variable factor with the other factor held constant. With the number of machines fixed at K^*, output increases as the number of workers increases, but after some point at a decreasing rate.

that is produced with L workers *given* a fixed number of machines. It is a function that relates total quantity produced to the number of workers when K is fixed at K^*.

$$\mathrm{TP}_L(L,K^*) = f(L,K^*) \qquad \text{(Total Product of Labor)} \qquad \textbf{(5-2)}$$

The **total product of labor** shows that the output produced changes as the number of workers changes with capital held constant at K^*. Equation 5-2 is a simplified production function because capital (machines) is fixed at K^*. The output produced by the workers is called the total product of labor because we are observing how output changes when the firm varies its employment of workers. An analogous total product function of machines can be defined if the number of workers is fixed and the number of machines is variable.

Figure 5-1 shows how the total product (output) increases when the number of workers increases with the number of machines fixed at K^*. Quantity increases at an increasing rate at first, and then at a diminishing rate when more workers are employed.[3] After some point, adding workers to the existing number of ma-

---

[3] In other words, $\partial^2 \mathrm{TP}_L(L, K^*)/\partial L^2 > 0$ at first, and later, becomes negative.

chines no longer increases output. The total product function illustrated in Figure 5-1 is only suggestive, however. For example, it is possible for the total product to decrease when the number of workers becomes large: worker productivity falls because workers get in the way of one another.

We can derive the average and marginal product functions of labor from the total product function. The **average product function** of labor, AP_L, measures output per worker, and is defined as

$$\text{Average product of labor} = \frac{\text{Total product of labor}}{\text{Number of workers}}$$

$$AP_L(L,K^*) = \frac{TP_L(L,K^*)}{L} \qquad \text{(Average Product of Labor)} \qquad \text{(5-3)}$$

The average product of labor is the measure of productivity often reported in newspaper articles that compare the productivity of U.S. and foreign workers.

The **marginal product function** of labor, MP_L, measures the change in quantity due to a change in the labor input, or the slope of the total product function of labor. For discrete changes in the number of workers, the marginal product of labor is defined as

$$\text{Marginal product of labor} = \frac{\Delta \text{ in total product of labor}}{\Delta \text{ in number of workers}}$$

$$MP_L(L,K^*) = \frac{\Delta TP_L(L,K^*)}{\Delta L} \qquad \text{(Marginal Product of Labor)} \qquad \text{(5-4)}$$

If we consider the number of workers fixed at L^* and allow the number of machines to be variable, we can define the marginal product of capital in an analogous way.[4]

$$MP_K(L^*,K) = \frac{\Delta TP_K(L^*,K)}{\Delta K} \qquad \text{(Marginal Product of Capital)}$$

Returning to the case where the fixed factor is capital, we reproduce the total product function in Figure 5-2*a* and derive the average and marginal product functions of labor in Figure 5-2*b*. The shape of the total product function of labor determines the shape of the average and marginal product functions. AP_L measures output per worker and is the slope of a ray drawn from the origin to any point on the TP_L function. When the firm employs L_1 workers, it produces q_1 units. $AP_L = q_1/L_1$ or the ratio $ab/0L_1$. The slope of the dashed line from the origin to point b is equal to $ab/0L_1$ or the average product of labor. The average product of labor for any given level of employment is equal to the slope of a straight line drawn from the origin to the total product function at that employment level. Remember that the steeper the straight line, the greater the slope.

---

[4] For infinitesimal changes in labor or capital, the marginal product of labor or capital is

$$MP_L(L,K^*) = \frac{\partial F}{\partial L} \quad \text{or} \quad MP_K(L^*,K) = \frac{\partial F}{\partial K}$$

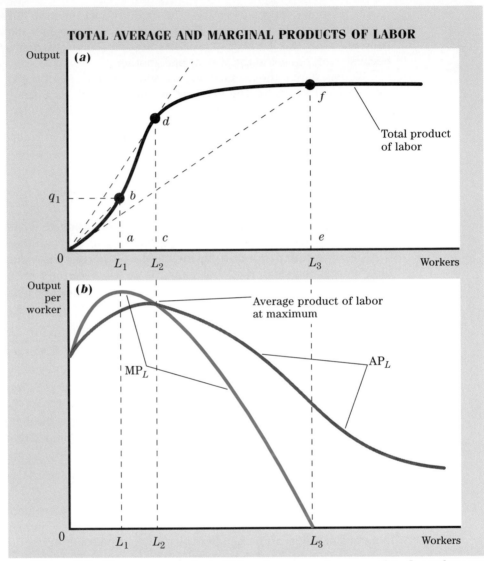

Figure 5-2   The average product of labor decreases when more than L_2 workers are added to a fixed amount of capital. As more workers are employed with a given number of machines, output per worker eventually decreases. The law of diminishing returns means that MP_L eventually falls as more workers are employed with the number of machines fixed. When the marginal product exceeds, equals, or is less than the average product, the average product increases, remains the same, or decreases, respectively.

As the number of workers increases, AP_L increases at first. For example, compare AP_L when the firm employs L_1 versus L_2 workers. The slope of the straight line from the origin to point b is less (i.e., flatter) than the slope of the straight line from the origin to point d. When the firm increases employment from L_1 to L_2

workers, AP_L increases because the slope increases to $cd/0L_2$ from $ab/0L_1$. So output per worker increases initially. What may be happening here is that workers can perform more *specialized* tasks as more are employed, and this raises the average product of labor. For example, instead of having a machine operator obtain raw materials as well as operate a machine, one worker can continuously be a machine operator while another supplies the material.

Further increases in employment reduce AP_L, for example, as employment increases from L_2 to L_3. With L_3 workers total output is equal to the distance ef, and the number of workers is equal to the distance $0L_3$. The slope of ray $0f$ is $ef/0L_3$ and is smaller than the slope of ray $0d$. Therefore, AP_L declines when employment increases to L_3 workers. As the firm adds more workers to the production line, this eventually may cause more machine stoppages for maintenance and a higher defect rate, both of which contribute to the declining AP_L.

Figure 5-2*b* shows that AP_L reaches a maximum when the firm hires L_2 workers, and then declines as the firm hires more workers. The slope of the ray $0d$ is larger than the slope of any other ray from the origin to any other point on the total product function. Therefore, AP_L reaches a maximum when the firm hires L_2 workers and is smaller when it employs fewer or more than L_2 workers.

There is a fundamental relationship between MP_L and AP_L. When MP_L is greater than, equal to, or less than AP_L, AP_L is increasing, constant, or decreasing, respectively.[5] A simple example may clarify this relationship between the marginal product and the average product. Let's say that you have a B or 3.0 average after completing 24 undergraduate courses. Put differently, you average 3 points per course and this is your average product. By the end of your junior year you are thinking seriously of attending graduate school. To improve your chances of acceptance, you apply yourself seriously during the first semester of your senior year and receive all A's. For the four courses you take during the semester, your marginal product for each course is 4.0 points. Because your marginal product (4.0) for each course in your senior year is greater than your average product (3.0), your average product increases above 3.0. This example just illustrates the principle that the average product increases whenever the marginal product is greater than the average product.

Figure 5-2 illustrates the same principle. In Figure 5-2*b* the marginal product of an extra worker is greater than the average product when L_1 workers are employed, and so the average product function increases (the slope of AP_L is

---

[5] The total product equals the product of the average product times the number of workers:

$$TP_L = AP_L(L)L$$

The marginal product is the slope of the total product function. Differentiating this equation with respect to L yields

$$\frac{d(TP_L)}{dL} = MP_L = AP_L + L\frac{d(AP_L)}{dL}$$

This equation says that $MP_L = AP_L$ plus a correction factor that depends on the slope of the AP_L function. When $d(AP_L)/dL = 0$, $AP_L = MP_L$ and AP_L is at a maximum. When $d(AP_L)/dL > 0$, MP_L is greater than AP_L and AP_L is increasing. When $d(AP_L)/dL < 0$, MP_L is less than AP_L and AP_L is decreasing.

positive). When the number of workers is L_2, $MP_L = AP_L$ and AP_L reaches a maximum. With L_3 workers MP_L is less than AP_L, and so output per worker is decreasing and the slope of the AP_L function is negative.

The **law of diminishing returns** describes the eventual decline in the marginal product of labor as more workers are employed with a given number of machines.

> The law of diminishing returns describes the eventual decline in the *marginal* product of the variable factor as the variable factor increases with other factors held constant.

The law of diminishing returns applies *only* to situations where one factor is increasing and the other factors are fixed. For example, applying more fertilizer to a farm of a given size will after some point reduce the marginal product of pounds of fertilizer.

APPLICATION **5-1**

Distinguishing between Marginal and Average Productivity

Michael Jordan is the exciting, famous professional basketball player for the Chicago Bulls. But even though they had the highest-scoring player in the National Basketball Association, the Bulls failed to win the league championship until the 1990–91 season when they finally were successful. Critics complained that Jordan shot too frequently and so opposing teams planned special defenses to guard him and ignored his teammates.

Let's compare his shooting performance with that of his teammates and see if we can conclude whether Michael Jordan shot too frequently or not enough. As a measure of shooting efficiency, we use points per shot. Table 5-2 shows the points per shot for Jordan and for the other Bulls from the 1987–88 season to the 1990–91 season.

Table 5-2   AVERAGE POINTS PER SHOT BY MICHAEL JORDAN AND TEAMMATES

SEASON	POINTS PER SHOT BY JORDAN (1)	POINTS PER SHOT BY OTHER BULLS (2)	JORDAN'S SHARE OF TOTAL SHOTS (3)
1987–88	1.060	1.008	0.299
1988–89	1.088	1.045	0.273
1989–90	1.100	1.065	0.284
1990–91	1.103	1.073	0.266

Source: Raw data obtained from the *Chicago Tribune.*

Columns 1 and 2 of Table 5-2 show that Michael Jordan's points per shot exceeded the points per shot of the other members of the team although the difference narrows over time. A shot by Jordan consistently produces more points, on average, than a shot by one of his teammates. The third column shows that Michael Jordan's share of total shots was lowest during the 1990–91 championship season. If the Chicago Bulls are using Jordan's talents optimally, shouldn't his share of total shots be increasing and not decreasing given that he scores more points per shot than his teammates?

To answer this question, we must distinguish between the AP and the MP of a player. The figures in columns 1 and 2 measure the *average* point productivity or AP of Jordan and his teammates and show that Jordan's AP is larger than that of the other Bulls. Given the AP figures, it is quite natural to believe that the Bulls would score more points per game if Jordan put up even more shots.

However, making decisions based on the AP rather than the MP of a player can lead to suboptimal results. What would happen to total points scored if the total shots were redistributed so that Jordan made one more shot per game and his teammates made one less shot?[6] To answer this question, you must know the *marginal* points or MPs of Jordan and his teammates. How many additional points would Jordan score if he took one more shot per game throughout the season and his teammates took one less shot? We can call this the marginal points per shot. We cannot assume that the marginal points per shot equal the average points per shot. Each player's marginal points per shot are likely to be less than his average points per shot, indicating that average points per shot is declining as more shots are taken. As Jordan's share of shots increases, the opposing team assigns more players to guard him, changes its defense, and forces him to take still more difficult shots. By using these tactics, opposing teams can reduce his effectiveness, and his marginal points per shot will be lower than his average points per shot.

To determine whether Michael Jordan should shoot more frequently, you have to compare the *marginal* points per shot for Jordan with those for his teammates. If Jordan's marginal points exceed those of his teammates, then total team points will increase if he shoots more frequently. If his marginal points equal those of his teammates, then the Bull's coach is using his talents optimally although the APs differ. The team maximizes total team points when the marginal points per shot are equal across players. Although the average points differ, the marginal points can still be equal across players.

In summary, the higher *average* point productivity of Michael Jordan does not imply that he should shoot more or less frequently.

Our investigation of the short-run properties of the production function is complete, and so we now turn to the long run when the firm can vary all factors of production.

[6] It is assumed that a redistribution of shots does not affect defensive performance.

5-4   THE LONG-RUN PRODUCTION FUNCTION

The production function described in Table 5-1 shows the quantity produced for different combinations of factors when both factors are variable. In the remainder of this section, we develop general expressions for the substitution of factors of production among each other and the returns to scale when all factors are variable. We use these general relationships later in the chapter to learn more about the firm's production and output decisions.

Substitution among Factors

Like a consumer who receives the same utility by substituting between goods, the firm usually can produce the same quantity by substituting between factors of production. What combination of factors should it use to produce q_1 units? You might think the answer can be found by asking production experts—those on the engineering staff with specialized expertise and on-the-job experience. However, they cannot answer this question because there simply is no single way to produce the product.

Figure 5-3 shows why. The number of machines is on the vertical axis, and the number of workers is on the horizontal axis. The curve with an output of q_1 is called an isoquant (*iso* means "equal," and *quant* signifies "quantity").[7] Output is constant along the isoquant, and the points along the isoquant $q = q_1$ represent the different combination of factors that can produce q_1 units per period. For example, the firm builds a capital-intensive plant, with many robots and few workers, to produce q_1 units. In Figure 5-3 the combination of K_1 machines and L_1 workers will produce q_1 units per period. However, this is just one way to produce q_1 units. The isoquant shows a menu of technical options: The company can use a more labor-intensive method of production to produce q_1 by substituting labor for machinery: it can reduce capital input by $\Delta K = K_2 - K_1$ and increase labor input by $\Delta L = L_2 - L_1$.

> An **isoquant** shows the different combinations of factors of production that can produce a given quantity of output.

The fundamental point is that there seldom is only one way to do something. The state of technology often offers alternative methods of production. To illustrate this point, consider the following examples.

1. A perceptive visitor from a developed country traveling in a less developed country is immediately struck by the different methods firms use abroad to produce goods and services. Labor substitutes for capital to supply domestic help, provide service in restaurants, and construct and maintain roads more than in developed countries. Workers substitute for bulldozers, and in factories labor is used instead of forklifts and conveyer belts to move material

---

[7] Table 5-1 shows three points on the isoquant $q = 600$ units. The firm can produce 600 units with 1 machine and 50 workers, 3 machines and 30 workers, or 5 machines and 20 workers.

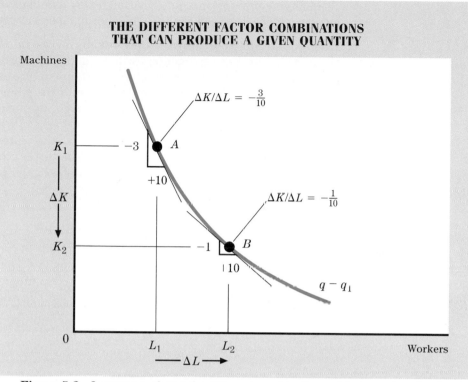

**THE DIFFERENT FACTOR COMBINATIONS
THAT CAN PRODUCE A GIVEN QUANTITY**

Figure 5-3   Isoquant q_1 shows the different combinations of factors of production for producing q_1 units. At point A the firm produces q_1 units per period with a more capital-intensive method of production. It uses K_1 machines and L_1 workers. At point B the firm produces q_1 units per period with a more labor-intensive method. It hires L_2 workers and uses only K_2 machines.

and inventories from one location to another. Companies in both types of economies usually are aware of the production options even though they adopt far different methods. Firms in less developed countries use more labor-intensive production methods, whereas those in developed countries use more equipment- or capital-intensive methods because labor is scarce and has a higher relative resource cost compared to capital goods.

2. Steel plants produce steel and undesirable by-products such as dust. Firms control dust particle emissions from smokestacks by installing filters. The larger the filter, the smaller the volume of dust emissions. Reducing emissions requires more sophisticated filters and a greater capital investment in filters. However, firms can control dust emissions by changing and maintaining filters more frequently. This is a more labor-intensive method of reducing air emissions. A company can attain a given volume of emissions by using either more capital-intensive methods (larger and more sophisti-

cated filters) or more labor-intensive methods (maintaining filters). The firm faces a tradeoff between capital- and labor-intensive methods.[8]

3. When you step into the shower in the morning, the last thing you are thinking about is the production function for hot water. Yet a production function produces water of a given temperature. The temperature of the water at the showerhead depends on (*a*) the temperature of the water as it leaves the water heater and (*b*) the heat loss as it travels through the pipe to the showerhead. The water temperature at the showerhead will be the same by substituting between the water temperature at the water heater and the amount of insulation surrounding the pipe. The thicker the insulation, the lower the required initial temperature at the water heater to achieve a given temperature at the showerhead.

The Marginal Rate of Technical Substitution

We can develop a measure that shows the technical options of producing the same output with different combinations of factors of production. The marginal rate of technical substitution (MRTS) measures the rate of substitution of one factor for another along an isoquant.

> The **marginal rate of technical substitution** is the rate at which a firm can substitute capital and labor for one another such that the output is constant.

For a discrete change in each factor of production, the definition of the marginal rate of technical substitution is

$$\text{MRTS}_{KL} = \left. \frac{\Delta K}{\Delta L} \right|_{q=c} \qquad \text{(Marginal Rate of Technical Substitution)} \qquad \textbf{(5-5)}$$

where $\Delta K / \Delta L$ is the slope between two points on a given isoquant.[9] The expression $|_{q=c}$ means output is constant at some level c.

An isoquant *cannot* have a positive slope because an increase in one factor that causes output to increase must be offset by a decrease in the other to keep output the same. In the usual case the MRTS_{KL}, the slope of the isoquant, is not constant but changes as the firm shifts from capital-intensive to labor-intensive methods of production. It uses more capital-intensive methods at point A than at point B on the isoquant in Figure 5-3 where it has more machines relative to workers. For a given increase of ΔL starting at point A, the firm is willing to reduce the number of machines by a larger quantity than it would starting at point B while keeping output constant. At point A the firm reduces the number of machines by 3 if it employs 10 more workers and still keeps output constant. For discrete changes in the number of workers and machines, the slope of the isoquant is

---

[8] For a more extended discussion of this situation and the general problem of controlling pollution, see Paul Downing, *Environmental Economics and Policy* (Boston: Little, Brown, 1984), chap. 4.
[9] For infinitesimal changes in each factor, the marginal rate of technical substitution is *dK/dL*, the slope of the isoquant at each point on the isoquant.

$\Delta K/\Delta L = -\frac{3}{10}$. At point B the firm has far fewer machines relative to workers. If it increases the number of workers by 10, it can reduce the number of machines by only 1 if the firm is to continue to produce q_1 units. At point B, $\Delta K/\Delta L$ equals $-\frac{1}{10}$.

As the firm moves down along the isoquant from the upper left to the lower right, the slope increases from $-\frac{3}{10}$ to $-\frac{1}{10}$. The firm substitutes labor for capital, but at a diminishing rate, as the firm moves along the isoquant. When this occurs, there is a **diminishing marginal rate of technical substitution.**[10] Throughout this chapter it is assumed that the production function exhibits a diminishing marginal rate of substitution.

Returns to Scale

In most industries the productivity of a firm changes as the quantity produced by the firm changes. **Returns to scale** relates the percentage change in output to a percentage change in inputs.[11] We distinguish among three cases.

1. When both inputs increase by m percent and output increases by more than m percent, there are *increasing* returns to scale.

2. When both inputs increase by m percent and output increases by m percent, there are *constant* returns to scale.

3. When both inputs increase by m percent and output increases by less than m percent, there are *decreasing* returns to scale.[12]

The ratio of capital to labor is constant along a ray from the origin like ray RR in Figure 5-4. We measure returns to scale for a given ratio of capital to labor.

How is the spacing of isoquants related to returns to scale? The six isoquants

---

[10] Given the production function $q = f(L,K)$, a diminishing marginal rate of technical substitution requires that

$$\frac{d(dK/dL)}{dL} > 0$$

The slope of the isoquant increases as the number of workers increases. Note, however, that the *absolute value* of the slope *declines*; hence the term *diminishing* rate of substitution.

[11] In Table 5-1 output more than doubles from 220 to 470 units when the firm doubles the number of workers from 10 to 20 and the number of machines from 1 to 2. There are increasing returns to scale. Output increases from 470 to 670 units, less than twofold, when the number of workers doubles from 20 to 40 and the number of machines doubles from 2 to 4. In this range there are decreasing returns to scale.

[12] There are constant returns to scale when

$$mf(L,K) = f(mL,mK)$$

An m percent increase in each factor increases total output by m percent. Geometrically, this condition says output increases by m percentage points, or $mf(L,K)$, when each factor increases by m percentage points. For example, if $m = 2$, the quantity of each factor doubles. If there are constant returns to scale, then $f(2L,2K) = 2f(L,K)$. A doubling of each input doubles total output. There are increasing returns to scale when $mf(L,K) < f(mL,mK)$ and decreasing returns to scale when $mf(L,K) > f(mL,mK)$. If there are increasing returns to scale, an m percent increase in each input increases output by more than m percent. If there are decreasing returns to scale, an m percent increase in each input increases output by less than m percent.

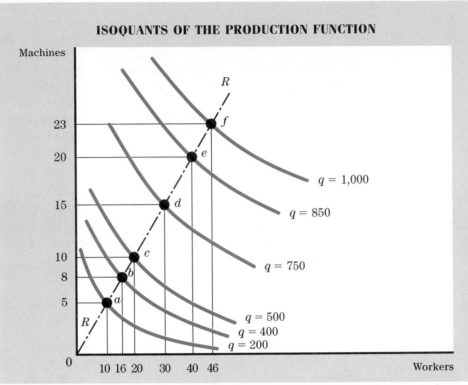

ISOQUANTS OF THE PRODUCTION FUNCTION

Figure 5-4 Between points *a* and *c* there are increasing returns to scale because inputs are doubled while output is more than doubled by increasing from 200 units to 500 units. To double output, the firm needs to have only 16 workers and 8 machines at point *b*. Between points *c* and *d* there are constant returns to scale since inputs increase by 50 percent and output increases by 50 percent from 500 units to 750 units. There are decreasing returns to scale between points *d* and *e*. Both inputs increase by 33.3 percent, but the increase in output is less than 33.3 percent from 750 units to 850 units. To increase output by 33.3 percent, the firm must employ 46 workers and 23 machines at point *f*.

in Figure 5-4 correspond to 200, 400, 500, 750, 850, and 1,000 units produced per year. The firm produces 200 units per year with 5 machines and 10 workers (point *a*). Output increases by 100 percent from 200 units to 400 units (point *b*) when both inputs increase by only 60 percent (workers increase from 10 to 16 and machines increase from 5 to 8). When there are increasing returns to scale, the isoquants are bunched closer together. If there were constant returns to scale, the isoquant with 400 units would have to be displaced to the northeast and go through point *c* so that output doubles when both inputs double relative to point *a*. However, with increasing returns to scale, a doubling of both inputs more than doubles output because output increases from 200 to 500 units.

Between points *c* and *d* there are constant returns to scale. When the firm combines 10 machines with 20 workers, it produces 500 units per year (point *c*). When it increases both inputs by 50 percent so that it uses 15 machines with 30 workers, output also increases by 50 percent to 750 units per year.

Between points *d* and *e* there are decreasing returns to scale. Both inputs increase by 33.3 percent, from 15 to 20 machines and from 30 to 40 workers, but firm output increases only from 750 to 850 units or by 13.3 percent. In this instance the percentage increase in both factors of production is greater than the percentage increase in output, and the space between isoquants is farther apart. If the isoquant with 1,000 units went through point *e* instead of point *f*, output and inputs would increase by 33.3 percent and there would be constant returns to scale. But the isoquant with 1,000 units goes through point *f*, where the percentage increase in inputs is greater than 33.3 percent.

When there are increasing returns to scale, a firm that produces more output requires fewer inputs relative to output than a firm producing less output. The larger firm is physically more productive than the smaller one. When there are constant returns to scale, the physical productivity of a larger firm is no greater than that of a smaller firm. Although the output of the larger firm is *m* times larger than that of the smaller one, so too are the input requirements of the larger firm. In this situation the smaller firm is just as productive as the larger firm. When there are decreasing returns to scale, a larger firm is physically less productive than a smaller firm. The larger firm must increase inputs by more than *m* percent just to produce *m* percent more output. The extent of returns to scale plays a key role in determining whether large or small firms are more productive and which can survive.

Returns to Scale and the Cobb-Douglas Production Function

A frequently used example of a production function is the **Cobb-Douglas production function.** The equation for this specific production function is

$$q = A\,L^a K^b \qquad \text{(Cobb-Douglas Production Function)} \qquad (5\text{-}6)$$

where A, a, and b are constants and are greater than zero. Output equals A times the product of labor raised to the power a and capital raised to the power b.

To determine the returns to scale for this production, let's change labor and capital by a factor m and then determine if output changes by more than, equal to, or less than m times.

$$q = A\,(mL)^a(mK)^b = A\,m^a L^a m^b K^b = m^{a+b}[AL^a K^b] \qquad (5\text{-}7)$$

Recognizing that the original output was $q = AL^a K^b$, this last equation says that output will increase by either less than m times if $a + b < 1$ (because $m^{a+b} < m$), by exactly m times if $a + b = 1$, or by more than m times if $a + b > 1$. Hence, we have found a very simple way of determining the returns to scale. First, calculate the sum of $a + b$. There are decreasing, constant, or increasing returns to scale depending on whether $a + b$ is less than, equal to, or greater than 1.

APPLICATION 5-2

Substitution and Returns to Scale for a Pipeline Production Function

In some industries engineering principles establish the link between inputs and output and help to identify the production function. As an example, consider the inputs and the output of an oil pipeline between two locations.

The output of an oil pipeline is the number of barrels of oil per day that flow through it. The inputs are the pipeline diameter and the amount of horsepower required to pump the oil through the pipeline. For a given pipeline diameter, more barrels of oil flow through the pipeline per day as the horsepower of the pump increases. For a given horsepower, more barrels of oil flow through the pipeline per day as the pipeline diameter increases. As expected, a given number of barrels of oil per day can flow through the pipeline with different combinations of diameter and horsepower. The firm can substitute a larger pipeline diameter for smaller horsepower, and when planning a pipeline, must be familiar with the marginal rate of technical substitution between the diameter of the pipeline and horsepower.

In a study of the production function of a pipeline, economist Leslie Cookenboo used a Cobb-Douglas production function[13]

$$T = AH^a D^b$$

where A, a, and b are constants, T is the number of barrels of oil per day, H is the horsepower, and D is the inside diameter of the pipeline. The numerical values of the constants depend on variables like the length of the pipeline, terrain variability from location A to location B, and the viscosity of the oil. Although technological advances will change the value of these constants over time, they do not alter the fundamental fact that the firm can substitute diameter for horsepower to produce a given flow through a pipeline.

Figure 5-5 shows the isoquants of the production function presented in Cookenboo's study. The firm can choose among several diameter-horsepower combinations to produce a given flow. In the figure selected isoquants of the production function correspond to different numbers of barrels of oil per day.[14] Each isoquant indicates how the marginal rate of technical substitution between pipeline diameter and horsepower changes as the firm substitutes between inputs. Like all isoquants, these isoquants have negative slopes and exhibit a diminishing marginal rate of

---

[13] Leslie Cookenboo, Jr., *Crude Oil Pipelines and Competition in the Oil Industry* (Cambridge, Mass.: Harvard University Press, 1955).

[14] The exact production function estimated by Cookenboo was $T = 5.4H^{0.37} D^{1.73}$. This production function exhibits increasing returns to scale:

$$T = 5.4(mH)^{0.37}(mD)^{1.73} = 5.4m^{0.37}H^{0.37}m^{1.73} D^{1.73}$$

$$= m^{2.1}(5.4H^{0.37}D^{1.73})$$

Because the exponent of m is greater than 1, an increase of m percent in each factor increases output by more than m percent. If $m = 2$, each input doubles. Output increases by $2^{2.1}$, or by slightly more than 3 times.

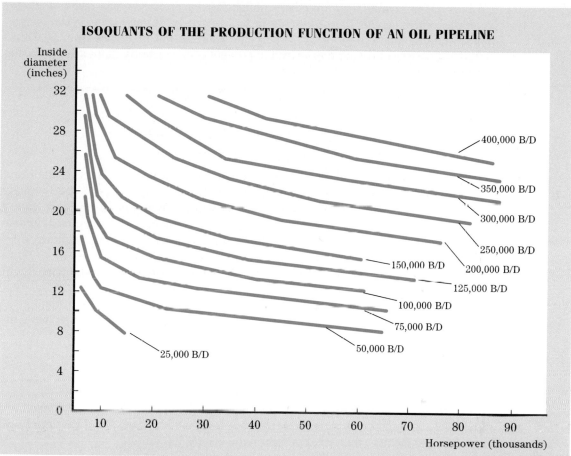

Figure 5-5   The isoquants of a pipeline production function show that the number of barrels of oil per day (B/D) that flow out of the pipeline depends on the inside diameter of the pipeline and the hydraulic horsepower. Pipelines with larger diameters require less horsepower to maintain a given flow of barrels of oil per day. [Leslie Cookenboo, Jr., *Crude Oil Pipelines and Competition in the Oil Industry*, Harvard University Press (Cambridge, Mass.: Harvard University Press, 1955), p. 15. Reprinted by permission of Harvard University Press, copyright 1955 by the President and Fellows of Harvard College.]

technical substitution. Only selected combinations of inputs are shown in Figure 5-5, and so it is not possible to hold the ratio of pipeline diameter to horsepower strictly constant. Still, Figure 5-5 indicates the presence of increasing returns to scale. When the diameter is approximately 13 inches and horsepower is approximately 7.5 (in thousands), 50,000 barrels of oil per day flow through the pipeline. The ratio of inches to horsepower (in thousands) is 1.73. When the diameter is 20 inches and horsepower is approximately 13, 125,000 barrels of oil per day flow through the pipeline. The ratio of inches to horsepower is 1.54. Although the two ratios are not equal, they are close enough for our purposes. The inside diameter increases from about 13 to 20 inches or by 54 percent. Horsepower (in thousands) increases from 7.5 to 13 or by 73 percent. Total output increases from 50,000 to 125,000 barrels of oil per day or by 150 percent. Consequently there are increasing returns to scale.

The Marginal Rate of Technical Substitution and the Marginal Product of Both Factors

The marginal rate of technical substitution and the marginal product of labor and capital may appear to be independent entities. However, it turns out that knowing any two allows us to determine the third. Starting at some point on an isoquant, we allow the firm to change both factors such that quantity is constant. Suppose it decides to substitute toward a more capital-intensive method of production by increasing the number of machines by ΔK and decreasing the number of workers by ΔL. What determines the size of the change in the numbers of machines and workers so that output is constant?

Let's begin by increasing the number of machines by ΔK with the number of workers fixed. Output will increase by Δq_K because the number of machines increases by ΔK. The increase in output is approximated by

$$\Delta q_K = \text{MP}_K \, \Delta K$$

Δq_K is approximately equal to the marginal product of an additional machine times the change in the number of machines. If the marginal product of a machine, holding the number of workers constant, is 120 units per year and the firm adds one more machine, then total output increases by 120 units.

Now let's hold the number of machines constant and decrease the number of workers by ΔL. For a given number of machines, output decreases by Δq_L when the number of workers decreases by ΔL. The decrease in output is approximated by

$$\Delta q_L = \text{MP}_L \, \Delta L$$

Δq_L is approximately equal to the marginal product of labor multiplied by ΔL. Let's say the marginal product of a worker, given the number of machines, is 60 units per year. Therefore, the loss of 2 workers decreases output by 120 units.

By moving along a given isoquant, output must be constant and the increase in output because of a ΔK increase in machines must exactly offset the decrease in output because of the ΔL decrease in workers. Therefore,

$$\Delta q_K + \Delta q_L = 0$$

After substituting the expressions for Δq_K and Δq_L, the condition becomes

$$\text{MP}_K \, \Delta K + \text{MP}_L \, \Delta L = 0$$

We solve for $\Delta K/\Delta L$,[15] which gives us an expression for the marginal rate of technical substitution in terms of the marginal products of the two factors.[16]

$$\text{MRTS}_{KL} \equiv \frac{\Delta K}{\Delta L} = -\frac{\text{MP}_L}{\text{MP}_K} \qquad \text{(Marginal Rate of Technical Substitution) (5-8)}$$

The marginal rate of technical substitution of K for L equals the negative of the ratio of the marginal product of L and K. If the marginal product of a machine is 120 units and the marginal product of a worker is 60 units, equation 5-8 says that the marginal rate of technical substitution of machines for workers is $-\frac{60}{120} = -\frac{1}{2}$. An increase in quantity because the firm adds one more machine is just offset by the decrease in quantity caused when the firm hires two fewer workers.

5-5   THE ISOCOST FUNCTION

The production function summarizes the technological options facing the firm. Assuming the firm knows its production function, can it determine what output to produce and what specific combination of factors to use? Unfortunately, the answer is no. There is an embarrassment of riches because there are too many technical options for producing any rate of output. The crucial variable is the **price of a factor.** To determine which particular combination of workers and machines should be used, the firm must know how expensive each factor of production is. Furthermore, we assume the firm's objective is to produce efficiently so that it minimizes the total cost of producing any given output.

To find the cost of a given output, the firm must know how much it costs to hire workers and machines. Assume that the annual earnings of each worker are w, and so the annual cost of one worker is w. What is the annual cost of the services of a machine? There are different ways of assessing this cost. If an organized rental market for machines exists, the annual cost of the machine is the rental value. There are rental markets for cars, workstations, large computers, office equipment, and so on; however, organized rental markets do not exist for many capital goods. For example, there is no organized market for specialized machinery that manufactures and dyes rugs. How should we value a machine when there is no organized rental market?

---

[15] Subtracting $\text{MP}_L \, \Delta L$ from both sides of the equation yields $\text{MP}_K \, \Delta K = -\text{MP}_L \, \Delta L$. Then, dividing both sides by ΔL and by MP_K produces the expression in the text.

[16] Recall the production function is $q = f(L,K)$ and that $\text{MP}_L = \partial f/\partial L$ and $\text{MP}_K = \partial f/\partial K$. Consider only those changes dL and dK such that output does not change, so $dq = 0$. Totally differentiating the production function and setting the result equal to zero, we have

$$0 = dq = \frac{\partial f}{\partial L} \, dL + \frac{\partial f}{\partial K} \, dK$$

Solve for dK/dL to obtain

$$\text{MRTS}_{KL} \equiv \frac{dK}{dL} = -\frac{\partial f/\partial L}{\partial f/\partial K} = -\frac{\text{MP}_L}{\text{MP}_K}$$

Assume that the price of a machine with an infinite life is M. Suppose the firm borrows funds and pays annual interest of i dollars per $100 of the amount borrowed. The cost of maintaining one machine in production for a year is the annual interest paid by the firm or i times M. Still another interpretation is possible. Suppose the firm has the funds to purchase the machine but chooses not to buy it and can earn a rate of return of i per $100 invested in the next best investment. If the firm purchases the machine, it forgoes an annual rate of return of i. The cost of maintaining one machine in production of the product for 1 year is iM. Let $r = iM$ be the opportunity cost of maintaining one machine in production. The opportunity cost is $18,000 if the rate of return is 5 percent and the price of a machine is $360,000.

The expression for the total annual cost C of producing the good is

$$\text{Total cost} = \text{Cost of labor} + \text{Cost of capital}$$

$$C = wL + rK \qquad \text{(Total Cost of Production)} \qquad \textbf{(5-9)}$$

The tradeoff between machines and workers can be seen more clearly by solving equation 5-9 for K:[17]

$$K = \frac{C}{r} - \frac{w}{r}L \qquad \text{(Isocost Line)} \qquad \textbf{(5-10)}$$

Equation 5-10 is called an **isocost line** because the total cost C is constant for all machine-worker combinations satisfying the equation. Hereafter, we will refer to total cost with the understanding that we mean total cost per period.

> An isocost line shows the different combinations of factors of production that can be employed with a given total cost.

Equation 5-10 is a straight line with K and L representing the two variables, while C, r and w are constants. For a given total cost C, the intercept of this straight line is C/r and is the number of machines the firm can purchase if it hires no workers. The slope of the straight line is $-w/r$ and, ignoring the sign, is equal to the factor price ratio, the annual cost of a worker divided by the annual cost of a machine. The slope is negative because, given total cost, the firm cannot hire more of one input without cutting back on the other.

To illustrate the isocost line, suppose the annual earnings of each worker are $36,000 and the annual cost of a machine is $18,000. How many machines can the firm purchase and how many workers can it employ if its total cost of production is $180,000? The y intercept of equation 5-10 is $180,000 divided by $18,000, or 10 machines. The x intercept is $180,000 divided by $36,000, or 5 workers. Since the cost of a worker is $36,000 and the annual cost of a machine is only $18,000, the slope of the isocost line is -2. For each additional worker hired, the firm purchases

---

[17] This equation is derived by subtracting wL from both sides of equation 5-9 to obtain $C - wL = rK$. Then, divide both sides of the equation by r and rearrange the equation to obtain equation 5-10.

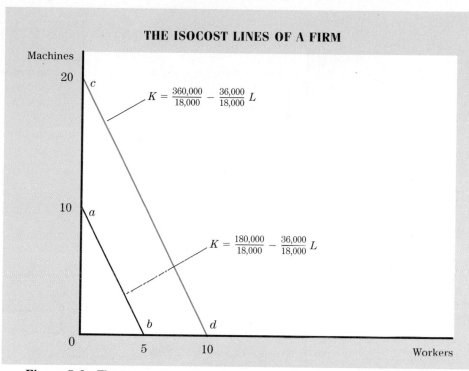

Figure 5-6   The isocost lines show how many units of each factor the firm can use while incurring the same total cost. If the total cost for the firm is $180,000, it can substitute machines for labor along the isocost line labeled *ab.* The firm could purchase 10 machines if it did not hire any workers, or it could employ 5 workers if it did not purchase any machines. If the total cost is $360,000, the firm can substitute machines for workers along the isocost line *cd.* It can now purchase 20 machines if it employs no workers and hire 10 workers if it purchases no machines.

two fewer machines so the total cost remains $180,000. The isocost line *ab* in Figure 5-6 has an intercept of 10 machines and a slope of −2.

Now that we know how to derive the isocost line, let's consider shifts in the isocost line. Equation 5-10 shows that a higher *C* increases the intercept but does not affect the slope of the isocost line. Therefore, the isocost line shifts outward in a parallel fashion and becomes the isocost line *cd* if total cost increases from $180,000 to $360,000. Any combination of factors on the new isocost line *cd* in Figure 5-6 will cost $360,000. Therefore, a change in total cost causes a parallel shift in the isocost line.

5-6   MINIMIZING THE TOTAL COST OF PRODUCING A GIVEN QUANTITY

Now we have all the ingredients to find which factor combination produces a given quantity at the lowest total cost. An isoquant of the production function and the

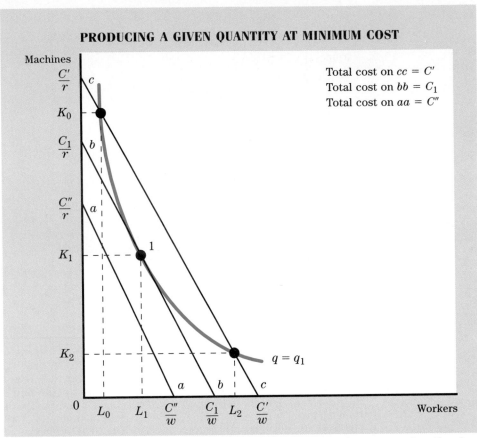

Figure 5-7   The minimum cost of producing a given quantity occurs when the slope of the isoquant equals the slope of the isocost line. At point 1 the slope of the isoquant for $q = q_1$ equals the slope of the isocost line bb. If the firm employs L_1 workers and purchases K_1 machines, it can produce q_1 units at the minimum total cost C_1. The firm could produce q_1 units by employing L_0 workers and using K_0 machines or by hiring L_2 workers and buying K_2 machines. However, the total cost would equal C', which is greater than C_1.

isocost lines aa, bb, and cc are displayed in Figure 5-7. Total cost increases by moving from aa to bb to cc. The firm can produce q_1 units at a total cost of C' on cc by using either L_0 workers and K_0 machines or L_2 workers and K_2 machines. Either of these combinations of factors will produce q_1 units with a total cost of C' but can q_1 be produced at a lower total cost?

The total cost of the different factor combinations along the isocost line bb equals C_1, which is less than C'. The firm can produce q_1 units if it employs K_1 machines and L_1 workers (point 1). This factor combination produces q_1 units at a minimum total cost of C_1. There is no other way of producing q_1 units at a lower total cost. The total cost on the isocost line aa is C'', which is less than C_1, but no machine-labor combination on aa can produce q_1 units. Therefore, the total cost of producing q_1 units cannot be less than C_1.

If the firm is producing q_1 units at minimum total cost, the slope of the isoquant equals the slope of the isocost line:[18]

$$\text{MRTS}_{KL} = -\frac{w}{r} \qquad \text{(Minimum Cost Condition)} \tag{5-11}$$

> A firm minimizes the total cost of producing a given quantity by selecting a combination of factors where the **slope of the isoquant equals the slope of the isocost line.**

There is another commonsense interpretation of the minimum cost condition. Earlier we showed that the marginal rate of technical substitution is equal to the negative of the ratio of the marginal products of the two factors. Let's replace the marginal rate of technical substitution in equation 5-11 by the negative of the marginal product of labor divided by the marginal product of capital:

$$-\frac{\text{MP}_L}{\text{MP}_K} = -\frac{w}{r}$$

If both sides of this equation are divided by $-w$ and both sides of the equation are then multiplied by MP_K, the equation becomes

$$\frac{\text{MP}_L}{w} = \frac{\text{MP}_K}{r} \qquad \text{(Minimum Cost Condition)} \tag{5-12}$$

Equation 5-12 says that the firm minimizes the total cost of producing a given quantity if the ratio of the marginal product of a factor to its price is the same for all factors.

---

[18] The firm minimizes total cost $C = wL + rK$ subject to the production function constraint $q = (L,K)$. The solution to this problem can be obtained by using the Lagrange multiplier method. For the reader who is already familiar with the Lagrange multiplier technique, we form the function $\pounds$

$$\pounds = wL + rK + \lambda[q - f(L,K)]$$

where λ is the Lagrange multiplier. $\pounds$ is a function of L, K and λ. To minimize $\pounds$, the firm selects L, K and λ to satisfy

$$w = \lambda\frac{\partial f}{\partial L}$$

$$r = \lambda\frac{\partial f}{\partial K}$$

$$q = f(L,K)$$

which are obtained by partially differentiating the Lagrangian function with respect to L, K, and λ and setting each of the resulting expressions equal to zero. Dividing the first equation by the second and then multiplying both sides by -1 yields

$$-\frac{w}{r} = -\frac{\partial f/\partial L}{\partial f/\partial K} = \text{MRTS}_{KL} \quad \text{or} \quad -\frac{w}{r} = -\frac{\text{MP}_L}{\text{MP}_K}$$

The slope of the isocost line equals the slope of the isoquant.

The ratio of the *marginal product of labor to the price of labor* represents the increase in output due to the last dollar spent on labor. To minimize total cost, the additional output due to the last dollar spent on labor must be equal to the additional output due to the last dollar spent on capital. If they are not equal, it pays the firm to reallocate its expenditure from one factor to another. The firm should spend more money on the factor with the higher marginal product per additional dollar spent on it because that factor gives the firm a greater boost in output for the extra dollar spent. Total output will increase while total cost does not change. If the last dollar spent on labor increases output by 3 units and the last dollar spent on capital increases output by just 1 unit, then the firm produces more output for the same total cost by transferring the last dollar spent on capital to labor. Total cost does not change, but total output increases by 2 units. Geometrically, this particular experiment is equivalent to moving southeast along isocost line *bb* in Figure 5-7 because total cost is constant in such a way that output increases as the machine-worker ratio decreases.

> The lowest total cost of producing a given quantity occurs when the ratio of the marginal product of a factor to the last dollar spent on it is equal for all factors of production.

Now that you know how the firm selects the combination of factors that minimizes the total cost of producing a given quantity, you can use this information to derive the long- and short-run total cost functions of the firm.

5-7   THE LONG- AND SHORT-RUN TOTAL COST FUNCTIONS

Once a firm knows how to produce a given output at minimum total cost, it can determine how minimum total cost varies with quantity. It cannot determine how many units to produce in the long run without knowing this relationship, which explains its interest in the shape of the long-run total cost function. We will derive a relationship between total cost and the quantity when both factors of production are variable and then when capital is the fixed factor and only the number of workers is variable.

The Long-Run Total Cost Function

The long-run total cost function indicates the lowest total cost of producing each quantity when all factors can be varied. Figure 5-8 shows two points of tangency of isocost lines with two isoquants. If the firm wants to produce q' units, it minimizes total cost by employing L' workers and purchasing K' machines so that total cost is C'. If the firm wants to produce q^* units at minimum cost, it combines L^* workers with K^* machines so that total cost is C^*.

The curve *ee* is called an expansion path. The **expansion path** is found by connecting all points of tangency between an isoquant and an isocost line. Each

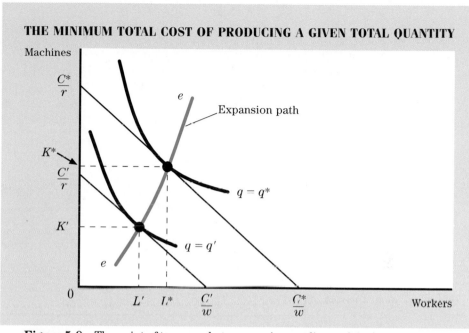

THE MINIMUM TOTAL COST OF PRODUCING A GIVEN TOTAL QUANTITY

Figure 5-8   The point of tangency between an isocost line and the isoquant determines the minimum total cost of producing a given quantity. The lowest total cost of producing q' units is C'. By hiring L' workers and purchasing K' machines the firm produces q' units at a minimum total cost of C'. The lowest total cost of producing q^* is C^*. The firm employs L^* workers and uses K' machines. The expansion path ee is formed by connecting all points of tangency between the isoquant and the isocost line. Associated with any total quantity is a minimum total cost of producing that quantity.

point on the path relates a quantity with a minimum total cost. For example, one point on ee pairs q' units with C'. The minimum total cost of producing q' units is C'. Another point on ee pairs q^* with C^* so that the minimum total cost of producing q^* units is C^*. Although it does not have to, the ratio of machines to workers can change at different points along ee. Consumers can purchase dresses at a small store that provides more service and is labor-intensive, or from a large discount store that sells dresses by using more capital-intensive methods—offering more square feet and less sales help.

To find the long-run total cost function, we take the many pairs of total cost and quantity on the expansion path ee and relate them on a different graph. Figure 5-9 shows the relationship between the quantity produced by a firm and minimum total cost. The long-run total cost function is

$$C_L = C_L(q) \qquad \text{(Long-Run Total Cost Function)} \qquad \text{(5-13)}$$

Equation 5-13 indicates that the long-run total cost depends on the quantity produced. It is a long-run total cost function because the firm varies all factors of production to produce each quantity at the lowest total cost.

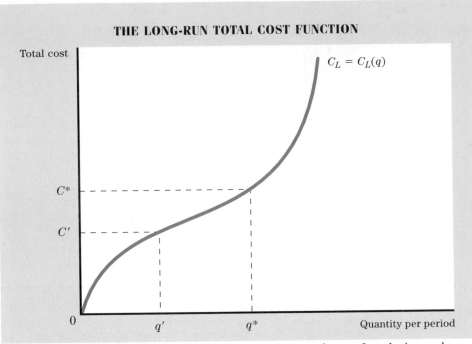

Figure 5-9   The expansion path relates a minimum total cost of producing each quantity. The long-run total cost function shows the lowest total cost of producing each quantity when all factors of production can be changed. The lowest total cost of producing q' units is C'. The lowest total cost of producing q^* units is C^*.

> The **long-run total cost function** shows the lowest total cost of producing each quantity when all factors of production are variable.

Returns to Scale and the Shape of the Long-Run Average Cost Function

The long-run total cost increases initially at a decreasing rate as the quantity increases. This moderate increase indicates that the firm is operating in a region of the production function where there are increasing returns to scale. Although output increases by m percent, total long-run cost increases by less than m percent. As the quantity of output becomes still larger, however, long-run total cost increases at an increasing rate however, and the firm experiences decreasing returns to scale.

The *long-run average cost* or cost per unit is equal to the long-run total cost divided by quantity:

$$\mathrm{AC}_L(q) = \frac{C_L}{q}(q) \qquad \text{(Long-Run Average Cost Function)} \qquad (5\text{-}14)$$

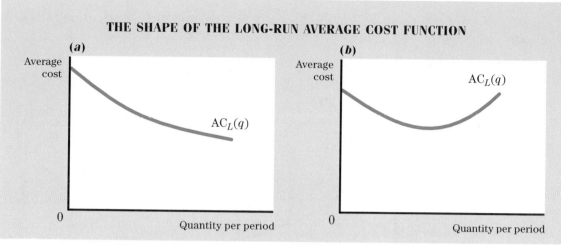

THE SHAPE OF THE LONG-RUN AVERAGE COST FUNCTION

Figure 5-10   (*a*) There are increasing returns to scale, so the long-run average cost is lower for a firm that produces a larger quantity than for a firm that produces a smaller quantity. (*b*) There are increasing returns to scale initially, and the long-run average cost decreases as the quantity produced by the firm increases. Long-run average cost reaches a minimum and then increases when there are decreasing returns to scale.

When there are increasing returns to scale, an m percent increase in output increases total cost by less than m percent. This means that the percentage increase in total cost is less than the percentage increase in quantity, and so long-run average cost declines as the firm produces a larger output. Figure 5-10*a* shows the shape of the long-run average cost function when there are increasing returns to scale. Notice that the larger the quantity produced, the lower the long-run average cost. In contrast, the long-run average cost function is U-shaped in Figure 5-10*b*. The long-run average cost decreases because of increasing returns and reaches a minimum where there are constant returns to scale; then decreasing returns to scale set in.

APPLICATION 5-3

The Long-Run Average Cost Function of a Pipeline

Figure 5-5 showed the isoquants of the production function of a pipeline with two factors of production: pipeline inside diameter and horsepower. The relative position of the isoquants in Figure 5-5 and footnote 14 indicates that there are increasing returns to scale. Cookenboo calculated long-run average cost (in cents per barrel) as a function of the flow of barrels of oil per day per thousand miles of pipeline. Figure 5-11 shows that long-run average cost decreases as the number of barrels per day increases. The decline in long-run average cost confirms the presence of increasing returns to scale.

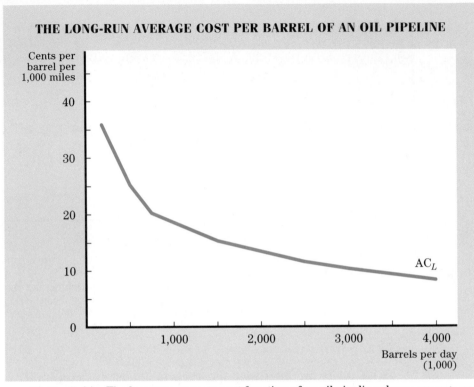

THE LONG-RUN AVERAGE COST PER BARREL OF AN OIL PIPELINE

Figure 5-11   The long-run average cost function of an oil pipeline shows average cost decreases as the number of barrels of oil per day increases. The larger the throughput, the lower the long-run average cost. [Graph is an approximation of chart 6 in Leslie Cookenboo, *Crude Oil Pipelines and Competition in the Oil Industry* (Cambridge, Mass.: Harvard University Press, 1955).]

The Short-Run Total Cost Function

Since one factor is fixed in the short run, the cost of this factor is fixed and does not vary with the quantity produced. Consequently the short-run total cost function of the firm includes a fixed cost plus the cost of the variable factor.

Short-run total cost = Total fixed cost + Total variable cost

$$C_s = C_s(q) = F + V(q) \qquad \text{(Short-Run Total Cost Function)} \qquad \textbf{(5-15)}$$

The **short-run total cost function** shows the lowest total cost of producing each quantity when one factor is fixed.

The fixed cost component is the total annual cost of the fixed factor. In this case the firm has K^* machines in place and must pay interest of $F = rK^*$ on the amount borrowed to pay for the machines. We assume that the firm must meet this expense even if it shuts its doors and stops production. The variable cost component

$V(q)$ represents costs that increase when the quantity produced increases. Because capital is fixed, total variable cost is composed only of total labor cost.

Let's see how the short-run total cost function is derived from the isoquants of the firm's production function by looking at Figure 5-12. In the long run the firm selects the factor combinations along the expansion path ee to produce any output at minimum cost (Figure 5-12a). It can produce q^* units at lowest cost C^* by selecting K^* machines and L^* workers. By combining K' machines with L' workers, it can produce q' units at a minimum total cost of C'.

In the short run the firm has K^* machines. The company's expansion path is the horizontal dashed line ss because the number of machines is fixed at K^* (Figure 5-12b).

If the firm wants to produce q' units in the short run with the number of machines fixed at K^*, it must employ L_2 workers and incur a total cost of C_2 (Figure 5-12b). The factor combination of L_2 and K^* is on the isocost line ff. The lowest total cost of producing q' is along the isocost line dd where total cost is C' (Figure 5-12b). Because the isocost line ff is to the northeast of dd, C_2 is greater than C'. It is more expensive to produce q' units in the short run when the number of machines is fixed at K^* than in the long run, when the number of machines is variable.

Figure 5-13 reproduces the long-run total cost function in Figure 5-9 and includes the short-run total cost function when the number of machines equals K^*. Figure 5-13 shows that the short-run total cost of producing q' units with K^* machines is C_2, while the long-run total cost of producing q' is only C'. If the firm wants to produce only q^* units in the short run, it would hire L^* workers and incur a total cost of C^* along the isocost line cc in Figure 5-12. While the company has K^* machines in the short run, this is the exact number it would select in the long run to produce q^* at the lowest cost. It just so happens that the K^* machines the firm has is exactly the number it would need to produce q^* units at the lowest total cost. Therefore, total short-run cost of producing q^* units is equal to the total long-run cost. In other words, having K^* machines is no constraint at all because the firm would use K^* machines to produce q^* units at the lowest cost anyway. Figure 5-13 shows that long-run total cost and short-run total cost are equal when the firm produces q^* units with K^* machines.

What happens if the number of machines is fixed at K^* and the firm wants to produce the smaller quantity $q^\bullet$? The firm employs L_1 workers to produce $q^\bullet$ units. The isocost curve bb in Figure 5-12b goes through the point where the firm has K^* machines and L_1 workers and incurs a total cost of C_1. The minimum total cost of producing $q^\bullet$ units is $C^\bullet$ on the isocost line aa in Figure 5-12a and requires a combination of $K^\bullet$ machines and $L^\bullet$ workers. Because C_1 is greater than $C^\bullet$, the short-run total cost of producing $q^\bullet$ units with K^* machines is greater than the total long-run cost $C^\bullet$. Figure 5-13 shows that the total short-run cost of producing $q^\bullet$ units is C_1 and is greater than the total long-run cost $C^\bullet$.

Let's pause here and restate some of our findings. We used the firm's production function and its isocost lines to derive the long-run cost function from the expansion path. In the short run the number of machines is fixed, and so the firm's expansion path is reduced to a horizontal line through K^*, the fixed number of

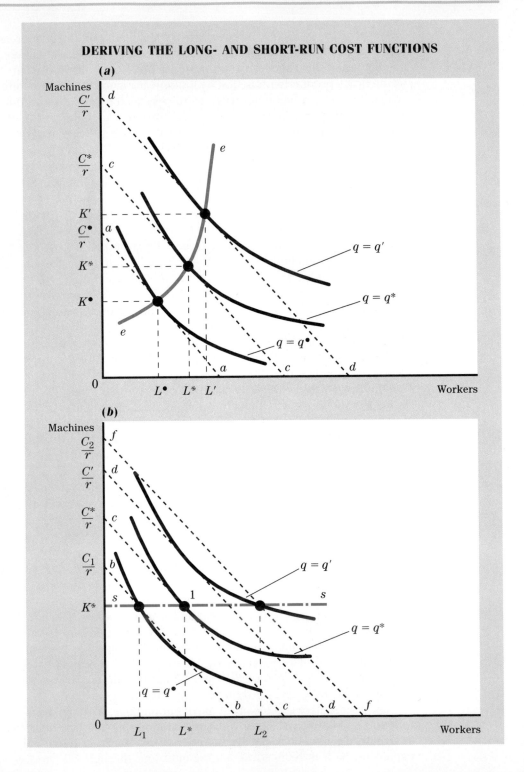

DERIVING THE LONG- AND SHORT-RUN COST FUNCTIONS

Figure 5-12   (*Opposite page*) In the short run the number of machines is K^*. If the firm wants to produce q' units, it employs L_2 workers (*b*). The short-run total cost of producing q' units is C_2. If the firm wants to produce q^* units, it employs L^* workers, the number it would employ in the long run if it wanted to produce q^* units at lowest total cost (*a*). The short-run total cost of producing q^* units is C^*, which also is equal to the long-run total cost of producing q^* units. If the firm produces $q^{\bullet}$ units, it employs L_1 workers in the short run and incurs a total cost of C_1 (*b*). In the long run it would produce $q^{\bullet}$ units with $K^{\bullet}$ machines and $L^{\bullet}$ workers at a lower total cost of $C^{\bullet}$ (*a*).

machines. We traced out the short-run total cost function when the number of machines is fixed at K^*. The short-run total cost function lies above the long-run total cost function for all quantities except one. At the quantity where the short run expansion path *ss* intersects the expansion path *ee* (point 1 in Figure 5-12*b*), short-run total cost equals long-run total cost (Figure 5-13).

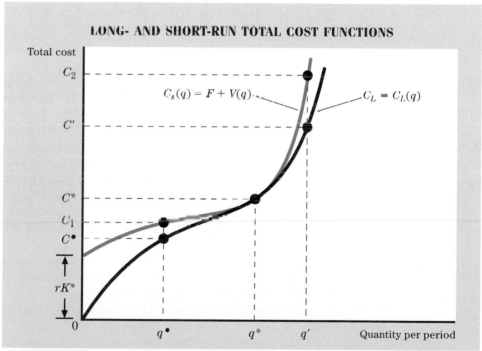

Figure 5-13   In the short run the number of machines is fixed at K^*. The firm can increase output only by increasing the number of workers. The total cost of producing any given rate of output will be greater in the short run than in the long run, except when the firm produces q^* units because q^* units can be produced at lowest cost by using K^* machines. Therefore, the short-run cost curve lies above the long-run total cost curve at all outputs except $q = q^*$. When the firm produces $q^{\bullet}$ in the short run, the short-run total cost is C_1, which is greater than the long-run total cost $C^{\bullet}$.

5-8   SHIFTS IN THE LONG-RUN TOTAL COST FUNCTION

The position of the long-run cost function will shift if the prices of the factors change or if technical progress makes the factors more productive. Such shifts in the position of the long-run cost function can affect the survival of different firms in the industry. If the prices of factors increase for some firms, those firms having to pay higher prices will have higher costs relative to other firms in the industry. For example, differential shifts in the cost of producing a good in different regions of the country can explain why the textile industry moved from New England during the 1930s and 1940s and relocated to North and South Carolina and Georgia. The more recent displacement of textile jobs from these states to Mexico is due to differential shifts in the cost of production and to changes in tariff barriers. The displacement of steel by aluminum in automobiles and in soft drink containers provides other illustrations of the effects of differential shifts in the cost of production.

A Change in the Price of a Factor

Suppose the price of a factor of production decreases. How does this decrease affect the behavior of the firm? If the firm continues to employ the same machine-worker combination as before, it can produce any given quantity at a lower total cost than before because the price of one factor is lower. However, it can reduce total cost even more by selecting a different machine-worker combination to produce the same output.

To demonstrate this change, let's assume that the market price of a machine decreases. Before the price decreases, the expansion path is ee in Figure 5-14. The firm produces q^* units at lowest total cost C^* by employing L^* workers and buying K^* machines. The slope of the isocost line aa' equals the slope of the isoquant at point 1. After the price of a machine decreases from M to M', the original isocost line aa' becomes $a'b$ in Figure 5-14. Because the annual cost of a worker is unchanged and the price of a machine falls, each isocost line rotates around the horizontal intercept. The cost of a machine decreases relative to the cost of a worker. Before the price of a machine decreases, the firm incurs a total cost of C^* if it purchases C^*/r machines and does not hire any workers. After the price of a machine is reduced, its annual cost falls and becomes $r' = iM'$. It is now able to buy $C^*/r' > C^*/r$ machines if it does not hire any workers. All the firm's isocost lines now have the same slope as isocost line $a'b$.

Therefore, the firm's new expansion path EE in Figure 5-14 is formed by connecting all points of tangency between each new isocost line and each isoquant. Because the price of a machine falls relative to the price of a worker, the new isocost lines are steeper and the ratio of machines to workers is higher than before at any new point of tangency. If the firm produces q^* units after the price of a machine decreases, it combines K' machines with L' workers and incurs a total cost of C'. The slope of the isocost line cc is tangent to the isoquant at point 2. The

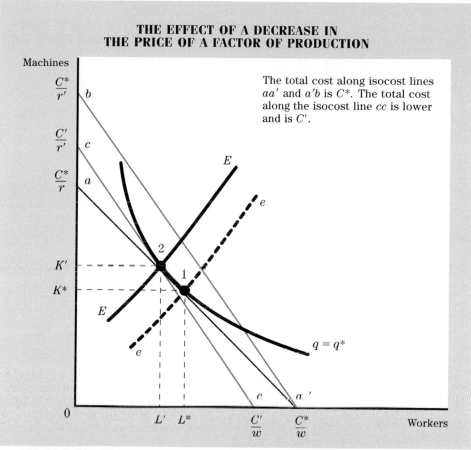

Figure 5-14 When the price of a machine decreases, the firm will substitute more capital for fewer workers to produce any given quantity. Initially, the firm uses K^* and L^* to produce q^* units (point 1). The slope of the isocost line aa equals the slope of the isoquant at point 1. The expansion path is the curve ee. After the price of a machine decreases, the isocost line becomes steeper and shifts from aa to ab. If the firm produces q^* units, it uses K' and L' to produce q^* units. A fall in the price of capital encourages the firm to substitute capital for labor. The new equilibrium is at point 2, where the slope of the new isocost line equals the slope of the isoquant. The new expansion path becomes EE.

firm uses relatively more capital than labor when the price of capital falls relative to the price of labor.

Because the isocost line cc lies below the isocost line $a'b$, the total cost C' associated with isocost line cc is less than the total cost C^* associated with isocost lines $a'b$ and aa'. Therefore, the total cost of producing q^* units is lower after the price of a machine decreases. By tracing along the new expansion path EE, we can derive the total long-run cost of production of each quantity. Figure 5-15 shows

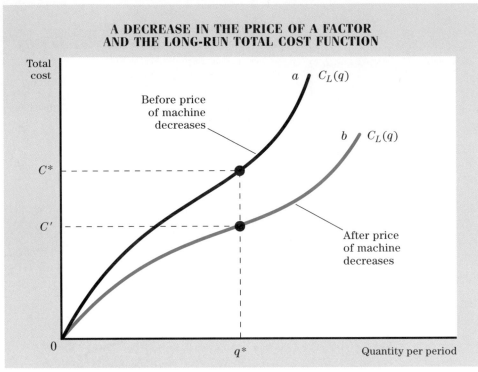

**A DECREASE IN THE PRICE OF A FACTOR
AND THE LONG-RUN TOTAL COST FUNCTION**

Figure 5-15   Before the price of a machine decreases, the long-run total cost function of the firm is the upper curve $0a$. After the price of a machine decreases, the new long-run total cost function is $0b$. At each quantity, the firm can produce that quantity at a lower total cost. If the firm produces q^* units, the total cost is C^* before the price of a machine decreases and C' after the price of a machine decreases.

that the new long-run total cost function lies below the original total long-run cost function. Not surprisingly, the total cost of producing each rate of output falls after the price of a machine decreases.

Technological Change

The long-run total cost function shifts downward when there are technological advances that allow the firm to produce a larger quantity with any given combination of factors. New ways of organizing factors of production permit the firm to produce a larger quantity with each combination of factors. The technological advance may cause the company to shift to relatively more or less capital-intensive methods depending on how the production function changes. What happens is that the technological advances allow the firm to produce a given quantity at a lower cost. Figure 5-16 shows the new long-run total cost function after a technological change. At each quantity the long-run total cost is lower after the technological change.

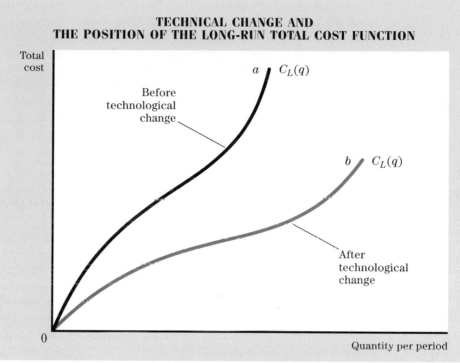

**TECHNICAL CHANGE AND
THE POSITION OF THE LONG-RUN TOTAL COST FUNCTION**

Figure 5-16   The long run total cost function shifts downward after a technical advance shifts the position of the production function. Each quantity can be produced at a lower total cost after the technical advance than before. The technical advance allows the firm to produce a larger quantity for each combination of factors.

APPLICATION 5-4

Substituting Aluminum for Steel in Autos

Aluminum and steel producers are constantly at war with each other to get more of their product used in automobiles. They bend the ears of automobile executives every chance they get, advancing their respective cases for the superiority of their metal in autos. An all-aluminum car would be lighter than an all-steel car so the aluminum car is more fuel efficient, an increasing concern for auto executives. Aluminum is easier to mold into different shapes so manufacturing costs can be lower. While aluminum has some advantages, it also has some distinct disadvantages. Most important, aluminum is more expensive than steel on a *per pound* basis. An aluminum body part will be lighter than a comparable steel part but might cost twice as much. Auto companies also have much more experience with and knowledge of the crash-resistant properties of steel than of aluminum, a major concern of the driving public.

It does seem that the advantages in the use of aluminum in cars are beginning to outweigh the disadvantages. There is evidence of growing use of aluminum in autos. Already, aluminum's share by weight is about 7 percent and may go higher. A virtually all-aluminum luxury car called the A-8 has been produced by the German auto maker Audi. Steel producers are worried about the inroads that aluminum is making and are concerned that an all-aluminum car will appear in the future. They do not want to lose the auto market, as they did the can market, to aluminum manufacturers. An unanswered question is how much of the growing use of aluminum is traceable to a declining relative price for aluminum and how much to technical changes that shift the production function for automobiles.

5-9   THE PRODUCTION FUNCTION AND LEARNING-BY-DOING

The production function relates the quantity of each factor to the output of the firm. Some reseachers suggest that firm output of some goods depends not only on the quantity of each factor but also on the total production history of the firm. They argue that the productivity of a firm also depends on the knowledge gained by producing the good. In some industries, companies learn by doing. The cumulative experience of the firm is a separate determinant of the quantity produced in addition to the quantity of each factor.

We can modify the production function to take into account the effect of learning-by-doing by adding the cumulative output of the firm as another input in the production function.

$$q = f(L,K,\Sigma q) \qquad \text{(Modified Production Function)} \qquad (5\text{-}16)$$

where Σq represents the cumulative quantity produced during the lifetime of the firm. In this formulation the production history of the firm is important.

Two firms with access to the same technology may currently employ the same number of workers and have the same amount of capital equipment. However, the cumulative production over the years may be greater for one firm than for the other. According to this modified production theory, the quantity produced in the current period by the more experienced firm will be higher than that produced by the other firm because of the difference in production experience. Learning-by-doing means that one firm can be physically more productive than another because it has produced more in the past. Other firms can duplicate the productive efficiency of this firm only over time and by producing more and learning more.

The learning-by-doing hypothesis appears to explain some of the differences in the efficiency of firms in selected industries, but some interesting questions about the hypothesis remain unanswered. Can other firms catch up to a firm with a larger cumulative output by hiring away some of its employees? Is learning at one firm transferable to another firm or is learning-by-doing firm-specific? Is learning-by-doing determined by cumulative firm output or is it related to cumulative industry output? For example, the cost of constructing an industrial plant may depend on the number of plants that have been built by all construction firms. In other words, all construction firms may gain information when a single construction firm builds another plant. If this does occur, each firm may have a tendency to wait and learn from the experience of others.

APPLICATION 5-5

Learning-by-Doing in the Semiconductor Industry

The semiconductor industry introduced seven generations of dynamic random access memory chips (DRAM) between 1974 and 1992. One common pattern for all generations is that prices decline as production experience increases, an indicator of the reduced cost due to learning-by-doing. Figure 5-17 shows price declines over time after each new generation of chip is introduced.

Economists Doug Irwin and Peter Klenow were interested in measuring the rate at which average costs fall with increases in cumulative output and whether

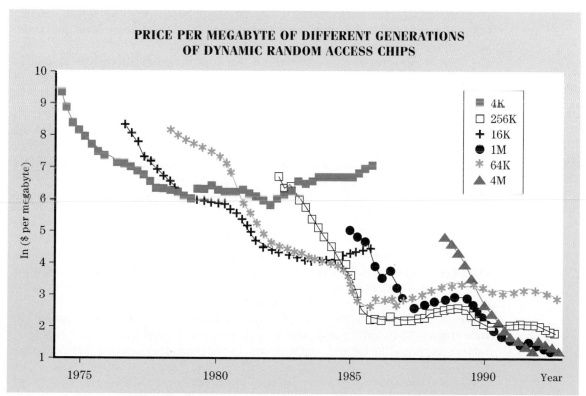

Figure 5-17   Prices of DRAM chips decline with increasing experience in producing the chip.

there are important *spillovers* from learning in this industry.[19] A positive spillover occurs when one producer's costs decline as another firm learns more about producing a chip. The first firm benefits from the activities of the second without actually paying any of its costs. This is not unlikely if, for example, engineers frequently talk with each other at industry meetings. Irwin and Klenow asked how much of the price decline could be explained by (1) cumulative firm production and (2) cumulative country production and cumulative production of foreign producers. Using statistical methods, they found that learning rates average about 20 percent so that a doubling of cumulative output reduces average costs by 20 percent. More interestingly, their results suggest that firms learn about three times more from an increase of their own output than from an increase in other firms' output. So, much of the benefits of learning are internalized within the firm. Apparently, but not surprisingly, national boundaries do not seem to be barriers to information flows. Spillover effects through learning from a unit increase in the output of other domestic rivals are about the same as from a unit increase in the output of foreign firms. Although much has been written of the head start that Japanese producers had in DRAM production, Irwin and Klenow found that the learning-by-doing gains of Japanese producers are not different from learning-by-doing of American producers. Of even greater importance is their finding that intergenerational learning appears to be low. Even though the firms in one country have a lower cost of producing one generation of DRAM chip there is no guarantee of continued success in producing the next generation.

This imaginative study demonstrates the importance of cumulative output in explaining the cost of production of DRAM chips and highlights the interesting and potentially important question of spillovers effects.

APPLICATION **5-6**

Learning-by-Doing at the Indianapolis 500

Another interesting example of the benefits of learning-by-doing comes from an unlikely source, the Indianapolis 500, the car race held annually on Memorial Day weekend. Consider miles per hour of the winner as the output of the race. Does learning-by-doing affect the miles per hour of the winner? We can determine if the cumulative number of times the Indianapolis 500 has been held affects the miles per hour of the winner. In other words, we can test to see how miles per hour depends on the cumulative frequency of the race.

Figure 5-18 shows the miles per hour of the winner of the Indianapolis 500 race from 1911 to 1972,[20] and there is a clear upward trend over time. Among the factors responsible for the increase are improvements in engine performance,

---

[19] Douglas A. Irwin and Peter J. Klenow, "Learning-by-Doing Spillovers in the Semiconductor Industry," *Journal of Political Economy* 102, no. 2 (1994); pp. 1200–27. © by The University of Chicago. All rights reserved.

[20] Restrictions were placed on racing cars after 1972, so that comparisons are more difficult to make after this year.

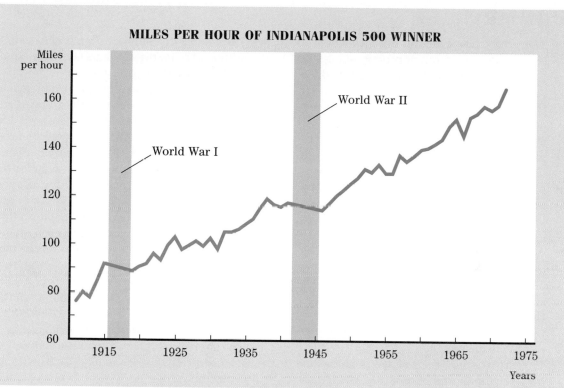

MILES PER HOUR OF INDIANAPOLIS 500 WINNER

Figure 5-18   Miles per hour of the Indianapolis 500 winner did not increase between the beginning and the end of the two world wars.

better car design, better suspensions, and improved gasoline quality. There is another interesting feature in Figure 5-18. Racing stopped during World War I and World War II. Note that a striking feature of the graph is that these improvements apparently stopped during each war. Miles per hour was not higher when racing resumed after each war. Racing stopped in 1942 because of World War II and did not resume until 1946, and Figure 5-18 indicates that learning stopped when racing stopped. Miles per hour of the winner at the end of the war is about the same as miles per hour of the winner before the war. If learning depends simply on time and not on experience, then the miles per hour of the winner would be higher at the end of each war than at the beginning.

Miles per hour could have increased over time because racing expands learning about the design of race cars and engine performance. Another explanation is that learning occurs in other industries during peacetime and that this learning benefits racing and increases racing performance during such times. Perhaps both factors are at work. The data do indicate that learning stops when racing stops, and so learning-by-doing appears to be an important determinant of performance in this sport.

SUMMARY

- The production function describes how a firm combines factors of production, given the current state of technology, to produce goods or services.

- When capital is the fixed factor, the average product of labor is output per worker and, after some point, decreases as more workers are employed. The marginal product of labor measures the increase in output due to an increase in workers. The law of diminishing returns means that the marginal product of labor eventually decreases as the firm hires more workers.

- An isoquant shows the different methods of producing a given quantity.

- The marginal rate of technical substitution is the slope of an isoquant and measures the required substitution between two factors of production so that the quantity produced is constant.

- Returns to scale describe the relationship between inputs and output for a given ratio of the two factors. A firm may experience increasing, constant, or decreasing returns to scale.

- In the long run a firm can vary each factor of production to the desired quantity. In the short run at least one factor is fixed and output can be increased only by increasing the other factors.

- The isocost line shows how a firm can substitute one factor for another with total cost held constant.

- The minimum total cost of producing a given quantity requires that the slope of an isocost line be equal to the slope of an isoquant. The minimum total cost of producing a given quantity occurs when the ratio of the marginal product of a factor to the price of the factor is equal for all factors.

- The long-run total cost function shows the lowest total cost of producing each quantity. If there are increasing returns, the long-run average cost decreases as the quantity increases.

- The long-run total cost function shifts downward if the price of a factor decreases or if there is a technical advance.

- The short-run total cost function shows the cost of producing each quantity when one factor is fixed.

- In some industries firms learn to be more productive through experience gained by producing. The cumulative output of the firm is a separate determinant in the production function.

KEY TERMS

production function
short and long runs
total product function
total product of labor
law of diminishing returns
isoquant
marginal rate of technical substitution
diminishing marginal rate of technical
    substitution
isocost function
isocost line

factors of production
state of technology
short-run production function
average and marginal product function of a
    factor
long-run production function
returns to scale
Cobb-Douglas production function
price of a factor
slope of an isoquant and slope of the
    isocost line

minimizing cost of producing a given output
expansion path
short-run total cost function

long-run total cost function
shifts in the long-run cost function
learning-by-doing

REVIEW QUESTIONS

1. Explain the concepts marginal and average product of labor. How are they related to each other?
2. What is the law of diminishing returns?
3. A student has a simple production function between the grade he receives in this course (the output) and hours per week spent studying for this course (the input). Assume an A = 5, B = 4, C = 3, D = 2, and F = 0. Suppose the production function is

STUDY HOURS PER WEEK	FINAL GRADE IN POINTS
0	0.00
1	1.50
2	2.75
3	3.75
4	4.25
5	4.50

   a. On a graph with output per hour of study time on the vertical axis and hours of study per week on the horizontal axis plot the student's average and marginal product functions.
   b. If the student tries to maximize average product, i.e., grade points per hour of study, how many hours will the student study for this course?
4. If the marginal product of labor is decreasing, the average product of labor is decreasing. Explain why you agree or disagree with this statement.
5. If the average product of labor is decreasing, then the marginal product of labor is

decreasing. Explain why you agree or disagree with this statement.
6. What is common along an isoquant?
7. Give two examples of substitution among factors of production.
8. The production function of a firm is

$$q = AL^{.23}K^{.57}$$

   a. Are there increasing or decreasing returns to scale?
   b. On a graph draw the shape of the resulting long-run average cost curve.
   c. If A increases, how does this change your answer to (a)?
9. What is the expansion path of a firm? What information is needed to derive an expansion path?
10. If a firm uses 20 units of labor and 20 units of capital, its marginal rate of technical substitution is -1. Explain why you agree or disagree.
11. If the firm uses 20 units of labor and 20 units of capital and the marginal product of labor and capital are 10 and 5 respectively, what is the marginal rate of technical substitution between capital and labor?
12. If a firm has 6 machines and 4 workers and the marginal rate of technical substitution is -6, would you expect the marginal rate of technical substitution to be -12 when the firm has 2 machines and 8 workers and is still producing the same output? Explain why or why not.
13. If the price of capital is $40 per period and the price of labor is $10, write an expression for the firm's isocost line. Show how the isocost line changes when (a) both

prices increase by 10 percent, (*b*) the price of labor decreases to $9, and (*c*) the price of capital increases to $50.

14. If the price of labor decreases by $2 per worker and the firm has 10 workers, the firm will take the savings of $20 and spend it to hire more workers. By doing this, the firm hires more labor relative to capital and can still produce the same output. Explain why you agree or disagree with this statement.

15. Two factors in the production of a good are unskilled labor and skilled labor. Suppose the price of skilled labor is 50 percent higher than the price of unskilled labor. Explain why you agree or disagree with each of the following conclusions.

a. The firm will hire 50 percent fewer skilled workers than unskilled workers.

b. The firm will hire 50 percent more skilled workers than unskilled workers.

c. The marginal product of a skilled worker will be one-half the marginal product of an unskilled worker.

d. The marginal product of a skilled worker will be twice the marginal product of an unskilled worker.

16. If there are learning-by-doing effects, what should happen to the quantity produced for a given quantity of labor and capital over time?

EXERCISES

1. In the short run a firm can increase output by increasing the number of workers. The average product of labor is shown in the accompanying table.

NUMBER OF WORKERS	1	2	3	4	5	6
AVERAGE PRODUCT OF LABOR	5	7	8	6	4	2

a. Derive the marginal product of labor.

b. Present an explanation of why the marginal product of labor increases and then decreases and becomes negative.

2. If the price of factor A is $20 per unit and the price of factor B is $300 per unit and the marginal product of factor A is 40 units and the marginal product of factor B is 60 units, the firm should increase the employment of A and decrease the employment of B to minimize the total long-run cost of producing existing output. Explain why you agree or disagree with this statement.

3. The estimated production function of a firm is

$$Q = AK^{.24}L^{.70}$$

If the firm expands output by 5 percent will its long-run cost increase by more than, equal to, or less than 5 percent? Explain.

4. The expansion path of country 1 is labeled #1 and the expansion path of country 2 is labeled #2 in the figure below. In which country is the price of labor higher relative to the price of capital?

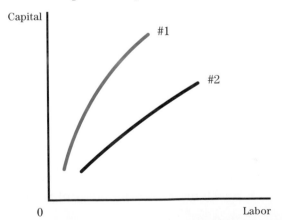

*5. Given the prices of the factors, the expansion path of a firm is *ee*. After the wage of workers increases, the new expansion path becomes *EE*. Can *EE* intersect *ee*? Explain why or why not.

6. A recent study estimated total farm output would remain constant if 20 tons of fertilizer were substituted for 1 acre of land. If the price of 1 ton of fertilizer is $175, what must be the lowest rental price of 1 acre of land before farmers will substitute fertilizer for land?

7. A large multinational textile firm is planning to open a new plant to produce cotton cloth for bed sheets. It has narrowed its choice to the United States and Malaysia. The wage rate for factory workers is lower in Malaysia than in the United States.

    a. If the firm is going to produce 20,000 sheets a month in its plant, no matter where it is opened, and the price of capital is the same in both countries, what can you say about the relative use of labor versus capital in the United States versus Malaysia? Show this with a graph

    b. Will the expansion paths of the two countries differ? Show the expansion paths for the two countries on a figure.

    c. If the price of capital is more expensive

in Malaysia than in the United States, what can you say about the relative use of labor and capital to produce 20,000 sheets? In which country would the cost of producing cotton sheets be lower?

8. The isocost line of a firm is *aa* in the accompanying figure (below). If the firm moves from point *B* to point *A* in (*a*), what is the relationship between MP_L/w and MP_K/r? If the firm moves from point *A* to point *B* in (*b*), what can you say about the relationship between MP_L/w and MP_K/r? (See figure below.)

9. Currently a firm uses 100 personal computers and employs 30 workers. To help the domestic computer industry the government gives a subsidy of 10 percent of the price for every *extra* computer the firm purchases from a domestic computer company. With the aid of graphs show how this subsidy affects the firm's isocost line.

10. A firm cannot change a fixed factor in the short run. Therefore, its total cost in the short run must exceed its total cost in the long run when it can vary all of its factors of production. Explain why you agree or disagree with this statement.

11. If there are constant returns to scale, the long-run total cost function will increase

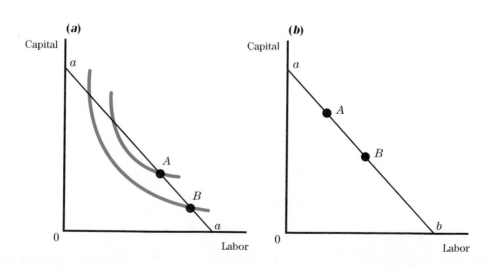

linearly with increases in output. Explain why you agree or disagree with this statement.

*12. Oil companies are drilling for oil at greater and greater depths in the Gulf of Mexico. One company will spend $1.45 billion to build a platform that will be 4,000 feet from the bottom of the Gulf—equivalent to three World Trade buildings placed end-to-end. Do you think the increased output from greater drilling depths occurs because oil companies are increasing total units of capital (with a given production function) or because technological change has shifted the production function? *Hint:* Real oil prices have been stable or declining over time. Explain.

*13. In Japan every 100 cars are produced with 8 workers while in the United States every 100 cars are produced with 10 workers. Given this information alone, can you conclude that Japanese auto producers are technically more efficient than U.S. auto producers? *Hint:* Describe how relative factor cost in the two countries affects the combination of factors used in the two countries.

THE COST FUNCTIONS OF THE FIRM

■ **6-1   Defining Costs**

■ **6-2   The Short and Long Runs**

■ **6-3   The Short-Run Cost Functions of the Firm**

Graphing the Short-Run Cost Functions

The Marginal and Average Cost Functions

The Area under the Marginal Cost Function

■ **6-4   Identifying the Relevant Costs When Solving Short-Run Cost Problems**

Application 6-1: How to Schedule Production between a New Plant and an Old Plant

Application 6-2: Why "Never Give Up" Is Not Always the Best Advice

Application 6-3: Inefficient or Efficient Environmental Regulation

Application 6-4: Why Are Fewer Sellers of Used Homes Using Brokers?

■ **6-5   Deriving the Long-Run Average Cost Function from the Short-Run Average Cost Functions**

The Long-Run Average Cost Function with a Limited Choice of Plants

The Long-Run Average Cost Function with a Continuum of Plant Sizes

■ **6-6   The Number of Firms and the Long-Run Cost Function**

Diseconomies of Scale and Industries with Many Firms

Economies of Scale and Industries with Few Firms

Application 6-5: The Emergence of the Standard Oil Company

Application 6-6: Size of Firm and Technological Change in the Steel Industry

■ **Summary**

■ **Key Terms**

■ **Review Questions**

■ **Exercises**

This chapter is about the costs of the firm. We begin by asking a basic question: What should be included in a firm's costs? As you will see, economists define costs in a special way that requires some adjustment in your thinking about the meaning of costs. Among the different cost concepts defined in this chapter, two are particularly important. The first is *opportunity cost* and the second is *marginal cost*. No firm can hope to be an efficient producer without an understanding and appreciation of both cost concepts. After introducing the firm's different short-run cost functions, we explore the relationship between the firm's short- and long-run costs. The chapter ends with a discussion of how the shape of the long-run cost function affects the number of firms that can produce efficiently in an industry.

The many new cost concepts introduced in this chapter are the building blocks for the development of the subject of firm supply that we will take up in the next chapter. Learning about these new cost concepts and the relationships between them will require extra attention on your part. Mastering the new vocabulary and working with these new cost concepts may be challenging even for an attentive reader. Studying this more technical material is—to use the familiar analogy—like going to the dentist. Few of us enjoy the visit but go because it is the lesser of two evils. It is necessary that you have a thorough understanding of the different cost concepts we discuss in Chapter 6 if you wish to avoid trouble when you move on to Chapter 7.

6-1 DEFINING COSTS

Before studying the firm's cost functions, we must decide precisely what to include as a cost of the firm. Most people would agree to including payments for raw materials and labor and rent paid for land and buildings as costs of the firm. We call these *explicit costs.*

> **Explicit costs** are payments for factors of production, such as wages and rents, and purchases of goods and services.

Even for explicit costs, however, you must exercise care about measurement. Suppose you purchase lumber at $400 per 1,000 board feet to sell in your lumber yard. The day after you receive delivery, the price jumps to $450. If you sell 1,000 board feet to a customer at a price of $425, are you making a profit? You might say you are because you paid $400. However, that ignores what you can now in fact get for the lumber, the opportunity cost. By selling lumber for less than the current price, you forgo the $450 that the lumber is now really worth. Hence the proper measure of cost is the *opportunity cost* of using the resource, in this case, $450 per 1,000 board feet. The correct way to measure the cost of a resource is its opportunity cost. For explicit costs, the purchase price of the resource may usually be the correct measure of cost, but at times the purchase price can differ from the opportunity cost of the resource; and so economists consider all opportunity costs to derive the firm's total costs.

> **Opportunity costs** represent the forgone earnings or income when a firm employs a resource for a specific use.

To demonstrate what economists include in opportunity cost, let's assume that you start your own business by opening a bookstore near a university. If you hadn't gone into business for yourself, you could have earned a salary in some capacity, perhaps managing someone else's bookstore, and this forgone salary is an opportunity cost. However, your decision to start your own business is even more costly. When you own and manage your own bookstore, you not only forgo the salary you could have earned but also the earnings on funds you would have invested elsewhere had you not invested in the bookstore. Another opportunity cost is the return on investment that you forgo by investing in the bookstore.

In summary, the total cost for the firm encompasses all explicit and opportunity costs.[1] Hereafter, we assume that the cost functions of the firm include all explicit and opportunity costs.

You may wonder why economists include opportunity costs as part of the total cost of the firm. Suppose the firm's cost did not include opportunity costs and total revenue from the bookstore just equaled total explicit costs. The bookstore would appear to have neither earned a profit nor incurred a loss. However, this is an unwarranted conclusion because you are not as well off as you would have been had you worked for someone else. You would have received a salary and earned a rate of return on the funds that you invested in the bookstore, and so you are worse off operating your own bookstore. Economists argue that the firm breaks even only if total revenue equals the sum of all explicit and opportunity costs and earns profits only if total revenue exceeds total explicit and opportunity costs.

6-2   THE SHORT AND LONG RUNS

The cost that the firm incurs is different in the short run from in the long run. As you recall, all factors of production are variable in the long run, and so the firm can change the amount of labor and capital it employs. In the short run, however, it operates under a constraint because at least one factor of production is fixed. We continue to assume that capital is the fixed factor.

---

[1] Accountants treat some costs differently than economists do. They consider advertising and research and development expenses as costs in the year incurred, although this practice is changing. Economists suggest that some types of advertising expenditures have long-term effects and contribute to the goodwill of the firm, providing an intangible asset. In short, some types of advertising create goodwill, and goodwill is an asset just as expenditures on plant and equipment are. Just as the cost of a physical asset is a depreciation in its value, the cost of intangible goodwill is its depreciation. For example, Coca Cola has built considerable goodwill by advertising its name. The value of the name is enormous. But suppose Coca Cola completely stopped advertising for one year. An accountant would say that the cost of advertising is zero. An economist would say that the firm incurs a cost equal to the decline in the value of goodwill because Coca Cola did not maintain the intangible asset by continuing to advertise. Many accountants agree with economists in principle but are quick to point out the practical difficulties of estimating a decline in the value of goodwill.

> In the short run at least one factor of production is fixed.

In reality the distinction between the long run and the short run is not quite so clear-cut. There are many short runs, each of a different length. As time elapses, the firm is able to change more factors of production. At this instant, all factors of production are fixed because the firm cannot change any factor. In a week's time the firm may be able to hire more unskilled workers and purchase more supplies, and by the end of the month it may find and hire more skilled workers. By the end of a year the firm may receive delivery on more machines, and in two years' time, it may expand the size of the plant. More factors of production become variable as time passes, and fewer and fewer constraints are binding on the firm. For the purpose of the analysis here, however, the simpler distinction between the short and the long run allows us to study the firm's behavior when at least one factor is fixed and all factors are variable.

The duration of the short run depends on how long it takes or how expensive it is to vary the amount of capital employed and differs from one industry to another. In one industry the short run could span just a few months, while it might extend over several years in another. If the capital good is a personal computer, delivery of a new computer may take no more than a week. If the capital good is a specialized die, it may take six months before the die becomes available. If the capital good is a nuclear generating plant, the short run could involve a decade or more before the plant becomes operational.

6-3   THE SHORT-RUN COST FUNCTIONS OF THE FIRM

Suppose the fixed factor is the size of plant so that the firm cannot change plant size in the short run. For example, suppose the company signs a five-year lease to rent a specialized factory. It is committed to this production facility for the duration of the lease and cannot change the terms of the lease.[2] Alternatively, if the firm finances the construction of a plant by borrowing, it incurs a fixed annual interest cost. It pays interest regardless of the number of units it produces. These **fixed costs** do not change with the quantity produced, but they are also sunk in the sense that the firm cannot escape them. On the other hand, if you rent a building and include a clause in the rental agreement allowing you to break the lease, the rent is a fixed cost because it is independent of output but not a sunk cost because you can break the lease at no cost. For the most part throughout this book, it is assumed that a fixed cost is also a sunk cost.

> A **sunk cost** is a past expenditure or a contracted expenditure that a firm cannot avoid.

---

[2] We assume the firm leases a specialized production facility and cannot subcontract the lease to some other firm.

As we discussed in Chapter 5, the short-run total cost function $C_s(q)$ shows the total cost of producing each quantity with a given plant size. The short-run total cost function is the sum of the fixed and variable cost functions.

$$C_s(q) = F + V(q) \qquad \text{(Short-Run Total Cost Function)} \qquad \textbf{(6-1)}$$

The *short-run total cost function* shows the lowest total cost of producing each quantity when at least one factor is fixed.

The subscript s in equation 6-1 refers to the short run. F is a constant amount and equals the total cost of the **fixed factor.** The firm pays F per period no matter what, if any, output it produces. $V(q)$ represents the **variable cost** function and includes those costs that change with the quantity produced. If labor is the only **variable factor,** variable cost equals total cost of labor. As the firm hires more workers, output and variable cost increase.

Graphing the Short-Run Cost Functions

We can graph total fixed and total variable cost functions and then sum these two functions vertically to derive the short-run total cost function. Figure 6-1*a* shows the total variable and total fixed cost functions and the derived short-run total cost function. Cost is on the vertical axis and quantity is on the horizontal axis. F is a horizontal line since it does not change with quantity produced. Total variable cost $V(q)$ increases at first at a decreasing rate as quantity increases but then at an increasing rate. The vertical sum of the total fixed cost and total variable cost functions forms the short-run total cost function.

From the short-run total cost, the variable and fixed cost functions, we can derive several average cost functions and a new cost function called **marginal cost.** Here, we discuss what each cost function represents and explain the relationships among these functions. The seven basic cost functions are:

- Short-run total cost function, $C_s(q)$
- Short-run total variable cost function, $V(q)$
- Total fixed cost, F
- Short-run marginal cost, $\text{MC}_s(q)$

- Short-run average cost function, $\text{AC}_s(q)$
- Average variable cost function, $\text{AVC}(q)$
- Average fixed cost function, $\text{AFC}(q)$

Figure 6-1*b* shows the firm's short-run average cost function $\text{AC}_s(q)$, average variable cost function $\text{AVC}(q)$, average fixed cost $\text{AFC}(q)$, and short-run marginal cost function $\text{MC}_s(q)$. Each of these functions can be derived from the cost functions in Figure 6-1*a*. After defining each of these functions, we will explain how to graph each one.

The **short-run average cost function** of the firm is defined as

$$\text{AC}_s(q) = \frac{C_s(q)}{q} \qquad \text{(Short-Run Average Cost Function)} \qquad \textbf{(6-2)}$$

$$= \frac{F}{q} + \frac{V(q)}{q}$$

$$= \text{AFC}(q) + \text{AVC}(q)$$

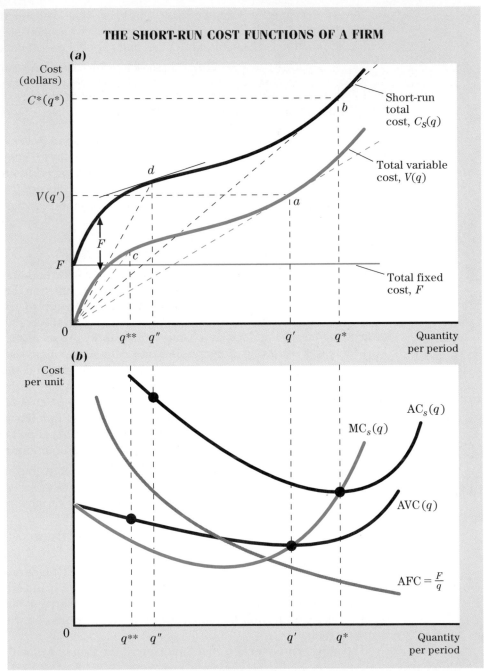

Figure 6-1 (*a*) The short-run total fixed cost, total variable cost, and total cost functions of the firm. (*b*) The short-run average variable, average fixed, average and marginal cost functions of the firm.

At each quantity short-run average cost is the sum of average fixed cost F/q and average variable cost $V(q)/q$.

The average variable cost function is

$$\text{AVC}(q) = \frac{V(q)}{q} \qquad \text{(Average Variable Cost Function)} \qquad \text{(6-3)}$$

The **short-run marginal cost function** is the change in total cost when quantity changes by Δq. For discrete changes in quantity,

$$\text{MC}_s(q) = \frac{\Delta C_s(q)}{\Delta q} \qquad \text{(Short Run Marginal Cost Function)} \qquad \text{(6-4)}$$

$\Delta C_s(q)$ is the change in fixed cost plus the change in variable cost, but since fixed cost is constant, we can express marginal cost in a different way:

$$\text{MC}_s(q) = \frac{\Delta V(q)}{\Delta q}$$

The short-run marginal cost is the *slope* of either the short-run total cost function or the variable cost function since the two functions differ by F, a constant.

Just how are the short-run average and marginal cost functions derived from the short-run total cost function? The short-run average cost at any quantity is the slope of a straight line drawn from the origin to the point on $C_s(q)$ associated with that quantity. For example, short-run total cost of producing q^* units is C^*. The ray $0b$ from the origin has a slope equal to total cost, the distance between b and q^*, or q^*b, divided by the quantity produced, the distance from the origin to q^*, or $0q^*$. The slope of the ray is $\text{AC}_s(q^*)$, or C^*/q^*. To recapitulate, the slope of the straight line from the origin to any point on the short-run total cost function is $\text{AC}_s(q)$ for that quantity.

You can tell whether $\text{AC}_s(q)$ increases or decreases when quantity changes by determining how the slopes of the successive rays to different points on the total cost curve change. You can see that the slope of the ray $0b$ is smaller (flatter) than the slope of the ray $0d$ in Figure 6-1a. Therefore, the average cost of producing q^* units is less than the average cost of producing q'' units.

What makes the ray $0b$ unique is that it alone is *tangent* to the short-run total cost function. The slope of ray $0b$ is smaller than the slopes of all other rays from the origin to points on the short-run total cost function. Therefore, short-run average cost reaches a minimum when the firm produces q^* and is higher for smaller or larger quantities.

There is now enough information to describe the general shape of the short-run average cost function. As output increases, the short-run average cost function decreases until it reaches a minimum when the firm produces q^* units and then increases when output exceeds q^*.[3]

Now consider the shape of the average variable cost function. For a given quantity, AVC is the slope of a ray from the origin to the total variable cost function. In Figure 6-1a the ray $0a$ is just tangent to $V(q)$ and the slope of the ray $0a$ is

---

[3] As q approaches 0, $\text{AC}_s(q)$ approaches infinity since F/q becomes ever larger.

$q'a/0q'$. The slope of ray $0a$ is smaller than that of any other ray from the origin to any other point on the variable cost function. For example, ray $0c$ is steeper than ray $0a$. Thus, its slope is larger than the slope of ray $0a$. Figure 6-1b shows that AVC initially decreases as quantity increases, reaches a minimum value when the firm produces q' units, and increases as output expands beyond q' units. Given $V(q)$, AVC(q) reaches a minimum at a smaller quantity than the quantity where AC$_s(q)$ reaches a minimum. The reason that average variable cost increases at quantities above q' is that labor becomes relatively less productive as the firm adds more workers with a given amount of capital.[4]

The Marginal and Average Cost Functions

You will recall that Chapter 5 derived a fundamental relationship between marginal and average products of a factor of production. The same quantitative statements apply to the relationship between the marginal and average cost functions.

1. When marginal cost is less than average cost, average cost decreases.

2. When marginal cost equals average cost, average cost is constant.

3. When marginal cost is greater than average cost, average cost increases.[5]

These relationships may appear more complicated than they really are. In reality, they are something any baseball fan from 7 to 77 understands. To borrow an example from America's favorite pastime, let's consider a baseball player who has a season batting average of .300. What this means is that he gets 3 hits on average for each 10 times at bat. Let's suppose the player gets 1 hit in 3 times at bat in the next game. For this one game, his *marginal* batting average is .333. Because his marginal batting average of .333 is greater than his season or *average* batting average of .300, his season batting average rises to over .300. When the marginal exceeds the average, the average increases.

Returning to our discussion of the short-run cost functions, we know that marginal cost is equal to the slope of the short-run total cost function. In Figure

---

[4] Short-run marginal cost is equal to the cost of an additional unit of the variable factor divided by its marginal product. If the firm hires another worker, it pays a wage of w. As explained in Chapter 5, the marginal product of labor is MP$_L$ = $\Delta q/\Delta L$ and measures the increase in output that the firm produces by adding another worker. Therefore, w/MP$_L$ measures the additional cost incurred per unit increase in output, or short-run *marginal cost*, holding capital constant. In other words, MC$_s$ = $\Delta V(q)/\Delta q$ = $\Delta(wL)/\Delta q$, but w is a constant, so we have MC$_s$ = w $\Delta L/\Delta q$ = w/MP$_L$.

[5] Although the relationship between the marginal and average cost functions holds in both the short and long runs, only the relationship for the short-run cost functions is shown here. Short-run total cost equals short-run average cost times quantity: $C_s(q) = $ AC$_s(q)q$.

Marginal cost equals the slope of the total cost function. Using the relationship between $C_s(q)$ and AC$_s(q)$ above, if we consider an infinitesimal change in q, the change in total cost is given by

$$\text{MC}_s(q) = \frac{dC_s(q)}{dq} = \text{AC}_s(q) + q\frac{d\text{AC}_s(q)}{dq}$$

This equation says that MC$_s(q) = $ AC$_s(q)$ plus a correction factor that is the product of quantity and the slope of the AC$_s(q)$ function at that quantity. When dAC$_s(q)/dq = 0$, the slope of the short-run average cost function is zero, and so AC(q) is at a minimum and the equation indicates AC$(q) = $ MC$_s(q)$. When dAC$_s(q)/dq > 0$, the slope of the short-run average cost function is positive, and so AC$_s(q)$ is increasing and MC$_s(q)$ is greater than AC$_s(q)$. When dAC$_s(q)/dL < 0$, the slope of the short-run average cost function is negative, and so AC$_s(q)$ is decreasing and MC$_s(q)$ is less than AC$_s(q)$.

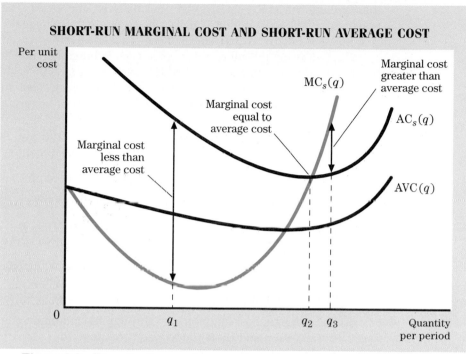

Figure 6-2   When the firm produces q_1, short-run marginal cost is less than short-run average cost, and so short-run average cost declines. At output q_2 short-run marginal cost equals short-run average cost, and so the average is constant. At output q_3 short-run marginal cost is greater than short-run average cost, and so short-run average cost increases.

6-2 short-run marginal cost is less than short-run average cost when the firm produces q_1 units, and so short-run average cost is declining. When the firm produces q_2 units, short-run marginal cost equals short-run average cost, and so the slope of the short-run average cost function is zero in Figure 6-2. For any quantity larger than q_2, the slope of the short-run average cost function is positive, and so short-run marginal cost is *greater* than short-run average cost. For example, short-run marginal cost exceeds short-run average cost when the firm produces q_3 units, and so short-run average cost is increasing. There is a corresponding relationship between the marginal and average variable costs,[6] and when marginal cost is less

---

[6] Total variable cost is equal to average variable cost times quantity: $V(q) = \text{AVC}(q)q$. Short-run marginal cost equals the slope of the total variable cost function. Differentiating this equation with respect to q yields

$$\text{MC}_s(q) = \frac{dV(q)}{dq} = \text{AVC}(q) + q\,\frac{d\text{AVC}(q)}{dq}$$

$\text{MC}_s(q) = \text{AVC}(q)$ plus a correction factor equal to the product of quantity and the slope of the $\text{AVC}(q)$ function. When $d[\text{AVC}(q)]/dq = 0$, $\text{AVC}(q)$ is at a minimum and $\text{AVC}(q) = \text{MC}_s(q)$. If $d[\text{AVC}(q)]/dq > 0$, $\text{AVC}(q)$ is increasing and $\text{MC}_s(q)$ is greater than $\text{AVC}(q)$. When $d\text{AVC}(q)/dL < 0$, $\text{AVC}(q)$ is decreasing and $\text{MC}_s(q)$ is less than $\text{AVC}(q)$.

than average variable cost, average variable cost decreases. The slope of the average variable cost function is zero when marginal cost equals average variable cost and it is positive when marginal cost exceeds average variable cost.

When drawing the short-run average cost, average variable, and marginal cost functions, you need to exercise care so that your graphs meet the conditions that we have described. You will be using graphs of these cost functions to solve problems, and so you must learn to draw these curves accurately. At the risk of being repetitive, let's restate the salient points. Your graphs of the short-run cost functions should meet the following five conditions, and you should be able to explain to yourself why the curves in Figure 6-1*b* satisfy each of these conditions.

1. Short-run average cost approaches infinity when q approaches zero.

2. Short-run average cost declines as quantity increases until it reaches a minimum, and then it increases.

3. The difference between $AC_s(q)$ and AVC decreases as the quantity increases because AFC $= F/q$ decreases.

4. Average variable cost normally reaches a minimum at a smaller quantity than the quantity where short-run average cost reaches a minimum.[7]

5. The marginal cost function goes through the minimum points of the average variable cost and short-run average cost functions.

The Area under the Marginal Cost Function

Before we use the short-run cost functions to solve some problems, we need to establish that the area under the marginal cost function between any two quantities equals the increase in variable cost when the firm's output increases from one quantity to the other.

Let's show this first by way of a numerical example. Table 6-1 lists the quantity produced in column 1, variable cost in column 2, and short-run marginal cost in column 3. Column 4 shows the sum of the marginal costs for each unit up to and including the last unit produced.

Figure 6-3*a* shows the marginal cost of a unit increase in output. Total variable cost is $80 when the firm produces 1 unit, and the marginal cost of producing the first unit is also $80. When the firm produces 1 unit, the sum of the marginal cost in column 4 is just $80. If the firm produces 2 units, column 2 shows that variable cost equals $140. Figure 6-3*a* shows that the marginal cost of the second unit is $60, and so the sum of the two values of marginal cost is $80 + $60 or $140. The marginal cost of the first unit plus the marginal cost of the second unit equals total

---

[7] $AVC(q) = V(q)/q$. As q approaches zero, $V(q)$ gets smaller and smaller, as does q. Therefore, the ratio of $V(q)$ to q is indeterminate. To evaluate this indeterminate form, we differentiate both the numerator and the denominator and evaluate each as q approaches zero. The numerator is $dV/dq = MC_s(q)$ or marginal cost as q approaches zero, and the denominator is 1. Therefore, as q gets smaller and smaller, $AVC(q)$ approaches marginal cost. Since the *slope* of the total variable cost function is marginal cost and approaches some limiting nonzero value as q approaches zero, AVC approaches that value as q approaches zero. Therefore, AVC $= MC_s$ as q approaches zero.

Table 6-1 TOTAL VARIABLE COST AND THE SUM OF MARGINAL COSTS

QUANTITY PRODUCED (1)	TOTAL VARIABLE COST($) (2)	SHORT-RUN MARGINAL COST($) (3)	SUM OF SHORT-RUN MARGINAL COSTS ($) (4)
1	80	80	80
2	140	60	140
3	240	100	240
4	380	140	380

variable cost of producing 2 units or $140. Geometrically, taking the sum of the values of marginal cost in this manner is equivalent to calculating the area under the marginal cost function up to 2 units. Now skip to the fourth unit. The variable cost of producing 4 units is $380, and the marginal cost of producing the fourth unit is $140. The sum of the marginal costs is $380 ($80 + $60 + $100 + $140). Here again, the sum of the marginal costs equals total variable cost of producing 4 units.

This numerical example can be extended one step further. Suppose you want to determine the incremental cost the firm incurs by increasing production from 2 to 4 units. Column 1 in Table 6-1 shows variable cost increases from $140 to $380 or by $240. However, we reach the same conclusion by taking the area under the marginal cost function between 2 and 4 units, the shaded area in Figure 6-3*a*. The area under the marginal cost function is equal to $100 + $140 = $240. Therefore, the increase in variable cost equals the area under the marginal cost function between 2 and 4 units.

Figure 6-3*b* shows the average variable and the marginal cost functions when the quantity variable is continuous. To calculate the increase in variable cost from increasing production from q' to q^*, we take the area under the marginal cost function from q' to q^*, or area 2.[8] To measure the increase in variable cost caused by increasing the production from zero to q', we take the area under the marginal cost function from $q = 0$ to $q = q'$, or area 1.

The area under the marginal cost function between q' and q^* units is equal to the increase in total variable cost from increasing output from q' to q^* units.

[8] Mathematically, the area under the marginal cost function MC(q) between q' and q^* units is

$$\int_{q'}^{q^*} MC(q)\, dq = \int_{q'}^{q^*} \frac{dV(q)}{dq} = V(q^*) - V(q')$$

The area under the marginal cost function equals the *change* in total variable cost when output increases from q' to q^*.

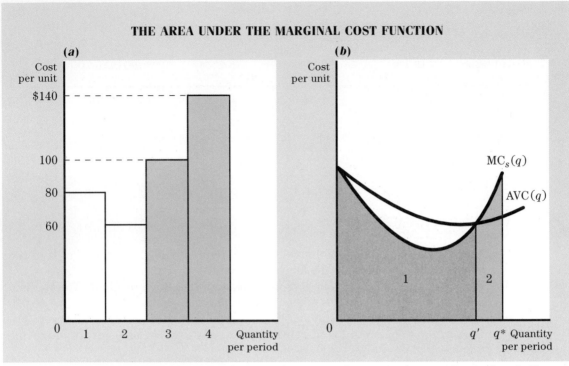

Figure 6-3   (*a*) Marginal cost for unit changes in the quantity produced. The area under the rectangles up to any quantity is the variable cost of producing that quantity. In (*b*) quantity is assumed to be continuous. The increase in variable cost from increasing output from q' to q^* is the area under the marginal cost function between q' and q^*, or area 2. The variable cost of producing q' is the area under the marginal cost function up to the quantity q', or area 1.

6-4   IDENTIFYING THE RELEVANT COSTS WHEN SOLVING SHORT-RUN COST PROBLEMS

With these preliminaries established, we can use the short-run cost functions to show how a firm that uses marginal analysis is more likely to minimize cost than one that does not.

APPLICATION **6-1**

How to Schedule Production between a New Plant and an Old Plant

A firm has two plants which it constructed at different times so they have different cost functions. Plant 1 is 30 years old and located in a northern city. Plant 2 is only

3 years old and located in the South. The short-run average cost functions of the two plants are shown in Figure 6-4. Cost per unit is on the vertical axis, and quantity is on the horizontal axis. Plant 2, the younger plant, has a lower average cost at each rate of output and is much more efficient than plant 1.

The responsibility of the production manager is to minimize the total cost of producing the monthly quota, which for the next month is q^* units as shown on the horizontal axis of Figure 6-4. The manager realizes that he cannot minimize total cost by producing the entire quota in plant 2 because short-run average cost would be much too high. Given the monthly quota, the production manager recognizes that he must use both plants. He schedules production at both to minimize the simple average of the short-run average cost for the two.

To achieve this objective, the production manager decides to assign q_1' units to plant 1, minimizing its average cost, and to assign q_2' units to plant 2 so that q_1'

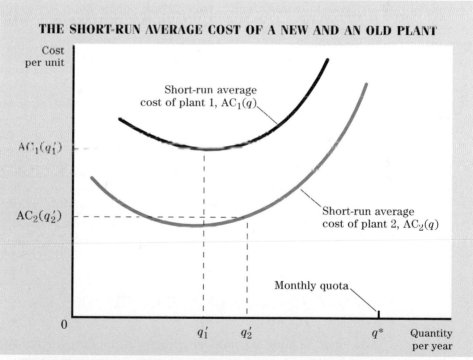

Figure 6-4   The monthly production requirement of the firm is q^* units. The firm has an old plant with a short-run average cost function AC_1 and a new plant with a short-run average cost function AC_2. The production manager schedules q_1' units at plant 1 and thereby guarantees that the average cost at plant 1 is at a minimum. The remainder of the monthly requirement, q_2', is scheduled for plant 2. The production manager says this schedule will minimize the simple average of the short-run average costs and meet the production quota. Does this schedule minimize total cost?

$+ q_2' = q^*$. The production manager believes this production schedule makes the simple average of the short-run average cost of the two plants as low as possible while meeting the monthly quota.

Some members of the management team are very upset when they learn about the production schedule. By scheduling q_1' units at plant 1 and only q_2' units at plant 2, the firm ends up with a production schedule where short-run average cost at plant 1, $AC_1(q_1')$, is greater than short-run average cost at plant 2, $AC_2(q_2')$. They cannot fathom how this can be the cost-minimizing solution and why the new plant is not producing more since its average cost is less than the average cost for plant 1. During several heated meetings, the production manager defends his policy by noting that average cost at both plants will increase if plant 2 produces more and plant 1 less. He asks his critics, "How can total cost decrease if average cost increases at each plant?" He points out that his responsibility is to produce the monthly quota at the lowest total cost—not to show a special preference for plant 2.

Has the production manager found the cost-minimizing solution or do the members of the management team have a valid point in advocating greater output at plant 2? The first step in finding the lowest cost solution is to identify what costs are affected by the manager's decision. The production manager should totally ignore fixed cost because the fixed cost at each plant is a bygone that the firm incurs no matter what the production manager decides. The production schedule affects only the variable cost of each plant. Therefore, the production manager should find a schedule that minimizes Z, the sum of total variable costs,

$$\text{Minimize } Z = V_1(q_1) + V_2(q_2)$$

and meets the monthly quota.

What condition must the manager satisfy if he minimizes the sum of total variable costs? Shifting production from one plant to another will raise the variable cost at the plant where output rises and lower the variable cost at the plant where output falls. The marginal cost of producing Δq_2 units at plant 2 is $\Delta V_2/\Delta q_2$, and the marginal cost of producing Δq_1 units at plant 1 is $\Delta V_1/\Delta q_1$. Suppose the production manager schedules production so that the marginal costs for the two plants are not equal:

$$MC_1 = \frac{\Delta V_1}{\Delta q_1} \neq \frac{\Delta V_2}{\Delta q_2} = MC_2$$

Then, the firm does not produce q^* units at the lowest cost. For example, at q^* units of output, suppose the marginal cost of producing another unit is $6 at plant 1 and $3 at plant 2. By producing one more unit at plant 2, the firm incurs an additional cost of $3. By producing one less unit at plant 1 the firm saves $6. The sum of variable costs falls by $3, and the firm is still meeting the production quota. As long as marginal cost differs across plants, the firm does not minimize the sum of total variable costs. The cost-minimizing solution requires *marginal cost* (not average cost) to be the same at all plants.

Minimum total cost occurs when **marginal costs are equalized at all plants.**

Let's use a graph to show why the equality of marginal costs minimizes the sum of variable costs.[9] In Figure 6-5 the length of the horizontal axis is q^* units, the total production quota. The origin for plant 1 is 0 on the left-hand side of the graph. The output of plant 1 increases on moving from left to right. The marginal cost function of this plant goes through the minimum point of its short-run average cost function. The quantity of plant 2 increases from right to left with $0'$ as the origin. Plant 2's short-run average and marginal cost functions start with $0'$ as the origin. Each point on the horizontal axis in Figure 6-5 represents an allocation of production between the two plants that satisfies the monthly quota of q^* units.

The production manager's proposed schedule assigns q_1' units for plant 1 and thereby minimizes the short-run average cost of this plant. When plant 1 produces q_1', plant 2 produces q_2', and Figure 6-5 shows that the marginal cost of plant 1 exceeds the marginal cost of plant 2. Clearly, the production manager's schedule does not minimize the sum of variable costs. Plant 2 should be producing more and plant 1 less, although this will increase the average cost of production at both plants.

Figure 6-6 reproduces the marginal cost functions of the two plants. The firm minimizes total production cost when marginal costs are the same at both plants and plant 1 produces q_1'' while plant 2 produces q_2''. We can measure the cost savings by showing that the variable cost of plant 1 decreases by more than the variable cost increases at plant 2 when plant 2 produces more and plant 1 less. Area 2, the area under the marginal cost function of plant 2 between q_2' and q_2'', is equal to the increase in variable cost when plant 2 produces more. The sum of areas 1 and 2, the area under the marginal cost function of plant 1 between q_1' and q_1'', is equal to the decrease in variable cost at plant 1. The net cost saving is equal to area 1. Therefore, there is merit to the management team's suggestion that plant 2 should produce more.

Why did the production manager fail to find the cost minimizing solution? His first mistake was to focus on average cost at each plant. This proved to be a serious error because the average cost includes average fixed cost and the production

---

[9] The production manager must satisfy $q_1 + q_2 = q^*$ and minimize

$$Z = V_1(q_1) + V_2(q_2).$$

The condition for minimizing Z can be found by substituting $q_2 = q^* - q_1$ for q_2 in the equation for Z. Z becomes:

$$Z = V_1(q_1) + V_2(q^* - q_1)$$

The first-order condition for a cost minimum is

$$\frac{dZ}{dq_1} = \frac{dV_1}{dq_1} + \frac{dV_2}{dq_2}\frac{dq_2}{dq_1} = \frac{dV_1}{dq_1} - \frac{dV_2}{dq_2} = 0$$

since the constraint $q_1 + q_2 = q^*$ requires $dq_2/dq_1 = -1$. Marginal cost must be the same in all plants.

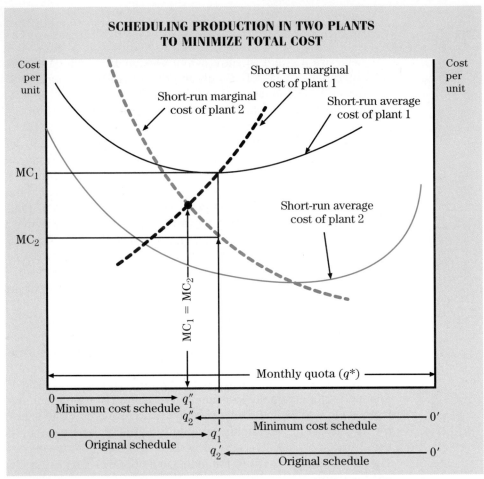

Figure 6-5 Total cost of scheduling q^* units in two plants is minimized if the firm schedules production so that marginal costs are equal in the two plants. The schedule proposed by the production manager underutilizes plant 2 and overutilizes plant 1. Marginal costs of the two plants are not equal. By expanding the quantity produced in plant 2 to q_2'' and reducing the quantity in plant 1 to q_1'', total cost decreases although the average cost of both plants increases.

manager has no control over fixed cost. In the short run he should have completely ignored fixed cost and just concentrated on minimizing the sum of variable costs. The production manager was allowing past decisions that determined fixed cost to influence future decisions. This example shows why it is critical for a manager to identify those costs which will be influenced by his decision and concentrate on minimizing these costs. His second mistake was not thinking in incremental terms. By failing to do this, the production manager advanced the superficially plausible but defective criterion of minimizing the average of the two short-run

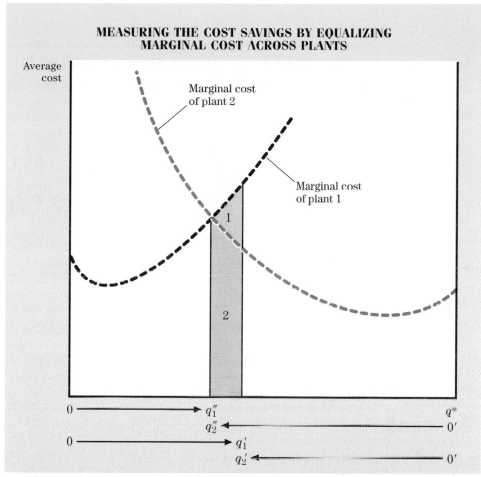

MEASURING THE COST SAVINGS BY EQUALIZING MARGINAL COST ACROSS PLANTS

Figure 6-6 Total cost is minimized when marginal cost is the same at both plants. By increasing the quantity from q_2' to q_2'' at plant 2, total cost increases by area 2. By decreasing the quantity from q_1' to q_1'' at plant 1, the cost savings become equal to the sum of areas 1 and 2. Therefore, the cost savings from equalizing marginal costs equal area 1.

average costs. If he had thought in terms of marginal cost, he would have recognized why the average cost criterion is defective.

The management team deserves only faint praise, however. They are so enamored of the new plant that they want to produce everything at it. It is true that the new plant is more efficient than the old one *at each quantity*. However, this is an irrelevant consideration as well because the plants do not have to produce the same quantity. At the cost-minimizing solution the two plants are *equally efficient at the margin* since marginal costs at both plants are equal.

APPLICATION 6-2

Why "Never Give Up" Is Not Always the Best Advice[10]

Everyone has received advice at some time from a friend or a parent to never give up. Such advice involves the "fixed cost fallacy." Suppose you plan to major in engineering, perhaps because one of your parents did. However, after you have completed several engineering courses, you find the subject uninteresting and wonder if history is more your calling. You may receive advice from your friends or parents to keep working and not to give up because you have put so much time into the engineering courses. This advice is based on the sunk cost fallacy. The time that you have spent in successfully completing the engineering courses is a sunk cost that you cannot recover. It is a bygone and should not affect your future decisions. Saying "Never give up" says that you should let past decisions affect your current decision.

Richard Nesbett and two colleagues surveyed University of Michigan faculty members and seniors and asked them whether they had ever walked out of a bad movie, refused to finish a bad meal, or terminated a bad research project with less promising prospects. Those students and faculty who had not let past decisions affect their future behavior avoided the sunk cost fallacy. If you walk out of a bad movie, you are saying that there are better things to do with your time than sit through the rest of the film. Moreover, your decision to walk out should not depend on how much you paid: the price of admission is a sunk cost and should not affect your decision to leave.

Nesbett et al. found that faculty members who used cost-benefit reasoning had higher salaries relative to their age and department and that economics faculty members used this reasoning more often than faculty members in the humanities or in biology. Interestingly, they also found that seniors who used this reasoning had higher SAT scores and had taken more economics courses.

APPLICATION 6-3

Inefficient or Efficient Environmental Regulation

The Environmental Protection Agency imposes detailed emission standards on manufacturing plants. These standards, designed to improve air quality, impose pollution limits on emission sources within a plant. At first glance this regulatory policy sounds eminently sensible and even reasonable. To improve air quality, each source should contribute to the effort.

Let's examine the economic consequences of this source-by-source regulation for a plant that has two sources of dust emissions. In Figure 6-7a the total tons of emissions from source 1 are plotted on the horizontal axis, and the marginal cost

[10] Based on Alan L. Otten, "Economic Perspective Produces Steady Yields," *The Wall Street Journal,* March 31, 1992, p. B1.

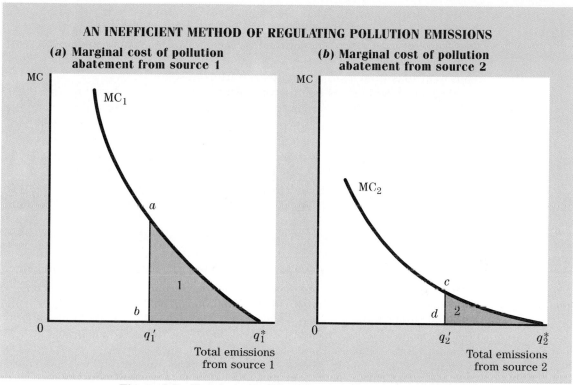

AN INEFFICIENT METHOD OF REGULATING POLLUTION EMISSIONS

(a) Marginal cost of pollution abatement from source 1

(b) Marginal cost of pollution abatement from source 2

Figure 6-7   Dust is emitted from two sources in a plant. Source 1 emits q_1^* tons of dust per day and source 2 emits q_2^* tons of dust per day without regulation. Source by source regulation requires source 1 to reduce emissions to q_1' and source 2 to reduce emissions to q_2'. The incremental cost of reducing emissions from source 1 is equal to area 1, and the incremental cost of reducing emissions from source 2 is equal to area 2. The source-by-source regulation does not equate the marginal cost of reducing emissions across sources.

of reducing emissions from source 1 on the vertical axis. Figure 6-7*b* shows the relationship between total emissions and the marginal cost of reducing emissions from source 2 at the same plant. (The two sources could be two smokestacks at the same plant.) We assume that source 1 would emit q_1^* tons of dust per day and source 2 would emit q_2^* tons without any regulation. Suppose a source-by-source regulatory program requires source 1 to reduce emissions from q_1^* tons per day to q_1' tons per day, and source 2 to reduce emissions from q_2^* tons per day to q_2' tons per day. The total cost of reducing emissions by $q_1^* - q_1'$ tons of dust per day is equal to the area under the marginal cost function for source 1, or area 1. The total cost of reducing emissions by $q_2^* - q_2'$ tons per day from source 2 is equal to the area under the marginal cost function for source 2, or area 2.

Source-by-source regulation of emissions can be very costly because it ignores the different marginal cost functions for pollution abatement across different locations, and even within the same plant. The marginal cost of reducing the last ounce of dust at source 1 when the plant removes q_1' tons is ab in Figure 6-7*a* and is greater than cd in Figure 6-7*b*, the marginal cost of removing the last ounce of dust from source 2 when the plant removes q_2' tons. Differences in marginal cost occur because source-by-source regulation mandates that the plant reduce emissions to q_1' tons from source 1 and to q_2' tons from source 2.

Regulatory authorities require total plant emissions be reduced by $(q_1^* - q_1')$ + $(q_2^* - q_2')$ tons. Is there a more cost-efficient way of reducing emissions by the same amount? Instead of using command and control regulations and specifying how much to remove from each source, suppose the firm is instructed to reduce emissions by the same total amount as before, but that the management can decide what is the most cost-efficient method. This method of regulation is called the *bubble concept* because it is as if a giant bubble surrounds the plant so that the regulator does not know how many sources there are. The regulator's only concern is with the total emissions escaping from the bubble.

How would the management of the plant respond under the bubble concept? They would find the solution where the marginal cost of reducing a ton of dust from source 1 equals the marginal cost of reducing a ton of dust from source 2. In Figure 6-8 the total mandated reduction of emissions for this plant is on the horizontal axis. The marginal cost of reducing tons of dust per day from source 1 is on the left vertical axis, and from source 2, on the right vertical axis. MC_1 and MC_2 are the marginal cost functions of reducing emissions from the two sources. The marginal cost of reducing a ton of dust emissions from each source increases as the plant removes more tons of dust, and it becomes increasingly expensive to remove dust from a given source as the amount removed increases. It is in the self-interest of management to minimize the cost of removing emissions. Management must find a solution where the marginal cost of dust removal at both sources is the same. The firm removes q_1'' tons of dust from source 1 and q_2'' tons of dust from source 2. Because the marginal cost of reducing emissions is equal for all sources, the bubble concept results in a more cost-efficient solution for a *given* reduction of emissions than the more detailed source-by-source method of regulation. Check your understanding of the analysis by presenting a geometric measure of the firm's cost savings if the regulator shifts from source-by-source regulation to the bubble concept.

Are the cost savings from implementing the bubble concept likely to be large? Robert Hahn has studied innovative environmental policies like the bubble concept and estimates that the 40 bubble plans that received federal approval saved firms about $300 million.[11]

Marginal analysis is useful not only for firms but also for regulatory authorities. Inefficient regulatory programs just create more political opposition to these programs. Some but not all environmental organizations recognize this fundamental point and support efforts to introduce more efficiency into regulatory design. The bubble concept and other innovative regulatory policies are gradually gaining more acceptance as preferable forms of regulation.

[11] For a summary of incentive-based mechanisms in the implementation of environmental policies, see Robert W. Hahn, "Economic Presciptions for Environmental Problems: How the Patient Followed the Doctor's Orders," *Journal of Economic Perspectives* 3, no. 2 (Spring 1989), pp. 95–114.

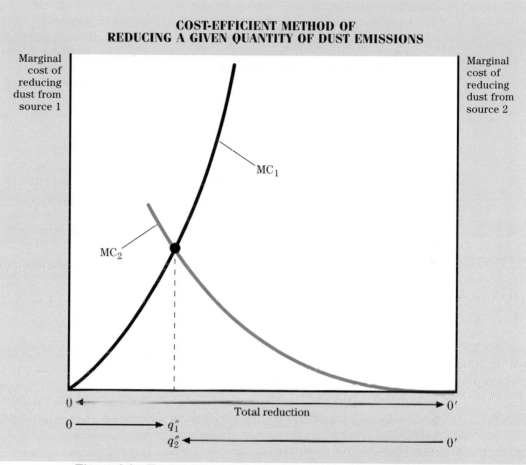

**COST-EFFICIENT METHOD OF
REDUCING A GIVEN QUANTITY OF DUST EMISSIONS**

Figure 6-8   The lowest cost of reducing a given amount of emissions is to equalize the marginal costs across all sources. Source 1 reduces emissions by q_1'' tons of dust per day. Source 2 reduces emissions by q_2'' tons of dust per day. The bubble concept allows each firm to decide what is the cost-efficient method to achieve a given reduction in the total quantity of emissions.

APPLICATION 6-4

Why Are Fewer Sellers of Used Homes Using Brokers?

In the 90s fewer sellers of used houses are willing to pay the 6 percent commission to full-service real estate agents and, instead, are either selling their houses without a broker or using discount brokers. Why are more owners selling their own homes? A real estate analyst suggests that more sellers are selling their own homes because house prices are not increasing as rapidly in the 90s as in the 80s. Instead of having a 50 percent capital gain after five years of occupancy, as was more common in the 80s, sellers in the 90s have moderate, and in some cases, no capital gains to report. Without the anticipation of large capital gains, more owners are selling their own houses to save on broker commissions. How valid is this explanation for the increase in do-it-yourself house selling? A seller should not let the size of a prospective capital gain determine whether the seller should hire a full-service broker. Whether the capital gain is likely to be large, moderate, or small is a bygone. To decide whether or not to hire a broker, the seller should compare the value of the time that will be saved and the higher price that will be received if a broker's services are used to the broker's commission cost. It is this comparison that should determine whether an owner should hire a broker, not the size of the prospective capital gain. A minority of sellers may not have any capital gains and cannot write off broker commission cost on their taxes, so they would be more likely to go it alone, but most sellers still report capital gains. The declining use of full-service brokers in the 90s may have more to do with a lower value of time in the slower-growth 90s and the emergence of discount real estate brokers or other emerging sales channels including the Internet.

6-5   DERIVING THE LONG-RUN AVERAGE COST FUNCTION FROM THE SHORT-RUN AVERAGE COST FUNCTIONS

In the long run a firm selects a plant size and a number of workers such that it produces each quantity at the lowest total cost. How does the company determine which plant size produces a given quantity at the lowest long-run total and average costs?

Let's begin with a description of how the firm identifies the long-run average cost function when it has a choice of just three plant sizes. Then we will demonstrate how to derive the long-run average cost function when the firm selects from a continuum of plant sizes.

The Long-Run Average Cost Function with a Limited Choice of Plants

The graphs of the short-run average cost functions for three different sizes of plants are shown in Figure 6-9. $AC_1(q)$ is the average cost function of the smallest plant, $AC_2(q)$ is the average cost function of the medium-sized plant, and $AC_3(q)$ is the average cost function of the largest plant. If the firm expects to produce any quantity between 0 and q_1 units indefinitely, it will build the smallest plant with the short-run average cost function of $AC_1(q)$ because this plant has the lowest short-run average cost for producing any quantity less than q_1. The firm will build a medium-sized plant with $AC_2(q)$ if it expects to produce any output between q_1

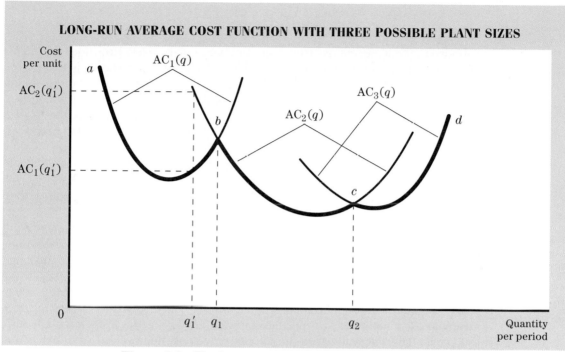

LONG-RUN AVERAGE COST FUNCTION WITH THREE POSSIBLE PLANT SIZES

Figure 6-9 The long-run average cost function shows the lowest average cost of producing each quantity. If the firm can select among only three plant sizes, the long run average cost function becomes the scalloped curve *abcd*. Plant 1 with AC_1 has the lowest average cost of producing any quantity less than q_1. Plant 2 with AC_2 has the lowest average cost of producing any quantity between q_1 and q_2. Plant 3 has the lowest average cost of producing any quantity greater than q_2.

and q_2 indefinitely, and the largest plant with $AC_3(q)$ if it plans to produce an output greater than q_2.

Although all three plants can produce any quantity less than q_1, the smallest plant produces it at the lowest short-run average cost. For example, if the firm decides to produce q_1' in Figure 6-9, the average cost of producing q_1' with the smallest plant is $AC_1(q_1')$, the short-run average cost. If the firm errs and builds the medium-sized plant, the mistake is costly because the short-run average cost, $AC_2(q_1')$, is higher. Clearly plant 1 has a lower short-run average cost and is the cost-efficient plant for producing q_1'.

The procedure for finding the long-run average cost function from the firm's short-run average cost functions is relatively simple. For *each quantity* on the horizontal axis, move up vertically until you reach the first short-run average cost function. The plant with that average cost function produces that quantity at the lowest average and total costs in the long run. In the present case the firm has just three choices for plant size, and so the long-run average cost function becomes the scalloped average cost function *abcd* in Figure 6-9.

The Long-Run Average Cost Function
with a Continuum of Plant Sizes

Suppose the firm can choose from a continuum of plant sizes. How does the shape of the long-run average cost function change? Figure 6-10a shows just three of *many* short-run total cost functions. The short-run total cost function of one plant is $C_1(q)$. This plant produces the quantity q_1^* and only q_1^* at the lowest total cost. A larger plant with the cost function $C_2(q)$ produces the quantity q_2^* at the lowest total cost. Finally, the plant with the short-run total cost function $C_3(q)$ produces q_3^* at the lowest total cost. Other short-run total cost functions exist, but we do not draw them to keep Figure 6-10 from becoming totally incomprehensible. Each plant would have the lowest total cost for producing some specific quantity. The long-run total cost function $C_L(q)$ is formed by connecting all the points that identify the minimum total cost of producing each quantity.

Given the long-run total cost function, we derive the **long-run average and marginal cost functions** and include them in Figure 6-10b. The long-run average cost function becomes the smooth U-shaped function labeled $AC_L(q)$, and the long-run marginal cost function is $MC_L(q)$. When there is a continuum of plant sizes, each plant has the lowest average cost for producing a unique quantity—not a range of quantities. If the firm expects to produce q_1^*, the plant with the short-run average cost function $AC_1(q)$ produces q_1^* and only q_1^* at the lowest average and total costs. This means that the short-run average cost function $AC_1(q)$ touches the long-run average cost function only when the firm produces q_1^* units. At any other quantity the short-run average cost function $AC_1(q)$ lies above the long-run average cost function because other plant sizes can produce these other quantities at a lower average cost than plant 1 can. Plant 1 can produce only q_1^* at the *lowest* average and total costs. If the firm wants to produce q_2^*, the plant with the average cost function $AC_2(q)$ produces q_2^* and only q_2^* at the lowest total and average costs. The average cost function labeled $AC_2(q)$ touches the long-run average cost function only when the quantity is q_2^*. Here again, plant 2 cannot produce any other output at lowest average cost. Finally, the plant with the short-run average cost function $AC_3(q)$ can produce q_3^* at the lowest average cost.

The procedure for deriving the long-run average cost function remains the same. For each quantity, find the plant with the lowest short-run average cost. There is a minimum average cost for each quantity. We form the long-run average cost function by connecting all such points. The long-run average cost function shows the lowest average cost of producing each quantity. The long-run marginal cost function in Figure 6-10b shows the incremental cost of producing another unit.

We have already described the relationship that must exist between the short-run average and marginal cost functions and between the long-run average and marginal cost functions. However, we have not discussed how to relate the short- and long-run marginal and average costs to each other.

When the firm produces q_2^*, Figure 6-10b shows that the long-run average cost is at a minimum and $AC_L = MC_L = AC_s = MC_s$. This set of equalities holds only at the minimum point of a U-shaped long-run average cost function.

At all other quantities two separate sets of equalities hold: $AC_L = AC_s \neq MC_L = MC_s$. At any quantity other than q_2^* the two separate equalities are (1)

THE LONG-RUN TOTAL AND AVERAGE COST FUNCTIONS WHEN PLANT SIZE IS CONTINUOUS

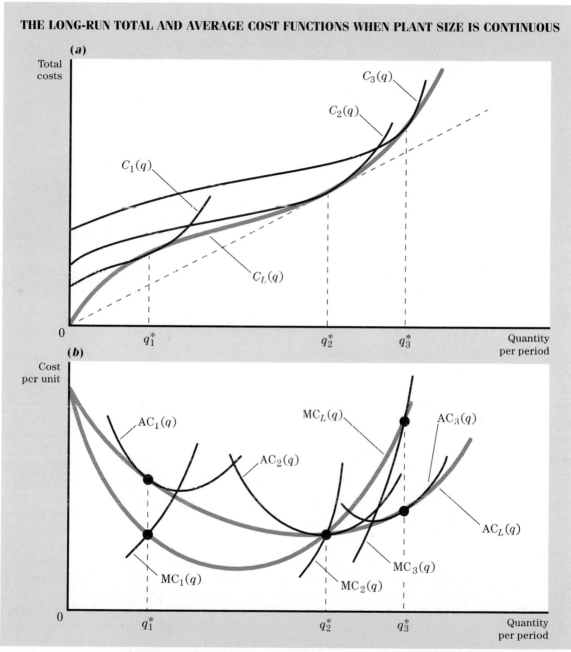

Figure 6-10   The long-run average cost function is derived by finding the plant size that can produce each quantity at the lowest average cost. Each plant size can produce a specific quantity at the lowest average cost. For example, the plant with $AC_1(q)$ can produce q_1^* at the lowest average cost.

short-run and long-run average cost are equal because the particular plant produces that output at the lowest average cost and (2) short-run and long-run marginal cost are equal because the marginal cost of expanding output is the short-run marginal cost of that plant. However, the average cost does not equal the marginal cost.

The three situations can be summarized as follows.

1. If $q < q_2^*$, $AC_L = AC_s > MC_L = MC_s$.

2. If $q = q_2^*$, $AC_L = AC_s = MC_L = MC_s$.

3. If $q > q_2^*$, $AC_L = AC_s < MC_L = MC_s$.

For example, in Figure 6-10b the short-run average cost function $AC_1(q)$ is tangent to the long-run average cost function when the firm produces q_1^*, and so short-run average cost equals long-run average cost. Because the slope of the short-run total cost function equals the slope of the long-run total cost function when $q = q_1^*$, long-run marginal cost equals short-run marginal cost. However, short- and long-run marginal costs are less than short- and long-run average costs.

6-6   THE NUMBER OF FIRMS AND THE LONG-RUN COST FUNCTION

The shape of the long-run average cost function limits the number of firms that can exist in an industry. The long-run average cost function in Figure 6-10 is U-shaped. When long-run average cost decreases, the firm experiences **internal economies of scale.** When all factors are variable, a k percent increase in output increases total cost by less than k percent. After the firm reaches a certain size, long-run average cost increases and the firm experiences **internal diseconomies of scale.** A k percent increase in output increases costs by more than k percent.[12]

The shape of the long-run average cost function plays an important role in explaining why there are many firms in some industries and only a few in other industries. The number of firms is large when the long-run average cost function is U-shaped and the market size is large. With a U-shaped long-run average cost function internal diseconomies of scale place a limit on the size of a firm; when the market is large, the quantity corresponding to the minimum of the long-run average cost function does not account for a significant proportion of the total market. A company that is too large will have higher average cost than a smaller firm. Why are there many and not just a few farms producing wheat? Internal diseconomies of scale must set in after a firm reaches a certain size. Just imagine the severe management problems that would emerge if all wheat farms in the United States became one huge collective farm. How could such a large farm be managed? The existence of many companies in an industry is an indication that internal diseconomies of scale set in at a relatively low level of output.

---

[12] The expression "internal economies of scale" as used here is synonymous with the expression "returns to scale" used in Chapter 5. Given factor prices, the two expressions refer to the same phenomenon—a k percent increase in output requires a less than k percent in the increase in inputs. Therefore, long-run average cost decreases as the firm produces a larger quantity.

Diseconomies of Scale and Industries with Many Firms

How do economists know that there are internal diseconomies of scale? Usually they draw this inference by looking at the number of firms and the size distribution of firms in industries. Many industries have a large number of producers, and so the market share of even the largest is quite small. For example, in 1982 there were 1,824 firms producing women's blouses and 853 producing fluid milk. The large number of firms in these industries suggests that diseconomies of scale limit the size of any one firm.

Economies of Scale and Industries with Few Firms

In some industries the technology creates persistent economies of scale. The larger the output produced by a firm, the lower the long-run per unit cost. The sources of these economies usually spring from the indivisibility of a factor of production. There may be a minimum efficient level of output such that plant size cannot be scaled down to produce one unit of a product. Advertisers buying time on network television used to face this situation because a company would have to purchase a network package rather than air time in specific broadcast areas. A small regional firm that sold its product in only one region of the country had to pay the national rate and was at a substantial cost disadvantage compared to a national company that sold its product in all regions of the country. Another example of indivisibility involves the minimum size of an automobile dealership. In small rural local markets only the largest manufacturers have automobile dealerships. Not every brand exists in these markets because of the indivisibility of the size of a dealership.

Another source of internal economies of scale is the relationship between a volume and an area. In Chapter 5 we saw that the long-run average cost of a pipeline decreased with quantity and so there were internal economies of scale. The cost of the materials for the construction of a pipeline increases with the diameter of the pipeline. The output of the pipeline depends on the area of its cross-section, which increases with the square of the diameter. As the diameter increases, total cost increases less than proportionally with output, and these physical relationships create internal returns to scale.

Finally, specialization of functions fosters economies of scale. In large firms there is greater specialization of functions than in smaller firms. Specialists perform such diverse functions as advertising, quality control, welding, and purchasing within the firm.

Industries with continual internal economies of scale are natural monopolies, which exist when the total cost of producing a given quantity is lowest if only one firm produces the product.

A **natural monopoly** exists when a single firm can produce a given quantity at lowest total cost.

Many public utilities are said to have this type of cost structure. Where there are persistent internal economies of scale, the lowest total cost of producing any quantity requires just one firm in the industry. The total cost of producing a given quantity increases when there is more than one firm. An industry in which there are continual internal economies of scale evolves into a single-firm industry. In some industries internal economies of scale exist but become less important and disappear beyond a certain quantity. In some industries the number of firms in the industry is typically small. For example, there were only nine chewing gum manufacturers in 1982 and the leading four companies accounted for 95 percent of sales. The breakfast cereal industry had 32 producers but the leading 4 companies accounted for 86 percent of sales. It is not an accident that the number of firms is relatively small in these industries. The internal economies of scale in the manufacture, promotion, and distribution of these products limit the number of firms that are cost-efficient. It is quite likely that the shape of the long-run average cost function explains the small number of producers in these cases.

Now that we have introduced the concept of the long-run average cost function, let's see what can and cannot be explained by the shape of this function.

APPLICATION **6-5**

The Emergence of the Standard Oil Company

One of the most prosperous firms in the history of American business was the Standard Oil Company of New Jersey. Standard Oil and its founder, the much vilified John D. Rockefeller, were so successful that the government sued the company in 1911 in a landmark antitrust case for monopolizing the market for refined petroleum products. At the time of the antitrust suit Standard Oil's market share exceeded 75 percent.[13] Standard Oil lost the case, and the firm was subdivided into several smaller regional companies.

Why was this company so successful and why did this industry change so much in such a short time? Many historians and economists view John D. Rockefeller as an unscrupulous businessman who used unfair methods to eliminate competitors. Why didn't firms in other industries have as much success? Surely, there were other businessmen in America at the time whose desire for wealth was as intense as Rockefeller's and who would have been willing to adopt unscrupulous methods of competition. Why didn't they succeed?

One interesting fact uncovered by John McGee in his study of the antitrust case is that Standard Oil was not always a dominant player in the refining market. McGee reports that the company was one of many in the industry and had only about 10 percent of the market in 1870. Between 1870 and 1890 the company went on a merger binge. The government claimed that Standard Oil acquired 123 refineries from 1870 to 1890 or 1900, although there is some disagreement as to when these acquisitions occurred.

Standard Oil had only a small share of the refining market in 1870, but 20 years later the industry was far different. A dominant leader had emerged with more than 75 percent of the market. Increasing any company's market share from 10 to more than 75 percent over 20 years is a remarkable feat, a rare event in the annals of American business. How can we explain this transformation?

One hypothesis that might explain this change is the presence of economies

---

[13] John S. McGee, "Predatory Price Cutting: The Standard Oil (NJ) Case," *Journal of Law and Economics* I (October 1958).

of scale in oil refining. Figure 6-11*a* shows the long-run average cost function of a firm in the refining business, and the shape of this function indicates that there are economies of scale. One could argue that the average cost of most firms was relatively high in 1870 because the typical refiner was small and produced only (say) q_1^* units. Suppose Rockefeller was the first to understand and take advantage of economies of scale. Expanding through acquisitions, he achieved internal economies of scale in the industry, and by 1890 many other firms had disappeared.

What does the internal economies of scale hypothesis leave unexplained? It does not explain why so many firms were in the industry in 1870. If there are internal economies of scale, one would not expect to observe so many firms in an industry because they would be unable to minimize the total cost of producing any given quantity. If there are internal economies of scale, just a few firms would be in the industry from the very beginning.

Let's consider an alternative hypothesis. Suppose firms in the industry up to 1870 had U-shaped long-run average cost functions. Therefore, no company could become very large because long-run average cost increased if a firm became too large. In that era no firm could control a large share of the market because it would have become an inefficient high-average-cost producer. Figure 6-11*b* shows that the long-run average cost function *aa* is U-shaped and that the lowest average cost occurs when the firm produces q_1^*.

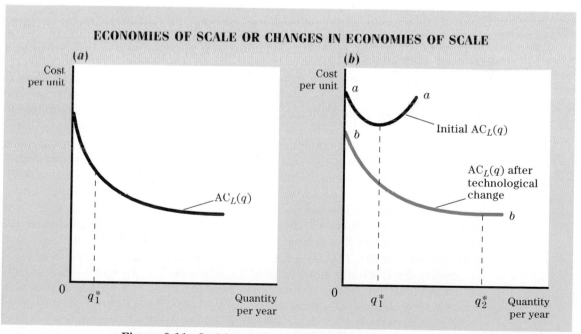

ECONOMIES OF SCALE OR CHANGES IN ECONOMIES OF SCALE

Figure 6-11   In (*a*) it can be seen that there are economies of scale in this industry. Few firms should exist in the industry if there are economies of scale. In (*b*) a change in technology shifts the long-run average cost function down and increases the extent of economies of scale. The optimal size of the firm increases from q_1^* to q_2^*.

Now assume that one or several technological changes occurred in the refining and transportation of crude oil. The long-run average cost function of the firm shifted down, and the extent of economies of scale became more pronounced. Because internal economies of scale are more important now, there is a greater incentive to merge and grow to q_2^*. In the past the U-shaped average cost function discouraged such mergers and growth.

How did the industry evolve? The technological changes caused firms to merge, output to become more concentrated, and the real prices of refined products to decline. Do we have any evidence that technological changes occurred? Alfred Chandler reports that the reorganization of Standard Oil Trust's refining facilities and coordination of the flow of raw materials from the oil field to the refinery to the consumer brought a sharp reduction in the average cost of producing a gallon of kerosene, the major product at the time. In 1880 the average cost of kerosene was 2.5 cents per gallon, and by 1885 it had fallen to 1.5 cents, a 40 percent reduction.[14] It appears that significant cost reductions occurred in this industry.

The technological and managerial change hypothesis gives a more consistent explanation of the facts than the simple economies of scale hypothesis does. It is probably one reason John D. Rockefeller was so successful. He was the first to recognize the significance of the changes in the industry and to understand the implications of these changes for firm size.

APPLICATION 6-6

Size of Firm and Technological Change in the Steel Industry

The steel industry in the United States has been transformed because of technological changes in the production of steel. Historically, the integrated U.S. steel companies produced steel using the open hearth method combining coke and iron ore to make liquid steel, which is poured into continuous casting machines. The resulting slabs of steel are then driven through huge capital-intensive rolling mills that produce steel sheets, heavy structural steel, and many other products. Some experts suggest that economies of scale were achieved by a firm producing steel in this manner when producing up to 6 to 8 million tons of steel per year. Consequently, most steel companies such as U.S. Steel, Bethlehem, National, and other integrated steel companies are large firms. Figure 6-12 shows the hypothetical long-run average cost function of a large integrated steel firm. Long-run average cost declines until the firm reaches a size where 8 million tons of steel are produced.

During the 1980s new firms entered the steel industry at a much smaller scale by using a new technological process to produce steel. The so-called minimills convert scrap into steel products directly by melting scrap steel at very high temperatures in electric furnaces. The minimills avoid the huge capital cost of blast

---

[14] Alfred D. Chandler, Jr., *Scale and Scope: The Dynamics of Industrial Capitalism* (Cambridge, Mass.: Harvard University Press, 1990), p. 25.

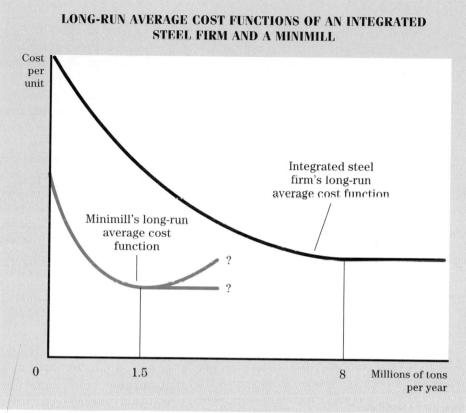

Figure 6-12   The long-run average cost function of an integrated steel firm indicates economies of scale until 8 million tons of steel are produced annually. Minimills are much smaller, suggesting economies of scale may be fully achieved with perhaps only 1.5 million tons of steel produced annually.

furnaces that the integrated producers must incur. The minimills are much smaller and frequently produce less than 1.5 million tons per year. As long as the prices of scrap steel remain low, the minimills can produce many steel products at the same or lower long-run average cost than the integrated steel mills. The long-run average cost function of a minimill is shown in Figure 6-12 where minimum long-run average cost is reached at a much smaller scale.

The technological advance has changed the structure of the industry. Entry into the steel industry has become easier. As a consequence, the combined market share of the integrated steel companies has declined. Furthermore, minimills are now building larger mills and expanding their product mix. They have improved the quality of the steel they produce and are selling more steel to appliance and auto manufacturers. In the steel industry technological change has not only reduced the cost of producing steel products but lowered the optimal size of a firm.

SUMMARY

- In the short run a firm has at least one fixed factor of production. All factors are variable in the long run.
- The short-run total cost function shows the lowest total cost of producing each quantity when at least one factor is fixed. The short-run total cost function is equal to the sum of fixed and variable costs.
- Short-run average cost declines with increases in quantity, reaches a minimum, and then increases. Average variable cost also declines with increases in quantity, reaches a minimum, and then increases.
- Short-run marginal cost goes through the minimum points of the average variable cost function and the short-run average cost function.

- A necessary condition for efficient production of a given total quantity by a multiplant firm is that all plants have the same marginal cost.
- In the long run a firm selects each factor of production so that it can produce each quantity at the lowest total and average costs.
- The shape of the long-run average cost function determines whether there are many or a few firms in an industry. When there are diseconomies of scale, there are a large number of firms in the industry when the size of market is large. When there are economies of scale, there will be one or a few firms in an industry.

KEY TERMS

explicit cost
sunk cost
fixed factor
short and long runs
variable cost
short-run average and marginal cost
    functions
equalizing marginal cost at all plants
internal economies and diseconomies of
    scale

opportunity cost
variable factor
fixed cost
marginal cost
area under marginal function
long-run average and marginal cost
    functions
natural monopoly

REVIEW QUESTIONS

1. The short-run total cost function of a firm is shown in the table below.

   a. What is fixed cost?
   b. Can you derive the variable cost func-

QUANTITY	SHORT-RUN TOTAL COST	QUANTITY	SHORT-RUN TOTAL COST
0	$1,200	40	$2,400
10	1,400	50	3,500
20	1,800	60	4,800
30	2,100	70	6,300

tion from the information in the table?

c. Derive and plot the short-run average cost function on a graph.

d. Calculate the marginal cost of increasing output for successive 10 unit increments in quantity.

2. The rental contract signed by a mall tenant with a shopping center developer specifies:

Rent = $50,000 if sales < $1,000,000

Rent = $50,000 + .05

(Sales − $1,000,000) if sales > $1,000,000

Is the rent paid by the tenant a fixed cost? Explain.

3. How does a fixed cost differ from a sunk cost?

4. Your parents present you with a graduation gift—a new car that costs $20,000. They agree to pay for all your expenses for the first year. Your parents say, "You have a free car for the first year."Is the car "free" during the first year? Explain why or why not.

5. Suppose a firm purchases a specialized die for $20,000 to manufacture a product. The die will last 1 year, and the manufacturer

can sell it to another manufacturer for only $500 within the year. What is the opportunity cost of the die before purchase? What is the opportunity cost of the die after the firm purchases it?

6. If short-run marginal cost is increasing, then short-run average cost is increasing. If short-run average cost is increasing, short-run marginal cost is increasing. Explain why you agree or disagree with these two statements.

7. Average cost decreases as output rises because a firm can spread a fixed cost over more units. Explain why you agree or disagree with this statement. Does this statement apply to the short or to the long run?

8. The area under the average variable cost function up to a prespecified quantity is equal to the variable cost of producing that quantity. Explain why you agree or disagree with this statement.

9. The area under the marginal cost function up to a prespecified quantity is equal to the variable cost of producing that quantity. Explain why you agree or disagree with this statement.

EXERCISES

1. At each quantity the marginal cost at plant 1 is 20 percent lower than the marginal cost at plant 2. Total cost will be minimized if total output is produced at plant 1. Explain why you agree or disagree with this statement.

2. The first table on page 250 shows the fixed cost (F), variable cost (V), total cost (C), average cost (AC), and marginal cost (MC) at two plants. The average cost at plant 1 is greater than the average cost at plant 2 at each quantity.

Suppose the monthly quota of the firm is 9 units. The production manager schedules 4 units at plant 1 because she minimizes AC_1

at $90 per unit, and plant 2 provides the remaining 5 units at an average cost of $15.20.

a. Fill in the values in the second table on page 250 and show whether the production manager's solution minimizes the total cost of production.

b. Explain why the simple average of the average cost at each plant does or does not minimize total cost.

3. A firm has two plants with marginal cost functions:

$MC_1(q_1) = \$50 + \$5q_1$

$MC_2(q_2) = \$25 + \$5q_2$

The firm schedules 25 units per month so $q_1 + q_2 = 25$. How many units should the

	Plant 1					Plant 2				
QUANTITY	F_1 (1)	V_1 (2)	C_1 (3)	AC_1 (4)	MC_1 (5)	F_2 (6)	V_2 (7)	C_2 (8)	AC_2 (9)	MC_2 (10)
1	300	10	310	310.00	10	50	5	55	55.00	5
2	300	15	315	157.50	5	50	8	58	29.00	3
3	300	35	335	111.67	20	50	12	62	20.67	4
4	300	60	360	90.00	25	50	18	68	17.00	6
5	300	180	480	96.00	120	50	26	76	15.20	8
6	300	340	640	106.67	160	50	46	96	16.00	20
7	300	520	820	117.14	180	50	90	140	20.00	44

firm produce in each plant so that it minimizes total cost?

4. You decide to buy a block of tickets to all Football U. home games including the homecoming game for $4 per game. The day before the homecoming game, you learn that the game is sold out and that you can sell your ticket for $50. If you go to the homecoming game, what is the cost of attending? Would you predict that the percentage of students with season tickets who attend the homecoming game is higher or lower compared to other games, all other things equal?

5. A company operates two oil wells in a state. Well A is capable of producing 1,000 barrels per day, and well B is capable of producing a maximum of 900 barrels a day. The state government regulates the rate of oil extraction from each well in the state. These restrictions are expressed in terms of the percentage of the maximum flow of oil from

each well (method 1). Currently, the government restricts output of each well to 50 percent of maximum output, and so the total allocation for the company is 950 barrels a day. Suppose the government is considering a different method of regulating the industry. Under method 2 it simply restricts the company's output to 950 barrels per day. Compare the two methods of regulation and explain whether they would result in the same rate of utilization of the two wells.

*6. At the end of August, a manufacturing firm receives an order from a retailing firm for q^* units that the firm must deliver to the store on November 1 for the Christmas season. Let $C = C(q_t)$ be the total cost of producing q_t units in either September or October. Let h be the per unit monthly inventory cost of storing one unit for a single month.

a. How many units should the manufacturing firm produce in September and Oc-

$q_1 - q_2 = 9$	AVERAGE COST AT PLANT	SUM OF VARIABLE COST, $V_1 + V_2$	SUM OF TOTAL COST, $C_1 + C_2$
$q_1 = 4, q_2 = 5$	$AC_1 = ? \ AC_2 = ?$		
$q_1 = 3, q_2 = 6$	$AC_1 = ? \ AC_2 = ?$		
$q_1 = 2, q_2 = 7$	$AC_1 = ? \ AC_2 = ?$		

tober so that the firm ships q^* units on November 1 and minimizes the sum of production and storage costs?

b. If the firm minimizes total production and storage costs, what condition must it satisfy?

c. Explain why it will not be efficient to produce one-half of the order in September and one-half in October.

d. How will the firm change its production decision if h increases?

*7. A firm operates a plant in state A and another plant in state B.

a. Show graphically how the firm allocates production between the two plants so that it produces q^* units per period at minimum total cost.

b. Suppose that officials in state B try to entice the company to schedule all of its production in state B. With the aid of graphs show the minimum size of a *lump sum subsidy* that the state would have to offer the company before it would shift all production to state B.

8. The short-run total cost function is shown in figure a below. The short-run average,

average variable, and marginal cost functions are shown in figure b. Using figure a as a standard of reference, point out three errors in figure b.

9. The number of U.S. beer manufacturers has declined over time. The accompanying table shows the number of manufacturers from 1947 to 1987.

YEAR	NUMBER OF COMPANIES	YEAR	NUMBER OF COMPANIES
1947	404	1972	108
1954	263	1977	81
1958	211	1982	67
1963	171	1987	101
1967	125		

a. How would you explain the 83 percent decline in the number of companies between 1947 and 1982?

b. How would you explain the growth of companies between 1982 and 1987?

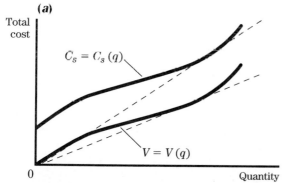

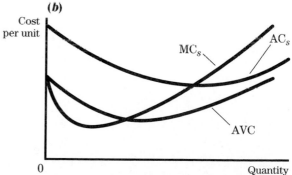

FIRM AND
MARKET
BEHAVIOR

- **Chapter 7**
  The Supply Functions
  of a Competitive Firm
- **Chapter 8**
  Price Determination
  in a Competitive Industry
- **Chapter 9**
  Monopoly
- **Chapter 10**
  Oligopoly and Monopolistic
  Competition
- **Chapter 11**
  Monitoring the Corporation:
  Corporate Governance

C H A P T E R 7

THE SUPPLY FUNCTIONS OF A COMPETITIVE FIRM

■ **7-1 The Competitive Firm**

The Price-Taking Assumption

The Price Elasticity of Demand of a
   Competitive Firm

Application 7-1: The Price Elasticity
   of Demand of Firms in Eastern
   Europe and Russia

■ **7-2 The Short-Run Supply
Function of a Competitive Firm**

Finding an Output That Maximizes
   Total Short-Run Profits

The Short-Run Supply Function of a
   Competitive Firm

Application 7-2: Short-Run Costs,
   Break-Even Analysis, and Profit-
   Maximizing Behavior

Application 7-3: When to Lay Up an
   Oil Tanker

■ **7-3 The Long-Run Supply
Function of a Competitive Firm**

Finding an Output That Maximizes
   Long-Run Profits

The Long-Run Supply Function of a
   Competitive Firm

■ **Summary**

■ **Key Terms**

■ **Review Questions**

■ **Exercises**

■ **Problem Set: Should Your
Company Honor a Contract?**

How does a firm decide how many units to produce? This chapter answers this question for a special type of firm—a competitive firm. In everyday usage, "competitive" often means rivalry between firms. Economists forsake common usage to give the term a completely different meaning. To an economist, the distinguishing feature of a **competitive firm** is that it is a *price taker*. A competitive firm is one that does not determine price. Rather, it can sell as many units as it wants without affecting the market price, and this is why it is called a price taker. The competitive firm's key decision is not what price to charge but how much to produce and sell at the current market price.

This chapter focuses on the short- and long-run supply decisions made by a **price-taking firm.** How many units will a price-taking firm supply at different prices? In what way is a price taker's short-run supply decision different from its long-run decision? How low does the price have to fall before a competitive firm will close its doors and refuse to produce anything? Before we can answer these questions, we must state what the goal of the firm is. In this and subsequent chapters we assume the firm's goal is to maximize profits. Besides the notion of *profit maximization*, we introduce a new and important concept—*marginal revenue*—the additional revenue received by selling another unit. By repeatedly using the marginal revenue concept, we are able to derive a competitive firm's short- and long-run supply functions.

7-1   THE COMPETITIVE FIRM

The Price-Taking Assumption

We begin by assuming the firm is one of many producing a homogeneous good. The hallmark of a competitive firm is that the quantity it supplies has no effect on the market price. A competitive firm behaves as if the market price is independent of the number of units sold by the firm, which explains why it is called a price taker.

> A competitive firm acts as if the market price is independent of the number of units sold by the firm.

The price-taking assumption implies that the firm's demand function is a horizontal line at the market price. Figure 7-1a shows the market demand and supply functions, where the horizontal scale is in millions of units. If the market price is P_1, the horizontal line dd in Figure 7-1b is the firm's demand function, where the horizontal scale is in thousands of units. A competitive firm can sell as much as it desires without affecting the market price P_1. The slope of a competitive firm's demand function is zero.

Because a competitive firm responds to but does not singularly determine the market price, it cannot affect the fortunes of any other firm in the industry. As a result, rivalry between any two competitive firms is distant and impersonal. If this

MARKET AND FIRM DEMAND FUNCTIONS

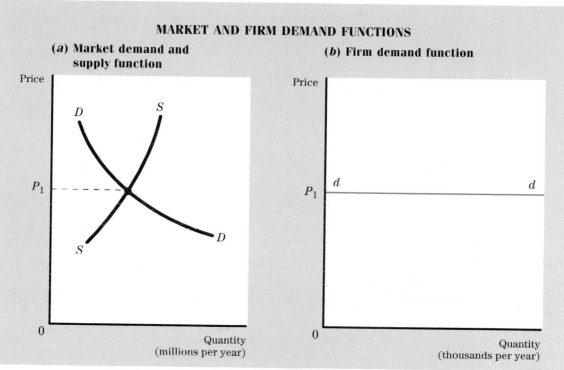

Figure 7-1   (*a*) The market demand and supply functions. The horizontal scale is in millions of units. When the market price is P_1, *dd* in (*b*) is the demand curve facing a competitive firm. The horizontal scale in (*b*) is in thousands of units. A competitive firm is a price taker and acts as if the quantity sold has no effect on the market price. The firm sells each unit at the existing market price of P_1.

sounds surprising or paradoxical, it is only because competition is usually associated with rivalry. To an economist, a competitive firm is a price taker so the rivalry among price-taking firms must be impersonal.

For example, there are thousands of wheat farmers. If we ask a farmer why the price of wheat is low, a knowledgeable one will not claim that a neighbor is producing too much wheat and flooding the market. The price of wheat is unaffected by the quantity a neighbor produces because the neighbor is only one of thousands of wheat farmers. Similarly, if a tornado destroys a paint factory and puts the company out of commission for a year, the increase in the price of a gallon of paint will be imperceptible. The same argument applies to restaurants, video stores, car washes, and other industries with many firms. Note that a firm can still be a price taker even if the entry of other firms is blocked by law. Entry restrictions limit the number of peanut producers. Barriers to entry into peanut farming are substantial. Nevertheless, existing peanut producers still are price takers because any one producer supplies a small share of the market.

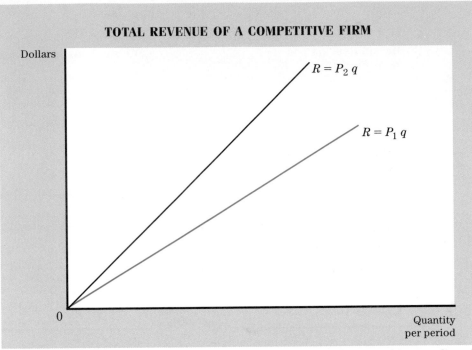

TOTAL REVENUE OF A COMPETITIVE FIRM

Figure 7-2   Because a competitive firm is a price taker, total revenue increases linearly with the quantity sold. The firm can sell each additional unit at the market price. If the price is P_1, total revenue function is $R = P_1q$. If the price rises to P_2, the total revenue function becomes $R = P_2q$.

Given the market price, a competitive firm's total revenue increases proportionally with the quantity sold.

$$R = Pq \qquad \text{(Total Revenue of a Price-Taking Firm)} \qquad (7\text{-}1)$$

where R is total revenue received by the firm, P is market price, and q represents units sold by the firm.

Figure 7-2 shows two total revenue functions, one for each price. Dollars are on the vertical axis, and quantity is on the horizontal axis. The total revenue function is a straight line for a given price. If the price is P_1, the total revenue function is $R = P_1q$ and so each unit sold increases total revenue by P_1. At a higher price of P_2, the firm's total revenue function becomes $R = P_2q$. Now, each unit sold increases total revenue by still more since P_2 is greater than P_1. The total revenue function rotates upward around the origin in Figure 7-2 as the price increases.

For a price-taking firm, the additional revenue from selling another unit equals the market price. If a video store rents cassettes at \$3 per cassette, the rental of each additional cassette brings in additional revenue of \$3. **Marginal revenue** (MR) is defined as the change in total revenue, ΔR, due to a change in quantity sold, Δq. For a competitive firm marginal revenue equals the price of the product.

Therefore,

$$\text{MR} = \frac{\Delta R}{\Delta q} = P \qquad \text{(Marginal Revenue for a Competitive Firm)} \qquad \text{(7-2)}$$

$\Delta R/\Delta q$ is the expression for marginal revenue, and for a price-taking firm, $\Delta R/\Delta q$ equals price.[1]

The Price Elasticity of Demand of a Competitive Firm

As noted above, the demand function of a competitive firm is virtually flat with a slope approaching zero. A change in the quantity demanded, Δq, barely changes the market price, ΔP. Therefore, $\Delta P/\Delta q$ is slightly negative but very close to zero and, consequently, $\Delta q/\Delta P$ approaches negative infinity. The point price elasticity of demand for a firm's demand function, E_d, approaches negative infinity. Economists say the price elasticity of demand of a price-taking firm is infinitely elastic.

> The price elasticity of demand for a competitive firm is infinitely elastic.

While we concentrate on a competitive firm in this chapter, we might momentarily expand the analysis to identify three factors that determine a firm's price elasticity of demand whether or not it is a competitive firm. The three factors are:

1. *Market share.* As the number of firms increases and the market share of a firm declines, a given percentage increase in the quantity produced by the firm causes a smaller percentage increase in the total quantity supplied by the market and therefore a smaller percentage decrease in the market price. If a firm with 1 percent of the market supplies 10 units and increases output by 10 percent, it increases the quantity by 1 unit. If the firm has 50 percent of the market and therefore supplies 500 units and increases output by 10 percent, the increase in the quantity supplied of 50 units causes a larger percentage decline in the market price. So, the smaller the firm's market share, the more elastic the firm's demand function. Since the quantity supplied by a competitive firm represents a small share of the total quantity supplied, an increase in the quantity sold by a competitive firm has an imperceptible effect on the price.

2. *Price elasticity of market demand function.* In the vicinity of the current market price, the more elastic the market demand function, the smaller the decrease in market price caused by an increase in the quantity produced by a firm. The more elastic is the industry demand function, the more elastic

---

[1] Marginal revenue is derived from the total revenue function, $R = Pq$. For a given P, the revenue equation is a straight line. Define the derivative of the total revenue function as marginal revenue. The change in total revenue due to a change in q is

$$\text{MR} = \frac{dR}{dq} = P$$

This equation says that the slope of the total revenue function is equal to the price of the product. For a price taker, MR equals average revenue (AR), since $\text{AR} = \text{TR}/q = P$.

is the firm's demand curve. An increase in firm output causes an even smaller decline in the market price, the more elastic is the market demand curve.

3. *Supply elasticity of other firms.* When a firm produces more units, the size of any price decline depends on the supply response of *all* other firms in the industry. If the other firms respond by reducing their combined output, the decline in the market price will be smaller than if they keep producing the original amount. For example, the price decrease will be smaller when a firm increases output if total imports into a country decrease when the domestic price falls. The **supply elasticity of other competitive firms** measures the percentage change in the quantity supplied by other producers for a given percentage change in the market price. The larger the *supply* elasticity, the larger the percentage decrease in the output of other firms, the smaller the price decline due to the increase in the firm's quantity, and therefore the more elastic the *firm's demand function.*

The above three factors determine the firm's price elasticity of demand.

APPLICATION **7-1**

The Price Elasticity of Demand of Firms in Eastern Europe and Russia

The three determinants of the firm's price elasticity of demand have a direct bearing on the restructuring of industry in the former Soviet Union and in Eastern European countries. One important concern is what will keep prices under control if new firms are free to set any price during the transition from a centrally controlled economy toward a more market-driven economy.

In some Eastern European countries and in Russia there is a popular distrust of capitalism. Some think that a market system will merely replace the monopoly and bureaucracy of the communist party with firms that will raise prices because of the absence of competitors. This is not an empty concern, especially in some industries where Soviet planning authorities built a few massive industrial complexes and factories rather than many smaller plants.

A critical question is what will be the price elasticity of demand for each of the new firms. The larger the supply elasticity of competitive firms, the more elastic the demand function of a firm will become. Because the number of current domestic competitors in Eastern Europe and Russia is relatively small, the supply from other firms must come from the rest of the world. By keeping tariffs low so that imports can enter their markets and by allowing firms to enter, the existing firms in Eastern European nations and Russia will face more elastic demand curves. These firms will behave more like competitive firms than as the sole suppliers of a product. Competitive supply from abroad and, perhaps later, from within will prevent domestic firms from setting higher prices in domestic markets. However, there is no assurance of this. The established domestic firms will probably use their considerable political power to gain protection, as has occurred in many Western economies. Then, the concern about high prices will not be an empty one.

7-2   THE SHORT-RUN SUPPLY FUNCTION OF A COMPETITIVE FIRM

The short-run supply function of a competitive firm shows the quantity supplied by the firm at each price given one fixed factor of production. In this discussion capital is still the fixed factor, so the firm cannot change plant size in the short run, and the cost of the fixed factor is a sunk cost.

The quantity supplied by a competitive firm cannot be determined until the firm's objective is specified. This chapter assumes that the management of the firm attempts to maximize total profits. There are two reasons why a competitive firm will have difficulty surviving if it does not maximize profits. First, if other firms in the industry find ways to reduce costs and to increase profits, a company that does not will earn lower profits and ultimately suffer losses. A nonmaximizing firm has a lower probability of surviving in the industry. The second reason is more subtle: A management that does not maximize profits invites a takeover. Other firms or shareholders will seek to acquire the inefficiently run company and improve its performance. A takeover attempt could either so weaken the position of the firm's top management that they resign or change managerial policies, reduce costs, and increase firm profits. The possibility of a takeover serves as a disciplinary device and circumscribes the behavior of management. Because of these two reasons, we adopt the assumption of profit maximization, and our derivation of the firm's short- and long-run supply functions rests on this assumption.

The expression for the firm's short-run profits is

$$\text{Profits} = \text{Revenues} - \text{Costs} \qquad \text{(Short-Run Profits of a Competitive Firm)}$$

$$\pi(q) = Pq - V(q) - F \tag{7-3}$$

In the short run, total cost equals total variable cost, which depends on the quantity produced, plus total fixed cost, which is independent of the quantity produced. $V(q)$ represents total variable cost, and F is total fixed cost. If the company doesn't produce anything, $q = 0$. When $q = 0$, the firm loses $-F$; that is, $\pi = -F$. If the firm decides to produce any quantity, it will do so only because it expects $\pi(q) > -F$. If it produces q units, total revenue is Pq and total variable cost of producing q units is $V(q)$. The firm would be foolish to produce these q units if Pq is less than $V(q)$ because its losses would be larger than F. Therefore, in the short run, the firm will operate only if total revenue either equals or exceeds total variable cost. Because total fixed cost is sunk, a bygone, the quantity produced in the short run does not depend on the size of fixed cost.

> In the short run the firm produces only if $Pq \geq V(q)$.

For example, suppose sunk costs equal \$40,000. The market price might be so low that the firm receives only \$50,000 from selling 5,000 units and incurs \$60,000 in total variable cost. Consequently, the firm would rather shut down and lose \$40,000 than produce 5,000 units and lose \$50,000.

Finding an Output That Maximizes Total Short-Run Profits

Let's derive a rule that a competitive firm will follow when it determines the quantity to produce in the short run and then apply this rule to find the quantity supplied at any price.

In the short run, the firm must make do with its current plant. The company's short-run marginal cost function shows the incremental cost of producing another unit with a given plant. To maximize short-run profits, the firm selects an output where MR, which equals P, equals short-run marginal cost.[2]

$$\text{MR} = P = \text{MC}_S(q) \qquad \text{(Determination of Quantity in the Short Run)} \qquad \textbf{(7-4)}$$

where $\text{MC}_S(q)$ is short-run marginal cost.

> A competitive firm produces a quantity where price equals short-run marginal cost, and marginal cost is rising.

Figure 7-3 shows the firm's horizontal demand function dd when the market price is P_1, the average variable cost (AVC) function, and the short-run marginal cost (MC_S) function. The firm maximizes short-run profits by producing q_1 units where $\text{MR} = P_1 = \text{MC}_S$. Total profits will decrease if the firm produces either a larger or a smaller output than q_1. In either case price will no longer equal short-run marginal cost, and so the firm will not earn maximum profits. For example, if the firm is producing q_0 units and increases output to q_1, the marginal revenue from selling $q_1 - q_0$ more units equals area abq_1q_0 under the firm's demand function, while the marginal cost of producing $q_1 - q_0$ more units is area cbq_1q_0 under the marginal cost function. Since the increase in revenue is greater than the increase in total cost, total profits increase.

The Short-Run Supply Function of a Competitive Firm

We have found one point on the firm's short-run supply function since the firm supplies q_1 units when the price is P_1. By applying the price equals marginal cost rule, the quantity the firm supplies at any price can also be found. What we discover is that the firm's short-run marginal cost function is the firm's short-run

---

[2] The firm would like to find a quantity that maximizes short-run total profits. If the profit function is differentiated with respect to q, a necessary first-order condition for profit maximum is

$$\frac{d[\pi(q)]}{dq} = P - \frac{d[C_S(q)]}{dq} = 0$$

The firm selects an output where market price equals short-run marginal cost. The second-order condition for a profit maximum requires

$$\frac{d^2[\pi(q)]}{dq^2} = -\frac{d^2[C_S(q)]}{dq^2} < 0$$

The slope of the marginal cost curve must be positive (i.e., marginal cost curve is rising) at the output at which price equals short-run marginal cost.

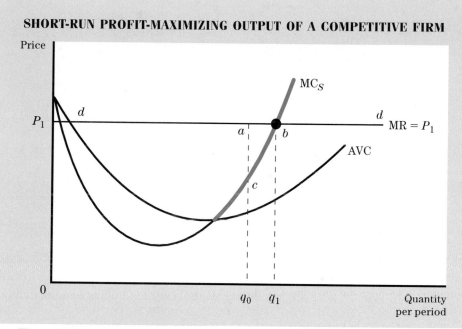

Figure 7-3 The firm maximizes profit by producing q_1 units, where P_1 equals short-run marginal cost. By increasing output from q_0 to q_1, the firm increases total profits.

supply function as long as **total revenue equals or exceeds total variable cost.**

> The firm's short-run marginal cost function is the firm's short-run supply function as long as total revenue $\geq$ total variable cost.

Figure 7-4 shows the firm's demand functions for two possible prices, P_1 and P_2, as well as the firm's short-run average variable and marginal cost functions. You may wonder why Figure 7-4 does not show the short-run average cost curve. In order to determine whether the firm is making a profit or incurring a loss in the short run, you need to know the position of the short-run average cost curve. However, the firm can determine its short-run profit-maximizing output *without* knowing whether it is earning a profit or suffering a loss. The size of fixed cost determines whether profits are high or low but has no bearing on what output the firm produces in the short run. If the firm sets output where price equals short-run marginal cost, it is doing as well as it can, given the price at which it can sell its product. Whether it ends up losing $10 or $10 million will have no effect on the quantity it produces in the short run as long as total revenue equals or exceeds total variable cost.

**THE SHORT-RUN SUPPLY CURVE
OF A COMPETITIVE FIRM**

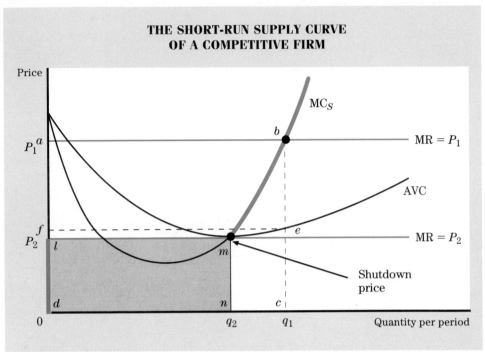

Figure 7-4   In the short run firm profits are maximized at an output where price equals short-run marginal cost. The firm supplies q_1 units if the price is P_1 and q_2 if the price is P_2. The firm will not supply any quantity if the price is less than the minimum average variable cost. The short-run marginal cost function is the firm's short-run supply curve for prices equal to or above P_2. The thick lines are the firm's short-run supply function.

When the price equals or exceeds minimum average variable cost, the firm maximizes profits by producing an output at which price equals short-run marginal cost. When the market price is P_1, the firm supplies q_1 units. P_1 exceeds average variable cost, which is equal to the distance ec. Therefore, total revenue is equal to the area $abcd$ and is greater than total variable cost, which is equal to the area $fecd$. At a lower price of P_2 the firm supplies only q_2 units. P_2 equals short-run marginal cost *and* minimum average variable cost. Therefore, total revenue (the shaded area $lmnd$) just equals total variable cost.

If the market price is less than P_2, total revenue is less than total variable cost. Therefore, the firm would rather close its doors and lose F in the short run than produce any amount and incur still larger losses. At any price less than P_2, the firm supplies nothing. In Figure 7-4, P_2 is the **shutdown price** because the firm will not produce anything in the short run if the price is less than P_2.

In summary, the firm's short-run supply function has two segments. The first segment is the thick vertical line centered on zero for all prices less than P_2. Then, the short-run supply curve jumps across horizontally to q_2 units when the price is

P_2. The second segment of the firm's short-run supply curve is the short-run marginal cost curve for prices above P_2.

APPLICATION **7-2**

Short-Run Costs, Break-Even Analysis, and Profit-Maximizing Behavior

Managers of firms often use a planning tool called break-even analysis to estimate how many units they must sell to break even, that is, how many units the firm must sell so that total revenue equals total cost. Break-even analysis projects revenue and total cost at different levels of production to find the break-even quantity. After demonstrating the use to which break-even analysis is put, we point out some of the underlying assumptions and indicate some important reservations concerning its utility as a planning tool.

Typically, break-even analysis applies to a short-run situation where some costs are sunk and others variable. On the revenue side, the firm takes the market price as given and projects total revenue as a linear function of the quantity sold. On the cost side, total cost is divided into fixed and variable costs. A common simplifying assumption is that total variable cost increases linearly with the quantity produced up to plant capacity. This linear function can be expressed as $V(q) = vq$, where v is a constant.[3] For example, if $v = \$100$, total variable cost increases by $100 a unit no matter how many units the firm produces, and so short-run marginal cost is $100. Another assumption of break-even analysis is that the firm has a fixed capacity that prevents it from producing more than q_c units per period.

Figure 7-5 shows total revenue, total cost, and total variable cost as a function of the quantity produced. Initially, we assume the market price is $150, and so total revenue is $R = \$150q$. Total cost is $C_S = F + \$100q$, where F is fixed cost. The break-even quantity is q_1 units where total revenue equals total cost. The firm must sell more than q_1 units before total revenue exceeds total cost—before profit is positive.

Break-even analysis appears to be a more impressive tool than it really is. If the firm is truly a price taker, it maximizes profits by producing at capacity output. Every unit sells for $150, the market price, and the short-run marginal cost is only $100. Since price exceeds short-run marginal cost, the firm wants to sell as much as it can produce in order to maximize short-run profits. If the firm produces q_c units, total variable cost will total $100q_c$ and profit will be $50q_c$. Note that the decision to produce the profit-maximizing quantity, q_c, does not depend on knowing the break-even quantity q_1.

Sometimes the claim is made that firms find break-even analysis useful in deciding by how much total variable costs should be cut when the price declines and the break-even quantity increases. Suppose market conditions worsen and the

---

[3] When $V = vq$, $AVC = V/q = v$. Therefore, average variable cost is constant up to capacity output.

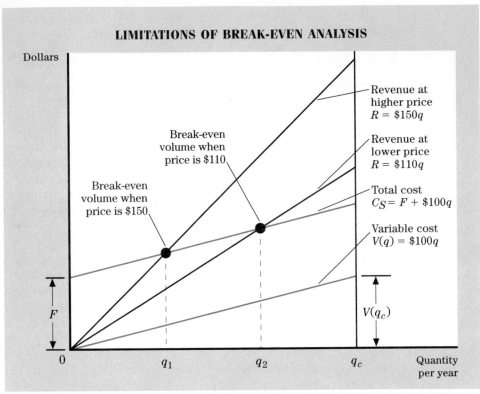

Figure 7-5   Total revenue increases linearly with quantity sold, and variable cost increases linearly with quantity produced. If the price is $150, the break-even volume is q_1, where total revenue equals total short-run cost. Total profits are maximized when the firm produces q_c. If the price falls to $110, break-even volume increases to q_2, but the firm continues to produce q_c.

market price falls to $110. The break-even point increases to q_2. How does knowing the new break-even point help the firm determine the quantity to produce and by how much to reduce total variable cost? Since marginal revenue is now only $110 but is still greater than the short-run marginal cost of $100, the firm still maximizes short-run profits by producing at capacity output. Although the price has declined, the firm will still produce q_c units and will still incur total variable cost of $100q_c$. Although price falls, total variable cost does not decrease because the firm maximizes profits by producing q_c units. Profit-maximizing behavior indicates that the firm should not reduce total variable cost if the market price declines. Economic analysis indicates that the firm either produces q_c or shuts down if the price is less than $100 a unit. Break-even analysis has some limitations because it does not provide answers to the important questions the firm faces.

When to Lay Up an Oil Tanker

When charter rates fall, an owner of an oil tanker must decide whether the vessel should be kept in operation or laid up. The owner must project whether the revenues from chartering the tanker will cover total variable cost. This prediction is difficult to make because tanker charter rates are volatile and are very sensitive to world economic and political events. When charter rates decline and stay low, owners will place some tankers in dry dock. How do the theoretical principles that determine the shutdown point in the short run apply in the tanker market?

To answer this question, let's classify the costs of a tanker into capital and operating costs. Huge capital costs are incurred in constructing a large tanker, and once built, it may have a useful lifetime of about 20 years. In the short run, we treat the capital cost of a tanker as a sunk cost and concentrate only on the operating cost. The position of the average variable cost function of a tanker depends on the age and size of the vessel, whether it is powered by steam or by a diesel engine, the cost of the crew, the insurance for the cargo, and so on. New tankers with more deadweight tons of rated capacity tend to be more capital-intensive and to have a lower average variable cost function. Many older tankers were built in the 1970s, are usually smaller, and are more likely to be steam-powered. Steam-powered tankers use more fuel for a given trip length, and therefore older tankers have a higher average variable cost function than newer, larger ones. Figure 7-6 shows the hypothetical average variable and short-run marginal cost functions of an old and a new tanker. The minimum average variable cost of the old vessel is higher than the minimum average variable cost of the newer one. The thick curves represent the short-run supply functions of the two tankers. Because of the differences in the average variable cost functions of the two types of tankers, the older tankers with higher average variable cost would probably be the first ones withdrawn from the fleet and placed in dry dock when charter rates fall.

An interesting situation occurred during and after the Persian Gulf crisis. Following the invasion of Kuwait in July 1990, charter rates rose—reaching a peak in February 1991. After rates increased, only 5 of the 50 tankers that remained in dry dock were the new very large or ultralarge tankers.[4] What makes the period between February 1991 and July 1992 especially interesting is the significant 54 percent fall in charter rates, a large percentage drop even for the volatile charter market. By July 1992, 14 of the 74 tankers laid up were very large or ultralarge tankers.

To minimize short-run fluctuations in charter rates, a simple average of charter

---

[4] These were American-flagged vessels that transport Alaskan oil to U.S. gulf ports and must use higher-paid American crews and conform to higher American safety standards.

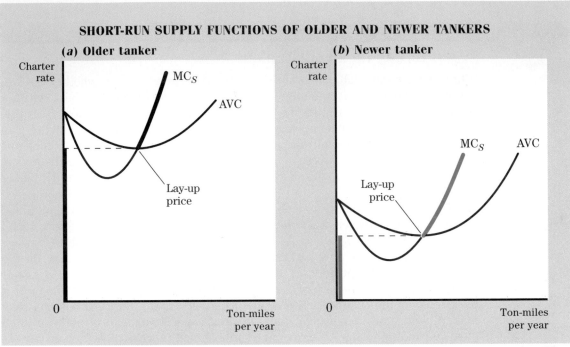

Figure 7-6   (*a*) An older tanker has a higher lay-up price than a newer one. When rates decline, the tanker with the higher minimum average variable cost will be the first to be taken out of service.

rates during the last three months was calculated. Figure 7-7 shows the average charter rates by month for a trip from the Persian Gulf to northwestern Europe by a very large tanker and the number of tankers of all sizes laid up. Because charter rates were so high at the beginning of 1991, the fall in rates that began in February 1991 and continued to May 1992 did not initially cause a large increase in the number of ships in dry dock until March 1993 when the number of ships withdrawn from the fleet rose rapidly. As charter rates fell, owners first withdrew tankers with higher minimum average variable cost, just as the theory predicts. The older steam-driven tankers with higher minimum average variable cost were first placed in dry dock. As charter rates continued to fall, owners then placed newer tankers with somewhat lower minimum average variable cost in dry dock.

This analysis of the tanker market shows that owners are aware of the different shapes of the variable cost functions for the different types of tankers and respond as the theory predicts. As a first approximation, the short-run model of the behavior of a competitive firm seems to explain firm behavior in the tanker market. Yet, this short-run model has its limitations. First, it does not take into account the one-time lay-up cost that an owner incurs when placing a tanker in dry dock. The owner might keep the tanker operating although the current charter rate is less than the minimum average variable cost if he thinks the rate will increase or will not fall

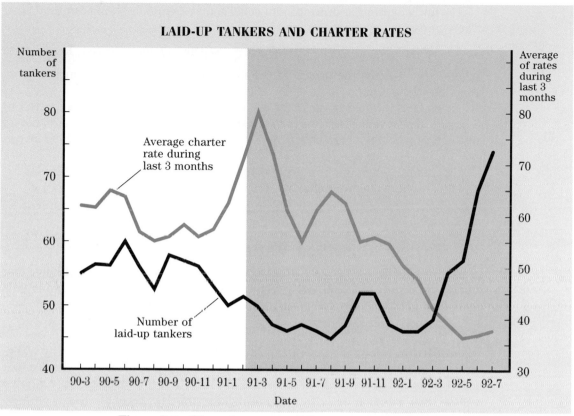

LAID-UP TANKERS AND CHARTER RATES

Figure 7-7   When charter rates fall, owners withdraw higher variable cost tankers. [From Lloyds' of London, *Lloyds' Monthly Shipping Economist.*]

much below minimum average variable cost. In this way the lay-up cost can be avoided.

7-3   THE LONG-RUN SUPPLY FUNCTION OF A COMPETITIVE FIRM

In the long run all factors of production are variable, and so the firm can select any combination of factors to produce each quantity. We continue to assume that the firm is a price taker and maximizes profits in the long run. A useful way of thinking about long-run supply decisions of a competitive firm is to visualize it as starting from scratch. It devises a plan that describes (1) the profit-maximizing quantity at each market price that might prevail in the long run and (2) what combination of factors it will use to produce that quantity at the lowest total cost.

In the long run the firm's profits equal total revenue less long-run total cost. The expression for total profits is

$$\pi(q) = Pq - C_L(q) \qquad \text{(Profits of a Competitive Firm in the Long Run)} \qquad \textbf{(7-5)}$$

where $\pi(q)$ denotes the profits of the firm and $C_L(q)$ is the long-run total cost function of the firm.

A company would never enter an industry in the long run if it expected to incur a loss. If revenues are less than total long-run costs, the potential shareholders of the firm would not earn as much as they would earn from the next-best investment.

Therefore, when the firm decides to enter an industry by building a plant, it expects profits to be **nonnegative.**

$$\pi(q) \geq 0 \qquad \text{(Nonnegative Profit Constraint in the Long Run)}$$

Finding an Output That Maximizes Long-Run Profits

A price-taking firm maximizes profits by **equating price to marginal cost,** that is, by producing the quantity at which marginal revenue equals long-run marginal cost. Since MR $= P$, the condition for profit maximization becomes

$$\text{MR} = P = \text{MC}_L(q) \qquad \text{(Determination of Quantity in the Long Run)} \qquad \textbf{(7-6)}$$

where $\text{MC}_L(q)$ is long-run marginal cost.[5] If the firm is producing a quantity where price is greater than marginal cost, it should produce more units since the last unit sold brings more revenue than it costs to produce, and so profits increase. If price is less than marginal cost, the last unit sold brings less revenue than it costs to produce and causes profits to decrease.

In Figure 7-8 price is on the vertical axis, and quantity is on the horizontal axis. The firm's demand function is the horizontal line labeled MR $= P_1$ if P_1 is the market price. The long-run average (AC_L) and marginal cost (MC_L) functions are included in Figure 7-8. Total profits are equal to area $abcd$ when the firm produces q_1 units where $P_1 = \text{MC}_L$.

The Long-Run Supply Function of a Competitive Firm

The firm's long-run supply function can be derived by repeatedly applying the $P = \text{MC}_L$ rule. We have already derived one point on the long-run supply curve of

---

[5] The firm selects an output that maximizes its profits. The firm's profits are $\pi(q) = Pq - C_L(q)$. The first-order condition for profit maximization is

$$\frac{d[\pi(q)]}{dq} = P - \frac{d[C_L(q)]}{dq} = 0 \qquad \text{or} \qquad \text{MR} \equiv P = \text{MC}_L(q)$$

A necessary condition for profit maximization is that the firm selects an output where price equals long-run marginal cost. The second-order condition for profit maximization is

$$\frac{d^2[\pi(q)]}{dq^2} = -\frac{d^2[C_L(q)]}{dq^2} < 0$$

For this condition to be satisfied, the slope of the marginal cost curve, $d^2C_L(q)/dq^2$, must be positive at the output where price equals long-run marginal cost.

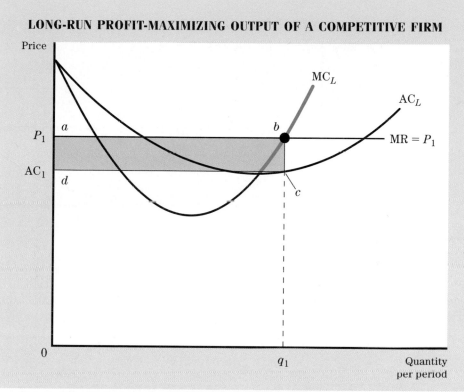

Figure 7-8   In the long run a competitive firm maximizes profits by producing q_1 units where price equals long-run marginal cost. The firm produces q_1 units at lowest cost by building a plant that produces q_1 units at a long-run average cost of AC_1. Total profits equal the area *abcd*.

a competitive firm because we know the firm supplies q_1 units when the price is P_1. Figure 7-9 shows the firm supplies a larger quantity of q_2 units when the price is P_2. Total profits are equal to the area *efgh*. At the lower price P_3, the firm will supply only q_3 units. When the firm produces q_3 units, long-run marginal cost equals long-run average cost, and long-run average cost is at a minimum. Therefore, profits are zero and the firm earns the same return on the capital invested as the shareholders would have earned from the next best investment. Shareholders are neither better nor worse off. If the price is less than P_3, the firm does not supply any output because it would incur losses at any quantity and so would not remain in the industry in the long run.

Like its short-run supply function, the firm's long-run supply function has two segments. The first segment is the vertical line in Figure 7-9 centered on zero for prices less than P_3. When the price is P_3, the supply curve jumps across horizontally to the second segment at q_3 units, and the second segment is the firm's long-run marginal cost function for higher prices.

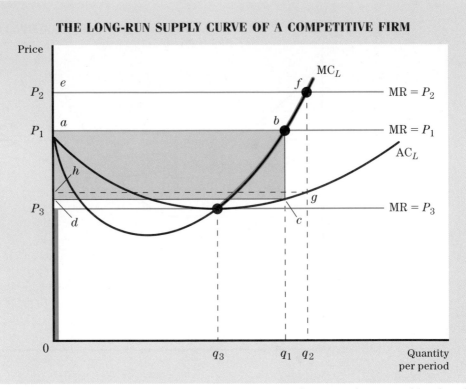

THE LONG-RUN SUPPLY CURVE OF A COMPETITIVE FIRM

Figure 7-9   The thick lines show the long-run supply curve of a competitive firm. If the price is P_2, the firm supplies q_2 units where P_2 equals long-run marginal cost. Total profits equal the area *efgh*. If the price is P_3, the firm supplies q_3 units and does not earn profits.

The firm's long-run marginal cost function is the firm's long-run supply function for prices above the minimum of the long-run average cost function.

We can draw an important implication from knowing the firm's long-run supply function. Our analysis implies that a competitive firm exhausts all internal economies of scale in the long run. A profit-maximizing competitive firm never knowingly produces an output between zero and q_3 units in the long run (and this is precisely the output range over which average cost declines). A competitive firm **exhausts all internal economies of scale.** Consequently, falling prices in a competitive industry cannot be explained by saying that the firms in the industry are achieving greater economies of scale. Such an explanation implies that a price-taking firm was not maximizing profit before. If a price-taking firm is maximizing profits, it will produce q_3 or more units and exhaust all internal economies of scale. Therefore, economies of scale cannot explain why prices decline in a competitive industry. Chapter 8 will explain how technological change or a fall in the price of a factor of production shifts the firm's cost functions downward and could explain why prices fall in a competitive industry.

SUMMARY

■ A firm in a competitive industry faces a horizontal demand curve. The market price is virtually unaffected by the quantity sold by a competitive firm.

■ The price elasticity of demand facing a firm depends on (1) the market share of the firm, (2) the price elasticity of market demand, and (3) the supply elasticity of the other firms in the industry.

■ When the firm is a price taker, its marginal revenue equals the market price.

■ In the short run a competitive firm determines output where price equals short-run marginal cost.

■ The short-run marginal cost curve of a competitive firm becomes the short-run supply curve of a competitive firm for prices equal to or above minimum average variable cost.

■ In the long run a competitive firm determines output where price equals long-run marginal cost.

■ The long-run marginal cost curve is the long-run supply curve of a profit-maximizing competitive firm for prices equal to or above minimum long-run average cost.

■ A profit maximizing competitive firm completely exhausts all internal economies of scale.

KEY TERMS

competitive firm
price-taking firm
supply elasticity of competitive firms
total revenue equals or exceeds total variable cost
the firm's short-run supply function
exhaustion of economies of scale in the long run

marginal revenue
price elasticity of demand for a competitive firm
equating price to marginal cost
shutdown price
the firm's long-run supply function
nonnegative profits in the long run

REVIEW QUESTIONS

1. What are the three factors that determine a firm's price elasticity of demand?

2. If market demand is very elastic, a firm will be a price taker, but if market demand is not very elastic, the firm will no longer be a price taker. Explain why you agree or disagree.

3. Explain why a competitive firm determines output such that price equals marginal cost.

4. In the short run a firm determines output where price equals short-run marginal cost as long as revenue exceeds fixed cost. Explain why you agree or disagree with this statement.

5. If a price-taking firm determines output where price equals long-run marginal cost but marginal cost is decreasing, the firm is not maximizing profits. Explain why you agree or disagree with this statement.

6. Draw a graph and present a geometric measure of the decrease in profits if a competitive firm increases output by Δq above the profit-maximizing quantity.

7. A profit-maximizing competitive firm will never produce in the region where average variable cost is declining. Explain why you agree or disagree with this statement.

8. A profit-maximizing competitive firm will never produce in the region where short-run average cost is declining. Explain why you agree or disagree with this statement.

9. To determine the profit-maximizing quantity in the short run, a firm must equate price to short-run marginal cost but does not need to know its average cost function. To determine output in the long run, the firm equates price to long-run marginal cost but must know its long-run average cost function. Explain why you agree or disagree with these statements.

10. As the production of television sets has increased over time, the price of a television set has fallen. This implies that producers of television sets have not yet exhausted all of these respective internal economies of scale. Explain why you agree or disagree with this conclusion.

EXERCISES

1. Explain why you would expect the price elasticity of demand facing a firm to be more elastic in the long run than in the short run. Clearly specify the factors that would increase the price elasticity of demand in the long run.

2. If a profit-maximizing competitive firm equates price to long-run marginal cost and produces in the range where long-run marginal cost is increasing, it is maximizing total profits. Explain why you agree or disagree with this statement.

3. If the French government prevents any more firms from producing bottled water, the firms already in the industry will no longer behave as price takers. Explain why you agree or disagree with this statement.

4. When the price is P^*, a competitive firm produces q^* bushels of apples. After price falls, the firm cuts output and suffers losses. Later, after demand increases and the price increases to P^*, the apple supplier will produce more than q^* bushels so that it can recoup its losses. Explain why you agree or disagree.

5. The variable cost function of a firm is shown in the following table.

QUANTITY	TOTAL VARIABLE COST ($)
1	6
2	10
3	12
4	20
5	28
6	40

The market prices for the next 6 years are as follows:

YEAR	1	2	3	4	5	6
MARKET PRICE ($)	8	6	3	2	5	1

In which years will a profit-maximizing firm produce, and what quantity will it produce each year?

6. Suppose the price is $40 per unit and the short-run cost function of a firm is $1,000 + $20q$ where the firm has a capacity to produce 100 units per period.

   a. What is the firm's break-even point?

b. What is the profit-maximizing output?

*7. A firm that maximizes profit per unit will maximize total profit. Explain when this statement is correct and when it is incorrect.

*8. A competitive firm has 12 cement plants. As the economy slips into a recession and the cement price begins to decline, the firm shuts down its smallest plant first. As price continues to decline, the firm closes 4 more plants. Later, demand revives but price does not increase by much initially so the firm opens its smallest plant first because it wants to increase output by only a little. Later, when the price increases by still more, the firm opens the remaining 4 closed plants. Explain why this shut-down

and open-up policy does or does not maximize the profits of the company.

9. Recently, a newspaper reported that a number of farmers shot and killed young calves in their herds: Waste of this kind is inconsistent with profit-maximizing behavior. Explain why you agree or disagree with this statement.

10. A price-taking firm signs a 5-year contract to lease a building. The owner of the building requires annual rent increases based on the rate of inflation. Suppose inflation increases the general price level by 5 percent in the last year and so the annual rent increases by 5 percent. How will this affect the price of the product made by the firm that leases the building?

PROBLEM SET

Should Your Company Honor a Contract?

In July of this year, your company signed a contract to deliver q_c units by the end of December of next year at a per unit price of P''. The contract will occupy all of your production capacity for next year. The cost function of your firm is

$$C = F + V(q) = F + aq \qquad q \le q_c$$

where F denotes fixed cost and variable cost is aq, where a is a constant and equals short-run marginal cost. Variable cost increases linearly with quantity up to capacity output q_c. Your company must pay a franchise tax of T dollars per year to the local government if it receives any revenue during the year. The firm can waive the franchise tax if it does not receive any revenue during the year.

Between July and the end of December of the current year, the price of a critical raw material the firm uses to manufacture the product soars, and average variable ($=$marginal)

cost increases from a to b, with $b > a$. Variable cost becomes $V(q) = bq$. Much to your horror, you learn that the contract does not include an inflation clause, which would have allowed you to increase the price if the price of the raw material increased. Now b is greater than P''. If your company fulfills the contract, the per unit price, P'', will be less than the marginal cost of producing the last unit, b. You face a quandary. Should you fulfill the contract or not?

You ask your attorney what liability you will face if your company does not fulfill the contract. She says that your company will be liable to the tune of any excess the customer will have to pay to purchase the product elsewhere. Your market research people say that a buyer who searches carefully probably could find a price of P^* in the current market but that there is little incentive to search that diligently. The customer is therefore more likely to get a price of P' that is well above P'' and above P^*, that is, $P' > P^* > P''$. Your attorney advises you that you will probably be liable for a penalty of $P' - P''$ for each unit not delivered.

In December of the current year another customer approaches you and asks you whether you would be willing to allocate all of your capacity to supply his firm with q_c units in the coming year. He is willing to pay you a price of P^*, where $P' > P^* > b$. Because you have only enough plant capacity to fulfill one of the contracts, you can satisfy the original contract or the new contract, but not both.

Questions

1. Write out an expression for the losses your company will incur if it fulfills the original contract.

2. Write out an expression for the losses your company will incur if it does not fulfill the original contract and rejects the new contract.

3. Write out an expression for the losses your company will incur if it does not fulfill the original contract but fulfills the new contract.

4. If you do not fulfill the original contract, under what conditions will you sign and fulfill the new contract?

5. Should you decide not to fulfill the original contract and to sign the new contract? How will F and T affect your decision?

CHAPTER 8

PRICE DETERMINATION IN A COMPETITIVE INDUSTRY

■ **8-1   Requirements for Long-and Short-Run Industry Equilibria**
Long-Run Industry Equilibrium
Short-Run Industry Equilibrium
Typical Competitive Industries

■ **8-2   Price Determination in a Constant-Cost Industry**
Two Assumptions of a Constant-Cost Industry
The Long-Run Industry Supply Function in a Constant-Cost Industry
Long-Run Industry Equilibrium in a Constant-Cost Industry

■ **8-3   Moving from One Long-Run Equilibrium to Another**
The Short-Run Industry Supply Function and Equilibrium Price
High Prices Cure High Prices
The Role of Profits
Application 8-1: Helping the Victims of Hurricane Andrew

■ **8-4   Price Determination in an Increasing-Cost Industry**
A Rising Factor Price When Industry Output Expands
Economic Rent or Producer Surplus
Differences in Firm Costs Due to Differences in Managerial Ability

Long-Run Industry Equilibrium When Managerial Ability Differs

■ ***8-5   Adoption of a Cost-Reducing Innovation**
Application 8-2: Higher Jet Fuel Price Downs the Boeing 707
Application 8-3: Regularities in the Evolution of Industries

■ **8-6   Raising the Costs for New Entrants**
How Licensing Changes the Shape of the Long-Run Industry Supply Function
Application 8-4: The Value of a License

■ **8-7   The Effect of Taxes, Trade Limitations, and Market Restrictions on Total Surplus**
Imposing a Per Unit Tax on a Competitive Firm
Long-Run Effects of a Per Unit Tax
Banana Wars: Total Surplus and the Gains from Trade
The Effect of a Per Unit Tax on Consumer and Producer Surplus

■ **Summary**
■ **Key Terms**
■ **Review Questions**
■ **Exercises**

* More difficult material.

In this chapter we analyze how price is determined in a competitive industry when firms are free to enter and leave the industry. To predict the price, firm output, and industry output, we introduce the invaluable concept of an *industry equilibrium* and explain why firms enter or leave an industry. After specifying the requirements for an industry equilibrium, we will develop a baseline model of a competitive industry where firms enter an industry when price is relatively high and profits exist, and leave it when price is relatively low and the industry is unprofitable. We will extend this baseline model to show how a shift in market demand disrupts the industry and causes the industry to pass through a series of short-run equilibria before settling down once again.

We make the analysis more descriptive of reality by relaxing some supply-side assumptions of the baseline model and analyzing (1) how a competitive industry performs when the costs of firms differ, (2) when firms should adopt a cost-reducing innovation, (3) how established suppliers benefit when entry barriers prevent new firms from entering the industry, and (4) how a competitive industry adjusts when trade restrictions and taxes are imposed.

After reading this chapter, you should have a better understanding of how price is determined in a competitive industry and the role that profits and losses play in causing resources to flow into or out of an industry in response to demand or cost changes. In all the models analyzed in this chapter, the entry or exit of firms plays a critical role in limiting the magnitude and duration of firm profits or losses. Throughout, the analysis highlights the role that price plays in transmitting messages from consumers to producers that consumers are demanding more or less of a product and how producers respond to these price signals.

8-1   REQUIREMENTS FOR LONG- AND SHORT-RUN INDUSTRY EQUILIBRIA

This chapter examines how price is determined in a competitive industry in either the short or long runs. To describe the requirements for an industry equilibrium, we must expand our definitions of the short and long runs. In Chapters 5 through 7 the fixedness of a firm's capital distinguished the short run from the long run. This distinction served our purpose since our objective was to analyze the behavior of only a single firm. Now we are enlarging our analysis to study the equilibrium of an industry, where we have to describe the behavior of firms inside and outside the industry. When economists speak of an industry equilibrium, they refer to an industry that is at rest—where price and quantity are stable given the market demand and supply functions. Consequently an industry equilibrium requires that firms outside the industry have no incentive to enter the industry. The specific requirements for an industry to be in short- or long-run equilibrium are summarized below.

Long-Run Industry Equilibrium

First let's consider the **long-run industry equilibrium.** Recall that all factors of production are variable in the long run. To this requirement we append the condition that firms can enter or exit from the industry in the long run. It's as if every firm is starting from scratch in the long run and can decide whether to produce a product, how much to produce, and how to produce that quantity.

Therefore, a competitive industry is in long-run equilibrium if:

1. Each firm in the industry has no incentive to change its method or its scale of production.

2. Profits are zero, and so no firm desires to enter or exit the industry.

Since no firm inside or outside the industry desires to change its behavior, the industry is said to be at rest or in long-run equilibrium.

Short-Run Industry Equilibrium

The **short-run industry equilibrium** differs from the long-run industry equilibrium because two restrictions apply in the short run. In the short run no current producer can change the fixed factor of production and no more firms than are currently outside the industry can enter. Therefore, a short-run analysis examines the behavior of firms already in the industry. Consequently, a short-run industry equilibrium exists if the firms currently in the industry have no incentive to change the quantity produced.

Typical Competitive Industries

It is perhaps redundant to point out that the supply behavior of price-taking firms will be analyzed throughout this chapter. Each firm's price elasticity of demand is infinitely elastic, and this condition is more likely to occur when there are many firms in the industry and each firm's market share is relatively low. Let's consider some examples that might fit the price-taking assumption of a competitive industry. In some industries there are many firms, and no firm has a large share of the market; many retailing and wholesaling industries satisfy these conditions. Table 8-1 lists some less glamorous, little-known manufacturing industries comprising more than 100 firms, in which the concentration ratio (the combined market share of the four largest firms) is less than 20 percent of the market. Not only are there many firms in these industries, but the industry leaders do not command a large share of the total market.

The models discussed in this chapter apply directly to industries like these where firms are price takers and where entry into the industry is free.

8-2 PRICE DETERMINATION IN A CONSTANT-COST INDUSTRY

The baseline model is that of a **constant-cost industry.** This model illustrates how price is determined in a long-run industry equilibrium and how a competitive industry progresses through a succession of short-run equilibria after a demand shift before reaching a new long-run industry equilibrium.

Table 8-1 NUMBER OF FIRMS AND MARKET SHARE OF THE LEADING FOUR FIRMS

INDUSTRY	NUMBER OF FIRMS IN 1987	CONCEN- TRATION RATIO (%)	INDUSTRY	NUMBER OF FIRMS IN 1987	CONCEN- TRATION RATIO (%)
Women's, misses', and juniors' dresses	1,406	6%	Plastic foam products	653	19%
Sawmills and planing mills, general	5,252	15	Aluminum foundries	557	16
Metal heat-treating	631	20	Metal doors	1,428	13
Bolts, nuts, rivets, and forgings	834	16	Conveyers and conveying equipment	703	17
Textile machinery	475	20	Printed circuit boards	950	14
Blowers and fans	445	14	Fresh and frozen prepared fish	579	18

Source: 1987 Census of Manufacturers, "Concentration Ratios in Manufacturing," Subject Series, MC87-S-6.

Two Assumptions of a Constant-Cost Industry

The baseline model makes the following two strong supply-side assumptions, and these two assumptions lead to a long-run **horizontal industry supply function.**

1. All firms in the industry have the same long-run total cost function and therefore the same long-run average and marginal cost functions.

2. The position of each firm's long-run average cost function does not shift as industry output changes.

Assumption 1 says that all firms are alike—each one is a clone of another. New firms entering the industry have the same cost functions as existing firms.

Assumption 2 requires a somewhat longer explanation. It implies that a change in industry output does not (*a*) change the prices of factors of production used to produce the product or (*b*) alter the firm's production function. Assumption 2 applies when an industry is small relative to the size of the economy and purchases general-purpose factors that many industries use. For example, the match industry no doubt satisfies assumption 2. If the total production of matches increases, the price of lumber, a factor in the production of matches, is probably unaffected because the match industry accounts for only a tiny fraction of the total demand for wood products. The match industry can expand or contract without affecting the price of lumber. Assumption 2 also applies when the industry employs factors of production in the same proportion that the other firms in the economy do. Then,

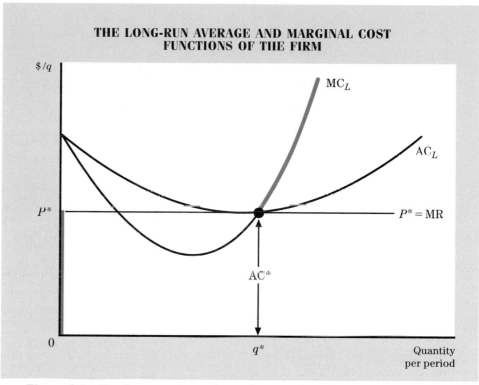

Figure 8-1   The firm experiences internal economies of scale and then internal diseconomies of scale. Minimum long-run average cost equals AC^* when the firm produces q^* units. The heavy lines show the long-run supply function of a competitive firm.

a change in an industry's output causes the industry either to employ more or to release factors of production in the same proportion as other industries employ or release the factors, thereby leaving relative prices of factors unaffected.[1]

The Long-Run Industry Supply Function in a Constant-Cost Industry

From the two assumptions of a constant-cost industry, we can deduce that the long-run industry supply function is horizontal. Let's explain why this conclusion follows from these two assumptions. The first assumption states that existing firms and new entrants have the same long-run average and marginal cost functions as those in Figure 8-1. This figure shows the long-run average (AC_L) and marginal

---

[1] Assumption 2 also rules out the possibility that a change in industry output alters the production function of the firm and causes the firm's long-run average cost function to change position. For example, as the total catch in a fishery increases because more boats are plying the waters, each boat finds that its catch declines and its long-run average cost function shifts upward. More fishing leads to a smaller catch per boat. This type of industry is excluded from this analysis.

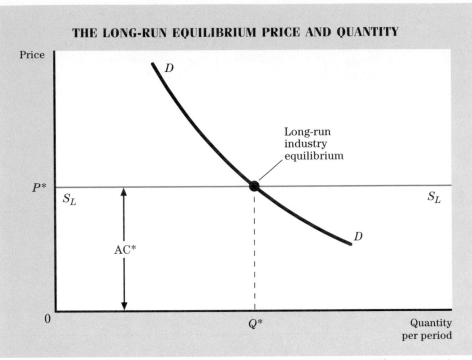

Figure 8-2   In long-run industry equilibrium the market price is P^* and the industry produces Q^* units. No existing producer wants to change the amount produced, and no firm wants to enter the industry if the market price is P^*.

cost (MC_L) functions of a representative firm in a competitive industry. The long-run average cost function of the firm has a typical U-shape, and minimum long-run average cost is AC^* when the firm produces q^* units. If the market price is P^*, the firm maximizes profits by producing q^* units.

The second assumption means that the position of the firm's long-run average cost function does not shift upward or downward as industry output changes. In the long run new firms can enter, and each firm will be willing to supply q^* units at a price of P^*. In this industry an indefinite quantity will be supplied at this price because equally efficient firms are each ready to supply q^* units at a price of P^*. In Figure 8-2 the long-run supply function is the horizontal line $S_L S_L$.

The long-run industry supply function is horizontal in a constant-cost industry.

Long-Run Industry Equilibrium in a Constant-Cost Industry

Given the long-run industry supply function, let's determine what the equilibrium price and quantity are if the industry is in long-run equilibrium. In Figure 8-2 the long-run industry supply function is $S_L S_L$, and the market demand function is DD. The long-run equilibrium price is P^*, and the equilibrium quantity is Q^* units. Given P^*, each competitive firm maximizes profits by producing q^* units, the level of output at which $P^* = \text{MR} = \text{MC}_L = \text{AC}_L$, as shown in Figure 8-1. When the price is P^*, no firm earns profits in long-run equilibrium.

How many firms are in the industry if it is in long-run equilibrium? If the industry supplies Q^* units and each firm produces q^* units, the number of firms in the industry must be $N^* = Q^*/q^*$. If the equilibrium industry quantity is 800,000 units and each firm produces 8,000 units, then 100 firms will be in the industry when it is in long-run equilibrium.

It's fairly easy to check that this is a long-run industry equilibrium. First, none of the N^* firms in the industry desires to change the quantity produced because each one is producing q^* units where $P^* = \text{MC}_L$ and would suffer losses by producing any other quantity.

$$P^* = \text{MR} = \text{MC}_L = \text{AC}_L^* \qquad \text{(Long-Run Equilibrium of the Firm)} \qquad \text{(8-1)}$$

Second, no firm desires to enter the industry since no firm in the industry is earning profits. The industry is at rest. Similarly, no firm desires to exit since no firm is suffering a loss.

8-3 MOVING FROM ONE LONG-RUN EQUILIBRIUM TO ANOTHER

So far, this analysis has been rather mechanical. You are probably asking yourself why any firm would want to be in an industry where profits are zero. What attracted these firms to this industry in the first place? We can enrich the analysis by disrupting the initial long-run industry equilibrium when demand increases.

When market demand increases, consumers are sending signals to producers that they will pay a higher price for each quantity demanded or are demanding more units at each price than before. How do firms inside and outside the industry know that consumers now value the product more highly? To answer this question, let's frame our analysis in two steps. First, let's determine how the existing firms in the industry respond to a shift in demand by creating a new short-run industry equilibrium before new firms can enter. Then, we can trace the supply behavior of existing firms as new firms gradually enter the industry and the industry passes through a series of short-run equilibrium positions en route to a new long-run equilibrium.

The Short-Run Industry Supply Function and Equilibrium Price

Before market demand increases, each one of N^* firms has a plant that produces q^* units at minimum long-run average cost of AC^*. This plant is the only one that can produce q^* at AC^*. Figure 8-3 shows the short-run average cost function AC_S

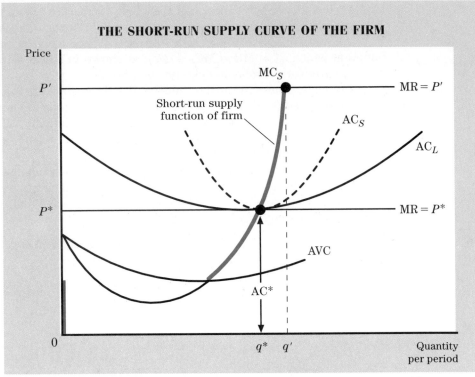

Figure 8-3   The short-run marginal cost function above the average variable cost curve is the short-run supply curve of the firm. In the short run the firm supplies q' units if the price is P'. The heavy lines trace out the firm's short-run supply function.

and the short-run marginal cost function MC_S of a plant that can produce q^* units at minimum cost.

As Chapter 7 demonstrated, each firm maximizes short-run profits by producing q' units if the price is P', and q^* units if the price is P^*. The firm's short-run marginal cost function is the firm's short-run supply function. The **short-run industry supply function** is ss in Figure 8-4, the horizontal sum of the short-run supply functions of the N^* firms.[2] The short-run industry supply function shows the quantity that existing firms in the industry supply at each price. For example, the total quantity supplied in the short run is $Q^* = q^*N^*$ when the price is P^*. Therefore, the short-run industry supply function intersects the long-run industry supply function at $Q = Q^*$.

---

[2] The short-run industry supply function has a horizontal segment because the short-run price cannot fall below minimum average variable cost. Enough firms leave the industry so that the price does not fall below minimum average variable cost, and the remaining firms in the industry produce at minimum average variable cost. However, once price exceeds minimum average variable cost, all firms produce.

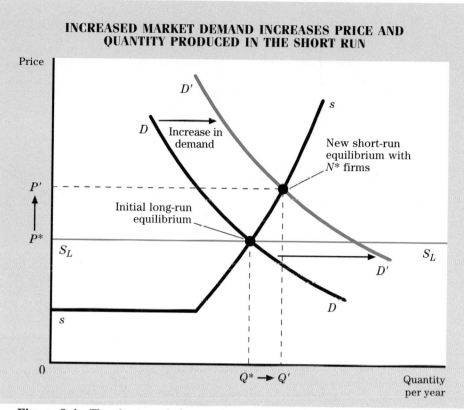

INCREASED MARKET DEMAND INCREASES PRICE AND QUANTITY PRODUCED IN THE SHORT RUN

Figure 8-4   The short-run industry supply curve is *ss* when the number of firms is fixed at N^*. Because demand increases from DD to $D'D'$, the initial long-run equilibrium is disrupted and price rises to P' in the short run so that the quantity demanded equals the quantity supplied by the N^* firms.

The industry's short-run supply function is the horizontal summation of each firm's short-run supply function.

Notice the short-run supply function *ss* is less elastic (steeper) than the long-run supply function S_LS_L. In other words, the short-run response of quantity supplied to a price increase is smaller than the long-run response because the number of firms can only change in the long run. This implies that any demand shift will cause price to change more in the short than in the long run.

Figure 8-4 shows the original and the new market demand functions and the short- and long-run industry supply functions. Because the market demand increases from DD to $D'D'$, price rises to P' to establish a new short-run equilibrium.

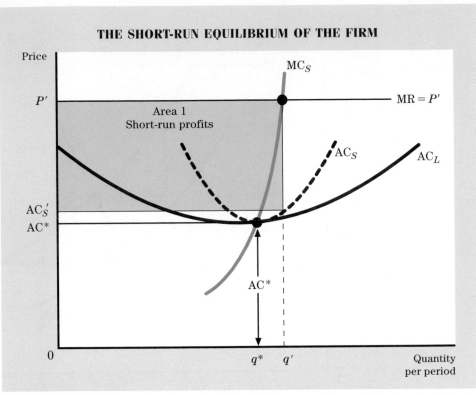

THE SHORT-RUN EQUILIBRIUM OF THE FIRM

Figure 8-5   The increase in market demand increases the market price to P' in the short run. The firm increases output to q' where P' equals short-run marginal cost. Area 1 measures the short-run profits of the firm.

The intersection of $D'D'$ with ss is a short-run equilibrium, in the sense that the market clears with the existing firms.

How does this increase in demand affect each competitive firm? At the higher price of P' each firm maximizes its profits by producing q' units (see Figure 8-5). The firm's short-run average cost increases from AC^* to AC'_S when the firm increases output from q^* to q' units. The firm earns profits equal to area 1, or $(P' - AC'_S)q'$.

> An unexpected increase in market demand increases price, firm and industry output, and firm profits in the short run. Each firm's revenue now exceeds the minimum payments necessary to retain factors in this industry.

High Prices Cure High Prices

The increase in market demand has increased price, made this a profitable industry to enter, and sets off alarms throughout the economy. Because the industry is now

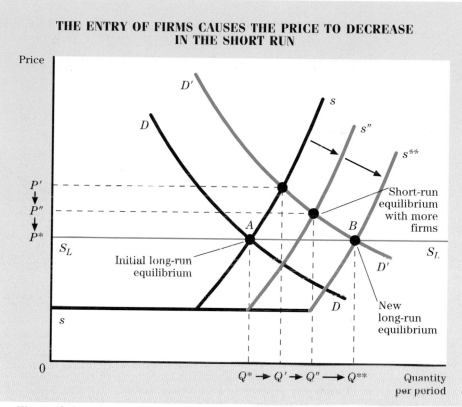

Figure 8-6   The short-run profits of firms in the industry attract more firms to the industry. As more firms enter, the short-run supply shifts to the right and becomes *ss″*. The market price decreases to *P″*, and quantity produced increases to *Q″*. As still more firms enter, the short-run supply curve becomes *ss***, the price decreases to *P**, total output increases to *Q***, and a new long-run equilibrium is reached.

profitable, new firms contract to build plants so that they can enter and sell at the currently attractive price. How long short-run profits persist depends on how long it takes new firms to enter the industry.

After a time, whose duration differs from industry to industry, new firms enter the industry and price declines. As these firms build comparable plants and enter, the short-run industry supply function shifts to the right and becomes *ss″*. Figure 8-6 shows that the rightward shift in the short-run supply function causes price to fall to *P″*.

Figure 8-7 indicates that each existing firm reduces output from *q′* to *q″* when the price declines from *P′* to *P″*. Firm profits decline as price falls and are now only equal to area 2 in Figure 8-7. The total quantity supplied increases from *Q′* to *Q″* in Figure 8-6 because the additional output supplied by the new firms more than offsets the lower output by the existing firms.

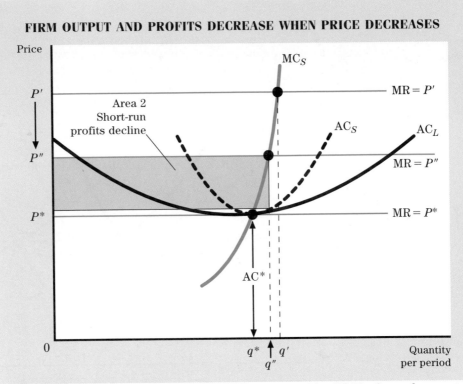

FIRM OUTPUT AND PROFITS DECREASE WHEN PRICE DECREASES

Figure 8-7   The entry of firms reduces the price from P' to P''. The firm reduces output from q' to q'' where P'' equals short-run marginal cost. The firm's profits decline and are equal to area 2.

The entry of firms shifts the short-run supply function to the right and causes price and firm profits to decline.

Later, as still more firms build plants and enter the industry, the short-run supply function shifts further to the right until it becomes ss^{**} in Figure 8-6 and price drops back to the long-run equilibrium price of P^*. The entry of new firms ultimately competes away the profits of the firms in the industry. There are more firms in the industry now, but each one of the larger number is producing only q^* units, the amount produced by each firm in the initial equilibrium.

An increase in market demand causes equilibrium industry output to increase but does not change the long-run equilibrium price in a constant-cost industry.

Now that our description of the adjustment process to a new long-run equilibrium is complete, let's pause here for several general comments about the constant-cost model and the adjustment process. This explanation of the **adjustment of an industry to a shift in market demand** gives some clues to how firms in the industry and throughout the economy in fact learn that consumers are demanding more units of the product. It is through the behavior of prices and profits that companies learn of the increased demand. Higher prices and resulting profits attract firms to the industry, cure high prices, and increase the supply of the product that consumers are now demanding in larger quantities than before. A search for profits motivates firms to enter the industry and causes price to fall back to the original long-run value where $P = \mathrm{MC}_L = \mathrm{AC}_L$.[3]

One implication of the constant-cost model is that growth in market demand cannot explain growth of the firm. In a constant-cost industry the increase in market demand causes the number of firms to increase but not firm size. Therefore, the constant-cost model cannot explain why firm size grows in some industries over time. Since firms do grow over time, however, a different model is needed to explain firm growth. Later in this chapter you will see how firm size can increase when a technological innovation increases the quantity at which long-run average cost reaches a minimum.

The Role of Profits

The increase in market demand is the reason that price and profits suddenly increase and ultimately causes more resources to shift into an industry from elsewhere in the economy. While the profits are only transitory, they serve an important function in enticing more firms to enter the industry and in shifting resources into the industry. If an edict prevented price from rising or if profits were hypothetically subject to a 100 percent tax, then there would be little incentive to enter the industry. The increase in demand would not trigger the entry of firms and the supply response. A firm outside the industry might do just as well by remaining in the industry it is already in.[4] If a market system is to respond to the changing demands of consumers, then the profit motive plays a vital role in reallocating resources from industries where demand is decreasing to industries where demand is increasing. Calls to eliminate profits reflect a misunderstanding of the critical role that they play in causing resources throughout the economy to respond to changes in consumer demands.

APPLICATION 8-1

Helping the Victims of Hurricane Andrew

On August 24, 1992, Hurricane Andrew ripped through southern Florida, causing severe flooding, blocked roads, and damage to houses, businesses, and telephone and public utility services. The disruption in electric service kept refrigerators from

---

[3] Chapter 18 discusses the socially optimal properties of an economy where firms are price takers and entry into all industries is free.

[4] Chapter 11 discusses the incentive for firms to let costs increase when regulation limits profits.

functioning, and fresh and frozen food spoiled. Residents could not purchase food and ice from grocery stores or plywood from hardware stores to repair their damaged houses and roofs because many stores closed. After the hurricane had passed, the demand for ice, flashlights, food, and plywood increased.

Out of the wreckage came opportunity. Many individuals from outside the area hit by the hurricane set up roadside stands selling food, flashlights, generators, and so forth. Many came from out of state—some to help and some to help and earn income. Florida officials became incensed when they learned of price increases throughout the damaged area. Bags of ice that normally cost $1 suddenly were being sold for $5. Motel rooms that ordinarily were $35 a night went for over $100 a night. Plywood prices doubled. Some restaurants raised prices. Some officials said that there was no difference between a looter and a price gouger. The Attorney General's office issued subpoenas for the records of firms, including those of seven plywood manufacturers.

Let's try to analyze this bleak situation objectively. After any major hurricane, private and public agencies begin to organize relief efforts. Typically, these agencies respond sluggishly and require several days to a week to take action. The victims have immediate needs, however, and they must fend for themselves during the first week after a hurricane. Will a more flexible and rapid supply response occur if prices are prevented from increasing or if prices are allowed to increase?

The demand for many goods increases after a hurricane passes, and the supply of these goods provided by local merchants decreases because of the damage caused by the storm. The increase in market demand and the decrease in market supply are the root causes of the price increases. Higher prices make it attractive for outsiders to come into the area and increase the supplies of ice, flashlights, chain saws, and work gloves. Especially during the first few days after the hurricane when public and private relief is not yet organized, the profit incentive can be the most effective way to expand supply quickly. It may appear callous to allow price increases after victims have already suffered substantial losses, but it is even more callous to *prevent* supplies from increasing, thereby preventing prices from *falling* just when victims are demanding and purchasing essential goods.

When the threat of prosecution holds prices down, outsiders will have less incentive to increase the supply of badly needed goods. If firms expect lawsuits because prices increase, they will have less incentive to ship goods into the state. The profit motive encourages suppliers to offer goods that are in greater demand and to allocate badly needed goods among different locations. Prices are reduced by increasing supplies, not by preventing supplies from increasing.

You have already seen how a competitive industry moves from one long-run equilibrium to another after market demand increases. Demand can shift inward, as the makers of typewriters learned when the personal computer arrived. A competitive industry goes through a similar adjustment process after market demand decreases. You can test your understanding of the equilibrating process by drawing graphs for the industry and the firm after market demand decreases and demonstrating why the short-run market price falls and later increases as firms suffer losses and leave the industry.

8-4 PRICE DETERMINATION IN AN INCREASING-COST INDUSTRY

The two assumptions of the baseline model of a constant-cost industry do not apply in many industries, particularly in those where firms differ in efficiency and size. For example, some firms have more capable managers or chief executive officers (CEOs) than others and can manufacture a product at a lower minimum long-run average cost than others can. Whether firm differences are caused by **differences in managerial ability** or differences in the productivity of land, we assume that there is an underlying factor that is not perfectly elastic in supply, be it managerial talent or land. To increase the total quantity supplied by producers in this industry, the product price must be increased in order to pay for the increasing cost of the factor, as progressively larger amounts of it are employed in the industry. This means that firms in the industry do not each have the same long-run average cost function (assumption 1 of the baseline model).

The second assumption of the model of a constant-cost industry—that the position of the firm's long-run average cost function does not shift as industry output changes—is also violated if the industry uses a specialized factor. In this case, an increase in industry output drives up the prices of some factors of production and causes the firm's long-run average and marginal cost functions to shift upward. While the firm is a price taker, the industry is not because an increase in its demand for the specialized factor causes the price of the factor to increase. In an increasing-cost industry the quantity supplied will increase in the long run only if the industry receives a higher price.

> The long-run industry supply function has a positive slope in an increasing-cost industry.

A Rising Factor Price When Industry Output Expands

In an **increasing-cost industry** the price of a factor of production increases as industry output expands, and so the industry's long-run supply function slopes upward. When factor prices increase, economists say there is an **external pecuniary diseconomy of scale.** Let's analyze the case of an external pecuniary diseconomy of scale since it is more common than an external pecuniary economy of scale—where an increase in industry output causes a factor price to decrease.

Figure 8-8*a* shows two pairs of long-run average and marginal cost functions of a competitive firm. AC_L is the firm's long-run average cost function when *industry output* is Q^* units (Figure 8-8*b*), while AC_L' is the firm's long-run average cost function when *industry output* increases to Q' units. After demand increases,

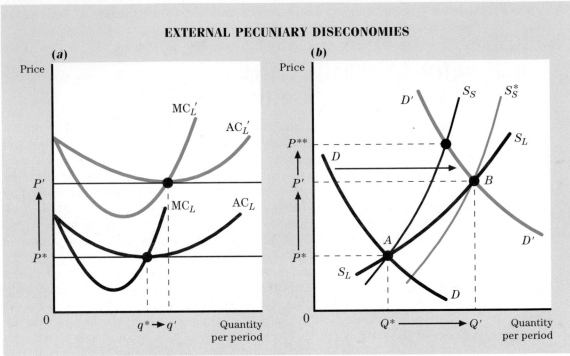

Figure 8-8   (*a*) The firm's long-run average and marginal cost curves shift upward when the industry output increases from Q^* to Q' because factor prices increase. (*b*) The equilibrium price and industry output increase in the long run after market demand increases. The increase in industry output causes the price of a factor of production to rise and shifts the firm's cost functions upward.

the firm's long-run average cost function shifts upward because a rise in industry output increases the price of a factor of production and causes every firm's long-run average and marginal cost functions to shift upward. In Figure 8-8*a* the quantity where long-run average cost reaches a minimum increases from q^* to q' because of the increase in the price of a factor. However, this is merely an illustration. The quantity where long-run average cost reaches a minimum may increase, stay the same, or decrease.

> When the price of a factor increases as the industry expands output, there are external pecuniary diseconomies of scale.

Let's trace out the effects of an increase in demand when there is an external pecuniary diseconomy. Initially, market demand is DD, and so the long-run equilibrium price is P^* and the total quantity supplied is Q^* in Figure 8-8*b*. Each firm produces q^* units, and there are N^* firms in the industry. After market demand increases from DD to $D'D'$, the price increases to the new short-run equilibrium price of P^{**} and the existing firms earn profits. This causes more firms to enter the industry, and the short-run supply function shifts to the right and becomes S_s^*. The price falls from P^{**} to P'. The new short-run supply function intersects the long-run supply function at point B where the new long-run equilibrium price is P', industry output increases to Q', and firm output increases to q' units. When there are external pecuniary diseconomies, an increase in market demand increases the long-run equilibrium price and industry output. In both the old and the new long-run industry equilibria the firms in the industry earn zero profits because the higher price of P' is equal to long-run marginal cost and the minimum average cost of the firm's new long-run average cost function.

The principal difference between a constant-cost industry and this example of an increasing-cost industry is that the equilibrium price increases when market demand increases. Price necessarily increases because the cost of production increases when industry output expands.

When is an industry likely to be an increasing-cost industry? External pecuniary diseconomies are more likely to appear when production requires the use of a specialized factor of production. Land is often considered a specialized factor because the quality of land varies from one acre to another or where natural resources are found. Natural resources and agricultural products require the use of land, and they are likely to be harvested or produced under external pecuniary diseconomies.

Economic Rent or Producer Surplus

You have seen that firm profits are zero in long-run industry equilibrium in both a constant-cost and an increasing-cost industry. While the profits of firms increase temporarily, entry of new firms competes these profits away in the long run. The main beneficiaries of an increase in market demand are the owners of the specialized factor of production who benefit because the price of the factor increases. If the specialized factor is land, land owners benefit because they can now rent out their land at a higher price. For example, an increase in the demand for wine benefits the owners of the specialized land on which the grapes grow. When the demand for gasoline increases, the owners of crude oil deposits benefit.

The benefits received by the owners of a scarce resource can be measured by studying the market for a factor of production that is not perfectly elastic in supply. In Figure 8-9 the supply function of a factor of production, $S_f S_f$, has a positive slope. More of this factor is supplied at higher prices. Therefore, an increase in the market demand for the good shifts the demand function for the factor from $D_f D_f$ to $D_f' D_f'$ and the factor price increases from P_f^* to P_f'.

When the supply function of a factor of production has a positive slope, the factor earns an economic rent and the price is above the minimum price required for it to be supplied. In Figure 8-9 the equilibrium price and quantity of the factor are P_f^* and F^*, respectively. The total amount paid to employ F^* units is $P_f^* F^*$. To simplify the explanation, assume that single units of the factor are supplied at different prices. The first unit of the factor will be supplied if the factor price is only P_1, the second unit at a slightly higher price of P_2, etc. The difference between

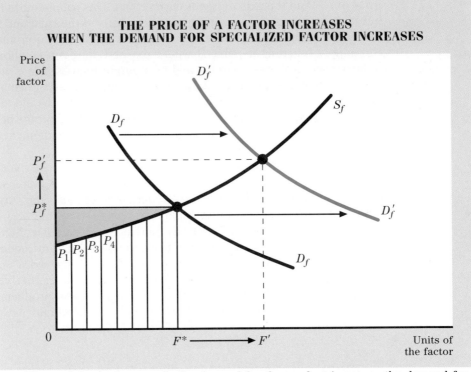

THE PRICE OF A FACTOR INCREASES
WHEN THE DEMAND FOR SPECIALIZED FACTOR INCREASES

Figure 8-9   An increase in the demand for the product increases the demand for a specialized factor of production. The price of the factor and total employment of the factor increase. The total rent received by the owners of the factor equals the price received less the minimum price at which each unit would be supplied. When F^* units of the factor are used to produce the product, total rent is equal to the shaded area.

the price and the minimum price required before that unit will be supplied is $P_f^* - P_1$ in Figure 8-9. The excess of $P_f^* - P_1$ is called an **economic rent** or **producer surplus** for the first unit. The difference $P_f^* - P_2$ is the economic rent or producer surplus for the second unit. The sum of these differences for all units up to F^* units is producer surplus, which is equal to the shaded area in Figure 8-9.

> An economic rent or producer surplus exists when the price received for a factor exceeds the minimum price required to employ the factor.

Some noteworthy examples of economic rent come from professional sports. In a recent interview a quarterback for a professional football team, who had recently signed a long-term contract paying him approximately $3 million annually, mentioned how much he enjoys playing football and how fortunate he is that someone is willing to pay him $3 million a year to play a game that he might be willing to play for perhaps $30,000 a year—his opportunity cost or what he could earn annually in another occupation. The rent he earns is the difference between his compensation and what he would earn in another occupation, or $2,970,000!

Differences in Firm Costs Due to Differences in Managerial Ability

Thus far it has been assumed that all firms are alike, but now it is time to modify this assumption. Here we assume the long-run average cost functions of firms differ because of differences in managerial ability. In the model the position of a firm's long-run average cost function depends on who manages the firm. Some CEOs are skillful at keeping a firm's costs low, whereas others manage companies that are in a perpetual struggle to survive. Because of differences in managerial ability, firms with less efficient managers can supply the product only at higher prices.

Figure 8-10 shows the long-run average cost functions of three of many firms from left to right according to the firm's minimum long-run average cost. The dif-

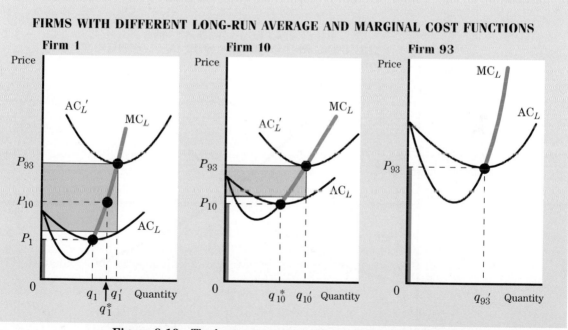

FIRMS WITH DIFFERENT LONG-RUN AVERAGE AND MARGINAL COST FUNCTIONS

Figure 8-10   The long-run average and marginal cost curves of the three firms differ because of differences in managerial ability. Each firm's long-run supply function is the thick segment. Each firm supplies more at a higher price. If the price is P_{93}, firm 1 supplies q'_1, firm 10 supplies q'_{10}, and firm 93 supplies q'_{93}. Competition for managers will increase managerial compensation above opportunity cost. The shaded area represents the increase in managerial compensation. After managerial compensation increases, the average cost curve of the firm shifts upward and becomes AC'_L.

ferent positions of the long-run average cost functions are due to the different abilities of the firms' managers. When a particular manager runs firm 1, it has the lowest minimum long-run average cost in the industry. Firm 1 enters this industry if the price of the product equals or exceeds P_1. Firm 10 has the tenth lowest minimum long-run average cost and enters the industry if the market price equals or exceeds P_{10}. Firm 93 has the ninety-third lowest minimum long-run average cost in the industry and enters the industry if the price equals or exceeds P_{93}.

Because the firm's long-run marginal cost function is its long-run supply function, the industry's long-run supply function can be derived by summing the individual firms' long-run supply functions horizontally. For example, at a price of P_{10}, firms 1 through 10 supply the product, with firm 1 producing q_1^* units and firm 10 producing q_{10}^* units. If the price is P_{93}, firm 1 produces q_1', firm 10 produces q_{10}', and firm 93 enters the industry and produces q_{93}'. When the price of the good increases, the total quantity supplied in the long run increases because (1) each existing firm in the industry is willing to supply more units in the long run and (2) less efficient firms enter the industry and increase the total quantity supplied. The long-run industry supply function $S_L S_L$ in Figure 8-11 has a positive slope.

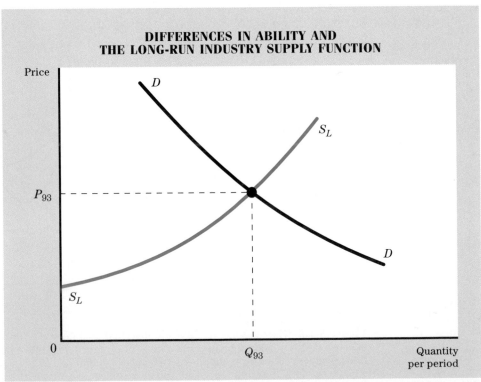

**DIFFERENCES IN ABILITY AND
THE LONG-RUN INDUSTRY SUPPLY FUNCTION**

Figure 8-11 When managers have different abilities, the long-run industry supply curve has a positive slope. As the price increases, each existing firm supplies more units and less efficient firms enter the industry. When market demand is DD, the long-run equilibrium price is P_{93} and firms 1 through 93 supply the product.

The long-run industry supply function has a positive slope when managers differ in ability.

Long-Run Industry Equilibrium When Managerial Ability Differs

In Figure 8-11, given the market demand function DD and the long-run supply function $S_L S_L$, the long-run equilibrium price is P_{93}, the equilibrium quantity is Q_{93}, and there are 93 firms in the industry. Firm 1 produces q'_1, firm 10 produces q'_{10}, and firm 93 produces q'_{93}. Each firm builds a plant that allows it to produce its profit-maximizing output at lowest total cost.

At a price of P_{93} it appears that all firms except firm 93 earn profits. For the moment, let's think of the two shaded color areas in Figure 8-10 as the profits of the respective firms. Firm 1 is very profitable and the envy of other companies in the industry. What is the profitability of firm 1 due to? It is due to the ability of the manager to run a tight ship and keep costs down. Who benefits from these unique talents? Apparently, the shareholders of the firm are the beneficiaries of the manager's successful cost-reducing efforts.

Would this situation persist if it occurred? Suppose you are the manager of firm 1 and your compensation is currently \$150,000 a year, the salary that you would earn managing a firm in another industry. What is likely to happen? You receive phone calls from headhunters who want to know what it would take for you to switch to another firm in the industry. Each firm is willing to offer you a more attractive compensation package because each expects you to reduce the costs of their firm so that it can earn profits. Clearly, firm 1 must match the competing offers if it is to retain your services; if you leave the costs of the firm will increase. You have specialized talents, and so you are in an enviable position. How high can your salary go? If there is a competitive market for managers, your compensation will increase until the "apparent" profits of firm 1 in Figure 8-10 disappear. If you received less for your services, whichever firm that employed you would earn profits and other firms would bid more for your services. Competition in the market for managerial talent will increase your salary by the shaded color area for firm 1 in Figure 8-10. The same forces are at work for firm 10. The salary of the manager of firm 10 will increase by the shaded color area for firm 10.

When there are differences in managerial ability, an increase in market demand benefits managers with scarce talents and not the shareholders of the firms.

If the market for managers is competitive and managerial compensation increases, the profits of each firm numbered from 1 to 92 will disappear. The average cost function of each firm shifts upward in a certain way when managerial compensation increases, but the firm's marginal cost function does not change. The rise in salary shifts the firm's total cost function upward by the amount of the higher compensation. Figure 8-12 shows the total cost function of the firm before

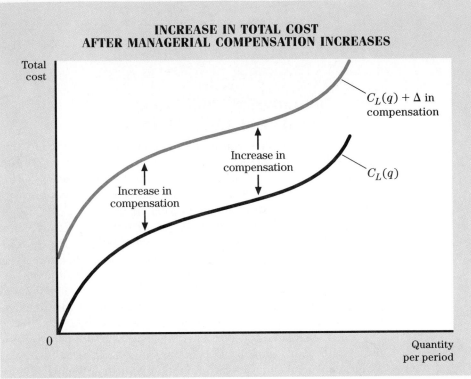

Figure 8-12   The firm's total cost function shifts upward by the increase in compensation of the manager. The slope of each total cost function for a given quantity is the same. This means the two total cost curves have the same marginal cost function. Therefore, the marginal cost of increasing output does not change when the compensation of the manager increases.

and after the manager's salary increases. The difference between the two total cost functions is the increased compensation paid to the manager, which resembles an increase in fixed cost and therefore does not affect the slope of the total cost function. At each quantity the slopes of the two long-run cost functions are the same, and so the two total cost functions have the same marginal cost function. Therefore, the marginal cost function does not shift when the compensation of the manager increases.

In Figure 8-10 the average cost functions of firms 1 and 10 shift upward and become AC'_L when executive compensation increases. Minimum average cost on the new average cost function occurs at q'_1 for firm 1. Because the marginal cost function does not shift, the firm produces q'_1 units before and after compensation increases since P_{93} is still equal to the firm's long-run marginal cost. The same is true for firm 10. Minimum long-run average cost including the higher salary still occurs when the firm produces q'_{10}.

There is a subtle message in this analysis that is easy to miss. When there is a factor with a rising supply price, the firm's average cost *does not* determine the price of the product, but rather, the product price determines the firm's average cost. If price exceeds average cost for any firms in the industry, these firms' apparent profits are dissipated in increased managerial compensation. The market price does not increase once again because the manager's compensation increases since the added compensation is like a fixed cost and consequently does not affect the firm's marginal cost function. If each firm's marginal cost does not change, the industry supply function does not change. Consequently, price does not increase by still more because compensation increases.

*8-5 ADOPTION OF A COST-REDUCING INNOVATION[5]

Like an unexpected increase in demand, costs can change unexpectedly. Technological change is often unforeseen and creates new production methods that reduce the cost of production and shift the supply functions outward. This section investigates how a competitive industry reacts to a technological change that lowers the firm's long-run average cost function. We will assume that firms outside the industry are the first to adopt the cost-reducing innovation and to begin supplying the product to the market. Once the new firms adopt the new technique, there are two sources of supply—companies using the old technology and companies using the new technology. The existing firms in the industry will face a critical decision: Should they junk old plants and immediately switch over to the new technology or wait until their old equipment and plants wear out?

Before considering a graphical treatment of when to **switch over to a new technology,** let's look at a numerical example. A competitive firm already has an existing plant that uses the old technology. Table 8-2 shows the fixed (sunk) cost of a firm using the old technology in column 2, its total variable cost in column 3, and its short-run marginal cost in column 4. If the firm builds a plant that uses the new technology, the long-run total cost is in column 5 and long-run average cost is in column 6. One point to notice is that the firm's total variable cost is less than the long-run total cost of the new plant at each quantity. Another point is that the firm will incur the sunk cost of the old plant whether it uses the old plant or builds a new one. Therefore, sunk cost can be ignored.

If the market price is $32 and the firm builds a new plant with the new technology, it will produce 4 units of output where price equals the firm's long-run marginal cost. At a price of $32 revenues are $128 ($32 × 4) and the total cost of producing 4 units with the plant using the new technology is $128, and so the profits of the firm are zero (ignoring sunk cost of the old plant). On the other hand, if the firm does not build a new plant but produces 4 units with the old plant, its total variable cost would be only $80. Therefore, the firm's profits must be higher because total variable cost of the old plant is less than the long-run total cost of using the new plant. If the firm does not build a new plant but continues to use the old plant, it will produce 6 units where the price of $32 equals the short-run

---

[5] This section borrows from unpublished writings of R. L. Bishop.

Table 8-2   COMPARING TOTAL VARIABLE COST OF AN OLD PLANT WITH THE TOTAL LONG-RUN COST OF A NEW PLANT

QUANTITY (1)	SUNK COST OF OLD PLANT ($) (2)	VARIABLE COST OF OLD PLANT ($) (3)	MARGINAL COST OF OLD PLANT ($) (4)	LONG-RUN TOTAL COST OF NEW PLANT ($) (5)	LONG-RUN AVERAGE COST OF NEW PLANT ($) (6)
1	200	35	35	65	65
2	200	44	9	80	40
3	200	60	16	96	32
4	200	80	20	128	32
5	200	106	26	180	36
6	200	138	32	240	40

marginal cost of the old plant. Total profits will be $192 − $138 = $54 (ignoring sunk cost). The firm's profits will be higher if it continues to use the old plant whenever the total variable cost of the old plant is less than the long-run total cost of the new plant. Equivalently, we can say that the firm will keep the old plant when its average variable cost is less than the long-run average cost of the new plant.

This numerical illustration brings out the importance of comparing the average variable cost of the old plant with the long-run average cost of the new plant when making the switch-over decision. Those are the costs under the manager's control. Now let's consider a graphical analysis of the switch-over decision. To illustrate the theory in its simplest form, our analysis starts with a constant-cost industry in long-run industry equilibrium. Figure 8-13a shows the long-run average cost function of an established firm using the old technology. The firm has built a plant with a short-run average cost function (AC_S) and a short-run marginal cost function (MC_S). In Figure 8-13c the market demand function is DD and the horizontal long-run industry supply function is S_L, with all firms using the old technology. There are N^* firms in the industry, and the short-run industry supply function is ss. The initial equilibrium price and quantity are P^* and Q^*, respectively, and each firm produces q^* units.

Figure 8-13b shows the long-run average and marginal cost functions of a new firm that uses the new technology. At each quantity the long-run average cost function of this firm is *lower* than the long-run average cost function of a firm that uses the older technology. Any firm starting from scratch prefers to use the new lower-cost technology.

A cost-reducing innovation lowers the firm's long-run average cost function.

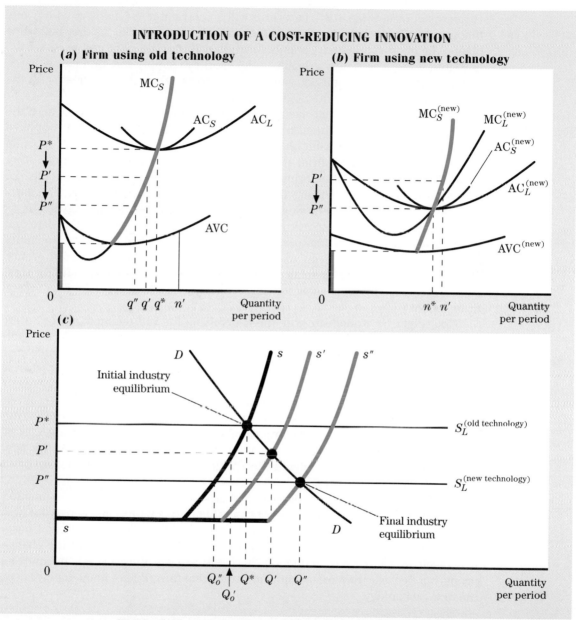

INTRODUCTION OF A COST-REDUCING INNOVATION

(a) Firm using old technology

(b) Firm using new technology

(c)

Figure 8-13   A cost-reducing technology is introduced by a new entrant (*b*). The price falls from P^* to P' as the short-run supply function shifts to the right (*c*) and becomes ss'. As more firms enter with the new cost-reducing technology, the price falls to P''. Later, the firms using the old technology (*a*) adopt the new technology when their old plants and equipment must be replaced.

Given the current price of P^*, new firms will quickly enter the industry with plants that use the new technology because they expect to earn profits. As they build new plants, the short-run industry supply function shifts to the right and becomes ss' in Figure 8-13c. The rightward shift in the short-run supply function causes price to fall to P' and total industry output to rise to Q'. During this adjustment, the firms adopting the new technology earn profits.

Figure 8-13a shows that each existing firm reduces output to q' where the lower price P' is equal to the firm's short-run marginal cost. Total output supplied by all existing firms still using the older technology decreases from Q^* to Q'_o in Figure 8-13c. The entry of firms using the new technology lowers the price from P^* to P' and causes existing firms to incur losses. To keep the graph simple, the losses sustained by an existing firm are not shown in Figure 8-13a. The early entrants earn profits after entering the industry with the new technology. Later, as still more firms enter, the short-run supply function shifts further to the right and becomes ss''. The equilibrium price falls to P'', the equilibrium industry quantity increases to Q'', and the firms using the new technology no longer earn profits. Each firm using the old technology reduces output by still more to q'', and the total quantity supplied by firms using the old technology falls to Q''_o. The losses of these firms mount.

You might be wondering why the firms using the old technology don't shift over to the new technology immediately since they are suffering losses. The reason is that an existing firm can produce each quantity at a lower average variable cost with the old plant. It incurs only the average variable cost of the old plant when it produces any given quantity since the fixed cost of the old plant is a sunk cost. If it adopts the new technology, the cost that it will incur to produce any given quantity will be the long-run average cost of using the new technology because the firm is starting from scratch. The firm should compare the average variable cost of the old plant with the long-run average cost of the new plant using the new technology before deciding whether to continue to use the old technology or to shift immediately to the new.

On the other hand, if the innovation shifts the long-run average cost function down such that the old plant's average variable cost function lies above the new long-run average cost function, the firm should switch over immediately. Consequently, firms cannot be expected to switch over immediately unless the change will result in a large cost reduction. It is not because they are not maximizing profits but because they are maximizing profits that firms do not immediately adopt the new technology.

> A firm will continue to use old technology if the average variable cost function of the old plant lies below the long-run average cost function of the new plant.

After a time, as the old plants wear out, the firms that remain in the industry adopt the new technology since the long-run average cost of the new technology is less than the long-run average cost of the old technology. When the firm makes the reinvestment decision, all costs are variable and none are sunk. The theory predicts that the proportion of industry output that firms supply with the new technology will gradually increase until all firms are using the new technology. During this conversion process the price remains at P'' since the reduction in output by firms that were using the old technology is offset by the added output of firms adopting the new technology.

How does a cost-reducing innovation affect the size of a firm? A cost-reducing method could either increase or decrease the quantity where long-run average cost reaches a minimum. In Figure 8-13b, n^* could be substantially larger than q^*. If so, an innovation would increase firm size after the industry reaches the new long-run equilibrium. One way of explaining why firms grow as equilibrium industry output increases is that technological change favors larger firms by increasing the quantity at which long-run average cost reaches a minimum.

APPLICATION 8-2

Higher Jet Fuel Price Downs the Boeing 707

If an airline is going to make cost-efficient decisions about when to retire aircraft, it should compare the average variable cost of an old airplane with the long-run average cost of a new airplane. Airlines introduce new planes over time; in particular, after jet fuel prices increased sharply in the 1970s, they brought along more fuel-efficient planes. Table 8-3 shows the fuel efficiency of selected aircraft measured in seat miles per gallon. The Boeing 707 was at the bottom of the list in 1975. Fuel efficiency was of lesser concern for the airlines when jet fuel prices were low. The price was about 60 cents per gallon in 1978 but began to increase in 1979 and

Table 8-3   THE FUEL EFFICIENCY OF SELECTED COMMERCIAL AIRCRAFT, 1975

TYPE OF AIRCRAFT	SEAT MILES PER GALLON
B-747	52.9
DC-10-10	51.8
B 737-200	41.1
B 727-200	39.7
B-707-300	35.2

Source: Civil Aeronautics Board, Airline Operating Costs and Performance Report, 1975.

peaked at \$1.25 in 1981. In a short span of two years jet fuel price doubled. Suddenly, older planes like the B-707 became much less cost-effective. The airlines moved as rapidly as possible to retire it. Figure 8-14 shows the stock of 707s and 747s in the fleet. The number of B-707s was declining gradually before the fuel price increased but notice the more rapid decline in the number of B-707s and the increase in the number of B-747s when fuel prices increased after 1978.

In terms of our theory we can say that the average variable cost of the B-707 in 1978 was sufficiently low because of lower fuel prices that airlines continued to operate B-707s even though more fuel-efficient planes such as the B-747 and other planes could have been purchased. There is no doubt that airlines would have gradually retired the B-707 even if the price of fuel had not risen after 1978. At the time the average variable cost of operating the older plane was lower than the long-run average cost of a new, more fuel-efficient plane, so airlines did not abandon all B-707s immediately but kept flying some B-707s.

Rising jet fuel prices after 1978 changed their calculations. Now the average

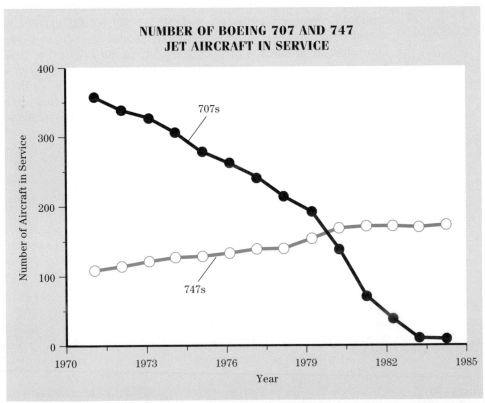

Figure 8-14   Because of the rapid increase in the price of jet fuel after 1978, airlines quickly retired the remaining, less efficient Boeing 707s in favor of more fuel-efficient planes.

variable cost of flying a B-707 shifted up by more than the upward shift in the long-run average cost of a new B-747 and other more fuel-efficient planes. With a much higher jet fuel price the optimal decision was to replace the B-707, and the airlines moved quickly to retire the remaining B-707s.[6]

APPLICATION **8-3**

Regularities in the Evolution of Industries

Cost-reducing innovations cause prices to decline. Looking at the *rate* of decline in prices, especially in mature industries, can provide an indication of the frequency with which firms introduce cost-reducing innovations. Michael Gort and Steven Klepper examined the evolution of 46 industries after a firm introduced a major innovation in each one.[7] While these major changes were made in different decades, the authors hoped to discover regularities in the way industries evolve after an initial major innovation. How did prices behave over time? Did the innovator maintain its market share and charge a relatively high price, or was the more common pattern one of declining prices and the entry of competitors? Did the number of firms grow steadily over time, or more rapidly in different stages as the industry evolved? Did major cost reductions primarily occur early in the development of these industries or did they continue to occur as the industry evolved? What happened to the number of firms and total industry output as the industry matured? These are some of the questions raised in this interesting study.

While there was considerable variability among the industries, Gort and Klepper identified five stages in the evolution of a representative industry. Table 8-4 shows the average percentage change in the inflation-adjusted price, output, and entry in each of the five stages.

In the first stage, industry output grows rapidly and price declines at a rapid annual rate although the number of firms grows modestly. In the second stage, entry of firms increases dramatically, price continues to drop rapidly, and the growth rate of output, while still substantial, begins to decline. During the third stage there is virtually no growth in the number of firms, prices continue to decline, but at a slower rate, and the growth rate of output declines. The fourth stage is the "shake-out" stage. From the end of the third stage to the end of the fourth stage Gort and Klepper report that the number of firms in the industry declines by an average of 40 percent, a dramatic decline, even though industry output continues to grow, but at a slower rate. In the fourth stage prices fall at a faster rate than in the third stage. In the last stage, the number of firms has stabilized again, but at a lower level, prices decline at the slowest rate, and industry output has virtually stabilized.

---

[6] From a more extensive discussion of the retirement of the B-707 by Austan Goolsbee, "Evidence on the Endogenous Retirement of Capital Goods," March 1996 (unpublished manuscript).
[7] Michael Gort and Steven Klepper, "Time Paths in the Diffusion of Product Innovations," *Economic Journal* 92 (September 1982), pp. 630–53.

Table 8-4   REGULARITIES IN THE EVOLUTION OF INDUSTRIES

STAGE OF INDUSTRY DEVELOPMENT	AVERAGE ANNUAL RATE OF DECREASE IN REAL PRICE (23 INDUSTRIES)	AVERAGE ANNUAL RATE OF INCREASE IN TOTAL OUTPUT (25 INDUSTRIES)	AVERAGE NUMBER OF ENTRANTS PER YEAR (46 INDUSTRIES)
First	− 13.6	56.6	0.5
Second	− 13.0	35.1	5.67
Third	− 7.2	12.3	0.13
Fourth	− 9.0	8.1	− 4.84
Fifth	− 5.2	1.0	− 0.47

Source: Reprinted with permission of Blackwell Publishers for the Royal Economic Society.

Change continues in these industries after the initial major innovation. There is not simply one major innovation which firms adapt to. The evidence is not at all consistent with a "big bang" theory of industry development. Prices decline continually, at a faster rate at first but nevertheless continually. Following the initial major innovation, it appears that firms continue to introduce cost-reducing innovations and learn to produce the product more efficiently in all stages. In the shakeout stage these cost-reducing innovations are of sufficient importance that the rate of price declines increases, the size of firms increases, and the number of firms in the industry decreases dramatically.

Entry of firms was discontinuous in these industries. What is somewhat surprising is that the number of entrants per year did not peak in the first stage. Some new firms did enter during this stage; however, it was not until the second stage that the number increased rapidly. In a particularly interesting finding the authors report that the duration of the first stage has been decreasing over time (see Table 8-5). In industries where the major innovation occurred before 1930, the first stage

Table 8-5   DURATION OF FIRST STAGE

YEAR WHEN MAJOR INNOVATION OCCURRED	DURATION OF FIRST STAGE (YEARS)
Before 1930	23
Between 1930 and 1939	10
After 1939	5

Source: Reprinted with permission of Blackwell Publishers for the Royal Economic Society.

lasted about 23 years, a lengthy period. In industries where major innovations occurred from 1930 to 1939, the first stage lasted about 10 years. And in industries where the innovation occurred after 1940, the first stage lasted only 5 years. So, the length of the period before the entry rate of competitors speeds up is shortening. Assuming short-run profits from an innovation are higher in the early stages of development of an industry, the Gort and Klepper results suggest that the period over which firms earn these short-run profits is decreasing.

Perhaps one of the most important lessons of this study is the persistence of price reductions throughout the evolution of an industry. This pattern of declining prices indicates that large and small cost reductions are occurring continually as an industry grows and matures.

8-6 RAISING THE COSTS FOR NEW ENTRANTS

It is the entry of firms that competes away short-run profits of firms in the industry. By limiting the entry of firms into the industry, established firms can prevent their profits from being competed away. The next question is. What are the economic consequences of raising barriers to entry? To answer this question, we consider the economic effects of licensing that prevent firms from entering a profitable industry.

How Licensing Changes the Shape of the Long-Run Industry Supply Function

Entry into some industries is blocked. In most cities, new firms cannot enter the taxicab business legally. Likewise, not everyone can open a retail establishment that serves alcoholic beverages or become a doctor, a veterinarian, a beautician, or a mortician. In most cities you must have a license, and the license is valuable— very valuable in some cases. In this section the constant-cost model is used to analyze the impact of licensing on long-run equilibrium price and quantity in a competitive industry.

Figure 8-15a shows that a price-taking firm produces q^* units when the equilibrium price is P^*. Figure 8-15b shows the market demand function DD and the horizontal long-run industry supply function $S_L S_L$. The long-run equilibrium price and quantity are P^* and Q^*, and there are N^* firms in the industry.

Assume that a regulatory commission issues a license to each existing firm in the industry and decides that only a firm with a license can supply the product. Licensing blocks further entry into the industry.

To determine how licensing affects the long-run equilibrium price and quantity, let's first determine how licensing alters the long-run industry supply function. In the long run each price-taking firm determines output where price equals long-run marginal cost. In Figure 8-15a the heavier portion of the long-run marginal cost function above the long-run average cost function is the firm's long-run supply function. If the price is P', the firm will supply q' units in the long run at a long-run average cost of AC'. Figure 8-15b shows that the new long-run industry supply

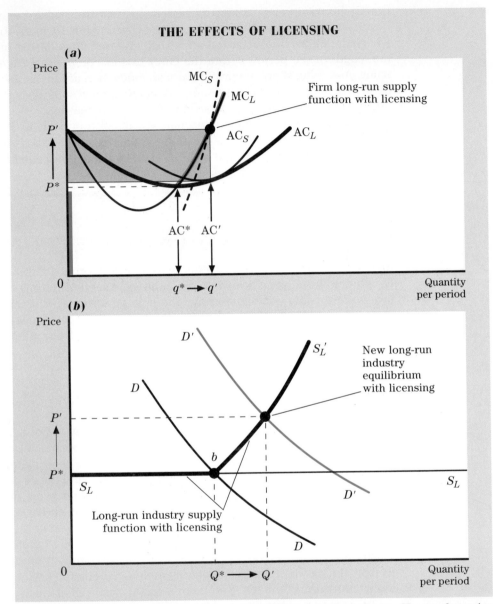

Figure 8-15   Licensing blocks the entry of firms into the industry. The market price increases to P' and the quantity supplied increases to Q' when demand increases to $D'D'$. (*a*) Each firm increases output from q^* to q'. The shaded area represents firm profits. The firm no longer produces at the minimum point of the long-run average cost function. Limiting entry causes a cost inefficiency since Q' is not produced at the lowest total cost.

function has the same horizontal segment as before, running from S_L to point b. Industry output can expand from zero to Q^* because firms with licenses can enter and each firm supplies q^* units in the long run. Once the industry supplies Q^* units at a price of P^*, all N^* licensed firms are producing in the industry. Increases in industry output can occur only if each licensed firm produces more units by supplying more output along its long-run marginal cost function. Consequently, the long-run industry supply function includes the horizontal segment from S_L to point b and the segment from point b to S'_L.

The simple act of licensing the existing N^* firms does not change the equilibrium price P^*. If each of the N^* firms continues to act as a price taker, no firm can increase price just because new firms cannot enter. Each firm knows that consumers will shift to the perfect substitutes supplied by competitors if it *alone* raises price.

What happens when demand increases from DD to $D'D'$? In Figure 8-15b the equilibrium price increases to P' and total quantity supplied increases to Q'. Figure 8-15a shows that the long-run output of each firm increases from q^* to q'. The increase in market demand creates long-run firm profits equal to the shaded area in Figure 8-15a. Normally, the entry of firms would compete these profits away, but with entry restricted the profits of the license holders persist. Each firm produces q' at the lowest long-run average cost of AC' by building a larger plant. The larger plant has a short-run average cost function AC_S that is just tangent to the long-run average cost function at q'. For example, the owner of a taxi may purchase a more expensive and more durable automobile so that it can remain on the road longer and is less likely to break down. A restaurant owner with a license to serve alcoholic beverages may build a larger retail establishment so she can serve more customers even if long-run average cost increases.

The restriction on entry creates a cost inefficiency. Total output of Q' is no longer being produced at the lowest total cost. The lowest total cost of producing Q' units would have each firm produce q^* units at AC^* but have more than N^* firms in the industry. If each of the N^* firms reduces output by $q' - q^*$ units but more firms enter the industry so that all firms produce q^* units, then Q' units will be produced at a lower total cost than under licensing. Therefore, licensing not only raises the price to consumers but creates a cost inefficiency by raising the total cost of producing Q'.

> Licensing prevents new firms from entering, harms consumers because price increases, creates profits, and does not minimize the cost of producing industry output.

APPLICATION 8-4

The Value of a License

You must own a medallion (license) to operate a taxicab legally in New York City. Medallions sell for considerable sums, sometimes for more than $170,000. The reason that they are so valuable is that new firms cannot enter the industry and the demand for taxi services in New York has increased to the point where the price of the service is well above the long-run average cost of operating a taxi. In contrast, if market demand equaled DD or there was free entry into the industry, the long-run equilibrium price would be P^* in Figure 8-15a. Profits would vanish, and the medallion would be worthless. This is exactly what happened in Washington, D.C., where entry into the taxicab industry is free and profits are competed away. The medallions in New York City are valuable because entry is restricted and demand is greater than DD.

The theory predicts that a decrease in the demand for the product will reduce the value of the license. Consider this supporting evidence. California has limited the number of licenses permitting the sale of alcoholic beverages in local bars and hotels. In Los Angeles County, the value of a license to sell alcoholic beverages in local bars or in hotels declined to $12,000–$13,000 in 1989 from $23,000–$30,000 in 1984.[8] In San Francisco the value of a license dropped to $16,000 from $32,000 over the same period. The decrease in the value of the license is due in part to the declining popularity of bar hopping and the increased concern about the potential liability incurred by bar owners.

The value of a license is the most sensitive barometer of changes in demand, cost, and entry conditions.

8-7   THE EFFECT OF TAXES, TRADE LIMITATIONS, AND MARKET RESTRICTIONS ON TOTAL SURPLUS

We can use the concepts of consumer surplus and producer surplus and show that a competitive industry equilibrium **maximizes total surplus, the sum of consumer and producer surpluses.** This is an important result because it implies that either private behavior or public policies that cause price to be above or below the competitive equilibrium price reduce total surplus. If we think of the sum of consumer and producer surplus as a pie, the competitive equilibrium maximizes the size of the pie from a social point of view. While a higher or lower price may benefit particular groups of producers or consumers, from a social point of view society is worse off because total surplus is lower. Of course, some qualifications must be appended to this blanket claim. Prices above or below the equilibrium price may be preferable if there are external efforts so that third parties are harmed or benefit from the output produced by a competitive industry. For example, if farmers use pesticides to control weeds but this lowers water quality and harms other firms or consumers, a case can be made to reduce agricultural output below the competitive equilibrium so that water quality can be improved. The fascinating

---

[8] Lawrence M. Fisher, "Old Standby, the Corner Bar, Falling Victim to New Values," *New York Times*, November 18, 1989.

topic of externalities will be discussed more thoroughly in Chapter 19. For now, our discussion assumes that external effects are not important.

We begin our analysis by determining the effect of a per unit tax on a competitive industry. After spelling out the consequences of this tax, we use the total surplus concept to evaluate the wisdom of trade restrictions, the consequences of levying a tax on an industry, and the setting of minimum and maximum prices.

Imposing a Per Unit Tax on a Competitive Firm

Suppose a per unit tax of t dollars per unit sold is imposed by the government. What impact will the tax have on the firm's cost functions and its profit-maximizing output? To answer this question, we need to determine the effect of the tax on the firm's long-run average and marginal cost functions.

After the government levies a per unit tax of t, the firm's profit function becomes

$$\text{Total profits} = \text{Total revenue} - \text{Total long-run cost} - \text{Total taxes}$$

$$\pi(q) = Pq - C_L(q) - tq \tag{8-2}$$

Total taxes paid by the firm to the government are tq. The firm's output that maximizes profits must satisfy the following condition.[9]

$$P = \frac{\Delta C_L(q)}{\Delta q} + t \tag{8-3}$$

The firm considers the per unit tax a cost of doing business, and so it determines output where price equals the sum of long-run marginal cost and t. The marginal cost of producing and selling another unit equals the pretax marginal cost of production plus the per unit tax paid to the government.

When the firm considers the per unit tax as another cost of the firm, the long-run average cost of the firm including the tax t becomes $AC_L + t$. The new long-run average cost function of the firm is the firm's pretax long-run average cost function shifted upward by the per unit tax. If the long-run average cost of producing a million units is $67 and the per unit tax is $8, then the new long-run average cost will be $67 + $8 = $75. The marginal cost function also shifts upward and becomes $MC_L + t$. If the marginal cost of producing the last unit was $5, it is now $13 with the tax included. Figure 8-16 shows the initial average and marginal cost functions and the new average and marginal cost functions with the per unit tax included.

Because the average and marginal cost functions shift upward by t, the new and the old long-run average cost functions reach a minimum at the same quantity. In Figure 8-16 long-run average cost reaches a minimum at $q = q*$ before and after the government levies the per unit tax. Figure 8-17 shows that the long-run industry supply function, S_L, shifts upward by t to become $S_L + t$.

[9] A profit-maximizing firm determines quantity so that

$$\frac{d\pi(q)}{dq} = P - \frac{dC_L(q)}{dq} - t = 0$$

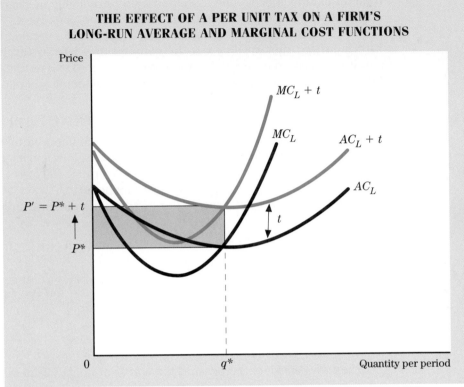

Figure 8-16   The firm's long-run average and marginal cost functions shift upward by the per unit tax.

Long-Run Effects of a Per Unit Tax

It is easy to trace the long-run effects of a per unit tax. Figure 8-17 shows that the long-run equilibrium price increases from P^* to P'. The equilibrium quantity declines from Q^* to Q'. By raising the per unit tax, the government increases the price of the product and decreases the quantity demanded. This confirms the old adage, "The power to tax is the power to destroy." Total tax collections are $T = tQ'$, the shaded color area in Figure 8-17.

How much price increases depends on the price elasticity of demand and of supply. Let's first consider how the price elasticity of demand affects the price increase. Figure 8-18a compares the effect of imposing a per unit tax when the two market demand functions are D_1D_1 and D_2D_2. The initial long-run equilibrium price is P^*. In the immediate neighborhood of the initial equilibrium price of P^*, D_1D_1 is more elastic than D_2D_2. After the government levies the tax and the long-run supply function shifts upward by t, the equilibrium price increases by only $P_1 - P^*$ when the demand function is D_1D_1, and from P^* to P_2 when the demand function is D_2D_2. This shows that the greater the price elasticity of the demand function, the smaller the price increase caused by a per unit tax.

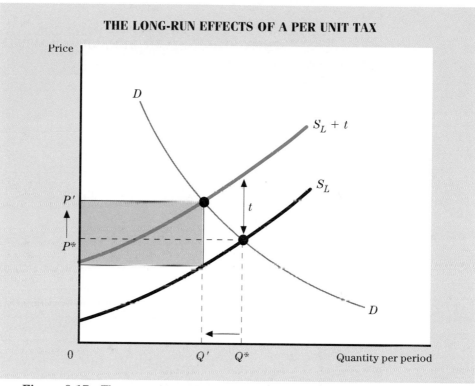

Figure 8-17   The per unit tax shifts the long-run industry supply function up by the tax. The long-run equilibrium price increases from P^* to P' and total quantity decreases from Q^* to Q'. The shaded area $T = tQ'$ represents total tax revenue collected by the government.

> The greater the price elasticity of the demand function, the smaller the price increase caused by a per unit tax.

Imposing a per unit tax forces consumers to buy more nontaxed substitutes when the market demand function is more elastic. The tax reduces industry output and the fall in industry output reduces the demand for the scarce factor and lowers the price of that factor. In an increasing-cost industry, when industry output falls, the production cost of the remaining sellers also falls. Therefore, some of the effects of the tax are borne by the owners of the scarce factor of production.

The effect of a per unit tax on price and on industry output also depends on the price elasticity of supply in the neighborhood of the initial equilibrium price. In Figure 8-18b two alternative supply functions are S_1S_1 and S_2S_2. Starting from the initial equilibrium price of P^*, the greater the price elasticity of the supply function, the greater the price increase caused by a per unit tax. The price increases from P^* to P_1 if the supply function is S_1S_1, and by a smaller amount to P_2 if the supply function is S_2S_2.

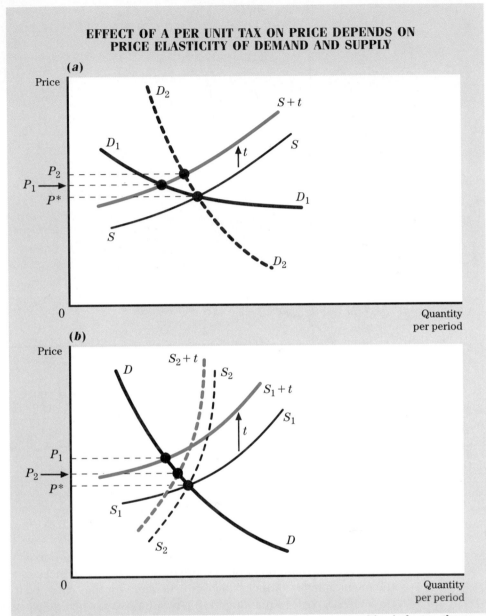

**EFFECT OF A PER UNIT TAX ON PRICE DEPENDS ON
PRICE ELASTICITY OF DEMAND AND SUPPLY**

Figure 8-18   (*a*) When a per unit tax is imposed on a competitive industry, the more elastic the price elasticity of demand, the less the price increases. (*b*) The less elastic the price elasticity of supply, the less the price increases.

> The greater the price elasticity of the supply function, the greater the price rise caused by a per unit tax.

As the industry supply function becomes more elastic, it begins to resemble a constant-cost industry. In the latter case, the price rises by the amount of the tax. Although industry output and the number of firms in a constant-cost industry decrease, factor prices do not change when industry output falls. Since the cost functions of the firm do not shift, the price of the good must increase by the amount of the tax if the industry is to reach a new long-run equilibrium. In contrast, when the industry supply function is almost vertical, a small change in industry output causes a larger change in the price of at least one specialized factor. As industry output decreases, its demand for specialized factors falls, as do the prices of those specialized factors. Because the per unit tax causes a decrease in industry output, factor prices fall, and this lowers the firm's long-run average cost function. Therefore, the price of the good does not need to rise as much to pay for the tax as the supply function becomes less elastic. Here again, the tax lowers the rent earned by the owners of specialized factors.

This analysis indicates that a per unit tax is not necessarily paid by the agent who collects it or that only consumers pay the per unit tax. A per unit tax can be completely shifted to consumers so that the price rises by the amount of the tax (constant-cost case), or it can fall entirely on a factor of production if the industry's supply function is perfectly inelastic.

Banana Wars: Total Surplus and the Gains from Trade

We can use the consumer and producer surplus concepts to show how trade restrictions reduce total surplus and to analyze the social cost of trade restrictions.

The European Union seems to be no friend of low marginal cost banana producers in Latin America. It has placed strict quotas on Latin American banana imports and given preference to imports from higher-cost producers in Europe's former African and other colonies. For Latin American producers this is a serious matter for they had been selling over 50 percent of their crop to Europe. The profound impact of the European restriction is reflected in a large drop in plantation land prices in Latin America.

To analyze the effect of this trade restriction, we assume that there are just two consuming markets—the United States and Europe—and just two sources of supply—Latin America and Africa. The supply and demand functions for the U.S. and European markets are shown in Figure 8-19.

First, we will analyze the no-trade situation where no trade means that all bananas produced in Latin America are banned from Europe and therefore are shipped to the American market. Because African suppliers are higher-cost suppliers, they ship only to the nearby European market.

In Figure 8-19a P_{US} is the equilibrium price in the American market and Q_{US} is the quantity of Latin American bananas shipped to the American market. In Figure 8-19b the equilibrium price in Europe is P_E and the equilibrium quantity of African

**SEPARATE MARKETS FOR BANANAS
WHEN TRADE IS BANNED**

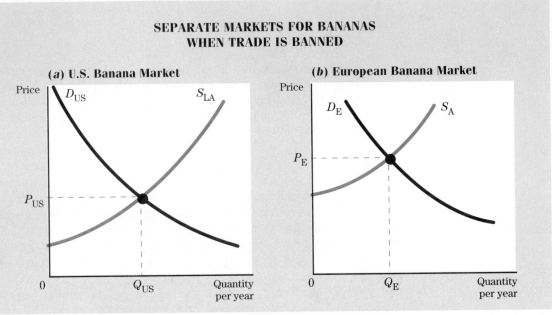

Figure 8-19   When trade in bananas is banned, the European price is higher than the American price. World output of bananas is produced inefficiently.

bananas shipped to Europe is Q_E. Because Latin American producers are more efficient producers, the equilibrium U.S. banana price is lower than the equilibrium European price.

One consequence of the trade ban is that world banana production is inefficiently produced. How can we infer this from Figure 8-19? Since each price-taking supplier in Latin America sets price equal to marginal cost, the marginal cost of the last ton of Latin American bananas equals P_{US}. Similarly, the marginal cost of producing the last ton of African bananas is P_E. Since $P_E > P_{US}$, the marginal cost of the last ton of bananas produced in Africa is greater than the marginal cost of the last ton of bananas produced in Latin America. Consequently, the total cost of producing the sum of $Q_{US} + Q_E$ is not minimized. The ban encourages production by high marginal cost suppliers and prevents production by low marginal cost suppliers.

Now let's assume that the barriers to banana trade are removed so that Latin American bananas can again be consumed by Europeans. There is now just one worldwide market with one aggregate market demand function and one aggregate supply function. What will be the common equilibrium price of bananas in America and Europe and how many bananas will Latin American suppliers ship to Europe? For the worldwide banana industry to be in equilibrium, the price must be the same in the American and European markets. For example, a higher or lower European price would mean that Latin American producers would ship all or none of their bananas respectively to Europe. However, this would either depress or raise the European price and raise or lower the American price. So, an equilibrium cannot exist with a price difference.

What will the common equilibrium price be in America and in Europe? At any price lower than P_E in Figure 8-20*b*, a European excess demand appears and increases the lower that the price is. Europe's quantity demanded is greater than Africa's quantity supplied. At any American price above P_{US} in Figure 8-20*a*, an excess supply of Latin American bananas appears and increases the higher that the price is. Latin American quantity supplied is greater than American quantity demanded. For a market equilibrium to exist, the price must be between P_E and P_{US} so that the excess supply of Latin American bananas equals the excess demand for bananas by European consumers. When the price increases to P', the excess supply is the distance *ab* in Figure 8-20*a* and equals the excess demand *de* in the European market shown in Figure 8-20*b*. The excess supply represents bananas that are shipped from Latin America to Europe to meet the excess European demand. At any lower price the excess demand exceeds the excess supply and at a higher price the opposite occurs. When trade is allowed, American consumers pay a higher price while European consumers pay a lower banana price. Latin American production increases from Q_{US} to Q'_{LA} but less is shipped to America

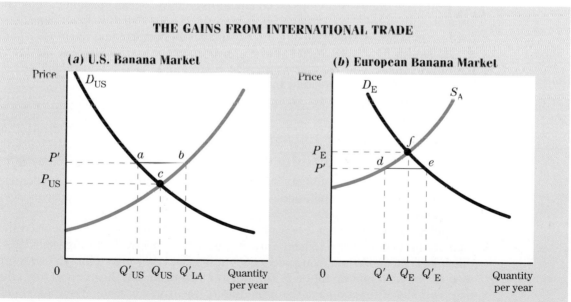

Figure 8-20   When trade in bananas is permitted, the world price becomes P'. Consumer surplus in the American market decreases by $P'acP_{US}$. Producer surplus of Latin American producers increases by the area $P'bcP_{US}$. The net increase in producer plus consumer surplus equals the area *abc*. In Europe the net increase in total surplus equals the area *def*. Trade increases total surplus in both markets.

and *ab* bananas are shipped to Europe while African production decreases from Q_E to Q'_A.

By using the concepts of consumer and producer surplus, we can show how integration of two markets into one market through international trade increases total surplus. In the U.S. market the price increase reduces consumer surplus by the area $P'acP_{US}$ in Figure 8-20a. More than offsetting this loss is the increase in producer surplus of area $P'bcP_{US}$ so net surplus increases by the approximate triangle area *abc*. In the European market consumer surplus increases by the area P_EfeP' in Figure 8-20b. However, producer surplus decreases by the area P_EfdP' so the net surplus increases by area *def*. The sum of the two triangles equals the increase in net surplus due to the opening up of trade. What we can say is that collectively Latin American producers could, in principle, pay American consumers for their loss in consumer surplus because of the increased price and still come out ahead by triangle *abc* and that collectively European consumers could afford to pay African producers for their loss in producer surplus because of the price decrease and still come out ahead by triangle *def*. In practice, such compensation is seldom paid. With free trade the price is the same in both countries. The marginal cost of producing a ton of bananas is the same throughout the world. World production becomes cost-efficient with free trade and this is one of the reasons that total surplus increases. With free trade consumers' willingness to pay for the last unit produced as reflected in the price of P' equals the marginal cost of the last unit. Consequently, total surplus is maximized.

How have trade restrictions on bananas affected European consumers? Recent estimates place the price of bananas in the United States slightly less than $1,000 per ton. In contrast, the price of a ton of bananas in Portugal and Spain is around $2,200 and in Italy over $2,500. Since transportation costs cannot explain these large differences, you can see that trade restrictions have a substantial effect. Bananas sell for premium prices in Europe.

The Effect of a Per Unit Tax on Consumer and Producer Surplus

As our analysis of the per unit tax has shown, taxes alter the behavior of consumers and producers. We can build upon that analysis to show the social consequences of imposing a per unit tax.

Before the government levies a per unit tax, the long-run equilibrium price and quantity in a competitive industry are P^* and Q^*, respectively, in Figure 8-21. At this long-run equilibrium, consumers benefit because they are willing to pay more than P^* for each unit up to the Q^*th. Chapter 3 showed that the area between the market demand function and the price line P^* measures consumer surplus. Each consumer receives a surplus because the market price is only P^* for each unit. Therefore, the gray area under the demand function and above the price line represents consumer surplus.[10] Producers receive P^* for all the units they sell,

---

[10] Assuming that income effects are negligible.

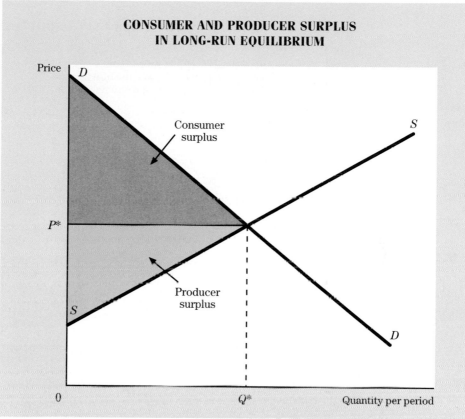

**CONSUMER AND PRODUCER SURPLUS
IN LONG-RUN EQUILIBRIUM**

Figure 8-21   The long-run equilibrium price and quantity are P^* and Q^*, respectively. Consumer surplus equals the gray shaded area between the demand function and the price line P^*. Producer surplus equals the shaded color area between the price line P^* and the supply function.

although they are willing to supply all units up to the Q^*th unit at lower prices. Therefore, the area between the price line P^* and the industry supply function, or the shaded color area, represents producer surplus when producers sell Q^* units at P^*.

Let's show how the sum of consumer and producer surpluses decreases when the government levies a per unit tax on a competitive industry. The market price increases to P', and the equilibrium quantity decreases to Q' in Figure 8-22. In the pretax situation consumer surplus is equal to the sum of areas 1, 2, and 3. The reason for dividing consumer surplus into these different areas will soon be evident. Producer surplus is the sum of areas 4, 5, and 6 so total surplus equals areas 1–6.

Because the price increases to P' and the quantity demanded falls to Q' after the tax is imposed, consumer surplus decreases by area 2 (the rectangle) plus area

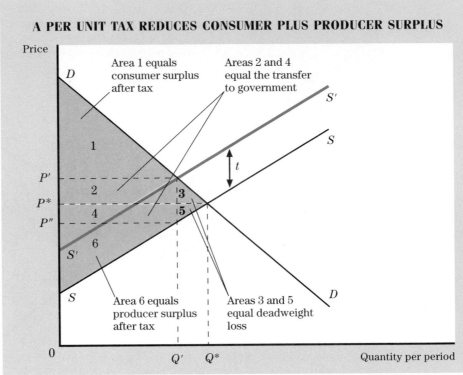

A PER UNIT TAX REDUCES CONSUMER PLUS PRODUCER SURPLUS

Figure 8-22   A per unit tax shifts the supply function and increases the market price to P'. Consumer surplus decreases to area 1. Producer surplus is equal to area 6 since the government collects the sum of areas 2 and 4 from producers. Areas 3 and 5 represent the deadweight loss of a per unit tax.

3 (the triangle). What happens to producer surplus? Producer surplus is now equal to area 6. Producers receive P' for all Q' units, but they must pay the sum of area 2 and area 4 to the government in taxes. Area 2 plus area 4 represents a transfer from consumers to the government with producers acting as tax collectors. Therefore, producer surplus is equal to area 6, and producer surplus decreases by area 4 plus area 5.

To sum up, the consumer surplus is now equal to area 1. The government receives a transfer from producers and consumers equal to areas 2 and 4, and producers receive a surplus equal to area 6. Area 3 represents the net loss in consumer surplus because it is not matched by a corresponding increase in tax payments, and area 5 represents the loss in producer surplus. The two triangles are a **deadweight loss** and are equal to the loss in surplus that is not offset by an increase in value to some other group. A deadweight loss occurs because the tax reduces consumption from Q^* to Q'.

A per unit tax reduces total surplus.

How would our analysis change if producers were able to get together and raise price or use the power of the government to levy quotas so that total output falls to Q' in Figure 8-22? Now the areas 2 + 4 represent profits received by producers. These areas are transfers from consumers to producers instead of tax transfers to the government. However the decrease in total surplus is still the same deadweight loss of areas 3 and 5 in Figure 8-22. Whether the restriction in industry output is caused by an increase in a per unit tax or by the introduction of quotas, the loss in total surplus equals deadweight loss. The only difference is who gets the transfer, the government or producers.

Sometimes, governments set prices below the equilibrium price of P^*. For example, rent control of apartments places limits on what rent can be charged for an apartment, and price controls are sometimes placed on natural gas. How is our analysis of consumer and producer surplus affected when price controls are imposed? In Figure 8-22 we can think of P'' as the controlled price. If we assume, somewhat unrealistically, that this price is effectively enforced, then producers will supply Q' units and areas 2 and 4 become transfers to consumers from producers. With minimum prices, consumer surplus increases by area 4 (rectangle) less area 3 (triangle) which is presumably positive if consumers who will continue to consume the good are the demanders of price controls. This example also demonstrates the danger of thinking that the loss in total surplus is only the deadweight loss triangles. In Chapter 1 we noted that minimum prices are often circumvented by charging more for other items or through a competition by potential renters to bribe owners of rent-controlled apartments to lease to them. Still another consequence is that resources must be applied to enforce the regulations. All of these efforts require real resources. Prized apartments will not be advertised. Landlords will try to rent to those renters who will give the landlord less trouble, making it more costly for some renters to find apartments. The cost of finding and obtaining a rent-controlled apartment will rise. The apartments are worth P' so renters would be willing to pay up to P' to obtain a rent-controlled apartment. In this case all of areas 2 + 4 could disappear if consumers use more and more resources to search for and obtain an apartment or, in a different context, if buyers evade natural gas price controls. If resources are used in this way because of the introduction of price controls, then the social cost of price controls is much larger and includes some or all of the rectangles 2 and 4 and not simply triangles 3 and 5.

SUMMARY

- In long-run industry equilibrium each firm has no incentive to change the method and scale of production and no firm has an incentive to enter the industry.
- In short-run industry equilibrium no existing firm desires to produce a different quantity.
- In a constant-cost industry all firms have

the same cost functions and the cost function does not shift when industry output changes. The long-run industry supply function is horizontal in a constant-cost industry. An increase in demand increases industry output but not the long-run equilibrium price.

- An unexpected shift in demand causes

short-run profits or losses in the industry. In the short run each firm maximizes profits by equating price to short-run marginal cost. The profits or losses encourage new firms to enter or existing firms to leave the industry. Price and profits decline as new firms enter, or price increases and losses decrease as firms leave.

■ The industry supply function has a positive slope in an increasing-cost industry.

■ An increase in market demand increases the long-run equilibrium price and industry output.

■ If there are differences in managerial ability, an increase in market demand increases managerial compensation so that each manager appropriates an economic rent. The firm earns zero profits.

■ A cost-reducing innovation causes price to fall as new firms enter the industry using the new technology. Existing firms will not adopt the innovation immediately if the av-erage variable cost function of the old technology lies below the long-run average cost function of the new technology.

■ Restricting the entry of firms into an industry through licensing changes the shape of the long-run supply function. A subsequent increase in market demand increases the profits of the holders of licenses. Market price and industry output increase, and each firm produces a larger output at the higher price. A firm will build a larger plant to produce the larger output and operates in the region where there are internal diseconomies of scale.

■ A per unit tax increases the market price and reduces industry output. The less elastic the demand function and the more elastic the supply function, the greater is the increase in equilibrium price.

■ Total surplus decreases when the government levies a per unit tax or imposes limits on trade.

KEY TERMS

long-run industry equilibrium
constant-cost industry
short-run industry supply function
the role of profits
external pecuniary diseconomy of scale
differences in managerial ability
changing the shape of the supply function
    through licensing and entry barriers
gains from trade
maximizing the sum of consumer and
    producer surpluses

short-run industry equilibrium
horizontal industry supply function
adjustment of an industry to a shift in
    market demand
increasing-cost industry
economic rent or producer surplus
switching over to a new technology
imposing a per unit tax on a competitive
    firm
deadweight loss

REVIEW QUESTIONS

1. What two conditions must be satisfied for an industry to be in long-run equilibrium?

2. If the price of a factor of production increases when industry output expands, the industry supply function will be upward sloping. Explain why you agree or disagree with this statement.

3. If all firms have the same long-run total cost

function, the industry will have a perfectly elastic long-run supply curve. Do you agree or disagree with this statement?

4. The equilibrium long-run price in a competitive industry must occur in the region where market demand is price-elastic; if market demand is price-inelastic, each firm in the industry can reduce output and increase its total revenue. Explain why you agree or disagree with this statement.

5. The theory of a competitive firm predicts that companies with more efficient managers will operate larger firms than less efficient managers. Explain why you agree or disagree with this statement.

6. Under what conditions will existing firms in an industry immediately adopt a cost-reducing innovation?

7. Restricting the number of producers through licensing implies that each firm in the industry no longer behaves as a price taker. Explain why you agree or disagree with this statement.

8. When a per unit tax is imposed, the equilibrium price increases, while equilibrium industry and firm output decrease. Explain why you agree or disagree with this statement.

9. The price elasticity of demand is -1.3 in industry A and -4.2 in industry B. The price elasticity of supply is 8.2 in industry A and 0.5 in industry B. If the government levies the same per unit tax in the two industries, in which industry will the price increase be larger?

EXERCISES

1. The long-run total cost function of a price-taking firm is presented in the table below.

QUANTITY	LONG-RUN TOTAL COST
10	$ 60
20	100
30	120
40	140
50	180
60	240

a. If this is a constant-cost industry, what will be the long-run equilibrium price?

b. What quantity will the firm produce and what will be the firm's short-run average cost if it produces this output efficiently?

2. Use graphs to show how the existing firms in a constant-cost industry adjust in the short and long runs when the market demand function shifts inward.

3. Managerial ability differs among the firms in an industry. Show the long-run equilibrium price, industry output, and output of the most efficient and the least efficient firms currently operating in the industry. Show the profits of the firm and the compensation of the manager for these two firms.

4. Suppose the domestic citrus market can be described by the following market demand and supply functions:

$$Q_d = 20,000 - 250P$$
$$Q_s = 5,000 + 200P$$

Also, assume that the supply of citrus produced outside the domestic country is perfectly elastic at a price of $5.

a. Determine the total quantity demanded, domestic supply, and the imports of citrus.

b. Suppose that a quota of 5,000 units is imposed on citrus imports. What will be the domestic equilibrium price?

c. Graph the demand and supply curves

and show the deadweight loss due to the quota.

5. Most of world cranberry output is produced in the United States on many farms located in Massachusetts and Wisconsin. Cranberry plants cannot be grown anywhere and are finicky, requiring lots of water and exacting nutrients from the soil to thrive. The demand for cranberries has been increasing as more are being used in mixed juices. U.S. output of cranberries has steadily increased from 1.4 million barrels (one barrel equals 100 pounds) in 1973 to 3.6 million barrels in 1993. The U.S. price of cranberries increased from $13.50 per barrel in 1973 to $50.50 per barrel in 1993. The rental price for renting an acre of land to produce cranberries has increased between 1973 and 1993. Develop a model of a competitive industry that can explain why the price, the total output of cranberries, and the rental price of an acre of land increased between 1973 and 1983.

6. Any firm that is incurring losses should try to emulate the policies of profitable firms. If the profitable firms are using the latest cost-reducing innovation, the loss-ridden firm should try to catch up with the profitable firms by adopting the new technology immediately. It is always more profitable to be at the vanguard of technology. Explain why you agree or disagree with this statement.

7. As more and more firms adopt a new cost-reducing innovation, the price will steadily decline until all firms are using the new innovation. Explain why you agree or disagree with this statement.

8. A local government pases a law that prohibits additional firms from entering a constant-cost industry. Assume that the firms in the industry have U-shaped long-run average cost functions and that the industry was in long-run equilibrium before entry was blocked. Show the new long-run equilibrium of the industry and a representative firm after market demand increases.

*9. Managerial ability differs among the firms in a domestic industry. The market demand function for the product is *DD*. Currently, the total compensation of the manager with the most efficient firm is $100 million.

The huge compensation packages of executives have incensed Congress. Congress decides to crack down on excessive increases in managerial compensation. It passes a law that prohibits firms in this industry from increasing compensation by more than 10 percent per year. Members of Congress argue that by keeping compensation down each firm's average cost and price will be held down so more firms will be able to compete in the industry.

a. Show the long-run equilibrium price, the industry output, and the outputs of the most efficient firm and the least efficient firm *currently* producing in the industry before any restriction was put on compensation. Show the profits of each firm and the manager's compensation at these two firms.

b. After the 10 percent restriction is imposed, market demand increases and the price of the product increases by 20 percent. Show the effect of the law, after demand increases, on the compensation of executives, the profits of firms, and the number of firms in the industry.

c. Will new firms enter the industry after market demand increases?

*10. A competitive constant-cost industry is in long-run equilibrium. The firms in this industry manufacture a product essential for national security. In response to complaints of excess competition, the government announces it will purchase only from the existing firms in the industry except under the following conditions: If demand increases so that the price of the product would otherwise increase by more than 10 percent, the government will allow enough firms to enter so that the price will not increase by more than 10 percent.

A congressional committee investigates the firms in the industry and finds that profits are excessive. It proposes that a per unit tax equal to the recent 10 percent price increase be imposed on the industry. It concludes that a per unit tax of this magnitude will only eliminate the excess profits of firms and will not raise the price of the product.

a. Suppose demand increases and the government permits enough new firms to enter the industry so that price cannot increase by more than 10 percent. Show the long-run equilibrium position of a representative firm and of the industry and the new long-run industry supply function.

b. With the use of graphs, show the long-run effects of the proposed per unit tax on the price, industry output, and profits of a representative firm. Do you agree with the claims of the congressional committee?

11. Price declines when demand decreases in an increasing-cost industry or when a technological change occurs. Can you name another variable that decreases when demand declines and increases when a technological change occurs?

12. A recent study has found that the average size of a firm increases when the price of a product declines. Which of the models of competitive behavior can explain this?

13. When the yen rises relative to the dollar, the price of cars imported from Japan increases. Because of this appreciation, U.S. auto companies will be slower to automate factories because they believe they're getting a breather from Japanese competition. Explain why you agree or disagree with this statement.

*14. A domestic competitive industry produces a product under increasing cost. Foreign suppliers produce under constant cost and are willing to supply an indefinite amount at the world price of P_w. The price elasticity of demand in the domestic market was recently estimated to be -1. With the aid of graphs show the equilibrium output, q, of a representative domestic supplier, total domestic output, Q_D, and total imports, Q_I.

*15. The dependence on foreign imports of a product is a growing political issue. Continuing Exercise 14, two plans are being considered to reduce domestic consumption and total imports by 20 percent each.

- *Plan 1.* Permit no imports unless accompanied by an import ticket and issue only $0.8Q_I$ import tickets to importers.
- *Plan 2.* Impose an import duty of t dollars per imported unit.

a. With the aid of graphs, show how plan 1 affects the combined supply function of domestic and foreign producers, total units consumed, total imports, and domestic output. Will this plan reduce imports and domestic consumption by 20 percent?

b. How large should the import duty in plan 2 be relative to P_w if total consumption declines by 20 percent?

c. With the aid of graphs show the effect of plan 2 on the combined supply function of domestic and foreign producers, total units consumed, total imports, and domestic output. Which plan will reduce total imports by a larger amount?

16. Who benefits and who loses from the trade restrictions on bananas?

*17. Arbitrageurs buy in a low-price market and sell in a high-price market. Suppose the manufacturer of Power Rangers, a popular toy, produces a limited supply of R units. They sell R_1 units to higher-income families at a price of P_1 and R_2 units to lower-income families at a price of P_2 where $R_1 + R_2 = R$ and $P_1 > P_2$. If arbi-

trageurs enter the market and buy Power Rangers from lower-income families and sell them to higher-income families until the prices are equal, will total surplus increase or decrease? Explain.

CHAPTER 9

MONOPOLY

■ 9-1 Assumptions of the Pure Monopoly Model

■ 9-2 The Monopolist as a Price Maker

The Demand Function of a Monopolist

The Total and Marginal Revenue Functions

Measuring the Change in Revenue by the Area under the Marginal Revenue Function

■ 9-3 The Theory of Monopoly Pricing

Application 9-1: Are Firms in the Cigarette and Oil Industries Monopolists?

Application 9-2: Privatizing a Near Monopoly in the Czech Republic

Application 9-3: Using a Quota to Create a Partial Monopolist

■ 9-4 Adjusting from One Long-Run Equilibrium to Another

■ *9-5 Adoption of a Cost-Reducing Innovation

■ 9-6 Competing to Be a Monopolist

Application 9-4: Alternative Methods of Selling a Monopoly

■ 9-7 The Tyranny of Durability

Actions the Monopolist Can Take to Reassure Buyers

Application 9-5: Disney Limits the Sales of *Fantasia* to 50 Days

■ 9-8 Taxing a Monopolist

■ 9-9 The Social Objection to Monopoly

Application 9-6: Will a Merger of Two Hospitals Decrease Total Surplus?

■ Summary

■ Key Terms

■ Review Questions

■ Exercises

* More difficult material.

327

A pure monopolist is the antithesis of a competitive firm. A competitive firm has no control over price and that is why it is called a price taker. On the other hand a monopolist is the only supplier of the product so it is a **price maker.** It sets price without fear of entry. This enviable position is not, however, without limits. While a monopolist's price is not constrained by competition, it is constrained by the law of demand. A monopolist can sell more units only by lowering price. It is this ever-present constraint that limits the behavior of the monopolist.

After stating the assumptions of the monopoly model, we explain how a monopolist sets price and output to maximize profits. Then we extend the theory in several directions, among which are how a monopolist responds to a demand shock or to a cost-reducing innovation and how competition to become a monopolist eliminates profits. We also study the effect of product durability and reach a surprising conclusion about what a monopolist can charge when selling a durable good. The chapter ends with a comparison of price and output under monopoly and under competition and discusses the social objection to monopoly.

9-1   ASSUMPTIONS OF
THE PURE MONOPOLY MODEL

This chapter begins by specifying two rather stringent assumptions if a firm is to behave as a pure monopolist.

1. *Competitors cannot enter the industry.* A pure monopolist has no immediate rivals and determines the quantity and price without fear of attracting other firms to the industry.

2. *No close substitutes.* There are no close substitutes for the product produced by a monopolist. Under the theory of pure monopoly the monopolist does not worry about the effect of its price policy on the price response of firms producing other goods because the other goods are distant substitutes for the monopolist's product.

Pure monopoly rarely occurs, because few industries satisfy these two stringent assumptions completely. Nevertheless, the theory of pure monopoly is useful as a standard or point of reference. The theory indicates what price a monopolist would charge, what quantity it would produce, and the profits it would earn. By comparing the monopoly solution with the competitive solution, we can better understand and rationalize the social opposition to monopoly in many countries.

In some industries a firm has a short-run monopoly, but the monopoly erodes eventually with the entry of other firms. Some examples of a short-run monopoly position that eroded with time include DuPont (nylon), Alcoa (aluminum), and the German joint sales agencies of the nineteenth century that permitted firms to coordinate output and price through legally enforced contracts. Another is the New York Stock Exchange, which for many years controlled over 90 percent of stock trading on organized exchanges but has lost market share in recent years.

Professional sports provide other examples of monopoly. In each major sport—baseball, football, hockey, and basketball—there is a single organization that determines the number of teams in each league, competition for players, and other important matters. Infrequently, new leagues are formed and attempt to enter the football, hockey, and basketball markets, but after a time they either fail or are merged into a single league. Some economists consider the National Collegiate Athletic Association a monopoly organization because it prevents bidding for high school athletics and prohibits member schools from independently negotiating television contracts.

In some instances, monopoly is a by-product of patent policy. The purpose of patent policy is to foster inventive activity by granting a monopoly for a limited duration—17 years in the United States. Because patent policy prevents firms from quickly copying the inventions of others, a firm is more likely to invest in research and development when the prospects of enjoying the fruits of the effort are greater. In the pharmaceutical industry patent protection is important because drug research is expensive and companies would not make an investment if they could not expect to profit from it. While patent policy promotes innovative activity, it also has a downside—monopoly pricing.

This chapter will have much more to say about the consequences of monopoly than about why a monopoly emerges in a particular industry. A theory as to why monopoly emerges is still in an embryonic stage, with much research yet to be completed. Some economists believe monopoly emerges when there are perpetual internal economies of scale, a situation where one firm can produce any output at a lower total cost than two or more firms can, as in a so-called natural monopoly. Many economists believe that monopoly can emerge when one firm has a large cost advantage over others, so that it can set a profit-maximizing price without attracting other firms to the industry.

9-2   THE MONOPOLIST AS A PRICE MAKER

Because a monopolist is the sole supplier of the product, the monopolist's demand function is the market demand function. Unlike a competitive firm, which takes the market price as given, the mind-set of a monopolist is completely different. A monopolist is always considering whether the tradeoff between a lower price and a larger quantity demanded will increase or decrease profits, something a competitive firm never considers. Before determining how a monopolist sets the price and determines quantity, let's explore this mind-set and determine how total revenue changes as the monopolist sells more units.

The Demand Function of a Monopolist

To illustrate the mind-set of a monopolist, let's consider the demand function for first class mail faced by the postal service. Table 9-1 shows a hypothetical market demand function for first class mail. Column 1 shows the price per letter; column 2 shows the number of pieces demanded by users; column 3 shows total revenue of the postal service; and column 4 shows the additional revenue received by the postal service for each 2 cent reduction in the price of a letter. Table 9-1 clearly shows the tradeoff between a higher price and a lower quantity demanded because

Table 9-1   MARKET DEMAND FUNCTION FOR FIRST CLASS MAIL

PRICE OF STAMP (cents) (1)	QUANTITY DEMANDED (billions of pieces) (2)	TOTAL REVENUE ($ billions) (3)	ADDITIONAL REVENUE ($ billions) (4)
36¢	130	$46.8	
34	150	51.0	$4.2
32	170	54.4	3.4
30	190	57.0	2.6
28	200	56.0	−1.0

consumers shift to other, albeit distant, substitutes. Column 3 shows the total revenue at each price and indicates total revenue increases as price falls from 36 to 30 cents per letter. A further price reduction from 30 to 28 cents reduces total revenue received by the postal service. Column 4 shows the additional revenue the monopolist receives by lowering the price in 2 cent increments. The postal service pulls in an additional $4.2 billion by lowering the price from 36 to 34 cents. By working down column 4, you can see that each price reduction brings in additional revenue to the postal service until the price is reduced from 30 to 28 cents and total revenue falls by $1 billion. Clearly, a monopolist's pricing decision cannot be made intelligently if it fails to recognize the tradeoff between price and the quantity demanded.

This numerical example is illuminating but special. Let's try to analyze the situation more generally by considering the inverse demand function of a monopolist. This demand function corresponds to the industry demand function discussed in Chapter 8 since the monopolist supplies the whole market. The **monopolist's inverse demand function** shows what consumers are willing to pay for each quantity.

$$P = D(Q) \qquad \text{(Inverse Demand Function of a Monopolist)} \qquad \textbf{(9-1}a\textbf{)}$$

Note that, unlike the demand function faced by a competitive firm, the demand function of a monopolist *is* a function of the quantity sold by the firm. The slope of the monopolist's demand function is negative since the quantity demanded increases as the price falls.

$$\frac{\Delta P}{\Delta Q} = \frac{\Delta[D(Q)]}{\Delta Q} < 0 \qquad \textbf{(9-1}b\textbf{)}$$

Figure 9-1 shows that the monopolist can sell more units but only by lowering the price along the demand curve *DD*. Throughout this chapter it is assumed that the monopolist sells all units at a single price. This means that the monopolist can increase the total units sold only by selling all the units at the lower price. For instance, the monopolist sells Q_1 units at a price of P_1 (point *a*) and receives

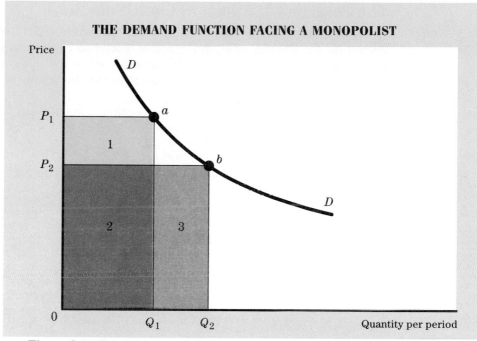

Figure 9-1   Because a monopolist faces a downward-sloping demand function, it can increase the quantity demanded from Q_1 to Q_2 by lowering the price from P_1 to P_2. Area 1 measures the loss in revenue because the price is reduced, and area 3 represents the gain in revenue because more units are sold.

P_1Q_1 in total revenue, or the sum of areas 1 and 2 in Figure 9-1. To sell Q_2 units (point b), the monopolist lowers the price to P_2 and receives P_2Q_2 in total revenue, or the sum of areas 2 and 3.

Figure 9-1 illustrates the perpetual tug-of-war that a monopolist faces. Areas 1 and 3 are the source of this tug-of-war. By lowering the price, the monopolist is trading off the additional revenue it receives by selling $Q_2 - Q_1$ more units against the lower revenue received, because all Q_1 units (which the monopolist could sell at the higher price of P_1) now sell for P_2. Area 1 measures the loss in revenue from the Q_1 units because price falls from P_1 to P_2, and area 3 is the gain in revenue from selling $Q_2 - Q_1$ more units at a price of P_2.

Areas 1 and 3 change size as the monopolist lowers price and moves down the demand function. Over one range of prices area 1 wins the tug-of-war, and over another, area 3 wins. Starting with a high price, area 3 is usually greater than area 1, and so total revenue increases when price falls. As the price falls further, there will usually be some price change where area 1 just equals area 3, at which point total revenue does not change. At still lower prices area 1 becomes larger than area 3, and so total revenue decreases. By lowering price and moving down the demand function, a monopolist's total revenue usually changes, first increasing and then decreasing.

The Total and Marginal Revenue Functions

It would be very tedious to determine how total revenue changes by repeatedly comparing the sizes of different rectangles. Fortunately, there is a more effective way of finding out how total revenue changes when the monopolist sells more units. Economists rely on the **marginal revenue function** to determine how revenue changes.

You can derive the marginal revenue function by starting with the monopolist's total revenue function. The total revenue received by the monopolist is

$$R = PQ \qquad \text{(Total Revenue of Monopolist)} \qquad \textbf{(9-2a)}$$

where R is total revenue. Substituting $D(Q)$ for P yields

$$R = D(Q)Q \qquad \textbf{(9-2b)}$$

$D(Q)$ is the price charged by the monopolist when Q units are sold. Figure 9-2 shows the total revenue function of a monopolist. Initially, total revenue increases as the monopolist lowers the price and sells more units, reaches a maximum when

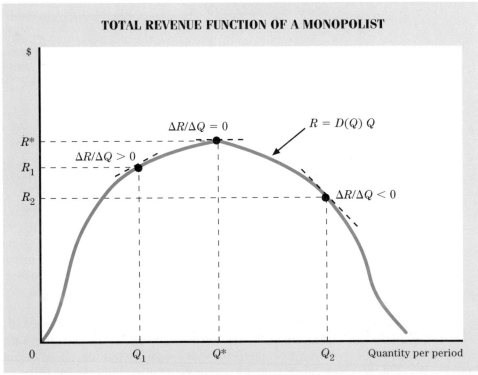

Figure 9-2   Total revenue increases, reaches a maximum, and then declines as the monopolist sells more units. The slope of the total revenue function equals marginal revenue. Marginal revenue is positive when the quantity is less than Q^*, equals zero when the quantity sold equals Q^*, and is negative when the quantity sold exceeds Q^*.

the monopolist sells Q^* units, and then declines when the monopolist lowers price and sells more than Q^* units. As you can see, the monopolist's revenue function is completely different from the linear revenue function of a price-taking competitive firm shown in Figure 7-2. Unlike a competitive firm, a monopolist can spoil the market by selling too many units and reducing total revenue.

Marginal revenue is the slope of the total revenue function, the change in the monopolist's total revenue ΔR when the quantity sold increases by ΔQ, or $\Delta R/\Delta Q$. Figure 9-2 shows that the slope of the total revenue function is positive as long as the quantity sold is less than Q^*, is zero when the quantity sold is Q^* units, and is negative if the firm sells more than Q^* units.

> The marginal revenue function shows the change in revenue ΔR when the quantity sold changes by ΔQ

An expression can be derived for marginal revenue MR at each point on the demand function that relates marginal revenue to the price of the product and the point price elasticity of demand.[1] To begin, suppose the monopolist changes output by ΔQ so that total revenue changes by

$$\Delta R = P \, \Delta Q + Q \, \Delta P \qquad \text{(Change in Revenue)} \qquad \textbf{(9-3)}$$

Change in total revenue equals price times change in quantity (or area 3 in Figure 9-1) plus quantity times change in price (or area 1 in Figure 9-1). Dividing both sides of equation 9-3 by ΔQ results in an expression for $\Delta R/\Delta Q$, or marginal revenue, MR(Q).

$$\text{MR}(Q) - \frac{\Delta R}{\Delta Q} = P + Q\frac{\Delta P}{\Delta Q} \qquad \textbf{(9-4)}$$

Equation 9-4 says that marginal revenue equals $P + Q(\Delta P/\Delta Q)$. The last term is negative since $\Delta P/\Delta Q < 0$ unless $Q = 0$ when MR $= P$. Therefore, marginal revenue is less than the price when $Q > 0$.

$$P > \text{MR} \qquad \text{(Price Is Greater than Marginal Revenue)} \qquad \textbf{(9-5)}$$

---

[1] Total revenue equals price times quantity: $R = D(Q)Q$. Marginal revenue is the slope of the total revenue function.

$$\frac{dR}{dQ} = D(Q) + Q\frac{d[D(Q)]}{dQ} = P + Q\frac{dP}{dQ}$$

Multiplying and dividing the second term by P and rearranging the equation for marginal revenue yields

$$\frac{dR}{dQ} = P\left(1 + \frac{Q}{P}\frac{dP}{dQ}\right) = P\left[1 + \frac{1}{(P/Q)(dQ/dP)}\right]$$

The expression for marginal revenue becomes

$$\frac{dR}{dQ} = P\left(1 + \frac{1}{E_P}\right)$$

This equation says that marginal revenue equals the price of the product times a correction factor of $1 + (1/E_P)$ which depends on the point price elasticity of demand.

After some algebraic manipulation, marginal revenue can then be expressed as

$$MR(Q) = P\left(1 + \frac{1}{E_P}\right) \tag{9-6}$$

where E_P is the point price elasticity.[2]

Equation 9-6 says that marginal revenue equals the price of the product times a correction factor of $1 + (1/E_P)$, which depends on the point price elasticity of demand.

Figure 9-3 shows the demand and the marginal revenue functions. For any Q less than Q^*, demand is price-elastic, and so $E_P < -1$ and $1 + (1/E_P) > 0$. Therefore, equation 9-6 indicates that marginal revenue is positive when demand is price-elastic. Notice that the marginal revenue function in Figure 9-3 lies above the horizontal axis for $Q < Q^*$ because demand is price-elastic. When price is P^*, $E = -1$, and so $1 + (1/E_P) = 0$ and marginal revenue is zero. The marginal revenue function intersects the x axis when $Q = Q^*$ and $P = P^*$. Finally, if the firm sells more than Q^* units, demand becomes price-inelastic, and so $-1 < E_P < 0$ and $1 + (1/E_P) < 0$. Marginal revenue is negative, and so the marginal revenue function lies below the x axis in Figure 9-3 when $Q > Q^*$.

Table 9-2 summarizes the relationship between the price elasticity of demand and marginal revenue for different ranges of the price elasticity.

Measuring the Change in Revenue by the Area under the Marginal Revenue Function

The marginal revenue function is a quick way to determine how revenue changes when the quantity sold changes. The area under the marginal revenue function between any two quantities measures the change in the monopolist's revenue when the quantity sold changes from one quantity to another.

For example, the *change* in the firm's revenue resulting from an increase in the quantity sold from Q_1 to Q_2 units is equal to the area under the marginal revenue function between Q_1 and Q_2 or the colored area in Figure 9-4.[3]

---

[2] Multiplying the right-hand side by P/P and rearranging the equation yields

$$MR(Q) = P\left[1 + \frac{Q}{P}\frac{dP}{dQ}\right] = P\left[1 + \frac{1}{\frac{P}{Q}\frac{dQ}{dP}}\right]$$

[3] The integral of the marginal revenue curve between two quantities, say Q_1 and Q_2, is the area under the marginal revenue function.

$$R(Q_2) - R(Q_1) = \int_{Q_1}^{Q_2} \frac{dR(Q)}{dQ} dQ$$

The area under the marginal revenue function from Q_1 to Q_2 is the difference between the total revenue from selling Q_2 units and the total revenue from selling Q_1 units, or the increase in total revenue due to the increase in units sold from Q_1 to Q_2 units. If $Q_1 = 0$, then $R(Q_1) = R(0) = 0$. Integrating from 0 to Q_2 gives the total revenue from selling Q_2 units.

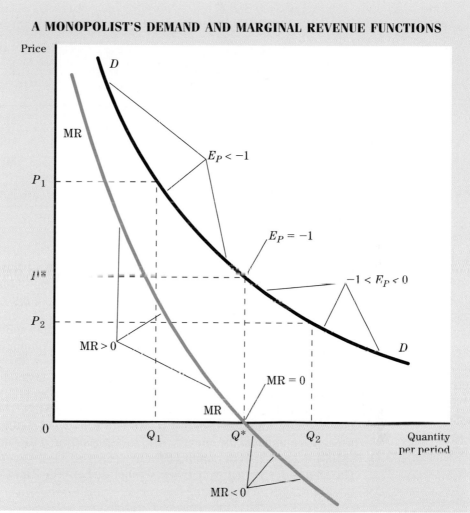

Figure 9-3   Marginal revenue is positive when the quantity sold is less than Q^*, is zero when the quantity sold equals Q^*, and is negative when the quantity sold exceeds Q^*. If demand is price-elastic, then marginal revenue is positive. If demand is unit-elastic, marginal revenue is zero, and if demand is price-inelastic, marginal revenue is negative.

The change in total revenue resulting from increasing the quantity sold from Q_1 to Q_2 units is equal to the area under the marginal revenue function between Q_1 and Q_2 units.

A simple numerical example demonstrates why the area under the marginal revenue function between any two quantities is equal to the change in total revenue.

Table 9-2   PRICE ELASTICITY AND MARGINAL REVENUE

PRICE ELASTICITY OF DEMAND, E_P (1)	VALUE OF PRICE ELASTICITY (2)	SIGN OF CORRECTION FACTOR, $1 + (1/E_P)$ (3)	MARGINAL REVENUE, $\Delta R/\Delta Q$ OR SLOPE OF TOTAL REVENUE FUNCTION (4)
Price-elastic	$E_P < -1$	> 0	$\text{MR} > 0$
Unitary	$E_P = -1$	$= 0$	$\text{MR} = 0$
Price-inelastic	$-1 < E_P < 0$	< 0	$\text{MR} < 0$

Consider unit changes in the quantity sold. Table 9-3 shows quantity demanded in column 1, price in column 2, total revenue in column 3, marginal revenue in column 4, and the sum of marginal revenues up to and including the last unit sold in column 5. Summing the marginal revenue values is equivalent to adding the areas under the marginal revenue function.

If the firm sells just 1 unit, it charges a price of $100 and receives $100 in total revenue. Marginal revenue obviously equals $100. Column 5 shows the marginal revenue of the first unit sold. The firm sells 2 units if the price is $90, and total revenue is $180. Marginal revenue from selling the second unit is only $80. Summing the marginal revenue from selling the first unit ($100) and the second unit ($80) yields the total revenue of selling 2 units, or $180. The area under the marginal revenue function between $Q = 0$ and $Q = 2$ is equal to the increase in the firm's revenue when the quantity sold increases from 0 to 2 units. We compute $(1 \times \$100) + (1 \times \$80)$ to obtain $180.

The area under the marginal revenue function between 2 and 4 units represents

Table 9-3   USING THE AREA UNDER THE MARGINAL REVENUE FUNCTION TO MEASURE THE CHANGE IN REVENUE

QUANTITY DEMANDED, Q (1)	PRICE, P ($) (2)	TOTAL REVENUE, PQ ($) (3)	MARGINAL REVENUE, MR ($) (4)	SUM OF MARGINAL REVENUES ($) (5)
1	100	100	100	100
2	90	180	80	180
3	75	225	45	225
4	60	240	15	240

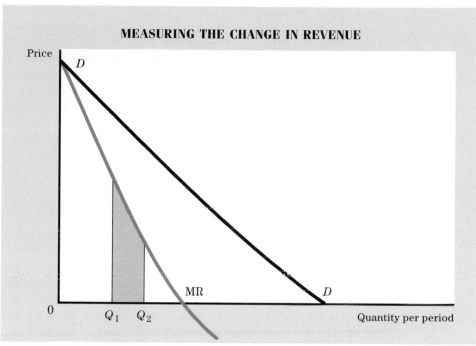

Figure 9-4   If the monopolist increases the total units sold from Q_1 to Q_2 units, the shaded area under the marginal revenue function between the two quantities represents the increase in total revenue.

the additional revenue received when the firm increases units sold from 2 to 4. In Table 9-3 the increase in total revenue by increasing the quantity sold from 2 to 4 units is $45 + $15 = $60. The $45 represents the area under the marginal revenue function when the quantity sold increases from 2 to 3 units, and the $15 represents the area under the marginal revenue function when the quantity sold increases from 3 to 4 units. The monopolist's revenues increase by $60 when the quantity sold increases from 2 to 4 units.

9-3 THE THEORY OF MONOPOLY PRICING

With these preliminaries out of the way, let us now consider how a profit-maximizing monopolist determines which price and quantity maximize total profits. For the moment let's simply assume that the monopolist maximizes profits and defer discussing why until Chapter 11.

The expression for long-run total profits of a monopolist is

$$\text{Total profit} = \text{Revenue} - \text{Long-run total cost}$$

$$\pi(Q) = D(Q)Q - C_L(Q) \qquad \text{(Total Profits of Monopolist)} \qquad \textbf{(9-7)}$$

where $\pi(Q)$ represents total profits. Total profit equals total revenue less long-run total cost. The monopolist selects output Q (and indirectly price P through the inverse demand function) to maximize total profits.

To make the **output decision,** that is, to find the long-run profit-maximizing output in Figure 9-5, the monopolist compares the marginal revenue from selling another unit with the marginal cost of producing the last unit. How much more revenue does the monopolist receive from selling one more unit and how much more cost does the monopolist incur in producing one more unit? If $MR > MC_L$, then profits increase, but they decrease if $MR < MC_L$. A profit-maximizing monopolist expands output until **marginal revenue equals long-run marginal cost.**[4]

$$MR(Q) = MC_L(Q) \qquad\qquad (9\text{-}8)$$

> A monopolist selects an output where the marginal revenue obtained from selling the last unit equals the marginal cost of producing the last unit.

The monopolist reaps maximum profits equal to area 3 by producing Q_m units where marginal revenue equals marginal cost. If the monopolist maximizes total profits by producing Q_m units, then profits decline if output is increased from Q_m to $Q_m + \Delta Q$. To demonstrate this, we must show that the additional revenue received is less than the additional cost incurred when output increases by ΔQ. Area 1 measures the additional revenue received, and the sum of areas 1 and 2 measures the additional cost of producing ΔQ units. Since the additional cost is greater than the additional revenue, total profits decrease by area 2 when the monopolist increases output by ΔQ. By using a similar argument, you should be able to show that profits decrease if the monopolist produces less than Q_m. Consequently, the monopolist maximizes total profits by producing an output where $MR = MC_L$.

The condition that profits are maximized when marginal revenue equals marginal cost has two hidden implications. To uncover these hidden implications first substitute $P[1 + (1/E_P)]$ for marginal revenue in equation 9-8:

---

[4] A profit maximum requires

$$\frac{d[\pi(Q)]}{dQ} = D(Q) + Q\frac{d[D(Q)]}{dQ} - \frac{d[C_L(Q)]}{dQ} = 0$$

or

$$D(Q) + Q\frac{d[D(Q)]}{dQ} = \frac{d[C_L(Q)]}{dQ} \qquad \text{or} \qquad MR(Q) = MC_L(Q)$$

For a profit maximum, the second derivative of profits with respect to Q must be negative.

$$\frac{d^2[\pi(Q)]}{dQ^2} = 2\frac{d[D(Q)]}{dQ} + Q\frac{d^2[D(Q)]}{dQ^2} - \frac{d^2[C_L(Q)]}{dQ^2} < 0$$

The first two terms on the right-hand side of the equation represent the slope of the marginal revenue function. The last term on the right-hand side is the slope of the marginal cost curve. The difference between the slope of the marginal revenue function and the slope of the marginal cost curve must be negative at the output where marginal revenue equals marginal cost. The marginal revenue function must cut through the marginal cost function from above.

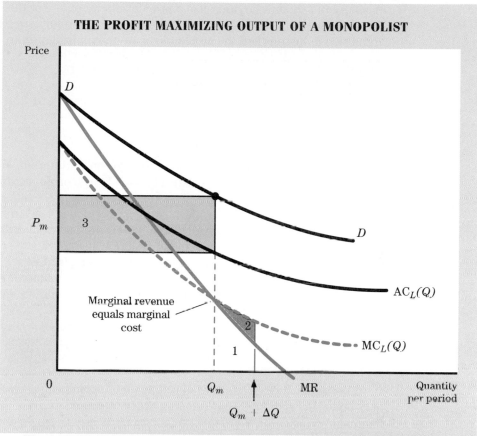

Figure 9-5 A monopolist maximizes profits by producing Q_m where marginal revenue equals marginal cost. The monopolist's total profits decrease if the monopolist increases output to $Q_m + \Delta Q$. The additional cost of producing ΔQ equals the sum of areas 1 and 2, the area under the marginal cost function. The additional revenue from the sale of ΔQ units equals area 1, the area under the marginal revenue function.

$$P\left(1 + \frac{1}{E_P}\right) = \mathrm{MC}_L \tag{9-9a}$$

By dividing both sides by MC_L and then by $1 + (1/E_P)$, the rearranged equation becomes

$$\frac{P}{\mathrm{MC}_L} = \frac{1}{1 + (1/E_P)} \tag{9-9b}$$

Equation 9-9b says that the ratio of monopoly price to marginal cost depends on the price elasticity of demand. The more elastic the demand function at the profit-maximizing price, the smaller the ratio of price to marginal cost. For example, suppose there are two demand functions where one demand function has a price elasticity of -5 and the other has a price elasticity of -2 at the monopoly price. The accompanying table shows what the ratio of monopoly price to marginal cost in the two industries is if the monopolists are maximizing profits.

PRICE ELASTICITY	$1/E_P$	P/MC_L
-5	-0.2	1.25
-2	-0.5	2.00

The price policies of the two monopolists are quite different. When the market demand function is more price-elastic ($E_P = -5$), the profit-maximizing monopoly price is just 25 percentage points above marginal cost. In the other industry, where demand is less elastic ($E_P = -2$), the monopoly price is twice marginal cost. This monopolist is able to elevate price well above the marginal cost. Therefore, the more elastic the monopolist's demand function in the vicinity of the monopoly price, the smaller the percentage **markup over marginal cost.** These two situations can be illustrated with graphs. Figure 9-6*a* shows a market where demand is more price-elastic at the monopoly price and where the markup over marginal cost is smaller than in the market shown in Figure 9-6*b*.

> The greater the price elasticity of demand, the smaller the markup of price over marginal cost.

The second hidden implication is that a monopolist will set the monopoly price at a point along the demand function where demand is *price-elastic*. The right-hand side of equation 9-9*a* is marginal cost, which must be positive. For marginal revenue to be positive, $1 + (1/E_P)$ must be positive, and this requires that E_P be less than -1. Therefore, the theory of monopoly pricing says that a pure monopolist will set a price on the demand function where demand is price-elastic. This point is often unappreciated by the student who casually and mistakenly refers to an inelastic demand of a monopolist. Demand is price-elastic at the profit-maximizing monopoly price.

> A profit-maximizing monopolist always operates along the demand function where demand is price-elastic.

APPLICATION 9-1

Are Firms in the Cigarette and Oil Industries Monopolists?

Many individuals, industry experts and others, believe the demand for cigarettes and gasoline is price-inelastic. A reasonable inference is that the average percentage reduction in the quantity demanded will be less than the average percentage increase in price if the price of either a pack of cigarettes or a gallon of gasoline

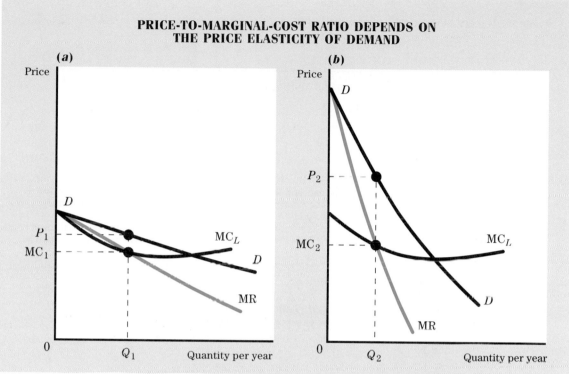

**PRICE-TO-MARGINAL-COST RATIO DEPENDS ON
THE PRICE ELASTICITY OF DEMAND**

Figure 9-6   The price-to-marginal-cost ratio is lower in (*a*) because demand is more price-elastic at the price of P_1 in (*a*) than at the price of P_2 in (*b*).

increases. There is considerable statistical support for these beliefs. Table 9-3 shows estimates of the *long-run* price elasticity of demand for cigarettes and oil from recent studies. Demand studies by economists find that the long-run price elasticity of demand is between -1 and 0, and so demand is price-inelastic in the *vicinity of the market prices* for these two products.

Along with the conviction that the demand for these products is price-inelastic is another strongly held conviction that the firms in these two industries act like a monopolist would, by coordinating their price and output policies to raise price and to maximize their joint profits. A frequently heard charge is that companies in these industries act in concert as if they were "collective" monopolists to increase price and therefore revenues because demand is price-inelastic.

What is wrong with this type of reasoning? We concluded that a profit-maximizing monopolist never operates in a region of the demand function where demand is price-inelastic because this implies that marginal revenue is negative. Figure 9-7 shows a monopolist's total revenue function. When the monopolist sells Q_2 units, total revenue is R^*. Envision the total revenue function as being shaped like a hill with the monopolist producing a quantity on the right side of the hill.

Table 9-3   ESTIMATES OF THE LONG-RUN PRICE ELASTICITY OF DEMAND

INDUSTRY	SOURCE OF ESTIMATE	ESTIMATED VALUE OF LONG-RUN PRICE ELASTICITY
Cigarettes	Becker, Grossman and Murphy (1991)	-0.7 to -0.8
Oil	MacAvoy (1982)	-0.29
	Griffin (1979)	-0.71 to -0.85
	Marquez (1984)	-0.25

Source: Cigarettes: Gary Becker, Michael Grossman, and Kevin M. Murphy, "Rational Addiction and the Effect of Price on Consumption," Center for the Study of the Economy and the State, Working Paper No. 68, February, 1991. Oil: Paul MacAvoy, *Crude Oil Prices as Determined by OPEC and Market Fundamentals*, (Cambridge, Mass.: Balinger Press, 1982); James Griffin, *Energy Conservation in the OECD: 1980 to 2000*, (Cambridge, Mass.: Balinger Press, 1979); Jaime R. Marquez, *Oil Price Effects and OPEC's Pricing Policy*, (Lexington, Mass.: Lexington Books, 1984).

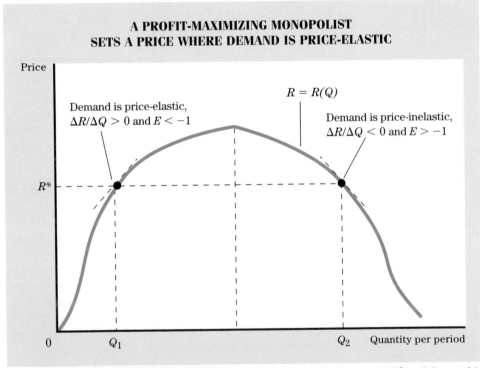

Figure 9-7   If a monopolist produces Q_2 units, total revenue equals R^* and demand is price-inelastic. The monopolist could receive the same revenue by producing only Q_1 units where demand is price-elastic. Total profits are higher when the monopolist sells Q_1 units because total cost of producing the smaller quantity must be lower.

Because the slope of the total revenue function is negative when the firm is selling Q_2 units, marginal revenue is negative and demand is price-inelastic. The monopolist can receive the same revenue R^* by producing Q_1 units, a smaller quantity. While total revenue is the same whether the monopolist produces Q_1 or Q_2, the total cost is smaller when Q_1 units are produced and total profit is higher. Therefore, a profit-maximizing monopolist will operate on the left side of the hill where total revenue increases when more units are sold by lowering the price. The theory predicts demand will be price-elastic for a monopolist.

If the firms in the cigarette and oil industries behave collectively as a profit-maximizing monopolist would, the price elasticity of demand should not be inelastic, for that is inconsistent with profit-maximizing behavior. One cannot claim that the demand for each of these products is price-inelastic and that the firms in each of these industries get together and act like a profit maximizing monopolist. It appears that the oil and cigarette firms are unable to coordinate their policies effectively and to charge a monopoly price. If they do get together, they do so imperfectly. They appear to be operating on the right side of the revenue hill. Chapter 10 examines why this might be so.

APPLICATION 9-2

Privatizing a Near Monopoly in the Czech Republic[5]

An effective way of obtaining a monopoly or near monopoly is to use the powers of the state to prevent entry. As privatization progresses in Eastern Europe, some Western firms have bought formerly state-sponsored monopolies and in the process managed to block other firms from entering. In the Czech and Slovak markets Philip Morris purchased the state-owned cigarette company, Tabak SA. With a substantial duty on imported cigarettes Philip Morris faces little competition from imported cigarettes. At the time of the sale the government promised to allow other companies to enter sometime later. However, Philip Morris used its advantage as the first post-communist entrant to strengthen its own brand names and to increase its market share. It has redesigned the packages of the brands previously sold by Tabak SA and has introduced new cigarettes. Its market share in the Czech market is said to exceed 70 percent. By being in the market before other competitors could enter, Philip Morris obtained a sizable advantage that may be difficult for later entrants to overcome. While privatization has worked well for Philip Morris, potential competitors are very upset. They say the government promised to end the monopoly on cigarettes when Tabak SA was sold to Philip Morris. Potential entrants are not impressed with the Czech privatization effort.

---

[5] Janet Guyon, "Czechs Play a Tough Game of Monopoly," *The Wall Street Journal*, October 12, 1993. Reprinted by permission of *The Wall Street Journal*, © 1993 Dow Jones & Company, Inc. All Rights Reserved Worldwide.

Using a Quota to Create a Partial Monopolist

In some markets foreign competition prevents domestic firms from increasing price. The discipline of foreign competition is a constant irritant to domestic producers, especially in markets with few domestic sellers. It is hardly surprising that domestic firms favor import limitations. But what about importers? Are importers harmed when limits are placed on imports? Surprisingly, importers can benefit from import limitations as the following analysis shows.

To show why importers can be better off, let's use the theory of competition and the theory of simple monopoly to show the effect of an import quota on price and output. Assume a sole domestic producer has the long-run average and marginal cost functions shown in Figure 9-8a. Figure 9-8b shows the importer supply curve is perfectly elastic. The many foreign suppliers, each of which is a price taker, supply indefinite quantities of the product to the American market at a price of P_I. It is this foreign supply that prevents the sole domestic supplier from raising the price in the American market. In Figure 9-8c the market demand in the United States is DD, and the long-run supply function of the American producer and the foreign suppliers is $S_L a S_L$. For any price between the minimum long-run average cost function of the domestic producer and P_I, the domestic firm would be the only supplier. At P_I foreign suppliers are willing to supply an indefinite quantity. With no restrictions on imports, the partial monopolist cannot sell any units at a price above P_I since importers are willing to supply indefinite amounts at P_I. Therefore, the domestic firm's demand function is flat at the price of P_I. Consequently, the equilibrium price is P_I, and total consumption is Q_c. The sole domestic producer supplies Q_d units, and total imports are $Q_c - Q_d$.

Suppose the domestic producer persuades Congress to impose a quota equal to the current quantity of imports, $Q_c - Q_d$. Figure 9-8b shows that the foreign supply function becomes vertical because foreign firms can only supply $Q_c - Q_d$ units if the price is P_I or higher. How does the quota affect the demand function of the domestic firm? In Figure 9-8d the demand function facing the domestic firm is $D'a$ up to the quantity Q_d, or the total quantity demanded less the quota. $D'a$ shows the quantity the domestic firm can sell at each price. For example, if the price is P_m, the *residual* quantity demanded is Q_m units, the difference between the total quantity demanded and the import quota. Therefore, the domestic firm knows the quantity demanded for its product will be Q_m units when the price is P_m, and this is one point on its demand function $D'D'$. At any price less than P_I, the foreign supply drops to zero, and so the firm's demand function jumps across and becomes the colored segment on DD at prices less than P_I. With a quota the partial monopolist's demand function becomes $D'abD$.

The domestic firm faces a downward sloping demand function for prices above P_I. It behaves like any firm that faces a downward sloping demand function. It maximizes profits by selling Q_m units at a price of P_m where marginal revenue

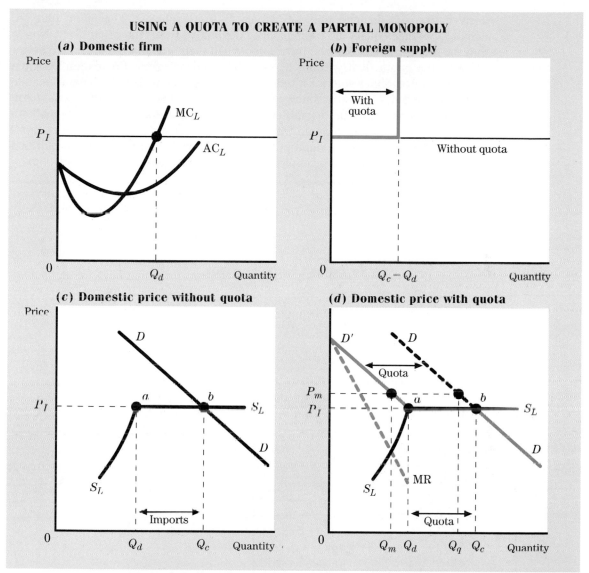

USING A QUOTA TO CREATE A PARTIAL MONOPOLY

(a) Domestic firm

(b) Foreign supply

(c) Domestic price without quota

(d) Domestic price with quota

Figure 9-8 The government converts a competitive industry into a partial monopoly by imposing a quota on imports. When imports are unrestricted, the domestic firm produces Q_d. When imports are limited to $Q_c - Q_d$, the demand facing the domestic firm becomes $D'abD$. The domestic firm maximizes profits by producing Q_m units and increases the price to P_m. The total quantity sold by the domestic firm plus foreign firms is Q_q.

derived from *its* demand function equals its marginal cost. The quota plus Q_m equals Q_q, which equals the total quantity demanded when the price is P_m. Notice that the foreign producers who have a quota sell their quantity at P_m and are better off with the quota than without it, as is the domestic firm. For example, when American automobiles sold for a relatively high price compared to Japanese-made cars, the Reagan administration urged the Japanese government to impose a voluntary export restraint that resembled a quota. Japanese auto companies benefited. In terms of this analysis, a quota transforms the domestic market from a competitive industry into a partial monopoly where the price and profits of the foreign suppliers and the domestic producer increase immediately.

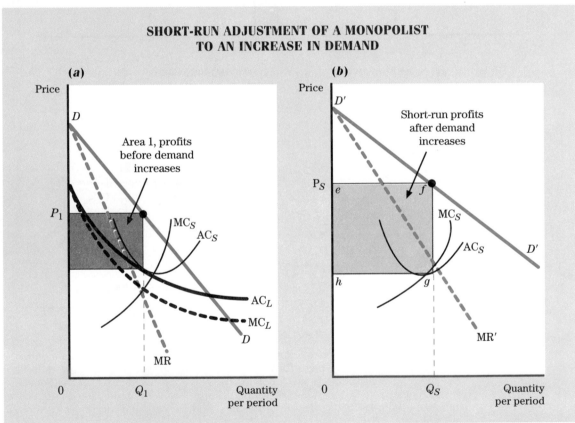

**SHORT-RUN ADJUSTMENT OF A MONOPOLIST
TO AN INCREASE IN DEMAND**

Figure 9-9   Before demand increases (*a*), the monopolist produces Q_1 units and sells each unit at a price of P_1. Profits equal the gray area. After demand increases to $D'D'$ (*b*), the monopolist increases output to Q_S where marginal revenue of the new demand function equals short-run marginal cost. The price rises to P_S. Total profits increase and equal the rectangle *efgh*.

9-4 ADJUSTING FROM ONE LONG-RUN EQUILIBRIUM TO ANOTHER

Just as a competitive industry adapts to a shift in demand, so too will a monopolist. To illustrate the short- and long-run adjustments, let's trace out how a monopolist responds to an increase in demand.

Initially, the monopolist is selling Q_1 units at a price of P_1 as shown in Figure 9-9a. The monopolist produces Q_1 units at lowest cost using a plant with a short-run average cost function AC_S and a marginal cost function MC_S. Here AC_S is tangent to the long-run average cost function AC_L when $Q = Q_1$. The monopolist's profits are equal to area 1. When demand increases from DD to $D'D'$, the monopolist makes do with its existing plant in the short run. It increases output to Q_S units where the new marginal revenue function MR' intersects the short-run marginal cost function. Price increases to P_S, and short-run profits are equal to area *efgh* in Figure 9-9b.

The monopolist can increase profits by still more in the long run by expanding plant size. Figure 9-10 shows that the new marginal revenue function MR' intersects the long-run marginal cost function at a quantity of Q_2 units. Therefore, when the monopolist expands, it builds a larger plant that produces Q_2 units at lowest total cost. Figure 9-10 shows the new short-run average cost function AC'_S and the short-run marginal cost function MC'_S of the larger plant. Again, the short-run average cost function of the larger plant is just tangent to the long-run average cost function when the monopolist produces Q_2 units. In the long run the monopolist lowers the price from P_S to P_2, and profits equal area *abcd*. The monopolist earns higher profits in the long run since area *abcd* is greater than area *efgh* in Figure 9-9b.

To summarize, a monopolist adjusts to an increase in demand along the same lines that a competitive industry does. In the short run the firm produces an output where marginal revenue equals short-run marginal cost with a given plant. In the long run, when firm size is variable, the monopolist produces a quantity where the new marginal revenue function intersects the long-run marginal cost function.

*9-5 ADOPTION OF A COST-REDUCING INNOVATION[6]

When a cost-reducing process innovation occurs in a competitive industry, new firms adopt the innovation and enter the industry. The increased supply lowers the price and creates losses for the firms using the old technology. Ultimately, all firms must adopt the cost-reducing innovation if they are to avoid losses. With monopoly entry is not possible. A monopolist does not have to worry that it will fall behind if a rival firm adopts a cost-reducing innovation since the monopolist has no rivals. Therefore, it might appear that a cost-reducing innovation would be adopted less readily under monopoly than under competition. However, this reasoning is faulty. A profit-maximizing monopolist has the same incentive to introduce the innovation

---

[6] This section borrows from the unpublished writings of R. L. Bishop.

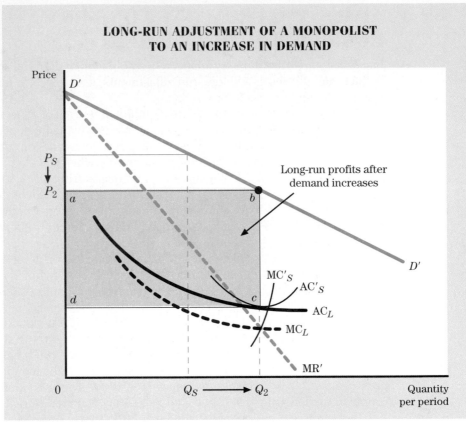

Figure 9-10   In the long run the monopolist produces Q_2 units where marginal revenue of $D'D'$ equals long-run marginal cost. To produce Q_2 units at lowest total cost, it builds a larger plant. Price falls from P_S to P_2. Long-run total profits equal the area *abcd*.

because the innovation reduces the cost of production and thereby increases the monopolist's profits.

This analysis focuses on the speed with which a monopolist adopts the new technology. A monopolist must decide whether it should scrap the existing plant and equipment immediately or whether it should wait until the old plant wears out. If this sounds familiar, it is because the monopolist makes the same decision as a competitive firm does. Because this analysis compares a monopolist's response to a cost-reducing innovation to the response of firms in a competitive industry, certain assumptions are adopted that make the two situations analogous. In the previous analysis of a competitive industry, the industry was a constant-cost industry where the long-run industry supply function was horizontal. To compare apples with apples, we assume that the long-run average and marginal cost functions of the monopolist are horizontal. Perhaps the easiest way to think about this is to assume that the monopolist operates a multiplant firm with identical plants. Each plant is comparable to an individual firm in the analysis of a competitive industry. The monopolist's long-run average and marginal cost functions are horizontal because the monopolist simply builds more equally efficient plants in the long run to produce a larger output. We continue to assume that all fixed costs are sunk. With this interpretation we can directly compare the analysis of the adoption of a cost-cutting innovation by a monopolist with the analysis of a competitive industry in Chapter 8.

Figure 9-11a shows the long-run average cost function AC_L of one representative plant that uses the existing technology. The monopolist operates each plant at the minimum point of its long-run cost function so that each plant produces q_0 units at a minimum long-run average cost of AC_0^*. In Figure 9-11c the demand function is DD, and the marginal revenue function is MR. The monopolist sells Q_0 units where the marginal revenue function MR intersects the long-run marginal cost function MC_L and charges P_1. To produce Q_0 at lowest total cost, the monopolist builds m plants so that each one operates at the minimum point of its long-run cost function and $mq_0 = Q_0$. Figure 9-11a shows each plant's short-run average AC_S and marginal cost MC_S functions.

The monopolist has m plants, and each has the short-run marginal cost function MC_S in Figure 9-11a. In the short run the total cost of producing any quantity is minimized by allocating production among its plants so that all m plants have the same short-run marginal cost. (If you need to refresh your memory, re-read section 6-4 of Chapter 6.) The monopolist's short-run marginal cost function MC_S is the horizontal summation of the short-run marginal cost functions of the m plants. In Figure 9-11c MC_S is the monopolist's marginal cost of increasing output in the short run.

After a cost-reducing innovation becomes available, the long-run average and marginal cost functions of a new plant become $AC_L^{(new)}$ and $MC_L^{(new)}$ in Figure 9-11b. At each quantity the long-run average cost of the new plant lies below the long-run average cost of an old plant. Starting from scratch, the monopolist prefers to use the new technology in all of its plants. However, the monopolist is not starting from scratch because it already has m operating plants. As in the analysis of a competitive industry, assume that the average variable cost function of the old plant lies below the long-run average cost function of a plant using the new technology. Therefore, it is cheaper for the monopolist to produce q_n units with an old plant than with a new plant, and so it continues to use the m old plants until they wear out.

> A monopolist will continue to use the old technology if the average variable cost function of the plant with the old technology lies below the long-run average cost function of the plant with the new technology.

Although the monopolist continues to use the old plants, it also builds new plants. Once the new technology becomes available, the marginal cost of expanding output is the new long-run marginal cost function MC_L'. The monopolist's pseudo–long-run marginal cost function is the horizontal summation of the short-run mar-

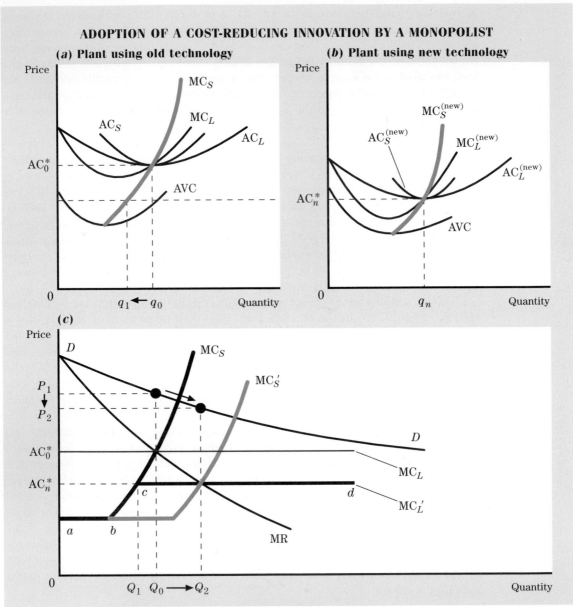

ADOPTION OF A COST-REDUCING INNOVATION BY A MONOPOLIST

(a) Plant using old technology

(b) Plant using new technology

(c)

Figure 9-11   A monopolist will expand output and lower price when a cost-reducing innovation becomes available. The price declines from P_1 to P_2, and the quantity produced increases to Q_2 where marginal revenue equals the modified long-run marginal cost function. The monopolist produces $Q_2 - Q_1$ with new plants using the new technology. Q_1 units are produced by plants using the old technology. These plants are later replaced by plants using the new technology.

ginal cost functions of the m old plants along MC_S up to the minimum long-run average cost function of the new plant, AC_n^*. At AC_n^* the monopolist can expand output along MC_L' by building more new plants and operating each one at q_n. Therefore, the monopolist's new pseudo–long-run marginal cost function is *abcd* in Figure 9-11c.

All the tools are now in place to analyze the monopolist's response to a cost-reducing innovation. At Q_0 marginal revenue now exceeds the new long-run marginal cost of MC_L'. The monopolist can increase profits by increasing output to Q_2 units where MR equals MC_L'. To produce Q_2 units at minimum total cost, the monopolist must make sure that marginal cost is the same for all the old plants and all the new plants that are built. This is accomplished by reducing the output of each old plant to q_1 (Figure 9-11a) so that the short-run marginal cost of each old plant equals the long-run marginal cost of a new plant when the new plant produces q_n units at the minimum long-run average of $AC_n^* = MC_n^*$. Because the old plants reduce their outputs, the monopolist adds more new plants to take up the slack. Therefore, the total output of the m old plants falls to Q_1, and the total output of all new plants is $Q_2 - Q_1$. By assigning Q_1 units to the m old plants and $Q_2 - Q_1$ units to the new plants, the monopolist produces Q_2 units at minimum total cost. After the new plants become operational, the monopolist's new short-run marginal cost function MC_S' is the horizontal sum of the short-run marginal cost functions of the m old plants and of the new plants, so that it intersects MC_L' and MR at $Q = Q_2$.

Because of the new technology, the monopolist's long-run marginal cost of expanding output is lower now than in the past. So it produces more units and reduces price to P_2. This analysis suggests that a monopolist has the same incentive as a competitive industry to adopt a cost-reducing innovation, and it does so as soon as it can. In this regard the incentives that lead new competitive firms to enter the industry with new technology apply equally to the monopolist. Instead of the entry of new firms, entry takes the form of new plants that the monopolist builds. As in the analysis of a competitive industry, the monopolist ultimately replaces the m old plants with new plants once they wear out. During this conversion process the price remains at P_2 since the total quantity produced by the monopolist remains at Q_2 units.

In summary, this analysis suggests that a monopolist will not delay introducing a cost-reducing innovation because it is not in its interest to do so. In this regard the behavior of a monopolist is qualitatively no different from that of firms in a competitive industry.

9-6   COMPETING TO BE A MONOPOLIST

This chapter has assumed that the firm is a monopolist and has not asked how it came to be one; however, this is a little artificial. If it is profitable to be a monopolist, firms will strive to become one. This rivalry can take many forms. For example, when a government issues a franchise that gives a firm the sole operating authority in a market, firms will go out of their way to secure the franchise. A cable franchise to service a local community can be very profitable. Rivalry among potential hopefuls is usually fierce as each aspirant lobbies, wines and dines officials, and contributes to reelection campaigns. The following Application shows how the design of a bidding process for a contract affects price, profits, and the number of subscribers to cable TV.

APPLICATION 9-4

Alternative Methods of Selling a Monopoly

A city will award a franchise to a cable company to send television signals by coaxial cable to homes for a monthly fee. There are economies of scale in providing these services. Rather than several companies offering the cable service, each laying a separate underground cable to service a community, the cost of providing the service will be lower with one firm providing a single underground cable.

The city is considering two ways to award the contract:

- *Proposal 1.* Allow competitive bidding for the contract and award it to the company that offers the largest payment to the municipality. The city learns that several established cable firms are opposed to this proposal. They argue that competitive bidding will increase the total costs of the firm that wins the contract and so the monthly fee will be higher.

- *Proposal 2.* Award the contract to the company that offers to charge the lowest monthly fee for the specified service.

Let's use the theory of monopoly pricing to evaluate the likely consequences of the two proposals.

Evaluation of Proposal 1   In Figure 9-12 the demand function for the cable service is *DD*. The demand function shows the number of hookups as a function of the monthly fee. The long-run average and marginal cost functions are AC_L and MC_L for all cable firms. Because there are economies of scale in providing cable service, AC_L decreases with the number of hookups.

Which bid will win the contract? To answer this question, you must determine what a firm will charge for the service. After a firm wins the contract, its bid is like a sunk cost, a bygone, and should not affect MR or MC or the monthly fee. The firm maximizes profits by charging a monopoly price P_m and hooks up Q_m homes. The total profits of the firm are equal to area 1 in Figure 9-12. We assume that many firms submit independent bids. If they compete among themselves by offering progressively higher bids, the highest possible bid is equal to area 1, or total profits, in Figure 9-12. Any firm that bids an amount equal to area 1 will win the contract. Therefore, competitive bidding transfers the profits to the municipality.

The firm that wins the contract will find that its long-run average cost function inclusive of its bid shifts upward and becomes AC′, which is just tangent to the demand function at the monopoly price. The marginal cost curve of the firm does not change because the bid is a lump sum amount and is like a fixed cost. While

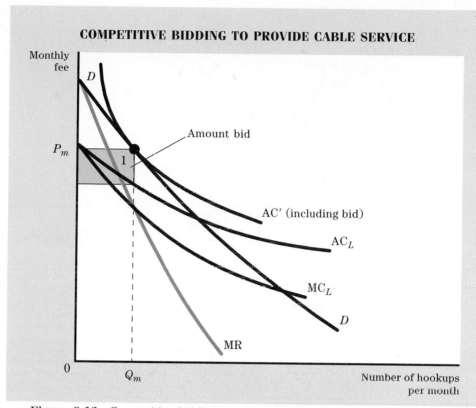

Figure 9-12   Competitive bidding for a monopoly of cable services increases the average cost function from AC_L to AC'. The marginal cost function is unaffected by the amount bid. Area 1 represents the amount bid and received by the municipality. The monthly fee is unaffected by the amount bid for the monopoly.

the average cost function shifts upward, the marginal cost of providing the service does not change. Therefore, the firm will continue to produce Q_m because marginal revenue still equals marginal cost at this quantity.

The argument that the high cost of the bidding process will raise the monthly fee is a specious one. The *average* cost curve of the winner is now higher. What is more important is that the *marginal* cost function is the same. The additional cost of serving one more customer is the same as it was before the firm submitted a bid. Therefore, the argument made by the cable companies rings hollow, and the claim that competitive bidding will increase the monthly fee is invalid.

Competitive bidding has one desirable feature. It discourages spending resources to win the contract. As long as the size of the bid determines the winner, each contestant has no incentive to use resources to lobby politicians. Profits are transferred to the local government and not eliminated through costly expenditures to win the contract.

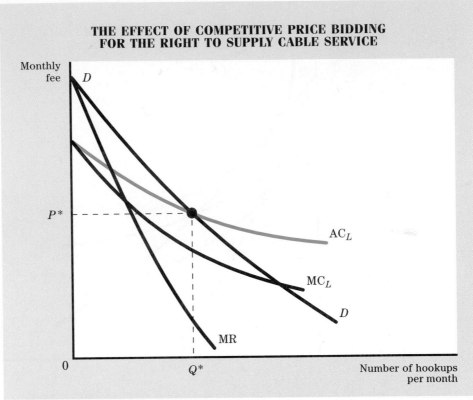

**THE EFFECT OF COMPETITIVE PRICE BIDDING
FOR THE RIGHT TO SUPPLY CABLE SERVICE**

Figure 9-13   If the contract is awarded to the firm that offers the lowest price, the winner will charge a monthly fee of P^* and the total number of hookups equals Q^*. At Q^* the monthly fee still exceeds marginal cost because of internal economies of scale of providing cable services. The winning firm does not earn any profits.

Evaluation of Proposal 2   Proposal 2 requires that the contract be awarded to the firm that offers the lowest monthly fee. In Figure 9-13 the lowest fee that is consistent with zero profits for the winner is the price P^* where $P^* = AC_L$. Any higher monthly fee would be undercut by other bidders, and any lower monthly fee would result in losses for the firm. If the firm offers P^* as the monthly fee, the number of subscribers is Q^*. The monthly fee will be lower and the number of hookups will be larger under proposal 2. Here again, the winning firm earns no profits, but consumer surplus is larger under proposal 2 than under proposal 1. While P^* is not equal to marginal cost, it is closer to marginal cost than the monopoly price in proposal 1. Therefore proposal 2 has more consumer benefits than proposal 1.

This analysis assumes that the city can monitor the firm so that it provides the quality of service specified in the contract. More advanced analyses investigate the consequences of pricing in this manner when it is costly to monitor the quality of service provided by the firm.[7]

9-7 THE TYRANNY OF DURABILITY

The analyses of monopoly implicitly assume that the monopolist produces a certain quantity of a nondurable good in each period and sells it at the monopoly price. This section shows how product durability affects the price policy of a monopolist.

The issue of the **effect of product durability on monopoly pricing** was first raised by Nobel Prize winner Ronald Coase.[8] Let's consider the Coase problem in the context of an example. A relative leaves you 80 acres of land on the Oregon coast with a beautiful view of the Pacific Ocean. This is an especially prized possession because the state owns all nearby land. You are the sole owner of this unique parcel of land, which is in great demand. Competitors cannot enter and increase the supply of land. You are a monopoly supplier should you decide to sell the land. A real estate consultant estimates that this exquisite parcel of land will have maximum value if you develop and sell 50 of the 80 one-acre oceanfront lots. To maximize the value of the parcel, you agree to sell one-acre lots and supervise the types of residential structures that the new owners can place on the lots.

The consultant sketches the likely demand function for the lots and estimates the inverse demand function for the lots as shown in the accompanying table.

QUANTITY OF LOTS DEMANDED	PRICE PER LOT ($)	TOTAL REVENUE ($)
30	$700,000	$21,000,000
40	600,000	24,000,000
50	500,000	25,000,000
70	300,000	21,000,000
80	200,000	16,000,000

Total revenue is maximized by selling 50 lots, each at the monopoly price of $500,000, and leaving 30 acres unsold.

Equation 9-10 represents the inverse demand function for lots.

$$P = \$1,000,000 - \$10,000Q \qquad \text{(9-10)}$$

[7] For a discussion of this and other issues related to cable television, see W. Kip Viscusi, John M. Vernon, and Joseph E. Harrington, Jr., *Economics of Regulation and Antitrust*, (Lexington, Mass.: D. C. Heath, 1992), pp. 399–415.

[8] R. H. Coase, "Durability and Monopoly," *Journal of Law and Economics* XV, no. 1 (April 1972), pp. 143–50.

where P is the most consumers will pay per lot for Q lots. The linear demand function DD and the marginal revenue function MR are shown in Figure 9-14. You own 80 one-acre lots. If the cost of selling the lots is negligible, the monopoly price per acre is $500,000, and marginal revenue is zero when you sell 50 acres. However, if you sell all 80 lots, the market-clearing price is $200,000 per lot where the demand function intersects the vertical supply function S at 80 lots.

You expect to become a multimillionaire by selling 50 acres at a price of $500,000 each. Although you are a monopolist, Coase claims that no one will pay $500,000 and you will be able to sell the land only at a competitive price! This claim rests on the following reasoning. After you sell 50 acres, what will you do with the remaining 30 acres? He says you will sell the remaining 30 acres if you want to maximize profits. The marginal cost of selling another acre is zero. If you sell the remaining 30 acres, the price per acre falls to $200,000 per lot for all 80 lots. Do you care? Others own the first 50 acre-lots and they, not you, will suffer a loss. Based on your own narrow self-interest you are better off selling 80 acres.

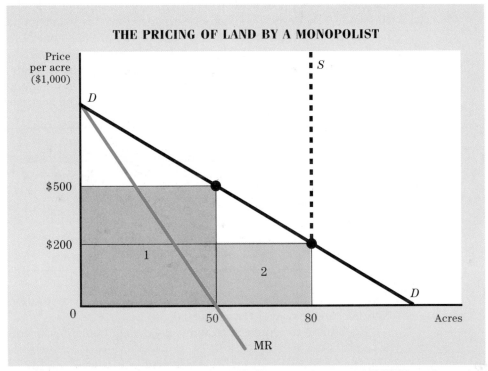

Figure 9-14   The sole owner of 80 acres of land will want to sell all 80 acres, not just the 50 acres. After 50 acres are sold, the owner has an incentive to sell the remaining 30 acres. Area 1 represents the revenue from selling the first 50 acres, and area 2 represents the revenue from selling the remaining 30 acres. The key point is that the owner has an incentive to sell all the acres.

Total profits are now equal to area 1 plus area 2 in Figure 9-14, or $25 million plus 30 more acres at $200,000 per acre for a total of $31 million. Therefore, you have an incentive to sell additional acres as long as you own any acres.

Because of this incentive to sell more units, potential buyers of the first bundle look ahead and will be reluctant to purchase at a price of $500,000 because they anticipate that price will fall to $200,000. They recognize that your profits will be higher if you sell all 80 lots. They, not you, will suffer losses when you do. No rational buyer would commit to buying at the monopoly price, fully realizing that the price will be lower in the future. Realizing this, buyers are unwilling to purchase an acre of land unless you sell all 80 acres at once at a competitive price of $200,000. Then, you will have no more lots to supply to the market and the buyer need not fear a future price reduction. Coase advances the proposition that a monopolist selling a durable good can charge only a competitive price unless it finds a way to protect the interests of buyers.

> With infinitely durable goods the market price is independent of the number of sellers in the market. A monopolist can sell a durable good, but only at a competitive price.

Actions the Monopolist Can Take to Reassure Buyers

Unless the monopolist can protect the buyer from subsequent price depreciation, the monopolist stands to lose $9 million. A creative manager may decide to lease rather than sell the land. The monopolist could develop each acre, charge a monopoly rent for each acre, and rent out 50 acres of land. Because the monopolist owns all the land, there is less of an incentive to rent the 50 acres and later rent 30 more acres at a lower rent because of the effect on future rents. If the monopolist increases the number of acres leased above 50 by lowering the rent on the additional units, it will not be able to charge the monopoly rent in future periods. In the next leasing period renters will not trust the monopolist and will not be willing to pay a monopoly rent. If the monopolist tries to obtain larger total rents by leasing still more acres later at a lower rent, the monopolist acquires a tarnished reputation.

Leasing rather than selling is a preferable option for the monopolist as long as the cost of negotiating the leases is not high and the cost of monitoring the behavior of lessors is not high. Leasing can be costly, however, because a lessor typically exercises less care over the property than an owner would.

The management might try to sell 50 acres but add a number of clauses to reassure buyers of the lots. For example, there could be a clause requiring the owner to give each buyer the best price if the owner sells any acre of land for less than $500,000. The firm commits to give any buyer a discount if the seller reduces the price. Or the owner could place a clause in the contract mandating repurchase of the land at the original price at the buyer's request. In this way any attempt by the monopolist to sell more units will be self-defeating because total profits will decrease. Introducing these provisions into a contract serves a useful purpose, but sometimes they have drawbacks. If demand conditions are highly variable, a buy-back provision could become very costly if demand declines and the value of the land decreases. The monopolist would then suffer a capital loss.

Another solution may require the monopolist to donate the 30 acres to a nonprofit agency or to the government with the provision that land use be noncommercial. After donating 30 acres to an environmental group or to a government, you can charge a monopoly price of $500,000 per acre.

This theory of the pricing of durable goods explains why a firm might publicly announce a limited production run for a product. For example, a firm may sell a special commemorative lithograph. The producer could promise to destroy the plate after producing a specified quantity. By adopting this policy the firm is posting its reputation as a bond and is signaling that it will not produce more units after selling the original quantity. Limited production runs of automobiles and rare or specialized books are examples of a firm signaling the buyer that the quantity sold will not increase. The goal of the sole supplier is to increase the confidence of the buyer that no subsequent price reduction will occur.

APPLICATION 9-5

Disney Limits the Sales of *Fantasia* to 50 Days[9]

In November 1991 Disney sold *Fantasia* on videocassette and laserdisc for only 50 days. To increase desirability, Disney limited sales to 50 days before Christmas. After December 20, 1991, the original film would never again be sold by Disney in a home video format but would be available at rental stores. Disney priced *Fantasia* from $24.99 to $99.99. The lowest price was for the basic videotape, while the top price was for the movie plus the story of the making of the film, a commemorative lithograph, a large 16-page souvenir book, and a certificate of authenticity signed by Roy Disney, vice president of the Disney board of directors. Disney reported advance orders of 9.25 million units for the videocassette, and 200,000 units for the laserdisc.

Why did Disney place a 50-day limit on sales of *Fantasia?* One explanation is that it wanted to publicly inform collectors that it would not sell more units at a lower price in the future. Collectors would trust Disney's announcement because the company has other classics that it may one day release and it would not want to spoil its reputation by later selling more units of *Fantasia* at a lower price.

9-8   TAXING A MONOPOLIST

This section investigates the long-run response of a monopolist to a per unit tax. After the government levies a per unit tax, the long-run average and marginal cost functions shift upward by the tax t. In Figure 9-15 the monopolist treats the per

---

[9] Based on Richard Christiansen, " 'Fantasia' a Hit with Video Audience," *Chicago Tribune*, October 31, 1991.

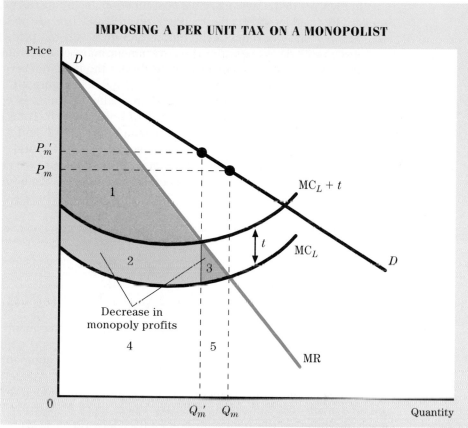

IMPOSING A PER UNIT TAX ON A MONOPOLIST

Figure 9-15   The pretax profit of a monopolist is equal to the sum of areas 1, 2, and 3. After the per unit tax of t is imposed, the profits of a monopolist decrease and equal area 1. Total profits decrease by the sum of areas 2 and 3.

unit tax as another cost of doing business. With the per unit tax, the additional cost of producing and selling one more unit equals the original long-run marginal cost plus the per unit tax paid to the government. A profit-maximizing monopolist finds an output where marginal revenue equals the sum of the marginal cost of production and t.[10] Therefore, a monopolist responds to a per unit tax by reducing output and raising price.

$$MR(Q) = MC_L(Q) + t \qquad (9\text{-}11)$$

[10] After the per unit tax is imposed, the profit function of the monopolist is

$$\pi(Q) = D(Q)\,Q - C_L(Q) - tQ$$

The monopolist selects Q, so that total profits are maximized, or

$$\frac{d[\pi(Q)]}{dQ} = D(Q) + Q\frac{d[D(Q)]}{dQ} - \frac{d[C_L(Q)]}{dQ} - t = 0$$

This expression can be rearranged to yield $MR(Q) = MC_L(Q) + t$.

In Figure 9-15 the new marginal cost function, including the per unit tax, shifts upward by t and intersects the marginal revenue function at the smaller output of Q'_m. The per unit tax reduces the output and increases the price to P'_m. The monopolist's profit decreases after the government imposes a per unit tax. Without a per unit tax total revenue equals the area under the marginal revenue curve up to the quantity Q_m, or the sum of areas 1, 2, 3, 4, and 5, in Figure 9-15. When all factor inputs are continuous, the total cost of producing Q_m units is equal to the area under the marginal cost curve or the sum of areas 4 and 5. Total profits equal the difference between the two areas or the sum of areas 1, 2, and 3. With a per unit tax, total revenue is equal to the sum of areas 1, 2, and 4. The total cost of producing Q'_m equals the sum of areas 2 and 4. Total profits decline and are now equal to area 1. The imposition of a per unit tax decreases the monopolist's profits by the sum of areas 2 and 3.

> A per unit tax increases the monopoly price and reduces the quantity produced and total profits.

9-9   THE SOCIAL OBJECTION TO MONOPOLY

Now that you know how a monopolist determines price and quantity, let's compare prices and quantities under monopoly and competition and consider the **social cost of monopoly.** In order to compare monopoly with competition, we want to be sure that the monopolized market can function as a competitive market. To make the two situations comparable, assume that the monopolized industry can be a constant-cost competitive industry where more firms enter the industry and each produces at the minimum point of its long-run average cost function. To maintain comparability, assume that the long-run supply function of the competitive industry becomes the monopolist's long-run average and marginal cost function. For example, assume a situation where a monopolist can merge the competitive firms and operates each firm as a plant. Assume that the monopolist can add identical plants so that it can increase total output at constant long-run average and marginal costs.

Figure 9-16a shows the competitive price and output in a competitive industry. Consumer surplus is equal to area 1. Because the long-run supply function is horizontal, producer surplus is zero. In Figure 9-16b the monopoly price P_m is higher and output Q_m is lower. Consumer surplus is smaller and is equal to area 2. Because price is higher, a monopoly transfers part of consumer surplus to the monopolist through the profits earned by the monopolist. Area 3 represents the transfer. Because output is smaller, monopoly creates a **deadweight loss of monopoly** equal to area 4. Deadweight loss is the loss in surplus suffered by some group (consumers or producers) that is not offset by a rise in surplus to some other group.

> The social objection to monopoly is that it creates a deadweight loss so total surplus is not maximized.

THE EFFECT OF MONOPOLY ON CONSUMER AND PRODUCER SURPLUSES

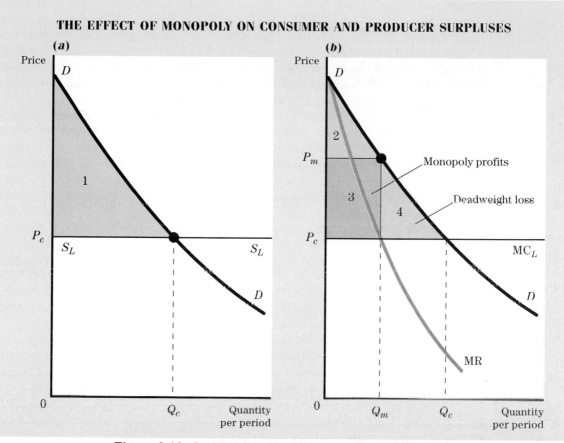

Figure 9-16 In (*a*) the competitive price and output are P_c and Q_c, respectively. Consumer surplus is equal to area 1. In (*b*) price increases to P_m and output contracts to Q_m in a monopolized industry. Consumer surplus decreases to area 2. Producer surplus increases and is equal to area 3. The deadweight loss is area 4.

The complaint about monopoly is that the monopolist produces too few units, not that it earns profits. If the government expropriated the profits of the monopolist through a special levy so that it earned no profit, the objection to monopoly would remain. Because the monopolist produces less than a competitive industry would produce, it employs too few factors of production. The unused factors find employment elsewhere in other industries, with the consequence that too many resources are being employed in other competitive industries scattered throughout the economy. The outputs of the other competitive industries in the economy are larger than they would otherwise be if the monopolist had to set a competitive price. Chapter 18 presents a more general analysis of the consequences of monopoly.

The government uses an antitrust policy and occasionally direct regulation of price to eliminate or attenuate deadweight loss caused by monopoly. Ideally, the monopolist should behave as a price taker instead of a price maker. The monopolist can be transformed into a price taker by setting a price ceiling at the competitive price where the demand function intersects the long-run marginal cost function. The regulated monopolist determines output where the competitive price (ceiling) P_c equals long-run marginal cost and quantity demanded equals quantity supplied in Figure 9-16b. With a competitive price ceiling areas 2, 3, and 4 equal consumer surplus and the deadweight loss of monopoly disappears.

Because a monopolist sets price above marginal cost, the marginal value of the last unit sold by a monopolist exceeds the marginal resource cost of the last unit produced. It is this discrepancy that the antitrust laws are designed to eliminate or reduce. The Sherman Antitrust Law is the elder statesman of antimonopoly legislation in the United States. It is designed to prevent contracts and conspiracies that restrain trade and commerce; it makes it illegal to monopolize or to attempt to monopolize a market.

The Sherman Act has played an important role in eliminating the most effective methods of maintaining price discipline among industry members. For example, a joint sales agency requires all members of a cartel to sell their product through a single sales agency and is an effective way of preventing member firms from cheating on production quotas. Early on, the joint sales agency was adopted by firms in several industries. This practice was challenged and declared illegal under the antitrust laws.

Some subtle and difficult issues that arise in antitrust cases are illustrated in Application 9-6: the size of the relevant market, cost efficiencies from a merger, and whether a proposed merger between two hospitals will increase the price of medical care.

APPLICATION 9-6

Will a Merger of Two Hospitals Decrease Total Surplus?[11]

Throughout the country, more and more hospitals are merging. This consolidation trend has alarmed the Antitrust Division of the Justice Department, which fears the trend will raise hospital prices just when the federal government is trying to control health expenditures. The Justice Department brought suit to prevent a merger between Mercy Health Center and Finley Hospital, two hospitals located in Dubuque, Iowa. Mercy Health Center specializes in cardiac care and Finley Hospital specializes in cancer treatment. The hospitals argued that the declining use of hospital beds required a merger. They claimed they would be able to obtain cost reductions by not having to duplicate certain facilities and equipment, such as a CT scanner, computer and billing systems, and so on.

To bolster its case, the Justice Department interviewed many businesses, including two health maintenance organizations (HMOs). The HMOs opposed the merger, saying it would reduce the discounts they had obtained from the hospitals because the two had had to compete for HMO business.

---

[11] For a more detailed discussion of this case, see Bryan Gruley and Laurie McGinley, "Antitrust Lawyers Fail to Stop Hospital Deal, with Big Implications," *The Wall Street Journal*, January 4, 1996. Reprinted by permission of *The Wall Street Journal*, © 1996 Dow Jones & Company, Inc. All Rights Reserved Worldwide.

The Justice Department claimed that services provided by the merged firm would account for 78 percent of the local health care services market and that the merger would eliminate discounts and contribute to hospital cost inflation. As in most antitrust cases, there was a serious disagreement over the size of the market. The Justice Department defined the geographical size of the market as Dubuque County plus a small portion of Illinois and Wisconsin. The hospitals argued that the geographic market was much larger and that if they raised prices, users would drive 50 to 70 miles to other hospitals and save $400 in out-of-pocket cost. They said that patients were paying a larger fraction of their hospital bills today and therefore were more sensitive to price differences. Some patients were already driving 100 miles to the hospital at the University of Iowa and 80 miles to the University of Wisconsin. In an important decision, the judge favored the hospitals' arguments.

This antitrust case raises several difficult issues that deserve our consideration. First, why do the hospitals have to merge to achieve any cost economies? Second, is the merger motivated by efficiency considerations, as the hospitals claim, or the anticipated reductions in discounts, as the Justice Department claims? Third, if the hospital merger reduces costs but also results in monopoly pricing, will total surplus increase or decrease?

SUMMARY

- A pure monopolist determines the price without attracting other firms to the industry or considering the price response of other firms because the products of other firms are not close substitutes.
- The marginal revenue of a monopolist is less than price because the monopolist reduces the price on all previous units that could have been sold at the higher price.
- A profit-maximizing monopolist never produces in the region where demand is price-inelastic.
- A profit-maximizing monopolist determines the quantity where marginal revenue equals marginal cost.

- In the short run an increase in demand causes profits to rise. Profits rise by still more in the long run when plant size can change.
- An innovation that reduces the cost of production lowers the monopoly price, raises output, and increases total profits.
- The sole producer of a durable good can sell a durable good only at the competitive price unless the producer can commit to the monopoly output.
- Levying a per unit tax will reduce the quantity produced by a monopolist.
- Total surplus is smaller under monopoly than under competition.

KEY TERMS

monopolist's inverse demand function
marginal revenue function
equating marginal revenue to marginal cost
competing to be a monopolist
effect of product durability on monopoly
    pricing

price maker
monopolist's output decision
markup over marginal cost
deadweight loss of monopoly
social cost of monopoly

REVIEW QUESTIONS

1. Under what conditions can a firm behave as a pure monopolist?
2. In the short run a monopolist should expand output until marginal revenue is zero. Explain why you agree or disagree with this statement.
3. The monopoly price and the long-run equilibrium price in a competitive industry always occur in the region of the demand function where demand is price-elastic. Explain why you agree or disagree with this statement.
4. Evaluate the following: I would rather be selling a good where demand is price-inelastic than price-elastic. Then, I can raise price and increase total revenue. If demand is price-elastic, revenue decreases when I raise the price.
5. Why is it correct to say that the price is always on the monopolist's demand function and never on the monopolist's marginal cost function?
6. Which foreign firms would favor and which would oppose a voluntary export restraint program that allows those importers who have exported goods to continue to do so?

7. In either a monopoly or a competitive industry a cost-reducing innovation reduces the price as soon as the new technology is introduced. However, in a competitive industry price continues to decrease when the new technology completely replaces the old technology, while a monopolist maintains the price when it replaces the old technology with the new technology. Explain why you agree or disagree with these statements.
8. Competitive bidding for the right to be a monopolist harms consumers because it raises the costs of the winner. Explain why you agree or disagree with this statement.
9. Would you rather have a monopoly of lemons or of rust-proof steel garage doors? Explain your answer.
10. When the government levies a per unit tax against a monopolist, the total revenue of the monopolist may either rise or decline. Explain why you agree or disagree with this statement.
11. Why is the price-cost ratio of monopoly smaller when the demand function is more elastic at the monopoly price?

EXERCISES

1. The market demand for macadamia nuts is the straight line

$$P = 200 - 5Q$$

where Q is measured in tons of macadamia nuts per year. There is a monopoly producer of macadamia nuts in this country.
   a. If the monopolist produces 5 tons of nuts, what would total revenue be? Construct a table of total revenue at 5, 10, 15 tons, and so on up to 40 tons.
   b. Make a table of the change in total revenue as the producer moves from 0 to 5 tons and so on. Graph the *change* in total revenue for successive 5 ton increments.
   c. If the marginal cost of producing a ton of macadamia nuts is $25, how many tons would the monopolist produce and sell?
2. Since a monopolist equates marginal revenue to marginal cost, an upward shift in the marginal cost function will increase a monopolist's marginal revenue and marginal cost by the same amount so total profits will not be affected. Explain why you agree or disagree with this statement.
3. The size of fixed cost will not affect the

quantity produced by the monopolist in the short run. Explain why you agree or disagree.

4. A monopolist with a price elasticity of -10 will have a smaller price–marginal cost margin *and* lower total profits than a monopolist with a price elasticity of -3. Explain why you agree or disagree.

5. At the monopoly price the price elasticity of demand is -2 and the ratio of price to the firm's average cost is 1.3. Can you tell from this information whether the firm is operating in the region where there are economies or diseconomies of scale? Explain.

6. Before a monopolist introduces a new process innovation, it produces Q_0 units. After a new process innovation is introduced, the monopolist increases output to Q_1 and lowers the price. The monopolist produces $Q_1 - Q_0$ units in new plants that use the new technology since the average variable cost of the old plant is less than the long-run average cost of a new plant. Is the monopolist maximizing profits? With the use of graphs explain why or why not.

*7. Suppose the long-run equilibrium price in a constant-cost competitive industry is P_c. An invention lowers the cost of production for just one new firm so that it can produce each rate of industry output by 20 percent less than the current equilibrium price. The new firm will be the sole producer in the industry as long as it sets the price below the long-run equilibrium competitive price. What is the largest value for the price elasticity of demand at the monopoly price that the new firm can charge and not attract competitive firms into the industry?

*8. Instead of assuming that there is only one domestic producer in the industry as in Application 9-3, suppose there are many domestic suppliers. Consider the effect of introducing a quota that allows the current level of imports to continue as in Appli-

cation 9-3. Predict the effect of the quota when there are many domestic suppliers and compare your results with the situation in Application 9-3 where there is a single domestic supplier. Can you determine whether the domestic industry behaves competitively or not by the response of price to the introduction of the quota? Explain.

9. Suppose the price a monopolist can charge is regulated by the government. Find the regulated price that maximizes the total number of units sold. *Hint:* At the regulated price, the firm's marginal revenue equals price up to the quantity demanded on the demand function.

Assume the government sets the price ceiling so that the regulated monopolist sells the maximum quantity. Then, a regulator allows competitive bidding for the right to be a monopolist.

  a. With the use of graphs determine how much a firm would pay for the right to be a monopolist under these circumstances.

  b. Does the amount the regulated monopolist pays tell you whether long-run average cost is decreasing or increasing?

*10. Countries enter into long-lived tariff agreements with each other. Suppose that country A exports product 1 to country B with a tariff of $50 per unit imposed by country B and country B exports product 2 to country A with a tariff of $100 per unit imposed by country A. Many of these agreements contain a most-favored-nation clause that requires a country to give the lowest tariff to all countries exporting the product to the country. Why would you expect these kinds of agreements to include a most-favored-nation clause?

11. A monopolist produced 1 million units last year. If a $10 per unit tax is imposed, the profits of the monopolist will decrease by $10 million. Explain why you agree or disagree with this statement.

12. If the government levies a per unit tax on a monopolist, the monopolist increases price and reduces the total quantity sold. Total revenue may either increase or decrease. Explain why you agree or disagree with this statement.

*13. The figure below shows AC_1 as the average cost of supplying health care when there are two independent hospitals. Assume competition between the hospitals lowers the price to $P_1 = AC_1$. Assume a merger between the two hospitals lowers the average cost of supplying health services to AC_2. P_2 is the monopoly price per unit of health services after the two hospitals merge. Calculate how consumer, producer, and total surplus change because of the merger. Under what condition will the merger reduce total surplus?

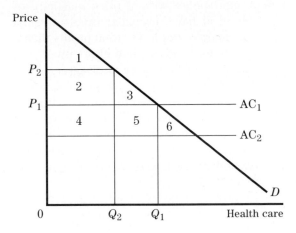

CHAPTER 10

OLIGOPOLY AND MONOPOLISTIC COMPETITION

■ **10-1 Cooperation among Price-Taking Firms: Cartel Behavior**
Application 10-1. Trouble in the Orange Cartel

■ **10-2 Price and Output with Oligopoly**
Cooperative Behavior and the Incentive to Cheat

■ **10-3 Models of Noncooperative Behavior**
The Cournot Model
The Reaction or Best Response Function of Each Cournot Rival
The Nash Equilibrium
Application 10-2: More Suppliers of Fine Caviar
The Cournot Model with n Competitors
The Bertrand Model
Application 10-3: Encouraging Competition among Suppliers

■ **10-4 The Effect of the Number of Rivals on Price**
Application 10-4: Retail Tire Prices
Application 10-5: Auction Markets

■ **10-5 Facilitating and Preventing Collusion**
Meeting Competition
Application 10-6: Detecting the Effects of Facilitating Practices

Preventing Collusion

■ **10-6 A Case Study: The Electrical Manufacturers' Conspiracy**
Collusion and Cheating
Product and Industry Characteristics and Successful Collusion
The Cost of Detecting Price Chiseling

■ **10-7 Game Theory and Noncooperative Strategies**
Dominant Strategies
A Dominant Strategy for Only One Firm
Application 10-7: Which Brands Enter Late and Which Enter Early?
Nash Equilibria
Repeated Games
Sequential Games
Application 10-8: Credible Commitment for *Independence Day*

■ **10-8 Monopolistic Competition**

■ **Summary**

■ **Key Terms**

■ **Review Questions**

■ **Exercises**

■ **Appendix: How the Number of Rivals Affects Firm Output and Price in the Cournot Model**

In some markets there is neither monopoly nor competition. What does it mean to say that there is neither monopoly nor competition? If the market is not monopolized, two or more independent firms are in the market. If firms do not behave competitively, they are not price takers. How is price arrived at in markets where there is more than one firm but where the firms are not price takers? Does it follow that in such markets price is above the competitive price but below the monopoly price, or could price equal either the competitive or the monopoly price? These are some of the questions that we answer in this chapter.

We consider a variety of different markets. In the first section of the chapter we look at a market where many price-taking firms escape the discipline of competition by forming a *cartel* that reduces each firm's output and increases the market price. In other industries with just a few firms, the *strategic interaction* among firms is the key to understanding how prices are determined. In these markets that are intermediate between monopoly and competition economists have developed different models and unambiguous answers are not presently available. The results of the models differ because of the assumptions about the strategic interaction among firms. In such a setting the price set by one firm depends on what price is set by a rival. What are the pricing implications if firms are in a one shot–single period situation or interact repeatedly with each other? Can consumers expect to benefit if firms compete with each other by agreeing to match a rival's price reduction? These are some of the questions that will be discussed in this chapter. The last section of the chapter considers industries with many firms but where firms are not price takers because each sells a slightly different product. Because each firm's product is slightly differentiated from those of other firms, each firm's product is an imperfect substitute for the products sold by its rivals. Consequently, a firm faces a downward sloping demand curve when it competes with its many rivals.

10-1   COOPERATION AMONG PRICE-TAKING FIRMS: CARTEL BEHAVIOR

Competitive firms sometimes seek to escape competition by cooperating rather than competing. A **cartel** is an arrangement among price-taking firms in an industry whose objective is to reduce output and raise price.

Let's demonstrate how a perfectly functioning cartel operates and then consider the special problems it faces. The analysis begins with a constant-cost competitive industry with n firms in long-run equilibrium. Figure 10-1a shows the long-run equilibrium output of a firm, and Figure 10-1b shows the long-run industry equilibrium. The long-run equilibrium price is P_e, and total industry output is Q_e. Each firm produces q_e at minimum cost by building a particular size plant with the corresponding short-run average and marginal cost curves.

Suppose all firms in the industry agree that they must seek relief from price competition. So, they agree to form a cartel whose purpose is to reduce output and raise price. The n firms in the industry would take this step because new firms cannot enter the industry immediately after price increases. If new firms could enter the industry

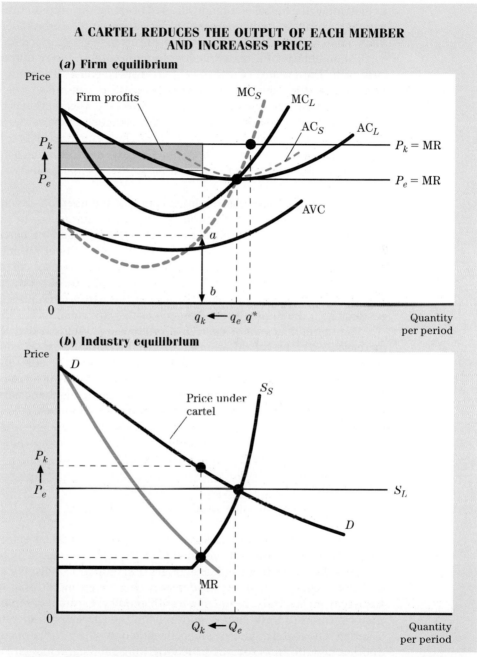

Figure 10-1 (*a*) When firms in an industry form a cartel, each reduces output from q_e to q_k. (*b*) The total quantity supplied decreases from Q_e to Q_k and increases the market price from P_e to P_k. At a price of P_k each member of the cartel would prefer to produce q^*, where P_k is short-run marginal cost in (*a*). The cartel can be successful only if it prevents firms from cheating on the quota of q_k.

immediately, the cartel could not succeed because the output cutback by the cartel members would be nullified by the output increase of the entrants. A successful cartel must be able to limit the entry of new firms at least temporarily.

The members of a cartel must determine total industry output, market price, and each firm's share of cartel output, usually called its quota. As a collective organization, the cartel, unlike a price-taking firm, can raise price by selling fewer units. To maximize industry profits, the cartel equates marginal revenue, derived from the market demand curve, to its marginal cost. Because the short-run supply function is the horizontal summation of the short-run marginal cost curves of the n firms, it becomes the cartel's short-run marginal cost function. The cartel behaves like a monopolist and determines output so that its marginal cost equals marginal revenue.

Figure 10-1b shows that the intersection of the marginal revenue function and the cartel's marginal cost function occurs at the output Q_k. In the short run the cartel reduces industry output from Q_e to Q_k. How should the cartel determine the output of each member? If it wants to produce Q_k units at minimum total cost, it will equalize the short-run marginal cost of production for all n members (see Chapter 6). If each firm's quota is q_k, the marginal cost of production of each one equals the distance ab in Figure 10-1a and the cartel minimizes the total cost of producing Q_k. Each member's short-run profits are equal to the shaded area.

The cartel succeeds if each firm produces q_k units so that the market price increases to P_k. But the difference between the market price P_k and each member's short-run marginal cost ab when each firm produces q_k units portends trouble. Because each firm is a price-taker, it maximizes profits by producing q^* units where P_k is equal to the firm's short-run marginal cost. Each member's narrow self-interest warrants an output of q^* units since each price-taking firm maximizes profits by producing more than the assigned quota. This is the fundamental dilemma faced by every cartel. What is in the interest of the cartel organization is not in the interest of each member.

> Each price-taking member of the cartel has an incentive to produce more than its assigned quota because price exceeds its marginal cost.

A cartel must resolve this conflict between individual self-interest and the collective interest or it will eventually fail. Cartels use several methods to discourage individual firms from increasing sales. For example, they may assign customers to firms because it is easier to detect a cheater by monitoring the customers it attracts from its rivals. In the nineteenth century, German companies used formal legal contracts to form cartels, and some of the agreements specified penalties for cheating. The cartel could sue and collect damages from violators of the agreement. Another favorite enforcement device was joint sales agreements. These agreements stipulated that each firm must sell its output to the cartel, which became the sole sales agent for all firms in the cartel. By establishing a joint sales agreement, the cartel discouraged individual firms from increasing output.

The antitrust laws of the United States prohibit cartels from using the more explicit and effective devices of maintaining cartel discipline. These laws force cartel members to use tacit and less effective methods to police and maintain the cartel and thus reduce the probability of cartel success. Cartels are fragile because monitoring compliance is costly and new firms can enter.

APPLICATION **10-1**

Trouble in the Orange Cartel[1]

Sunkist Growers Inc. is an association of orange growers and packing houses operating under a federal marketing order that assigns quotas to individual growers to prop up the price of fresh oranges. Marketing orders, which are a product of the depression decade of the 1930s, raise price and the income of growers by placing limits on the output of individual growers. A marketing order is a legal mechanism for restricting output of a product and raising price just as the theory of cartels predicts. In the marketing order for oranges, a committee of members, often the larger growers and packers, determines total output and assigns individual quotas. Membership in the marketing order is compulsory. If a member ignores the quotas, he or she is subject to a federal fine and imprisonment.

Although the committee has assigned quotas for years under the auspices of the government, it is only lately that charges of cheating by some members of the Sunkist association have surfaced. Many Sunkist directors are affiliated with the larger Sunkist packing houses. The charges indicate that the vexing problem of cheating that faces any cartel exists even in cartels operating under federal jurisdiction. Several dozen citrus packers are accused of exceeding their quotas and reaping profits that exceed $60 million because they were able to sell at the inflated cartel price. The charges allege that some Sunkist directors knew of the violations and that some were affiliated with those who were involved.

10-2   PRICE AND OUTPUT WITH OLIGOPOLY

You have seen how a cartel with price-taking firms attempts to coordinate production and increase its profits by raising the price to the monopoly price. Now let's investigate price and output when the number of firms in the market is relatively small and the market shares of the leading firms are large. These firms also can increase their profits by raising price to the monopoly price, and in some ways they should have less difficulty cooperating.

Table 10-1 lists some industries where the *concentration ratio*, the combined market share of the four leading firms, is over 80 percent. In these industries the leading firms have relatively large market shares. In several cases the number of firms in the industry seems large, but most firms appear to be specialty producers selling relatively low volumes.

---

[1] Based on Ralph T. King, Jr., "Navel Battle Poses Threat to Sunkist, Raising Prospect of Lower Retail Prices," *The Wall Street Journal*, March 18, 1993.

Table 10-1   COMBINED MARKET SHARE OF THE FOUR LARGEST FIRMS IN SELECTED INDUSTRIES, 1987

INDUSTRY	COMBINED MARKET SHARE OF FOUR LARGEST FIRMS	NUMBER OF COMPANIES IN INDUSTRY
Chewing gum	96%	8
Household laundry equipment	93	11
Cigarettes	92	9
Electric light bulbs	91	93
Household refrigerators and freezers	85	40
Primary batteries, dry and wet	88	59

Source: 1987 Census of Manufacturers, "Concentration Ratios in Manufacturing," Subject Series, MC87-S-6.

Cooperative Behavior and the Incentive to Cheat

The critical feature of markets with few firms is the interdependence among firms. When firms make price or output decisions, the outcomes of their decisions depend on their rivals' corresponding decisions. No oligopolistic firm is an island unto itself. Let's illustrate this interdependence with a game called the **prisoner's dilemma.**

In the original version of the prisoner's dilemma, two separated prisoners have to decide whether to confess to a crime. We change the context of the game to the problem of whether each of two identical firms should or should not cooperate. Consider the industry demand function in Table 10-2. The price, quantity, and total

Table 10-2   INDUSTRY DEMAND FUNCTION AND TOTAL PROFITS

PRICE (1)	QUANTITY DEMANDED (2)	TOTAL REVENUE OR PROFITS (3)
$8	4	$32
7	10	70
6	**14**	**84**
5	16	80
4	18	72
3	20	60

revenue for the industry are in columns 1–3 for selected prices and quantities. Column 3 shows that total industry profits (costs are ignored) are maximized at $84 if total industry output is 14 units. Assuming the two firms in the market cooperate, they would share the market by each supplying 7 units so that each firm's profits equal $42. With a **cooperative solution** the two firms divide maximum industry profits.

Before we predict that this will be the solution to the pricing problem, we need to ask whether it is in the self-interest of each firm to honor this agreement. Table 10-3 shows the market price and firm 2's profits for different quantities that firm 2 produces, *given* that firm 1 produces 7 units. To keep the calculations simple, we assume that firm 2 must add 2 units at a time if it decides to deviate from the cooperative agreement. Look at the output decision from firm 2's perspective. If firm 1 honors the collusive agreement and produces 7 units, what is firm 2's best response? Profits *increase* by 7.1 percent to $45 if firm 2 increases output from 7 to 9 units. It is in firm 2's self-interest to violate the agreement and produce 9 not 7 units. We conclude that firm 2 will deviate from the agreement and produce 9 units. When an agreement is in the self interest of both parties, we call the agreement a **self-enforcing agreement.** In this case the agreement to produce 7 units is not self-enforcing since at least one party will gain by violating the agreement.

A self-enforcing agreement exists when each party maximizes profits given the behavior of its rival.

We can repeat the analysis for firm 1. If firm 2 produces 7 units, then firm 1's profits will increase to $45 if firm 1 produces 9 units. Herein lies the catch. If both firms produce 9 units, Table 10-2 shows that the price falls to $4 and each firm's profits equal $36 ($4 × 9) or 14.3 percent less than the profits of $42 under the cooperative solution.

In Figure 10-2 we look at the same problem slightly differently by presenting a profit payoff matrix. Figure 10-2 shows that each firm's profit payoffs of the game depends on the decision of its rival. Each firm can decide to cooperate by producing 7 units or to cheat by producing 9 units. Firm 1's profit payoffs are in the lower

Table 10-3   PROFITS OF FIRM 2 IF FIRM 1 PRODUCES 7 UNITS

PRICE	OUTPUT OF FIRM 2	TOTAL PROFITS OF FIRM 2
$6	7	$42
5	**9**	**45**
4	11	44
3	13	39

PROFIT PAYOFF MATRIX FOR THE STATEGIES OF DUOPOLISTS

Firm 1 \ Firm 2	Share the Market	Cheat
Share the Market	π_2 = \$42; (Cooperative solution); π_1 = \$42	π_2 = \$45; π_1 = \$35
Cheat	π_2 = \$35; π_1 = \$45	π_2 = \$36; (Noncooperative solution); π_1 = \$36

Figure 10-2 In a prisoner's dilemma game the optimal strategy for each firm is to cheat on a cooperative agreement. Whether firm 1 cheats or cooperates, firm 2's best strategy is to cheat. The same can be said of firm 1. What is privately rational is not collectively rational.

left-hand corner of each cell while firm 2's profit payoffs are in the upper right-hand corner of each cell. Each firm's profits equal \$42 if both cooperate and share the market (northwest cell). If either firm cheats by producing 9 units while the other produces 7 units, the cheater earns \$45 while the noncheater earns only \$35 (southwest and northeast cells). If both firms cheat, each firm earns \$36 (southeast cell).

We already know that each firm's profits are higher if it cheats while knowing that its rival cooperates. If firm 1 cheats, firm 2's best response is to cheat by producing 9 units and increasing profits by \$1 to \$36 from \$35. So firm 2's best response is to cheat and produce 9 units. The same argument applies to firm 1. Both will produce 9 units so their individual profits equal only \$36 (southeast cell).

This solution does appear paradoxical. Clearly, both firms would have higher profits if neither cheats. The profit pie is largest if both rivals cooperate. Yet, private self-interest drives both firms to cheat. By striving to increase their share of profits, each firm contributes to shrinking the size of the profit pie. The essential implication of the prisoner's dilemma game is that what is individually rational behavior is not collectively rational.

This **propensity to cheat** has general applicability. In Figure 10-3 a monopolist produces Q_m, its profit-maximizing output, where marginal revenue is 0 because

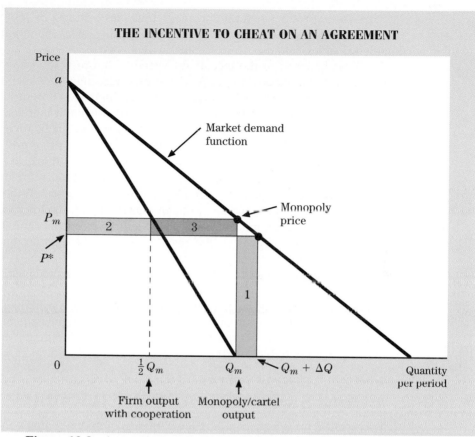

Figure 10-3 A monopolist maximizes profits by producing Q_m and charging P_m assuming marginal costs are zero. If the monopolist increases output by ΔQ, the price decreases to P^*. Area 1 represents the increase in the monopolist's revenue and the sum of area 2 and 3 measures the loss in revenue because the price falls. Because profits are maximized at the monopoly output of Q_m, area 1 must be less than the sum of areas 2 and 3. If two firms share the market and each produces $Q_m/2$, the two firms sell each unit at P_m. Suppose firm 2 cheats on an agreement by increasing output by ΔQ and causing price to fall to P^*. Total revenue of firm 2 increases by area 1 less area 3 where area 3 represents the loss in revenue suffered by firm 2 because the price falls. Area 2 is the loss in revenue suffered by the other firm because the price falls by ΔP. A duopolist has more of an incentive to cheat and to expand output while a monopolist does not.

costs are ignored. Figure 10-3 shows each firm shares the market by producing one-half of the monopoly output. If a monopolist increases output above Q_m by ΔQ, total profits decrease. Area 1 represents the increase in revenue because consumers purchase ΔQ more units. The sum of areas 2 and 3 represents the loss in revenue because Q_m units sell at a lower price. The reason for distinguishing between areas 2 and 3 will soon become self-evident. Because a monopolist maximizes total profits when producing Q_m units, area 1 must be less than the sum of areas 2 and 3, and so total profits decrease. This is why the monopolist produces only Q_m units.

What happens to the incentive to produce more when two sellers share the market at the monopoly price? A cooperative agreement between two firms would have each firm produce $Q_m/2$ units. If firm 2 increases its output by ΔQ, area 1 equals the increase in revenue received by firm 2 when it increases output by ΔQ. What does firm 2 lose? Area 3 represents the loss in firm 2's revenue. The units it previously sold (50 percent of the total) at the higher price are now sold at the lower price. Firm 2's loss equals only one-half of the total loss in revenue because firm 1 incurs the other half of the loss. So, a duopolist has more of an incentive to expand output by ΔQ, while a monopolist does not. Furthermore, the larger the number of firms in the industry, the greater the incentive to cheat. If there are n identical firms in the industry, a firm that increases output by ΔQ incurs only $1/n$ of the total loss in revenue that results because the existing quantity sells at a lower price. This explains why the cooperative solution becomes still more difficult to achieve as the number of firms increases. The gains from cheating increase with the number of firms that have signed the agreement.

Because cheating on the cooperative solution is profitable, members must either find ways to prevent others from cheating or recognize the futility of reaching a cooperative solution. Often it is so costly to prevent cheating that firms recognize that the cooperative solution is unattainable and behave noncooperatively.

10-3 MODELS OF NONCOOPERATIVE BEHAVIOR

This section presents two well-known models of duopoly. Each one starts with the premise that cooperative behavior is too costly to achieve. We want to show what price and quantity emerge from each model when firms behave noncooperatively. Then, we show what the two theories say about price and output when the number of rivals increases. Once we know what these theories predict about the relationship between the number of firms and price, we can turn to some evidence and see how accurate the predictions are.

The Cournot Model

The first model of a noncooperative duopoly is called the **Cournot model,** named after the pioneering French mathematical economist.[2] In this model two firms sell identical products and face a linear inverse market demand function, $P = a - bQ$. They have the same total cost function with a constant marginal cost of c.

In the Cournot model the two firms decide what quantity to produce independently but simultaneously. The output of firm 1 is q_1, and the output of firm 2 is q_2. Given the combined output of the two firms, the market-clearing price is $P = a - bQ = a - b(q_1 + q_2)$, where $q_1 + q_2$ replaces Q in the demand function so that all units sell at the market-clearing price.

[2] Augustin Cournot, *Researches into the Mathematical Principles of the Theory of Wealth*, Nathaniel T. Bacon (trans.) (New York: Macmillan, 1897).

The profit function of firm 1 is

$$\text{Profits} = \text{Revenue} - \text{Cost} = Pq_1 - cq_1$$

$$\pi(q_1) = (a - bq_1 - bq_2)q_1 - cq_1 \qquad \text{(Profit Function of Firm 1)} \qquad \textbf{(10-1)}$$

$$= aq_1 - bq_1^2 - bq_2q_1 - cq_1$$

Total profits of firm 1 depend on how many units it produces *and* how many units firm 2 produces. Therefore, firm 1's profit-maximizing quantity depends on the quantity that firm 2 produces. The same is true of firm 2's profit-maximizing quantity. Suppose that firm 2 is producing quantity q_2. Then, firm 1 decides that it will produce one quantity if it believes firm 2 will not change its output, and quite another quantity if it expects that firm 2 will increase or decrease its output when firm 1's output increases. An important assumption of the Cournot model is that firm 1 believes that firm 2 will *not* change its output when firm 1 changes its output.

$$\frac{\Delta q_2}{\Delta q_1} = 0 \qquad \text{(Cournot Assumption)} \qquad \textbf{(10-2)}$$

Equation 10-2 says that firm 1 expects the output of firm 2 to remain constant when it changes its own output.

> Each Cournot competitor assumes that it can change its output without causing its rival to change its output.

With the Cournot assumption the demand function facing firm 1 becomes

$$P = (a - bq_2^*) - bq_1$$

where firm 1 considers $a - bq_2^*$ a constant because of the Cournot assumption.

Let's use a graph to illustrate firm 1's demand function given that firm 2 produces q_2^*. *DD* is the inverse market demand function in Figure 10-4*a*. If firm 2 produces q_2^* units, the demand function for firm 1 becomes *d'd'* in Figure 10-4*b*. If firm 1 produces nothing, the price will be $a - bq_2^*$. Each unit that firm 1 produces reduces price by b, and so the slope of *d'd'* is the same as the slope of *DD*. Therefore, *d'd'* represents the quantity demanded for firm 1's product at each price after firm 2 supplies q_2^* units; *d'd'* is called a *residual demand function*.

The Reaction or Best Response Function of Each Cournot Rival

Instead of assuming that firm 2 is producing q_2^* units, a specific quantity, let's derive a more general relationship between firm 1's output conditional on firm 2's output. Given q_2, firm 1 selects q_1 to maximize its profits.

$$\frac{\Delta \pi}{\Delta q_1} = 0$$

$$a - 2bq_1 - bq_2 - c = 0$$

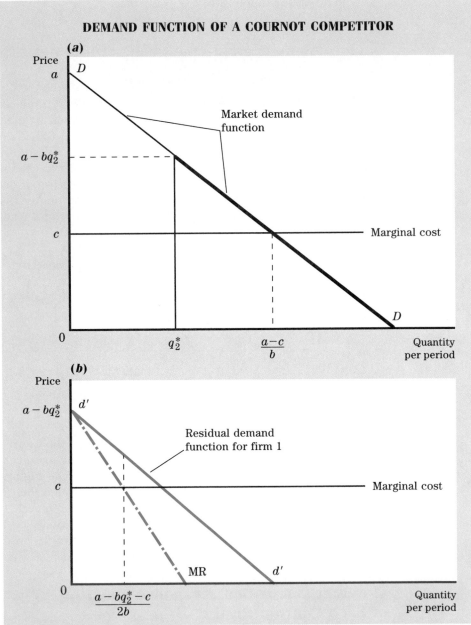

Figure 10-4   If firm 2 produces q_2^*, the residual demand function of firm 1 is the heavy line labeled $d'd'$ in (b). It is the demand function facing firm 1 given that firm 2 produces q_2^*. If firm 1 produces nothing, the price is $a - bq_2^*$. Each unit produced by firm 1 reduces price by $-b$. The marginal revenue function of the residual demand function is MR, the dashed line. Firm 1's marginal revenue equals marginal cost when it produces $(a - c - bq_2^*)/2b$.

We solve this equation for q_1 in terms of q_2.[3]

$$q_1 = \frac{a - c - bq_2}{2b} \qquad \text{(Firm 1's Reaction Function)} \qquad \textbf{(10-3)}$$

Equation 10-3 is called firm 1's **reaction function.** It shows the profit-maximizing quantity of firm 1 for any quantity that firm 2 produces. If the intercept of the inverse market demand function is $a = \$24$, while $b - \$1$, and $c = \$10$, firm 1 maximizes profits if it produces 5 units when firm 2 is producing 4 units.

> The reaction function of firm 1 shows firm 1's profit-maximizing quantity for each quantity produced by firm 2.

Because the coefficient of q_2 is negative in firm 1's reaction function, the larger q_2, the smaller the profit-maximizing quantity of firm 1.[4]

Figure 10-5 shows the reaction or best response function of firm 1. The quantity produced by firm 2 is on the vertical axis, and the quantity produced by firm 1 is on the horizontal axis. The intercept on the vertical scale is $(a - c)/b$, which is the competitive output.[5] This means that firm 1 will produce nothing if firm 2 is already producing the competitive output because profits are zero. Firm 1 is better off producing nothing rather than producing any positive quantity and lowering the price below marginal cost. The horizontal intercept shows that the firm will produce $(a - c)/2b$, which is the monopoly output if firm 2 produces nothing.[6] As you can see from these two extreme cases, the best response function gives plausible quantity responses for firm 1.

Everything said about firm 1 applies to firm 2 as well. Under the Cournot assumption firm 2 assumes that firm 1's output is constant and will not change

---

[3] This equation is derived by adding $2bq_1$ to both sides of the equation above and then dividing both sides by $2b$.

[4] The larger the quantity produced by firm 2, the smaller the intercept of the demand function facing firm 1. The residual demand function facing firm 1 shifts inward as firm 2's output increases. The profit-maximizing output for firm 1 decreases as its demand function shifts inward.

[5] With a competitive solution, output is determined where price equals marginal cost or

$$P = a - bQ = c$$

Therefore, the competitive industry output equals $Q_c = (a - c)/b$.

[6] A monopolist selects a quantity to maximize

$$\pi = PQ - cQ = (a - bQ)Q - cQ = aQ - bQ^2 - cQ$$

$$\frac{d\pi}{dQ} = a - 2bQ - c = 0$$

To find the marginal revenue = marginal cost solution, we first remind the reader that the derivative of aQ is a, of bQ^2 is $2bQ$, and of cQ is c. Marginal revenue is MR $= a - 2bQ$. Equating marginal revenue to marginal cost yields

$$a - 2bQ = c$$

Therefore, the monopoly output equals $Q_m = (a - c)/2b$.

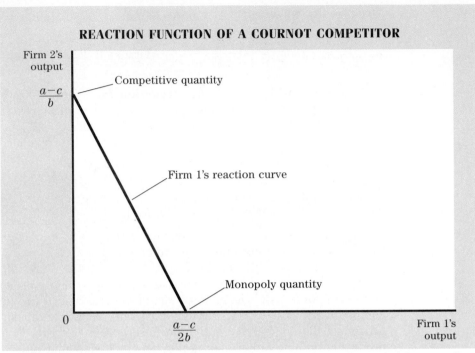

Figure 10-5   The reaction function of firm 1 shows the profit-maximizing quantity of firm 1 for each quantity produced by firm 2.

when firm 2 changes its quantity. Given q_1, firm 2 selects q_2 to maximize its profits. Firm 2's reaction or best response function is symmetrical.

$$q_2 = \frac{a - c - bq_1}{2b} \qquad \text{(Firm 2's Reaction Function)} \qquad \textbf{(10-4)}$$

Figure 10-6 shows both reaction functions on the same graph. Each one indicates the profit-maximizing output of one firm given the output of the other.

The Nash Equilibrium

We have determined the profit-maximizing output of each firm given the output of its rival. Before we can find what quantity each firm produces, we must define what constitutes an equilibrium. A *Nash equilibrium*, named after the famous mathematician John Nash, requires each firm to maximize its profits given the quantities produced by its rivals. Each firm must satisfy this condition simultaneously in a Nash equilibrium. So, when no firm has an incentive to change its behavior, a Nash equilibrium exists. In the duopoly case, finding a pair of quantities that satisfies a Nash equilibrium means we have also found a self-enforcing agreement.

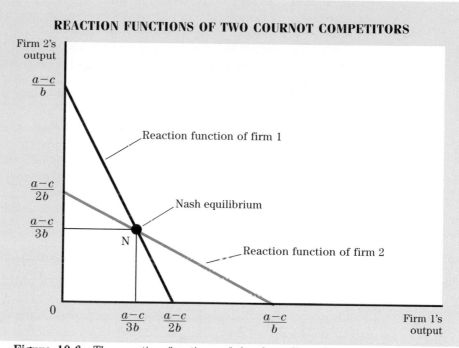

Figure 10-6   The reaction functions of the duopolists show the profit-maximizing output of each firm given the output of the rival. At point C-N each duopolist is maxi mizing its profits given the rival's output. Each firm produces $(a - c)/3b$. The quantities produced by both firms satisfy the conditions for a Cournot Nash equilibrium.

A **Nash equilibrium in quantities** requires each firm to choose a quantity that maximizes its profits given the quantity produced by a rival.

What pair of quantities satisfies a Nash equilibrium? Each duopolist must be maximizing its profits given the output of a rival in a Nash equilibrium. For this to be true, each must be on its reaction function. There is only one pair of outputs that satisfies this requirement. At point N in Figure 10-6 the two reaction functions cross, and each firm produces $(a - c)/3b$.[7] If duopolist 2 produces $(a - c)/3b$, firm

---

[7] This quantity is derived by substituting the expression for q_2 in equation 10-4 into equation 10-3 to obtain

$$q_1 = \frac{a - c - b[(a - c - bq_1)/2b]}{2b}$$

Multiplying both sides by $4b$ yields $4bq_1 = 2a - 2c - a + c + bq_1$. Collecting terms and simplifying leads to

$$q_1 = \frac{a - c}{3b}$$

Then, substitute $(a - c)/3b$ for q_1 in equation 10-4 and derive a similar expression for firm 2.

1 expects firm 2 to keep output constant while it produces its profit-maximizing output of $(a - c)/3b$ units. If firm 1 produces $(a - c)/3b$, firm 2's best response is to produce $(a - c)/3b$.

Each firm assumes its rival's output will not change, and this assumption is realized at point N and only at point N. At this point each firm is producing its profit-maximizing output given the output of its rival, and so a Nash equilibrium exists. Other points on either reaction function do not satisfy the conditions of a Nash equilibrium.

In summary, each firm produces $(a - c)/3b$ in a Nash equilibrium. The total output of two Cournot firms is $\frac{2}{3}(a - c)/b = \frac{4}{3}(a - c)/2b$. Footnotes 5 and 6 showed the cooperative (monopoly) output is $(a - c)/2b$, and the competitive output is $(a - c)/b$. So, two Cournot competitors produce one-third more than a monopolist would, or two-thirds of the competitive output.

Because total output is higher, price is lower when two firms rather than one are in the market in the Cournot model. The market price is

$$P = a - b\left[2\left(\frac{a - c}{3b}\right)\right] = \frac{a}{3} + \frac{2c}{3} \qquad \text{(Price with Two Cournot Rivals)} \qquad \textbf{(10-5)}$$

Because price is lower with two rather than one firm in the market, the combined profit of the two firms is lower than monopoly profit.

To recapitulate, the Cournot model says that total output is greater and price and total profits are lower when the number of sellers increases from one to two.

APPLICATION 10-2

More Suppliers of Fine Caviar[8]

For many years a state cartel in the former Soviet Union determined the amount of caviar that Western countries received. In a typical year the catch of Soviet sturgeon, whose eggs make the finest caviar, yields about 2,000 tons of caviar, of which the West received only about 150 tons. By controlling the quantity sold abroad, the former Soviet government was able to prop up the price of caviar and earn hard currency. The large difference between the price of caviar in Moscow and in New York indicates how effective control has been over shipments of caviar to the West. In Moscow a state-supplied kilogram of top-grade black caviar sold for about $5 on the black market, while the price in New York was more than $500.

The break-up of the Soviet Union disrupted the Soviet monopoly, and the autonomy of the former Soviet states has created more competitors. The two largest Soviet fisheries are now in different republics, one in Russia and one in Kazakhstan. Each republic wants to produce caviar for export. In addition, individual fishermen are entering the business and establishing export channels. The price of fine caviar has dropped with an increase in the number of competitors. The Soviet news agency Interfax reported a 20 percent drop in the official caviar export price from the previous year. As one official remarked, "All of these small

---

[8] Based on Jane Mayer, "Horrors! Fine Caviar Now Could Become as Cheap as Fish Eggs," *The Wall Street Journal*, November 18, 1991.

rivals mean that the price will fall and the market will be ripped apart. This is a delicacy—we need to keep it elite."

The Cournot Model with n Competitors

The results for two Cournot competitors can be extended to n Cournot competitors, where n is any positive integer. This extension indicates how an increase in the number of rivals affects price and quantity. If price falls when the number of sellers increases from 1 to 2, how much lower will it be if there are 10 or 1,000 sellers?

To answer this question, assume that there are n identical Cournot competitors in the market and each one assumes that the output of all rivals is constant when setting its output. Total quantity demanded equals total quantity supplied by the n Cournot competitors, and so $Q = q_1 + q_2 + \cdots + q_i + \cdots + q_n$. The profit function of the ith Cournot competitor becomes

$$\pi(q_i) = (a - bQ)q_i - cq_i$$

$$- (a - bq_1 - \cdots - bq_i - \cdots - bq_n)q_i \quad cq_i$$

The appendix at the end of this chapter shows that the quantity that maximizes the profits of firm i is related to n rivals in the market by

$$q_i = \frac{1}{n+1} \frac{a-c}{b} \qquad \text{(Output of a Firm with } n-1 \text{ Rivals)} \qquad \textbf{(10-6)}$$

Each Cournot competitor produces $1/(n+1)$ of the competitive output $(a - c)/b$. As the number of Cournot competitors increases, the quantity produced by each seller decreases. For example, if $n = 1$, we have a monopolist and $q_i = (a - c)/2b$, the monopoly solution. If there are 3 Cournot competitors, each firm produces $\frac{1}{4}(a - c)/b$ or one-quarter of the competitive output. The reason this occurs is that the residual demand function facing a firm shifts to the left as the number of rivals increases. The profit-maximizing output of any one firm decreases as the number of rivals increases.

Although each Cournot competitor produces less, the total quantity supplied increases as the number of rivals increases, and so price falls. Since $Q = nq_i = (n/n - 1)([a - c]/b)$, the price is related to the number of rivals by

$$P = \frac{a}{n+1} + \frac{nc}{n+1} \qquad \text{(Price with } n \text{ Cournot Rivals)} \qquad \textbf{(10-7)}$$

As the number of competitors increases, price decreases at a decreasing rate. The first term $a/(n + 1)$ becomes negligible as n increases, and the second term approaches c because $n/(n + 1)$ approaches 1.

> The Cournot model predicts that price decreases and approaches marginal cost as the number of rivals becomes large.

Let's review the major features of the Cournot model. With our demand and cost assumptions the Cournot model predicts that price decreases at a decreasing rate as the number of Cournot rivals increases and ultimately approaches the competitive price. It correctly predicts the monopoly price and output when $n = 1$ and the competitive solution when n becomes large. What remains in doubt is whether the Cournot model can accurately predict actual price behavior when n is between these extremes.

The Bertrand Model

The second noncooperative duopoly model to be considered is the **Bertrand model.** The structure of the Bertrand model of duopoly is fundamentally different from that of the Cournot model.[9] The sequence of firm and consumer decisions in the Bertrand model is as follows: Identical firms move first by independently announcing *prices.* For example, two catalog firms announce prices when they send out their fall catalogs. Then consumers respond to the price quotations by purchasing from the low-price seller. In the Bertrand model, unlike the Cournot model, the low-price supplier supplies the whole market because Bertrand assumes that consumers shift to this seller without cost. This assumes that the low-price seller is able to supply the entire market. If price quotations are identical, the firms divide the market equally.

Let's see what each firm's demand function looks like when firms quote prices. In doing this, it is helpful to express the quantity demanded as a function of price. If the inverse demand function is $P = a - bQ$, the demand function becomes $Q = (a/b) - (1/b)P$. If the price quoted by firm 2 is P_2, firm 1's demand function is shown in the accompanying table.

RELATION BETWEEN P_1 AND P_2	FIRM 1'S QUANTITY DEMANDED
$P_1 > P_2$	0
$P_1 = P_2$	$0.5\left(\dfrac{a}{b} - \dfrac{1}{b}P_1\right)$
$P_1 < P_2$	$\dfrac{a}{b} - \dfrac{1}{b}P_1$

Duopolist 1 sells nothing if its price exceeds firm 2's price, shares the market when prices are equal, and attracts all consumers if it quotes the lowest price.

Figure 10-7 shows the demand function facing firm 1 when firm 2's price is P_2. The first part of the discontinuous demand function is the thick segment AB. Here, the quantity demanded is zero because $P_1 > P_2$. The two firms share the market when $P_1 = P_2$. Firm 1's demand function is the horizontal segment BC. The thick

---

[9] Joseph Bertrand, "Review of 'Theorie mathematique de la richesse social,'" *Journal des Savants,* 1883, pp. 499–508. Translated by James W. Friedman.

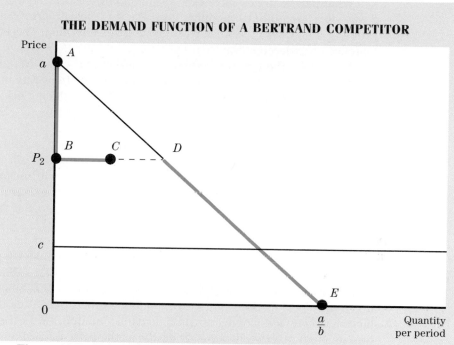

Figure 10-7   In the Bertrand model the demand function facing each duopolist is the discontinuous function *ABCDE*. If firm 2 sets a price of P_2, firm 1 sells nothing if its price exceeds P_2 (segment *AB*). If the two firms charge the same price, they share the market, and so firm 1 produces *BC* and firm 2 produces *CD*. If firm 1 lowers price, it captures the whole market (segment *DE*). What distinguishes the Bertrand model from the Cournot model is that the firm's demand function is horizontal at the price charged by its rival. With a slight price cut a firm can capture the whole market.

segment *DE* shows that firm 1 satisfies the whole market when $P_1 < P_2$. Therefore, firm 1's demand function runs from *A* to *B*, then from *B* to *C*, and then from *D* to *E*. Along the segment *CD*, demand is perfectly elastic. By offering a tiny price cut, firm 1 can double the quantity it sells.

Now you know what each duopolist's demand function looks like given the price of its rival. Next we determine the pair of prices that will exist in an equilibrium. As in the case of the Cournot model, we need to find an equilibrium and for this purpose we introduce the concept of a *Nash equilibrium in prices*. A Nash equilibrium in prices is a pair of prices such that each firm's price maximizes its profits given the opponent's price. A Nash equilibrium exists when both prices satisfy this condition.

A **Nash equilibrium in prices** requires each firm to choose a price that maximizes its profits given the price of its rival.

What pair of prices satisfies a Nash equilibrium? Let's begin by assuming firm 2 quotes a price above marginal cost: $P_2 > c$. Clearly, firm 1 is not maximizing profits if it charges more than P_2 because it sells nothing. Therefore, firm 1 either matches or undercuts firm 2's price.

If $P_1 = P_2$, the two firms share the market and each firm earns profits since price exceeds c. However, this particular equality of prices cannot represent a Nash equilibrium because firm 1 can increase profits by reducing price by a penny and double its market share. The demand function is perfectly elastic at the price quoted by the rival.

This argument extends to any price greater than c. A tiny price cut by one Bertrand duopolist is profitable. Based on this argument, all price pairs except $P_1 = P_2 = c$ can be eliminated as being inconsistent with a Nash equilibrium in prices. Therefore, the two price quotations must be equal to marginal cost in a Nash equilibrium. The noncooperative solution with two Bertrand sellers in the market is the competitive price and output!

In summary, the Bertrand model predicts that the competitive result emerges just by going from one to two sellers! With the Bertrand model any rivalry produces a competitive price. As you can see, this implication is far different from the one in the Cournot model. The different results are due to differences in shape of the firm's demand functions in the two models. In the Cournot model each duopolist faces a downward sloping residual demand function. In the Bertrand model the firm demand function is perfectly elastic at the price quoted by a competitor, and so a price cut is always profitable as long as price exceeds c.

Table 10-4 compares price and output for monopoly, the Cournot and Bertrand models of duopoly, and competition.

Table 10-4   A COMPARISON OF PRICE AND OUTPUT FOR EACH MODEL

MODEL	PRICE	INDUSTRY QUANTITY
Monopoly	$\dfrac{a + c}{2}$	$\dfrac{a - c}{2b}$
Cournot ($n = 2$)	$\dfrac{a}{3} + \dfrac{2c}{3}$	$\dfrac{4}{3}\left(\dfrac{a - c}{2b}\right)$
Bertrand ($n = 2$)	c	$\dfrac{a - c}{b}$
Competition	c	$\dfrac{a - c}{b}$

APPLICATION 10-3

Encouraging Competition among Suppliers

During the 1980s and early 1990s large firms began to purchase services from specialized firms rather than perform these services internally. Larger firms realized that specialized firms could provide services at a lower price than they could. Examples of some services that large firms disposed of include mail delivery, maintenance, and accounting functions.

Imagine that you are a purchasing agent for a large company that has many offices throughout the country requiring frequent cleaning. Suppose there are two well-established national cleaning services and you are planning to select one or both of them for this task. You have to decide how many square feet of office space to clean per week and whether one or both firms will provide the services. Like all demand functions, your demand function for cleaning offices slopes downward. If the price per 100 square feet cleaned is high, you will reduce the cleaned area. During informal discussions with representatives of the two companies, you provide information about the area to be cleaned at each price, and so each firm knows your demand function.

You must decide how to structure the bidding process and how to award the contract. Should you award it to just a single firm or divide it between the two? One concern of yours is not to be at the mercy of any one firm, and so you are leaning toward dividing the contract between the two firms.

You are considering three methods of assigning the contract.

- *Method 1.* Each supplier offers a bid to clean a certain number of square feet per week. You reveal the two bids at a joint meeting with both parties present. The price per 100 square feet is found by summing the quantities and reading off the price from your demand function. Each firm receives this price per 100 square feet cleaned, and each firm cleans the quantity of space bid. You favor this contract because both firms will supply the services and you will not be at the mercy of a single company.

- *Method 2.* Each firm bids a price per 100 square feet. The firm that bids the lower price wins the whole contract and cleans all units. The total area cleaned is determined by your demand function at the lowest bid price. If the bids are the same, the firms share the market and clean the same number of square feet. You are reluctant to use this method because you fear that you will be at the mercy of one firm.

- *Method 3.* This method is the same as method 2 except that the two firms share the task at the lowest price bid. You are more comfortable with this method because you will not be at the mercy of a single firm.

Given these three alternatives, which method would you select? Would you have the firms bid an area to clean (method 1) or bid a price (method 2 or 3)?

What can you say about the idea of dividing the contract between the two bidders at the lowest bid price?

There are two issues to consider: First, the two firms could cooperate and charge a profit-maximizing price. If they get together, they could estimate what it would cost you to perform the service internally and charge a slightly lower price. Because they might get together, you want to adopt the method that puts the greatest strain on any agreement to cooperate. Second, if the firms fail to cooperate with one another, which method will yield the lowest price?

What lessons can you learn from the Cournot and Bertrand models of duopoly? The first assignment method describes the Cournot model. Under method 1 each firm selects a quantity. Method 2 describes the Bertrand model. If the two firms act noncooperatively, price will be lower with method 2 than with method 1. You hope the inducement to win the whole contract will cause the two firms to compete and to bid the competitive price. You want to offer the supplier a carrot—obtaining a large increase in the quantity by offering a lower price. Anything you can do to increase the total area cleaned will encourage a rival to cut price. With a Nash equilibrium in prices, both firms will quote a price equal to marginal cost so that you will not have to rely on a single firm. Therefore, method 2 puts a greater strain on any possible agreement between the two suppliers than method 1 because the gain from offering a lower price is greater. Conversely, you do not want to divide the contract between the firms unless there are compelling reasons to do so. The drawback of method 3 is that it discourages a firm from offering a lower price. No matter what price is bid, the firm receives only 50 percent of the market. By dividing the contract between the two suppliers, you will structure the bidding to discourage independent pricing. If the firms act independently, method 2 has more to recommend it.

10-4   THE EFFECT OF THE NUMBER OF RIVALS ON PRICE

The Cournot and Bertrand models make strikingly different predictions of how the number of rivals affects price. As the appendix at the end of this chapter shows, price declines in the Cournot model at a decreasing rate as the number of rivals grows. In the Bertrand model price falls to marginal cost when there are two or more competitors. Figure 10-8 compares prices and the number of competitors in the two models. You can see that the price declines at a decreasing rate to marginal cost as the number of Cournot competitors increases. In the Bertrand model the price falls abruptly from the monopoly price to the competitive price as soon as the number of competitors is two.

Now let's turn to some evidence and see whether one or the other theory gives a closer approximation to the real world by surveying some of the empirical studies that explicitly examine this question.

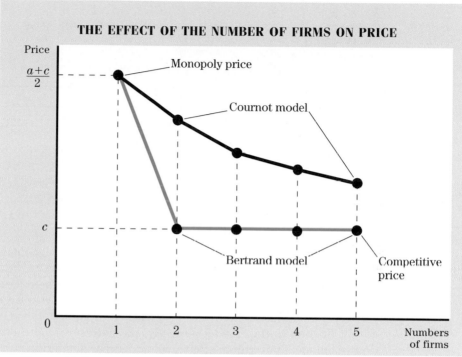

Figure 10-8   Price declines systematically toward marginal cost as more Cournot competitors enter the market. In contrast, the Bertrand model yields the competitive result with two or more Bertrand competitors.

APPLICATION 10-4

Retail Tire Prices

Timothy Bresnahan and Peter Reiss studied retail tire prices in numerous local markets with different numbers of sellers.[10] They tried to adjust for differences in the cost of operating in small versus large markets, although this was not always easy to do. They found that prices declined with an increase in the number of retail sellers but not in a continuous manner. Median prices for a specific tire are shown in Table 10-5 for towns with one to five sellers and, separately, for large urban markets.

A statistical analysis of the price data shows that prices fall but not continuously with increases in the number of dealers in the market. The difference between the median price in monopoly and duopoly markets is not statistically significant.

[10] Timothy F. Bresnahan and Peter C. Reiss, "Entry and Competition in Concentrated Markets," *Journal of Political Economy* 99 (October 1991), pp. 977–1009.

Table 10-5   MEDIAN RETAIL TIRE PRICES AND NUMBER OF RETAILERS IN MARKET

| | Monopoly | Number of Tire Dealers | | | Competition |
	1	2	3	4	5	URBAN
Median price ($)	53.9	55.0	52.9	50.9	49.8	43.2

Median prices in markets with three to five dealers are significantly lower than in monopoly and duopoly markets. In urban markets where the number of retailers is larger, prices are still lower.[11] If urban markets with more sellers approximate competitive markets, then we can say that the median price exceeds the competitive level in markets with five or fewer sellers. Although these empirical findings do not fit the Cournot model perfectly, the pattern is more consistent with the Cournot model than with the Bertrand model. The similarity of prices in monopoly and duopoly markets is inconsistent with the predictions of both models. The findings suggest that duopolists can and do reach the cooperative solution. The results of this study flatly contradict the prediction of the Bertrand model since the price appears to be above the competitive price when two or more sellers are in the market.

APPLICATION **10-5**

Auction Markets[12]

In a comprehensive investigation of the effect of the number of sellers or buyers on price, Leonard Weiss reviewed several studies of auction markets as well as other markets. We report results for auctions of tax-exempt bonds, offshore oil, and timber sales by the National Timber Service. Just as sellers can collude to raise price, buyers can collude to purchase a product at a lower price. Our interest is in determining how many bidders must be in the market before price rises to the competitive price.

    Table 10-6 summarizes the findings of these different studies. In all the auction markets the price paid by bidders increased but at a decreasing rate as the number

[11] Some of the differences between the median prices in urban markets and in smaller markets may be due to unmeasured cost differences and to differences in the services offered.
[12] Based on Leonard Weiss, ed., *Concentration and Price* (Cambridge, Mass.: MIT Press, 1989), Table 4.1. © 1989 Massachusetts Institute of Technology.

Table 10-6   MAXIMUM NUMBER OF BIDS WITH SIGNIFICANT INCREASE IN PRICE

Tax-Exempt Bonds		Offshore Oil Auctions		Timber Sales	
GENERAL OBLIGATION BONDS	REVENUE BONDS	1954–1971	1972–1975	SEALED BID	ORAL BID
8	5	7	7	4	8

of bidders increased. For each type of auction Table 10-6 shows the maximum number of bidders in the market where there was a statistically significant effect of the number of bidders on price. For example, in offshore oil auctions, the winning bid increased until the number of bidders at the auction exceeded seven. At this auction it is likely that the competitive price was paid when eight or more bidders participated.

This summary indicates that price approximates the competitive price with at most seven or eight bidders in four of six cases and four or five bidders in the other two cases. Therefore, the Cournot model approximates price behavior at these auctions better than the Bertrand model does since price increases with the number of bidders. What these studies suggest is that cooperation becomes increasingly difficult to achieve when there are more than eight members. Successful collusion with more sellers or buyers appears unlikely.

The results of these empirical studies suggest that the Cournot model gives a better, but still imperfect, accounting of itself than the Bertrand model does. Prices in auction markets appear to rise significantly until the number of buyers reaches eight. From then on, the number of rivals does not have a significant effect on price. So, the predictions of the Cournot model fit the data better than those of the Bertrand model.

10-5   FACILITATING AND PREVENTING COLLUSION

Although cooperation is difficult to achieve, sellers have an incentive to collude and to prevent profits from being competed away. This is particularly true in the Bertrand model where an increase from one to two sellers causes price to drop abruptly to the competitive price. This section considers how sellers or buyers can benefit by changing the rules of the game.

Meeting Competition

Let's modify one assumption of the Bertrand model and assume instead that one firm announces a price policy of "meeting competition." A stereo store or a bookstore is not going to be undercut by a rival and announces that it will compete aggressively by offering to match any price cut.

Let's see if a price policy of **meeting competition** creates greater rivalry among sellers and lowers price or raises price. If each firm knows that a rival will immediately match its price, the incentive to offer a lower price evaporates. Instead of lowering price, a policy of meeting competition will maintain higher prices.

While sellers benefit by adopting a policy of meeting competition, they will not find it a cure-all for the cheating problem. For one thing, the policy is often difficult to administer. There must be an objective, low-cost way of determining quoted prices. How do you know that a competitor is offering the product at a lower price? This policy can be a nuisance and can result in disgruntled consumers and even lawsuits.

APPLICATION **10-6**

Detecting the Effects of Facilitating Practices

David Grether and Charles Plott studied the effect of certain facilitating practices on price in an experimental setting.[13] The facilitating practices included (1) meeting the lowest price of a competitor, (2) delivering the product to the buyer at the lowest price received by any other buyer, and (3) providing the buyer with a 30-day notice of any price change. In 1979, the Federal Trade Commission (FTC) challenged these practices in an action against the Ethyl Corporation, E. I. DuPont, Nalco Chemical Company, and PPG Industries. The FTC asked the four producers of lead-based antiknock compounds to cease and desist from using these market practices. The FTC argued that these facilitating practices (1) lowered the incentive of firms to cut price by ensuring that competitors match price decreases, (2) eliminated any incentive for secret price cutting, and (3) ensured simultaneous price changes.

Grether and Plott assessed these claims by creating a market in a laboratory setting. They recruited subjects for participation in several experiments in which each became either a buyer or supplier. Buyers received a different reservation (maximum) value for each unit they purchased. The difference between the reservation value and the actual price paid in the experimental market was their per unit profit. Sellers received a reservation (minimum) value for each unit they supplied. The difference between the price at which they sold each unit and the reservation value was their profit on the unit. Buyers benefited most by buying at the lowest possible price, and suppliers benefited most by selling at the highest possible price. Figure 10-9*a* shows the demand and supply functions created by Grether and Plott, given the reservation values for buyers and sellers, and the equilibrium price. The dots in Figure 10-9*b* are the average transaction prices in each period. During periods 1 through 11 the sellers could not communicate or use the facilitating practices. As is true in many experiments of this kind, price

---

[13] Reprinted with permission from Charles R. Plott, "Laboratory Experiments in Economics: The Implications of Posted-Price Institutions," *Science* 232 (May 9, 1986), pp. 732–38. Copyright 1986 by the American Association for the Advancement of Science.

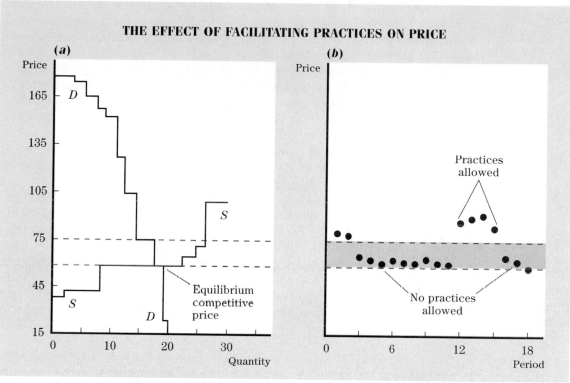

Figure 10-9 Market demand and supply functions are constructed by assigning reservation values to units demanded by buyers and units supplied by sellers. During periods 1 through 11 no facilitating practices are allowed, and the price settles close to the competitive equilibrium price. During periods 12 through 15 suppliers introduce and use facilitating price policies. The price rises and then declines again during periods 16 through 18 when the facilitating practices are prohibited.

settled quickly toward the competitive equilibrium price. The facilitating practices were permitted during periods 12 through 15 and then eliminated during periods 16 through 18. Figure 10-9b shows that price increased above the competitive equilibrium when the firms adopted the facilitating practices 1 through 3. Price declined toward the competitive price when the participants discontinued these practices.

The results of these experiments indicate that facilitating practices raised price above the competitive price but not to the monopoly price. They suggest that meeting competitors' prices, preannouncing prices, and guaranteeing a buyer the lowest price raise price.

Preventing Collusion

What can a buyer do to prevent a conspiracy among suppliers from functioning successfully? Kenneth Hendricks and Robert Porter have offered several suggestions to make life difficult for conspiring suppliers where contracts are awarded by a bidding system.[14] A buyer benefits by reducing the amount of price information that suppliers have. This can be done by announcing the identity of the winning bidder but not the bid. If suppliers continually submit identical bids, the buyer can refuse to pick randomly among bids when awarding the contract but always award it to the same firm. This will certainly create confusion among the members of a conspiracy. They will suspect price chiseling by the innocent but favored firm that repeatedly lands the contract. The buyer hopes that this will lead to price chiseling by others. If the purchaser finds the bids are different but still suspects a conspiracy, she can periodically select the second-lowest bid as the winner but fail to disclose the price. Here again, the buyer's strategy is to sow seeds of distrust among the members of the conspiracy.

When collusion is suspected, the buyer can set a reservation price and announce that no bid above this price will be acceptable. She can also affect the success of any conspiracy by the way she awards the contract. If many short-term contracts are being offered, it may be preferable to combine them all into one large contract rather than offering contracts sequentially. Instead of offering a sequence of five yearly auctions, the buyer can arrange to have one auction covering all five years. When she offers five annual auctions, the cartel can punish a firm that cheats on price in year 1 during subsequent years. The cartel members can lower price in year 2, for example, to punish the price chiseler. However, by offering one 5-year contract, the buyer tempts members of the cartel to offer a price cut to win the whole contract and prevents the cartel from punishing the renegade immediately. As we discuss later in this chapter, an important general message here is that repeated interaction among sellers tends to reduce cheating.

These suggestions by Hendricks and Porter show that a buyer does not have to stand idly by but can adopt policies to reduce the effectiveness of a supplier conspiracy. By structuring the form and type of an auction, the effectiveness of any suspected conspiracy can be reduced.

10-6 A CASE STUDY: THE ELECTRICAL MANUFACTURERS' CONSPIRACY

As noted before, a cooperative agreement among a small number of firms is not easily reached. What is perhaps most surprising is that cooperative agreements are difficult to reach even under the most favorable conditions. The problems that firms have in reaching a cooperative solution can be illustrated in a revealing case study of the electrical manufacturers' conspiracy. In 1960 the principal executive officers of General Electric Company, Westinghouse Electric Company, Allis-Chalmers, and other major electrical manufacturers pleaded guilty to charges of conspiring to fix prices. Seven officers received 30-day sentences—stiff sentences for the time. Numerous lawsuits followed these guilty pleas, and the awards to plain-

---

[14] Kenneth Hendricks and Robert Porter, "Collusion in Auctions," *Annals D'Economie et de Statistique*, N 15/16, 1989, pp. 217–30.

tiffs reached approximately $900 million, or $3.9 billion in 1990 dollars, hardly a trifling sum.[15]

During the investigation the government learned that representatives of these firms met frequently to discuss prices, to assign contracts to particular suppliers, and to determine the market shares of members of the conspiracy. These meetings affected numerous products sold to public and private utilities, ranging from transformers to switchgear to turbines. The orders submitted by utilities are usually large, especially for turbines, and are specific to the particular requirements of each utility. Meeting and discussing prices with competitors is a violation of U.S. antitrust laws.

Collusion and Cheating

By recounting the events and practices of the conspiracy, we hope to identify the critical factors that caused this conspiracy to break down periodically. Representatives of the firms discussed prices and market shares and developed an elaborate system, called the "phase of the moon," which assigned each order to a particular firm. In some lines of business conspirators met to determine which firm would submit the lowest bid on each contract and what bids each loser would submit. The phase-of-the-moon mechanism determined the price each conspirator would submit on each order, with the low price rotating among competitors to create the illusion of competitive bidding. Between December 5, 1958, and April 19, 1959, the position rotated among the competitors every two weeks. For example, during one two-week period ITE, a member of the conspiracy, submitted the low bid and quoted a price of $200 below the book price. Westinghouse offered a $100 discount off the book price, Federal Pacific was $50 below book, General Electric was 0.1 percent off book, and Allis-Chalmers quoted the book price.

The firms adopted a phase-of-the-moon system intermittently from 1953 to 1959. Although the representatives of the different firms who attended these meetings solemnly agreed to abide by these prices, they often cheated on each other. Frustrated by this cheating, General Electric expressed displeasure at its declining market share and began pricing independently. The fragile price agreements became especially vulnerable whenever demand decreased. Price cutting became rampant during the 1954 recession and culminated in what became known as the "white sale" in January 1955 when some units sold at 45 percent off book price.

In May 1955 company representatives began to meet again to try to raise prices. Forty-two meetings took place over the next 18 months where the firms assigned a bid price for every switchgear order to each firm in hopes of raising prices. Prices increased but it is unclear how much of the rise was due to the circulation of memoranda or to the rise in backlogs. The next pricing crisis occurred in 1957. A large public utility order was to be split between General Electric and Westinghouse but Westinghouse offered a secret price discount to win a still larger order. The public utility conveniently informed General Electric of the offer, and General

---

[15] This account follows Ralph G. M. Sultan, *Pricing in the Electric Oligopoly*, vol. 1 (Cambridge, Mass.: Harvard University Press 1974), chaps. 2 and 3.

Electric matched the secret price cut and won the whole contract. This episode proved fatal to the conspiracy. It triggered another wave of deep price cutting by other firms in the industry. Westinghouse responded by cutting price on the next order. And on the next order Allis-Chalmers offered a still larger price cut. More meetings followed, but they became shouting matches with each firm accusing the others of cheating on agreements. The smaller companies claimed the larger companies were pricing to drive them out of the market. The larger companies charged the smaller companies were increasing their market share by aggressive bidding.

By late 1958 the larger firms agreed to surrender market share to small firms in hopes of increasing prices. This agreement collapsed when prices began to crumble again in the middle of 1959. The meetings stopped when rumors of an investigation by the Department of Justice began to circulate.

Product and Industry Characteristics and Successful Collusion

This case study reveals the difficulties firms have in reaching a cooperative solution even when the industry has a small number of firms—five firms in the switchgear market—even when firms discuss individual orders. Under conditions that can only be described as favorable to collusion, firms nevertheless cheated on the agreement.

The facts of the case suggest that the number of sellers in the market isn't the only or necessarily the most important determinant of successful collusion. Characteristics of the product and the industry appear to affect the success of an agreement. In the electrical manufacturers' case the Bertrand model seems more applicable than the Cournot model because one firm usually wins the order and firms submit prices. Because each order is large, the desire of a firm to win the order by offering a lower price is difficult to resist. This is especially true when demand declines and the discrepancy between current price and short-run marginal cost increases. Price cutting broke out whenever demand decreased, excess capacity appeared, and backlogs decreased.

Collusion also appears to be less successful when the buyer can suppress or distort price information. In this industry, a utility can conceal a price reduction. Negotiations with private utilities are private, and a private utility can play one firm off against another by revealing or distorting the price information received from other sellers. Given the large size of a typical order, a private utility encourages price chiseling by a conspirator by awarding the whole contract to any firm that will undercut the others. In contrast, public utilities adopt sealed bidding where the prices of all bidders become public knowledge with the announcement of the winning bid. It is easier to determine which firm violated the price agreement when the contract is awarded. Sultan reports the average percentage reduction off-the-book price was 9.5 percent higher for private utilities than for public utilities. By publicly revealing bids, public utilities reduce the incentive to cut prices.

In short, fluctuating demand, secret price negotiations, and the absence of hard information about prices are all responsible for the difficulties experienced by the electrical manufacturers. These are unfavorable conditions for a successful conspiracy. Perhaps these unfavorable circumstances were the reason the conspirators had to meet and discuss individual orders if the conspiracy was to achieve even a modicum of success.

The Cost of Detecting Price Chiseling

The case study of the electrical manufacturers' conspiracy indicates that the success of collusion depends more on the characteristics of the product and industry conditions and less on the number of sellers. Recent developments in the theory of oligopoly have focused on the conditions that make price cutting easy or difficult to detect. The rationale for this approach is that collusion is more successful when the colluding firms can quickly detect price chiseling and can do so at a low cost. When the cost of detection is low, members of a conspiracy can respond quickly to a price cut by matching the price reduction and limiting the gains of a renegade. When the cost is high, the gain from price cutting is larger and price agreements will either be unsuccessful or firms will not even attempt to collude in the first place.

This line of research has focused on the determinants of the **cost of detecting price chiseling.** Nobel Laureate George J. Stigler identified the following factors in an important early contribution to these studies.[16] In Stigler's analysis, a firm suspects price chiseling when the quantity that it sells decreases inexplicably. If it can lose only a small quantity to a competitor before inferring that some firm is cutting price, then the gains from price chiseling will be correspondingly small and a price agreement has a better chance of succeeding.

Stigler identifies the following three determinants of the cost of detecting price cutting.

1. *Number of buyers.* When there are many small buyers of a product, keeping a price cut secret is no small achievement. The likelihood of a firm learning of a price cut can be predicted with a simple analysis of the probability that customers will reveal their prices. To see why this is so, consider the likelihood that a rival learns about a price cut that you offer to all n of your customers. Let p be the probability that a rival will hear about your price cut from a buyer. Then $1 - p$ is the probability that the rival will not learn about your price cut to one buyer. If you offer a price cut to all n customers, the probability that all n buyers will not inform is $(1 - p)^n$. The probability of detection is therefore $1 - (1 - p)^n$. If $p = .01$, the probability that a buyer will tell is only one chance in a hundred. If you offer a price cut to 100 buyers, then the probability that your rival will learn of the price cut is $1 - (.99)^{100} = .63$. In 63 chances out of 100 your rival will learn of your price cut. The larger the number of buyers, the larger the probability that your rivals will detect the price cut.

2. *Customer turnover.* In some industries there is considerable turnover of customers in the normal course of business, while in others customers tend to always purchase from the same seller. When the probability of a repeat

---

[16] George J. Stigler, "A Theory of Oligopoly," *Journal of Political Economy* 72, no. 1 (February 1964), pp. 44–61.

sale to a customer is low, customers move from one seller to another for a host of random reasons. The quantity that a firm sells will fluctuate randomly from period to period from the normal turnover of customers. It will be difficult for a firm to infer whether its sales are down because another firm is chiseling on price or because many customers are purchasing from other sellers for random reasons that have nothing to do with price cutting. A price chiseler can hide behind this smoke screen and take more customers away from rivals by cutting price without being detected. Price agreements are less likely to succeed in this inhospitable environment.

3. *Availability of price information.* If information about prices paid or received is readily available, the gains from price cutting are smaller. Often, government agencies must make all submitted prices publicly available. The identity of the renegade and the magnitude of the price reduction become public knowledge. This suggests that collusion will be more successful when suppliers are selling to government agencies than to private firms.

In summary, recent developments in oligopoly theory place greater emphasis on the characteristics of the product, demand stability, and the characteristics of the buyers as determinants of successful collusion.

10-7   GAME THEORY AND NONCOOPERATIVE STRATEGIES

We have seen that in markets with few firms interdependence among firms is pronounced. What strategy a firm adopts depends on what it thinks the opponent's strategy is. We formalize these notions in an introduction to game theory. **Game theory** is the study of the strategic interaction among a small number of players whether they are firms, nations, employers, or employees. A *game* is a situation of mutual interdependence among agents. Game theory helps economists identify the options available to the firms in an oligopoly and in some cases to deduce what strategy the firm should adopt. This section introduces some of the concepts and methods used in game theory to determine the strategies of two firms. Our discussion of game theory concentrates on noncooperative games where each firm maximizes its profits given the strategy of a rival.[17]

As you will see, every game has three components: (1) a set of players, (2) a set of strategies, and (3) a listing of payoffs. In the following examples there are two players and two strategies for each player with the corresponding payoffs.

Dominant Strategies

In some situations a firm can select a profit-maximizing strategy that does not depend on what strategy its rival adopts. A **dominant strategy** is the firm's best strategy no matter what strategy its rival selects. The idea of dominant strategy

---

[17] For a thoroughly enjoyable introduction to strategic thinking, the reader should consult Avinash Dixit and Barry Nalebuff, *Thinking Strategically* (New York: W. W. Norton, 1991).

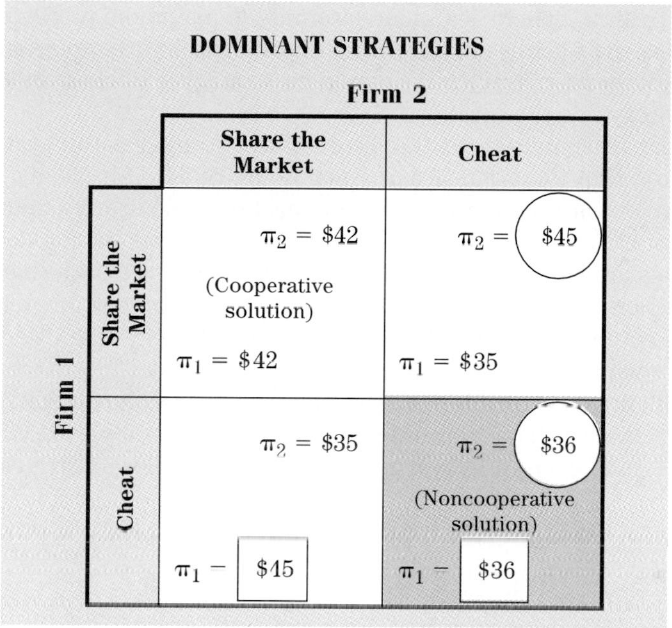

DOMINANT STRATEGIES

Firm 2

		Share the Market	Cheat
Firm 1	**Share the Market**	$\pi_2 = \$42$ (Cooperative solution) $\pi_1 = \$42$	$\pi_2 =$ $\$45$ $\pi_1 = \$35$
	Cheat	$\pi_2 = \$35$ $\pi_1 -$ $\$45$	$\pi_2 =$ $\$36$ (Noncooperative solution) $\pi_1 -$ $\$36$

Figure 10-10   The dominant strategy of firm 1 is to cheat no matter which strategy firm 2 selects. Similarly, firm 2's profits are higher if it cheats no matter what strategy firm 1 selects.

can be illustrated by reconsidering the duopoly problem. In the prisoner's dilemma game the optimal strategies of the two duopolists were dominant strategies. In Figure 10-10 we reproduce the payoff matrix in Figure 10-2.

Recall that firm 1's payoffs (profits) are in the lower-left-hand corner of each cell, while firm 2's payoffs are in the upper-right-hand corner of each cell. Profits of each duopolist are $42 if they share the market (northwest cell). If either firm cheats while the other does not, the cheater earns $45 and the noncheater earns only $35 (southwest and northeast cells). If both firms cheat, each firm earns $36 (southeast cell).

The special feature of this game is that the strategy that maximizes the profits of each firm is independent of the strategy adopted by its rival. When your profit-maximizing strategy is independent of your rival's, you have a dominant strategy.

> A dominant strategy is the firm's best strategy no matter what strategy a rival adopts.

To verify this, look at the game from firm 1's viewpoint. If firm 2 shares the market at the monopoly price, firm 1's profits are higher and equal $45 if it cheats (southwest cell). If firm 2 cheats, firm 1's profits are higher by cheating too, and so both firms end up in the southeast cell. No matter which strategy firm 2 adopts, firm 1's profits are higher if it follows the cheating strategy. For each strategy adopted by firm 2, there is a square around the maximum profits that firm 1 earns. Notice that the squares around firm 1's profits are in the same row, the southwest and the southeast cells. Firm 1's dominant strategy is to cheat on output no matter what strategy firm 2 selects.

Similar reasoning shows that firm 2's best strategy is to cheat. If firm 1 shares the market, firm 2's profits are at a maximum of $45 if it cheats. If firm 1 cheats, firm 2's profits are $36 if it cheats (southeast cell). So firm 2's dominant strategy is to cheat no matter what firm 1 does. When both firms have a dominant strategy, two circles are in the same column and two squares are in the same row. The cell with a square and a circle identifies the dominant strategy of each rival. In Figure 10-10 the southeast cell identifies the dominant strategy where each firm cheats on the agreement.

If both firms could enforce an agreement to share the market, each would earn $42. Yet both firms cheat on output, and each earns only $36, as happened in the electrical manufacturers' conspiracy. This example illustrates the prisoners' dilemma.

A Dominant Strategy for Only One Firm

In some games only one firm has a dominant strategy. The question becomes: What strategy should the firm without a dominant strategy follow?

Consider the following game. Firm 1 is an auto company with prowess in engineering. It is more adept at introducing technical innovations like sophisticated suspension systems or more responsive engines, while firm 2 has more capable designers and is successful when introducing styling changes. Both firms are planning to introduce a new model automobile. Should each bring out a new model that favors its strength with firm 1 introducing a technically advanced model and firm 2 bringing out an automobile with a new design?

The profits for each combination of strategies are in Figure 10-11. Firm 1 plays to its strength, engineering. Its dominant strategy is to introduce a technical model change. For each strategy adopted by firm 2, firm 1 earns higher profits by introducing a technical model change. Firm 2 does not have a dominant strategy. Firm 2's best strategy depends on what strategy firm 1 follows. If firm 1 introduces a technical model change, firm 2's best strategy is to copy and introduce a technical model change as well. If firm 1 adopts a styling change, firm 2's best strategy is to adopt a styling change.

What strategy should firm 2 adopt given that it does not have a dominant strategy? At this point it should put itself in firm 1's shoes. It knows that firm 1 is a technical colossus. Therefore, it is quite likely that firm 1 will pick a strategy that exploits this strength because its profits will be higher. Therefore, firm 2 expects firm 1 to introduce a technical change. Given this, the best strategy for firm 2 is to adopt a technical change as well, although it cannot match firm 1's strength in this area. If firm 2 adopts a styling change when firm 1 adopts a technical change, it earns only $15 million in profits while it can earn $20 million if it introduces a new model with technical innovations. Unfortunately for firm 2, consumers value a technical change more than a styling change.

The lesson to be learned from this example is clear. If you do not have a

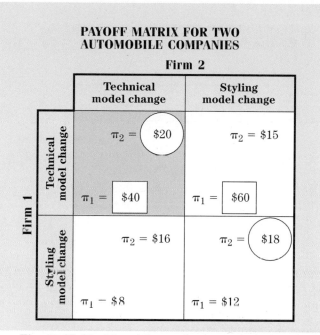

Figure 10-11   Firm 1 has a dominant strategy. It introduces a model change with numerous technical advances. If it introduces technical innovations, it earns profits of $40 million if firm 2 follows the leader and introduces a new auto with technical changes. Firm 1 earns profits of $60 million if it introduces a technical change and firm 2 introduces a styling change. Consumers place a greater value on technical than on styling changes. On the other hand, firm 2 does not have a dominant strategy. If firm 1 introduces a technical change, then firm 2's best strategy is to introduce a technical change. If firm 1 introduces a styling change, firm 2's best strategy is to introduce a styling change. The profit-maximizing strategy of firm 2 depends on what strategy firm 1 adopts.

dominant strategy, see if you can infer your rival's dominant strategy. If your rival has a dominant strategy, assume that your rival is rational and will adopt this strategy. Then select the strategy that maximizes your profits given the favored strategy of your rival.

Let's consider another example. Firms have a choice of when to introduce a new brand. Should a company try to introduce a brand early or late in the evolution of the market? And does this depend on whether the brand name is new or borrowed? Suppose two firms are planning to enter a market. Firm 1 has a well-established, well-recognized brand-name product in another market. Firm 1 wants to take advantage of the recognized name that it has already created and to introduce a product in this new market by using the existing name. Marketing professionals call this a *brand extension strategy*. For example, Coca Cola introduced Diet Coke. This is a brand extension in a new market, the diet soft drink market. Firm 2 is a new firm and will introduce the product with a new brand name.

By using a brand extension, the firm hopes that consumers who are familiar

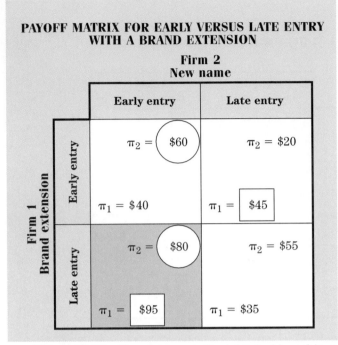

PAYOFF MATRIX FOR EARLY VERSUS LATE ENTRY WITH A BRAND EXTENSION

Firm 2
New name

	Early entry	Late entry
Early entry	$\pi_2 = \$60$ $\pi_1 = \$40$	$\pi_2 = \$20$ $\pi_1 = \$45$
Late entry	$\pi_2 = \$80$ $\pi_1 = \$95$	$\pi_2 = \$55$ $\pi_1 = \$35$

Firm 1 Brand extension

Figure 10-12   Firm 1 has a well-established brand in another market. It decides to adopt a brand extension strategy when entering a new market. It does not have a dominant strategy. If firm 2 enters early, firm 1 enters its brand extension late so that it can judge the market better. It wants to minimize the probability that its brand extension will fail and damage the reputation of its established brand name. If firm 2 enters late, firm 1 will take a chance and enter early since it earns \$45 million rather than \$35 million when it enters late. Firm 2 has a new brand, and its dominant strategy is to enter early. Therefore, firm 2 enters the market early with its new brand, and firm 1 enters late with its brand extension.

with the brand name will try the new product. Firm 1 has to be careful not to damage the reputation of the existing brand if the brand extension fails in the new market. Therefore, having an existing brand can be a help or a hindrance in the new market. One strategy that firm 1 can follow is to wait and learn more about the market before modifying some features of its brand extension to increase its chance of success. Firm 2 does not have an existing brand name. So if its product fails, it does not damage the reputation of an existing brand name. For firm 2 the relative payoff from entering the market early is greater than from entering late. The payoffs of the two firms are shown in Figure 10-12. Firm 2's dominant strategy is to enter the market early. Both circles are in the same column. Firm 1 does not have a dominant strategy because the two squares are in different rows. Firm 2 enters early with a new product and name, and firm 1 enters later with a brand extension.

Table 10-7   DISTRIBUTION OF ENTRY TIMES BY TYPE OF BRAND

	EARLY ENTRY	LATE ENTRY
New name	35 (81.4%)	8 (18.6%)
Brand extension	13 (25%)	39 (75%)
Total	48 (50.5%)	47 (49.5%)

APPLICATION 10-7

Which Brands Enter Late and Which Enter Early?

Are the predictions of the theory consistent with the behavior of firms that introduce brand extensions? Mary Sullivan examined the entry decisions of firms entering the market with new product names and firms entering with brand extensions.[18]

She found that firms introduced brand extensions later than new name brands. The probability of entering either late or early is a function of whether a firm used a brand extension or a new name. Table 10-7 shows the number of products and the percentage of brands that were introduced either early or late for new name and brand extensions. Seventy-five percent of brand extensions entered late, while 81 percent of new names entered early. Sullivan also found that products with brand extensions that entered late had a higher probability of surviving six years or more than brand extensions that entered early.

Nash Equilibria

Unfortunately, not all games have dominant strategies. Let's return to our example of two automobile companies introducing technical or styling changes for their new cars. However, let's change the payoff matrix so that each benefits if each has no competition and therefore is the sole innovator, be it a technical or a styling model change. In Figure 10-13 the profit payoff is $60 for firm 1 if it offers a technical advance while firm 2 earns a profit of $55 if it offers a styling advance (northeast quadrant). The numbers are reversed if firm 1 offers a styling advance while firm 2 offers a technical advance (southwest quadrant). If both offer a styling model change or both offer a technical model change, competition among the firms results in lower profits.

[18] Mary W. Sullivan, "Brand Extensions: When to Use Them," *Management Science* 38 (June 1992), pp. 793–806. Reprinted by permission of Mary W. Sullivan, The Institute of Management Sciences, 290 Westminister Street, Providence, Rhode Island 02903.

**PAYOFF MATRIX FOR TWO
AUTOMOBILE COMPANIES**

Firm 2

		Technical Model Change	Styling Model Change
Firm 1	**Technical Model Change**	$\pi_2 = \$20$ $\pi_1 = \$20$	$\pi_2 = \$55$ $\pi_1 = \$60$
	Styling Model Change	$\pi_2 = \$60$ $\pi_1 = \$55$	$\pi_2 = \$25$ $\pi_1 = \$25$

Figure 10-13   There are two Nash equilibria in this game. Profits are higher if the firms bring out different types of model changes. Firm 1's decision depends on the decision of firm 2 and vice versa. Each firm would like to move first by announcing a technical model change.

In this game there are two Nash equilibria. In a Nash equilibrium each firm is doing the best it can *given* the strategy of the rival. If firm 2 is offering a technical model change, then firm 1's best strategy is to offer a styling model change. Conversely, if firm 1 is offering a styling model change, firm 2's best strategy is to offer a technical model change. In Figure 10-13 the northeast and the southwest cells satisfy the requirements for a Nash equilibrium. In either equilibrium neither firm has an incentive to change its strategy given the strategy of the rival. Which equilibrium will prevail? We cannot say. It could depend on which firm is the first mover. Each firm would like to move first by offering a technical model change. The first mover will receive $60 in profits while the second mover will offer a styling model change and earn only $55. If there is no first mover advantage, it is in the best interest of both firms to coordinate policies so that the firms do not offer the same type of model change.

Repeated Games

Limited horizons are confining. In the Bertrand single period game we found that two or more Bertrand firms compete and a Nash equilibrium in prices requires price to equal marginal cost. We mentioned at the time that one reason that this outcome occurred was because each firm's demand function was perfectly elastic at the rival's price. There is another more important explanation for this result. In a single period game there is neither an opportunity nor a value to punishing a price-cutting firm.

With repeated interaction among firms richer strategies can be adopted to discourage price competition. Let's describe the consequences of repeated inter-action. Suppose one duopolist adopts a **punishment strategy** whereby it will reduce price to marginal cost indefinitely whenever a rival sets price below the cooperative monopoly price. How will this punishment strategy affect the thinking and decisions of a rival that is considering a price cut? By cutting price by a penny, a Bertrand competitor can still steal the complete market for *one* period and earn approximately π_m, monopoly profits. In a single period game this temptation is irresistible. But in a multiperiod game, the potential price cutter must consider the long-term consequences of a price cut. Price will fall to marginal cost thereafter so profits in all future periods will be zero. So, a potential price cutter's total profits over the indefinite future equal π_m. A potential price cutter should compare the one period profits with the sum of per period profits that the firm would earn indefinitely by cooperating and sharing the market. In the first period a cooperative rival receives $\pi_m/2$, only one-half of monopoly profits, but that stream of profits continues indefinitely. Figure 10-14a shows the profit stream from competing and 10-14b shows the profit stream from cooperating. Price chiseling yields immediate

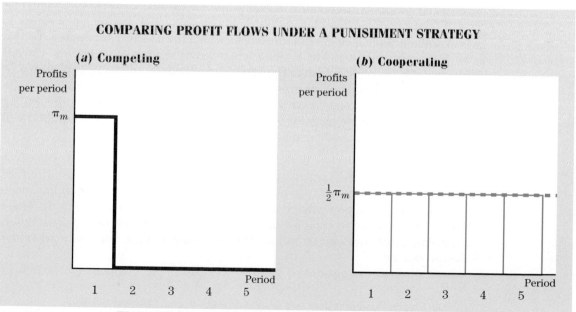

COMPARING PROFIT FLOWS UNDER A PUNISHMENT STRATEGY

(a) Competing

(b) Cooperating

Figure 10-14   (*a*) By cheating on an agreement the firm earns π_m for one period. (*b*) By cooperating, a duopolist earns $1/2\pi_m$ indefinitely.

and sizable profits but nothing thereafter; cooperative behavior results in smaller immediate but persistent profits over time.

To determine which strategy to follow, a potential price cutter must determine how valuable future profits are compared to current profits. If a dollar received tomorrow is just as valuable as a dollar received today, we can see that the potential price cutter will not cut price. The firm's share of cooperative profits in just the first two periods already equals the first period profits from price chiseling. Even if a future dollar is worth somewhat less than a current dollar, it may still not pay to cut price. So we reach an important conclusion: *repeated interaction* among firms makes cooperative behavior more likely. Of course this does not mean that punishment strategies always work. If future profits are far less important than current profits, then the potential price cutter may deviate and grab short-run profits even when a punishment strategy is in place.[19] An important point is to recognize that the opportunity to punish is a valuable tool for members of a duopoly.

A punishment strategy that cuts price to marginal cost indefinitely is a very drastic strategy. It's akin to announcing that you will drop the bomb if your opponent doesn't behave. You would announce such a policy only if you thought that you would never have to implement the policy. Economists have proposed other less drastic policies in the repeated prisoner dilemma game. One of the more appealing strategies is called "*tit for tat.*" In the first period you play the cooperative strategy. In the second round you play the cooperative strategy if your rival played the cooperative strategy, but you cut price to marginal cost if your opponent chiseled in the first period. In each subsequent period you play the cooperative strategy if your opponent cooperated in the previous period, or set price to marginal cost if your opponent chiseled. A desirable feature of the "tit for tat" strategy is that it combines the element of punishment with a reward for cooperating. You let your rival know that cheating is not a free good by cutting price but you reward your rival for cooperative play. The strategy is superior to the drastic policy of setting price equal to marginal cost indefinitely in situations where you know little about your opponent and where you think that your opponent will make pricing mistakes or where it is costly for you to credibly convince your rival that you will implement a drastic punishment strategy.

Sequential Games

In some situations decisions are made in sequence. A firm is the first to introduce a speedier chip, or a new advertising campaign, or a new movie using the latest graphics programs, or to enter a market. Soon after, other firms may copy or enter. In deciding what strategy to follow, the first mover must anticipate what the follower will do.

Let's illustrate a **sequential game** with an example. Suppose an incumbent

---

[19] Later, in Chapter 14, we will show how to convert profits at some future period into their current or present value so that the firm will be indifferent between receiving profits at some future date or a smaller sum today.

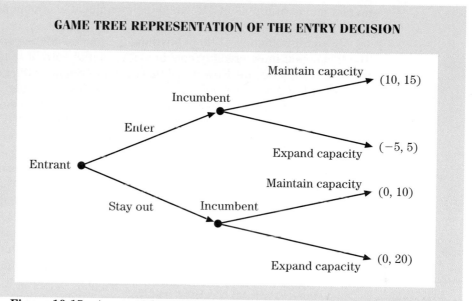

GAME TREE REPRESENTATION OF THE ENTRY DECISION

Figure 10-15   A potential entrant enters the industry and the incumbent maintains capacity. The potential entrant does not view the incumbent's threat to expand capacity as credible.

has one plant. It thinks the market is expanding and must decide whether to add a second plant or to stay with one plant. A potential entrant aspires to enter the industry. The incumbent knows that the entrant is considering entry into the market and has dropped some hints that it plans to add a second plant. How should the potential entrant evaluate this rumored expansion? Will the incumbent preempt the market by expanding capacity?

To analyze the decisions made by the entrant and the incumbent, we must specify the sequence of decisions. It is easier to do this by presenting the payoffs in the form of a *game tree*. In Figure 10-15 moving from left to right shows the order of play. First, the entrant decides whether to enter or not. Then the incumbent decides whether to expand or maintain capacity. The payoffs at the right show the potential entrant's profits followed by the incumbent's profits for each branch of the tree.

From the incumbent's perspective, the best situation is for the entrant to stay out. Then, the incumbent will expand capacity to meet a growing demand and earn profits of $20. If the potential entrant does enter, the profits of the incumbent are higher if it maintains capacity given the new capacity added by the entrant. Assuming the entrant knows this, it will not consider the incumbent's rumored threat to expand output as credible. The incumbent would only be shooting itself in the foot if it expanded capacity after the new firm entered. Consequently, the potential entrant assumes that the incumbent will not expand capacity. It will enter the market and earn profits of $10 while the incumbent accommodates the entry and earns profits of $15.

Given this situation, is there anything the incumbent can do to prevent entry? The incumbent must credibly convince a potential entrant that it will expand its capacity if entry occurs. How might this be done? Suppose the incumbent commits to staffing the new plant and to paying the workers whether they do or do not produce before the potential entrant makes its entry decision. For example a union agreement may require the firm to pay 95 percent or more of a worker's compensation whether the firm produces or not. Further, assume the additional hiring cost equals $12 whether the workers produce or not. Figure 10-16 shows the game tree with the revised payoffs. Now the entrant must take the incumbent's threat to expand seriously. If the new firm enters, the incumbent's profits are $5 if it expands and only $3 if it maintains its capacity and has to pay compensation to the newly hired employees. If the incumbent expands, the entrant suffers losses of $5. Hence the entrant stays out, and the incumbent expands and earns profits of $20.

This illustration shows the importance of **credible commitment.** The firm earns $20 rather than $15 by making a credible commitment. A commitment must be believable if it is to work. Sometimes that might mean that the firm making a commitment must burn a bridge. The firm may have to demonstrate its commitment. Perhaps the firm will build such a specialized plant that no other use for the plant is possible. Once built, the marginal cost of operating the plant is negligible. In a different context a corporate raider may deliberately insert a clause that

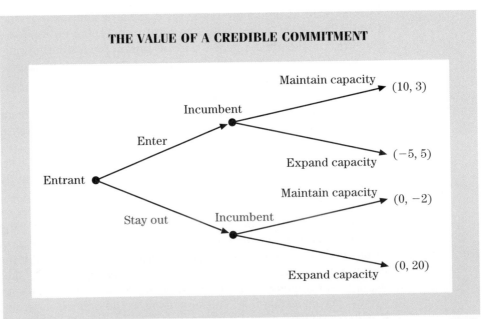

THE VALUE OF A CREDIBLE COMMITMENT

Figure 10-16 By hiring the staff for the second plant and committing to a payroll, the incumbent alters the entry strategy of a potential entrant.

requires the raider to pay a higher interest rate on the financing if the raider raises the bid price for a target. In doing this, the raider makes a commitment that would destroy the deal if the bid price is raised. This ties the raider's hand and weakens the bargaining position of the target to get a higher price. The danger of a credible commitment is that a second bidder enters with a more favorable bid.

APPLICATION 10-8

Credible Commitment for *Independence Day*

Movie producers introduce many movies during the summer season, especially movies that appeal to young audiences. They often jockey with one another for the best opening day. If at all possible, they don't want to launch a new movie with a first screening on the same day another movie is opening. Studios try to preempt certain dates by announcing opening day for a movie prior to the summer season. An illustration of this commitment to an opening date was the announcement for *Independence Day*, a movie expected to be enormously popular. The studio announced that the movie would open on July 2, two days before Independence Day. The studio could credibly preempt this day because other studios knew that the timing would be perfect for maximizing interest in and audience size for the film. Given the prerelease publicity for the movie, no other studio was willing to release a new movie around this date. As you may remember, *Independence Day* did box-office business after its release with some movie theaters staying open around the clock.

10-8 MONOPOLISTIC COMPETITION

Some industries have many firms but each firm offers a product that is not a perfect substitute for the other products in the market. The products sold by these firms are called **differentiated products.** While the number of firms is large, the firms are not price takers. There are many restaurants in major metropolitan areas and no two are alike. If Giordano's Pizzeria in Chicago raises the price of its deep dish pizza, not all of its customers will flee to other pizza restaurants even in the long run. Bookstores, specialty clothing stores, and beauty shops are some other examples that come to mind.

These industries are different from competitive industries because the products sold by firms are not perfect substitutes, but they are similar to competitive industries because entry into these industries is relatively easy. How can we model the behavior of firms in these industries aptly called by economists *monopolistically competitive* industries?

Figure 10-17*a* shows the demand and cost functions facing Giordano's, a pizza restaurant. The demand function for Giordano's Pizzeria is downward sloping, perhaps because some of its customers are located nearby and will not go to more

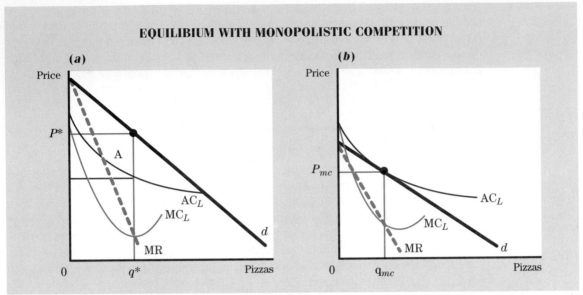

Figure 10-17 (*a*) In the short run the pizza restaurant earns profits equal to area A. (*b*) Entry by other pizza restaurants shifts the demand curve inward and eliminates profits.

distant pizza establishments if Giordano's raises its price. In the short run, before other firms can enter the industry, the firm sets a price of P^* and sells q^* pizzas where marginal revenue equals marginal cost. The restaurant's profits equal area A.

These profits are temporary because there are no barriers to entry. Other similar firms can enter and sell pizzas. The profits in the retail pizza industry attract new firms that supply slightly different pizzas and ambiance. As firms enter, they cause Giordano's demand function to shift inward. Figure 10-17*b* displays a situation where enough of these new firms have entered so that Giordano's demand function has shifted inward such that Giordano's profits are competed away. In the long run the pizza price P_{mc} equals long-run average cost. The restaurant sells q_{mc} pizzas where the restaurant's marginal revenue equals its marginal cost.

In monopolistically competitive industries profits are competed away with entry as they are in competitive industries. While each firm sells a differentiated product and, therefore, faces a downward sloping demand function, this does not guarantee long-run profits. How does a monopolistically competitive industry differ from a competitive industry? Each monopolistically competitive firm is a price maker and therefore price exceeds marginal cost while it equals marginal cost in a competitive industry.

Under monopolistic competition each firm produces a smaller quantity than a competitive firm would. Long-run average cost is higher than minimum average cost. While a monopolistic competitor produces too few units because $P > $ MC, it does not follow that fewer firms in the industry would increase total surplus. It is true that a smaller number of firms in the industry would increase the output of each remaining firm and thereby lower long-run average cost of the remaining firms. However, the question cannot be answered simply by concentrating solely on production efficiency. While production efficiency would increase by reducing the number of firms in the industry, consumers would be harmed since the variety of products produced decreases. Each firm offers a different variety and therefore caters to the particular demands of some consumers. Consequently, limiting the number of firms reduces consumer surplus since some consumers are forced to purchase products with less desirable attributes. It is necessary to compare the benefits of variety with the costs of variety before an informed assessment can be made. It is not possible to conclude that the variety of products sold when firm profits are zero is either too much or too little without much more detailed information.

SUMMARY

- A cartel is an arrangement among Independent firms whose objective is to raise price by restricting the output of its members. A cartel cannot succeed unless it enforces compliance by members.

- The cooperative solution to the duopoly problem is for both firms to share the market and charge the monopoly price. This solution is subject to cheating because it is profitable for a firm to produce more if its rival abides by the agreement.

- In the Cournot model of duopoly each firm selects its profit-maximizing output assuming that the output of its rival is constant.

- A Nash equilibrium in quantities requires each firm to choose a quantity strategy that maximizes its profits given the quantity strategy of its rival. As compared to the cooperative solution, in a Nash equilibrium the price is lower and total output is higher with two Cournot competitors.

- In the Bertrand model of duopoly each firm selects a price. In a Nash equilibrium in prices price falls to marginal cost when the

number of sellers increases from one to two.

- Observations on prices appear to fit the predictions of the Cournot model more closely than those of the Bertrand model.

- A competitive policy of meeting a rival's price maintains high prices, not lowers them.

- A price conspiracy among sellers will be less successful when the turnover of customers is large, the number of buyers is small, price information is scarce, and the size of the order is large.

- Game theory is the study of strategic interaction between players.

- Games may be structured to involve a single or repeated interaction among players and the result of the game is sensitive to this specification.

- In a monopolistically competitive market there are many firms with each producing a differentiated product. Each firm faces a downward sloping inverse demand curve.

KEY TERMS

cartel
prisoner's dilemma
self-enforcing agreement

cooperative solution
propensity to cheat
Cournot model

noncooperative behavior
reaction function
Bertrand model
meeting competition
game theory
dominant strategy
punishment strategy
sequential game
monopolistic competition

Nash equilibrium in quantities and prices
effect of number of competitors on price
the cost of detecting price chiseling
repeated games
credible commitment
differentiated products

REVIEW QUESTIONS

1. The larger is the number of members in a cartel, the less stable the cartel. Explain.
2. Why doesn't the cartel immediately shut down some firms so that the remaining ones can produce a quantity where long-run average cost is at a minimum?
3. Why doesn't a competitive firm behave strategically with respect to another competitive firm?
4. What prevents Cournot duopolists from sharing the market at the monopoly price?
5. What is a firm's reaction curve and what does it describe?
6. What prevents Bertrand duopolists from sharing the market at the monopoly price?
7. What are the principal differences between the Cournot and Bertrand models?

8. How do the predictions of the Cournot and Bertrand models differ with respect to the effect of the number of rivals on price?
9. How does the prisoner's dilemma capture the essential feature of the oligopoly problem?
10. What factors determine the probability of successful collusion?
11. What policies would you adopt as a buyer if you suspect collusion by sellers?
12. Why do repeated games often give different results from single period games?
13. How does a monopolistic competitor differ from a firm in a competitive industry?

EXERCISES

1. If members of your class tried to form a study-reduction cartel, what problems would such a cartel have?
2. A cartel includes large and small companies, each with different long-run average and marginal cost curves. A cartel requires each member to reduce output by 15 percent in the short run from the total output produced. The authority assigns a quota to each firm that is 15 percent less than the output produced by the firm in long-run competitive equilibrium.

   a. Explain why the 15 percent reduction rule will or will not maximize total profits of the cartel.
   b. How would you assign the quota of each firm to maximize total cartel profits?
   c. Can you explain why the cartel would adopt the 15 percent rule?
3. There are only two cellular telephone companies in the Los Angeles area. We can think of them as duopolists when they set their per minute prices for a telephone

call. Assume that consumers can change firms costlessly. The market demand function is $P = 60 - Q$ and marginal costs are zero.

   a. What does firm 1's demand curve look like?

   b. What is the Nash equilibrium in this situation? How many units does each firm produce and what is the price?

   c. If each firm has a fixed cost of $50, what are firm profits?

   d. If the firms merged, what would be the equilibrium price? If you were an economist working for the Federal Trade Commission, would you recommend that the merger take place? Explain why or why not.

4. Can you explain why two Bertrand competitors would build a plant with a fixed production capacity? What size would the plant be?

5. Suppose you are the purchasing agent of a firm and you believe that the suppliers are colluding. What actions might you take to increase the cost of collusion?

6. A construction firm is negotiating with two cement firms for one of them to supply $1 million of concrete per year over the next three years. Discuss how the construction company should structure the contract so that it costs the construction firm the least amount over the three years.

7. If 50 percent of the firms in an industry produce 50 percent of the output of the industry, the industry cannot be an oligopoly. Explain why you agree or disagree with this statement.

8. Five couples agree to meet for dinner. Before they order, each couple agrees to pay the average of the total bill. After each couple returns home, they complain about how much dinner cost and how much they overate. Can you explain the basis of their complaint? How is this related to the prisoner's dilemma?

9. If both firms in a duopoly have a dominant strategy, neither achieves maximum profits. Explain why you agree or disagree with this statement.

10. If a firm has a dominant strategy and its opponent does not, the firm with the dominant strategy maximizes its profits. Explain why you agree or disagree with this statement.

11. Two duopolists may either collude or cheat. The payoffs are summarized in the accompanying matrix. Suppose one duopolist announces a policy of meeting the competitor's price. How will the new entries in the payoff matrix change? Explain how the policy of meeting a competitor's price changes the behavior of duopolists.

*12. The payoff matrix that follows shows the payoffs of two firms if they do or do not cooperate. (For example, if they both cooperate, they each earn a.) What must be the relationship between a, b, c, and d under the prisoner's dilemma? (*Hint:* Show the required set of inequalities between a, b, c, and d so that noncooperative behavior is the dominant strategy of each player.)

13. Local officials of a major city in Eastern Europe hope to increase tourism. After years of neglect, they decide to beautify the city. One of the projects is to clean 75 historic statues in the city. Suppose city officials ask you how they should allocate the job among a small number of high-quality firms. Briefly describe what advice you would give to determine how the contract should be structured.

*14. The exclusive right to supply cable television to a community is awarded to a cable company. The monthly fee that the cable company charges is inversely related to the number of subscribers. The cable company charges each subscriber a uniform monthly fee for the service. There are economies of scale in providing cable services.

   a. With the aid of graphs show how a cable monopolist determines the monthly fee.

Suppose local telephone companies develop a new technology to transmit TV programs over telephone lines. Local telephone companies want to use the new technology and enter the cable market. There are economies of scale if the telephone company adopts the new technology. The long-run average cost function of the local telephone company lies below the long-run average cost function of the cable company. Congress is considering a proposal that would allow the local telephone company to enter the cable market.

   b. If the telephone company and the local cable company act like Bertrand competitors, what monthly fee would be charged for the service? Show the profits of the cable company and the telephone company.

15. Why can a firm be better off if its rivals have the capability to harm the firm than if they do not?

CHAPTER 10 APPENDIX

How the Number of Rivals Affects Firm Output and Price in the Cournot Model

The profit function of the ith Cournot competitor is $\pi(q_i) = P(Q)q_i - cq_i$: substituting the inverse demand function $P = a - bQ$, we have

$$\pi(q_i) = (a - bQ)q_i - cq_i$$

$$= (a - bq_1 - \cdots - bq_i - \cdots - bq_n)q_i - cq_i$$

The profit-maximizing quantity for the ith Cournot competitor satisfies

$$a - bq_1 - \cdots - 2bq_i - \cdots - bq_n - c = 0$$

Solving for q_i by adding $2bq_i$ to both sides of the equation and dividing by $2b$ yields

$$q_i = \frac{a - c}{2b} - \frac{q_1 + \cdots + q_{i-1} + q_{i+1} + \cdots + q_n}{2}$$

Because all firms are alike, all n Cournot competitors must produce the same profit-maximizing quantity that firm i produces, and so $q_1 = \cdots = q_i = \cdots = q_n$. Therefore, we can substitute q_i for the quantity produced by each of the other $n - 1$ firms on the right-hand side of the above equation and rewrite it as

$$q_i = \frac{a - c}{2b} - \frac{(n - 1)q_i}{2}$$

Adding $[(n - 1)q_i]/2$ to both sides of this equation, simplifying, and then multiplying both sides by $2/(n + 1)$ results in equation 10-6.[20]

Although each firm produces less as the number of competitors increases, total output increases. Total output equals $Q = nq_i$

$$Q = nq_i = n\left(\frac{1}{1 + n}\right)\left(\frac{a - c}{b}\right)$$

$$= \frac{n}{1 + n}\frac{a - c}{b}$$

Total output of n Cournot competitors is $n/(n + 1)$ times the competitive output. If $n = 3$, total output equals three-quarters of the competitive output. As n increases, $n/(n + 1)$ increases and approaches 1. Therefore, we can say that the Cournot model predicts that total output approaches the competitive output as the number of competitors becomes large.

The expression for price is[21]

$$P = a - bQ$$

$$= a - b\left(\frac{n}{n + 1}\right)\left(\frac{a - c}{b}\right)$$

Simplifying this equation yields equation 10-7.

---

[20] Adding $[(n - 1)q_i]/2$ to both sides yields

$$q_i\left(1 + \frac{n - 1}{2}\right) = \frac{a - c}{2b}$$

$$q_i\left(\frac{2 + n - 1}{2}\right) = \frac{a - c}{2b}$$

$$q_i\left(\frac{n + 1}{2}\right) = \frac{a - c}{2b}$$

The expression in the text is obtained by multiplying both sides by $2/(n + 1)$.

[21] This expression for price is obtained with the following operations:

$$P = a - b\left(\frac{n}{n + 1}\right)\left(\frac{a - c}{b}\right) = \frac{an + a}{n + 1} - \frac{na - nc}{n + 1} = \frac{a}{n + 1} + \frac{nc}{n + 1}$$

MONITORING THE CORPORATION: CORPORATE GOVERNANCE

■ 11-1 External Monitors: Product and Capital Markets

Application 11-1: The Effect of a Change in Management on Operations

■ 11-2 The Free Rider Problem and the Tender Offer

■ 11-3 Internal Monitors of Management

Expense Preference

Ex Post Settling Up

■ 11-4 The Principal-Agent Relationship and Ownership Structure

■ 11-5 Expense Preference under a Profit Constraint

The Profit Constraint

Deregulation and Import Competition

■ 11-6 The Unregulated Firm and Expense Preference

Application 11-2: Cummins Engine Company

■ 11-7 How the Market for Corporate Control Functions

The Effectiveness of Internal Monitors

The Effectiveness of External Monitors

Evidence about Takeovers

The Effect of Takeovers on the Stock Performance of Targets and Acquirers

■ Summary

■ Key Terms

■ Review Questions

■ Exercises

The pricing models that we developed in Chapters 8 through 10 rest on the common assumption of profit maximization. The principal mission of the firm's managers is to look after shareholder interests by maximizing firm profits. Just how valid is this assumption? The separation of the manager from shareholders, the suppliers of equity funding, is a central fact in large firms around the globe. Given this separation, why should a manager look after the interests of shareholders and not the manager's interests? Although the shareholders want managers to maximize firm profits, the firm's managers who are responsible for devising and implementing the firm's strategies can advance other agendas such as empire building, excessively handsome compensation packages, large support staffs, and so on. The interests of shareholders can conflict with those of managers. Who then monitors the manager's performance and how can these monitors align the interests of managers with those of shareholders?

Even with a separation of owners from managers, there are economic forces that constrain the behavior of managers. The product and the capital markets are **external monitors** that limit opportunistic behavior of managers. The capital market operates, whether the product market is competitive or monopolistic, to create the proper incentive for managers to maximize profits. In addition, there are **internal monitors** of managerial performance. The board of directors has the authority to reward the chief executive with various compensation packages for a good performance or to dismiss managers who do not maximize profits. These external and internal monitors constantly evaluate management performance. Some appear to work more effectively at some times and less effectively at other times. This chapter explains how these external and internal monitors operate and their effectiveness in inducing managers to act according to the best interests of shareholders.

11-1   EXTERNAL MONITORS: PRODUCT AND CAPITAL MARKETS

For firms in competitive markets, managers maximize profits by minimizing cost and by producing the profit-maximizing quantity. When an industry has many profit-maximizing firms in the market, any firm that does not do the same will not survive because price will be less than long-run average cost. This competition in the product market disciplines those managers who do not pursue the goal of profit maximization. If a manager errs by building too large or too small a firm, the firm's long-run average cost will exceed minimum long-run average cost and losses will eventually drive it out of the market. Therefore, the survival of the firm creates an incentive for a manager to maximize profits. Product market competition is an important external monitor in competitive industries.

The capital market also monitors management performance. When a firm is publicly owned, it offers ownership shares called common stock which are traded on organized stock exchanges. Investors who purchase stock become owners of the company, and their investment increases in value when the firm's profits increase and the stock price of the firm increases. Shareholders expect the management to maximize profits so that the stock price reaches a maximum. A manager who does not maximize profits causes the stock price to be lower than it would otherwise be. When firm profits are not maximized, an outsider or a group of existing shareholders may attempt to buy up enough shares to secure control of the firm and then replace management with new managers who will pursue profit-maximizing strategies.[1] Those who wish to control the firm can accomplish this either by a merger or by buying shares from the shareholders of the firm through a takeover. If outsiders or dissatisfied shareholders acquire control of the firm and increase profits, the rise in the price of the stock is the reward stockholders receive for replacing a management that fails to maximize profits. In this way the capital market penalizes inefficient managers by replacing them. The capital market serves as another external monitor whether the industry has one, a few, or many sellers.

APPLICATION **11-1**

The Effect of a Change in Management on Operations

Do economists have any evidence that firm performance changes after a management or ownership change? In a management buyout some members of the current management group and other investors purchase all the shares from the existing shareholders. The firm becomes privately owned, and shares are no longer traded on organized exchanges. Management buyouts became increasingly important during the 1980s. Buyouts create incentives for the new management team to reduce expenses and increase efficiency. Steven Kaplan analyzed 76 management buyouts of firms to determine their effect on financial performance of the firm.[2] In 19 of the 76 buyouts the chairman of the board or the CEO of a buyout firm left the firm and did not join the new firm. The turnover rate for the chairman and the CEO in buyout firms is significantly higher than the turnover rate for all firms and indicates that management buyouts often involve a change in the managers of the firm.

To evaluate the performance of firms before and after a management buyout, Kaplan used different measures of operating performance; only his results for the change in operating income relative to sales are reported here. He examined firms 2 years before and 3 years after a management buyout to determine if operating performance improved.

Table 11-1 summarizes his findings. The results show that operating income relative to sales declined modestly from 2 years to 1 year before the buyout (column 1). From 1 year before to 1 year after the buyout (column 2), operating income relative to sales increased by 7.1 percent, and from 1 year before to 3 years after the buyout (column 3), by 19.3 percent. The results are even more impressive when compared to changes in industry performance. After adjusting for industry changes, operating income relative to sales increased by 12.4 and 34.8 percent, respectively. Kaplan's results show a significant improvement in the operating performance of firms after a management buyout. It appears that a change in management and

---

[1] An early contribution to the study of corporate control is Henry G. Manne, "Mergers and the Market for Corporate Control," *Journal of Political Economy* LXXIII (April 1965), pp. 110–20.
[2] Steven Kaplan, "The Effects of Management Buyouts on Operating Performance and Value," *Journal of Financial Economics* 24 (1989), pp. 217–54.

Table 11-1   EFFECT OF MANAGEMENT BUYOUT ON OPERATING PERFORMANCE

OPERATING INCOME RELATIVE TO SALES	Measured from year i before buyout to year j		
	-2 TO -1 (1)	-1 TO $+1$ (2)	-1 TO $+3$ (3)
Percentage change	-1.7	7.1	19.3
Industry-adjusted percentage change	-1.9	12.4	34.8

Source: Reprinted with permission of Elsevier Sequoia, Lausanne, Switzerland, publishers of *Journal of Financial Economics.*

ownership coincides with an improvement in operating performance over a 4-year span.

In another study Frank Lichtenberg and Donald Siegal investigated how employment of production and nonproduction workers changes when there is a change in ownership.[3] Their goal was to assess the contention that CEOs tend to protect their immediate subordinates—administrators and supporting staff at central or regional headquarters. They compared firms that changed ownership from 1977 to 1982 with those that had not and found that employment growth at central and divisional offices declined by 16 percent for firms that changed owners compared to firms that did not, after controlling for industry changes

Both these studies indicate that a management change leads to an improvement in the operating performance of a firm. The results suggest that the capital market tends to replace managements that are incapable of improving the operating performance of firms.

To sum up, competition in the product and capital markets limits the permissible actions of managers of firms. While the chief executive officer of a large company exercises considerable authority within the firm, these external monitors circumscribe the CEO's authority.[4]

11-2 THE FREE RIDER PROBLEM AND THE TENDER OFFER

Although the capital market can penalize the managements of firms that do not maximize profits, the effectiveness of the capital market can be limited under

[3] Frank R. Lichtenberg, *Corporate Takeovers and Productivity* (Cambridge, Mass.: MIT Press, 1992), chap. 4.
[4] The terms "CEO" and "manager" are used interchangeably to refer to the individual with executive authority.

certain conditions. This section explains why an individual shareholder has little incentive to replace a management team that is not maximizing profits.

Although shareholders are the owners of a corporation, an individual shareholder has limited power over the management team appointed to represent shareholder interests. Most shareholders diversify their resources by investing in several companies or by buying shares in a mutual fund that in turn holds a stake in many corporations. In other words, most shareholders own a very small percentage of a given corporation, and many corporations have thousands of shareholders, with no one shareholder having a large ownership interest.

For firms with many small shareholders, a special problem arises when the capital market attempts to displace a management team that performs poorly. Let's assume that an individual or group of individuals concludes that the current management is not maximizing profits. They believe that a different management could raise the profits of the firm, and so they decide to replace management by soliciting a majority of the firm's shares through a **tender offer.**[5] The bidder hopes to acquire a majority of the shares and then vote to oust the existing management. In a tender offer, an individual or group offers to pay a price higher than market price for each share provided shareholders tender a specified number of shares.

Does an individual stockholder sell her shares to the bidder or wait to see if the bidder can replace management and install a new management that will maximize profits? To answer this question from the perspective of a stockholder, compare the profit and the stock price before the tender offer, during the tender offer, and after the new managers take control of the firm. Suppose profits are currently π^* under existing management and the current stock price is S^*. An individual or a group believes profits will increase after the existing management is replaced. With new management, this group projects a rise in profits to π' and predicts that the stock price will then rise from S^* to S'. The bidding group then offers a price of S'', where $S^* < S'' < S'$, to existing shareholders if (say) 50 percent of the firm's shares are tendered, so that the group can acquire the majority of the stock and turn out the current management. If the majority does not tender, the takeover fails and no shares change hands.

If you owned shares in the firm, would you sell your shares to the bidder? Economists Sanford Grossman and Oliver Hart, who have studied takeover bids, say no. To see why, consider the payoff matrix for an individual shareholder below. The shareholder may tender or not and the takeover is either successful or not. If the majority does not tender so the takeover is unsuccessful, the firm's profits do not change and no shares change hands so the share price remains at S^* whether the shareholder tenders or not. So, the shareholder is indifferent. If the takeover is successful, the new management increases profits and the stock price so the shareholder's capital gain is $S'' - S^*$, if the stock is tendered, and $S' - S^*$, if the stock is not tendered. A sophisticated shareholder will reason that the bidder will never offer a tender price as high as S' for the shares because the bidder will not gain anything if the tender offer succeeds. The tender price must be less than the

---

[5] This analysis follows Sanford Grossman and Oliver Hart, "Takeover Bids, the Free Rider Problem, and the Theory of the Corporation," *Bell Journal of Economics* 11 (Spring 1980), pp. 42–64.

		Tender offer	
		Successful	**Unsuccessful**
Shareholder decision	**Do not enter**	S'	$S*$
	Tender	S''	$S*$

price the bidder expects the stock price to reach. The bidder hopes to buy the shares at the tender price of S'' and later sell or retain them when the price reaches S'. Therefore, a sophisticated shareholder will not tender the shares but will wait until the price increases to S' before selling them. Of course, a sophisticated shareholder hopes that other shareholders tender their shares, the tender offer succeeds, and a new management increases profits so that the stock price increases from $S*$ to S'. In this way the shareholder experiences greater price appreciation by not tendering.

Shareholders get a free ride because of the tender offer. The bidder has done some research, and this research has yielded valuable private information that profits and the price of the stock will increase with a change in management. There is no simple way for the bidder to charge the other existing shareholders for this new information. Shareholders receive the benefits of a takeover without incurring the cost of obtaining the new information and initiating the tender offer.

> If one shareholder devotes resources to improving management, then all shareholders benefit. Other shareholders free-ride on the efforts of the shareholder.

If most shareholders behave this way, a takeover will fail and the ineffective managers will remain in their jobs. The free rider problem reduces the effectiveness of the capital market as a monitor of managerial performance.

An implication of this argument is that tender offers will fail unless the bidder receives some reward. Grossman and Hart suggest a solution. Corporate charters allow a raider to treat nontendered shares differently from tendered shares. If the raider succeeds and acquires a majority control of the firm, he or she can set the price of the merger or the liquidation of the firm at an unfavorable price for the minority shareholders who did not tender. In the meantime, the raider can change the management of the firm. Sometimes the target is merged with another company owned by the raider. The raider can even offer S' to purchase the majority of the shares. Then he or she can merge the target with the parent company, offer a price less than S' for the minority shares, and then sell these at S'. In this way the bidder earns a capital gain on the remaining shares.

There is another way for a raider to gain from the increase in the stock price. Grossman and Hart assumed that the bidder owns few if any shares to start with. There is nothing to stop him from quietly accumulating stock of the company before announcing a tender offer. With the passage of the Williams Amendment in 1968, an individual or a firm can acquire up to 5 percent of a target's shares before public disclosure of the acquired stake is required. Under this amendment a raider can quietly acquire a 5 percent or larger holding in a firm at S^*. Then, the bidder might even be willing to pay S' for a majority of the stock or, if required by law or a corporate charter, all shares in a tender offer and still earn a gain from the price increase on the 5 percent stake in the firm. Therefore, this is one way to attenuate the free rider problem.

The free rider problem reduces the effectiveness of the capital market in disciplining a grossly inefficient management but does not prevent the capital market from functioning. As you have seen, there are ways around the free rider problem. The rapid growth of tender offers in the 1980s indicates that the capital market still functions to remove inefficient managers from their positions.

11-3　INTERNAL MONITORS OF MANAGEMENT

Even if we ignore the free rider problem, the capital market is an expensive and cumbersome mechanism for disciplining management and can perhaps be described as the mechanism of last resort. Individuals attempt to gain control of a firm through the capital market when management performance is so poor that it attracts the attention of outsiders or existing shareholders. When the capital market must act, it indicates that the internal monitors are ineffective. This section explains how an internal monitor can affect management performance.

Two internal monitors are the existence of concentrated share ownership and the board of directors. A few shareholders who own 20 to 30 percent of the company have greater incentives to collect information and monitor management. While not common in the United States, there are numerous instances where concentrated ownership by a large family exists. Studies show that concentrated ownership is associated with a higher probability of takeover, a lower compensation package for management, and a higher turnover of managers if a takeover is unsuccessful.[6]

---

[6] For an extended discussion of these and other issues related to firm governance, see Andrei Shleifer and Robert W. Vishny, "A Survey of Corporate Governance," Working Paper No. 5554, National Bureau of Economic Research, April 1996.

An important function of the board of directors is to monitor, evaluate, and either reward or penalize management performance. The board of directors can be thought of as a first line of defense, protecting shareholders from actions of management that reduce profits and the value of the firm and that cause the capital market to act. In part, the board of directors exists because the individual shareholder has little incentive to incur the cost of monitoring management. The board of directors is an institution which in principle can attenuate the consequences of the free rider problem. How does the board serve this purpose?

Expense Preference

In theory the board of directors is the internal body that monitors and evaluates managerial performance and gives expert advice to management. The board can make the manager pay for decisions that reduce firm profits but increase the manager's utility, but in practice there are limits to what a board can accomplish. It does not have the detailed information or the time to monitor management day by day. Rather, it takes a more distant position by offering advice and periodically evaluating management performance, and, in view of this assessment, rewarding or penalizing the chief executive officer.

In many large corporations the chief executive officer has considerable authority and leeway. He decides what projects the firm will undertake and can indulge his own preferences for some kinds of expenses. The CEO has many opportunities to make decisions that can increase his utility and raise the firm's costs. A CEO may decide to act cautiously and pass up many potentially profitable projects because they would require greater effort by the whole management team. Profitability may be lower than otherwise, but the utility of the manager is higher. If he hires a friend to run the purchasing department when there is a more qualified candidate who would be willing to take the position at the same salary, the utility of the CEO is higher but the costs of the firm are also. For example, a manager with a technical-computer background can become enamored of the latest and most expensive computer system and have it installed for the company when a less expensive system would suffice. This decision lowers company profits but increases the manager's utility. The chief executive officer of RJR-Nabisco had apartments available for the management team, paid exorbitant fees to sports figures to induce them to attend company affairs, and had a fleet of 10 planes and 36 pilots available to fly him and other executives around the United States on official and personal business when the occasion arose.[7]

A CEO can raise expenses above the cost-minimizing amount for a given quantity produced. Let's call the excess of expenses above the cost-minimizing amount expense preference.

> **Expense preference** is the excess of expenses over the level that maximizes the firm's profits.

---

[7] Bryan Burrough and John Helyar, *Barbarians at the Gate* (New York: Harper and Row, 1990), pp. 92–96.

Ex Post Settling Up

The board of directors has a fiduciary duty to protect the interests of the owners of the firm. Usually, it cannot prevent expense preference of the manager, but it can make the manager pay for the expense preference. The board can adopt a policy of tying the CEO's compensation to expense preference. Periodically, it evaluates and settles up with the manager. For example, the board of directors could pay the manager a base salary and at the end of the year determine a bonus based on the results for the year. It might compare the cost performance of different-sized firms in the industry or in the economy and estimate how the manager's policies inflate costs. If the manager raises costs by indulging his or her tastes, the board reduces total compensation by reducing the bonus. **Ex post settling up** means that the board reduces compensation dollar for dollar for the increase in cost.[8] In this way an active, sophisticated board of directors can adopt a policy that makes the manager pay for any increase in expense preference.

A simple one-period model demonstrates how a manager maximizes utility by selecting a market basket of expense preference and compensation. Let's assume the board of directors sets the manager's compensation at C^* with the expectation that the manager will maximize profits. If the board later finds that the manager indulged her expense preference and did not maximize profits, it reduces the manager's compensation dollar for dollar with the increase in expense preference. In Figure 11-1 line aa is the manager's budget constraint between compensation and expense preference. The slope of aa is -1 because the compensation of the manager decreases by \$1 for every \$1 increase in expense preference.

To determine what combination of expense preference and compensation maximizes the manager's utility, you need to consider the manager's utility function. Assume the utility of the manager increases when either compensation or expense preference increases. Expense preference includes the excess expenditure above the expenditure that a profit-maximizing firm incurs for such items as thick carpets for the office, a large supporting staff, a large fleet of company planes, hiring more associates from the manager's fraternity or sorority, etc. Figure 11-1 shows several indifference curves of the manager. The manager maximizes utility at point A where the indifference curve U_1 is tangent to aa and expense preference is E' while managerial compensation is C'. The manager prefers the combination of C' and E' to C^* and no expense preference because his utility is only U_0. So, the manager chooses E', and the board matches the increase in expense preference by lowering managerial compensation from C^* to C'. The manager, not the shareholders of the firm, pays for the expense preference.

This analysis assumes that the board of directors is an independent body, has sufficient information, and is capable of an unbiased evaluation of CEO performance, but this is not always the case. The CEO often has a say in the makeup of the board, can subtly influence board members, and can shift business to the companies which the members of the board represent. Also, the board may have considerable difficulty observing and verifying whether the costs of the firm are

---

[8] Eugene Fama, "Agency Problems and the Theory of the Firm," *Journal of Political Economy* 88 (April 1980), pp. 288–307.

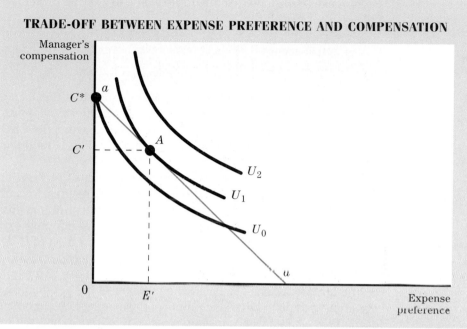

Figure 11-1   The manager's utility depends on compensation and expense preference. The board determines the manager's compensation so that it falls by a dollar for every dollar increase in expense preference. Line *aa* shows the manager's budget constraint and has a slope of −1. The manager maximizes utility when the slope of his indifference curve equals the slope of *aa*. He indulges in expense preference of E' and receives a lower compensation of C'. The manager would receive C^* if he maximized profits, but his utility would be only U_0. The manager pays for indulging his tastes by receiving lower compensation.

unusually high when it has neither the expertise nor the information to monitor the many activities of the company. Remember, evaluation of a CEO's performance is more of an art than a science where it is difficult to distinguish between expenditures that are expense preference and those that aid the firm in maximizing profits. Is a posh office an expense preference or a necessary expense to impress clients? Often, the board of directors lacks the information needed to make the necessary adjustments to the manager's compensation to offset increases in expense preference. It is more likely to act only when there are gross deviations from expected conduct.

11-4   THE PRINCIPAL-AGENT RELATIONSHIP AND OWNERSHIP STRUCTURE

The manager is the agent and the shareholders are the principals in a corporation. Often the principals cannot monitor the actions of the agent perfectly. When the agent makes decisions that affect the well-being of the principal, there is a principal-agent relationship.

> A principal-agent relationship exists whenever an agent makes decisions that affect the well-being of the principal.

In analyzing managerial behavior, we assumed that the manager did not supply any capital to the firm. In other words, management was separate from the owners of the firm. How does managerial behavior change when the CEO is also an owner of the firm? We can investigate this situation by slightly modifying the analysis of expense preference.

A sole owner of the firm holds the residual rights to the profits or losses of the firm. She receives any residual profit or incurs any residual loss. When the manager is the sole owner, she makes a tradeoff between the profits of the firm and expense preference instead of a tradeoff between compensation and expense preference. Assume the manager-owner would receive compensation of C^* if hired by another firm in the same capacity.

In Figure 11-2 total profits are on the vertical axis and expense preference is on the horizontal axis.[9] Because the manager is the residual owner, any expense preference simply reduces the profits of the manager-owner dollar for dollar. Costs of the firm are higher because of expense preference, and the owner's profits are lower. In Figure 11-2 line aa shows the tradeoff between profits and expense preference. The owner's indifference curve U_1 is tangent to aa at point A, and her utility is maximized when profits are π' and expense preference is E'. Here again, the owner who indulges her tastes pays for that indulgence through lower profits.

Figures 11-1 and 11-2 represent two extremes of owner or management types. In both instances it is the owner or the manager who pays for expense preference. The more relevant case is where the manager owns a fraction of the total shares and the board of directors uses ex post settling up to monitor management. In a large company the management team owns only a small fraction of the firm. As the share of ownership of the firm declines, the behavior of the manager changes.

Suppose the sole owner-manager sells $1 - \beta$ of the ownership claims on profits and retains a share β of any profits. β represents the manager's share of the rights to the profits of the firm. For example, she might sell the rights to 30 percent of the profits to outsiders and retain the remaining 70 percent.

If outsiders purchase 30 percent of the rights to profits, how much will they be willing to pay? To answer this question, let's reconsider Figure 11-2. When the manager is the sole owner of the firm, the profits of the firm are π'. It seems reasonable enough to say that outsiders will receive 30 percent of π'. However, this fails to take into account how a change from full to partial ownership affects the behavior of the manager. After selling 30 percent of the rights, she faces a different tradeoff between profits and expense preference than when she was the

---

[9] This section borrows from Michael C. Jensen and William H. Meckling, "Theory of the Firm: Managerial Behavior, Agency Costs and Ownership Structure," *Journal of Financial Economics* 3 (1976), pp. 305–60.

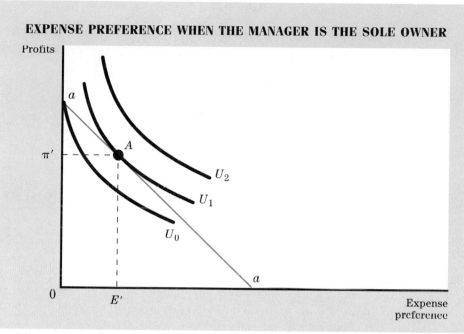

EXPENSE PREFERENCE WHEN THE MANAGER IS THE SOLE OWNER

Figure 11-2   When the manager is the sole owner of the firm, she can trade a dollar of firm profits for a dollar of expense preference along the budget line *aa*. The owner-manager maximizes utility at point *A* where the slope of the indifference curve U_1 equals -1. At point *A* expense preference is E' and profits are π'.

sole owner. Before outsiders purchase the rights, a $1 increase in expense preference costs the owner-manager $1 in profits. Now, she can indulge in expense preference of $1 and lose only 70 cents in profits since the new owners collectively suffer a loss of the other 30 cents. The partial owner-manager no longer faces a dollar-for-dollar tradeoff between expense preference and profits. This means that the relative cost of increasing expense preference declines for a partial owner. Therefore, a partial owner-manager behaves differently from a full owner by increasing expense preference and decreasing the profits of the firm by more than a sole owner would.

> A manager consumes more expense preference as the share of ownership declines.

If the new owners correctly anticipate the increase in expense preference, they will pay only 30 percent of π'' in Figure 11-3, where π'' is the profit of the firm after expense preference increases to E''. As a result, a reduction in the share of ownership moves the owner along the budget constraint *aa* from point *A* to a point like *B* in Figure 11-3. A consequence of dispersed ownership is that total profit declines. Two conditions must be satisfied if the manager maximizes utility. First,

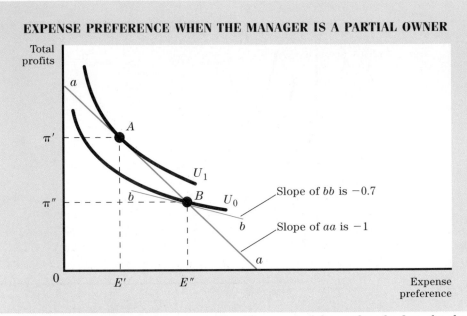

EXPENSE PREFERENCE WHEN THE MANAGER IS A PARTIAL OWNER

Figure 11-3   When the manager retains 70 percent of the profits of a firm, the slope of her budget constraint bb is -0.7. The manager maximizes utility by selecting E'' for expense preference and receives π'' in profits at point B. She increases expense preference as her ownership share decreases.

she must be on aa, which describes the firm's tradeoff between profit and expense preference, and second, she must maximize her utility so that the slope of her budget constraint equals the slope of her utility function.

Both conditions are satisfied at point B. The manager's budget line bb has a slope of -0.7 and is tangent to indifference curve U_0. At point B the slope of her indifference curve is -0.7, and her budget constraint bb is tangent to this indifference curve. The manager's utility at point B is U_0, expense preference is E'', and her profits from the sale of the shares and from the remaining shares are π''. Since bb intersects aa at point B, the manager is simultaneously on aa, which describes the firm's tradeoff between profits and expense preference. Therefore, we conclude that expense preference increases as the ownership share of the manager decreases.

Partial ownership increases expense preference and reduces firm profits by $\pi' - \pi''$. How much should outsiders pay for 30 percent of the rights to profits? They should anticipate that the partial owner-manager will increase expense preference and therefore should pay only 0.3 of π'', not 0.3 of π'.

Let's pause here and state the main conclusion. Greater separation of management from ownership increases expense preference and lowers the profits of the firm. The smaller the fraction of profits owned by the manager, the greater the incentive for the manager to indulge in expense preference. Since the interests of shareholders and managers diverge as managerial ownership share decreases, more careful monitoring of the manager by the board or by large shareholders should be observed as well as the greater use of performance-based bonuses or stock options.

11-5 EXPENSE PREFERENCE UNDER A PROFIT CONSTRAINT

The analysis has been applicable to an unregulated firm whether it is a competitive firm, an oligopolistic firm, or a monopolistic firm. We have assumed that the board of directors can enforce a dollar-for-dollar tradeoff between expense preference and either compensation or profits. Therefore, a manager pays for an increase in expense preference by a reduction in profits (or compensation).

Now let's turn to regulated firms to determine how a profit constraint changes the behavior of managers. You will see how profit regulation can allow a manager to escape paying for an increase in expense preference.[10] Examples of firms that operate under a profit constraint are public utilities, regulated commercial banks, and regulated insurance companies. This analysis can also apply to a private firm that might come under regulatory scrutiny if the firm's profits become too large. A critical assumption of this analysis is that these firms are scrutinized by regulatory agencies if they become too profitable.

How does the behavior of the manager change when the firm operates under a profit constraint? The following discussion assumes that the manager of a regulated monopoly is not an owner but receives a compensation package equal to C^*, her opportunity cost.

First, look at the behavior of the manager when the monopolist is unregulated. As a convenient starting point, assume that the manager's utility is maximized when total compensation is C^* and she does not indulge in any expense preference. This is merely a starting point and is not essential to the subsequent argument. Figure 11-4a shows the profit-maximizing price is P_m and the profit-maximizing quantity is Q_m. The profits of the unregulated monopolist are π^* or are equal to the area $abcd$. Line aa in Figure 11-4b is the budget constraint of the manager between compensation and expense preference. In this example, maximum utility of the manager occurs when compensation is C^*, expense preference is zero, and the firm's profits are π^*. The manager is on the indifference curve U_1. The profit function of the unregulated monopolist is cc in Figure 11-4c, and the firm maximizes profits by producing Q_m units.

The Profit Constraint

What happens when the firm becomes regulated and the regulator places a profit constraint of $\pi' < \pi^*$ on the monopolist? Assume that the regulator has enough

---

[10] This section is based on Armen A. Alchian and Ruben A. Kessel, "Competition, Monopoly and the Pursuit of Money," *Aspects of Labor Economics* (Princeton, N.J.: Princeton University Press, 1962), pp. 157–83.

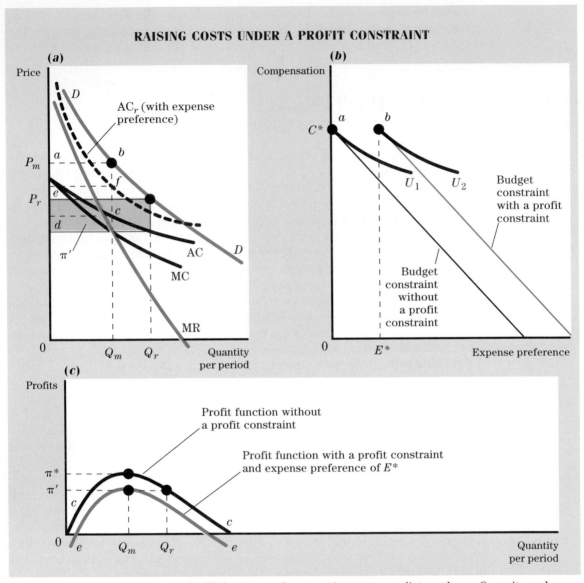

RAISING COSTS UNDER A PROFIT CONSTRAINT

Figure 11-4   Without a profit constraint a monopolist produces Q_m units and earns π^* in (c). The manager receives C^* in compensation and utility of U_1 in (b). With a profit constraint of π' the utility of the manager increases to U_2 when he or she receives the combined package of C^* and E^*. The regulated firm continues to produce Q_m, but the total cost of producing Q_m increases by E^*.

information to impose an effective profit constraint but does not have enough information to know whether the firm is producing any quantity at minimum total cost. If profits exceed the profit constraint π', the regulator will reduce price until profits equal π'. In effect, the regulator imposes a profit cap of π'. How does a profit constraint change the behavior of a manager?

The manager can satisfy the profit constraint in two ways.

- *Option 1.* The manager can lower the price from P_m to P_r and sell more units. Figure 11-4a shows that the price falls to P_r and profits fall to the mandated π', and Figure 11-4c shows that profits decrease to π' when price falls to P_r and output increases to Q_r. The firm is still a cost-efficient producer because it is producing Q_r units at the lowest total cost so that it remains on cc in Figure 11-4c. The manager receives C^* in compensation before and after the firm operates under a profit constraint.

- *Option 2.* The manager can indulge her tastes and allow costs to increase until profits fall to π' while still producing the profit-maximizing quantity Q_m. In Figure 11-4a the firm's average cost function shifts upward and becomes AC_r under a profit constraint. Area $efcd$ measures the increase in expense preference. Figure 11-4b shows that the tradeoff between profits and expense preference becomes bb and expense preference increases to E^*. Figure 11-4c shows that the profit function of the monopolist shifts downward and becomes ee because expense preference increases by E^*. At each quantity the difference between cc and ee is E^*. The increase in expense preference is like an increase in lump sum cost and can take different forms depending on the monitoring ability of the regulator. If the regulator can detect excessive compensation of the manager or the management team more easily than an increase in other types of expenses, the manager's compensation may not rise much, but staff size may increase, offices may be better equipped and furnished, etc.

When a firm operates under a profit constraint, the manager can increase expense preference without paying for the increase by a reduction in compensation. Therefore, the manager's utility increases when expense preference increases to E^*. Figure 11-4b shows that the budget constraint of the manager becomes bb under a profit constraint. Given C^*, expense preference increases to E^* and firm profit falls to π'. The manager moves from indifference curve U_1 to the higher indifference curve U_2. Clearly, the manager prefers option 2 to option 1.

A profit constraint increases expense preference and the utility of the manager.

With a profit constraint the cost of being inefficient decreases. The management of the firm has less incentive to operate the firm efficiently, and stockholders have less incentive to monitor the performance of the management team. Just what will shareholders gain if they replace the existing management? With the current management, the profits of the firm equal the profit constraint of π'. If a new management team operates the firm more efficiently, the firm will have to produce

Q_r and sell the larger quantity at a lower price so that total profit is still π'. Shareholders cannot benefit from a change in management. Therefore, a profit constraint reduces the incentive of shareholders or raiders to monitor the practices of management. The fundamental problem with a profit constraint is that current shareholders or outsiders can no longer benefit by penalizing wasteful management practices. Therefore, these practices will receive less scrutiny, and the firm will no longer minimize costs. A common criticism of regulated firms is that they are run inefficiently, have inflated cost structures, and are less demanding companies to work for.

A profit constraint raises the total compensation package of the current management group. Without a profit constraint the manager receives C^* and no expense preference. With a profit constraint she still receives C^* in compensation and increased utility because expense preference increases from zero to E^*. The utility of the manager is now higher than it would be if she managed a company in an unregulated industry. The manager of the regulated firm now holds a more desirable position.[11] Managers with the same qualifications in other industries receive only C^* in compensation and no expense preference. Yet, shareholders of the regulated firm have no incentive to reduce the manager's compensation or to replace the manager even if they could.

Deregulation and Import Competition

A profit constraint dulls the incentive to take over a regulated firm and to increase its efficiency. The theory predicts that firms operating under a profit constraint are less likely to be targeted for a merger or takeover. Not only will it be difficult to increase profits, but any takeover of a regulated firm must submit to regulatory scrutiny and receive regulatory approval.

However, the story changes when the government deregulates the firm. Even if deregulation is not accompanied by the entry of domestic and foreign competitors, the firm is subject to attack by raiders because its costs are not minimized. The problems of a deregulated firm are magnified when the entry of competitors forces price to fall and the market share of the deregulated firm to decline. In either case the profit function of the firm shifts downward because the entry of competitors reduces prices and the market share of the recently deregulated firm. Before deregulation, the profit function of the firm is *ee* in Figure 11-5 where the effective profit constraint is π'. As noted above, the regulated firm satisifes the profit constraint by increasing expense preference to E^*.

With deregulation, new firms enter the industry, prices fall, and the profit function of the formerly regulated firm shifts downward. Suppose the profit function shifts downward and becomes *ff* in Figure 11-5. Maximum profits are now

---

[11] Because others would like to hold the position, the existing management team will have to put obstacles in the path of would-be managers. The existing management can protect its position by making it more difficult for would-be managers to obtain control of the firm by owning enough stock so that a hostile takeover will not succeed.

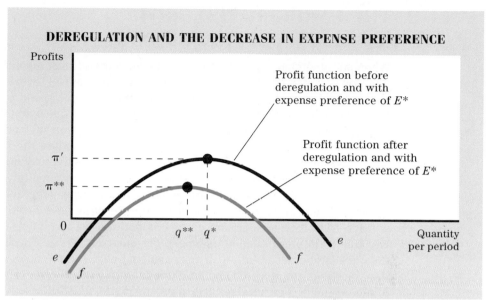

DEREGULATION AND THE DECREASE IN EXPENSE PREFERENCE

Figure 11-5   With deregulation new firms enter the industry and price falls. The profit function of the deregulated firm shifts downward, and becomes *ff*. Maximum profits decline and are π^{**} when the firm produces q^{**} units. The profit constraint of π' is no longer binding. A capital gain can be realized if the existing or a new management reduces expense preference below E^*.

only π^{**} and are less than π'. The profit constraint is no longer binding. Now, management practices come under scrutiny and attack. Total profits have declined, and dissident shareholders complain that the firm is being run inefficiently. If management responds by eliminating expense preference, profits will increase and the stock price of the company will increase.

What kind of reaction can be expected from the management? It might recognize the changed circumstances, accept the inevitable, and adjust to deregulation. Yet, evidence suggests that the existing management frequently does not adapt to these changes. Just why it often fails to respond is not fully understood by researchers. One explanation is that it has developed specialized skills over the years in negotiating with regulators and in providing service to customers, not in developing and introducing new products and in keeping costs down. The existing management has skills and abilities that are more suitable for a protected regulatory environment. It appears that some managements find the transition difficult to make and are incapable of restructuring their companies. The same puzzling behavior can occur when a successful unregulated firm suddenly faces import competition and must reduce the scale of operations. Some managements that are successful in an expanding market appear incapable of changing gears and making the difficult decision to reduce the size of the firm and to lower costs. These are the companies that are most subject to hostile takeovers.

11-6 THE UNREGULATED FIRM AND EXPENSE PREFERENCE

When an unregulated firm does not minimize costs, it must mean that the internal monitor is ineffective and product competition is relatively weak. A takeover attempt indicates that internal monitors are not functioning and outsiders believe that lower costs and higher profits are possible. A failed takeover attempt indicates that management has strong allies and cannot be displaced at low cost.

Often management policies receive less scrutiny when the firm manages to perform on par with other firms in the industry although it may not be maximizing profits. These policies are examined more closely when a major change occurs—such as a reduction in demand or the entry of new firms—that reduces the profitability of the firm. In some industries domestic firms have faced increased competition from foreign suppliers. Price competition was so intense that firms with enviable profit performance unexpectedly incurred losses. These losses focused greater shareholder attention on management policies. Shareholders began to question the size of the research and development program, the compensation packages of management, new product decisions, the deployment of assets, and so on.

The case of Cummins Engine Company aptly illustrates these issues.

APPLICATION 11-2

Cummins Engine Company[12]

Cummins Engine Company, founded in 1919, is a major American manufacturer of high-quality diesel engines for heavy-duty trucks. Historically, the company has supported an extensive research and development program. In 1979 it could report 43 consecutive years of profits, a proud achievement.

Cummins Engine has a history of remarkable public service. The company has sponsored or subsidized many public activities in Columbus, Indiana, the home of its headquarters. For many years it has paid recognized architects to design all public buildings in Columbus. It has built homeless shelters, financed drug counseling programs in local schools, and sent engines and generators to flood victims in South Carolina in 1989. It helped build a school in Brazil near its new factory. Henry Schacht, Cummins' chairman, says the company's goal is "being fair and honest and doing what is right even when it is not to our immediate benefit."

Most companies do not participate in these types of activities, but such activities can be consistent with profit maximization if the company creates goodwill with local and state governments. So, we cannot decisively conclude that the firm is not engaging in profit-maximizing activities just because it performs a public service.

---

[12] Based on Robert Johnson, "With Its Spirit Shaken but Unbent, Cummins Shows Decade's Scars," *The Wall Street Journal*, December 13, 1989; and Alison Leigh Cowan, "Cummins Thwarts Latest Threat," *New York Times*, May 11, 1990.

After years of relative prosperity, the decade of the 1980s was not kind to Cummins Engine Company. Besides a deep recession, competition from foreign suppliers heated up when Nissan Motor Company entered the U.S. market and offered engines at a substantial price discount. Prices fell. Cummins cut prices to maintain its market share and sustained losses. Still, the firm had to announce layoffs in 1983. The company continued to spend lavishly for R&D, about 5 percent of sales, and for its charity programs even at the expense of short-run profits. Among the Fortune 500 firms only 95 spend more on charity than Cummins does.

Cummins became a takeover target when Hanson PLC, a British conglomerate, acquired 8.8 percent of the stock in the fall of 1988. The takeover attempt suggests that the internal monitor was not functioning in this case. Fortunately for Cummins, it had a friend. The J. Irwin Miller family of Columbus, which had helped found Cummins, bought Hanson's stock for $72 million and returned it to the company in exchange for a package of high-yield securities.

Shortly afterward, Industrial Equity purchased 14.9 percent of the stock but in May 1990 agreed to end its battle with Cummins. It abandoned its efforts to obtain a seat on the board and agreed not to purchase more shares for 10 years. Some analysts speculated that Industrial Equity decided to become a passive shareholder because of the hostile attitude toward takeovers at the federal and state levels. Commenting on the management at Cummins Engine, Robert G. Sutherland, president of Industrial Equity, said, "We got tired of it. They're deeply entrenched. Shareholders should be concerned." In this example, the external monitor did not succeed in displacing management.

11-7 HOW THE MARKET FOR CORPORATE CONTROL FUNCTIONS

Although all monitors exert control over management performance, they are not all equally cost effective. As noted earlier, the capital market is a cumbersome and costly disciplinary mechanism. Therefore, we might expect it to be a last-resort monitor. If internal monitoring is less costly to apply, that is, more effective, then external monitors should play a minor role. Yet, evidence from the 1970s and 1980s indicates that external monitors played an important role in forcing managements to maximize profits and in replacing managements that did not. The role of external monitors increased throughout the 1970s and especially in the 1980s with the acquisition of firms through friendly and hostile takeovers. Therefore, we may infer that internal monitoring was not the cheapest method for monitoring management practices in recent decades. With the growing opposition of states to hostile takeovers that began in the late 1980s, the cost-effectiveness of external monitors has decreased and internal monitors appear to be playing a more active role. Some boards of directors are showing more independence and intervening directly in management practices, and mutual fund managers are now voting less frequently to support management positions. Dissident shareholders are bringing more proxy contests to obtain representation on the board.

The Effectiveness of Internal Monitors

This section documents changes in the performance of internal and external monitors and determines which monitors have functioned to limit deviations from profit maximization. As you read this discussion, recall that studies have already been cited showing that the operating performance of firms improves when ownership changes.

Let's look at the effectiveness of internal monitors over the years. Is there any evidence that they have changed over long periods of time? Researchers have begun to examine the role of internal monitoring only recently, and so we can give only a tentative answer to this question.

Michael Jensen and Kevin Murphy examined this question in an interesting study of the compensation of the chief executive officer in large corporations.[13] They wanted to determine by how much CEO compensation increases when the performance of the firm improves. What reward does the CEO receive for improving firm performance? If the CEO's compensation is very sensitive to the performance of the stock, then he or she has a greater incentive to increase profits and the stock price. These researchers used the annual change in the market value of a company's stock as a measure of firm performance. Total CEO compensation includes salary, bonus, and, when available, the value of stock options. They compared the annual change in total CEO compensation to the change in the market value of the firm. What makes this study particularly interesting is how the pay-performance relationship has changed over time. Jensen and Murphy estimated the sensitivity of managerial compensation to changes in the firm's market value over several decades. Their study indicates whether managerial compensation has become more closely tied to the stock price of the firm over time.

Over the 1974–1986 period, the lifetime wealth of an average chief executive increased on average by just $1.85 for each $1,000 increase in the market value of a large firm and $8.05 for each $1,000 increase in the market value of a small firm. Pay and performance appear to be more closely related in smaller corporations. Although these sums appear to be small, we cannot really tell whether they are large or small without a standard of reference. What is more interesting is the change over time in the pay-performance relationship. First, the researchers looked at the pay-performance of CEOs in the 1930s and then in the 1970s and 1980s. They found that executives in the top quartile of firms on the New York Stock Exchange received a 17.5 cent increase in salary and bonus for each $1,000 increase in market value in the 1930s, but only 1.9 cents in the 1974–1986 period. In other words, the reward for performance has declined over time.

Table 11-2 shows mean CEO compensation (adjusted for inflation), size of firm, mean and standard deviation of the annual change in salary, and bonus for the two periods. It indicates that CEO total salary and bonus have declined after adjusting for inflation, although firm size as measured by market value has more than dou-

[13] Michael Jensen and Kevin J. Murphy, "Performance Pay and Top-Management Incentives," *Journal of Political Economy* 98 (April 1990), pp. 225–64.

Table 11-2   CHANGE IN REAL COMPENSATION OF CEO IN LARGE CORPORATIONS FROM 1934–38 AND 1974–86 (1986 DOLLARS)

	1934–38	1974–86
Mean of CEO salary plus bonus	$813,000	$645,000
Mean market value of firm ($ billions)	1.6	3.4
Mean annual change in salary and bonus	31,900	27,800
Average standard deviation of annual change in salary and bonus	205,000	127,000

Source: Michael Jensen and Kevin J. Murphy, "Performance Pay and Top-Management Incentives," *Journal of Political Economy* 98 (April 1990), p. 256. Reprinted by permission of the University of Chicago Press, copyright 1990 by the University of Chicago. All rights reserved.

bled. This surprising finding contradicts the often heard complaint that CEO compensation has gone through the roof in recent years. Row 4 shows that the change in compensation from year to year is more stable now than in the past. The standard deviation of the annual change in compensation is a measure of dispersion and has been smaller in recent years. These data suggest that the tie between **compensation and firm performance** in large corporations is weaker now than it was in the past.

In a more recent study of executive compensation but covering a shorter period—just the 1970s and 80s—Joskow and Rose find that executive compensation became more sensitive to changes in accounting profit rates and to percentage stock price changes in the 80s relative to the '70s.[14] While the reasons for this change are not completely clear, the change in compensation policies indicates boards of directors are responding to align the interests of shareholders with the interests of managers.

The contention that managerial stake in the firm has declined over time has been questioned by some recent research results. In a recent study Holderness, Kroszner, and Sheehan compared stock ownership in the 1,500 firms listed on major exchanges in 1935 with approximately 5,000 listed firms in 1995.[15] Table 11-3 shows the median and mean percentages of stock ownership held by officers and directors of large firms in 1935 and 1995. The authors found that stock ownership by officers and directors has increased not decreased over this 60-year period. For

[14] Paul L. Joskow and Nancy L. Rose, "CEO Pay and Firm Performance: Dynamics, Asymmetries, and Alternative Performance Measures," Working Paper No. 4976, National Bureau of Economic Research, December 1994.

[15] Clifford G. Holderness, Randall S. Kroszner, and Dennis P. Sheehan, "Were the Good Old Days That Good? The Evolution of Managerial Stock Ownership Since the Great Depression," Working Paper No. 131, Center for the Study of the Economy and the State, University of Chicago, December, 1996.

Table 11-3   CHANGES IN STOCK OWNERSHIP BY OFFICERS OF LARGE FIRMS

	Percentage Ownership by Officers and Directors	
YEAR	MEDIAN	MEAN
1935	6.5%	12.9%
1995	14.4	21.1

Source: Clifford G. Holderness, Randall S. Kroszner, and Dennis P. Sheehan, "Were the Good Old Days That Good? The Evolution of Managerial Stock Ownership Since the Great Depression," Working Paper No. 131, Center for the Study of the Economy and the State, University of Chicago, December 1996.

the representative large listed firm, officer and director ownership of a firm's stock is at least as important, if not more so, now than in the past.

The performance of the board of directors as a monitor of management is mixed. Board members are often insiders, who favor management, or outsiders with too little information or time with which to make informed decisions, or sometimes individuals with financial reasons to side with existing management. This does not mean that boards are only figureheads. Research does show that a higher turnover of CEOs follows poor stock performance. And so the board does dismiss those CEOs that do not produce results. A recent trend to pay board members with the stock of the company reflects a desire to tie compensation of board members to firm performance.

The Effectiveness of External Monitors

After examining the available evidence on internal monitors, we cannot say the data unambiguously indicate that internal monitors have become less effective over time. On the other hand we do have some evidence that external monitors have become more important over time, which does suggest internal monitors have become less effective. A sign of this is the increase in acquisition activity. Acquisitions through friendly or hostile takeovers expanded throughout the 1970s and most of the 1980s. However, takeovers did decline in the early 1990s when state laws have made them more difficult to achieve and the growth of the economy has slowed.

Evidence about Takeovers

Let's summarize some of the better known findings about **takeovers.** The scale of the takeover wave is impressive. Takeovers drastically altered the U.S. economy throughout the 1980s. Economists Andrei Shleifer and Robert W. Vishny report that 143 of the Fortune 500 in 1980 were acquired by another company by 1989 in either a friendly or a hostile takeover. The total value of assets changing hands amounted to $1.3 trillion.[16]

It appears that a disproportionate share of takeovers took place in deregulated industries. Transportation and broadcasting accounted for 20 percent of all mergers and acquisitions from 1981 to 1984, and oil and gas accounted for 26.3 percent.[17] Also, the takeover wave appears to have concentrated on conglomerate firms— firms that produce a variety of products. The birth of many conglomerates occurred in the late 1960s through mergers of specialized independent firms.

Often, the breakup of a conglomerate follows a successful takeover. Parts of the conglomerate are sold off, and the remaining firm is focused on one or a few lines of business. Some researchers consider the takeover wave an antidote for the unsuccessful diversification wave of the late 1960s.

Another finding is that takeovers occur disproportionately in industries that are in decline or where some major change has occurred. The value of the firm has declined because the industry is in decline. It may be that management has failed to reduce the scale of the firm considering the decrease in product prices. Firms in these kinds of industries are subject to takeovers by corporate raiders that specialize in reducing the size of the firm by selling off parts of it.[18]

The Effect of Takeovers on the Stock Performance of Targets and Acquirers

An important question is whether a takeover increases or decreases the value of the combined firm by transferring managerial control from existing management to a new management group. Why should the combination be worth more? Among the reasons are (1) more efficient use of management resources, (2) redeployment of assets for more profitable uses, (3) greater earnings resulting from increases in monopoly power, and (4) greater responsiveness to changing demand and supply conditions. "Synergy" is the all-purpose term used to describe these effects. If there are synergistic effects, the value of the stock of the two firms combined is greater than the sum of the values of the stock of the separate parts.

Several research studies have focused on the magnitude of synergistic gains, and most have reached the same conclusion. The stock price of a target firm increases appreciably with the announcement of a planned takeover, and the stock price of the acquiring firm increases proportionately by much less at the same time. Indeed, in recent years the stock price of the acquirer has not increased significantly and may even have declined modestly. Increasingly, a takeover begins to resemble an auction with many firms entering the bidding for the target. Nevertheless, the total value of the target and the acquiring firms increases. On average, takeovers create wealth.

---

[16] Andrei Shleifer and Robert W. Vishny, "The Takeover Wave of the 1980's," *Science* 249, pp. 745–49.
[17] Gregg A. Jarrell, James Brickley, and Jeffrey M. Netter, "The Market for Corporate Control: The Empirical Evidence Since 1980," *Journal of Economic Perspectives* 2, no. 1, pp. 49–68.
[18] Andrei Shleifer and Robert W. Vishny, "Value Maximization and the Acquisition Process," *Journal of Economic Literature* 2 (Winter 1988), pp. 7–20.

**Table 11-4   MEAN PERCENTAGE CHANGE IN STOCK PRICE
IN 236 SUCCESSFUL TENDER OFFERS, 1963–84**

	Period			All Contests
	7/63–6/68	7/68–12/80	1/81–12/84	7/63–12/84
Target	18.9	35.3	35.3	31.8
Acquirer	4.1	1.3	−2.9	1.0
Combination	7.8	7.1	8.0	7.4
Number of contests	51	133	52	236

Source: Michael Bradley, Anand Desai, and E. Han Kim, "Synergistic Gains from Corporate Acquisitions and Their Division between the Stockholders of Target and Acquiring Firms," *Journal of Financial Economics*, May 1988, p. 11. Reprinted with permission of Elsevier Sequoia, Lausanne, Switzerland, publishers of *Journal of Financial Economics.*

Table 11-4 shows the mean percentage change in the stock price of the target, the acquiring firm, and the combination following the announcement of 236 successful tender offers between 1963 and 1984. The last column shows that the stock price of a target firm increases on average by 31.8 percent on announcement of a tender offer after controlling for other factors. The stock price of a typical acquirer increases by only 1.0 percent, and the combined revaluation increases by an average of 7.4 percent. The reason the combined percentage revaluation is closer to 1 percent and not 31.8 percent is that the acquirer was typically larger than the target.

The results for the subperiods are also of interest. From 1963 to 1968, there was little government regulation of tender offers. In 1968 Congress passed the Williams Amendment that brought tender offers under the purview of the Securities and Exchange Commission. Also, state anti-takeover acts had been passed in 36 states by 1978, which had the effect of lengthening the takeover process. It appears that the effect of greater government scrutiny was to lower the return to the acquirer. The last period was affected by the Reagan administration's more relaxed attitude toward takeovers and the development of management defenses against them. The mean return to acquirers has decreased over time, while the mean return to targets has increased.

The principal conclusion is that there are synergistic gains from takeovers. The market value of the two firms is higher after the proposed takeover is announced than before. The owners of acquired firms appear to benefit more than the owners of the acquiring firms. Shleifer and Vishny interpret this as evidence of transferring resources from less able managers to more able managers.

In summary, the market for corporate control is an intricate one with many monitors at work. Economists often simply assume that firms maximize profits without stopping to justify this assumption. In this chapter we have shown how external and internal monitors discipline managements who depart from maximizing profits. This does not mean that firms always maximize profits. However, the discipline of external and internal monitors places limits on these deviations from profit-maximizing behavior.

SUMMARY

▪ Competition in the product and capital market disciplines managers who stray from maximizing profit.

▪ If one shareholder devotes resources to improving management, then all shareholders benefit. The free rider problem lessens the effectiveness of the capital market.

▪ Expense preference is the excess of expenses over the level that maximizes the profits of the firm.

▪ Ex post settling up reduces the compensation of the manager by the amount of expense preference.

▪ A manager consumes more expense pref-

erence when ownership is separate from management.

▪ A profit constraint on a firm increases expense preference and the utility of the manager.

▪ The compensation of executives appears to be less closely related to firm performance over time, although this trend may have been reversed recently.

▪ Two internal monitors of management are concentrated share ownership and the board of directors.

▪ The total value of a target and an acquirer increases on average with the announcement of a takeover.

KEY TERMS

external and internal monitors
capital market
free rider problem and the tender offer
ex post settling up
market for corporate control
takeovers

product market
tender offer
expense preference
expense preference under profit constraint
compensation and firm performance
stock performance of targets and acquirers

REVIEW QUESTIONS

1. Explain the difference between an external and an internal monitor of a firm.

2. Does the diversification of stock holding through the purchase of mutual funds mean that an individual shareholder has little incentive to monitor management practices?

3. Pension funds have grown enormously over time. Would you expect pension fund managers to be effective monitors of firms? Explain why or why not.

4. Explain why you would or would not expect the capital market to be an effective monitor of management behavior.

5. What arguments would you make to suggest that internal monitors have become either less or more effective over time?

6. Explain why expense preference increases as the manager's share of ownership declines.

7. A profit constraint exists in every competi-

tive market. Therefore, competitive firms do not minimize the cost of producing any

EXERCISES

1. In a noncompetitive market managers can lead a quieter life by earning profits but not necessarily maximizing profits. What conditions must exist for this statement to be true?
2. The court system in Russia does not protect investors as extensively as does the court system in the United States. What does this imply about the financing of firms in the new Russian Republic?
3. The current profits of a partnership with two equal-share owner-managers equal π. Suppose one owner-manager decides to buy out the other. Would you expect the profits of the firm to change after the other partner leaves the firm? Explain.
4. During a recession a firm operating under a profit constraint becomes a more efficient producer. Use graphs to show why a demand reduction during a recession affects the behavior of a firm operating under a profit constraint.
5. Assume a private firm is not regulated.

rate of output. Explain why you agree or disagree with this statement.

However, the firm believes its profits will be regulated if they become too high. Would you expect this firm to produce each rate of output at the lowest total cost?
6. Suppose a regulator suspects a firm is not producing output at minimum cost. What benefits would accrue to the firm and the regulator if the regulator commits to a fixed regulated price over a certain number of years?
7. If a CEO engages in expense preference, he or she must pay for it. Explain what this statement means. Under what conditions is it true and when is it not true?
8. A recent study found that those domestic firms in an industry that also sold their products in global markets had lower long-run average cost functions than the firms that only sold in the domestic market. The study concluded that the discipline of international competition is required to make firms produce more efficiently. Explain why you agree or disagree with this conclusion.

PART V

PRICING: PRACTICES AND POLICIES

■ **Chapter 12**
Price Discrimination

■ **Chapter 13**
The Free Rider Problem and
Pricing

■ **Chapter 14**
Market Behavior with Asymmetric
Information

■ **Chapter 15**
Pricing under Uncertainty

CHAPTER 12

PRICE DISCRIMINATION

■ 12-1 Revenue Enhancement: The Goal of Price Discrimination

■ 12-2 First-Degree (Perfect) Price Discrimination

■ 12-3 Second-Degree Price Discrimination

■ 12-4 Third-Degree Price Discriminaiton

Methods of Grouping Consumers: Examples

Finding the Optimal Pricing Policy for a Given Total Quantity

Price Elasticity and Pricing Strategy

Application 12-1: Universities Are Learning More about Differences in the Price Elasticity of Demand of Their Students

Reconsideration of the Examples

Finding the Optimum Output to Produce and Prices to Charge

Application 12-2: Should a Firm Expand into the European Market?

Preventing Arbitrage

Application 12-3: Pricing a Renault in Belgium and in England

The Difference between Second- and Third-Degree Price Discrimination

■ 12-5 Bundling

■ 12-6 Two-Part Tariffs

Setting the Fixed Fee and Per Unit Price for Identical Consumers

Setting the Fixed Fee and Per Unit Price for Different Types of Consumers

Using Two-Part Tariffs to Price Consumer Capital Goods

Application 12-4: Why Did IBM and Xerox Lease Rather Than Sell Their Machines?

■ Summary

■ Key Terms

■ Review Questions

■ Exercises

Our models of monopoly and oligopoly pricing assumed that all consumers pay the same price for each unit of a product. Consequently, the models do not explain why coach passengers on the same plane pay substantially different prices for a seat or why some students in your class pay a lower net tuition than do others. In this chapter we study price discrimination—charging different prices for the same product.

The motivation for price discrimination cannot be understood without understanding consumer surplus. Recall that in Chapter 3 we introduced the concept of *consumer surplus*—the difference between what a consumer is willing to pay for a given quantity of a good and the amount he does pay. When there is a gap between the marginal value to the consumer and the price charged for that unit, we say that the consumer receives a surplus. The purpose of price discrimination is to reduce consumer surplus by making consumers pay more for each unit. What you will learn in this chapter is why firms want to charge different prices to different customers, the conditions under which they can do so, and the means by which they do it.

12-1　REVENUE ENHANCEMENT: THE GOAL OF PRICE DISCRIMINATION

There are some markets where identical items sell for different prices.[1] For example, a new car dealership may sell 75 new automobiles a week of the same make. Some consumers pay lower prices than others for the same automobile, depending on their knowledge of market prices and on their bargaining skills.[2] Each student in your class listens to the same lectures, reads the same textbook, and pays the same tuition. However, some receive fellowships and other aid and others do not, so the net tuition paid by students differs. These are just some of the types of pricing policies considered in this chapter.

This investigation assumes that the firm is a price maker. Just what does a price-making firm achieve by charging different prices? We have defined *marginal value* as the most that consumers would pay for each unit of a good. At the risk of repetition, let's state again that consumer surplus is the difference between the maximum that the consumer would pay to obtain a given quantity of a good and

---

[1] For a comprehensive and more advanced treatment of price discrimination the interested reader may consult Louis Phlips, *The Economics of Price Discrimination* (Cambridge: Cambridge University Press, 1983); and Dennis Carlton and Jeffrey M. Perloff, *Modern Industrial Organization* (Glenview, Ill.: Scott, Foresman/Little, Brown, 1990), chaps. 14 and 15.

[2] Not all price differences are due to price discrimination. Many differences are a result of differences in costs. When a firm charges a higher price for delivering nails to a distant customer, the nails are the same but the product is not. The nails sold to nearby consumers are a different product from the nails sold at a distant location. In a competitive industry a firm will charge a higher price to a consumer located at a distance than to one nearby because of the cost of transportation. The difference in price equals the cost of transportation between the distant and the nearby consumers. Another caveat is worth emphasizing: There is a danger of equating the absence of price differences with an absence of price discrimination. If a supplier sells lumber at the same delivered price throughout the United States when there are significant transportation costs, the seller is engaging in price discrimination. In this case the firm discriminates in favor of the more distant buyers.

the actual amount he pays. When the marginal value exceeds the price for each unit, the consumer's utility increases by buying each additional unit. Looked at in this light, each unit consumed is then viewed by the buyer as a bargain.

Firms recognize that consumers receive a surplus by purchasing a product and that consumers are often willing to pay more than the market price. In other words, firms know there is a direct line between **consumer surplus and revenue enhancement.** Let's consider a simple example that shows by just how much more a firm's revenues and profits can be increased.

A monopolist's inverse demand function is shown in Table 12-1. Marginal value, or the maximum amount that consumers will pay for successive units, is in column 1, quantity demanded in column 2, total revenue in column 3, and marginal revenue in column 4. As you can see from the table, the most that some consumer is willing to pay for the first unit is $24, and the second unit can be sold for at most $22, and so on. Total cost is in column 5 and increases linearly with quantity, and marginal cost of production equals $14. Column 6 of Table 12-1 shows that a monopolist maximizes profits of $18 by charging a uniform price of $20 for each unit.

Notice that even a monopolist does not collect all of the consumer surplus when charging a uniform monopoly price to all buyers. Consumer surplus equals $24 − $20 = $4 on the first unit and $2 on the second unit. Clearly, the monopolist's profits would increase by $6 if it could charge $24 for the first unit, $22 for the second unit, and $20 for the third unit. Thus, if the monopolist can charge different prices for successive units, the monopolist can raise profits over and above the profits earned by a monopolist that charges a uniform price. By charging the most that consumers are willing to pay for each unit, the monopolist will march down the demand curve by charging successively lower prices until price equals marginal cost. To sell the fourth unit, it charges $18, for the fifth unit, it charges $16, and so

Table 12-1   INCREASING REVENUE AND PROFITS THROUGH PRICE DISCRIMINATION

MARGINAL VALUE (PRICE) (1)	QUANTITY DEMANDED (2)	REVENUE (3)	MARGINAL REVENUE (4)	COSTS (5)	PROFITS WITH MONOPOLY PRICE (6)	PROFITS WITH PRICE DISCRIMINATION (7)
$24	1	$24	$24	$14	$10	$10
22	2	44	20	28	16	18
20	3	60	16	42	**18**	24
18	4	72	12	56	16	28
16	5	80	8	70	10	30
14	6	84	4	84	0	**30**
12	7	84	0	98	−14	28

on. If it sets prices equal to the respective marginal values, the marginal revenue of each successive unit becomes the price of the product. Revenue increases by $18 when the fourth unit is sold and by $16 when the fifth unit is sold. With perfect price discrimination a monopolist will produce a quantity where *price equals marginal cost* of $14. Table 12-1 shows that the monopolist will sell six and not more than six units because price would be less than marginal cost and profits would fall.

In column 7 we show total profit for each quantity sold when the firm engages in price discrimination. The marginal value of the first unit is $24 so profit equals $10 ($24 − $14). Profits from the sale of the second unit equal $8 ($22 − $14). So the total profit on the first two units equals $18. Proceeding in this manner we find that total profit equals $30, a 67 percent increase over the profits of $18 with a uniform price, when the monopolist produces 6 units and sets the price of successive units equal to the marginal value of the unit.

We can offer a different interpretation to the monopolist's price discrimination solution. We can think of the monopolist as setting a uniform price equal to marginal cost of $14 for each unit demanded and then imposing a declining surcharge for successive units. Since the price of $14 equals the marginal cost of production, the monopolist's profits come from the surcharges. The surcharge for the first unit is $10 so that the consumer who buys the first unit pays $24, her marginal value. The surcharge for the second unit is $8 and so on. The sum of the surcharges for six units equals consumer surplus and the monopolist's profits.

This is shown in Figure 12-1. The monopolist sets a base price equal to marginal cost of $14. Consumers demand a total of six units at this price. The monopolist extracts consumer surplus by imposing a declining surcharge. The shaded area equals consumer surplus and is now appropriated by the monopolist as profit.

Since a firm's revenue and profit can be increased by charging different prices to a consumer or to different consumers, let's look at the different ways revenue can be increased by reducing consumer surplus. How much of an increase in revenue a monopolist can obtain depends on the information it has about the consumer. As a result, there are **three types of price discrimination**—first-, second-, and third-degree—which are discussed in the following three sections.

12-2   FIRST-DEGREE (PERFECT) PRICE DISCRIMINATION

With first-degree price discrimination a firm captures all of a consumer's surplus because it has detailed information about how much the consumer is willing to pay for each unit. In Figure 12-2 the buyer is willing to pay P_1 for the first unit, P_2 for the second unit, and so on, and these are the prices the firm charges for successive units. With perfect price discrimination the firm captures all the consumer surplus and achieves maximum revenue enhancement.

As you might suspect, first-degree price discrimination requires such detailed information about consumers that it is seldom practiced. To capture all the consumer surplus, the company must know the demand curve of each buyer. Each

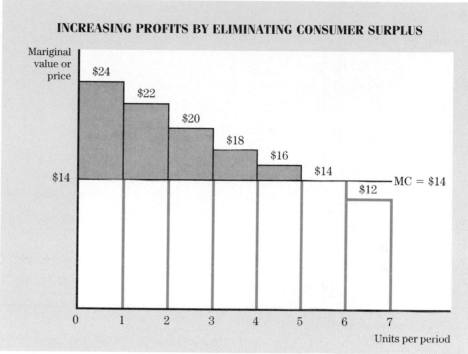

INCREASING PROFITS BY ELIMINATING CONSUMER SURPLUS

Figure 12-1   The marginal value of successive units declines. When the per unit price is $14, consumers demand 6 units. A monopolist maximizes profits by selling 6 units and charging a declining surcharge. Total profits equal consumer surplus, the shaded area. By charging a per unit price of $14 and a declining surcharge, the firm's profits increase to $30.

consumer has an incentive to feign disinterest in the firm's product or to camouflage information about his or her true demand function in hopes of retaining some consumer surplus. An example that approximates but does not replicate perfect price discrimination is the haggling between a consumer and a new car dealer. The salesperson sizes up the customer and attempts to find out what price he or she is willing to pay before deciding whether to quote the sticker price or to cut below the list price and eat into the dealer's profit margin. Acquiring detailed information about consumer demand is so costly that it prevents firms from practicing perfect price discrimination. Just imagine the insurmountable problems that would face Disney World if it had to identify the individual demand functions of the diverse group of visitors attending its entertainment parks.

12-3   SECOND-DEGREE PRICE DISCRIMINATION

With second-degree price discrimination the firm sets a price schedule, a limited number of prices for different blocks of units. In Figure 12-3 the firm charges a

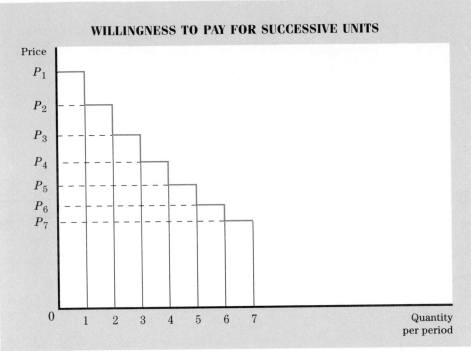

Figure 12-2   Under first-degree price discrimination, the price equals the willingness to pay for successive units. The consumer is willing to pay at most P_1 for the first unit, P_2 for the second unit, and so on. The firm captures all the consumer surplus in the form of higher profits. Firms seldom have the necessary information to implement first-degree price discrimination and to capture all the consumer surplus.

high per unit price of P_1 to those consumers who purchase Q_1 or fewer units, P_2 to those consumers who purchase between Q_1 and Q_2 units, and P_3 for consumers who purchase larger quantities, between Q_2 and Q_3.

We can interpret block pricing in another way. The firm announces a block price schedule where price depends on the quantity consumed. Each consumer then *self-selects* into one of the blocks depending on which block maximizes the consumer's surplus. Under second-degree price discrimination the firm does not have enough information to assign each consumer to a particular block. Consequently, in setting the block prices, the company must take into account some very complicated substitutions made by consumers who will shift from one block to another if the price of a nearby block is changed. For example, if the firm increases P_3, some consumers who buy more than Q_2 units at the lower price will reduce their quantity demanded to less than Q_2 because the consumer surplus of buying fewer than Q_2 units is now greater than the consumer surplus from buying more than Q_2 units. With second-degree price discrimination, the firm is unable to appropriate all of the consumer surplus.

For example, as we note below, libraries pay higher prices for professional

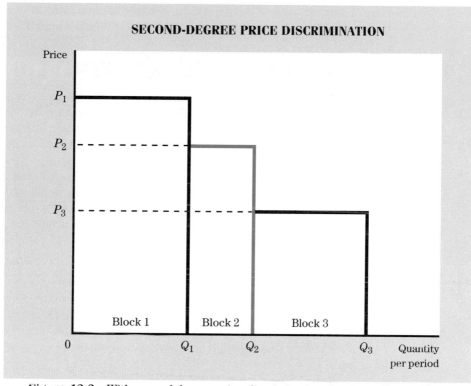

SECOND-DEGREE PRICE DISCRIMINATION

Figure 12-3 With second-degree price discrimination the firm offers a block price function. The first Q_1 units are purchased at a per unit price of P_1. The second block from Q_1 to Q_2 is purchased at a per unit price of P_2, and quantities between Q_2 and Q_3 are purchased at a per unit price of P_3. Second-degree price discrimination yields greater revenue and consumer surplus is smaller compared with a uniform price policy.

journals than do individual subscribers. For *third-degree* price discrimination buyers are separated into two groups, libraries and individuals. The suppliers of journals can separate the libraries from individual subscriptions by the address label. Libraries cannot pretend to be individuals when subscribing. In contrast, with second-degree price discrimination, the firm has no way of assigning consumers to a particular block or group. Telephone users or electricity buyers can shift from one block to another and therefore receive a lower or higher rate depending on whether their consumer surplus is higher or lower in one block than in another. This is not possible under third-degree price discrimination.

Regulated public utilities frequently use declining block pricing. The price paid for electricity depends on the quantity consumed per month. There are other examples where the price depends on the quantity purchased. Buying a monthly public transit pass costs less per ride than buying individual tickets. Quantity discounts offer consumers a lower per unit price for a larger quantity and may allow a firm to extract a greater surplus from smaller consumers than from larger ones. However, quantity discounts have other explanations and may be related to the cost savings of serving a consumer who buys larger quantities.

12-4 THIRD-DEGREE PRICE DISCRIMINATION

A price-making firm that practices first-degree and, to a lesser exent, second-degree price discrimination knows something about the buyer's demand function and benefits from this information by charging the consumer different prices. In the third type of price discrimination, the firm has no information on individual demand functions but knows from experience that different groups of consumers have different demand functions. With third-degree price discrimination the price-making firm uses a certain characteristic to divide consumers into groups. Then it picks different prices for the different groups that maximize its profit. With third-degree price discrimination the firm can sort consumers into groups so that most of those who pay a higher price cannot purchase in the lower-priced market.

Methods of Grouping Consumers: Examples

To illustrate some of the characterisics that a price-making firm uses to group consumers, we examine some situations where consumers pay different prices. As you read through the examples, try to identify the differences between different consumer groups to determine how a price-making firm can take advantage of the groupings.

1. The price of a professional journal is lower for an individual subscriber than for a library.

2. If a traveler returns home from a trip on Sunday instead of Saturday, the air fare is lower. Table 12-2 shows coach fares for a round-trip flight with a Wednesday departure and a Saturday or a Sunday return for March 1997. The fare for a round-trip from New York to Los Angeles is in column 2, and the fare for a round-trip from Chicago to San Francisco is in column 3. If you left New York for Los Angeles on Wednesday and returned on Saturday, the round-trip fare was $1,539, or 3.57 times higher than if you returned on Sunday when the round-trip fare was $431. The fare for a round-trip from Chicago to San Francisco with a Saturday return is 4 times that with a Sunday return. Why are coach fares so much higher for a Saturday return than for a Sunday return?

3. Doctors, lawyers, and tax consultants charge different fees to different customers. A doctor may charge me substantially more for an appendix operation than she charges you for the same operation.[3] Yet, we can both walk into a grocery store or dry cleaner and pay the same prices for the same merchandise or for the same cleaning service.

---

[3] For a classic, if dated, analysis of price discrimination in medicine, the reader is encouraged to read Reuben Kessel, "Price Discrimination in Medicine," *Journal of Law and Economics* I (October 1958), pp. 20–53.

Table 12-2 SELECTED ROUND-TRIP AIR FARES, MARCH 1997

DAYS OF THE WEEK (1)	NEW YORK–LOS ANGELES ($) (2)	CHICAGO–SAN FRANCISCO ($) (3)
Leave Wednesday and return on Saturday	1,539	1,511
Leave Wednesday and return on Sunday (nonrefundable)	431	378
Ratio of fare with a Saturday return to fare with a Sunday return	3.57	4.00

4. A child's haircut is less than an adult's haircut.

5. Some movie houses offer student discounts.

6. In many cities senior citizens receive discounts if they show a card when using public transit facilities.

7. Apparel prices are higher at the beginning of the season than at the end. Figure 12-4 shows the percentage of men's dress shirts that are sold on sale and the average percentage markdown of these shirts by month. The percentage of dress shirts that are sold on sale and the percentage reduction in price are lower at the beginning of the spring and summer season (April to June), and at the beginning of the fall and winter season (September through December). Markdowns increase during January and February and in July and August, the traditional sale months. The seasonal pattern for women's apparel is similar and even more pronounced.

8. Tourists usually pay higher prices for jewelry or souvenirs than do long-term residents of a city or town.

These examples illustrate four characteristics that firms use to separate consumers into groups:

- *Time*. Airlines and department stores use time of use or time of purchase to segment consumers. The supersaver rate applies only to flyers who stay over on Saturday. End-of-season shoppers receive discounted prices.

- *Age*. A discount for a child's haircut or a senior citizen's use of public transit depends on the age of the individual.

- *Income*. The income of the individual is the basis for lower medical fees for lower-income patients or for lower movie prices for students.

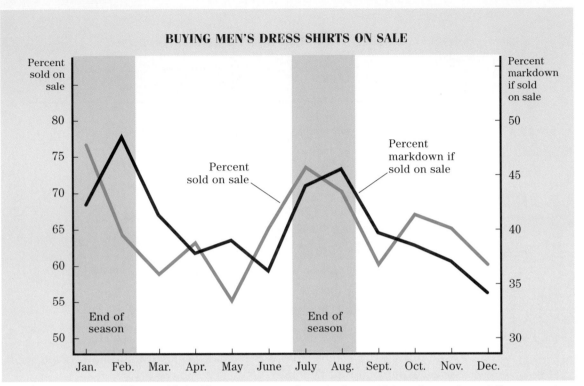

Figure 12-4   The percentage of men's dress shirts put on sale and the percentage markdown if the shirt is put on sale are larger at the end of seasons. [B. Peter Pashigian and Brian Bowen, "Why Are Products Sold on Sale? Explanations of Pricing Regularities," _Quarterly Journal of Economics_, November 1991, p. 1026. Reprinted with permission of Harvard University Press, copyright 1991 by the President and Fellows of Harvard University.]

- _Information._ The amount of information possessed by the consumer is another basis for discrimination. Long-term residents of an area have more information about alternative sellers than tourists do.

Whatever means a price maker uses to segment the market, the underlying goal is to increase profits by lowering consumer surplus. To show how a monopolist discriminates among groups of consumers, we divide the analysis into two parts—one in which the total quantity to be sold is fixed and the monopolist has to determine how much to sell to each group so total revenue is maximized, and another in which the monopolist determines the quantity as well as the allocation of the quantity to each group.

Finding the Optimal Pricing Policy for a Given Total Quantity

In the first part of the analysis the monopolist sorts consumers into two groups using some characteristic of consumers. For example, either an individual or a library subscription is being offered. Consumers in market 1 have a different group demand function than consumers in market 2. To start with the simplest case, assume that the monopolist has already produced Q^* units that it will sell in markets 1 and 2. Because the goods have already been produced, we can ignore the cost of production since it is a sunk cost. The monopolist wants to sell the total quantity in the two markets so as to maximize total revenue, and thereby also maximize profits since all costs are sunk.

Consumers in the two markets have different inverse demand functions. The demand functions in markets 1 and 2 are

$$P_1 = D_1(Q_1) \quad \text{and} \quad P_2 = D_2(Q_2) \qquad \text{(Inverse Demand Function in Markets 1 and 2)} \qquad \text{(12-1)}$$

Given each demand function, the marginal revenue functions in markets 1 and 2 are $MR_1(Q_1)$ and $MR_2(Q_2)$, respectively, where marginal revenue in each market is related to the price and the point price elasticity of demand in that market.

$$MR_1 = P_1\left(1 + \frac{1}{E_1}\right) \quad \text{and} \quad MR_2 = P_2\left(1 + \frac{1}{E_2}\right) \qquad \begin{array}{l}\text{(Marginal Revenue} \\ \text{Functions in} \\ \text{Markets 1 and 2)}\end{array} \qquad \text{(12-2)}$$

Total revenue of the firm is

Total revenue = Revenue from market 1 + Revenue from market 2

$$R = Q_1 D_1(Q_1) + Q_2 D_2(Q_2) \qquad \text{(Total Revenue)} \qquad \text{(12-3)}$$

In addition, the total number of units sold in markets 1 and 2 must equal Q^*. Once the quantity to sell in each market is known, the prices are determined from the market demand functions in equation 12-1. To find the number of units to sell in each market so that total revenue is maximized, the monopolist must decide:

1. Whether to charge a common price or a different price in each market.

2. Which group should get the lower price if the firm charges different prices.

Let's take up the first issue. Should the monopolist charge the same or different prices? If it charges a uniform price of P^*, it sells Q_1^* in market 1 and Q_2^* in market 2, so that $Q^* = Q_1^* + Q_2^*$ (Figure 12-5). Because the demand functions of the two groups differ, marginal revenue from selling the last unit in market 1, MR_1^*, is less than marginal revenue from selling the last unit in market 2, MR_2^*. Because of this difference, total revenue will increase if the firm sells fewer units in market 1 and more units in market 2.

To illustrate why the firm should sell fewer units in market 1 and more units in market 2, consider this numerical example. Suppose all units are currently sold at a uniform price of $100. At this price the point price elasticity of demand is -2 in market 1 and the point price elasticity of demand is -4 in market 2. Demand is therefore more elastic in market 2 than in market 1 ($E_2 = -4$ is less than $E_1 = -2$). Marginal revenue from the last unit sold in market 1 is $P_1[1 + 1/E_1)] = \$100[1 + (1/(-2)] = \$50$. In market 2 marginal revenue from the last unit sold is $P_2[1 + (1/E_2)] = \$100[1 + (1/(-4)] = \$75$. Transferring the last unit from

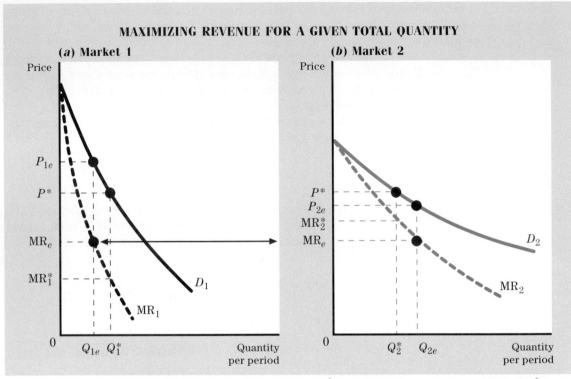

Figure 12-5   At a common price of P^* the marginal revenue in market 1, MR_1^*, is less than the marginal revenue in market 2, MR_2^*. The monopolist can increase total revenue by raising the price in market 1 to P_{1e} and raising marginal revenue to MR_e while lowering the price in market 2 to P_{2e} and lowering marginal revenue to MR_e. Of the Q^* units available for sale, Q_{1e} are sold in market 1 and Q_{2e} are sold in market 2. The firm maximizes total revenue when marginal revenue is the same in both markets.

market 1 to market 2 increases total revenue by $25 because revenue in market 1 decreases by $50 but revenue in market 2 increases by $75. To sell more units in market 2 and fewer units in market 1, the firm lowers the price in market 2 and raises the price in market 1. Total revenue is higher when the monopolist charges different prices rather than a uniform price.

As long as marginal revenue in the two markets differs, total revenue will continue to increase if the firm sells more units by lowering the price in the market with higher marginal revenue and raising the price in the market with lower marginal revenue. Although the prices in the two markets are moving in opposite directions, the difference between marginal revenues is narrowing and the firm always sells Q^* units. At some point the **marginal revenues will be equal.** Marginal revenues equal MR_e in both markets when the firm sells Q_{1e} at a price of P_{1e} in market 1 and Q_{2e} at a price of P_{2e} in market 2. While marginal revenues are now equal, prices are different in the two markets.

Total revenue reaches a maximum when the marginal revenues in the two markets are equal.[4]

$$MR_1(Q_1) = MR_2(Q_2) \quad \text{(Equality of Marginal Revenue in the Two Markets)} \quad (12\text{-}4)$$

> A firm maximizes total revenue from selling a fixed number of units so that marginal revenue is the same in each market.

Price Elasticity and Pricing Strategy

If a monopolist allocates Q^* so that marginal revenue is the same in both markets, which market will have the lower price? Substitute the expression for marginal revenue in each market in equation 12-2 into equation 12-4 to obtain

$$P_1\left(1 + \frac{1}{E_1}\right) = P_2\left(1 + \frac{1}{E_2}\right)$$

After dividing both sides of the equation by P_2 and then by $1 + (1/E_1)$ and simplifying, the equation becomes

$$\frac{P_1}{P_2} = \frac{E_1 E_2 + E_1}{E_1 E_2 + E_2} \quad \text{(Ratio of Prices that Maximize Profits)} \quad (12\text{-}5)$$

Equation 12-5 shows that the ratio of the prices that maximize the firm's profits depends on the two point price elasticities. The numerator and the denominator on the right-hand side of equation 12-5 have a common term, $E_1 E_2$. The product of the two price elasticities is positive since each price elasticity is negative. From $E_1 E_2$ we add a negative number E_1 in the numerator and E_2 in the denominator.

The price elasticity of demand is more elastic in market 2 than in market 1 if $E_1 > E_2$. Because the numerator is greater than the denominator, the right-hand side of equation 12-5 is greater than 1 and P_1 is larger than P_2. If $E_1 = -3$ while $E_2 = -5$, then the right-hand side of equation 12-5 is $(15 - 3)/(15 - 5) = 1.2$.

---

[4] Let $P_1 = D_1(Q_1)$ and $P_2 = D_2(Q_2)$ be the demand functions in the two markets. Suppose the firm has Q^* units to sell, so that $Q_1 + Q_2 = Q^*$. The firm wants to maximize $R = Q_1 D_1(Q_1) + Q_2 D_2(Q_2)$ subject to the condition that $Q_1 + Q_2 = Q^*$. Solve this constraint for Q_2 and substitute the result into the equation for total revenue: $R = Q_1 D_1(Q_1) + (Q^* - Q_1)D_2(Q^* - Q_1)$. The equation is now simply a function of Q_1. Using calculus, we find the first-order condition for a revenue maximum requires

$$\frac{dR}{dQ_1} = Q_1 \frac{dD_1}{dQ_1} + D_1(Q_1) + (Q^* - Q_1)\frac{dD_2}{dQ_2}\frac{dQ_2}{dQ_1} - D_2(Q_2) = 0$$

Because $Q_2 = Q^* - Q_1$, $dQ_2/dQ_1 = -1$, a unit increase in Q_1 must decrease Q_2 by a unit if the total output is Q^*. Therefore,

$$Q_1 \frac{dD_1}{dQ_2} + D_1(Q_1) = Q_2 \frac{dD_2}{dQ_1} + D_2(Q_2)$$

The first two terms on the left-hand side represent marginal revenue in market 1, and the two terms on the right-hand side represent marginal revenue in market 2. A firm maximizes the total revenue from selling a given quantity by making marginal revenue the same in the two markets.

P_1 is 20 percent higher than P_2. In which market segment will the price be lower? Equation 12-5 indicates that the price is lower in the market with the more elastic demand function. A profit-maximizing monopolist charges a lower price to the group with a more elastic demand function at the profit-maximizing price. The intuition behind this result is that a monopolist charges a lower price to the group for which the quantity demanded will decline by proportionally more for a given percentage increase in price. The quantity demanded of this group is more sensitive to a price increase than the quantity demanded of the other group, and so the price paid by its members is lower.

> The profit-maximizing price is lower in the market with the more elastic demand function.

It is clear that a monopolist receives greater revenue by charging different prices if the price elasticities of demand differ, that is, it will maximize revenue by **setting prices based on elasticity of demand.** We can also determine when a monopolist that can engage in price discrimination will not do so. If $E_1 = E_2$ at a common price, the price elasticities in the two markets are the same and equation 12-2 says that marginal revenues in the two markets are equal at the common price; $P_1/P_2 = 1$. Total revenue will fall if the firm charges different prices to the two groups of consumers. So, a monopolist will forsake price discrimination if the price elasticities of demand are the same for the two groups at the uniform profit-maximizing price.

APPLICATION 12-1

Universities Are Learning More about Differences in the Price Elasticity of Demand of Their Students

You want to enroll at your preferred university but you are uncertain about whether the university will accept your application. Should you apply for early admission to demonstrate your commitment to the university? In the past many students in a similar situation would commit to early admission. Lately, it has become less clear that this is a wise choice.

What has changed? More and more admissions officers are being told to allocate student aid so as to maximize net tuition revenue. By varying student aid universities can charge different net prices to their students. The goal is to maximize total net tuition revenue by charging lower tuition to those students with more elastic demand functions. With this goal in mind, universities and colleges across the land are becoming more aware of differences in demand elasticities among applicants and adjusting student aid based on these elasticities. Admissions officers do not want to give aid to students who would attend anyway. So schools seek information that might indicate whether an applicant's demand curve is less rather than more price-elastic. Schools take note of whether an applicant opted for early admission or initiated contact with the school or requested a campus interview or has other sources of income. Some schools believe that applicants exhibiting these behaviors or with these characteristics will enroll even if little or no student aid is offered. If a university receives many applications to its esteemed business school but relatively few to its lesser-known humanities school, the university may give larger student aid awards to humanities applicants and smaller awards to business school applicants to maximize net tuition revenue and achieve a well-rounded student body. Universities and colleges are learning more about differences in the price elasticities of demand of their students.

Reconsideration of the Examples

Price discrimination theory predicts that the group with the more elastic demand function pays a lower price. If we return to the previous examples, can a reasonable case be made that the group paying the lower price has the more elastic demand curve? Would you expect the demand function for individual journal subscriptions to be more elastic than the demand function for library journal subscriptions? Because faculty members and students expect a university library to subscribe to the important journals in each field, many but not all libraries will continue to subscribe if a journal raises the subscription price. On the other hand, proportionally more individual faculty members and graduate students will cancel subscriptions and rely on library holdings if the individual subscription price increases. It appears plausible that the demand function for individual subscriptions is more elastic than the demand function for library subscriptions.

Why is the round-trip fare substantially lower if a traveler returns on Sunday rather than on Saturday? Here the goal is to distinguish between the business traveler and the tourist. The tourist has flexibility in scheduling a flight, whereas the business traveler is eager to report back to the home office, catch up on office work, and rest over the weekend. The business traveler has a less elastic demand function for a Friday return trip than a tourist and finds it more costly to stay over until Sunday. On the other hand, the inconvenience of returning on Sunday or later is less for tourists, who have a more elastic demand function for travel on a particular day of the week. Why do airlines require a Sunday departure rather than a Saturday departure? A plausible answer to this question is that they can more effectively separate the business market from the tourist market by doing so.

At a higher price, lower-income patients are more likely to delay or to put off seeing a physician than higher-income consumers are. And so, the price elasticity of demand appears more elastic for lower- than for higher-income patients.

The demand for children's haircuts is likely to be more elastic than the demand for adults' haircuts. If the price of a child's haircut increases, parents are more likely to cut the child's hair themselves or to visit the barbershop less frequently.

The demand for films by students may be more elastic than the demand by the general public. The lower average income of students or the availability of substitute films at reduced rates on campus could explain why the students' demand function is more elastic.

It is less clear that price discrimination is the motivation for senior citizen discounts. Unlike the general public, senior citizens often do not have access to an automobile, an important substitute for public transit. This suggests that the demand function for senior citizens is less elastic. On the other hand, a fare increase might cause a larger decrease in the quantity demanded because senior citizens do not use public transit to journey to work but for more discretionary purposes. Overall, we cannot conclude that senior citizens have a more elastic demand function for public transit rides. Other hypotheses may better explain senior citizen discounts for public transit.

The prices for men's and women's apparel are higher in October and November, at the beginning of the fall-winter apparel seasons, than in January and February, the end of the fall-winter season. Early in the season buyers demand the latest creations, while late in the season they are less exacting in their demands. It is possible that early buyers have less elastic demands and late buyers have more elastic demands. Price discrimination could be the underlying reason for these long-standing pricing practices but is only one of several hypotheses that could explain this type of pricing pattern. One problem in applying the price discrimination theory is that merchandise sold at the beginning of the season is different from that sold at the end of the season. At the end of the season only the remnants that did not sell earlier remain on the shelves and only a limited selection is available. The second problem is that there are *many* sellers in most retail markets. Later in this chapter, we will discuss the difficulty of engaging in price discrimination when there are many sellers in the market. Chapter 15 considers a demand uncertainty explanation for these pricing practices.

When shopping in a foreign country, tourists have less information about alternative suppliers than the local population does. Because they know of fewer substitute suppliers and have less information about prices, they may have a less elastic demand function. The seller can usually determine if customers are tourists from the questions they ask and how they dress. Firms can then set prices based on the information possessed by the buyer.

Finding the Optimum Output to Produce and Prices to Charge

This section investigates how a monopolist determines the total quantity to produce and the distribution of that quantity between two markets. Before beginning the analysis, you should understand why this section focuses on profits while the last section focused only on revenue. In the last section all costs were sunk. By maximizing revenue, a firm automatically maximized profits. In contrast, production costs are variable in this section because the monopolist determines what quantity to produce.

First, we present an expression for the profits of the firm:

Profits = Revenue in market 1 and market 2 − Cost of production

$$\pi = D_1(Q_1)Q_1 + D_2(Q_2)Q_2 - C_L(Q) \qquad \text{(Total Profits of a Price-} \qquad \textbf{(12-6)}$$
$$\text{Discriminating Monopolist)}$$

In this case, total revenue depends on the units sold in the two markets, and total cost depends on the total number of units produced. The sum of the quantities sold in the two markets must equal total production Q.

$$Q = Q_1 + Q_2 \quad \text{(Total Output)} \tag{12-7}$$

You already know from the previous analysis that the monopolist will allocate total output so that the marginal revenue is the same in both markets. To decide how much to produce, the monopolist increases output until the marginal cost of production is equal to the marginal revenue from selling another unit in either market. To maximize profits, a price-discriminating monopolist equates marginal cost to marginal revenue in *both* markets.[5] The necessary conditions for profit maximization by a price-discriminating monopolist are

$$\text{MR}_1(Q_1) = \text{MC}(Q_1 + Q_2)$$
$$\text{MR}_2(Q_2) = \text{MC}(Q_1 + Q_2)$$

(Necessary Conditions for a Price-Discriminating Monopolist) $\quad$ **(12-8)**

Therefore,

$$\text{MR}_1(Q_1) = \text{MR}_2(Q_2)$$

> The firm expands output until the marginal revenue in each market equals the marginal cost of production.

The following graphical method can be used to find the total quantity produced and the profit-maximizing prices. After you become familiar with this technique, you can apply it in finding solutions to many price discrimination problems.

The first requirement is to find a way to equate marginal revenue across markets. To do this, pick a value for marginal revenue and then find the quantity that must be sold in each market so that marginal revenue in each market equals

---

[5] For the calculus-trained reader, we show the derivation of these profit maximization conditions. The firm maximizes $\pi = D_1(Q_1)Q_1 + D_2(Q_2)Q_2 - C_L(Q)$ subject to the constraint $Q_1 + Q_2 = Q$. After substituting this constraint and eliminating Q, the profits of the firm depend on Q_1 and Q_2. The two first-order conditions for a maximum are

$$\frac{\partial \pi}{\partial Q_1} = D_1(Q_1) + Q_1 \frac{dD_1}{dQ_1} - \frac{dC_L(Q)}{dQ} \frac{dQ}{dQ_1} = 0$$

$$\frac{\partial \pi}{\partial Q_2} = D_2(Q_2) + Q_2 \frac{dD_2}{dQ_2} - \frac{dC_L(Q)}{dQ} \frac{dQ}{dQ_2} = 0$$

where ∂ denotes partial differentiation. Because a unit increase in Q_1 or Q_2 increases Q by a unit, $dQ/dQ_1 = dQ/dQ_2 = 1$. The two first-order conditions become

$$\text{MR}_1(Q_1) = D_1(Q_1) + Q_1 \frac{dD_1}{dQ_1} = \frac{dC_L(Q)}{dQ}$$

$$\text{MR}_2(Q_2) = D_2(Q_2) + Q_2 \frac{dD_2}{dQ_2} = \frac{dC_L(Q)}{dQ}$$

Marginal revenue (the first two terms on the left-hand side) in market 1 or market 2 must equal the marginal cost of production. Because marginal cost is the same in both markets, it follows that marginal revenue across markets will be equal.

this prespecified value. Sum the two quantities and determine a point on a new graph that relates the prespecified marginal revenue to this total quantity.

Figure 12-6 shows that marginal revenue equals MR^* if the firm sells Q_1^* in market 1 (Figure 12-6a) and Q_2^* in market 2 (Figure 12-6b). The total quantity sold when MR^* is the marginal revenue in each market is $Q_1^* + Q_2^* = Q^*$ (point a on the ΣMR function in Figure 12-6c), where marginal revenue is on the vertical axis and total quantity is on the horizontal axis.

We derive the ΣMR function by repeating this procedure for all possible values of marginal revenue. To demonstrate this point, consider a second value of marginal revenue, MR', and determine how many units the firm can sell while achieving MR' in each market. If it sells Q_1' in market 1 (Figure 12-6a) and Q_2' in market 2 (Figure 12-6b), marginal revenue in each market is equal to MR'. In Figure 12-6c the total quantity Q' $(= Q_1' + Q_2')$ and MR' determine point b on the ΣMR function. The firm can sell a total of Q' units so that marginal revenue in each market is equal to MR'. Geometrically, ΣMR is constructed by summing the individual *marginal revenue functions* horizontally. Each point on the ΣMR function indicates what marginal revenue will be in each market when the firm produces a given total quantity.

The second requirement is to equate marginal cost to marginal revenue in each market. The long-run marginal cost function of the monopolist in Figure 12-6c intersects the ΣMR function at point a and determines the total quantity produced. If the firm produces Q^*, it knows that it can sell Q^* units so that marginal revenue is MR^* in each market. It sells Q_1^* units in market 1 at P_1^*, and Q_2^* in market 2 at P_2^*. Because MR^* in each market equals marginal cost of production, the firm selects a total quantity where marginal revenue in each market equals marginal cost of production. Therefore, the equalities in equation 12-8 are satisfied.

To review the two-step technique: The horizontal sum of the marginal revenue functions determines the ΣMR function. The intersection of the ΣMR function with the marginal cost function determines the total quantity produced and the marginal revenue, MR^*. The firm determines the quantity to sell and the price in each market so that marginal revenue equals MR^*. This graphical method can be used to find solutions to the exercises at the end of this chapter.

APPLICATION 12-2

Should a Firm Expand into the European Market?

The following situation is an opportunity for you to apply the graphical method and to test your understanding of price discrimination.

A company is the sole supplier of a product and sells it in the domestic market at a price of P_0. Because the firm has been successful in the domestic market, several members want the firm to expand into the European market. Others oppose the expansion. They feel that they know much more about domestic demand conditions than those in the European market. For example, their best guess is that the price elasticity of demand in the domestic market is -5 at the current

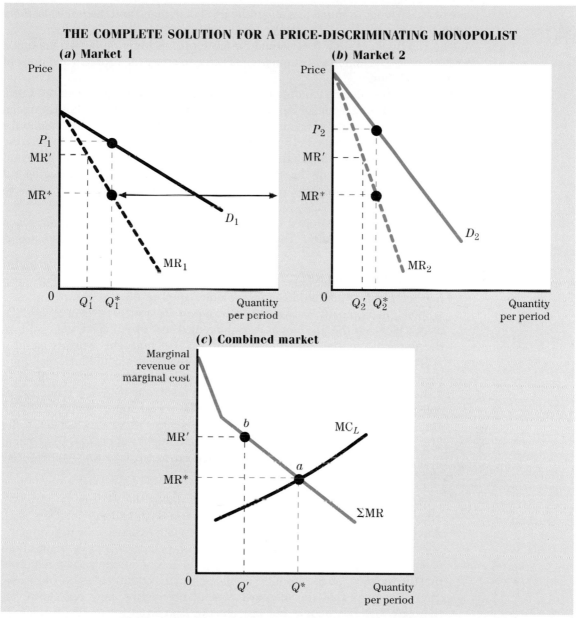

Figure 12-6   Marginal revenue is the same in both markets and marginal revenue in each market is equal to marginal production cost. The ΣMR function is the horizontal summation of the individual marginal revenue functions. It intersects the marginal cost function at point a. If the firm produces Q^* units, the ΣMR function indicates that the firm can obtain MR^* in each market. Of the Q^* units produced, Q_1^* are sold in market 1 at P_1 and Q_2^* are sold in market 2 at P_2. Marginal revenue is the same in both markets, and marginal revenue in each market equals marginal cost of production.

price of P_0. They know much less about the level of demand and the price elasticity of demand overseas.

The CEO believes the firm should obtain more information before making a decision, and so he appoints a committee of three to study the problem and present a recommendation.

The committee decides to obtain more information about the size of the European market by hiring a consulting firm. The consulting firm reports that European demand will not exist at a price of P_0, estimating that there will be no demand for the product unless the price is 15 percent lower than P_0. If the price is $0.75P_0$, the consulting firm estimates that European demand will be about 25 percent of current domestic demand. It appears that the firm can break into the European market but only if it is willing to offer the product at a price considerably lower than the domestic price.

After a lengthy discussion, it becomes clear that the committee cannot reach a consensus recommendation. The arguments of the committee members are as follows.

- *Group 1.* One member raises three objections to expansion into the European market. First, to obtain a foreign volume equal to 25 percent of domestic volume, the company will have to offer a price that is 25 percent lower. She asks, "Why sell the product at a 25 percent discount when we can sell it in the domestic market at a full price of P_0?" Second, she worries about a potential arbitrage problem. Some of the foreign sales could leak back into the domestic market. Third, she fears that diseconomies of scale will set in if the firm expands by 25 percent. This will inevitably lead to a reduction of sales in the profitable domestic market. She recommends a cost study be conducted to determine if diseconomies of scale will be experienced if the firm expands into the European market. She might support the expansion proposal if the study shows that marginal cost of production will not rise and if the firm can prevent arbitrage.

- *Group 2.* The other two members strongly favor the expansion proposal. They argue that expansion into foreign markets should not interfere with domestic output at all. They recommend a prudent expansion by the company into those foreign markets where sales can be made at a price higher than $0.8P_0$. They argue that the arbitrage problem can be minimized by requiring that the warranty on the product be valid only in the country of initial purchase. They recognize that the marginal cost of production may rise; however, they say that this should not prevent the firm from expanding prudently. They believe that the profits of the firm will increase with expansion.

By using the theory of price discrimination, you can evaluate the different points raised by the two groups. The member who objects to the expansion has made three points. First, she claims the price discount is too large to justify the expansion. Second, the potential arbitrage problem concerns her. Third, she says the decision to expand into the European market depends critically on the absence of diseconomies of scale.

How valid are these points? The first point fails to distinguish between price and marginal revenue. If the firm is a price maker, marginal revenue is less than price in both the export and the domestic markets. The 25 percent difference between the domestic and the export prices does not mean that the difference between the marginal revenues in the two markets is 25 percent. Marginal revenue from the *first* unit sold in the European market could be greater than marginal revenue from the *last* unit sold in the domestic market although the European price is less than the domestic price. If marginal revenue from selling the first unit in the foreign market exceeds marginal revenue from selling the last unit in the domestic market, total revenue will increase by increasing sales in the European market and reducing sales in the domestic market. Notice that the decision to enter the European market does *not* depend on knowing whether there are or are not diseconomies of scale. The expansion decision depends solely on whether marginal revenue from the first unit sold in the foreign market is greater than marginal revenue from the last unit sold in the domestic market. How much is produced, given entry, will depend on whether there are or are not diseconomies of scale.

Is marginal revenue from the first unit sold in the foreign market greater than marginal revenue from the last unit sold in the domestic market? At the current rate of domestic output the latter can be estimated from the expression for marginal revenue:

$$\text{MR} = P_0\left(1 + \frac{1}{E}\right) = P_0\left(1 + \frac{1}{-5}\right) = 0.8P_0$$

Marginal revenue from the last unit sold in the domestic market is 80 percent of the current price. For example, if $P_0 = \$80$ and $E = -5$, MR is $64. If marginal revenue from the first unit sold in the foreign market is greater than $64, then entry into the foreign market will increase total revenue.

The consultant study estimated that the quantity demanded becomes positive in the foreign market if the European price is 15 percent less than the domestic price or when the European price is $0.85P_0$, or $68. This means that the first unit will sell at $0.85P_0$. Although the foreign price is less than the domestic price, marginal revenue from the first unit sold abroad is greater than marginal revenue from the last unit sold at home. By reducing the number of units sold in the domestic market and increasing the number sold in the European market, total revenue can be increased for a given total quantity. Therefore, entry into the European market must *increase* total profits.

Figure 12-7a shows the domestic demand function, *DD*, the domestic marginal revenue function, MR, and the marginal cost function, MC. The original equilibrium price and output are P_0 and Q_0, respectively. The foreign demand and marginal revenue functions in Figure 12-7b are *dd* and mr, respectively. Note that the vertical intercepts of *dd* and mr are $0.85P_0$.

How many units should the firm sell in the domestic and in the foreign markets? Is it true that entry into the European market should not affect the quantity sold in the domestic market? We can answer these questions by finding the optimum quantities and prices that maximize firm profits. The first step is to sum the marginal revenue functions horizontally to obtain the function labeled ΣMR in Figure 12-7c.

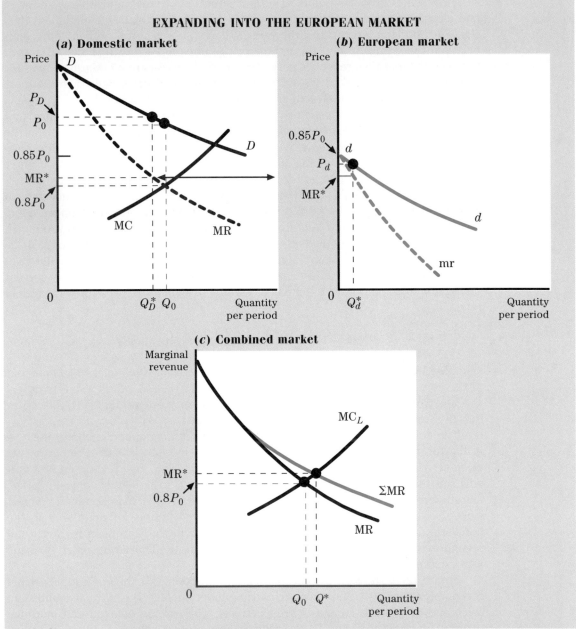

EXPANDING INTO THE EUROPEAN MARKET

Figure 12-7   The firm produces Q_0 units in the domestic market and sells each at a price of P_0. Marginal revenue in the domestic market is $.8P_0$ because the price elasticity is -5. The first unit can be sold only at a price of $0.85P_0$ in the European market, or 15 percent less than in the domestic market. Nevertheless, the firm should expand into the European market. The marginal revenue from the first unit sold in the European market is greater than the marginal revenue from the last unit sold in the domestic market. The firm should produce Q^* units and sell Q_d^* units at a price of P_d in the European market. The quantity sold in the domestic market decreases to Q_D^* units.

This function intersects the marginal cost function when total output is equal to Q^*. Expansion into the European market increases marginal revenue from $0.8P_0$ to MR^*. The firm allocates Q^* between the domestic and the European markets so that marginal revenue in each market equals MR^*. Therefore, the price rises to P_D and the total number of units sold in the domestic market decreases to Q_D^*. Penetration into the domestic market does decline (as one member predicted), and the domestic price rises to P_D. The firm sells Q_d^* units at a price of P_a in the European market, and total profits increase. If entry into the foreign market increases marginal cost of production, marginal revenue in the domestic market must also increase since at the optimum $MR = MC$. Entry into the European market increases the domestic price and reduces the quantity sold in the domestic market. What this analysis shows is that operations in the domestic market cannot and should not be isolated from those in the European market. Compartmentalizing operations will not maximize firm profits. Entry into the European market affects the price in the domestic market if the firm's marginal cost function is not flat.

A question about arbitrage is also raised. It is a serious problem and must be prevented if profits are to increase. The proposal to use a warranty deserves a more thorough investigation to determine if it would be effective.

How would you evaluate the suggestion by the two members who recommend that the firm enter any foreign market as long as the first sale is at $0.8P_0$? The overall conclusion of the two members of group 2 is correct, but the suggested criterion is faulty. There may be several foreign markets the company could enter. As it enters each market, total production increases and marginal cost of production rises. For example, suppose the company enters the European market and marginal cost of production increases to $0.83P_0 = MR_d = MR_f$. Then it would not pay to enter the Eastern European market, say, where marginal revenue from the first unit is $0.8P_0$. If marginal cost is increasing, the firm should not adopt a general policy of entering any market where at least one sale can be made at $0.8P_0$.

Preventing Arbitrage

This analysis of third-degree price discrimination assumes that the firm can separate markets. If it tries to practice price discrimination when the markets are not separated, it will find that it is selling units only in the low-priced market. Middlemen will appear who will purchase in the low-priced market, resell in the high-priced market, and earn a profit. This process is called *arbitrage*. When arbitrage occurs, price differences disappear and price discrimination cannot persist. Therefore, a firm must always be on guard to prevent arbitrage. It is less costly to prevent arbitrage for some products than for others. For example, services are more costly to arbitrage than are goods. It would be very expensive for you to resell an appendix operation or the specific advice you receive from a tax consultant. Tariff barriers and import controls also limit arbitrage. Firms can charge a different price abroad than in the home market if there are barriers preventing low-priced items sold abroad from being imported back into the domestic market. Companies sometimes sell products abroad at lower prices than in the home market. For example, American drug companies sometimes sell drugs at lower prices abroad than in the United States. Likewise, Japanese companies sell consumer electronic products abroad at lower prices than in Japan.

APPLICATION **12-3**

Pricing a Renault in Belgium and in England

New car prices are lower in Belgium than in England. An account in *The Economist* reveals that the price of a Clio RT hatchback was equivalent to £5,750 if purchased in Belgium, but £7,519 in England, or 30 percent more in England.[6] How can this difference persist? A correspondent for *The Economist* wished to purchase a Clio before returning to England, and so he ordered a right-hand-drive car in Belgium. Renault said that the only right-hand-drive model it could supply in Belgium was one destined for the British market and at the British price. The correspondent referred Renault to a ruling by the European Court of Justice in 1985 requiring Ford to supply its German dealers with right-hand-drive cars at prices close to those charged for left-hand-drive cars. Renault argued that the right-hand-drive Clio RT included fuel injection, tinted windows, a sun roof, and so on, and that these features were optional on the left-hand-drive versions sold in Belgium. The account in *The Economist* noted that the options could not explain the 30 percent price differential.

An auto manufacturer can therefore separate automobile markets by shipping cars with different features to the two markets. In this way, it prevents arbitrage and is able to practice price discrimination.

If arbitrage is prevented on the demand side of the market, third-degree price discrimination may still be impossible when there are many sellers in the market. The reason is that arbitrage can occur on the *supply side* as well. If there are enough other firms in the market that act as price takers, a discriminatory price structure will crumble because arbitrage on the supply side is difficult to prevent. Entry into the high-price segment of the market will eliminate any price differences between markets that cannot be explained by cost differences. Price-taking suppliers will respond to a higher price on the West Coast by shipping the product to the West Coast rather than to the East Coast, causing price to fall on the West Coast and to rise on the East Coast until any price difference disappears. This is why price discrimination is less likely to be observed in competitive markets where firms are price takers. Price discrimination can occur only if arbitrage on both sides of the market is prevented.

[6] Based on "Price Sensitive," *The Economist*, February 22, 1992, p. 66. © 1992 The Economist Newspaper Group, Inc. Reprinted with permission. Further reproduction prohibited.

> A firm will engage in price discrimination if (1) it is a price maker, (2) it can separate markets and prevent arbitrage, and (3) the price elasticities of demand differ between groups.

The Difference between Second- and Third-Degree Price Discrimination

Now that we have reviewed the different types of price discrimination, let's reconsider the difference between second- and third-degree price discrimination. With third-degree price discrimination the company can identify and assign consumers to groups based on some characteristic, for example, their age, student status, or mailing address. If a firm sells student subscriptions to a magazine at a relatively low price, it must identify students so that only students can subscribe. Or since the prices of journals are lower for individual subscribers, publishers must be on the lookout for the mailing address of a library to prevent a library's buying journals at lower prices. The assumption is that there is a low-cost way of identifying and sorting consumers. With second-degree price discrimination the firm cannot identify at low cost what type of customer each is beforehand. Therefore, consumers can shift into one group from another. The firm cannot sort consumers directly; however, it can quote prices that indirectly sort buyers into groups. The firm sets prices so that consumers self-select into different groups in a way that maximizes the firm's profits.

To illustrate the difference between second- and third-degree price discrimination, let's return to the example of airline travelers who must decide on their day of return. Until now, we have assumed that business travelers must return before Sunday and that tourists could return on Sunday or later. Now let's entertain the possibility that business travelers will shift and delay their return to Sunday if the price inducement is attractive compared to that for a pre-Sunday return. Several considerations go into calculating the prices the airline charges as a function of the day of return. To be specific, an airline must determine what prices to charge for Friday, Saturday, and Sunday returns. We already know that airlines charge substantially higher fares for travelers who do not stay over Saturday night, and we want to consider a numerical example that captures the essence of the pricing problem.

Assume the airline has only two classes of customers, business and tourist. Table 12-3 shows the willingness of each type of customer to pay for a return on each of the three days. The business traveler will pay up to $1,200 to return on Friday, $600 to return on Saturday, and only $400 for a coach ticket with a Sunday return. We assume that the tourist is indifferent about the return date and is willing to pay $350 for any of the three days.

If you could identify a customer as a businessperson or a tourist when he or she makes a reservation, you would charge the business traveler $1,200 no matter what day she returns, charge the tourist $350 no matter what day he returns, and receive a total revenue of $1,550, the maximum revenue because it leaves no

Table 12-3   WILLINGNESS TO PAY FOR BUSINESS AND TOURIST CONSUMERS

	FRIDAY RETURN ($)	SATURDAY RETURN ($)	SUNDAY RETURN ($)
Business	$1,200	$600	$400
Tourist	350	350	350

consumer surplus for either traveler. In this simple example perfect price discrimination and third-degree price discrimination are identical since there is only one type of customer in each class, and the firm maximizes profits by charging the willingness to pay for each class of customer.

Suppose you cannot identify the type of customer when the reservation is made. What prices should the airline charge for a return on each day? To answer this question assume that the traveler selects the return day that maximizes his or her consumer surplus, the difference between willingness to pay and the price charged by the airline.

$$\text{Consumer surplus of traveler} = \text{Willingness to pay} - \text{Price paid}$$

To keep matters simple, we ignore costs. Because the airline cannot identify consumers who are willing to pay more, it cannot practice third-degree price discrimination. Faced with this situation, it sets prices for each return day that induce the business traveler to self-select into a different return day from the return day of the tourist.

For the moment, let's ignore Sunday and just consider what will happen if the price is $350 for a Saturday return and $1,200 for a Friday return. Clearly, the tourist will return on Saturday because his consumer surplus is negative, $350 − $1,200 = −$850, when returning on Friday. Unfortunately, from the airline's perspective, the business traveler will also return on Saturday. We reach this conclusion because each traveler selects a return day that maximizes consumer surplus. The business traveler's consumer surplus with a Friday return is zero since price equals willingness to pay. She prefers to return on Saturday because consumer surplus is $600 − $350 = $250. Because both travelers return on Saturday, the prices charged by the airline produce a total profit of only $350 + $350 = $700.

To induce the business traveler to return on Friday, the price of a Friday return must be no higher than $949 so that consumer surplus is greater than $250. Then, consumer surplus with a Friday return is $1,200 − $949 = $251, and the business traveler selects a Friday return because consumer surplus is larger on Friday than on Saturday. The airline's profits increase to $949 + $350 = $1,299. The price for a Friday return is $949, and for a Saturday return, $350. With these prices both the business traveler and the tourist self-select into groups.

Because the difference in willingness to pay for a Saturday return between the business traveler and the tourist is large, the airline can entice the business traveler to return on Friday only by reducing the price of a Friday return. This suggests that it can do still better by getting the tourist to return on Sunday and the businessperson to return on Friday since the difference between the willingness to pay of the tourist and of the business traveler is smaller on Sunday. Suppose the airline announces a price of $350 for a Sunday return, a price above $549 for a Saturday return, say $550, and a price of $1149 for a Friday return. At these prices the consumer surplus of the business traveler with a Friday return is $1,200 − $1,149 = $51. Consumer surplus is $50 with a Saturday return and $400 − $350 = $50 with a Sunday return. Therefore, the business traveler will return on Friday. The tourist will return on Sunday since his consumer surplus is negative for any return day other than Sunday. The airline's profit is $1,149 + $350 = $1,499. Therefore, air fares are $1,149 for a Friday return, any price greater than $549 for a Saturday return, and $350 for a Sunday return. With these prices the business traveler and the tourist self-select into different return days so that the airline maximizes profits.

In summary, with second-degree price discrimination a company cannot identify which group customers belong to and therefore cannot sort them into groups at a low cost, while with third-degree price discrimination it can. Because the firm cannot sort consumers directly, its profits are lower than they would be if it could. Recall that airline profits would be $1,550 if the airline could identify business travelers, but are only $1,499 because it cannot.

12.5   BUNDLING

Some products are bundled together and sold as a package. You buy shoelaces with shoes. Microsoft sells Word with Excel and other software in a package. Matchbox sells miniature collector cars in bundles of eight. Why do firms *bundle* goods into a package and not sell the items individually?

In many cases the reason has to do with efficiency. The savings in transaction costs make selling shoelaces with shoes a more economical way of selling shoes than selling shoes and shoelaces separately. However, there are some cases in which the motivation for packaging goods together appears to be price discrimination. **Bundling reduces consumer surplus** and increases a firm's profits.

Let's show why and when this is true. Assume that a firm sells miniature replicas of classic cars. It could sell the cars either individually or as a package. Suppose the firm produces replicas of a 1955 Chevrolet and a 1955 Ford Thunderbird, two of the most distinctive and popular cars of the 50s. To keep matters simple, let's suppose there are two consumers: Consumer 1 owned a 1955 Chevrolet in his youth and has fond memories of the car. Consumer 2 can still remember the beauty of his 1955 Thunderbird. Table 12-4 shows their willingness to pay for the replicas.

Not surprisingly, each consumer is willing to pay more for a replica of the car that he owned in his youth. The willingness-to-pay values are *negatively correlated* across consumers. Consumer 1 values the Chevrolet more than the Thunderbird while consumer 2 values the Thunderbird more than the Chevrolet. If the firm

Table 12-4   NEGATIVELY CORRELATED WILLINGNESS-TO-PAY VALUES

	Willingness to pay		
CONSUMER TYPE	1955 CHEVROLET	1955 THUNDERBIRD	BUNDLE
Consumer 1: previous owner of 1955 Chevrolet	$30	$20	$50
Consumer 2: previous owner of 1955 Thunderbird	18	35	53
Total revenue if replicas are priced individually	36	40	

could charge a different price to each customer for each car, it would do so and its profits would be highest. Usually, the firm cannot engage in such perfect price discrimination because it cannot identify which consumer owned which car in his youth and hence cannot infer each consumer's willingness to pay. We will assume that the firm charges the same price to each customer for each car.

Notice that the firm maximizes profits by charging $18 for the Chevrolet and $20 for the Thunderbird when the replicas are priced individually. At these prices each consumer buys both cars because the surplus from each purchase is nonnegative. So, the firm's profits equal $76. We ignore the cost of producing the cars. Notice that both consumers end up with a positive surplus after purchasing both cars when the cars are priced individually and the willingness-to-pay values are negatively correlated. Consumer 1's surplus is $12 on the Chevrolet purchase and zero on the Thunderbird, and consumer 2's surplus is $15 on the Thunderbird and zero on the Chevrolet.[7]

Because both consumers would walk away with an aggregate positive surplus when the replicas are priced individually, the firm should consider bundling the replicas so as to reduce consumer surplus and raise profits. If the firm bundles the two replicas together and sells a package, it maximizes profits by selling the bundle at $50 to each consumer. Consumer 1 is willing to pay at most $50 for the bundle and consumer 2 is willing to pay at most $53 for the bundle. We assume that each buys the bundle as long as surplus is nonnegative, that is, as long as the willingness to pay for the bundle less the bundle price is nonnegative. So, bundling increases the firm's profits to $100, a 32 percent increase. By bundling the replicas, the firm exploits an opportunity to reduce consumer 1's surplus to zero and consumer 2's surplus to just $3. To summarize, bundling allows the firm to reduce consumer

---

[7] Strictly speaking, the firm may have to charge $17.99 for the Chevrolet replica and $19.99 for the Thunderbird replica for there to be a positive surplus from each purchase. We ignore these details in this analysis.

Table 12-5   POSITIVELY CORRELATED WILLINGNESS-TO-PAY VALUES

CONSUMER TYPE	Willingness to pay		
	1955 CHEVROLET	1955 THUNDERBIRD	BUNDLE
Consumer 1: previous owner of 1955 Chevrolet	$30	$40	$70
Consumer 2: previous owner of 1955 Thunderbird	18	35	53
Total revenue if replicas are priced individually	36	70	

surplus and increase its profits when the willingness to pay values are negatively correlated across consumers.

The benefits from bundling disappear when the willingness-to-pay values of the two consumers are positively correlated. Suppose we change the willingness-to-pay values so that consumer 1 is willing to pay more for both cars. Table 12-5 shows the new values.

Now, the willingness-to-pay values are *positively correlated.* Consumer 1 values both cars more highly than does consumer 2. If the replicas are sold individually, total profits equal $106. Both buyers buy the Chevrolet at $18 and the Thunderbird at $35. It is more profitable to sell two units of both cars at $18 and $35 respectively than to sell one each at $30 and $40 respectively. When the replicas are sold as a bundle, the profit-maximizing price for the bundle is $53 so profits are also equal to $106. Consumer 2 ends up with no surplus but consumer 1 has a surplus of $17.

Why don't the firm's profits increase by bundling the replicas? When they are sold individually, the firm maximizes profits when consumer 2 pays a total of $53 for both cars, $18 for the Chevrolet and $35 for the Thunderbird. So consumer 2's surplus is already zero when the replicas are priced individually. If the firm is going to increase its profits by still more, it must capture some of the surplus of consumer 1 without forcing consumer 2 from the market. But this is impossible. Profits will fall, not rise, if the firm tries to capture some of consumer 1's surplus by increasing the bundle price above $53. Any increase in the bundle price above $53 forces consumer 2 out of the market because consumer 2's surplus would be negative. The firm's profits would decline from $106 to $70. Hence, the firm cannot gain by bundling. For bundling to be the more profitable strategy with two consumers, both consumers must have positive surplus when the firm prices the replicas individually. This in turn implies that the consumers' willingness-to-pay values are negatively correlated. Then, the firm has a real opportunity to use bundling to lower consumer surplus and raise profits. Otherwise, pricing the replicas separately is the best that the firm can do.[8]

12-6   TWO-PART TARIFFS

A **two-part tariff** is a pricing technique that firms often use to reduce consumer surplus. It requires consumers to pay a fixed fee that gives them the right to purchase units of a good at a specified price. After paying the fixed fee, consumers can purchase as many units as desired at a specified per unit price. The consumer's total expenditure on the good is the fixed fee plus the per unit price times the quantity purchased.

Two-part tariffs are used at amusement parks, at health and golf clubs, and by firms renting specialized durable goods. In each case consumers pay a fixed fee and then an additional amount that depends on the number of units purchased. For many years Disneyland charged an entrance fee as well as a per ride cost in the form of a book of tickets. Health and golf clubs charge an annual membership fee to join the club and sometimes an additional charge that depends on the use of the facility or the course. If a firm rents a copying machine, the renter pays a monthly rental fee and an additional amount that depends on the number of pages copied.

Setting the Fixed Fee and Per Unit Price for Identical Consumers

This section examines how a monopolist sets the fixed fee and the per unit price to maximize the firm's profits and to extract some or all of the consumer surplus. We start with the simplest case where all consumers are alike. Let's see how a firm that rents a copying machine to a user determines the two-part tariff. The supplier of the machine needs to determine the monthly rental fee and the per copy price to charge. Assume that the number of copies made per month can be metered through a counting device on the copying machine.

The demand function for copies by the renter, *DD*, is shown in Figure 12-8. The price per copy is on the vertical axis, and the number of copies per month is on the horizontal axis. The marginal cost of producing each copy, mc, includes wear and tear on the machine and the cost of service. Suppose the firm charges a per unit price equal to mc. At this price the consumer demands q_1 units, and consumer surplus is $s_1 + s_2 + s_3$. Why consumer surplus is divided into three areas is explained below. If the supplier sets the monthly fee at $s_1 + s_2 + s_3$, or consumer surplus, total profits of the firm become $s_1 + s_2 + s_3$. Since each copy costs mc, the price of the copy, the firm does not earn any profits from the copies made by the user. The firm's profit comes from the monthly fee.

You may wonder whether total profits can be increased still more by charging a higher price per copy. At first glance this seems to be an attractive proposal. The

---

[8] More advanced analyses allow the firm to use mixed bundling where the firm sells a bundle and also individual items. For a more extensive discussion, see William J. Adams and Janet L. Yellen, "Commodity Bundling and the Burden of Monopoly," *Quarterly Journal of Economics* 90, August 1976, pp. 475–98.

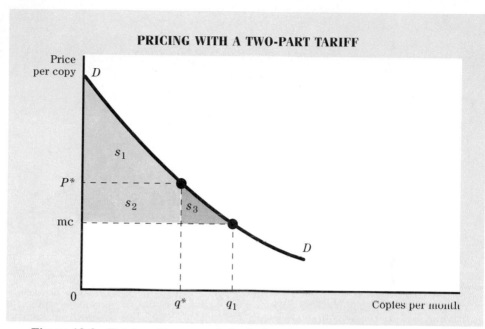

PRICING WITH A TWO-PART TARIFF

Figure 12-8   Total profits are maximized when the per unit price equals marginal cost and the fixed fee equals consumer surplus. The fixed fee is $s_1 + s_2 + s_3$ and represents the profits of the firm. If the per unit charge is P^*, the firm can charge a fixed fee of only s_1. The profits of the firm are equal to $s_1 + s_2$, and so total profits decrease by s_3.

firm would earn profits not only from the fixed fee but from copying as well. What this suggestion neglects is the inverse relationship between the per unit copying price and the monthly fee. The monthly fee must decrease if the copying price increases, or the consumer will not rent the machine.

To see why this is so, let's suppose the per unit copy price P^* is greater than mc. Because of the higher price, the number of copies demanded decreases to q^* units and consumer surplus to s_1. The user will not rent the copying machine unless the monthly fee decreases to s_1. Has the increase in the per unit price from mc to P^* increased profits? Total profits consist of the monthly fee, or s_1, plus the profits from making q^* copies. The per unit price is P^*, and the cost of each copy is mc. The profits from the copies made by the firm are $(P^* - mc)q^*$, or s_2. The total profits of the firm are now $s_1 + s_2$ and are lower by s_3. If all consumers are identical, maximum profits are obtained by setting the per unit price equal to marginal cost and the monthly fee equal to consumer surplus. This pricing policy eliminates all consumer surplus and is similar to first-degree price discrimination.

When there is a single consumer or many consumers of the same type, total profits are maximized by setting the per unit price at marginal cost and the monthly fee equal to consumer surplus.

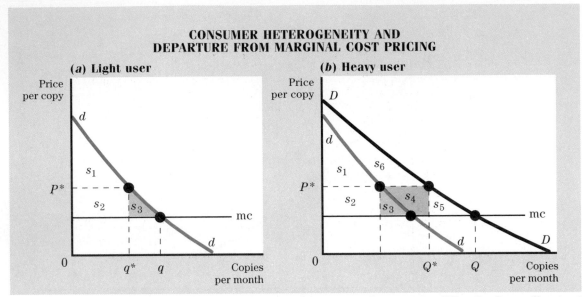

Figure 12-9   When the demand functions of consumers differ, the firm will not set the per unit price equal to marginal cost (mc) when the firm charges a uniform monthly fee. If the per unit price equals marginal cost, the heavy user retains a substantial portion of consumer surplus. When the price is raised to P^*, the increase in profit from the copies made by the heavy user more than offsets the reduced profit from the fewer copies made by the light user. When the price is increased from mc to P^*, the profit from the copies made by the light user decreases by s_3. The profit from the copies made by the heavy user increases by s_4. When s_4 exceeds s_3, the firm sets the per unit price equal to P^*.

Setting the Fixed Fee and Per Unit Price for Different Types of Consumers

Now let's examine a somewhat more typical case where there are different types of consumers. Suppose the firm rents a copying machine to two types of consumers, light and heavy users. In Figure 12-9a, dd is the demand function of a typical light user, and in Figure 12-9b, DD is the demand function of a heavy user. The demand function of the light user is also superimposed on Figure 12-9b. If the firm can charge different monthly fees for the same copying machine, maximum profits occur when the per unit price equals marginal cost and the monthly fee equals the consumer surplus of each user. The light user pays a monthly fee of $s_1 + s_2 + s_3$, and the heavy user pays a monthly fee of $s_1 + s_2 + s_3 + s_4 + s_5 + s_6$.

Assume that the supplier of the copying machine *cannot* charge a different monthly fee to the two types of users. The firm faces a dilemma. If the monthly fee is set too high, the small user will drop out of the market. On the other hand, a low monthly fee will allow the heavy user to retain a substantial portion of consumer surplus. By experimenting with the pricing of the monthly fee, the supplier will learn that $s_1 + s_2 + s_3$ is the maximum monthly fee the light user will pay.[9] Any higher monthly fee will cause this user to discontinue renting. Figure 12-9b shows that the heavy user retains $s_4 + s_5 + s_6$ as consumer surplus because each user pays a monthly fee of only $s_1 + s_2 + s_3$. The firm would like to obtain more of the consumer surplus of the heavy user even if the small consumer contributes less consumer surplus.

One way to do this is to raise the per unit price. Suppose the company raises the per unit price from mc to P^*. Will total profits increase? The light user will rent the machine only if the monthly fee falls to s_1. Therefore, the firm reduces the monthly fee paid by both users to s_1. The number of copies made by the light user is q^*, and the profit from these copies is s_2. The total profit from the light user is equal to $s_1 + s_2$. When the per unit price is raised from marginal cost to P^*, the profit on sales to the light user declines by s_3.

However, the profit earned on sales to the heavy user increases. The monthly fee paid by the heavy user also equals s_1 in Figure 12-9b. This user makes Q^* copies, and the profit from these copies is $s_2 + s_3 + s_4$. Total profit from the copies made by the heavy user is $s_1 + s_2 + s_3 + s_4$, and total profit from renting to the heavy user increases by s_4 when the copy price increases to P^*. Total firm profits increase if s_4 exceeds s_3. In Figure 12-9b, s_4 is larger than s_3, and so profit increases.

If the two demand functions are far apart, the firm will ignore the light user, setting the monthly fee equal to the consumer surplus of the heavy user and the price of each copy equal to marginal cost. When the demand functions are close together, the per unit price will depart from marginal cost. When there are many different groups of customers with different demand functions, the firm raises the per unit price above marginal cost.

> When consumers differ, a firm that charges a uniform fixed fee to two different buyers will not set the per unit price at marginal cost.

Using Two-Part Tariffs to Price Consumer Capital Goods

Often a consumer buys a capital good from a firm and then purchases another good to obtain the services from the capital good. For example, a firm may sell a camcorder and a special tape. Another example is a manufacturer that sells a razor and razor blades. The model of a two-part tariff can be used to determine the price of the consumer capital good as well as the price of the other product.

Assume that a firm develops a new camcorder that takes excellent pictures at a lower cost than any camcorder on the market. This camcorder requires a special tape that your firm alone produces at a marginal cost of mc per roll. The consumer receives utility directly from the home videos he or she shoots but not from the camcorder.

---

[9] For a pioneering and extended discussion of two-part tariffs, see Walter Oi, "A Disneyland Dilemma: Two-Part Tariffs for a Mickey-Mouse Monopoly," *Quarterly Journal of Economics* LXXXV (February 1971), pp. 77–96.

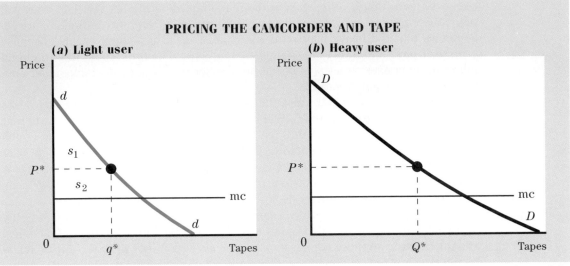

Figure 12-10   The firm must determine a separate price for the camcorder and for tapes. If the profit-maximizing price of a tape is P^*, the firm will charge a price of s_1 for the camcorder. As long as it is profitable to sell to both types of consumers, the firm cannot set the price of the camcorder above s_1.

There are two types of demanders, light and heavy camcorder users. (Figure 12-10 shows the two demand curves for tapes.) Your firm must determine what price to charge for the tape and what price to charge for the camcorder. In this discussion we assume that it is more profitable to sell to both consumers than just to the heavy user. Because the demands of the two consumers are different, the firm sets the price per tape above marginal cost, mc. In Figure 12-10 P^* is the price of a tape that maximizes the total profits of the company. Consumer surplus for consumer 1 (the light user) is s_1. What is the maximum amount the firm can charge for the camcorder? Clearly, it can charge at most s_1 and consumer 1 will still purchase the camcorder. If the fixed fee for the camcorder exceeds s_1 when the price of a tape is P^*, consumer 1 will not purchase the camcorder or any tapes.

Assuming the firm charges the same price for the camcorder, the price of the camcorder is s_1. If the marginal cost of producing the camcorder is C, the profits of the firm from the sale of the camcorder and tapes to consumer 1 are

$$\pi_1 = (s_1 - C) + (P^* - \text{mc})q_1 \qquad \text{(Profits from Sales to Consumer 1)} \quad \textbf{(12-9)}$$

where P^* is the price of a tape, mc is the marginal cost of producing tapes, and q_1 is the number of tapes purchased. The profits from the sale of the camcorder and tapes to consumer 2 (the heavy user) are

$$\pi_2 = (s_1 - C) + (P^* - \text{mc})q_2 \qquad \text{(Profits from Sales to Consumer 2)} \quad \textbf{(12-10)}$$

You can see from this analysis that the marginal cost of producing tapes affects the price of the camcorder. If the marginal cost of producing a tape falls, it will not only lower the price of a tape but will also increase the price of the camcorder. A decrease in the marginal cost of producing a tape increases the profits of the firm. It is less clear how the firm will fare if competitors can produce the tapes at a lower marginal cost. Exercise 13 at the end of this chapter raises the interesting question of whether the firm's profits increase or decrease when competitive producers of tapes introduce a lower-priced substitute for the company's tapes.

APPLICATION 12-4

Why Did IBM and Xerox Lease Rather Than Sell Their Machines?

In several instances firms with monopoly power are willing to rent a machine to a customer but refuse to sell the machine. Two well-known examples are IBM and Xerox. In the 1930s IBM manufactured tabulating equipment—punch card machines and sorters—but refused to sell it to customers. Similarly, in the 1960s Xerox refused to sell copying machines. Both companies were willing to rent tabulating or copying machines, and each charged a monthly fee and a per unit price based on usage of the equipment.

IBM had a near-monopoly on tabulating machines but did not have a monopoly on the perforated punch cards used with the sorting machines. Still, it sold approximately 81 percent of the cards used since it required each lessee to purchase tabulating cards only from IBM. It charged the same monthly lease to all users and set the per card price above marginal cost for renters who used more than a minimum number of cards per month. Charging a premium price for punch cards was a device IBM used to reduce the consumer surplus of large users.

The pricing policy of Xerox in the early 1960s was similar. It leased its copying machines at $25 per month, charged the user 3.5 cents per copy, a price which exceeded marginal cost, and required a minimum of 2,000 copies per month.[10] A renter who made 2,000 copies per month paid $25 + $70 per month, or $1,140 per year, or $5,700 over the 5-year lifetime of the machine. On the other hand, a renter who made 20,000 copies a month paid $43,500 over the 5-year lifetime of the machine. The same machine produced different levels of profit depending on who rented it. Table 12-6 shows the revenue Xerox received from two different customers.

These two examples raise the question of **leasing versus selling:** why these companies preferred to rent and would not sell the machines. Chapter 9 explained that a monopolist prefers leasing to selling in order to dispel the fears of consumers that it will act opportunistically. This is a possible explanation for the leasing preference of these companies.

Another explanation is that the firm can better control arbitrage by leasing. If

---

[10] E. A. Blackstone, "Restrictive Practices in the Marketing of Electrofax Copying Machines and Supplies: The SCM Corporation Case," *Journal of Industrial Economics* 23 (1975), pp. 189–202.

Table 12-6   REVENUE FROM LEASING

COPIES PER MONTH	MONTHLY FEE ($)	MONTHLY REVENUE FROM COPYING ($)	TOTAL REVENUE PER YEAR ($)	TOTAL REVENUE OVER FIVE YEARS ($)
2,000	$25	$ 70	$1,140	$ 5,700
20,000	25	700	8,700	43,500

Xerox sold the machines and arbitrage prevented it from selling them at different prices to different users, total profits would be lower. It would either sell a machine at $43,500 to only the large user (ignoring any cost of maintenance) or to both users but at a drastically lower price of $5,700 per machine. By leasing, it collected a combined total of $49,200 from both users.

In addition, there is another more subtle point here. Xerox did not know which customers were intensive users. Therefore, it did not know who was willing to pay a higher price for the machine. By leasing, the company relied on the actual use patterns of its clients to identify low- and high-intensity users and collected more from the intensive users. If more-intensive machine users had greater consumer surplus, Xerox could collect some of it by setting the copy price above marginal cost. So, leasing dominates selling for two reasons: First, it avoids the arbitrage problem on the demand side of the market. Second, it allows the firm to discover who is an intensive user and to collect more of the consumer surplus from these users.

In summary, leasing is a more profitable strategy when arbitrage in the sale market is costly to prevent and when the intensity of use differs across consumers and is unknown. Even if a firm can prevent arbitrage, it prefers leasing because leasing identifies the intensity of demand of users.

SUMMARY

- A firm charges different prices for the same good to reduce consumer surplus and increase its revenues and profits.
- First-, second-, and third-degree price discrimination are different methods of decreasing consumer surplus and raising the profits of a firm.
- Under third-degree price discrimination maximum profits of a firm occur when

marginal revenue is the same in all markets and marginal revenue equals marginal cost.
- A firm charges a lower price in the market with a more elastic demand function.
- Third-degree price discrimination requires (1) a price maker, (2) no arbitrage or resales, and (3) different price elasticities between markets.
- When willingness-to-pay values are nega-

tively correlated across consumers, bundling reduces consumer surplus and increases profits.

▪ Under a two-part tariff a consumer pays a fixed fee and a variable amount that depends on the number of units consumed. When all consumers are alike, the firm sets the fixed fee equal to consumer surplus and the per unit price equal to marginal cost. If the demand functions of consumers differ, the per unit price that maximizes profits will not equal marginal cost.

▪ Leasing is preferable to selling when arbitrage cannot be prevented or where the intensity of consumer demands is unknown.

KEY TERMS

consumer surplus and revenue enhancement
grouping consumers
setting prices based on clasticity of demand
bundling reduces consumer surplus
two-part tariff
leasing versus selling

three types of price discrimination
equating marginal revenue across markets
preventing arbitrage
setting the per unit price and the fixed fee

REVIEW QUESTIONS

1. Define first-degree price discrimination. Describe two price policies that will achieve the goal of first-degree price discrimination.

2. Price discrimination by physicians occurs because higher-income patients have inelastic demands and arbitrage on the demand side is costly. Are these two conditions sufficient when there are many suppliers in the market?

3. A monopolist that practices perfect price discrimination captures all the consumer surplus in the form of higher profits. Explain why you agree or disagree with this statement.

4. Why does third-degree price discrimination reduce consumer surplus?

5. How does second-degree price discrimination differ from third-degree price discrimination?

6. If consumer 1 is willing to pay $70 for A and $35 for B and consumer 2 is willing to pay $170 for A and $85 for B, the only way for the firm to maximize profits is to sell a bundle with a bundle price of $255. Explain why you agree or disagree.

7. Could a monopolist who does not find it profitable to expand abroad before demand decreases in the domestic market find it profitable to expand abroad after domestic demand decreases?

8. If the price elasticity is -2 in market A and -6 in market B, the price in market B is one-third the price in market A. Explain why you agree or disagree with this statement.

EXERCISES

1. Explain what third-degree price discrimination is and carefully identify the conditions under which a firm will engage in third-degree price discrimination. What

methods have been employed to separate customers into groups. Give two examples not listed in the text.

2. Vendors at Yankee Stadium know that Yankee fans and Boston Red Sox fans have different demand functions for hot dogs. For each vendor, the Yankee fans' inverse demand function is

$$P = 4 - .005Q$$

while the Red Sox fans' inverse demand function is

$$P = 2.25 - .01Q$$

The marginal cost of a hot dog is .15.

The vendors are instructed to look at the baseball cap the buyer is wearing (assume that every fan wears a cap). If the fan wears a Yankee cap, the fan pays one price and if the fan wears a Red Sox cap, the fan pays a different price.

a. What price will a vendor charge a Yankee fan and what price will a vendor charge a Red Sox fan?

b. How many hot dogs does each vendor sell and what is the profit of the vendor?

3. The theory of third-degree price discrimination predicts that a monopolist will charge a lower price in the market where demand is price-elastic and a higher price in the market where demand is price-inelastic. Explain what is wrong with this statement.

4. The following questions refer to the decision to expand into the European market (Application 12-2).

a. Show the optimal quantities and prices in the domestic and European markets if marginal cost of production is declining. Will the price in the domestic market stay the same if the firm enters the European market?

b. Assume the price elasticity of demand in the domestic market is -10 instead

of -5 and marginal cost is increasing. Explain why it would or would not be profitable to expand into the European market.

*5. (Hidden City Problem) An airline is the only firm offering service (1) between city A and city B, which is 300 miles away from city A; and (2) between city A to city C, which is 500 miles away from city A. See figure below.

The round trip fare from city A to city B is $254 and the round trip fare from city A to city C is $208.

a. With the aid of graphs present an explanation of the airline's pricing policy.

b. Last year's load factor (the fraction of seats that were filled) on flights from A to C was low so the airline is considering eliminating direct flights from A to C and adding a continuing flight from B to C without changing fares. Assuming the frequency of service does not change, will the profits of the firm rise if it drops direct service from A to C and offers indirect service to C through B? Identify the factors that you would look at before determining if firm profits will increase when it drops direct service to C.

*6. A monopolist is selling in a domestic market at a price of $100. At his price the price elasticity of demand is -2. The average cost of production is $40.

a. Will it be profitable for the monopolist to enter a separated foreign market if the price that the first unit can be sold for in the foreign market equals $60? Explain.

b. Is the firm currently operating under economies or diseconomies of scale? Explain.

c. If the firm enters a foreign market, will it raise the price in the domestic market? Explain.

7. A firm produces a product and sells it to two types of customers, C_1 and C_2. Normally, it offers a 25 percent discount to group C_2. Periodically, the company upgrades the quality of the product, and after a lag of a year, competitors copy the improvements. In those years when the firm has an advantage over competitors, the demand for the product by both groups increases. The company raises the price by 10 percent and eliminates the 25 percent discount to group C_2. Frequently, the firm has difficulty meeting orders, and does not feel that it should offer a discount when it can sell all that it can produce at a higher price. The price policy of the firm is summarized in the accompanying table.

	PRICE TO GROUP C_1	PRICE TO GROUP C_2
Year when no product upgrade is offered	P_1	$0.75P_1$
Year when product upgrade is introduced	$1.1P_1$	$1.1P_1$

Assuming the firm is a price-making firm, critically evaluate this pricing policy. Is it wise not to offer a price discount in those years when demand increases?

8. The willingness to pay of a business traveler and a tourist for a return on Friday, Saturday, or Sunday are shown in the next table. What price policy should the airline adopt to maximize profits?

	FRIDAY RETURN ($)	SATURDAY RETURN ($)	SUNDAY RETURN ($)
Business	$1,200	$1,000	$850
Tourist	600	600	350

*9. A book publisher thinks it would be a good idea to publish all 20 chapters of a book in a conventional textbook format suitable for a semester course in microeconomics. In addition it would like to offer a version that includes only the first 10 chapters for use in quarter courses and plans to publish chapters 11 through 14 separately for use in specialized courses in business schools. The publisher's estimates of the size of the market for each version, the willingness to pay for each market segment, and marginal cost of production for each version are shown in the accompanying table.

TYPE OF MARKET	SIZE OF MARKET (THOUSANDS)	VERSION 1 (MARGINAL COST = $10)	VERSION 2 (MARGINAL COST = $5)	VERSION 3 (MARGINAL COST = $2)
Semester course	30	$60	$45	$ 2
Quarter course	20	50	30	5
Specialized courses	5	10	5	30

a. Explain what price the publisher should charge for version 1, version 2, and version 3 when only one version is sold.

b. If the publisher decides to produce multiple versions of the book, which versions should be introduced and what prices should be charged? Explain how the publisher should determine the prices.

10. If an unregulated monopolist sells a bundle to consumers and all consumers who buy the bundle have a positive surplus, the firm is not maximizing its profits. Explain why you agree or disagree with this statement.

11. The willingness to pay for two miniature cars for three consumers is shown below.

	Willingness to pay		
CONSUMER TYPE	**1955 CHEVROLET**	**1955 THUNDERBIRD**	**BUNDLE**
Consumer 1	$15	$30	$45
Consumer 2	25	38	63
Consumer 3	20	32	52

a. What prices should the firm charge if the cars are priced individually?

b. What price should the firm charge for a bundle?

c. Explain why the firm's profits will or will not increase if it sells a bundle.

12. A monopolist supplies rides at an amusement park. The demand function for rides of a typical consumer is shown in the figure to the right. The per unit cost of supplying the rides has two components: c, the cost of supplying the equipment, and d, the cost of printing and collecting the tickets at each ride. The per unit cost is independent of the number of rides offered at the park. The capital letters in the figure represent areas. The monopolist is considering two pricing policies:

- *Policy 1.* An entrance fee and a per unit charge for each ride.

- *Policy 2.* Just an entrance fee. (The advantage of this policy is that the firm can save on printing and collecting tickets.)

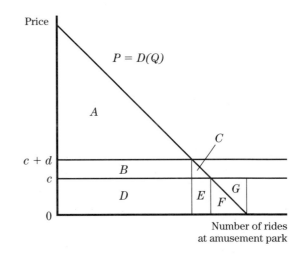

a. On the graph, show the entrance fee, per unit charge, total number of rides supplied, and total profits under each policy.

b. Under what conditions will the profits under policy 2 exceed the profits under policy 1?

c. What is the disadvantage of policy 2?

Can you think of another pricing policy that allows the firm to earn higher profits?

*13. This question extends the analysis of pricing consumer capital discussed in Section 12-6. You have developed a new camcorder that takes excellent pictures at a lower cost than any camcorder on the market and requires the use of a special tape that you alone produce at a marginal cost of c per tape. Your market research department predicts that the demand for tapes will come from small and large demand buyers. The demand curves for tapes of each type of customer are shown in the figure below. Assume that you have priced

the tape and camcorder to maximize total profits of the firm. Now suppose that competitors develop a lower-cost substitute for your tapes and sell the substitute at f per tape that is less than c per tape.

  a. How will the availability of the competitive supply of tapes affect the price of the camcorder? Explain.

  b. With the aid of graphs show how the supply of lower-cost tape affects the profits obtained from the small buyer and the profits gained from sales of the camcorder and tapes to the large buyer. Will total profits decrease?

14. In the accompanying figure, DD is the daily demand function of a customer for a good. A monopolist charges P_1 for each unit of the good and sells q_1 units; d denotes marginal cost, and MR represents marginal revenue. The letters A, B, and C denote areas. A consumer can store the product for a day, but the product spoils from then on. A market research firm reviews the pricing policy and recommends that the firm charge an entrance fee for each day if the consumer purchases the product, along with a per unit charge. It recommends a daily entrance fee equal to $A + B + C$ and a per unit fee of d. After this

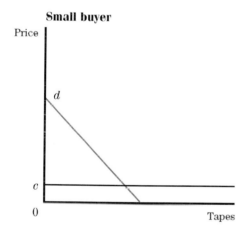

Small buyer

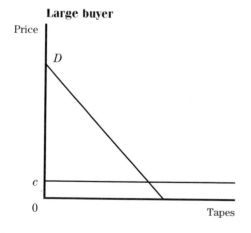

Large buyer

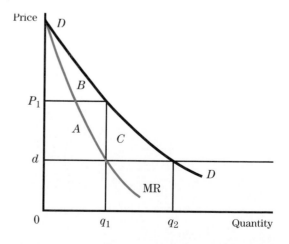

pricing policy is introduced, the purchases of the consumer follow a 2-day cycle. The consumer purchases q_2 units on the first day and nothing on the second day.

a. Will the profits with the new pricing policy be greater than the profits with the old policy over a 2-day period?

b. Suppose your answer to part a is that the profits with the old pricing policy are higher over a 2-day period. Would you then eliminate the two-part tariff and simply charge P_1 in each period? Can you suggest a different two-part pricing policy that will yield greater profits?

CHAPTER 13

THE FREE RIDER PROBLEM AND PRICING

■ **13-1 Free Rider Problems in Different Markets**
Application 13-1: IBM Sues a Former Employee

■ **13-2 Why Are Manufacturers Interested in the Retail Price?**
Case 1: GM's Restriction on Dealer Sales
Case 2: IBM and Apple Restrictions on Dealers
Case 3: Discounting Prince Tennis Rackets

■ **13-3 Benefiting from Retail Price Competition**
Allowing Free Entry of Retailers
Deriving the Inverse Wholesale Demand Function
Maximizing the Profits of the Manufacturer

■ **13-4 The Special Service Theory and the Free Rider Problem in Retailing**
The Special Service Theory
Resale Price Maintenance and the Special Service Theory
Applying the Theory to Explain Behavior

The Role of Each Assumption
Why Does Free-Riding Appear in Retailing?
Dealing with the Free Rider Problem without Using a Minimum Suggested Retail Price
The Objection to RPM: Facilitating a Cartel

■ **13-5 Free-Riding with Quality Certification**
Application 13-2: Testing New Toys at Small Toy Stores
Application 13-3: Toys "R" Us Wants Toy Manufacturers to Sell to It Exclusively

■ **13-6 Free Rider Problems between Manufacturers**
Application 13-4: Ben and Jerry versus Goliath

■ **Summary**
■ **Key Terms**
■ **Review Questions**
■ **Exercises**
■ **Problem Set: A Young Designer and the Free Rider Problem**

Free rider problems arise whenever the creators of valuable goods or information cannot protect the use of their creations. The creators, who have typically invested resources to develop and produce the new goods or new information, cannot fully appropriate the return on their investment. Instead, "free riders" who have not contributed to the development and production are able to profit from the creators' investment. Free rider problems appear in many markets. In today's global economy, companies may invest resources to create brand names and then find other firms producing unauthorized knockoffs and selling them under the brand names. Well-known designers see their unique clothing designs copied within days after they appear in Paris designer shows and sold under the brand name of the original designer. Software companies like Microsoft are constantly at odds with foreign governments that look the other way when foreign firms copy and sell software without paying royalties. One estimate is that between 40 and 50 percent of all software is pirated. In Chapter 11 we encountered a free rider problem when shareholders benefit from the efforts of one or several large shareholders to improve management performance without sharing the cost of the efforts. We will return to the free rider problem in Chapter 19 when we discuss the provision of public goods such as national defense. In the present chapter we survey the different forms that free rider problems can take and selectively examine how private markets cope with them.

"Free-riding" is worrisome because the collective failure to protect the investment required to develop new information and new products will cause firms to underinvest in such development. If enterprising firms invest resources to produce new products only to find that others quickly enter and produce the same products without incurring the new product development costs, the original firms are not able to recover their new product development costs and will be less likely to undertake other new product projects. Hence, some new products will not appear in the market, and society will not benefit from them.

This chapter begins by presenting an assortment of **free rider problems** that arise in various markets. Then, we consider two that commonly occur in retailing markets and one that involves manufacturers. Free rider problems are worth studying in order to comprehend the policies, which would otherwise appear puzzling and inexplicable, that firms adopt to combat them.

13-1   FREE RIDER PROBLEMS IN DIFFERENT MARKETS

Free rider problems crop up in a wide range of markets. This section describes four instances of such problems, demonstrating the scope and importance of the issue.

Free Rider Illustration 1:   Free rider problems can appear in labor markets. Companies often establish research and development (R&D) teams to work secretly on new projects. To benefit from R&D efforts, sponsoring firms must keep research results under wraps so that competitors cannot appropriate information which, as the research project evolves, the members of the project team accumulate. For example, team members know which approaches were successful and which were not. A rival firm working on a similar research project, or any competitor, may go to extraordinary lengths to acquire this knowledge. One way that competitors do this is by hiring the personnel on the research team. A free rider problem emerges because one firm has invested considerable resources to create valuable information that other firms can acquire in this way typically at a nominal cost.

How can firms prevent employees from leaving with trade secrets? Often they use contracts that require employees to remain with the company for a given number of years and not to sell or transmit information to competitors. However, the legal status of these contracts remains unclear. Another way firms can protect themselves is to parcel out parts of a project to different teams so that only the manager and a few other employees are fully aware of all the results. However, there are limits to this since the success of a project depends on the interchange of information and ideas. Still another way that firms protect themselves is by assigning employees with firm-specific knowledge and experience to a project. These individuals have been with the company for many years and are more valuable to their current employer than they would be to another firm. However, even this may not be a successful deterrent to members of a large, successful research team who may be enticed by large salary offers to leave the firm and take trade secrets with them.

APPLICATION **13-1**

IBM Sues a Former Employee

In 1991 Seagate Technology, Inc., hired away Peter Bonyhard, one of IBM's star engineers.[1] Bonyhard's specialty at IBM was developing disk-drive heads, and Seagate promptly told him to develop the next generation of disk-drive heads.

IBM sued Seagate to prevent its employee from skipping to the new company with trade secrets and in December 1991 won an injunction preventing Bonyhard from working on the Seagate project. IBM said the case was unique because Bonyhard took a similar job with a competitor. It claimed that Bonyhard could not help revealing IBM's secrets in his new job and wanted him not to work on disk-drive heads. Seagate's countersuit charged that IBM expected its top technical people "to remain in lifetime servitude" to the company. Bonyhard argued that a knowledge of heads was his specialty and that other work would not be suitable for him. In April 1992 an appeals court lifted the injunction, and Bonyhard began working on the Seagate project.

Free Rider Illustration 2:   In the agricultural sector firms also try to protect the "fruits" of their research and development efforts. For years seed-producing firms that create new seed varieties have complained about farmers who sell some

[1] Based on Michael W. Miller, "IBM Sues to Silence Former Employee," *The Wall Street Journal*, July 15, 1992.

or all of their crop as seeds packaged in "brown bags" for subsequent planting by other farmers. Company projects researching seed varieties can involve substantial research and development expenditures. Once the seeds of a new variety are sold, they can be reproduced cheaply by farmers for certain sexually reproducing crops such as soybeans. This substantially reduces the return on investment for the seed-producing firms. Often, soybeans, for instance, are more valuable as seed than as feed grain and so some farmers sell the crop as seed. This combination of high research and development costs of companies and low cost of reproducing the seed by farmers creates a fertile ground, we may say, for free rider problems to sprout.

The 1970 Plant Variety Protection Act protects inventors of seeds by giving them the exclusive right to market sexually reproducing seeds such as soybeans. Asgrow Seed, owned by Upjohn Company, learned that some farmers were selling their soybean crop as seed and brought suit charging that they were violating the Plant Variety Protection Act. The dispute is over the interpretation of vague wording in the law that exempts farmers who save seed from their crop and later sell the seed to farmers for the next season's plantings. The legal disagreement is over how much of the crop can be sold as seed by one farmer to other farmers.

The issue is an important one because by selling seed farmers reduce the return to the inventor of the new seed variety. Firms doing seed research claim that they invest substantial sums in research and development and they are unable to recover their expenditures if farmers can enter the market and sell seed to other farmers. Some firms claim that "brown-bagging" has so reduced their return that they have eliminated their seed research and development programs for hard winter wheat, cotton, and soybeans. The courts will have to decide the severity of this free rider problem as they clarify the property rights of current and potential creators of new seed varieties.[2]

Free Rider Illustration 3:   Free rider problems turn up when firms create intellectual property. Trademarks or brand names like Sanka reduce the cost of search for consumers, who associate some property of the product with the name.[3] Sanka, for example, denotes decaffeinated coffee made by General Foods. Manufacturers have an incentive to develop trademarks when they can produce a consistent quality over time. Then, consumers receive one or several desirable benefits with each use of the product. A manufacturer that maintains a trademark through advertising has an incentive to produce a product of consistent quality, and the producer of a consistent-quality product has an incentive to advertise the name.

The cost of creating a valuable trademark is high. A company spends considerable sums on quality control, quality of service, and advertising. On the other hand, the cost of duplicating a trademark—a label or a name—is small. Without legal restrictions, once a firm has developed a valuable trademark, competitive firms could easily copy it and earn profits temporarily. The competitors could

---

[2] Paul M. Barnett, "High-Court Battle Sprouts from Clash between Farmers and the Seed Industry," *The Wall Street Journal*, May 23, 1994. Reprinted by permission of *The Wall Street Journal* © 1994 Dow Jones & Company, Inc. All Rights Reserved Worldwide.

[3] This discussion is based on William M. Landes and Richard A. Posner, "Trademark Law: An Economic Perspective," *Journal of Law and Economics* XXX (October 1987), pp. 265–310.

produce the good and the label at a lower cost than the original producers, and unless the owner of the trademark could prevent this, there would be little incentive to develop a trademark or a brand name in the long run. In such cases, however, trademarks receive protection from the courts. The law prohibits them from being copied, although fraudulent use of trademarks remains a problem for many firms, especially in countries that do not enforce the copyright laws of other countries.

Free Rider Illustration 4:   The growing popularity of the Internet has created an important and perhaps intractable free rider problem.[4] Once a copyrighted work appears on the Internet, copying is so cheap that the Internet is becoming a huge worldwide copying machine. By using scanning devices to place copyrighted material on the Internet, digital technology enables the inexpensive dissemination of such material. The Internet can make copies that are generally as good as the original. The spectacular growth of the Internet means that millions of users around the globe are ready clients.

Copyright law grants rights for authorized reproduction and for authorized distribution of copies. The Internet has raised the following difficult and unresolved issues.

1. If a surfer calls up some copyright information from the Internet, should this be treated as a reproduction that violates a copyright?

2. Databases require considerable expenditures to compile. Now, when databases are copied on the Internet, the creator of the database does not receive any compensation. Should databases receive copyright protection?

3. Under copyright law the owner of the copyright controls the sale of the first copy but not the sale of the used copy. The sale of the initial copy may result in an endless supply of perfect copies. What restrictions on copying should be enforced and by whom?

4. Who is liable? If an undergraduate uses a university site and places copyrighted material on the Internet, is the undergraduate or the university liable for the copyright violation?

5. Of what value is greater copyright protection in developed countries if pirated copies can be obtained from countries that do not abide by international agreements?

The United Nations, the European Union, and governments especially of developed countries are struggling with these and related issues. Owners of intellectual property advocate a tightening of the copyright laws and stronger protection. They want to rewrite the copyright laws so that any type of electronic transmission of a copyrighted work requires permission. One point of controversy is the treatment of library copying. In some European countries libraries have the right to transmit an endless supply of copies. Copyright owners are demanding more stringent limitations on electronic copying privileges of libraries.

---

[4] This section is based on "Intellectual Property," *The Economist*, July 27, 1996. © 1996 The Economist Newspaper Group, Inc. Reprinted with permission. Further reproduction prohibited.

Even if the copyright laws are more precisely defined, there remains the difficult issue of how to compensate creators of intellectual property. Can feasible and low-cost mechanisms be created that will compensate owners of copyrights for the *use* of their property? At one extreme is the suggestion to do nothing. To protect themselves, authors would have to update material to keep one slight step ahead of the pirates, not easily implemented. For example, authors of textbooks would have to revise their books more frequently so that older versions become somewhat obsolete. Another option includes payment for each use. Each user would have to sign up and perhaps pay a signup fee using a credit card. Additional charges would be based on frequency of use. This pricing policy would not solve all free rider problems but would grant the copyright holder some protection. A lot of publishers, authors, artists, and companies are spending sleepless nights trying to find feasible and effective solutions to the Internet problem.

While these are only four illustrations, they demonstrate the diversity of situations where free rider problems appear, and they have two points in common. First, in each instance a firm or individual creates valuable *general* information that is valuable not only to its creator but to others as well. The information is not firm-specific. The more basic the research, the more general the information created. The second point is that other firms can appropriate the information without fully compensating its creator. Therefore, the owner cannot completely control the use of the information.

> Free rider problems occur when information is general and the creator of the information cannot establish property rights to it.

In these illustrations firms can design incentive mechanisms to prevent the free rider problem from emerging. For example, they could compensate the worker at the end of the project, rely on the courts to establish property rights to a brand name or to certain information (as in the case of a new seed variety or a trademark), or redesign the product to eliminate or reduce the severity of the free rider problem. This chapter concentrates on the policies companies use to prevent the free rider problem from arising.

13-2   WHY ARE MANUFACTURERS INTERESTED IN THE RETAIL PRICE?

We begin our investigation of the free rider problem somewhat indirectly by examining three cases of manufacturers in different industries limiting the quantities that retailers can sell and preventing retail price competition. The manufacturers' argument for such practices is that they mitigate the free rider problem.

Case 1: GM's Restriction on Dealer Sales

General Motors and other automobile manufacturers require their dealers to carry an adequate inventory, to employ a sales and service staff appropriate for the size of the market, and to provide after-sale service. However, a General Motors dealer on the outskirts of a large metropolitan area came up with an idea to reduce costs.[5] He cut the sales staff and inventories to the bone and advertised a very low price. The dealer was willing to take orders from customers who knew what kind of car and what options they wanted, and he promised delivery to each customer after the customary time required to obtain delivery. His advertising campaign was a success, and orders increased when consumers jumped at the opportunity to purchase GM autos at lower prices.

You might think that GM's management would eagerly embrace a more efficient way of operating a dealership since a lower retail price would not only increase the dealer's volume but GM's volume as well. But GM's reaction was decidedly cool, and the new strategy failed when the dealer could no longer obtain deliveries. The dealer claimed that GM forced him out of business by slowing delivery of orders to him because it disapproved of his new advertising and pricing policies.

What explains GM's hostility toward a policy that would lower the retail price of autos and increase the number sold?

Case 2: IBM and Apple Restrictions on Dealers

For many years IBM and Apple Computer policed and, if necessary, terminated dealers who regularly sold out of their marketing areas to gray marketers. Gray marketers are retail outlets that systematically sell outside their customary local market and include mail-order suppliers, some local computer stores, and other electronics stores.[6] Authorized IBM and Apple dealers that sold primarily in their own local markets complained to their respective manufacturers that discounters drove prices down and took customers away. These dealers claimed that customers who buy in the gray market are "tire kickers," individuals who frequent authorized IBM or Apple retail outlets but buy elsewhere.

Why did IBM and Apple discourage competition among dealers by preventing authorized retailers from selling outside their immediate local markets?

Case 3: Discounting Prince Tennis Rackets

Racket Doctor, a retail outlet selling Prince tennis rackets in Los Angeles, lowered the price of certain Prince rackets to just a few dollars below the lower bound of retail prices suggested by Prince Manufacturing, Inc.[7] Prince Manufacturing had sent each of its dealers a memorandum with suggested price ranges for six of its top lines. For example, the suggested range for Thunderstick, its best racket, was between $229.95 and $250. The memo included a warning that dealers who set prices below the guidelines would no longer receive Prince rackets. After other retailers complained, Prince Manufacturing terminated Racket Doctor. Why did the company prevent Racket Doctor from selling its tennis rackets at lower prices?

---

[5] D. Levin, "FTC Probes Charges GM Forced Dealer Out of Business over Discount Pricing," *The Wall Street Journal*, February 15, 1985.
[6] "Blue vs. Gray: IBM Tries to Stop the Discounters," *Fortune*, May 27, 1985, p. 79.
[7] Paul Barrett, "Anti-Discount Policies of Manufacturers Are Penalizing Certain Cut-Price Stores," *The Wall Street Journal*, February 27, 1991.

In each of these cases the manufacturer's policy attenuated retail price competition and encouraged retailers to maintain higher rather than lower prices. This behavior may strike you as odd since it seems logical for a manufacturer to encourage dealers to sell as many units as they can. Yet, in each instance, the manufacturer limited competition by preventing retailers from lowering prices. Why did these companies discourage competition among their dealers?

13-3   BENEFITING FROM RETAIL PRICE COMPETITION

The behavior of the manufacturers toward their retailers in the cases above appears puzzling because it seems to be inconsistent with profit maximization. Given the wholesale price, a manufacturer will sell fewer units the higher is the retail price. Therefore, we expect manufacturers to favor lower, not higher, retail prices.

We develop a model to show why manufacturers want lower retail prices. In the model, a monopoly manufacturer sells a product to many competitive retailers who in turn sell the product to final consumers. The manufacturer decides the total quantity to produce, sets the wholesale price, and allows free entry into retailing so that its profits are maximized. Initially, we assume that each retailer sells a product with which consumers are familiar. The retailer's primary role is to supply the inventory for consumers to buy. For example, virtually all supermarkets and drugstores carry Crest toothpaste, a product so familiar that consumers need little or no advice from a druggist before making a purchase decision. Later, we expand the model to consider products about which the retailer plays a key role in providing consumers information.

Allowing Free Entry of Retailers

Given the manufacturer's wholesale price, a manufacturer sells more units the lower is the retail price. Since the retail price will be lower by allowing free entry into retailing, a manufacturer prefers more competition among its retailers. With free entry retailers will enter until any retailing profits are competed away. At that point the retail price must equal the wholesale price paid by the retailer *plus* the retailer's long-run *minimum* average selling cost. Retailers earn the same return on their capital as they could obtain in the next best use. Accordingly, competition among retailers guarantees that the manufacturer's product is sold at the lowest feasible retail price.

A numerical example may help to clarify this point. In the retail market, assume the inverse retail demand curve for the manufacturer's product is downward sloping and is such that the manufacturer can sell 1 million units per year if the retail price is $25. Furthermore, assume each (identical) retailer's *minimum* long-run average selling cost equals $7 when each retailer sells 10,000 units per year. The highest wholesale price that the manufacturer can charge and still sell 1 million units is $18. The retailer sells each unit at $25 and the retailer's minimum long-run average cost, which equals the wholesale price plus the minimum long-run average selling cost, equals $18 + $7 = $25. Therefore, retailers do not earn any profits. If each retailer sells 10,000 units, retailers will enter until the manufacturer has 100 retailers selling the product and no retailer is earning a profit.

Let's illustrate this situation with a graph. Figure 13-1 shows a retailer's long-run average cost function, $AC_L(q)$, and long-run marginal cost function, $MC_L(q)$. The long-run average cost function has two components, the wholesale price, $18, and the long-run average selling cost $ASC_L(q)$. The retailer pays $18 for each unit shipped by the manufacturer to the retailer. Selling costs include labor, depreciation of the retail plant, and supplies, but excludes the wholesale price of the product. The long-run average cost function of the firm, $AC_L(q)$, is U-shaped in Figure 13-1. The retailer achieves economies of scale as volume increases, but then diseconomies of scale set in. When the retailer sells 10,000 units, long-run average selling cost reaches a minimum of ASC_0, or $7, and long-run average cost reaches a minimum value of $25.

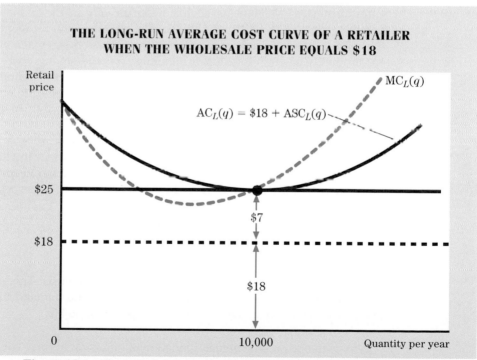

THE LONG-RUN AVERAGE COST CURVE OF A RETAILER WHEN THE WHOLESALE PRICE EQUALS $18

Figure 13-1   The long-run average cost function of a retailer is $AC_L(q)$ and equals the sum of the wholesale price and the long-run average selling cost function. The retailer's *minimum* long-run average cost equals $18 + $7 = $25 when the retailer sells 10,000 units per year. When the retail price is $25, the retailer does not earn profits. The retail price will be $25 when 1 million units are supplied by 100 retailers, each selling 10,000 units.

The long-run average cost function of the retail establishment is $18 + \mathrm{ASC}_L(q)$ and is U-shaped because $\mathrm{ASC}_L(q)$ is U-shaped.

$$\mathrm{AC}_L(q) = \$18 + \mathrm{ASC}_L(q) \qquad \text{(Long-Run Average Cost Function of Retailer)} \qquad \textbf{(13-1)}$$

If the retail price is $25, each price-taking retailer maximizes profits by selling 10,000 units where $25 is equal to *minimum* long-run average and long-run marginal cost.

Deriving the Inverse Wholesale Demand Function

Before we can determine how a manufacturer selects the wholesale price and indirectly the number of retailers in the industry, we must first derive the inverse wholesale demand function that faces the manufacturer. The manufacturer's wholesale demand function describes the highest wholesale price that the manufacturer can charge for each total quantity sold to all retailers.

If the manufacturer allows the free entry of retailers no matter what quantity the manufacturer produces, the long-run average selling cost of each retailer will be $7. If, as we assume, retailing is a constant-cost industry, each retailer that enters is just as efficient as each retailer already in the industry. Whether the manufacturer produces 1 or 2 million units, it wants each retailer to sell a quantity that *minimizes* long-run average selling cost. This occurs when each retailer sells 10,000 units and therefore has a minimum average selling cost of $7. What will vary is the number of retailers. If 1 million units are sold, the manufacturer requires 100 retailers so that each retailer's average selling cost is $7. If 2 million units will be sold, the manufacturer requires 200 retailers, each selling 10,000 units, so that each retailer's long-run average selling cost equals $7.

With this information we can derive the manufacturer's inverse wholesale demand. The highest wholesale price that a manufacturer can charge its retailers for any given total quantity is the retail price less $7. If the inverse retail demand function is $R = D(Q)$ where R is the retail price, the inverse wholesale demand function is

$$\text{Wholesale price} = \text{Retail price} - \$7$$

$$W = D(Q) - \$7 = N(Q)$$

where $W = N(Q)$ is the inverse wholesale demand function. The inverse wholesale demand curve is derived by shifting the inverse retail demand function down by minimum long-run average selling cost, or in this case $7.

> The inverse wholesale demand function of the manufacturer equals the inverse retail demand function less the retailer's *minimum* long-run average selling cost.

When there is **free entry into retailing,** the difference between the retail price and the wholesale price is just large enough so that the retailers cover their *minimum* long-run average selling costs. If a manufacturer restricted the number of retailers while still trying to sell 1 million units, each retailer would have to sell more units and its long-run average selling cost would increase. The manufacturer would have to lower the wholesale price to compensate each retailer for its higher per unit selling costs. Consequently, by restricting entry into retailing, the manufacturer's profits would decline and this is why the manufacturer favors free entry into retailing.

Maximizing the Profits of the Manufacturer

The profit function of the manufacturer is equal to total revenue from units sold to dealers less manufacturing costs.

$$\pi_m = WQ - M(Q)$$

$$= N(Q)Q - M(Q) \qquad \text{(Manufacturer's Profits)} \qquad \textbf{(13-2)}$$

where $M(Q)$ represents the manufacturer's total production costs.

The monopolist selects the profit maximizing output where marginal revenue from the last unit sold (derived from the inverse *wholesale* demand function) equals the marginal cost of production.[8]

$$\mathrm{MR}_m(Q) = \mathrm{MC}_m(Q) \qquad \text{(Equilibrium Condition for Manufacturer)} \qquad \textbf{(13-3)}$$

$\mathrm{MR}_m(Q)$ is the manufacturer's marginal revenue from selling another unit to retailers. MC_m denotes the marginal cost of producing another unit. In Figure 13-2 the manufacturer produces 1 million units where marginal revenue equals marginal cost. $18 is the profit-maximizing wholesale price, and equilibrium retail price is $25. Total profits of the manufacturer equal the area *abcd*.

The difference between the retail price and the wholesale price must equal minimum average selling cost ASC_0, of $7. So, the retailer's profits are zero. If the difference between the retail and the wholesale price is $7 and a retailer sold fewer or more than 10,000 units, it would incur losses because average selling cost would no longer be at the minimum. Because the retailer is operating at a point where

---

[8] More generally, since ASC_0 is the minimum long-run average selling cost, the wholesale demand function is derived by subtracting ASC_0 from the market demand function.

$$W = N(Q) = D(Q) - \mathrm{ASC}_0$$

Substituting this expression for W into the manufacturer's profit equation gives

$$\pi_m = [D(Q) - \mathrm{ASC}_0]Q - M(Q)$$

Using calculus, we find that profits are maximized when

$$\frac{d(\pi_m)}{dQ} = D(Q) + Q\frac{d[D(Q)]}{dQ} - \mathrm{ASC}_0 - \frac{d[M(Q)]}{dQ} = 0$$

The first two terms on the right-hand side represent marginal revenue of the retail demand function. The third term represents minimum long-run average selling cost, and the last term represents marginal production cost. Marginal revenue of the wholesale demand function is equal to the sum of the first three terms, or marginal revenue of the retail demand function less ASC_0. Therefore, the profit-maximizing quantity occurs where marginal revenue of the wholesale demand function equals marginal production cost.

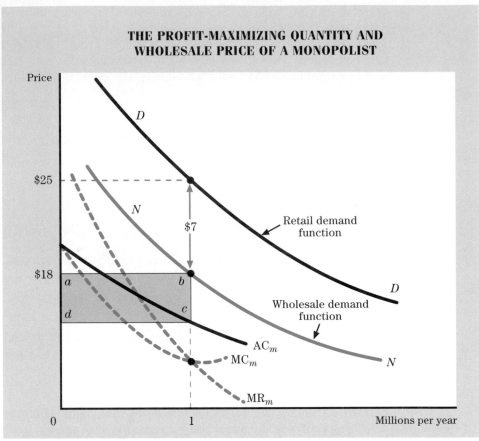

**THE PROFIT-MAXIMIZING QUANTITY AND
WHOLESALE PRICE OF A MONOPOLIST**

Figure 13-2 If the monopolist allows the free entry of retailers, the difference between the retail price and the wholesale price equals $7, the retailer's minimum long-
run average selling cost. The monopolist's wholesale demand function is *NN*. The
monopolist charges a wholesale price of $18 and produces 1 million units where the
manufacturer's marginal revenue equals marginal cost. The per unit retail price equals
$25 and the manufacturer's profits equal area *abcd*.

long-run average selling cost is at a minimum, the retailer's long-run average cost
equals its long-run marginal cost.

   In summary, the manufacturer receives the highest wholesale price for any
quantity the manufacturer sells by allowing free entry of retailers so that each one
operates at the minimum point of the long-run average selling cost function. It is
in the self-interest of the manufacturer to have the most cost-effective retailers so
that the total cost of selling 1 million units is minimized. The manufacturer then
determines the profit-maximizing quantity and the wholesale price by equating its
marginal revenue to its marginal cost of production.

13-4   THE SPECIAL SERVICE THEORY AND THE FREE RIDER PROBLEM IN RETAILING

Our analysis implies that a manufacturer's profits are higher when retailers are free to enter so that each operates at the minimum point on its long-run average cost function. However, we observed that General Motors, IBM, Apple, and Prince limited competition by preventing retailers from *lowering* price. Why is their behavior so different from what economic theory predicts?

The Special Service Theory

Lester Telser has advanced an interesting theory that focuses on the free rider problem to explain why and when a manufacturer resists retail price competition.[9] According to the special service theory retailers not only provide inventory but also supply educational services to consumers that shift the manufacturer's demand function outward. Recognizing the value of these services, manufacturers develop policies that encourage retailers to provide these educational services.

> A **special service** is a service that the consumer receives without charge and shifts the retail and wholesale demand functions outward.

The theory has four assumptions.

1. The retail and wholesale demand functions shift outward if retailers provide special (educational) services to consumers.

2. The retailer supplies the special service at the point of sale more cheaply than the manufacturer can through general promotion messages.

3. The information supplied by the retailer is brand-specific.

4. It is too costly for the retailer to charge separately for the special service.

Given these assumptions, how does the special service theory explain why manufacturers limit retail price competition and favor a minimum suggested retail price? Step back in time and consider the problem faced by computer manufacturers when PCs were first introduced in the early 1980s. They were a new and unknown product to most people and to many businesses, and customers required information about their possible uses. They wanted to know about the special characteristics of computers and how the manufacturer's computer would help solve their particular problems. To sell their products, manufacturers arranged to have dealers supply **educational information** to diverse consumers by providing detailed answers at the point of purchase.

Initially, each manufacturer adopts a general policy that guarantees retailers

---

[9] Lester Telser, "Why Should Manufacturers Want Fair Trade?" *Journal of Law and Economics* 3 (October 1960), pp. 86–105.

will supply the information. The manufacturer might insist that each dealer have a well-trained sales staff that understands the special requirements of each customer and conducts hands-on demonstrations. These services are costly to provide, and so the retail margin, the difference between the retail and wholesale prices, had to be large enough to cover the costs incurred by these service-rich retailers.

Let's suppose a computer manufacturer initially appoints a large number of service-rich retailers but then relaxes standards for retailers. Assume that you decide to enter the retail computer market but wonder how you can succeed in such a competitive business. You would wonder if the high retail markup could be the key to your success. Instead of operating a retail outlet with a large sales staff and an extensive and expensive inventory, your retail operation will be "lean and mean." If the customer knows what type of computer he or she wants, your sales staff will supply it promptly and at a lower price. Your retail operation will focus on customers who know what computer they want. Your business is not for the less informed customer who needs more prepurchase support, advice, and hand-holding. By managing a bare-bones operation, you expect to pass on significant cost savings.

Figure 13-3a shows the long-run average and marginal cost functions of a retailer that supplies special services, and Figure 13-3b shows the long-run average and marginal cost functions of one that does not. In both cases the wholesale price

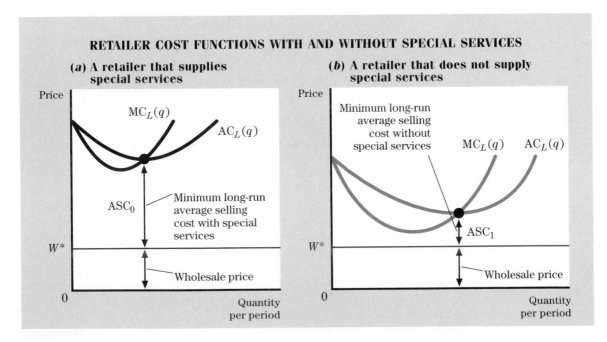

Figure 13-3   (a) Long-run average and marginal cost functions of a retailer who supplies special services. (b) Long-run average and marginal cost functions of a retailer who operates a bare-bones operation and does not supply special services.

is W^*. The minimum long-run average selling cost of the retailer that provides special services is ASC_0, and the minimum long-run average operating cost of the retailer that does not is ASC_1.

How do consumers react when this different type of retailer enters the market? More customers become "tire kickers." They visit service-rich computer stores and receive useful and valuable prepurchase educational services. But when the salesperson tries to close the transaction, they refuse to buy. Then they purchase at a lower price from a service-lean dealership.

These consumers receive and benefit from a free ride. They obtained valuable services from the service-rich dealer without having to pay for them. Because customers purchase from service-lean dealers, service-rich dealers suffer losses. They have incurred the cost of making these services available but do not recover this cost when customers purchase elsewhere. The market is no longer in equilibrium. Either the service-rich dealers will have to go out of business or they will have to convert their operations to service-lean dealerships.

If two retailers can choose whether to be service-lean or service-rich retailers, the dominant strategy of each retailer is to be a service-lean retailer. Figure 13-4 shows the payoffs for two among many retailers. If retailer 2 is service-lean, retailer 1's profits are higher if it also chooses to be a service-lean retailer. Retailer 1 does not earn profits by becoming a service-lean retailer because there is competition

**DOMINANT STATEGIES IN THE
FREE RIDER PROBLEM**

Retailer 2

	Service-lean	Service-rich
Service-lean	$\pi_2 = \$0$ $\pi_1 = \$0$	$\pi_2 = -\$50$ $\pi_1 = \$100$
Service-rich	$\pi_2 = \$100$ $\pi_1 = -\$50$	$\pi_2 = \$0$ $\pi_1 = \$0$

Retailer 1

Figure 13-4   The dominant strategy of retailer 1 is to be a service-lean retailer no matter which strategy retailer 2 selects. Similarly, retailer 2's profits are higher if it is a service-lean retailer no matter what strategy retailer 1 selects.

among all service-lean retailers. Nevertheless, it avoids the losses it would incur if it supplied special services that retailer 2 and other retailers can free-ride on. If retailer 2 provides special services, then retailer 1's profits are $100 if it does not and instead free-rides on the special services provided by the other retailers. If retailer 1 also provides special services when others do, competition among all service-rich retailers implies that retailer 1 does not earn profits. Hence, retailer 1's dominant strategy is to be a service-lean retailer. By similar reasoning, retailer 2's dominant strategy is to be a service-lean retailer. Consequently neither will provide special services and the manufacturer's profits are lower. The Nash equilibrium implies both retailers choose service-lean strategies.

Resale Price Maintenance and the Special Service Theory

Under *resale price maintenance* (RPM) or a more informal system where the manufacturer suggests a range of retail prices, a manufacturer sets the minimum price at which a retailer can sell the product.

> Under **resale price maintenance** a manufacturer prohibits its retailers from selling the product below a minimum suggested price.

How does a manufacturer benefit from the use of a minimum retail price? A service-lean store can no longer sell computers at prices below those charged by the service-rich retailer. Now the shoe is on the other foot. The service-lean dealer is at a disadvantage because customers have less incentive to visit his dealership. By shopping at the service-rich dealership, customers pay the same price as at the service-lean dealership *and* receive the valuable educational services. Now it is the service-lean dealer who must decide whether to leave the market or to revamp store operations and become a service-rich dealer.

When the manufacturer sets a minimum retail price, retailers must engage in *nonprice competition* by supplying special services. The demand function for the product shifts outward, as shown in Figure 13-5. In Figure 13-5*a* DD is the inverse retail market demand function and NN is the manufacturer's wholesale demand function if retailers do not supply special services. In Figure 13-5*b* $D'D'$ is the retail demand function, and $N'N'$ is the wholesale demand function when retailers supply special services. MR and MR' are the marginal revenue functions of the two wholesale demand functions, and MC_m is the marginal cost function of the manufacturer.

Because the wholesale demand curve shifts outward, the manufacturer's profits are higher if retailers supply special services. Then, the retail and wholesale prices that maximize these profits are R' and W', respectively. If retailers do not provide special services, the retail and wholesale prices that maximize profits are R^* and W^*. Under RPM the manufacturer will set the retail price at R'.[10] When

---

[10] The model considers only a monopoly manufacturer. However, studies show that firms in industries with many firms also use RPM, and it can be inferred that RPM is a feasible business arrangement even in industries with many firms. The existence of RPM in industries with many firms implies that special services for their products are brand-specific, even when the products are close substitutes.

OUTPUT AND THE DIFFERENCE BETWEEN THE RETAIL AND THE WHOLESALE PRICE ARE LARGER WHEN SPECIAL SERVICES ARE SUPPLIED

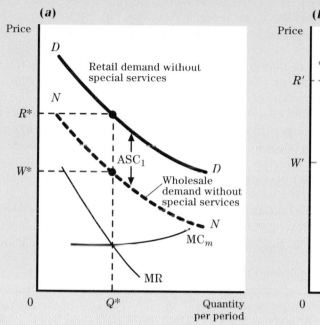
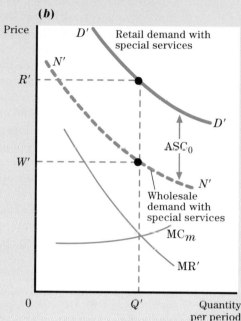

Figure 13 5 (*a*) If no special services are provided by retailers, the retail and wholesale demand functions are DD and NN and the monopolist sells Q^* units at a wholesale price of W^* and the retail price of R^*. (*b*) When special services are provided, the retail and wholesale demand functions shift outward and become $D'D'$ and $N'N'$. The manufacturer increases output from Q^* to Q' and increases the wholesale price from W^* to W'. The retail price rises to R' and the retail margin increases to $R' - W'$ to cover the increased selling cost of retailers.

retailers supply special services, the difference between the retail and wholesale prices must be large enough to cover the higher long-run average selling cost, ASC_0, of providing the special services.

> When the manufacturer enforces a minimum retail price, retailers have a greater incentive to provide special services.

Applying the Theory to Explain Behavior

Let's consider how the special service theory might explain why the manufacturers discouraged retail price competition in the three cases discussed in Section 13-2.

In the GM case the offending dealer was free-riding on the services supplied by other franchised dealers. These dealers offered customers a broad inventory of autos and a trained sales staff. The sales staff was available to answer questions about the automobile, option packages, and color choice and to take customers out for a test drive. Once they had this information, they purchased at a dealership that essentially took orders like a catalog operation. This type of dealership clearly has lower costs than those that provide a full range of informational services. In the long run the presence of service-lean dealerships would drive service-rich dealerships out of business, thereby reducing the demand for GM cars. If GM feels that the long-run demand for GM autos increases when dealers provide these informational services, it will disapprove of dealers who do not provide them.

IBM and Apple included clauses in their contracts that prevented dealers from becoming wholesalers selling to mass distributors or to mail-order houses. Initially, both manufacturers discouraged sales through mass distributors and mail-order firms and encouraged their dealers to provide prepurchase educational information to consumers. A mail-order operation that offers IBM or Apple computers has the potential for creating a free rider problem. Customers can obtain information from service-rich IBM and Apple dealers and then order computers at a lower price from the mail-order firm. The attempts by IBM and Apple to restrict price competition represent possible solutions to the free rider problem that these companies faced at the time.

Prince Manufacturing discouraged price competition for its new higher-priced tennis rackets. When selling expensive tennis rackets, it may want the retailer to spend time with the consumer describing the different features of the racket and determining which type of racket is the most suitable. Prince judges that consumers who purchase expensive tennis rackets value this information, and it wants to discourage other stores from free-riding by selling rackets below the minimum suggested price.

The Role of Each Assumption

Let's review each assumption of the special service theory to see how the conclusions would change if the assumption were relaxed.

1. If the wholesale demand function does not shift outward when retailers supply special services, the manufacturer's profits would be lower by requiring retailers to supply services that consumers do not value. The average selling cost function of the retailer shifts upward, and the wholesale demand function shifts inward. Under these circumstances the manufacturer has no incentive to impose a minimum retail price.

2. If the manufacturer could supply the special services at a lower cost than the retailer, it would provide them directly to consumers and the free rider problem would disappear. Dealers could not free-ride on other dealers because the manufacturer would provide the education function.

3. Special services are brand-specific. If the information provided by retailers is general, customers can obtain it from the retailers of one manufacturer and purchase from a retailer selling a different brand. Dealers of one man-

ufacturer can free-ride on the information supplied by the dealers of another manufacturer and consequently can underprice the dealers of a competitor. When the information supplied by retailers is brand-specific, this is impossible.

4. If transaction costs are small, the retailer can charge separately for the time the consumer spends with a salesperson. The buyer pays for the educational services separately and is then free to purchase the computer at the same store or elsewhere. The customer cannot free-ride on a service that must be paid for. The free rider problem exists because there is no cheap way to charge for special services.

Why Does Free-Riding Appear in Retailing?

A free rider problem can appear whenever there is a demand for prepurchase information by consumers. By recognizing these conditions in advance, a firm can prevent the problem from emerging by taking the appropriate steps. We list some of the conditions that cause free rider problems to develop.

1. Free rider problems are more severe for new products than for established products because consumers are less knowledgeable about new items than about established goods. If a manufacturer wants retailers to provide special services, it must anticipate the possibility of a free rider problem and protect retailers that provide these services. A manufacturer is more likely to discourage retail price competition by setting a minimum suggested price early in the product life cycle. Later, as the product ages and consumers gain more experience with it, the company can terminate the suggested minimum price.

2. A free rider problem is more likely to develop when a firm is selling a complex durable or technical good. In these cases consumers often lack information and need advice. For example, when buying nonprescription drugs, a person is likely to ask the druggist for advice when confronted with 20 alternative cold remedies. Drugs and small consumer durable goods were frequently sold under RPM when this practice was legal.

3. The free rider problem is more severe when the cost of time of the consumer is low relative to the cost of the product. A busy executive has a high cost of time. He or she is less likely to comparison-shop and more likely to purchase from a high-service store. Consumers are more likely to shop for a lower price when buying an expensive consumer durable good or appliance when the price of the good is high relative to the cost of the consumer's time.

Dealing with the Free Rider Problem without Using a Minimum Suggested Retail Price

The Supreme Court's attitude toward resale price maintenance has fluctuated over the years. In the 1980s, antitrust authorities and the courts softened their treatment of a minimum suggested retail price when evidence of a price conspiracy was absent. Firms like Prince Manufacturing suggest a range of prices at which retailers may sell a product rather than specifying a minimum suggested price. Retailers receive a warning that selling below this range will be grounds for termination. As long as the courts do not view this as price collusion between retailers or between manufacturers, this practice appears acceptable. While manufacturers have become more venturesome as they sense a more relaxed attitude toward minimum suggested retail prices by the courts and antitrust authorities, RPM remains a gray area in which some antitrust vulnerability exists.

Some firms have adopted other distribution policies to control the free rider problem. Some alternatives are the following.

1. Provide information at company-owned demonstration stores that do not sell products. Some examples are IBM in personal computers and, many years ago, Zenith in radio and television. Demonstration stores are expensive to operate, and so manufacturers limit their number and usually establish them in large metropolitan areas. They can help but do not fully solve the free rider problem. Major cosmetic companies purchase space in department stores and have their own personnel demonstrate products. In this way the manufacturer's role expands to include providing consumer information.

2. Limit the number of dealers and implicitly grant each dealer an exclusive territory to discourage customers from shopping around among competing dealers.

3. Select retailers who have a history of providing a service-rich environment. A high-quality department store is more likely to merchandise your product in a service-rich style than to adopt a service-lean method of retailing just for your product. Prescreening applicants prevents or at least reduces the probability that a free rider problem will arise. Given the high cost of terminating dealers, a prescreening policy is essential.

4. Design products with unique features or operating systems that make it more costly for other manufacturers to clone products and therefore to free-ride off your dealers. In an interesting illustration one company sells a game whose level of difficulty increases with each copy made. The game becomes hopelessly difficult if the owner makes several copies.

These alternatives are partial and often imperfect substitutes for direct limits on retail price competition. Limiting the number of dealers raises the cost of comparison shopping for consumers. This attenuates the free rider problem but reduces dealer density and encourages monopoly pricing by the dealer. There is much to be said for a policy of carefully screening potential dealers. The history of the retailer can provide clues about what type of retailer an applicant is likely to be. Is the candidate currently operating or has the candidate ever operated a service-rich retail establishment? Of course, an applicant with promise but little history is more difficult to assess. Clearly, the firm should seek expert legal advice so that contracts clearly specify which business practices will and will not be acceptable. Appointing dealers without an appreciation of the consequences of the free rider problem will lead to problems. Trying to rectify the problem by later changes in the terms of the contract leads to a quagmire of legal problems.

The Objection to RPM: Facilitating a Cartel

You may be wondering why the courts take a hostile attitude toward RPM if consumers benefit when retailers provide special services. Part of the objection is political, and part is intellectual. Most discounters oppose RPM. They argue that it raises retail prices and does not permit stores with fewer services to compete with full-service stores. This complaint is partly correct but is not a justification for a ban on RPM. Discount stores offer fewer services and lower prices and would be at a competitive disadvantage if they had to charge a higher price. On the other hand, a manufacturer seeks a more efficient method to distribute its product at the retail level. If the position of the inverse retail demand function is unaffected, the manufacturer always prefers the lowest-cost method of retailing the product and would rather rely on low-margin discount stores. The manufacturer has no reason to oppose a store offering the product with fewer services at a lower retail margin than a high-margin store. Indeed, there are many manufacturers that sell their products to discounters and would continue to do so even if RPM were permitted.

The case against RPM is that it can be a facilitating device to increase the effectiveness of a cartel. RPM can be used along with other devices to shore up an imperfect cartel. As noted in Chapter 10, a cartel is a fragile instrument subject to member cheating. To be effective, it must limit the increase in the quantity sold by a price cheater. With a fixed retail price a manufacturer who gives a secret wholesale price cut to its dealers will not experience an increase in sales because the retailer cannot lower the retail price. The gains from price cutting are smaller with than without RPM. RPM can be employed with other mechanisms that limit the increase in the quantity sold by a manufacturer who is a price chiseler. For example, the members of the cartel may agree to have exclusive retail dealers, not to raid the retailers of another cartel member, and to prevent secret price cheating at the retail level. All these arrangements reduce the increase in the quantity sold by a secret price cutter and therefore discourage price cutting. Therefore, opponents of RPM claim that manufacturers can use RPM to shore up a weak cartel and to make collusion more effective.

13-5   FREE-RIDING WITH QUALITY CERTIFICATION

Howard Marvel and Stephen McCafferty examined a different type of free rider problem where one type of retailer free-rides off another type of retailer.[11] They present the **quality certification** theory to explain why a manufacturer uses RPM and why it limits the number and kinds of dealers selling the product.

---

[11] H. Marvel and S. McCafferty, "Resale Price Maintenance and Quality Certification," *Rand Journal of Economics* 15 (Autumn 1984), pp. 346–59.

The three assumptions of the quality certification theory are:

1. Retailers incur costs to certify the quality or fashion characteristics of a product. Any up-front investment qualifies.

2. Retailers cannot charge separately for the certification function. If the certifying retailer could sell the information about quality to consumers separately, the free rider problem would disappear.

3. The decision to certify a brand by stocking it is general information. Consumers will purchase the brand elsewhere if it is available at a lower price.

The decision of a store to carry a brand is valuable information for consumers. If a store carries a certain brand, consumers infer it must meet the store's minimum specifications. When Marshall Field's, Neiman Marcus, or Macy's stocks a lesser-known brand, that decision reveals valuable information to consumers about either its quality or its fashion characteristics. The information is *general* in the sense that the value of the information does not depend on where the consumer ultimately purchases the product. Nevertheless, to the consumer this information is useful whether the consumer purchases the brand at Marshall Field's or at a specialty store.

Let's examine the free rider problem that appears when a store decides to carry a lesser-known brand following an investigation of the product and the reputation of the manufacturer. The retailer invests resources to identify brands that meet or surpass its minimum quality or fashion standards. That's the rub. The firm incurs the costs of certifying quality but cannot establish ownership over the information that it creates.

Suppose the manufacturer of the brand ships the brand to any retail store that orders it. Some of these stores simply copy the decision of the certifying retailer to carry the brand and can underprice the certifying store because they do not incur the costs of certification. They are free-riding on the decision of the certifying store to carry the brand. The certifying store incurred the cost but cannot appropriate the value of the information from the copying stores. If a majority of consumers are indifferent as to where they buy, they will purchase the brand at a lower price from stores that do not perform the certification function.

Clearly, a store will be reluctant to perform the certifying function if other firms can quickly free-ride on the decision. Suppose the demand for the manufacturer's brand decreases if a higher-quality store does not perform the certification role. The manufacturer must anticipate the consequences of allowing other stores to copy the adoption decision of the certifying store. It must guarantee that copying competitors will not receive the same merchandise as the certifying store does by limiting the distribution of the brand to only those stores that perform the certification function. The manufacturer can refuse to deal with lower-quality retailers and might agree to sell the product under RPM to prevent stores from underpricing the certifying store.

The quality certification theory can explain why manufacturers are reluctant to allow any retailer to sell their products but prefer to select similar types of stores to carry a brand. Just as the manufacturer selects retailers who will not free-ride on other retailers when it wants retailers to provide special services, so too does the manufacturer discourage retailers from free-riding on the information created by the certifying store.

APPLICATION 13-2

Testing New Toys at Small Toy Stores

With the growth of large discount stores such as Wal-Mart and Toys "R" Us, it is more difficult to introduce toys that require special handling, demonstrations, and instructions. Some manufacturers introduce new toys or reestablish older toys by relying exclusively on small toy shops for displays and demonstrations.[12] Many small stores associate with manufacturers that sell only to small toy stores because they cannot compete on price with the larger impersonal discount stores.

Small stores can claim partial credit for the success of such toys as Thomas the Tank Engine, Koosh balls, Erector sets, and Playmobile building sets. Massive advertising campaigns do not succeed with all types of toys. To be successful, some must be sold with demonstrations and displays that allow children to touch and play with them in the store. An example of this type of toy is Playmobile's playpens. Retailers are encouraged to set up playpens to give children a hands-on opportunity to play with them. No small toy store is likely to set aside space and encourage demonstrations if customers can then run down the street to a nearby discount store and purchase the toy in a box. Therefore, Playmobile limits its distribution to small specialty toy stores.

Small toy stores recognize that their exclusivity with a toy may end if the toy becomes too popular, because some toy manufacturers will then sell it in discount stores. Still, manufacturers give the smaller stores an opportunity to recoup their higher costs by preventing discount stores from immediately cashing in on toys that prove to be successful because of the efforts of small stores.

APPLICATION 13-3

Toys "R" Us Wants Toy Manufacturers to Sell to It Exclusively

Toys "R" Us, the discount toy retailer, is upset with low-price warehouse clubs and with some toy manufacturers.[13] Why is Toys "R" Us upset? The company

---

[12] Based on Joseph Pereira, "Toys 'R' Them: Mom-and-Pop Stores Put Playthings like Thomas on Fast Track," *The Wall Street Journal*, January 14, 1993.

[13] Bryan Gruley and Joseph Pereira, "FTC Says Toys 'R' Us Competes Unfairly," *The Wall Street Journal*, May 23, 1996. Reprinted by permission of *The Wall Street Journal*, © 1996 Dow Jones & Company, Inc. All Rights Reserved Worldwide.

carries and heavily promotes the toys of many manufacturers year round. When the Christmas holidays roll around, the warehouse clubs enter the market and order and sell only the most popular toys and sell them more cheaply than Toys "R" Us. So, Toys "R" Us has demanded that selected toy manufacturers not sell their more popular toys to discounters or it will not carry and promote the toys. For other toys, manufacturers would be free to sell to warehouse clubs and other retailers.

Is Toys "R" Us trying to eliminate competition so that it can sell toys at higher prices? Toys "R" Us has about 20 percent of the toy market with warehouse clubs growing rapidly. The Federal Trade Commission charged Toys "R" Us Inc. for illegally boosting prices by pressuring toy manufacturers not to sell certain toys to discount retailers. It wants Toys "R" Us to refrain from retaliating against toy manufacturers that sell popular toys to discount retailers at Christmas.

This antitrust case raises several interesting questions. Can Toys "R" Us set retail toy prices with 20 percent of the market? If it can set prices, will the profits of a toy manufacturer increase if Toys "R" Us behaves as a firm with some market power and limits the distribution of the product? As we have explained above, manufacturers benefit if retailers compete among themselves. Therefore, why would the major toy manufacturers such as Mattel and Hasbro agree to this restriction unless they expected to benefit? Indeed, when surveyed, toy manufacturers did not feel that they were being coerced by Toys "R" Us.

Our analysis suggests that a toy manufacturer may agree to a limitation on distribution or require a minimum retail price if there is a free rider problem that needs to be addressed. Does a year-round promotion of many toys by Toys "R" Us shift the demand curve for some toys outward at Christmas time, and, if so, is this year-round promotion subject to free-riding by warehouse and other discount houses? Because Toys "R" Us and the toy manufacturers have been subject to these agreements for several years, it should be possible to determine whether unit sales increased, as the free rider hypothesis predicts, or whether they declined, as the retailer monopoly hypothesis predicts.

13-6 FREE RIDER PROBLEMS BETWEEN MANUFACTURERS

Free rider problems can occur among manufacturers as well as among retailers. This section describes a free rider problem involving manufacturers.

In the following application, a manufacturer of premium ice cream requires a distributor to sell only the manufacturer's product and prevents the distributor from wholesaling the product of a new entrant into the industry. By restricting the distributor to only one brand, the manufacturer raises its cost of distribution. Why would a manufacturer adopt a policy that raises the per unit cost of distribution?

APPLICATION 13-4

Ben and Jerry versus Goliath

Originally, Ben and Jerry's Homemade, Inc., was a small maker of premium (and very rich) natural ice cream located in Vermont.[14] The company experienced considerable success first in Vermont and then throughout the Northeast and has become a nationwide supplier. However, Ben and Jerry's did not pioneer gourmet ice cream. Haagen-Dazs was one of the early entrants and is the industry leader. When Ben and Jerry's began to expand into other New England states, they signed on with some New England distributors who also distributed Haagen-Dazs ice cream. Haagen-Dazs did not take kindly to this turn of events and soon made it clear that distributors had to make a choice—either Haagen-Dazs or Ben and Jerry's. Since Haagen-Dazs outsold Ben and Jerry's at the time by 10 to 1, it was an easy though distasteful decision for the distributors. Ben and Jerry's decided to fight back in its own imaginative way. Jerry went to Minneapolis, the home office of Pillsbury, the owner of Haagen-Dazs, where he was the lone picket carrying a placard reading "What's the Doughboy Afraid Of?"

At first glance this appears to be a straightforward case of Haagen-Dazs, the industry leader, placing an entry barrier before a young upstart, Ben and Jerry's. However, there is more here than meets the eye. Why was Haagen-Dazs willing to forgo the economies of scale in distribution by restricting a distributor to just its brand? If there are economies of scale from joint distribution, as there appear to be, exclusive dealing restrictions lower the profits of Haagen-Dazs by raising the costs of distribution. In more typical cases manufacturers do not insist on exclusive distribution because they realize the cost of distribution will be higher.

Perhaps Haagen-Dazs was trying to establish a monopoly in premium ice cream. While possible, this does not appear plausible because other producers have entered the gourmet ice cream market. Could there be another reason for the behavior of Haagen-Dazs? Reuben Mattus, creator of Haagen-Dazs, recalled the problems he faced when he first tried to establish Haagen-Dazs in the marketplace. Haagen-Dazs certified the gourmet ice cream market. It entered the industry when the market was small and when few believed there was a demand for gourmet ice cream. It conducted formal and informal market studies, identified neighborhoods where there might be a demand, and persuaded store managers to stock premium ice cream. Haagen-Dazs invested considerable resources to identify and develop the market. The information produced was *general*, not firm-specific. Other competitors could free-ride on this information by copying some of the location decisions of Haagen-Dazs. The routes of the Haagen-Dazs distributors and the stores served by the distributors have provided valuable information to competitors about the locations of markets for gourmet ice cream.

---

[14] Based on Sanford L. Jacobs, "Gourmet Ice Cream Company Fights for Store Freezer Space," *The Wall Street Journal*, December 17, 1984.

This interpretation puts the exclusive distribution policy of Haagen-Dazs in a different light. One of several possible interpretations is that the company hoped to circumvent the free rider problem and to establish ownership of the valuable information it had created.

When firms cannot establish ownership of the information they produce, they allocate fewer resources to produce this information. Some markets will not develop or expand because of a free rider problem. Society recognizes the serious nature of the free rider problem by granting trademarks and issuing patents to protect the use of brand names and technical discoveries. This case illustrates the difficult dilemma that society faces. Should other firms be prevented from appropriating the general information that a firm creates if one consequence is either a short- or long-term monopoly?

SUMMARY

- If the position of the demand function does not depend on the number of retailers or the services provided by the retailer, the manufacturer's profits will be higher if retailers are free to enter the industry.
- A free rider problem exists if consumers obtain valuable services without paying for them.
- A special service is a service that consumers obtain without charge and which shifts the retail and wholesale demand functions outward.

- Resale price maintenance establishes a minimum retail price and prevents retailers from free-riding on the special services provided by other retailers.
- A firm that creates general information by investing resources to certify product quality or the fashion features of a product is subject to a form of free-riding. The quality certification theory explains why a manufacturer might use a minimum retail price and might refuse to deal with some retailers who would like to carry its product.

KEY TERMS

free entry of retailers
special services
resale price maintenance

free rider problem
educational information
quality certification

REVIEW QUESTIONS

1. A manufacturer that limits the number of retailers reduces the cost of distributing the product to consumers. Explain why you agree or disagree with this statement.
2. Evaluate the meaning and logic of the following statements: A major objective of our

firm is to have a profitable dealer group. A dealer who signs up with us rather than a competitor will over the years earn higher profits than with another manufacturer. What's good for our dealers is good for our firm.

3. State the four assumptions of the special service theory.

4. A special service is one that can be obtained free of charge. This definition is clear, but it is not always obvious whether a service is or is not special or whether a special service will cause a large shift in the demand function. Indicate which of the following are special services and explain why.

   - A store provides free delivery for all purchases.
   - A store stocks different sizes, colors, and styles of merchandise.
   - A store provides fitting rooms for customers to try on merchandise.
   - A store provides a pleasant shopping en-

vironment and an informed retail sales staff.

   - A store provides credit for customers who finance their purchases.

5. How would you test the special service theory? List two implications of this theory.

6. Would you expect automobile manufacturers to sell automobiles under resale price maintenance if it were legal? Explain.

7. State the three assumptions of the quality certification theory.

8. You would expect a firm to adopt exclusive dealing early in the life cycle of a product and adopt resale price maintenance as the product matures, assuming that RPM is legal. Explain why you agree or disagree.

EXERCISES

1. Suppose your instructor forms a group of five class members. The group is to present a half-hour presentation on the contents of this chapter before the entire class. Everyone in the group will receive the same grade. What type of free riding problem can appear? What would you recommend the instructor do to attenuate the free rider problem?

2. Suppose some firms in an industry use RPM while others do not. For example, firms selling higher-quality products use RPM, while firms selling lower-quality products do not. Would you expect some firms to use RPM while others do not under the special services or under the cartel argument?

3. A manufacturer wants a higher retail price so that it can increase its profits by raising the wholesale price. Evaluate this statement if the manufacturer is (a) a price-taking competitive firm and (b) a monopolist.

4. Present an explanation of why a manufacturer would voluntarily discontinue the

use of RPM. Describe a way of testing your explanation.

*5 Your company has developed a new microcomputer and is focusing on sales to the home market. You plan to sell your computer through a network of authorized dealers. The capital requirements for establishing a dealership are relatively modest, and so a plentiful supply of qualified applicants seems assured. Field tests reveal that you will have to rely on your dealers to perform two distinct and important educational functions. First, most buyers are unfamiliar with what your computer can do, and so potential customers must learn about its special properties as well as the general role of a personal computer. Second, customers will need help in learning the mechanics of using the microcomputer to perform such functions as database management, playing CDs, and other new features.

Members of your marketing staff think the problem of educating the consumer will disappear if the dealer sells the computer with a promise to supply 10 hours of free instruction time at the dealership after the consumer has purchased the machine. However, your staff is struggling with the problem of how the company can ensure that all dealers will offer the computer instruction package to customers. Some dealers might promise to and then not supply the prepurchase information, and some might promise to provide postsale instruction but then decide to save on costs by not delivering the lessons or by delivering fewer services. Everyone agrees that it will be prohibitively expensive for the company to monitor dealers individually. Moreover, they all believe that it would be beneficial in the long run to have a stable group of dealers and less dealer turnover.

Two proposals are being considered:

- *Proposal 1.* Select the wholesale price so that the difference between the retail and wholesale prices is large enough to cover the costs of providing educational and other dealer functions.
- *Proposal 2.* Let the company sell under resale price maintenance (assuming that it is legal).

Evaluate the two proposals in terms of ensuring that dealers supply pre- and postpurchase educational information.

6. Suppose there are both experienced and first-time buyers in an industry. The first-time buyers are willing to pay for dealer information services, but the experienced buyers demand fewer special services. A monopolist manufacturer sells to dealers at a uniform wholesale price and is considering two distribution policies:

- *Policy 1.* Adopt resale price maintenance.
- *Policy 2.* Sign up selected dealers who will sell under resale price maintenance to first-time buyers. A different group of

dealers will sell to experienced buyers at a market-determined price.
a. Will first-time buyers receive the information under each policy? Explain.
b. Will the two types of dealers earn the same rate of return under each policy? Explain.

*7. You operate a store that sells new CDs. The average price for a CD is around $11 and would-be buyers are not allowed to listen to the CD before purchase. Many of your customers have mentioned that they would buy more CDs if they could listen to the CDs before they decide whether to purchase. If you change your policy and allow would-be customers to listen to CDs prior to purchase, you plan to increase the average price to $15. The assistant manager is opposed to a blanket change in the policy and suggests that the new policy will be more successful if applied to classical music where the typical buyer is older.
a. What factors would you consider before you decide to change the policy?
b. What might be behind the assistant manager's suggestion to limit the policy to classical CDs?

*8. A cooperative association of newspaper publishers is formed to engage in the collection, assembly, and distribution of news to its members. Members of the association develop stories and quickly place them on the association's wire so that other members have access to news originating in other cities and can use the stories in their newspapers. Charter members are to be selected from newspapers in one- and multiple-newspaper cities and towns. The association faces two problems: Which newspapers should be members of the association, and what bylaws should the association adopt? A consulting firm recommends that only one newspaper from each market be included in the association. It also proposes the following bylaws:

- Members cannot supply news to non-members. Violators will be suspended from the association for not less than 3 months.
- Members will have veto power to block another newspaper in the same market from joining the association.

After the membership adopts the bylaws, the government sues the association for monopolizing the market for information and orders it to allow any newspaper to join.

    a. What is the purpose of these bylaws?

    b. Predict the economic effects of allowing all newspapers who desire to do so to join the association.

9. Which of the assumptions listed below apply to the quality certification hypothesis?

    a. Dealer-specific information is supplied by the retailer.

    b. The retailer incurs costs to determine the quality and brand characteristics of a product.

    c. The retailer cannot charge separately for performing certain functions at the retail level.

    d. The retail demand function shifts outward.

    e. The manufacturer supplies a list of potential consumers or "hot" prospects to dealers promoting the product.

    f. The dealer provides general information applicable for all dealers selling the product.

    g. The dealer influences the selection of the brand by the consumer.

    h. The demand function of the manufacturer shifts outward if the retailer verifies certain brand and quality characteristics of the product.

10. To prevent an opportunistic dealer from switching a customer from an advertised brand to a private label brand, a manufacturer should merchandise the advertised product under exclusive dealing and grant the dealer an exclusive territory. Explain why you agree or disagree.

PROBLEM SET

A Young Designer and the Free Rider Problem

A young aspiring designer of women's dresses has had little success persuading larger stores to feature her collection. She has gained recognition in the fashion industry because she has recently won several design contests. Her artistic successes attract the attention of Fashion Originators (hereafter called Fashion), a trade association whose members design, manufacture, and distribute women's fashion dresses to retail stores. The association invites her to join. She is eager to join because she knows her collection will appear in better stores.

Fashion was formed in 1993 by designers who wanted to improve their access to the retail market. Its members do market research and have earned a reputation for anticipating fashion trends. Fashion was very successful from 1994 to 1995, and there are high hopes for even greater success. Fashion has everything going for it—talented designers, rapid sales growth, and good relations with stores.

The designer becomes a member of Fashion at the end of 1995. The next two years prove disappointing to all members of the association. Sales growth slows down, and the market share of Fashion in the stores selling their products declines. The turnaround is baffling. Some members think that their present difficulties are transitory and caused merely by bad forecasting of fashion trends. Others are not so sure.

Fashion commissions you to do a study and to present some recommendations. You select a random sample of retail stores that have sold Fashion dresses since 1993 and obtain the data in the table below.

Use the information in the table to identify the reasons why Fashion did so poorly in 1996 and 1997. How can you explain why its market share dropped although real income, advertising, and size of market increased?

	1994–95	1996–97
Average price of Fashion dresses sold in stores that sell Fashion and the dresses of other manufacturers ($)	250	260
Average price of non-Fashion dresses sold in stores selling Fashion and other manufacturers' dresses ($)	225	210
Average dress volume per store ($1,000)	320	420
Advertising budget of Fashion ($1,000)	30	44
Fashion's market share of all dresses sold in stores selling Fashion dresses (%)	60	33
Number of fashion awards received by members of Fashion	4	12
Number of fashion awards received by other manufacturers selling dresses in stores featuring Fashion dresses	2	1
Per capita income (constant dollars)	11,750	12,120

CHAPTER 14

MARKET BEHAVIOR WITH ASYMMETRIC INFORMATION

■ **14-1 Consequences of Asymmetric Information**
Example: Health Insurance
Example: Automobile Insurance
Example: Borrowing in the Credit Market

■ **14-2 Asymmetric Information and Adverse Selection**
A Lemons Model
Equilibrium Prices and Quantities with Complete Information
Equilibrium Price and Quantity with Asymmetric Information
*A More General Treatment of the Lemons Problem
Overcoming Asymmetric Information
Identifying Markets for Lemons
Application 14-1: The Free Agency Market in Professional Baseball
Application 14-2: The Used Pickup Truck Market

■ **14-3 Moral Hazard**

■ **14-4 Asymmetric Information and Potential Cheating**
An Honest Monopolist?
Modeling Competitive Behavior under Asymmetric Information
Promising and Delivering a High- or a Minimum-Quality Product

Promising High Quality but Delivering Low Quality
Actual Quality Produced in Competitive Markets

■ **14-5 How Does a Competitive Industry Supply a High-Quality Product?**
Delivering a High-Quality Product with a Price Premium
The Incentive to Cheat
Cheating versus Honesty
Application 14-3: The Price Premium at McDonald's
Application 14-4: A Price Premium in Labor Markets
Nonsalvageable Investments
When the Required Price Premium is Unknown
Conclusions about the Klein-Leffler Model

■ **Summary**
■ **Key Terms**
■ **Review Questions**
■ **Exercises**
■ **Problem Set: Integration and Opportunistic Behavior**
■ **Appendix: Present-Value Calculations**

In earlier chapters we assumed for the most part that information was inexpensively acquired so that buyers and sellers were fully informed about the features of the product. Neither side had an informational edge because informational asymmetries could not exist. Consequently, neither side could cheat the other. As you can imagine, the information that buyers and sellers have plays an important role in the way markets function. In this chapter we show just how crucial information symmetry is by investigating how markets work when one side of the market has more information than the other.

In markets with **asymmetric information** buyers and sellers behave differently from what we have seen thus far. When consumers are poorly informed compared to sellers, how does their behavior change? Will they be less likely to buy those products about which they have less information, and, as a consequence, will some markets not even exist and will fewer sales occur in others? You might believe that sellers are better off if they can take advantage of poorly informed consumers. A surprising result is that some sellers are worse off when consumers have less information. The reason for this is discussed later in the chapter. Not surprisingly, consumers attempt to overcome their informational disadvantage by searching out sellers with reputations for trustworthiness. But how can consumers find trustworthy sellers? When consumers have less information, is it more profitable for a seller to cheat consumers by acting opportunistically or to resist such temptations and instead develop a reputation for honesty? These are some of the questions that we investigate in this chapter.

14-1 CONSEQUENCES OF ASYMMETRIC INFORMATION

Asymmetric information is more likely to exist in a new situation. A firm may be dealing with a customer for the first time, or an inexperienced consumer may be purchasing a complex product for the first time. Some examples of asymmetric information are the following.

Example: Health Insurance

Empire Blue Cross and Blue Shield is a nonprofit organization that provides health insurance to many New Yorkers.[1] In 1991 it dropped group coverage health insurance for several professional and trade groups, among them 700 lawyers who are members of the state bar association. By law Blue Cross must accept all members of the association without requiring a health checkup when it agrees to offer the association group health insurance. Blue Cross discontinued the policies after finding that the healthy younger members of the group purchased lower-priced insurance elsewhere. Empire Blue Cross was actually insuring older and sicker members who did not have alternatives.

In this instance asymmetric information exists because consumers know more

---

[1] Milt Freudenheim, "Associations' Coverage Cut by Blue Cross," *New York Times*, June 13, 1991, p.C1.

about their health than Blue Cross does. The fees set for the group insurance contract depend on the health status of the *average* member of the group. However, members of the New York bar may self-select into the bar association and are more likely to join the association when group rates are lower than the rates they face as individuals. However, individuals in poor health are more likely to join because they find the premium to be a bargain since the health of the average member of the association determines the premium and members can join without an examination. This creates a problem of *adverse selection* because those with fewer health problems leave the group and find lower-cost alternatives when they find their rates increasing as less healthy members join. These relatively healthy individuals prefer to pay insurance premiums which are based upon their *individual* health status rather than on the *average* of a relatively less healthy group.

From the company's perspective, adverse selection occurs because the sample of individuals who sign up for health insurance does not represent a random sample of all members of the New York State bar.

> **Adverse selection** can occur when members are not a random selection of the group.

Example: Automobile Insurance

I had purchased my automobile insurance from the same company for many years but decided to switch when the insurer replaced agents who provided service and advice with impersonal representatives. When I contacted a new company, the agent immediately asked me if I had a renewal form from my present company. I said that my renewal was not yet due. He replied that without a renewal form he would have to charge a substantially higher rate. He suggested that I wait until a renewal notice arrived, at which time he would offer me a policy at a considerably lower rate.

How was the insurance company's pricing policy affected by asymmetric information? The company knows less about the driving ability of an individual than the individual does. It suspects that walk-ins are not a random sample of drivers but an adverse selection of the general driving public with poor driving and accident records. Every insurance company wants to avoid signing up the rejects from other insurance companies. Because the company does not have information about each candidate, it assumes the worst. The company prices insurance higher to attenuate the adverse selection of walk-in candidates that results from asymmetric information. After I provided the renewal notice from my old company, the new company had more information about me, and so the asymmetric information problem became less serious and the insurance company lowered the premium.

Example: Borrowing in the Credit Market

A bank lending funds to a diverse set of borrowers must be on guard so that the quality of the loan does not change with the interest rate that it charges. By the quality of the loan we mean the probability that the borrower defaults. If a bank raises interest rates, it may find that the composition of borrowers changes. Chances are that borrowers who cannot get loans approved at other banks will apply for loans and make up a larger percentage of applicants. Another consequence is that the higher interest rate will attract more applicants that want to use the proceeds for high-risk ventures. Hence, the loan officer could find that average loan quality declines when the bank raises its interest rate.

14-2   ASYMMETRIC INFORMATION AND ADVERSE SELECTION

Before we consider the details of a formal "lemons model," let's consider the special problems that arise when sellers are better informed.[2] Let's suppose that you are in the market for a used car. Used cars vary in quality in ways that are often difficult to detect by the average used car buyer. Often, sellers know more about the quality of the used cars that they are selling than buyers do. Let's suppose that used cars can be either gems (high quality) or lemons (low quality). While buyers cannot determine whether a specific car is high or low quality, we assume that they know from either their previous experience or from the experiences of their parents and friends that a certain fraction, say 20 percent, of all used cars are lemons.

Buyers are wary about buying because they do not want to be stuck with a lemon. More to the point, while 80 percent of *all* used cars are gems, there is no guarantee that 80 percent of the cars on used car lots are gems. Why not? The fraction of cars on used car lots that are gems depends on used car prices. If used car prices are relatively low, suppliers of high-quality cars will not offer these cars for sale so used car lots will be populated with lemons. When there is asymmetric information, average car quality of the cars offered for sale decreases as used car prices decrease. Price and the quality of used cars sold are positively correlated. Consequently, the cars offered for sale are an adverse selection of all used cars because only the low-quality cars are supplied. A separate market for high-quality cars will not even exist and so high-quality used cars may not even be offered for sale. Some sales that would have occurred if both sides had complete information will not occur because of asymmetric information. So, some gains from trade, which would have been realized had buyers and sellers been equally informed, go unrealized.

To illustrate such a case, suppose that all gem owners are willing to supply used cars at a price of $11,000. Consumers are willing to pay $12,000 for a *known* gem but only $6,000 for a *known* lemon. Because buyers cannot tell the difference between gems and lemons, gems and lemons sell for the same price. A risk-neutral but uninformed buyer would be willing to pay a weighted average price of $12,000(.8) + $6,000(.2) = $10,800 for a used car picked at random. However, $10,800, the price that consumers are willing to pay for a used car, is less than

---

[2] George A. Akerlof, "The Market for 'Lemons': Quality Uncertainty and the Market Mechanism," *Quarterly Journal of Economics* LXXXIV (August 1970), pp. 488–500.

$11,000, the price at which gem owners are willing to supply their cars. Consequently, no gems will be supplied and there will be no transactions involving gems even though buyers are willing to pay $12,000 for known gems and sellers are willing to part with gems for $11,000.

Since only lemons and no gems are supplied, buyers will definitely not pay $10,800 for the certainty of getting a lemon. Because only lemons are supplied, buyers will pay only $6,000 for the lemons that appear on used car lots.

A Lemons Model

In this section we develop a more general lemons model for used cars. Buyers cannot distinguish between a high- and a low-quality used car so both qualities must sell at the same price. This is one consequence of asymmetric information: cars of different qualities can sell for the same price. We want to determine the equilibrium price and quantity of used cars that are sold and show how the used cars that appear in the market are not always a random selection of all used cars.[3]

The model assumes that all N individuals who own automobiles of a given vintage and of a particular brand are considering selling them. Some of the cars have never given their owners any trouble. The engine, the transmission, the suspension system, and the brakes operate flawlessly. Let's call these cars gems and assume that gems represent a fraction, f, of all N autos. On the other hand, the owners of the remaining cars have had one problem after another. These autos are lemons. Therefore, $1 - f$ is the fraction of the N autos that are lemons.

Owners of gems and of lemons each have minimum prices at which they are willing to sell their autos in the used car market. The lowest price at which all owners of gems will sell their autos is S_g, while owners of lemons will sell their autos at a minimum price of S_l, where $S_l < S_g$. On the demand side of the market buyers are willing to pay B_g for a known gem and B_l for a known lemon, where $B_l < B_g$. Assume that $B_g > S_g$ and $B_l > S_l$ so that both markets can exist.

Equilibrium Prices and Quantities with Complete Information

By first determining the equilibrium price and quantity when the market participants have complete information and then when information is distributed asymmetrically, we can show the consequences of asymmetric information on prices, quantities, and the sales of gems and lemons.

To simplify the analysis, assume that the demand functions for gems and for lemons are perfectly elastic. This means that the demand function for gems is horizontal at a price of B_g for gems and at B_l for lemons. These are the prices that consumers are willing to pay for each type of car when they know car quality.

Figures 14-1a and b show the separate demand and supply functions when

---

[3] The material in this section draws on the excellent chapter on asymmetric information in David M. Kreps, *A Course in Microeconomic Theory* (Princeton, N.J.: Princeton University Press, 1990), chapter 17. The interested reader who wants to delve deeper into the problems raised by asymmetric information should consult this source.

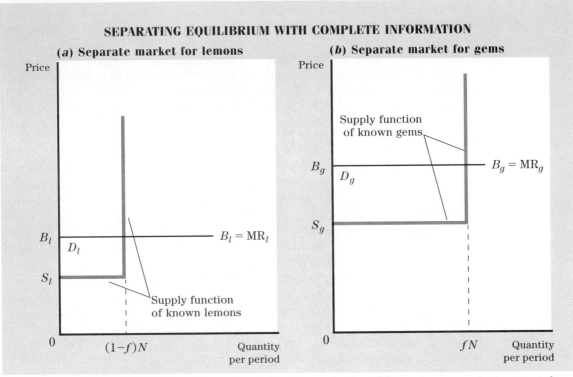

Figure 14-1   When the quality of a used automobile can be assessed prior to purchase, two markets emerge, one market for high-quality automobiles (gems) and a second market for low-quality automobiles (lemons). Some buyers purchase lemons and pay B_l for the lower-quality automobile. Other buyers purchase gems at a higher price of B_g. With complete information the used car market separates into two markets.

buyers have complete information about the quality of an automobile. Because a supplier of a lemon cannot pass it off as a gem, separate markets exist for lemons and for gems. The demand function is horizontal at the buyer's bid price of B_l for lemons in Figure 14-1*a* and is horizontal at the buyer's bid price of B_g for gems in Figure 14-1*b*. The quantity of lemons supplied is $(1 - f)N$ as long as the price of a lemon equals or exceeds S_l. In the market for gems the quantity supplied is fN if the price equals or exceeds S_g. The equilibrium prices are B_g for gems and B_l for lemons, and the market for gems is separate from the market for lemons.

Equilibrium Price and Quantity
with Asymmetric Information

Now let's see how the behavior of buyers and sellers changes when buyers cannot distinguish gems from lemons. What price are consumers willing to pay for a used car when all they know is that gems represent a fraction f of all used cars in the *population?* In this situation we assume that consumers are willing to pay a weighted average price of B_g and B_l based on the fraction f of gems in the used car population.

$$P_b = fB_g + (1 - f)B_l \qquad (14\text{-}1)$$

The bid price P_b is a weighted average of prices. For example, if $f = 0.9$, $B_g = \$12{,}000$, and $B_l = \$6{,}000$, consumers will pay at most $\$11{,}400 = .9(\$12{,}000) + .1(\$6{,}000)$ for an auto picked at random. Because consumers cannot tell the gems from the lemons, there is only one market. In that single market, market demand for used cars will be perfectly elastic at the price of $\$11{,}400$. Obviously, if f is smaller, then consumers would be willing to pay a lower price for a used car, so the fraction of gems in the population of used cars determines how high a price that consumers are willing to pay for the used cars offered for sale.

What does the supply function of autos look like when asymmetric information exists? If the market price is less than S_l, no owner is willing to supply a used automobile to the market. Lemon owners are willing to supply $(1 - f)N$ autos if the price is equal to or greater than S_l. If the price equals or exceeds S_g, owners of gems also supply autos to the market. Figure 14-2 shows that the "hybrid" supply function of autos is $S_l abcS'$. This is a hybrid supply function because the average quality of the autos supplied increases when the price equals or exceeds S_g since gems are supplied.

To describe the industry equilibrium completely, we must distinguish between two cases: (1) where both lemons and gems trade and (2) where just lemons trade. In the first case the fraction of gems in the population of autos is relatively high and P_b exceeds S_g. Owners of gems are willing to supply gems to the market, as of course are owners of lemons. In the second case, the fraction of gems is lower such that P_b is less than S_g and owners of gems will not supply any cars to the market. Only lemons will appear in the used car market. Consequently the cars sold in the market are an adverse selection of all used cars.

Let's determine what fraction of used cars must be gems before gems are supplied to the used car market. Owners are willing to supply gems to the market if

$$S_g \leq P_b$$

Substituting the expression for P_b from equation 14-1 gives

$$S_g \leq f(B_g) + (1 - f)B_l$$

or

$$S_g \leq f(B_g - B_l) + B_l \qquad \text{(Condition for Gems to Be Supplied)} \qquad (14\text{-}2)$$

Solve equation 14-2 for f by subtracting B_l from both sides of the equation and then dividing both sides by $B_g - B_l$ to obtain

$$f \geq \frac{S_g - B_l}{B_g - B_l} \qquad (14\text{-}3)$$

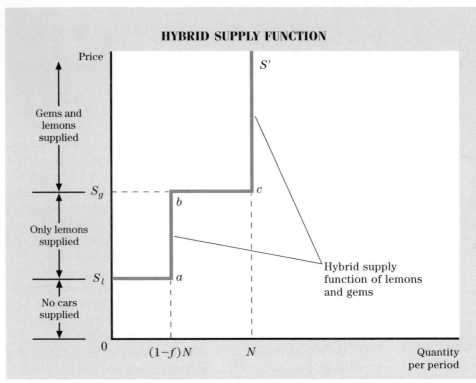

Figure 14-2   With asymmetric information, sellers have more information than buyers. Buyers cannot distinguish between high- and low-quality automobiles. If the price is less than S_g but equal to or greater than S_l, the quantity supplied equals $(1 - f)N$, the supply of lemons. If the price equals or exceeds S_g, all N automobiles are supplied. The total quantity supplied is a mixture of lemons and gems. The supply function is $S_l abcS'$.

If gem owners are to supply their cars to the market, f must equal or exceed the right side of equation 14-3. If the offer price for a gem is $10,000 ($S_g$), the bid price for a gem is $12,000 ($B_g$), and the bid price for a lemon is $6,000 ($B_l$), gems must equal or exceed 66.7 percent of used automobiles. Then, the price that consumers are willing to pay for a randomly selected car is $10,000 or more, equal to or greater than the price that owners of gems must receive to part with them. If gems make up *less* than two-thirds of all used cars, they will not be supplied because buyers are then unwilling to pay $10,000 for a used car. The used car market is therefore full of lemons. Because of asymmetric information, there is adverse selection because the autos that trade in the market do not represent a random selection of all used cars but consist only of lemons.

Adverse selection of used cars occurs when the price that consumers are willing to pay is less than the price at which owners are willing to supply gems. The traded autos are not a random selection of all used cars.

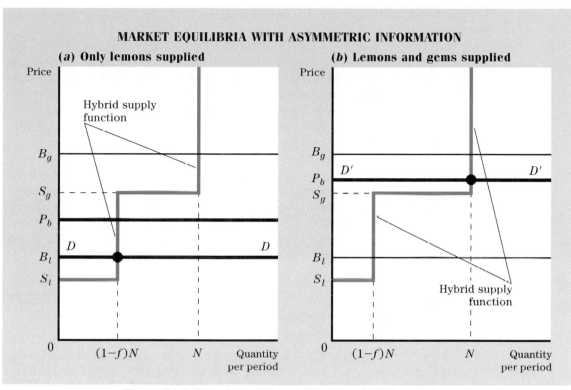

Figure 14-3   The demand function is DD in (a) where P_b is less than S_g. Only owners of lemons supply used cars to the market. When the share of gems is sufficiently high so that P_b is greater than S_g, the demand function is $D'D'$ in (b) and owners of gems and lemons supply autos to the market. Both types of autos sell at the higher value for P_b. One equilibrium has only lemons selling in the market, and the second equilibrium has lemons pooled with gems. The owners of lemons benefit, while the owners of gems are harmed.

Figure 14-3 shows two possible equilibria in the market. In Figure 14-3a the fraction of gems is such that $P_b < S_g$. Consumers realize that only owners of lemons are willing to supply used cars to the market and are only willing to pay B_l. The horizontal demand function DD at the price B_l intersects the hybrid supply function at the quantity $(1 - f)N$. The equilibrium price for a used car is B_l, and there is adverse selection because only lemons trade. However, notice that no one is fooled in this **equilibrium.** Buyers expect and find only lemons, and so they are willing to pay only the price of a lemon. This equilibrium occurs when there are too many lemons in the population of autos.

In Figure 14-3b f is such that $P_b \geq S_g$. The share of gems in the population of used cars is high enough so that the price that consumers are willing to pay is above the price that owners of gems must receive to supply them. The demand function $D'D'$ is horizontal at a price of P_b. Both types of autos trade in the used car market at the same price. Of those traded, fN have satisfied new owners, but disappointment is the rule for the unlucky buyers of the remaining cars. Consumers know the probability of buying a lemon is $1 - f$, and that is why they are willing to pay only P_b, not B_g, for a used auto. In this equilibrium both gems and lemons trade in the market, and so there is no adverse selection in the autos offered. Yet, this equilibrium is different from the equilibrium with complete information, where both gems and lemons trade at different prices. Here both gems and lemons sell at the same price and there is a **pooling equilibrium.** Because of the asymmetric information in the market, differentiation of lemons from gems proves impossible. Table 14-1 summarizes the two equilibria.

A surprising implication of our analysis is that some sellers are *worse* off when consumers are at an informational disadvantage. Owners of gems would receive B_g if buyers had complete information. But when consumers are at an informational disadvantage, owners of gems either do not bother to offer their cars for sale or, if they do, receive less than B_g. Clearly, owners of gems are worse off because asymmetric information does not allow gem owners to separate their cars from lemons, while owners of lemons are rewarded because they receive either B_l or more than B_l for their lemons.

*A More General Treatment of the Lemons Problem

Although our model captures some features of the lemons problem, it is somewhat restrictive. We can generalize the analysis in two directions. First, instead of having just gems and lemons, we assume more realistically that the qualities of used cars vary continuously, with higher qualities supplied at higher prices. Second, instead of assuming the demand for used cars is horizontal at the weighted average price, we can explicitly specify a market demand curve that not only takes account of the effect of price on the quantity demanded, given car quality, but accounts for changes in the quantity demanded when car quality decreases because price decreases. This modified model, unlike the previous model, can explain why the whole market for used cars might completely close down when information is distributed asymmetrically.

Table 14-1   PRICE AND QUANTITY TRADED FOR TWO EQUILIBRIA

FRACTION OF GEMS	BID PRICE RELATIVE TO S_g	MARKET PRICE	QUANTITY SOLD	TYPE OF AUTOS TRADED
$f \geq \dfrac{S_g - B_l}{B_g - B_l}$	$P_b \geq S_g$	P_b	N	Gems and lemons
$f < \dfrac{S_g - B_l}{B_g - B_l}$	$P_b < S_g$	B_l	$(1 - f)N$	Lemons

When there is asymmetric information, consumers sensibly recognize that average car quality will decrease as price decreases because fewer higher-quality cars are offered. So price and quality move in the same direction. Price affects the quantity demanded in two ways. The first is the traditional effect of price on the quantity demanded: the quantity demanded is inversely related to price, given car quality. In a market with asymmetric information price exerts a second effect on the quantity demanded. Lower used car prices reduce the average quality of used cars appearing in the market (adverse selection) and this second effect causes the quantity demanded to decrease since consumers are willing to pay less for the lower average quality of cars that will be offered by owners. If the second effect is large enough, the total quantity demanded will decrease when the price decreases.[4] Hence, when information is distributed asymmetrically, the market demand function can have a positive slope over a range of prices.

With this specification the quantity demanded may decrease when price decreases if the second effect dominates the first effect over a range of prices. Figure 14-4 shows a backward bending market demand function and two possible used car supply functions SS and $S'S'$. If the supply curve of used cars is $S'S'$, no equilibrium price exists and no cars trade. The adverse selection problem is so severe that no sales of used cars are made. With the supply curve SS the equilibrium price equals P^* but only Q^* units are supplied and car qualities with reservation supply prices above P^* do not trade in the market. There can even be multiple equilibria when the supply curve (not shown) happens to intersect the demand function at two prices.

The presence of asymmetric information creates special problems for a decentralized price system. As we noted above, some markets may not appear at all. In health care for the elderly, an insurance company must be careful when offering a group health policy so that it does not attract an adverse selection of the elderly. Those in poor health would find the policy cheap relative to the expected benefits and would join in greater numbers as described in the example at the beginning of this chapter. To avoid the adverse selection problem, the federal government

---

[4] Consider the market demand function for used cars where the quantity demanded depends on the price of the auto *and* the average quality of autos offered for sale, AvgQ(P). Note that the average quality of the autos in the market depends on price, increasing as price increases. The market demand function for autos is therefore

$$Q = D[P, \text{AvgQ}(P)]$$

Price affects the quantity demanded in two ways. First, there is the conventional effect. The quantity demanded increases when the price decreases. The second argument in the demand function captures the second effect. The quantity demanded increases because the demand function shifts outward when the average quality of autos increases. The average quality of all autos offered in the market increases because more higher-quality cars are offered at higher prices. Therefore, a decrease in price has two effects. The first effect represents a movement along a demand function for a given average car quality. The second effect captures the decrease in the quantity demanded because the demand function shifts inward when average car quality decreases at lower prices. The net effect of a price change on the quantity demanded is given by

$$\frac{dQ}{dP} = \frac{\partial D}{\partial P} + \frac{\partial D}{\partial (\text{AvgQ})} \frac{\partial (\text{AvgQ})}{\partial P} = (-) + (+)(+) = ?$$

Thus, a price decrease may either increase or decrease the quantity demanded depending on the sizes of the two effects.

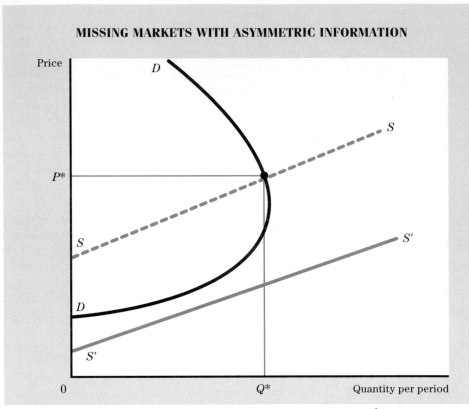

Figure 14-4   If the supply curve is *SS*, the equilibrium price is P^* and the quantity of used cars sold equals Q^*. Used cars with reservation prices greater than P^* will not be supplied. If the supply curve is $S'S'$, the market will not exist with asymmetric information.

may have to insure individuals older than 65. Another suggestion is for the government to mandate increased information provided by the better informed party or create more information, such as in this case, the health status of the insured, or in the lemons model, the condition of the used car. A modest attempt has been made in the industry to provide minimal information about used cars. Other market institutions have emerged to attenuate the asymmetric information problem and are described below.

Overcoming Asymmetric Information

There is an incentive for owners of gems to separate their autos from lemons, and several market institutions have developed to convey product information to potential customers. Three such mechanisms are warranties, testing, and reputation. These market institutions arise to deal with the consequences of asymmetric information, but they are expensive to create and do not always eliminate the problem completely.

1. Warranties   The owner of a gem can distinguish her gem from a lemon by offering a warranty. Suppose she offers to pay the buyer for repair expenses during the first year and the agreement can be enforced. The owner of a gem has a greater incentive to do this than the owner of a lemon does. Suppose the repair cost of a true gem is zero, while the buyer of a lemon has repair costs of $2,500 in the first year. If an expenditure of $2,500 transforms a lemon into a gem, buyers would be indifferent between purchasing a gem or a lemon if the difference between B_g and B_l is $2,500. Now an owner of a gem is perfectly willing to offer a warranty to the buyer and sells the auto for B_g. The owner of a lemon is in a bind. He must either sell his auto for B_g and issue a warranty or sell it for $B_g - \$2,500$ with no warranty. If he refuses to do the first, the buyer infers that the auto is a lemon. In any event, the market separates lemons from gems. Owners of gems sell them for B_g, and owners of lemons sell them for B_l.

A limitation of warranties is the cost of enforcement. What guarantees that the seller will comply with the terms of the warranty? Also, the coverage of the warranty must be clear because sometimes it is difficult to verify the cause of the defect. Is it due to the initial condition of the automobile or is it due to poor maintenance by the new owner? Warranties may solve one problem but create others. The buyer has less incentive to exercise care and to maintain the automobile if the warranty is all-inclusive. Economists call the reduced incentive to exercise care the *moral hazard* problem. Moral hazard deals with behavior after a contract has been entered into.

2. Testing   In some markets it is possible to pretest the product. A repair facility can pretest an auto and, perhaps, issue a guarantee. Usually, the cost of checking a car does not increase proportionally with its value. The testing cost is more like a lump sum. Tests of more expensive cars are therefore more likely, and so the lemon problem is likely to be more serious for cheaper automobiles because the cost of a test is a relatively larger proportion of the value of a car.

3. Reputation   The lemons problem is usually more severe when it involves a one-shot transaction between a buyer and a seller with no possibility of a repeat sale. With repeated transactions, the seller has less incentive to take advantage of the buyer because the buyer is less likely to return. In these situations you would expect a market institution to evolve that alleviates the problem, and one such institution is the **reputation** of the seller. An automobile dealer has greater expertise in evaluating automobiles than an individual buyer and wants to establish a reputation for fair dealing to attract repeat business.

Identifying Markets for Lemons

You might expect asymmetric information to be a more serious problem in a new market where buyers have little information to go on. We now investigate two situations where asymmetric information could be a potential problem.

APPLICATION 14-1

The Free Agency Market in Professional Baseball

The first example of a new market is the development of the free agency market in professional baseball which Ken Lehn studied.[5] With the arrival of free agency in 1976 a baseball player with six years of service could sign a new contract (usually a multiple-year contract) with his current team or become a free agent and sign with another team. Before free agency, the player could negotiate only with his current team. Free agency was a revolutionary change and presented a new challenge to team owners.

The management of a professional baseball team presumably knows more about the players on its team than about players on other teams. It has more information about the players' motivation, desire to win, conditioning, willingness to play with injuries, and so on. The existing management may also know more about how a particular player will respond to a lucrative long-term contract. If current owners know more about their own players, management is less likely to err when assessing the value of a player to the team.

Lehn assumed that after free agency arrived, current owners knew more about their players than other owners did, and so there was asymmetric information in the market for players. He reasoned that existing management would pay higher compensation to retain players who would be less likely to shirk after signing a long-term contract. Lehn used the number of days a player was on the disabled list per season before and after the arrival of free agency as a measure of player

[5] Kenneth Lehn, "Information Asymmetries in Baseball's Free Agent Market," *Economic Inquiry* XXII (January 1984), pp. 37–44.

Table 14-2   NUMBER OF DAYS ON DISABLED LIST

PLAYER STATUS	DAYS DISABLED BEFORE FREE AGENCY	DAYS DISABLED AFTER FREE AGENCY	PERCENTAGE CHANGE
Pitchers (58 in sample):			
Remained with team	3.66	9.57	167%
Became free agent	5.12	28.07	448
Nonpitchers (97 in sample):			
Remained with team	5.30	9.74	84
Became free agent	4.31	9.83	128

tendency to shirk—a higher number indicates a player is more likely to complain about injuries and not play.

Table 14-2 shows the number of days on the disabled list for players who did not become free agents and remained with their original team and those who became free agents and signed with other teams. Lehn considered pitchers separately from nonpitchers.

Lehn found that pitchers who remained with their teams, although eligible for free agency, had been on the disabled list for 3.66 days per season before the arrival of free agency. Pitchers who became free agents subsequently had missed 5.12 days per season before free agency. On the other hand, after free agency, pitchers who remained with their teams were on the disabled list 9.57 days per season, a 167 percent increase. However, pitchers who became free agents and signed with other teams were on the disabled list an average of 28.07 days per season, a 448 percent increase! These results suggest that current owners were better able to filter out those players who would take it easy after signing a longer-term contract. Those players signed with other less informed teams and subsequently complained about sore arms and other ailments so that they were on the disabled list for relatively more days under free agency.

Table 14-2 shows that pitchers are primarily responsible for the difference between players who remained with their teams and players who became free agents. The difference is smaller for nonpitchers. This suggests that asymmetric information is a more serious problem for a new owner when evaluating pitchers than when evaluating players of other positions.

This example provides evidence of asymmetric information in the free agency market.

APPLICATION 14-2

The Used Pickup Truck Market

The second application focuses on the used pickup truck market. Eric Bond tried to determine whether asymmetric information is a serious problem in the market for used pickup trucks by examining the repair history of these vehicles.[6] Bond reasoned that if there is asymmetric information in the market, pickup trucks with higher maintenance expenditures would be overrepresented in the used truck market. Used trucks purchased from their original owners should have higher average maintenance expenditures per truck before being sold in the used market than a random sample of trucks of the same age, mileage, and so on, that also included those that were kept by their original owners. Bond looked at major maintenance expenditures for the engine, transmission, brakes, and rear axle during the 12 months before the sale of the truck.

---

[6] Eric Bond, "A Direct Test of the 'Lemons' Model: The Market for Used Pickup Trucks," *American Economic Review* 72 (September 1982), pp. 836–40. Copyright © 1982 by the American Economic Association.

Table 14-3 shows the proportion of pickup trucks that required major engine maintenance in the past 12 months classified by whether they were purchased new or used by the current owner.

Bond assumed that adverse selection occurs because of asymmetric information in the market. Therefore, only lemons trade, and buyers of used pickup trucks incur maintenance expenditures after purchases. If so, trucks purchased used should have higher annual maintenance expenditures than trucks kept by their original owners. However, Bond did not find significant differences in repair expenditures between the two groups of trucks. The results of this study suggest that adverse selection is not a serious problem in this market, perhaps because so few lemons are produced, or because institutions such as warranties, testing, and seller reputations are well developed.

14-3   MORAL HAZARD

Suppose you live outside Los Angeles in a wooded area where wildfires spread rapidly and you are willing to pay a high premium to buy fire insurance. To determine the premium, the insurance company has to estimate the probability of a fire.

Is there any reason why the probability of a fire loss might depend on whether a homeowner has fire insurance? We can reason that if you do not have insurance, you will exercise more care about how you landscape your property, how frequently you prune dead branches from your bushes and trees, and how frequently you water. First, you know that a fire is more likely to cause damage if trees and brush are located near your house. Second, the probability of fire damage will decrease if you frequently cut and safely discard dead limbs and brush. Recognizing this, you will cut down nearby trees on your property and frequently cut away and cart off all dead limbs and brush that could help propel a fire, thereby decreasing the probability of a fire loss.

On the other hand, if you purchase a fire insurance policy with 100 percent coverage, your behavior will change *on the margin*. You might not cut down so many nearby trees and you might be more willing to plant attractive shrubs and

Table 14-3   PROPORTION OF TRUCKS REQUIRING MAJOR ENGINE MAINTENANCE

YEAR	PURCHASED NEW	PURCHASED USED
1976	0.08	0.05
1975	0.10	0.11
1974	0.11	0.13
1973	0.15	0.15
1972	0.13	0.15

bushes that improve the appearance of your house even though they add to the probability of a fire loss. We are assuming that the insurance company cannot monitor all of your efforts and therefore cannot base your premiums on the degree of care you exercise. Insurance changes your behavior. The insured does not bear the full cost of a fire and consequently does not take the proper level of care to prevent a fire. Economists call this a **moral hazard** problem. In this case the principal (the insurance company) takes an action (issues an insurance policy) that affects the agent's behavior (you remove fewer trees and clear less brush).

In Figure 14-5 we show your demand curve DD for cutting down trees or bushes on your property given that you have no insurance. It measures the private and (we assume) the social marginal value of cutting down successive trees or trimming dead branches from nearby trees and bushes. The marginal value decreases as more trees are cut down. Presumably, as more and more distantly located trees are cut down, the probability of a fire loss decreases but by a lesser amount. If the marginal cost of cutting down a tree is C, you will cut down T_1 trees where the marginal value of cutting down a tree equals the marginal cost of cutting down a tree. If you cut down fewer than T_1 trees, the marginal value that you place

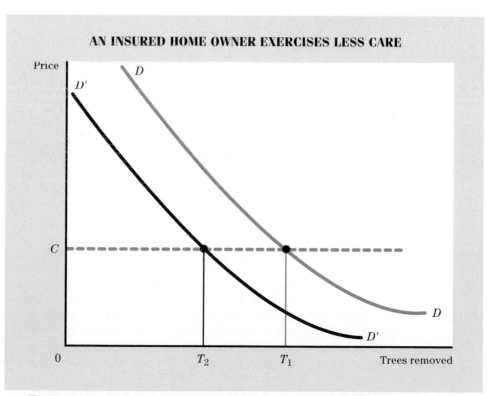

AN INSURED HOME OWNER EXERCISES LESS CARE

Figure 14-5   Without insurance the homeowner removes T_1 trees. With insurance the demand for tree removal decreases because of moral hazard, and the insured homeowner removes only T_2 trees.

on cutting down the last tree would be greater than the marginal cost of cutting down a tree and you would not be behaving optimally.

If you have insurance, you behave differently. You exercise less care because you have 100 percent fire coverage. In Figure 14-5 your demand for cutting down trees shifts inward and becomes $D'D'$. You still take some precautions to lower the probability of a fire, since insurance will not cover your intangible personal loss, but those precautions will be less extensive. You will cut down only T_2 trees, those nearest to your home, and trim fewer dead branches from the remaining trees and bushes. In a different context an insured driver will drive less carefully than an uninsured driver. Or, a person who rents a car might exercise less care by braking hard or flooring the pedal at each stoplight because the renter does not bear the full cost of his actions in terms of a lower resale value of the car.

If the insurance company could costlessly monitor the care you take, it could charge a higher premium if you chose to cut down fewer than T_1 trees, but charge a lower premium if you cut down T_1 trees. However, efforts of care are often hidden from the insurance company. While cutting down trees may be more easily detectable than clearing brush around your home, there are many other activities a homeowner can take that are costly for an insurance company to monitor.

> When there is a moral hazard problem, the insured agent takes less than the optimal amount of care.

14-4 ASYMMETRIC INFORMATION AND POTENTIAL CHEATING

In this section we consider how asymmetric information affects firm behavior, beginning first with monopoly and then moving on to a competitive market. As we have already noted, some markets may not exist because of "lemon" situations. Our purpose here is to determine if a monopolist and then a competitive firm have any incentive to acquire a reputation for reliability and honesty.

An Honest Monopolist?

Let's consider a monopolist and ask what prevents the monopolist from deliberately over-representing a product to the benefit of the firm and to the detriment of consumers. Your immediate response might be that the monopolist will act honestly because the seller wants consumers to return. There is more than a modicum of truth to this answer but you should not be completely satisfied with this answer.

Suppose a monopolist must *either* produce a high-quality product at a constant long-run per unit cost of $15 *or* a low-quality product (that consumers cannot recognize as inferior when they purchase) at a long-run per unit cost of $10. Because consumers cannot tell the quality of the product until *after* they have bought it, the monopolist can either promise and deliver a high-quality product or deceive consumers by promising a high-quality product but then delivering a low-quality product. If the monopolist produces and delivers a high-quality product, assume the profit-maximizing price is $20, at which it can sell 100 units. The monopolist's annual profits are ($20 − $15)100 = $500. Consequently, the monopolist earns $500 per year for the indefinite future and consumers reward the firm by becoming repeat buyers.

If the monopolist decides to act opportunistically by promising a high-quality product but delivering a lower-cost and lower-quality product that consumers cannot evaluate beforehand, the monopolist can deceive consumers for one year and earn profits in the first year of ($20 − $10)100 = $1,000. The monopolist earns more in the first year but does not make any future profits because consumers do not become repeat buyers after they have been ripped off.

Will the monopolist choose $1,000 for only one year or $500 per year forever? The answer depends on how the monopolist weights future profits relative to current profits. To answer this question, we must find the *present value* of the two profit streams. The **present value of a profit stream** is an amount which if received immediately would leave the firm indifferent between receiving this amount or receiving the profit stream. The appendix to this chapter shows how to derive the present value of an amount received in a future year. The present value $1,000 earned at the end of one year (followed by a stream of zero profits) equals $1,000 divided by $(1 + i)$ where i is the discount rate. The discount rate is the rate that the firm can earn on its investments. If the discount rate is 10 percent and next year's profits equal $1,000, the present value of future profits equals $1000/ 1.10 = $909.09. This means that a firm that receives $909.09 immediately could invest it for a year at 10 percent interest and would have $1,000 at the end of the year. Therefore, the firm is willing to receive $909.09 immediately, the present value of $1,000, or $1,000 a year later.

What is the present value of an annual income stream of $500 per year? To answer this question, we determine what a profit stream of $500 per year is worth today. The appendix to this chapter shows that the present value of an indefinite stream of $500 equals $500/$i$ where i is the discount rate. If the discount rate is 10 percent, the present value of an everlasting annual stream of $500 equals $500/.10 = $5,000. This means that a firm is indifferent between receiving $5,000 immediately or $500 annually for the indefinite future.

At a discount rate of 10 percent, the monopolist will choose to deliver the high-quality product and have consumers come back year after year.[7] Future profits

---

[7] Assume P_m is the profit-maximizing monopoly price for a high-quality product, C_h is the per unit cost of producing the high-quality product, C_l is the per unit cost of producing the lower-quality product, and the profit-maximizing quantity of the high-quality product is Q_m. A monopolist will produce high quality if

$$\frac{P_m - C_h}{i} Q_m > \frac{P_m - C_l}{1 + i} Q_m$$

The left-hand side is the present value of delivering high quality while the right-hand side is the present value of cheating. The inequality can be written as

$$\frac{P_m - C_h}{i} > C_h - C_l$$

The present value of per unit profit for a high-quality product must be greater than the immediate increase in profit from cheating.

from repeat sales play an important role in restraining any opportunistic behavior on the part of the monopolist in the immediate present. Of course, if the future is less important and the discount rate is very high, even a monopolist would select the opportunistic option.[8]

Modeling Competitive Behavior under Asymmetric Information

What happens when we extend this reasoning to a competitive industry where free entry eliminates firm profits? A competitive firm, faced with the choice of acting opportunistically and earning profits for a single year versus delivering a high-quality product but not earning profits, maximizes the present value of profits by promising a high-quality product but delivering a low-quality product. This argument implies that competitive firms will act opportunistically whenever the opportunity arises. Buyers lacking information about product quality and facing competitive firms will therefore assume the worst and will pay only for a low-quality product no matter how sincere the seller appears. Consequently, the theory implies that low-quality products drive out high-quality products in competitive markets!

Economists Ben Klein and Keith Leffler reject this implication and argue that a competitive market will adapt to supply a variety of qualities. They offer a competing model that stresses the value of reputation and explains when competitive firms will acquire reputations for honesty and reliability.[9] Let's examine their model, starting with its assumptions.

1. The total cost of production, C, depends on the quantity produced, X, and the quality, q, of the output; $C = C(X, q)$. We omit the subscript L since all the cost functions in this chapter are the firm's long-run cost functions. For a given X, the cost of production rises with increases in the quality of the product. Initially, we assume that there is a ready market for the assets of the firm, and so the company does not suffer losses if it sells these assets.

2. Each competitive seller supplies a product whose quality cannot be assessed before purchase (except for the minimum-quality product described below) and promises to supply a high-quality product at a price $P(q_h)$, where P is the price and q_h is the promised high-quality product. (An example of product quality is durability.) The seller charges a higher price for a higher-quality product.

3. Courts do not penalize firms that supply a lower-than-promised quality.

4. A seller can deceive existing customers for only one period before being detected. The tarnished reputation of such a seller precludes future sales to all current and future customers.

---

[8] In this case, for a monopolist to favor producing the low-quality product, the discount rate would have to be 55 percent or more. If the discount rate is greater than 100 percent, the monopolist would produce the low-quality product because the present value of profits from producing the low-quality product is higher.

[9] Ben Klein and Keith Leffler, "The Role of Market Forces in Assuring Contractual Performance," *Journal of Political Economy* 89 (August 1981), pp. 615–41.

5. There is a low-quality product, q_{min}, that consumers can assess accurately before purchase.

6. Consumers know the minimum per unit cost of producing each level of quality. For example, they know that an electric saw with a lifetime of two years with normal use costs $140 to produce, whereas one that lasts four years costs $300. Although all consumers have this information, they cannot tell prior to purchase whether the product purchased is a low- or a high-quality item.

Working with these assumptions Klein and Leffler identify the conditions under which competitive firms promise and deliver a high-quality product.

Promising and Delivering a High- or a Minimum-Quality Product

How will a competitive firm fare when it promises and delivers a high-quality product? Figure 14-6 shows the firm's long-run average cost function, $AC(X, q_h)$, and marginal cost function, $MC(X, q_h)$, if it produces the high-quality product. If the firm decides to produce the minimum-quality product, then the long-run average and marginal cost functions are $AC(X, q_{min})$ and $MC(X, q_{min})$, respectively. Figure 14-6 shows that the average cost of producing the high-quality product exceeds the average cost of producing the low-quality product at each quantity.

With free entry into the industry the long-run equilibrium price is P^* and the firm produces X^m units of the high-quality product. Although the firm does not earn profits, satisfied customers give it their repeat business.

A competitive firm that promises and delivers a high-quality product receives repeat business but does not earn profits.

If the firm promises and delivers q_{min}, the long-run equilibrium price is P_m with free entry and the firm produces X_m units. Again, consumers expect and receive the minimum-quality product. A competitive firm that supplies the minimum-quality product receives the repeat business of consumers but does not earn profits in long-run industry equilibrium.

Promising High Quality but Delivering Low Quality

Suppose a competitive firm promises a high-quality product but delivers a minimum-quality product. The cheating firm receives a per unit price of P^* because customers expect it will deliver a high-quality product. Figure 14-7 shows that the firm maximizes profits by producing X^{**} units where P^* equals the marginal cost of producing a minimum-quality product.

The firm earns profits but they last for only one year because consumers realize the firm has taken advantage of them and they will no longer patronize it. The company's annual profit is equal to the sum of areas C and D in Figure 14-7. Area C represents the profits from the first X_m units produced and is $(P^* - P_m)X_m$. P_m

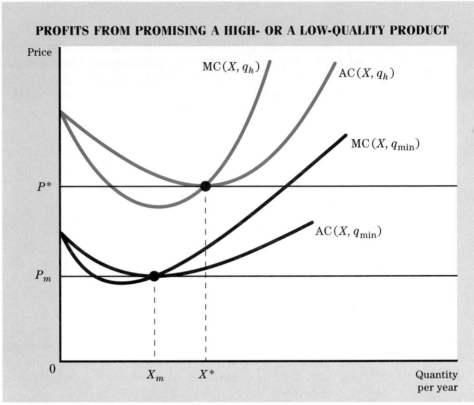

Figure 14-6   If a competitive firm produces a high-quality product, its average and marginal cost functions are $AC(X, q_h)$ and $MC(X, q_h)$, respectively. If the firm produces a minimum-quality product, the average and marginal cost functions are $AC(X, q_{min})$ and $MC(X, q_{min})$, respectively. At each quantity the average cost of producing the higher quality is higher.

is equal to the minimum long-run average cost of producing X_m units of a minimum-quality product. So, the difference between P^* and P_m equals the profit per unit from selling X_m units. Area D is the area between the P^* price line and the marginal cost function between X_m and X^{**} units and represents the additional profit the firm earns by increasing production from $X = X_m$ to $X = X^{**}$. Remember that area under the price line of P^* between X_m and X^{**} is equal to the increase in total revenue resulting from the increase in the quantity sold, and the area under the marginal cost function measures the additional cost of increasing production from X_m to X^{**}.

A competitive firm that promises a high-quality product but delivers a low-quality product does not receive repeat customers but earns profits for one period.

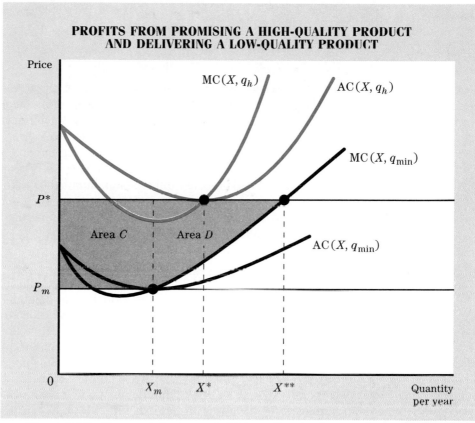

Figure 14-7   By promising to supply high quality, the firm receives a price of P^* for each unit. If the firm delivers low quality, the firm produces X^{**} units. The total profit from promising high quality while delivering low quality is equal to the sum of areas C and D.

To illustrate the relationships in Figure 14-7, suppose $P^* = \$10$, $P_m = \$5$, $X_m = 10$, and $X^{**} = 13$. The profit on the first 10 units produced is ($\$10 - \$5$) times 10 units, or \$50. If the marginal cost of producing the eleventh unit is \$8, the additional profit earned by producing and selling this unit is $\$10 - \$8 = \$2$. If the marginal cost of producing the twelfth unit is \$9, the additional profit from selling this unit is \$1. By proceeding in this manner and adding the difference between price and marginal cost for all units between the tenth and thirteenth, the increase in total profit from increasing production from 10 to 13 units can be measured.

The present value PV_1 of the profits earned at the end of one year (followed by a stream of zero profits) is equal to total profits divided by $1 + i$, where i is the discount rate (the rate the firm can earn on its investment). Therefore, the present value of annual profits that result from promising a high-quality product but delivering a low-quality product is[10]

$$PV_1 = \frac{1}{1 + i} (C + D) \qquad\qquad\qquad (14\text{-}4)$$

Because the present value of profits based on a cheating strategy is higher than the present value of profits based on a strategy of delivering the promised quality, a competitive firm will promise but not deliver a high-quality product. However, consumers will either anticipate this behavior or will learn from experience that these firms take advantage of them when consumers are unable to assess quality before purchase. They will refuse to purchase from vendors promising to deliver a high-quality product and purchase only the minimum-quality version of the product where they can evaluate the quality before purchase. Under asymmetric information the range of qualities that will be produced by competitive firms apparently shrinks to only the minimum quality.

Actual Quality Produced in Competitive Markets

How do we reconcile the prediction of the model—that competitive firms supply only minimum-quality goods to the market—with observations that firms do produce a range of qualities? You might reason that competitive firms can solve the problem by introducing warranties or other types of guarantees. Would warranties solve the quality problem? Not really. Here again, the same question arises: Why should the buyer believe that the seller will fulfill the terms of the warranty? If I receive a guarantee from my roofer that my roof will be watertight for five years, what assurance do I have that the roofer will still be in business in five years? Moreover, the roofer may claim that someone tampered with the roof or that a leak is due to a structural defect. As noted earlier in this chapter, warranties will not always solve the problem of deception in situations where legal sanctions are too expensive.

14-5   HOW DOES A COMPETITIVE INDUSTRY SUPPLY A HIGH-QUALITY PRODUCT?

For a competitive firm to supply a high-quality product, it must have a stake in the future, and so not have an incentive to grab short-run profits and then leave the industry. The firms in a competitive industry must receive a **price premium** so

---

[10] The present value of annual profits is

$$PV_1 = \frac{1}{1 + i} \left\{ (P^* - P_m)X_m + \sum_{X=X_m}^{X=X^{**}} [P^* - MC(X, q_{min})] \right\}$$

The first term in the curved braces, $(P^* - P_m)X_m$, equals area C and is the profit earned on the first X_m units produced since P_m equals the long-run minimum average cost of producing the X_m units of the minimum quality. The second term inside the brackets represents area D and is the additional profits the firm earns by increasing output from X_m to X^{**} units.

that there are long-run profits. Let's determine what the price premium must be if the firm is to act honestly.

Delivering a High-Quality Product with a Price Premium

If a competitive firm receives a price $P' > P^*$, it earns profits, and these profits are an incentive for it to supply a high-quality product. If the price is P' in Figure 14-8, a competitive firm that delivers high quality maximizes profits by producing X' units where P' is equal to the marginal cost of supplying a high-quality product. The firm earns profits equal to area A when it receives a price premium of $P' - P^*$. Area A is the sum of two smaller areas, just as the sum of areas C and D represents the total profits of a cheating firm. One part of area A is $(P' - P^*)X^*$ (not shown separately), the profits from sales when the firm produces X^* units. P' is price and P^* is equal to the minimum long-run average cost of producing X^*

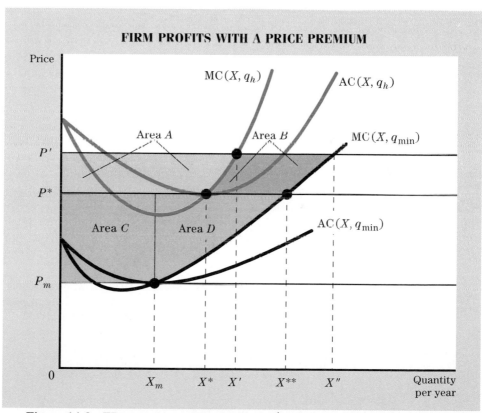

Figure 14-8   When a price premium of $P' - P^*$ exists, a firm that delivers high quality earns profits equal to area A indefinitely. A firm that promises high quality but delivers low quality earns profits equal to the sum of areas A, B, C, and D but only for a single period.

units. The second part of area A is the area between the price line, P', and the marginal cost function, $MC(X, q_h)$, from X^* units to X' units and is equal to the increase in profits gained from raising output from X^* units to X' units. Area A is the sum of these two areas and measures the firm's annual profits when a competitive firm delivers a high-quality product because it sells each unit at P'. Because the firm lives up to its promises, satisfied customers become repeat customers.

> A price premium gives a firm a greater incentive to forgo short-term profits in favor of future profits.

What is this indefinite profit stream worth today? The appendix at the end of this chapter shows that the present value of an indefinite profit stream equal to area A is area A/i, where i is the discount rate. Given demand and cost conditions, PV_2 is the present value of this infinite annual stream of profits when the price is P':[11]

$$PV_2 = \frac{1}{i} A \tag{14-5}$$

It is these future profits that create the incentive for the firm to deliver the higher-quality product so that consumers return. The opportunity cost of delivering a low-quality item is the loss of future sales and the future stream of annual profits.

The Incentive to Cheat

However, a premium price of P' also increases the profits gained using the cheating strategy. When the price is P', a cheating firm maximizes profits by producing X'' units, as shown in Figure 14-8 where P' equals the marginal cost of supplying a minimum-quality product. The total profits of the cheater now equal the sum of areas A, B, C, and D. Since the sum of areas C and D is equal to the cheater's profits when the price is P^*, profits increase by areas A plus B when the price rises from P^* to P'. A premium price raises the present value of a cheater's profits as well.

Because the firm earns these profits for only one year, their present value is the sum of areas A, B, C, and D multiplied by $1/(1 + i)$. The present value of profits when high quality is promised and low quality is delivered is[12]

---

[11] PV_2 can be written as

$$PV_2 = \frac{1}{i} \left\{ (P' - P^*)X^* + \sum_{X=X^*}^{X=X'} [P' - MC(X, q_h)] \right\}$$

The first term in the curved braces is the profits from the sale of X^* units and the second term is the profits from increasing sales from X^* to X'.

[12] PV_3 can be written as

$$PV_3 = \frac{1}{1 + i} \left\{ (P' - P_m)X_m + \sum_{X=X_m}^{X=X''} [P' - MC(X, q_{min})] \right\}$$

The first term in the curved braces is the profits from the sale of X_m units and the second is the profit from increasing sales from X_m to X''.

$$PV_3 = \frac{A + B + C + D}{1 + i} \tag{14-6}$$

Cheating versus Honesty

The firm must choose between these two strategies. With the trust strategy it delivers a high-quality product and earns profits equal to area A indefinitely. With the "grab-and-run" strategy the company promises a high-quality product but supplies a low-quality product and receives a one-year profit equal to the sum of areas A, B, C, and D. The annual profit from cheating is larger than the annual profit from acting honestly, but it lasts only one year.

When will a competitive firm adopt a strategy of delivering a high-quality product? Assuming the firm selects the policy that maximizes the present value of profits, it will supply a high-quality product when the price is P' if $PV_2 \geq PV_3$. Substituting the two expressions for the present values into this inequality yields

$$PV_2 \geq PV_3$$

$$\frac{A}{i} \geq \frac{A + B + C + D}{1 + i} \quad \text{(Condition for Providing High Quality)} \tag{14-7}$$

where the letters represent the areas in Figure 14-8. Multiplying both sides of the inequality by $1 + i$ gives[13]

$$\frac{A}{i} + A \geq A + B + C + D$$

$$\frac{A}{i} \geq B + C + D \tag{14-8}$$

If equation 14-8 is satisfied as an equality, a competitive firm maximizes the present value of profits by delivering a high-quality product at a price of P'.

Will there always be a premium price P' greater than P^* that satisfies equation 14-8 as an equality? Not necessarily. If P' is just slightly higher than P^*, then area A will be very small relative to the sum of areas C and D and 14-8 cannot be satisfied as an equality. As P' increases, area A, the profits from the production of a high-quality product, increase, and areas C and D do not change. Therefore, the ratio $(C + D)/A$ decreases as P' increases. As P' rises, areas A and B change at different rates that depend on the shapes of the marginal cost functions for producing high- and minimum-quality products. There is no guarantee that area B will increase at a slower rate than area A.

In some situations no price will satisfy the inequality (equation 14-8), and so there is no price premium that makes honesty the highest present value policy. Under these circumstances a competitive industry will not supply the higher-quality

---

[13] The firm earns profits equal to area A in the first year whether it cheats or delivers the high-quality product. Therefore, profits equal to area A in the first year have no bearing on the decision to supply a high-quality product. Equation 14-8 says that the firm will act honestly if the present value of future profits in year 2 and later from acting honestly exceeds the sum of areas B, C, and D received at the end of year 1.

product, and it is in these instances that the strongest case for government intervention exists. Otherwise, consumers will be willing to purchase only the minimum quality for fear of being taken advantage of. By imposing sanctions for misrepresenting a product, government regulation may introduce the proper incentive for firms to supply high-quality products.

In other cases P' is the smallest price above P^* that satisfies 14-8. $P' - P^*$ is therefore the smallest price premium that will induce a competitive firm to deliver the promised quality. By paying a premium price P', consumers are willingly paying protection money to bribe the firm to behave honestly. The seller receives the stream of future profits as long as it delivers the promised quality. So the opportunity cost of cheating is loss of this attractive profit stream.

APPLICATION 14-3

The Price Premium at McDonald's

We can look at the operating performance at McDonald's franchises to determine if McDonald's provides them with a price premium. McDonald's wants all of its stores to provide fast service, meals of a uniform quality, and a clean and cheerful atmosphere. Does McDonald's entice franchisees to meet these responsibilities with a price premium?

McDonald's determines the number of franchises and can limit this number so that each one receives P' and earns profits. If there is a price premium for McDonald's franchisees, it should be profitable to own and operate a franchise. Economists Patrick Kaufmann and Francine Lafontaine examined the profitability of McDonald's franchises in 1982 and 1989[14]. They present publicly available information about the profitability of 1,283 McDonald's-owned restaurants that have

[14] Patrick J. Kaufmann and Francine Lafontaine, "Costs of Control: The Source of Economic Rents for McDonald's Franchisees," *Journal of Law and Economics* XXXVII (October 1994), pp. 417–54.

Table 14-4   ESTIMATED PROFITABILITY OF MCDONALD'S FRANCHISES IN 1982

	Yearly Sales (in $ thousands)		
	900	1100	1300
Yearly profits ($ thousands)	3.4	62.8	107.7
Present discounted profits	44.5	821.7	1409.3
Up-front costs	371.5	404.5	535.5
Present value after subtracting up-front costs (before taxes)	(327.0)	417.2	873.8

been in operation for 13 months or longer. In 1982, 73 percent of these restaurants had annual revenues of $1.1 million or more. Kaufmann and Lafontaine then adjust the operating profits of company-owned stores for royalty payments of 11.5 percent of sales that a franchisee must pay to McDonald's, the security deposit, inventory, maintenance, and the opportunity cost of labor of the franchisee. Row 1 of Table 14-4 shows the estimated annual profits for franchises of three different sizes (as measured by annual sales) after making these adjustments.

For example, a restaurant with annual revenues of $1.3 million expects to earn $107,700 in annual profits in 1982. Row 2 shows the present value of the profit stream when the inflation-adjusted discount rate is 5 percent. For a franchise with annual revenues of $1.3 million, the present value of profits is $1.4 million. Row 3 subtracts the up-front costs that each franchisee incurs when starting a franchise—for equipment, for time spent in training, and the franchise fee. The net before-tax present value is $873,800 for such a restaurant. These calculations suggest that all but the smallest McDonald's franchises are very profitable. Because they are, McDonald's must be giving its franchisees a price premium.

APPLICATION 14-4

A Price Premium in Labor Markets

Paying a premium to ensure honest behavior has applications in markets other than product markets. The same issue arises in the labor market when a firm cannot monitor a worker and pays a premium wage to discourage him or her from shirking on the job. If a worker is found shirking and is terminated, he or she may not be able to find another job that pays a premium. By paying a premium wage, the employer makes the job a lucrative one that the worker wants to keep. The employee is then less likely to shirk on the job whether this involves the way the worker treats customers or the effort exerted by the worker. The employer is willing to pay a premium wage if it reduces the firm's cost of monitoring workers.

In an interesting case study Alan Kreuger[15] investigated the pay of managers and workers in company-owned and in operator-owned fast food outlets. He claims that an owner-manager has a greater incentive to exert effort in supervising workers because the owner's total reward is directly tied to the profits of the outlet. On the other hand, at company-owned outlets a manager receives a salary but does not share in the profits of the outlet. Therefore, he or she has less incentive to monitor employees closely since there are no direct benefits.

Because of the different incentives for monitoring workers, company-owned outlets can substitute higher pay for less direct monitoring. Is there any evidence that this occurs? Kreuger examined the average hourly wage of assistant and shift

[15] Based on Alan B. Kreuger, "Ownership, Agency, and Wages: An Examination of Franchising in the Fast Food Industry," *Quarterly Journal of Economics* CVI (February 1991), pp. 75–102.

Table 14-5   AVERAGE HOURLY WAGE RATE

TYPE OF WORKER	FRANCHISEE-OWNED ($)	COMPANY-OWNED ($)	PERCENTAGE DIFFERENCE
Assistant and shift manager	4.35	4.75	9.2
Crew worker	3.57	3.61	1.1

Reprinted by permission of President and Fellows of Harvard College and Massachusetts Institute of Technology, copyright 1991.

managers and crew workers in franchisee-owned and in company-owned fast food outlets. Table 14-5 shows his results.

Kreuger found that companies pay a premium wage to assistant and shift managers but not to ordinary workers in fast food outlets. Thus, it appears that in the fast food industry company-owned firms rely on a premium wage to discourage managers from cheating.

Nonsalvageable Investments

McDonald's may be able to limit the number of outlets, but this is not possible in a competitive industry. If entry into a competitive industry is unrestricted, how can a price premium and profits exist in the long run?

Ordinarily, entry into an industry reduces price. However, consumers will not purchase the product at a lower price than P' in Figure 14-8. No rational consumer will purchase from a seller promising to supply a high-quality product at a price less than P' because he or she knows it is more profitable for the firm to deliver the minimum-quality product. The demand for the high-quality model simply disappears at any price less than P'. What this means is that new entrants cannot enter the market by offering a lower price and realistically expect customers to switch sellers. Entry through *price* competition will not succeed.

Since price competition is not feasible, the only way firms can enter the industry is by competing through *nonprice* means. They can do this by making investments that will not only increase their costs and eliminate profits but also convince consumers that they will be around in the future. Their capital improvements must be firm-specific and, if possible, produce services for which customers experience some value. By making **nonsalvageable investments,** firms send a signal to consumers that they will suffer a large capital loss if they cheat on quality and must exit the industry.

These firm-specific investments are less valuable in alternative uses. Competing by investing in nonsalvageable capital raises the firm's cost, eliminates profits, and discourages cheating because the company becomes a hostage to consumers.[16] Each firm in the industry must participate in this type of competition if it expects to retain consumers since consumers receive some utility from the nonsalvageable investments made by the firm. If a company raises its costs by simply giving money to charity, it will lose customers to other firms that increase the utility of the consumer by investing in nonsalvageable assets. It is this type of nonprice competition among firms that eliminates profits and establishes a long-run industry equilibrium.

> *Nonsalvageable investments* eliminate profits and make a firm a hostage to the industry.

Perhaps the best example of a nonsalvageable asset is the development of a **brand name** through the firm's advertisements. By advertising, the company establishes goodwill or brand name capital. The brand name represents certain characteristics of the product that consumers are willing to purchase, and the goodwill is an asset, just as the firm's plant is an asset. Brand name capital helps the company make sales in the present and in the future. The value of the brand name depreciates and may become worthless if the firm cheats and must exit the industry.

Another example of a nonsalvageable investment is the purchase of distinctive fixtures for a store. The fixtures are firm-specific and elaborate and therefore are less valuable to other companies. For example, you might place a special logo on a rug or on the fixtures of your store. If your firm goes out of business, it suffers a **capital loss** when it sells the fixtures because the investment in fixtures is firm-specific.[17]

In each example the firm suffers a capital loss if it cheats and leaves the industry. It is for this reason that a grab-and-run policy is no longer attractive. We can determine the size of the capital loss that the firm would suffer in equilibrium if it did cheat. Let's consider the special case where firm-specific investments are like a fixed cost and so do not affect the position of the long-run marginal cost function of the firm. These investments shift the long-run average cost function upward until profits disappear where the firm produces X' units when the price is P' in Figure 14-8. If the firm invests in firm-specific projects and then cheats on quality, it gains the present value of the one-period profit, or $(A + B + C + D)/(1 + i)$. The opportunity cost of the cheating strategy is the capital loss on the firm-specific investment that it has made. The capital loss, β, must equal the present

---

[16] Deliberately creating a hostage to induce exchange is treated in Oliver E. Williamson, "Credible Commitments: Using Hostages to Support Exchange," *American Economic Review* 83 (September 1983), pp. 519–40.

[17] A firm can make specific investments that tie it to the industry but do not increase the utility of the consumer. The design of the factory building is specific to the production of a product. If you have to leave the industry and sell the building to a competitor, you will take a capital loss because your competitor will have to modify the layout of the building to suit its special requirements.

value of the profits gained from delivering the promised quality. In long-run industry equilibrium β is

$$\beta = \frac{A}{i} \qquad \text{(Capital Loss Incurred by Firm)} \qquad \textbf{(14-9)}$$

In order for the firm to be indifferent between cheating and not cheating, the capital loss must just equal the present value of the one-period profit obtained by delivering the promised quality since the price premium is determined where

$$\frac{A}{i} = \frac{A + B + C + D}{1 + i}$$

The value of the capital loss that the firm suffers if it cheats is on the left-hand side of this equality, while the present value of the gain from cheating is on the right-hand side. Therefore, the capital loss on the nonsalvageable assets is equal to the present value of the one-period profit gained from cheating.

For example, assume that a firm's total investment is $100,000. If the one-period profit obtained from cheating is $4,200 and the discount rate is 5 percent, then the capital loss that the firm suffers if it cheats must be $4,000. Therefore, the firm's total investment must be worth only $96,000 if the firm cheats and has to exit the industry. This implies that area A is equal to $4,000(.05) = $200.

When the Required Price Premium Is Unknown

The Klein-Leffler model assumes that consumers know the required price premium that discourages cheating. (Refer to earlier section, "Modeling Competitive Behavior under Asymmetric Information.") If we relax assumption 6 of the model and suppose that buyers do not know the exact quality–average cost relationship, firms must adopt policies that allow consumers to infer that a price premium exists. Consumers do this by observing signals that a firm has made specific investments. For example, they deduce that a company that advertises heavily and develops a brand name has made nonsalvageable investments. Firm- or brand-specific investments indicate the existence of a price premium. By observing what they believe to be brand-specific investments, they infer that the firm is selling the product at a premium price and that it will suffer a loss if it leaves the industry.

Obviously, uncertainty about the necessary price premium that ensures quality places an additional burden on consumers. They are even less capable of determining whether firms have made adequate brand-specific investments than of assessing the quality of the product. Moreover, the firm will have more difficulty convincing them that its brand-specific investments are large enough to prevent cheating. When there is uncertainty, there are more opportunities for firms to pretend that they have made the required nonsalvageable investments when they have not, and this presents more possibilities for cheating.

Conclusions about the Klein-Leffler Model

The Klein-Leffler model is one of several that economists have developed to explain why firms develop reputations for fair dealing and reliability. In their model the creation of a reputation is a consequence of the firm's profit-maximizing calculus. The authors do not assert that sellers will be either honest or unscrupulous. In their model sellers will be one or the other depending on their incentives. The lesson to take from this model is that the price system can develop incentive mechanisms to deal with difficult asymmetric information problems even when the threat of legal sanctions is absent.

SUMMARY

- Asymmetric information exists when one side of a potential transaction has more information than the other side.
- When asymmetric information exists, the owners of high-quality products suffer losses. When they offer high-quality products, and sell them in a pool that includes low-quality products, they receive a lower price.
- With adverse selection the products that appear in the market are different from the products that firms sell when both sides have complete information. When asymmetric information exists, market institutions such as warranties and testing arise, and there is greater reliance on the seller's reputation.
- A moral hazard problem exists when an

agent takes less than the socially optimal care in response to a principal's action.
- In long-run equilibrium competitive firms have a profit incentive to promise a high-quality product but supply a low-quality product. If there is nothing to tie the firm to the industry, it will supply only those qualities that consumers can assess before purchase. There will be an adverse selection of all product qualities in long-run industry equilibrium.
- A competitive firm may overcome the adverse selection problem if it receives a price premium and makes nonsalvageable investments. These nonsalvageable investments make the firm a hostage in the industry.

KEY TERMS

asymmetric information
separating versus pooling equilibrium
reputation
promising high quality and delivering high
    or minimum quality
brand name

adverse selection
moral hazard
present value of profits
nonsalvageable investments
price premium
capital loss

REVIEW QUESTIONS

1. If S_g = \$20,000, B_g = \$24,000, and B_l = \$12,000, what is P_b and what percentage of used autos must be gems before gems appear in the market?
2. When there is asymmetric information in

the market, all used cars sell at the P_b. Explain why you agree or disagree with this statement.
3. In a pooling equilibrium owners of lemons are able to sell their autos as gems, and

the only individuals harmed are the unfortunate purchasers. Explain why you agree or disagree with this statement.

4. Give an explanation for why a new car depreciates considerably immediately after its sale.

5. If there is asymmetric information, would you expect the prices paid for free agents to be lower than those paid for players who remained with their teams, with all other factors held constant? Explain why or why not.

6. Would you expect cheating by one department in a department store to be less likely because of the potential loss of sales in other departments? Does the Klein-Leffler theory address this issue?

7. Would you expect a tourist to be more vulnerable to cheating? Why would you expect this to be true? What market institutions have emerged to lessen the cheating problem?

8. What is the present value of $20,000 received at the end of the first year if the discount rate is 10 percent?

9. What is the present value of $1,000 per year indefinitely if the discount rate is 5 percent?

10. How does the price premium change when the discount rate increases? How does the price premium change if a firm can get away with cheating for two years instead of for one year?

11. If a manufacturer's total investment is $50,000, what information do you need to determine what the value of the investment will be if the firm goes out of business?

12. Suppose a competitive firm sells a product whose qualities consumers cannot assess before purchase. The firm tries to enter the industry by charging the market price and also offers free delivery after investing in a fleet of delivery trucks. Explain why consumers will or will not purchase the product from the firm.

EXERCISES

1. What is the lemons problem? When do lemons problems appear?

2. Suppose you are trying to determine whether a lemons problem exists in the market for used pickup trucks. Explain why each of the following tests would or would not reveal a lemons problem.

   a. The percentage of pickup trucks that trade in the first year.

   b. The percentage of trucks sold to dealers by the original owners is increasing over time.

   c. The maintenance cost of trucks after they are sold by the original owners is greater than the maintenance costs of trucks that original owners retain.

3. It is said that a market may not even exist when there is a lemons problem. Describe a demand and supply model and show how this can occur.

4. What is meant by the adverse selection problem? When do adverse selection problems appear?

5. Would you expect the adverse selection problem to be more serious for insurance firms offering insurance policies to employers with minimum-size groups than to trade associations? Explain why or why not.

6. What is the moral hazard problem? When does it occur?

7. A monopolist will not cheat consumers because the monopolist earns profits on repeat sales. Explain why you would agree or disagree with this statement.

8. If the consumer knows the total quantity

produced by the firm before purchasing the product, he or she can tell if the firm will deliver a minimum-quality product or a high-quality product, and so the cheating problem disappears. Explain why you agree or disagree with this statement.

*9. You have invented a new home burglar alarm system. You plan to franchise the system to independent retail outlets. Customers purchase alarm systems infrequently, and so they have little information. You are fearful your franchisees will strive for short-run profits by saving on installation costs and thereby ruin the reputation of the alarm system. While you could try to monitor the installations of individual franchisees, it would be very expensive. Assume that the retailers are price-taking firms and use the Klein-Leffler theory to explain how many franchises you would issue to prevent cheating.

*10. Suppose you are planning to open a health club. Customers have been burned in the past because a few of these clubs have closed abruptly without refunding unused memberships. You know that consumers are wary of joining a new health club. Evaluate whether the following policies will overcome the problem of consumer wariness.

a. Raising the price of a membership to obtain a premium price.

b. Prohibiting the sale of lifetime memberships.

c. Starting a trade group with local and nationwide clubs and extending reciprocal privileges to individual members. If a club goes out of business, the members may use the facilities of another club. What kinds of problems would you face if you joined such a club? Would you place any restrictions on reciprocity?

d. Investing in health equipment with your own distinctive label on the equipment.

11. China has attempted to deal with consumer fraud by allowing consumers that purchase fakes to receive twice the price for a refund by proving consumer deception. Comment on the effectiveness of this mechanism to promote honest business dealings.

*12. Your company produces an advanced model of a PC every year. Assume that you are a monopolist. A market research study reveals that two types of consumers use the computer. Type 1 buyers are sophisticated and use all the new features that the new model offers. Type 2 users are computer-phobic, are intimidated by the latest technology, and are content to use older, familiar models. Your company wants to sell the new computer to the sophisticated users, but they complain about the cost of finding buyers and selling their old computers in the used computer market. As the CEO, you know that more consumers will purchase the new model if they can sell their used computers at the end of the year to a type 2 user. Any arrangement facilitating the transfer will increase the demand for the new model. (Assume that firms cannot lease the equipment.) Two possible policies are being considered:

- *Policy 1.* Rent a large facility once a year where these two types of consumers can meet and a type 2 consumer can purchase a used computer from a type 1 user.
- *Policy 2.* Give exclusive rights to a limited number of dealers who act as intermediaries between the two types of consumers.

a. Present a brief discussion of the advantages and disadvantages of these two policies.

b. Which policy would you select? Defend your decision against the alternative policy.

PROBLEM SET

Integration and Opportunistic Behavior

There are times when a buyer or a supplier is vulnerable when fulfilling the terms of a contract. One party to a transaction must make an up-front investment that is specific to the transaction. Once made, that party is in a vulnerable position because the other party can threaten to pull out unless the terms of the contract are made more favorable retroactively. If these situations can reoccur, it may be more efficient for firms to integrate (make rather than buy the product) and to eliminate the market transaction.

Firm X has supplied a part to firm Y for many years. At the beginning of each year the two firms sign a contract whereby X agrees to supply its total production to Y at a competitive price negotiated by the two parties before production begins. Because X signs a contract before production begins, it insisted long ago that a safety margin be built in just in case X's costs rise after it signs the contract. Y agreed to include a clause in the very first contract that X would always have the right to increase prices by at most P percent above the cost-based competitive price without giving Y any special explanation. The two firms have been doing business for many years, and X has only infrequently increased price and then only when it appeared justified.

Relations between the two firms had always been amicable. X was a reliable supplier, delivered goods on time, and supplied uniform quality. Two years ago, however, there was a change in the management at X, and since then X has increased the price retroactively by P percent each year. Y began to suspect that X was taking advantage of the relaxed and amicable long-term relationship between the two firms and was acting opportunistically by raising the price even though the increase was not cost-justified.

Y forms a committee to reevaluate the arrangement and to suggest alternative courses of action. The committee estimates X's per unit cost of production at capacity output, q^*, is A in the accompanying figure.

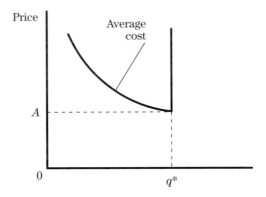

The committee also investigates whether Y should consider producing the part. There isn't much information to go on, but a recent research study of Y's operations in other areas, where it produces other parts, concluded that Y is not a particularly efficient producer of parts. The report concluded that Y's average cost of production averaged I percent above the market prices for a sample of eight parts.

Given this unimpressive experience with producing parts internally compared to buying in the open market, the committee is not too optimistic and is reluctant to recommend that Y produce this particular part internally. It decides to make use of the price system and recommends that Y offer X a premium price of more than A dollars, the cost-based competitive price. It recommends that X be told clearly that if it raises the price above this premium price in the future without justification, Y will terminate purchases from X in all future years.

Questions

1. Use the Klein-Leffler analysis to develop an expression for the present value of X's profits if it raises price by P percent above A dollars in the coming year without justification.

2. What price should Y offer X to discourage X from raising price by P percent above A dollars (assuming no unforeseen contingency)? Let that price be $(1 + k)A$ (where $k > 0$). Derive an expression for k and show how it depends on the discount rate i and the maximum price increase P.

3. What determines how high the discount rate can rise before it pays Y to make the part rather than buy it?

■ CHAPTER 14 APPENDIX

Present-Value Calculations

A dollar received at the end of the year is worth less than a dollar received today because a dollar in hand earns interest. At the end of one year a dollar has increased in value to $1 + i$ if the interest rate is i percent per year. A dollar becomes \$1.05 if the interest rate is 5 percent. The 5 percent is a real return if it is assumed that the general price level neither increases nor decreases. This appendix evaluates two profit streams by calculating the present value of each one. The present value of profits in a future year is an amount, if received today, that is equivalent to the profits received in some future year. The procedure for determining the present value of a future dollar is called *discounting*.

> The present value of future profits is an amount received immediately that is equivalent to the stream of profits received in future years.

In the chapter one strategy a firm can pursue is to cheat and receive profits at the end of the first year. Let's consider the present value of the profit stream consisting of profits of π_1 at the end of the year 1. What is the present value of π_1? What amount received at the beginning of the year is equivalent to receiving π_1 at the end of year 1? You should be indifferent between receiving π_1 at the end of the year or $\pi_1/(1 + i)$ at the beginning of year 1. For example, receiving \$1,000 at the end of year 1 is equivalent to receiving $1000/(1 + 0.05) = \$952.38$ immediately if the interest rate is 5 percent. Why are these two equivalent alternatives? If you receive $\pi_1/(1 + i)$ at the beginning of year 1 and earn an annual interest rate of i on this amount, you will have $[\pi_1/(1 + i)] (1 + i) = \pi_1$ at the end of year 1. There is an exact equivalence between receiving $\pi_1/(1 + i)$ at the beginning of year 1 and receiving π_1 at the end of the year. We say that the present value of π_1 is $\pi_1/(1 + i)$. Therefore, to calculate the present value of the one-time profits at the end of the year from cheating, the firm divides these profits by $1 + i$.

What is the present value of a profit stream of A_1 in the first year, A_2 in the second year, and so on? The present value of this steady stream of profits is equal to the sum of the present value of the profits in each year. If the profits in year 1 are A_1, we already know that the present value of the profits in year 1 is $A_1/(1 + i)$. What is the present value of

Table 14A-1   PRESENT VALUE OF A STREAM OF PROFITS

YEAR	PROFITS	PRESENT VALUE OF PROFITS RECEIVED AT END OF YEAR
1	A_1	$\dfrac{A_1}{1+i}$
2	A_2	$\dfrac{A_2}{(1+i)^2}$
3	A_3	$\dfrac{A_3}{(1+i)^3}$
.	.	.
.	.	.
.	.	.
n	A_n	$\dfrac{A_n}{(1+i)^n}$

profits of A_2 received at the end of year 2? What sum received immediately is equivalent to receiving A_2 2 years from now? If you receive an amount equal to $A_2/(1+i)^2$ immediately and invest it in year 1 and again in year 2 along with the interest earned in year 1, at the end of year 2 you will have $[A_2/(1+i)^2](1+i)(1+i) = A_2$. At the end of year 1, you will receive $[A_2/(1+i)^2](1+i)$, or $A_2/(1+i)$. Then, if you earn interest on this amount in year 2, you will have $A_2/(1+i)(1+i) = A_2$ at the end of year 2. The present value of A_2 received at the end of year 2 is $A_2/(1+i)^2$.

The algorithm for calculating the present value of profits received at the end of some future year should be clear by now. Say you want to determine the present value of A_n received at the end of year n. Divide A_n by $(1+i)$ raised to the power n, or $A_n/(1+i)^n$.

The last column of Table 14A-1 shows the present value of future profits in each year when the firm receives profits at the end of the year.

The present value of a profit stream is equal to the sum of the present value of each year's profits. The present value of an indefinite profit stream is

$$\text{Present value} = \frac{A_1}{1+i} + \frac{A_2}{(1+i)^2} + \cdots + \frac{A_n}{(1+i)^n} + \cdots \qquad \textbf{(14A-1)}$$

The present value, PV, of an indefinite stream of a constant amount A is

$$\text{PV} = (D + D^2 + \cdots + D^n + \cdots)A$$

where $D = 1/(1+i)$. Multiply and divide the right-hand side of the expression by $1-D$ to obtain

$$\text{PV} = (1-D)(D + D^2 + \cdots + D^n + \cdots)\frac{A}{1-D}$$

Multiplying through by $1 - D$ yields

$$PV = (D - D^2 + D^2 - D^3 + D^3 + \cdots)\frac{A}{1 - D}$$

$$= \left(\frac{D}{1 - D}\right)A$$

Since $D = 1/(1 + i)$ and $1 - D = i/(1 + i)$, $D/(1 - D) = 1/i$. Therefore, the present value of an indefinite profit stream A is

$$PV = \frac{A}{i} \qquad \text{(Present Value of a Perpetual Constant-Profit Stream Received at the End of Each Year)} \qquad \textbf{(14A-2)}$$

CHAPTER 15

PRICING UNDER UNCERTAINTY

■ **15-1   Seasonal Variation in Men's and Women's Apparel Prices**

■ **15-2   The Growth in Markdowns over Time**

■ **15-3   Uncertainty about Consumer Tastes**

Pricing Fashion Apparel: A Numerical Example

A Model with More Colors

■ **15-4   Selecting a Price Policy**

A Single-Price Policy

A Two-Price Policy

Selecting the Initial and Markdown Prices to Maximize Expected Revenue

Changing the Probability Distribution of Prices

■ **15-5   Using the Theory to Understand Markdown Pricing Practices**

Application 15-1: Markdowns by Merchandise Group

Differences in Equilibrium Prices under Certainty and Uncertainty

When to Apply the Uncertainty Theory

■ **Summary**

■ **Key Terms**

■ **Review Questions**

■ **Exercises**

Unlike the other chapters in this book in which a general theory has been followed by relevant applications, this chapter reverses the process. We first present some interesting pricing practices in the retail clothing market, beginning with the observation that women pay relatively higher prices for apparel compared to men at the beginning of a season and relatively lower prices at the end. What model can explain this pricing behavior? Are retailers engaging in price discrimination that is more pronounced for women's than for men's apparel? Why should women's demand function for clothing be much less elastic at the beginning of the season and much more elastic at the end of the season compared to men's demand functions? A more fundamental issue is whether the price discrimination model should be applied to an industry in which there are so many competitive retail sellers. If price discrimination is not the explanation for the phenomenon, is there a substitute explanation for the seasonal patterns in apparel pricing?

A second interesting pricing regularity is the dramatically increasing frequency of markdowns over time. We show this in a graph in Section 15-2. Are stores offering so many more sales now than 30 years ago because there is greater competition among retailers now than in the past? But then why should increased competition affect only end-of-season and not beginning-of-season prices?

To explain these pricing regularities, we develop a simple pricing model. As you read this chapter, you will gain a better appreciation of how economists extend their understanding of markets by developing and testing theories that explain interesting phenomena.

15-1   SEASONAL VARIATION IN MEN'S AND WOMEN'S APPAREL PRICES

Figure 15-1 illustrates the price behavior observed during the fall-winter season for both men's and women's clothes—higher initial prices are followed by a sharp decline in January and February. The fall-winter season starts sometime in September and continues through February, after which the spring-summer season begins. The horizontal line in Figure 15-1 represents the average price for the year set equal to 1.00. Notice the different price behavior for women's and men's clothing. Women's prices are higher initially but drop more than men's prices by the end of the season.[1] For example, in October 1988 the price index for women's clothing was about 5.5 percent higher than the yearly average price and about 4 percentage points below the yearly average in January 1989. Between October and January there is a seasonal swing in prices of about 9.5 percentage points.

In contrast, the seasonal swing in men's apparel prices is more modest, about 3.5 percentage points. Women's apparel prices are higher relative to the average compared to men's apparel prices at the beginning of the season and fall by a larger percentage during January and February when clearance sales are held.

---

[1] The rise in prices from September to October may partially reflect early season sales. However, the price increases are more likely to reflect the sales offered on remaining summer clothing and the lighter-weight clothing sold in early fall.

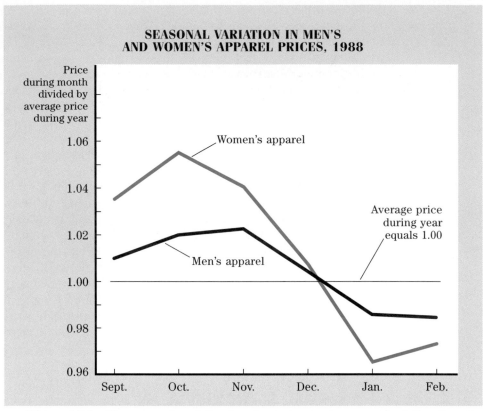

**SEASONAL VARIATION IN MEN'S
AND WOMEN'S APPAREL PRICES, 1988**

Figure 15-1   The seasonal variation in price is greater for women's clothes than for men's clothes.

Another example of this seasonal price change was discussed in Chapter 12. In Figure 12-4 the percentage markdown for men's dress shirts followed a seasonal pattern, with larger markdowns offered at the end of the fall-winter and spring-summer seasons. What causes this **seasonal variation** in apparel prices and why is it greater for women's than for men's apparel?

15-2   THE GROWTH IN MARKDOWNS OVER TIME

Figure 15-2 shows the percentage markdown on merchandise sold in American department stores from 1948 to 1985. The graph reveals that a distinct change occurred in the late 1960s. After many years with no trend in the series, in the late 1960s department stores began to give larger markdowns and/or to mark down a larger percentage of merchandise. Why did department stores change their pricing policies?

After observing the pervasiveness of sales and markdowns in the 90s, some analysts have suggested the cause is the excessive number of retail stores selling

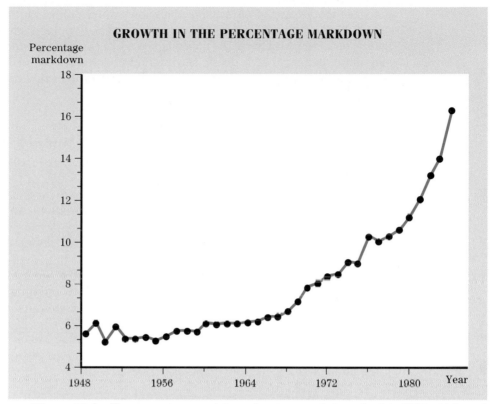

Figure 15-2 The percentage markdown has increased since the late 1960s. [Adapted from B. Peter Pashigian, "Demand Uncertainty and Sales: A Study of Fashion and Markdown Pricing," *American Economic Review*, December 1988, fig. 1, p. 941.] Copyright © 1988 by the American Economic Association.

clothing—the over-storing of America. According to this argument, competition among stores has so increased that stores are forced to mark down clothing prices more frequently and to offer larger percentage discounts. A glance at Figure 15-2 indicates this is not a convincing explanation, because markdowns began to grow much earlier. If an explanation for the growing frequency of sales is to be found, it needs to explain why this growth began in the late 60s.

15-3   UNCERTAINTY ABOUT CONSUMER TASTES

If we are to better understand these pricing regularities, we want to build a model that can explain why retailers offer clearance sales at the end of the season and why in recent times retailers have been offering larger markdowns. During a clearance sale the store reduces prices on merchandise that did not sell earlier in the season at higher prices. To explain these pricing practices, we begin by noting that in some cases a store buyer must place an order for a line of dresses a year or more before the start of the season. She knows which colors and styles are popular now but is uncertain which colors and styles will be popular a year from now. The source of this uncertainty is the unpredictability of consumer tastes in color, length, silhouette, and style of a dress. Buying decisions that were made one year ago under considerable uncertainty are the root cause of the price reductions offered during clearance sales.

Pricing Fashion Apparel: A Numerical Example

Let's start with a comparatively simple situation that nonetheless captures the essence of the pricing problem facing a store selling a line of fashion dresses. A store sells a dress line with three colors. In each season one of the three is the "hot" color, the "fashion hit" of the season, and a dress with a hot color can be sold for at most $500. Another color will be an "acceptable" color during the season and can be sold for at most $300. The third color is the "unpopular" color of the season, a "fashion disaster," and can be sold only for $100. The probability that a particular color is the fashion hit color of the season is $\frac{1}{3}$; the probability that it is an acceptable color is $\frac{1}{3}$; and the probability that it is the unpopular color is $\frac{1}{3}$. For example, mauve dresses are fashion hits in $\frac{1}{3}$ of the seasons, acceptable in $\frac{1}{3}$ of the seasons, and unpopular in $\frac{1}{3}$ of the seasons.

The store must set the price at the beginning of the season before it knows which color will be the fashion hit of the season. If the firm can set only a single price throughout the season, its price choices are

1. *High-Price Policy:* Set a relatively high price of $500 and therefore sell only dresses with the season's hot color. That is, a mauve dress will be the hot color only $\frac{1}{3}$ of the seasons, and in those seasons a mauve dress can fetch $500. Two-thirds of the seasons the store cannot sell a mauve dress because mauve is either an acceptable or unpopular color so consumers value a mauve dress at less than $500. Therefore, the expected or average revenue from selling mauve dresses equals $\frac{1}{3}$ ($500) + $\frac{2}{3}$ ($0) = $166.67. Over many seasons the average revenue that a store receives from selling a mauve dress equals $166.67.

2. *Medium-Price Policy:* If the firm charges $300 for all of its dresses throughout a season, it will sell those colors that are either hot or acceptable in that season. A mauve dress has a probability of $\frac{2}{3}$ of selling at a price of $300. One-third of the seasons mauve is a hot color and $\frac{1}{3}$ of the seasons it is an acceptable color. In either case, a mauve dress can be sold for $300. In the remaining seasons mauve is the unpopular color and the store cannot sell a mauve dress at a price of $300 since consumers are willing to pay only $100 for this color. The expected revenue equals $\frac{2}{3}$ ($300) + $\frac{1}{3}$ ($0) = $200 per dress with this color.

3. *Low-Price Policy:* If the firm charges $100 per dress, it will sell a mauve dress in every season. One-third of the seasons mauve is a hot color, $\frac{1}{3}$ of the time it is acceptable, and $\frac{1}{3}$ of the seasons it is an unpopular color, but

in all seasons, the store can sell a mauve dress at $100. The expected revenue equals $\frac{1}{3}$ ($100) + $\frac{1}{3}$ ($100) + $\frac{1}{3}$ ($100) = $100.

If a firm must charge a single price throughout the season, it maximizes expected revenue by charging a price of $300 per dress. By the end of each season, it learns which two of the three colors are either hot or acceptable but its price policy is not based on and does not reveal which is the hot color and which is the acceptable color among the three colors that the firm sells.

Can the firm increase expected revenue by getting consumers to reveal which is the hot color? Suppose that it charges a higher price at the beginning of the season and then lowers the price at the end of the season? For example, it could adopt a high-medium price policy by charging $500 for all colors at the beginning of the season and, consequently, selling only the hot color. Then, it could sell the acceptable color at a sale price of $300. Let's calculate the expected revenue from the three possible pricing combinations.

1. *High ($500)–Medium ($300) Price Policy:* The initial price is $500 so only the hot color sells and the markdown price at the end of the season is $300 so only the acceptable color sells. Expected revenue equals $\frac{1}{3}$ ($500) + $\frac{1}{3}$ ($300) − $266.67.

2. *High ($500)–Low ($100) Price Policy:* The initial price is $500 so only the hot color sells and the remaining two colors sell at the end of the season since the markdown price is $100. Expected revenue equals $\frac{1}{3}$ ($500) + $\frac{2}{3}$ ($100) − $233.33.

3. *Medium ($300)–Low ($100) Price Policy:* The initial price is $300 so both the hot and acceptable color sell and the unpopular color is sold at the end of the season at a price of $100. Expected revenue equals $\frac{2}{3}$ ($300) + $\frac{1}{3}$ ($100) = $233.33.

The firm maximizes expected revenue by adopting a high-medium price policy. At the beginning of the season it charges $500 for all colors. At this relatively high price, consumers are willing to buy dresses only with the hot color. Then, the store lowers the price to $300 and consumers are willing to buy only the acceptable color at this price. The firm learns which of the colors is the hot color through the timing of purchases since only the hot color sells in the initial period. By the end of the season the firm also knows which is the season's acceptable color from the timing of purchases. By adopting a *two-price policy* the firm has raised the expected revenue from $200 to $266.67. Hence, markdown pricing is superior to a constant pricing policy.

A Model with More Colors

We can generalize this numerical illustration by allowing the store to order more than three colors. Assume a line of fashion dresses in 10 bright, bold colors. A year ago, the buyer for the store ordered the line of dresses in 10 bright, bold colors. Once the dresses arrive, the store manager or department manager must decide

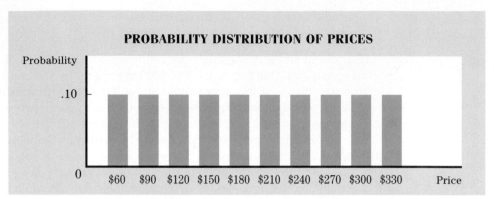

Figure 15-3   The probability of selling a dress at each of the 10 prices is .10.

what price to charge for them. The store manager faces uncertainty because he doesn't know what value consumers will place on each color. Are consumers willing to pay $300 for a coral dress this season? The manager cannot answer this question with certainty because he doesn't know which of the 10 colors will prove to be more popular.

Of course the manager is not a babe in the woods and has some experience to fall back on. Experience tells him that dresses of this quality in the most popular color of the season could sell as high as $330. On the other hand, a dress in the color disaster of the season will not sell for anything more than a distress price of $60.

Figure 15-3 shows the probability distribution of prices that consumers are willing to pay. Table 15-1 shows that the manager anticipates the most popular color of the season will sell for $330, the second most popular color for $300, the third most popular for $270, and so on. The probability that any one of the 10 colors will be the most popular is $\frac{1}{10}$ = .10. At the other extreme there is a probability of $\frac{1}{10}$ that one of the colors will sell for only $60. If you think of the store selling a coral dress season after season, the probability distribution of prices says coral will be the most popular color 10 percent of the time and sell for $330. Another 10 percent of the time consumers will value a coral dress at $300, and so on. Another interpretation of the probability distribution is that one of the consumers will value one of the 10 colors at $330, another at $300, and so on.

According to Table 15-1, 6 of the 10 colors will sell if the price is $180 per dress. Some consumers are willing to pay up to $330 for 1 of the 10 colors. Similarly, one other color will prove to be slightly less popular, and so consumers are willing to pay $300 for a dress of that color. Consumers will gladly purchase a dress in either of these colors if the price is $180. Table 15-1 indicates that they value 4 of the colors at less than $180, and therefore these colors will not sell if the price of each dress is $180.

The values in Table 15-1 can be used to derive the **inverse demand function for colors.**

$$P = \$360 - \$30C \qquad\qquad \text{(15-1)}$$

Table 15-1   PROBABILITY DISTRIBUTION OF PRICES

PRICE ($) (1)	NUMBER OF COLORS SOLD AT EACH PRICE (2)	PROBABILITY THAT A COLOR PICKED AT RANDOM WILL NOT SELL AT THIS PRICE (3)
$360	0	1.00
330	1	.90
300	2	.80
270	3	.70
240	4	.60
210	5	.50
180	6	.40
150	7	.30
120	8	.20
90	9	.10
60	10	.00

where C is the number of colors demanded. This function is shown in Figure 15-4. Figure 15-4 shows that the firm expects to sell 5 of the 10 colors if the price is $210. Assuming there are 10 colors in the line, the expected revenue per dress ordered equals $5 \times \$210/10 = \$105$ per dress. If the price is $180, 6 of the 10 colors in the line will sell. The average revenue per dress ordered equals $6 \times \$180/10 = \$108$ per dress. By lowering the price by $30 from $210 to $180, the firm sells one more color in the line and increases revenue by $180 or by $18 per dress ordered. However, the firm loses revenue because 5 of the colors which could be sold for $210 are now sold for $180 for a total reduction in revenue of $150 or by $15 per dress ordered. On balance *average revenue per dress* ordered increases by $3 when the firm lowers the price from $210 to $180.

Solving equation 15-1 for C gives the number of colors that consumers demand at each price.

$$C = \frac{\$360 - P}{\$30} \tag{15-2}$$

P varies from a low of $60 to a high of $330, and C can equal 1, 2, 3, . . . , 10. According to equation 15-2, when $P = \$210$, $C = (\$360 - \$210)/\$30 = 5$, and so 5 of the 10 colors will sell. The store manager does not know which 5 colors will sell, only that 5 colors will sell when the price is $210.

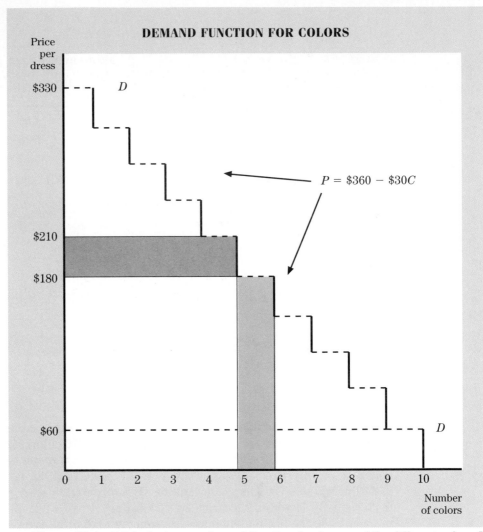

Figure 15-4   *DD* is the inverse demand function for dresses of the different colors. If the price equals $210, consumers demand 5 of the 10 colors. If the price is lowered by $30 to $180, consumers demand 6 of the 10 colors. The firm gains $180 by selling one more color at the lower price but loses $150 by selling the 5 colors at $180 rather than $210 each.

Since the demand function for colors indicates how many colors will sell at each price, we can use that information to derive an expression for the probability that a color picked at random will not sell at each price. Column 3 of Table 15-1 shows the probability that the color will not sell at a price of $150 is (1) the probability that the color will sell only at $60 ($=\frac{1}{10}$) plus (2) the probability that the color will sell only at $90 ($=\frac{1}{10}$) plus (3) the probability that consumers will value the color at \$120 ($=\frac{1}{10}$). Therefore, the probability that a color will not sell when the price is \$150 is the sum of these probabilities, or .30.

More generally, the cumulative distribution of prices shows the probability that a color picked at random will not sell at each price and is equal to the sum of the probabilities that consumers will value a color at less than the price charged.

> The **cumulative distribution of prices** gives the probability that a color picked at random will not sell at each price.

The cumulative distribution of prices can be derived by subtracting the number of colors that sell from the total number of colors in the line and then expressing this difference as a fraction of the total. Let $F(P)$ be the probability that a dress picked at random will not sell at each price. $F(P)$ is defined by

$$F(P) = \frac{10 \quad C}{10} \qquad (15\text{-}3)$$

The number of colors that sell, C, depends on the price. The number of colors that do not sell is $10 - C$. By dividing $10 - C$ by 10, we express the probability that a color will not sell as a function of C, which in turn depends on P.

Substituting the demand function for colors in equation 15-2 for C in equation 15-3 yields[2]

$$F(P) = \frac{P - \$60}{\$300} \qquad (15\text{-}4)$$

where $P - \$60, \$90, \$120, \ldots, \$360$. $F(P)$ is the probability that a color picked at random will not sell if the price is P. For example, equation 15-4 says the probability that a color will not sell is .4 if the price is \$180. Figure 15-5 shows a graph of $F(P)$, the probability that a color will not sell at each of the 10 prices.

15-4 SELECTING A PRICE POLICY

How does the manager set a price when facing this uncertainty, and what goal does he have in mind when setting the price? This section compares two possible pricing policies that could be adopted. First, we look at a single-price policy where the store charges a single price throughout the season. Then, we show how the store can earn higher revenues by charging two prices during a season, an initial price and a markdown price.

When the manager determines the price under either pricing policy, the cost of purchasing the dresses is a sunk cost. It is also assumed that the other costs of

---

[2] Substituting equation 15-2 into equation 15-3 gives

$$F(P) = \frac{10 - [(\$360 - P)/\$30]}{10} = \frac{\$300 - \$360 + P}{\$300}$$

from which equation 15-4 is obtained.

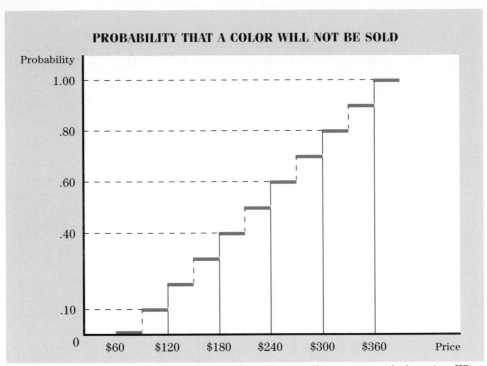

Figure 15-5   The probability that a color will not sell increases with the price. When the price of a dress is $180, the probability that a color will not sell is .40. If the price is $300, the probability that a color will not sell is .80.

the store are fixed at this point. Therefore, the store manager can ignore these costs when determining the price and focus only on the revenue side in order to maximize expected profits.

A Single-Price Policy

Under a **single-price policy** the store charges a single price throughout the season. We assume the firm selects a price that maximizes *expected revenue* per dress ordered. In selecting a price that maximizes expected revenue per dress ordered, the firm keeps lowering the price until the additional revenue from selling another color because of a lower price just equals the lost revenue from selling those colors, which would have been sold at a higher price, at the lower price. Table 15-2 shows the revenue per dress ordered for each possible price that the firm may select. Expected revenue per dress ordered reaches a maximum when the price is $180 per dress and 6 of the 10 dress colors in the line are sold.

   While the price is $180, average revenue per dress is only $108. The reason for this difference is that 40 percent of the colors do not sell; only 60 percent of the colors sell. Averaging the revenue from the 6 of 10 dresses that sell for $180 each

Table 15-2   AVERAGE REVENUE PER DRESS ORDERED

PRICE (1)	QUANTITY SOLD (2)	TOTAL REVENUE FROM DRESSES SOLD (3) (1) × (2)	AVERAGE REVENUE PER DRESS ORDERED (4) (3)/10
$330	1	$ 330	$ 33
300	2	600	60
270	3	810	81
240	4	960	96
210	5	1050	105
180	**6**	**1080**	**108**
150	7	1050	105
120	8	960	96
90	9	810	81
60	10	600	60

and no revenue from the four colors that do not sell yields a revenue of $108 per dress ordered.[3]

A Two-Price Policy

The main shortcoming of this single-price policy is that the manager learns little about willingness to pay for the different colors. When the price of a dress is $180 throughout the season, 6 of the 10 colors sell. What troubles the manager is know-

---

[3] The expected revenue per dress is

$$ER = P[1 - F(P)]$$

where $F(P)$ is the probability that a dress will not sell if the price is P, so $1 - F(P)$ is the probability that a dress will sell if the price is P. Expected revenue per dress equals price times the probability of selling a color picked at random. When setting a price that maximizes expected revenue, the manager has to consider two effects that price has on expected revenue. The firm receives more revenue per unit sold because of the higher price, but the probability that a dress will sell declines since fewer colors sell at a higher price. The manager selects a price that strikes a balance between a lower price and a higher probability that a color will sell. After substituting the expression for $F(P)$ in equation 15-4 into the equation for expected revenue and simplifying, we find

$$ER = \frac{1}{\$300} (\$360P - P^2)$$

The firm maximizes expected revenue by selecting a price so that

$$\frac{d(ER)}{dP} = \frac{1}{\$300} (\$360 - 2P) = 0 \quad \text{or} \quad P = \$180.$$

ing that 5 of these 6 colors could be sold for more than $180 if only he knew the values consumers placed on each color.

> A fundamental defect of a single-price policy is that it does not allow the manager to sort consumers into those who are willing to pay still more for certain colors and those who are not.

A single-price policy does not isolate the more popular colors for which consumers are willing to pay much more than $180 from colors for which they are willing to pay $180 or slightly more. The manager never finds out which of the colors that sell are the more highly valued colors.

A more informative pricing policy would allow the manager to learn more about what consumers are willing to pay for the different colors. Instead of charging a single price over the season, the store could use a **two-price policy** and charge two prices—a higher initial price and a later markdown price.[4] At the higher initial price, only those colors that consumers value highly will sell. The remaining colors will simply sit on the racks throughout the first period. However, customers will reveal to the manager what the more popular colors are by the colors they purchase at the higher price. For example, if the initial price is $270, only 3 of the 10 colors will sell. The manager learns that these 3 colors are the more popular colors this season and that consumers are unwilling to pay $270 for the remaining 7 colors. Later, the store will sell some or all of the remaining colors at a lower markdown price.

Selecting the Initial and Markdown Prices to Maximize Expected Revenue

Before developing a formal expression for expected revenue, it is useful to consider the following thought experiment. Let's pick a color at random and ask what expected revenue is from selling dresses of this color under a two-price policy. Let the initial price be P_i and the markdown price be P_m. For a color picked at random, three outcomes are possible. First, it may be one of the more popular colors of the season and all dresses of that color sell at the initial price of P_i. The probability that this will occur is $1 - F(P_i)$. Recall that $1 - F(P_i)$ is the probability that consumers will value a color at P_i or higher. A second possible outcome is that consumers may not value the color that highly, and so dresses of that color do not sell at the price P_i but do sell at a markdown price of P_m. In other words, consumers value the color at less than P_i but equal to or greater than P_m. The probability that this will occur is $F(P_i) - F(P_m)$.[5] The third possible outcome is that consumers will value the color at less than P_m and dresses of this color do not sell even during

---

[4] This section is based on Edward P. Lazear, "Retail Pricing and Clearance Sales," *American Economic Review* 76 (March 1986), pp. 14–32; B. Peter Pashigian, "Demand Uncertainty and Sales: A Study of Fashion and Markdown Pricing," *American Economic Review* 78 (December 1988), pp. 939–53.

[5] The probability that a color will sell in the markdown period is the probability that it will not sell in the initial period, $F(P_i)$, times the conditional probability that it will sell in the markdown period, $F(P_i)[F(P_i) - F(P_m)]/F(P_i)$, or $F(P_i) - F(P_m)$.

the markdown period. The color is the color disaster of the season, and dresses of this color just remain on the racks. The probability of this outcome is $F(P_m)$. The three outcomes are summarized in the accompanying table.

VALUE PLACED ON COLOR	COLOR VALUED AT A PRICE GREATER THAN P_i	COLOR VALUED AT A PRICE LESS THAN P_i BUT EQUAL TO OR GREATER THAN P_m	COLOR VALUED AT A PRICE LESS THAN P_m
Probability color will sell at price	$1 - F(P_i)$	$F(P_i) - F(P_m)$	$F(P_m)$
When dress sells	In regular season	On sale in markdown season	Does not sell

Let's see what a two-price policy might look like on a graph of the inverse demand function for colors. The store has 10 dresses, each of a different color. In Figure 15-6 price is on the vertical axis and number of colors is on the horizontal axis. If the firm sets the initial price at $300, only 2 of the 10 colors will sell. Area 1 represents the revenue received in the first period. If the markdown price is $150, 5 of the remaining 8 colors sell and the total revenue from selling these colors is equal to area 2. Throughout the season 7 of the 10 colors sell. The total revenue is 2($300) + 5($150) = $1,350. Revenue per dress ordered is only $1,350/10 = $135, although the initial price is $300, and the markdown price is $150 because 3 colors do not sell.

To find the optimal initial and markdown prices, we must first develop a general expression for expected revenue. As described above, expected revenue is P_i times the probability of selling a color when the initial price is P_i plus P_m times the probability of selling a color at the markdown price of P_m. The expression for **expected revenue** is

$$ER = P_i \text{ (probability of selling color at } P_i)$$
$$+ P_m \text{ (probability that color will be valued between } P_i \text{ and } P_m)$$
$$= P_i[1 - F(P_i)] + P_m[F(P_i) - F(P_m)] \tag{15-5}$$

Substituting the corresponding expressions for $F(P_i)$ and $F(P_m)$ from equation 15-4 into equation 15-5 yields

$$ER = P_i\left[1 - \left(\frac{P_i - \$60)}{\$300}\right)\right] + P_m\left[\left(\frac{P_i - \$60}{\$300}\right) - \left(\frac{P_m - \$60}{\$300}\right)\right]$$

$$= P_i\frac{\$360 - P_i}{\$300} + P_m\frac{P_i - P_m}{\$300}$$

$$= \frac{1}{300}(\$360P_i - P_i^2 + P_iP_m - P_m^2) \tag{15-6}$$

Equation 15-6 shows that expected revenue depends on the initial and markdown prices. The manager selects P_i and P_m to maximize expected revenue of selling a color picked at random.

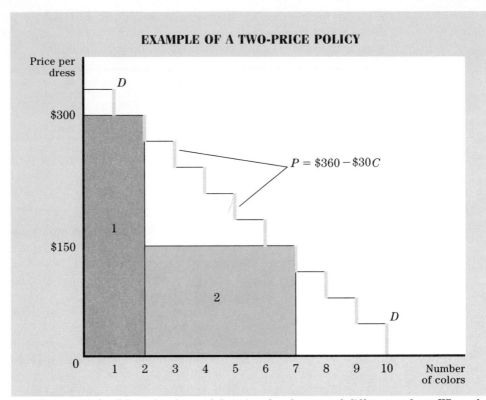

EXAMPLE OF A TWO-PRICE POLICY

$P = \$360 - \$30C$

Figure 15-6 *DD* is the demand function for dresses of different colors. When the initial price is $300, 2 of the 10 colors sell. In the second period the markdown price is $150 and 5 of the remaining 8 colors sell. Area 1 is the revenue received in the first period, and area 2 is the revenue received in the second period.

Care must be exercised when using the expression for expected revenue to find the optimal prices. The first point to note is that the optimal markdown price depends on what initial price the store charges. The lower the initial price, the lower the markdown price. Because of this, how the markdown price changes when the initial price changes must be taken into account when determining the optimal initial price.

To find the optimal initial and markdown prices, we work backward by first considering the second period. When a retail store sets the markdown price, it has already set the initial price. We want to derive a *relationship* that shows the store's optimal markdown price for each initial price. Once this relationship is known, we can return to the first period and find the optimal initial price, taking into account how the initial price affects the optimal markdown price.

With this suggested procedure in mind, the first step is to derive a relationship between the firm's markdown price and its initial price. Having already selected the initial price, the manager now wants to select the markdown price to maximize expected revenue.

The markdown price that maximizes expected profit in equation 15-6 satisfies[6]

$$P_i - 2P_m = 0 \qquad (15\text{-}7)$$

Solving this equation for P_m, we derive a relationship between the markdown price and the initial price,

$$P_m = \frac{P_i}{2} \qquad \text{(Optimal Markdown Price Policy)} \qquad (15\text{-}8)$$

Equation 15-8 describes a decision rule for the manager to follow and says the optimal price policy is to set the markdown price at 50 percent of the initial price.

Now that the optimal markdown *price policy* is known, we can go back to the initial period and find the initial price that maximizes expected revenue while explicitly taking account of the optimal markdown pricing policy. Substitute $P_m = P_i/2$ into equation 15-6 to obtain

$$ER = \frac{1}{\$300}\left[\$360P_i - P_i^2 + P_i\frac{P_i}{2} - \left(\frac{P_i}{2}\right)^2 \right]$$

$$= \frac{1}{\$300}(\$360P_i - \tfrac{3}{4}P_i^2)$$

Now, expected revenue depends only on P_i, and the firm maximizes expected revenue[7] when P_i satisfies

$$\$360 - \tfrac{3}{2}P_i = 0 \qquad (15\text{-}9)$$

Solving equation 15-9 for P_i yields the initial price that maximizes expected revenue.

$$P_i = \tfrac{2}{3}(\$360) = \$240 \qquad \text{(Optimal Initial Price)} \qquad (15\text{-}10)$$

Notice that the initial price is two-thirds of the vertical intercept of the inverse demand function for colors in equation 15-1. Since the optimal markdown price is one-half of the initial price, it is one-third of the vertical intercept of the inverse demand function for colors, or $120.

$$P_m = \$120 \qquad \text{(Optimal Markdown Price)} \qquad (15\text{-}11)$$

When the store charges these two prices, Table 15-1 shows that 80 percent of the dresses sell by the end of the markdown period. Forty percent of the colors sell at a price of $240 per dress, another 40 percent sell at the markdown price of

---

[6] The firm maximizes expected revenue by selecting the markdown price so that

$$\frac{d(ER)}{dP_m} = \frac{1}{\$300}(P_i - 2P_m) = 0$$

[7] To maximize expected revenue, the firm selects P_i so that

$$\frac{dER}{dP_i} = \frac{1}{\$300}(\$360 - \tfrac{3}{2}P_i) = 0$$

$120, and only 20 percent are unsold. The expected revenue from a dress picked at random is $240(.4) + $120(.4) = $96 + $48 = $144. The expected revenue from a two-price policy is 33 percent higher than $108, the expected revenue from a single-price policy. The two-price policy is far superior to the single-price policy.

> Expected revenue for the two-price policy exceeds expected revenue for the one-price policy.

With a two-price policy, some consumers purchase dresses at the higher initial price and reveal which colors are more highly valued this season. The store manager learns more about what consumers are willing to pay for selected colors by implementing this more sophisticated pricing policy. This kind of within-season learning does not occur with a single-price policy.

Changing the Probability Distribution of Prices

The preceding example shows why a two-price policy is superior to a single-price policy. However, it is also somewhat misleading. It appears to say that stores will always mark down goods by 50 percent when the inverse demand function for colors is a straight line (equation 15-1). Now, you know from observation that this is not always true. As an example, the different patterns of men's and women's apparel prices indicate that the percentage markdown is larger for women's than for men's clothing.

Can the uncertainty theory be extended to include markdown policies different from 50 percent? The optimal percentage markdown depends on the range of the probability distribution of prices. Uncertainty is greater for clothing where consumer preferences change rapidly, especially for fashion clothing sold to younger customers. For other types of clothing, there is less price uncertainty.

When there is less dispersion in the probability distribution of prices that consumers are willing to pay, the store maximizes expected revenue by reducing price by less than 50 percent. To demonstrate this, consider this example where the probability distribution of prices has the same expected or mean price ($195) as that observed for dresses in the discussion above but has a smaller range of prices that consumers are willing to pay. Therefore, we keep the expected price constant while changing the range of prices that consumers will pay. In this case the probability distribution of colors is a *mean-preserving spread*.

Let's assume that the store sells a very conservative line of solid black and blue dresses that the store manager knows from experience will sell for either $210 or $180. Consequently, the expected price is still $195, as in the example involving fashion colors. Table 15-3 shows the price, the probability that a color will not sell at each price, and the probability that a color will sell at each price.

Here the store's optimal two-price policy is to charge $210 in the first period and sell 50 percent of the dresses, and then to charge $180 in the markdown period, the minimum price that consumers are willing to pay for the least preferred color. Expected revenue is ER = .5($210) + .5($180) = $195.

All dresses sell, and the expected revenue from the sale of a color picked at

Table 15-3   PROBABILITY DISTRIBUTION OF PRICES

PRICE ($)	PROBABILITY THAT A COLOR PICKED AT RANDOM WILL NOT SELL AT THIS PRICE, $F(P)$	PROBABILITY THAT A COLOR PICKED AT RANDOM WILL SELL AT THIS PRICE, $1 - F(P)$
210	.50	.50
180	0	1.00

random equals the expected price. In this case the percentage markdown is only ($30/$210)100% = 14.3%. When the dispersion in the prices of the probability distribution is sufficiently small, the store will mark down price by less than 50 percent and the optimal markdown price will equal the minimum price that consumers are willing to pay for the least desirable color.

As the dispersion in prices that consumers are willing to pay for different colors diminishes, the percentage markdown decreases. The theory predicts that firms selling more conservative clothing where consumer tastes are easier to forecast will give smaller percentage markdowns. An important implication of this uncertainty theory is that a store's pricing policy will be determined by the type of merchandise it sells. Generally, merchandise with greater price uncertainty will have higher percentage markdowns.

15-5 USING THE THEORY TO UNDERSTAND MARKDOWN PRICING PRACTICES

This chapter began by documenting two empirical regularities. We noted that women's apparel prices start higher at the beginning of the season and end lower at the end of the season than men's apparel prices. The uncertainty theory presented here can explain the different price movements. We can think of men's clothing as being more akin to conservative clothing and having a smaller dispersion in the prices that consumers are willing to pay since fashion has historically played a lesser (though growing) role in men's clothing. As you will recall in the last example above, the price was $210 at the beginning of the season and $180 at the end of the season for an average price of $195. The initial price of 210 is 7.7 percent higher than the average price and the markdown price of $180 is 7.7 percent below the average price. Women's clothing is more like the fashion line where the optimal initial price is $240 and the markdown price is $120. The average price is $180. For this line the initial price is 33 percent higher than the average price and the markdown price is 33 percent below the season average. Hence, our uncertainty theory can explain why women's apparel prices start higher relative to the average price and end lower compared to men's apparel prices.

This uncertainty theory also offers a useful clue as to why the size of markdowns has increased over time. The theory tells us that the percentage markdown is larger where there is greater uncertainty about the prices that consumers will pay for merchandise. A natural extension of this implication is that markdowns will increase if stores begin selling more fashion and less conservative merchandise over time. For example, if consumers began to wear clothing with more colors and prints by the end of the 1960s, then uncertainty would increase. There is some evidence of such changes. There was a shift away from the use of whites and to greater use of prints and colors in women's and men's clothing. For example, men's dress shirts and bed sheets, which were invariably white in the early 60s, took on all sorts of colors and stripes by the end of the 60s. Also, consumers shifted away from more formal and tailored clothing to greater reliance on sportswear and casual wear for which there are fewer hard-and-fast guidelines. Women began mixing coordinates on their own. Each of these changes increases uncertainty and makes it more difficult for firms to predict the demand for colors and styles and helps explain the growth of markdowns over time.

APPLICATION 15-1

Markdowns by Merchandise Group

There are other differences in price behavior based on merchandise group that for the most part are consistent with the uncertainty hypothesis. Department stores report the dollar value of all markdowns as a percentage of the total value of goods sold by merchandise group. For example, in the first example involving fashion colors the price of four of eight colored dresses decreases by $120 from an initial price of $240 to $120. Total dollar markdowns are 4($120) = $480. The store's total sales volume equals four colors sold at $240 each and four colors sold at $120 each, for a total of $960 + $480 = $1,440. The ratio of dollar markdowns to total dollar sales is $480/$1440 = 0.333.

Table 15-4 shows dollar markdowns as a percentage of total sales volume of department stores by merchandise groups in 1965, 1977, and 1984. Columns 2 and 3 list dollar markdowns relative to sales volume for women's fashion merchandise (shoes, dresses, coats, and so on) and for women's standard merchandise (undergarments) where fashion changes have been less important. Column 4 shows the percentage for men's apparel, and column 5, the percentage for junior and teens' clothing and accessories.

Style and fashion changes are more frequent in some merchandise lines than in others. In 1965 markdowns relative to dollar sales were higher for women's fashion apparel than for women's standard apparel, where uncertainty is lower. Markdowns were also higher in the teens' and junior clothing group.

These long-standing historical differences began to change slowly after 1965. By 1984 markdowns had exploded in the teens' and junior merchandise group, where fashion has become so much more important and where fashion successes are very transient. One surprising change was the rapid growth of markdowns for men's apparel. By 1984 markdowns relative to sales volume were slightly less than

Table 15-4   DOLLAR MARKDOWNS AS A PERCENTAGE OF TOTAL DOLLAR VOLUME

YEAR (1)	WOMEN'S FASHION APPAREL AND ACCESSORIES (2)	WOMEN'S STANDARD APPAREL (3)	MEN'S APPAREL AND ACCESSORIES (4)	TEENS' AND JUNIOR APPAREL (5)
1965	10.2%	4.5%	6.6%	10.8%
1977	11.8	8.2	10.8	18.2
1984	19.8	13.8	19.3	27.0

Source: Adapted from B. Peter Pashigian, "Demand Uncertainty and Sales: A Study of Fashion and Markdown Pricing," *American Economic Review* 78 (December 1988), table 3, p. 947. Copyright © 1988 by the American Economic Association.

the markdowns for women's apparel, although well below the relative markdowns for teens' and junior clothing. While fashion has become more important over time in the selling of men's apparel, the size of the change is puzzling. More research is required before all these changes can be fully explained.

A reasonable interpretation of these broad trends is that department stores are selling more fashion merchandise in recent years than they did in 1965, and so greater uncertainty is present now than before. Now it is more difficult than before to predict which styles, colors, and silhouettes will sell, and this rise in uncertainty has caused an increase in percentage markdown.

Differences in Market Equilibrium Prices under Certainty and Uncertainty

Let's contrast the market equilibrium under uncertainty and certainty. Instead of assuming the store does not know what prices consumers will pay for each color, assume that every store manager in a competitive industry is clairvoyant and knows what price customers are willing to pay for each color. As long as there is free entry into the industry, competition among stores lowers the price to the marginal cost of the dress. All identical dresses sell at the same price and at marginal cost. For example, if the store faces a price distribution for the fashion line and the long-run average and marginal cost of producing a dress is $180, the store manager orders only the six colors for which consumers are willing to pay $180 or more. He never orders dresses that consumers value at less than their marginal cost because they will not sell. Free entry of stores and competition among stores guarantee that all ordered dresses sell at a price equal to marginal cost. There is a single price of $180 and no clearance sales. Prices are stable throughout the season. Consequently, uncertainty plays a critical role in explaining the seasonal behavior of prices and the incidence of clearance sales.

Another explanation for the seasonal variation in prices is that each store practices third-degree price discrimination. It discriminates between consumers who buy early in the season and who have less elastic demand functions and those who buy late in the season and have more elastic demand functions. The price discrimination theory can also explain why prices fall throughout the season. However, this hypothesis does not explain why product selection is so different in the two periods. The uncertainty hypothesis predicts that product selection will be different in the two periods. The price discrimination with certainty hypothesis says that early demanders have less elastic demand functions for all colors carried by the store. If a store practices price discrimination under certainty, it will charge early buyers higher prices because they have less elastic demand functions and end-of-season buyers lower prices because they have more elastic demand functions. However, there is no reason why the color selections made at the beginning of the season should differ from the color selections at the end of the season under the certainty hypothesis. Another reason to question the validity of the price discrimination hypothesis is the presence of many sellers of clothing in retail markets so that monopoly is difficult to achieve.

When to Apply the Uncertainty Theory

The uncertainty theory developed in Sections 15-3 and 15-4 should be applied only in certain market situations. First, the firm must be uncertain about consumer tastes—the prices that consumers will pay for different colors or styles. Therefore, the theory applies to products subject to periodic changes in tastes such as fashion clothing. Another market in constant change with frequent new product introductions is the toy industry. In this industry manufacturers develop many new toys each year under uncertainty and have considerable difficulty predicting which will be successful.

The uncertainty theory does not explain the pricing of most hardware and canned grocery products. The designs of hammers, for instance, are very stable from season to season or from year to year. If hardware dealers increased prices at the beginning of the year and lowered them later, most consumers would refuse to buy at the beginning of the year. They know that the same product will be available later in the year at a lower price. Indeed, a season has little meaning. This is what distinguishes some but not all clothing from hardware. Automobile manufacturers face the same problem when they discontinue offering rebates in the middle of a model year. Consumers stop purchasing until the rebates are restored because they know that they will be able to purchase the same auto if they wait.

In the fashion market consumers buy early rather than late because they will not be able to purchase the same merchandise later at a lower price. The successful styles sell early. By waiting, consumers risk not being able to purchase a particular color or style later during the markdown period. If they were assured of purchasing a favorite color in the markdown period, some would indeed delay their purchases. The uncertainty model applies when the merchandise sold during the initial period is different from the merchandise sold during the markdown period.

In contrast, consider a classic blue blazer or a cashmere topcoat. Since the style does not change from year to year, some consumers will wait and purchase these items during the markdown period. Therefore, the theory applies less to a blazer or to more conservative or basic clothing. If this is true, we would expect less seasonal variation in the prices of blue blazers.

SUMMARY

- Uncertainty about consumer tastes is the primary cause of clearance sales.
- Uncertainty about consumer tastes is described by a probability distribution of prices that consumers are willing to pay for different colors.
- Expected revenue per dress is higher if a firm charges an initial and a markdown price rather than a single price throughout the season.

- The uncertainty theory predicts that the percentage markdown will be larger and the fraction of goods sold will be lower for fashion goods as uncertainty increases.
- The uncertainty theory applies to products subject to frequent new product introductions such as fashion clothing.

KEY TERMS

uncertainty about consumer tastes
inverse demand function for colors
cumulative distribution of prices
single-price policy

seasonal variation
expected revenue
two-price policy

REVIEW QUESTIONS

1. What is expected revenue?
2. Describe in your own words what the expected revenue of a store is when it charges a single price thoughout the season.
3. Describe in your own words what the expected revenue of a store is when it charges two prices throughout the season.

4. Explain why expected revenue can be less than the price at which dresses are sold.
5. Predict how the seasonal variation in prices of made-to-order men's suits would differ from prices for ready-made suits.

EXERCISES

1. The number of colors sold depends on price as shown in the following table. There are 11 colors in the clothing line.

Fill in columns 3 and 4 and determine the optimal single price that maximizes expected revenue over the season.

PRICE (1)	QUANTITY SOLD (2)	TOTAL REVENUE FROM DRESSES SOLD (3) (1) × (2)	AVERAGE REVENUE PER DRESS ORDERED (4) (3)/11
$450	1		
420	2		
390	3		
360	4		
330	5		
300	6		
270	7		
240	8		
210	9		
180	10		
150	11		

2. The demand function for colors is

$$P = \$450 - \$30C$$

where $C = 1, 2, \ldots, 15$. If a firm charges only a single price, what price maximizes expected revenue? What is expected revenue? Do all the colors sell?

3. The demand function for colors is

$$P = \$450 - \$30C$$

where $C = 1, 2, \ldots, 15$. What are the optimal initial and markdown prices? What is the expected revenue per dress? Do all colors sell?

4. Explain why you would expect the percentage markdown to be lower for men's white shirts than for striped shirts.

5. Suppose a department store decides to compensate the firm's buyers of merchandise by the formula

$$C = a + b \text{ (total retail sales of the line)} + c \text{ (percentage of units not sold)}$$

where C is annual compensation and a, b, and c are constants; a and b are positive; and c is negative. What effect will this compensation formula have on the behavior of employees whose responsibility is to purchase merchandise a year in advance?

6. A few years ago Sears announced and adopted an "everyday low price" policy. The goal was to charge a stable price for each item and to eliminate sales. The company also announced a new policy of selling brand name women's clothing. Comment on the wisdom of this policy. Under what conditions will an "everyday low price" policy be justified and when will it fail?

7. Explain why you would expect to find a higher percentage markdown for imported goods than for domestically produced goods, other factors being constant.

*8. A recent study found that men's dress shirts, men's sweaters, women's blouses, and women's sweaters that had a higher initial price sold at a higher average percentage markdown than the clothing in each category that had a lower initial price. Use the theory of pricing under uncertainty to explain these pricing patterns.

*9. A study of men's dress shirts found that

the average initial price for shirts not sold on sale was $19.24, and for those subsequently sold on sale, $24.89. Present an explanation for these findings.

10. Sellers of mansions often have more difficulty selling their houses than sellers of standardized tract housing. Sellers of mansions often have to reduce the initial price to sell the mansions. Can you explain why mansions take longer to sell and why the average markdown on mansions is higher than the average markdown on tract housing?

INTER-TEMPORAL EQUILIBRIUM AND FACTOR MARKETS

- **Chapter 16**
  Consumer and Supplier Behavior over Time
- **Chapter 17**
  Wage Determination in Labor Markets

CHAPTER 16

CONSUMER AND SUPPLIER BEHAVIOR OVER TIME

■ **16-1   Telescoping the Future into the Present**
Application 16-1: Mustering Out of the Military

■ **16-2   Consumption Spending over Time**
The Intertemporal Budget Constraint
Intertemporal Preferences
Intertemporal Utility Maximization of the Consumer
The Importance of Present Value of Income
The Effect on Saving of an Increase in Current or Future Income
Application 16-2: Personal Bankruptcy
Saving, Borrowing, and the Interest Rate
The Equilibrium Interest Rate

■ **16-3   Depletion of a Natural Resource**
When to Sell a Nonrenewable Resource
Application 16-3: Freeing Prices in Russia
Market Equilibrium Prices
The Effect of the Interest Rate on Equilibrium Prices
Application 16-4: The Historical Trend in Crude Oil Prices
A Renewable Resource
■ **Summary**
■ **Key Terms**
■ **Review Questions**
■ **Exercises**

With a few exceptions most of this book has dealt with the choices of consumers and producers who maximize utility or profits over a single period. The time horizon of these agents, be they consumers or producers, was a single period. In the models the consumer maximized utility as if there were no tomorrow, and so too did the profit-maximizing producer. We deliberately avoided some difficult but interesting questions about behavior over time, for the greater simplicity of the single-period analysis.

Economists can justify this apparent tunnel vision when the consequences of ignoring the future are not serious. If the determinants of the demand for a perishable good are of interest, the one-period model presented in Chapters 2 through 4 describes the consumer's actual consumption decisions. But the future cannot always be ignored. In any explanation of saving and borrowing behavior, there must be a tomorrow, otherwise the motivation for savings would evaporate. To explain saving and borrowing over time, we formulate a theory that, among other things, explains why a consumer chooses to save and therefore consumes less today in order to consume more tomorrow. The intertemporal theory of consumer behavior explains how the consumer decides how much to spend and save over time and creates a link between current and future spending.

There is a link between the present and the future on the supply side of the market as well. The number of bushels of tomatoes that a competitive producer supplies this year depends primarily on this year's price because tomatoes are costly to store from one season to another. The quantity supplied this year does not depend on what the price will be next year. In contrast, an owner of a gold mine or an oil well thinks differently. He or she needs to know the future as well as the current price to decide how much gold or oil to sell this year. Knowing what to do today requires knowledge of current *and* future prices. In the second half of this chapter prices are linked over time in an intertemporal market equilibrium as consumers and suppliers determine the depletion of a non-renewable resource.

This chapter expands the theory of consumer and producer behavior under perfect foresight and shows how foreseen changes in future demand and supply conditions affect the present behavior of consumers and suppliers.

16-1   TELESCOPING THE FUTURE INTO THE PRESENT

Most individuals would prefer to receive a dollar today than a dollar in some future year because a dollar in hand earns interest if invested. (See the appendix to Chapter 14 for a discussion of present value and its calculation.) At the end of one year a dollar increases in value to $1 + i$ if the real interest rate is i percent per year. A dollar today becomes \$1.05 if the annual interest rate is 5 percent. The 5 percent is a real return because it is assumed throughout the chapter that there is neither inflation nor deflation.

This chapter considers a series of two-period problems where an individual receives income I_1 at the *beginning* of period 1 and I_2 at the beginning of period 2. Because the consumer receives income at the beginning of each year, the present value calculations are slightly different from those described in Chapter 14. To find the amount you would accept today instead of receiving I_2 at the beginning of year 2, you must calculate the present value of this truncated stream of income. As we noted in Chapter 14, present value is an amount received today that is equivalent to a specified amount received in some future year. The procedure for determining the present value of a future dollar is called *discounting*.

> The **present value of future income** is an amount received immediately that is equivalent to the income received in a future year.

The present value of I_1 is simply I_1, because income is received at the beginning of year 1 and no lesser amount can be equivalent to I_1. What is the present value of I_2? What amount received at the beginning of year 1 is equivalent to receiving I_2 at the beginning of year 2? You are indifferent between receiving I_2 in year 2 or receiving $I_2/(1 + i)$ in year 1. If you receive $I_2/(1 + i)$ at the beginning of year 1 and earn an annual interest rate of i on this amount, you will have $[I_2/(1 + i)]$ $(1 + i) = I_2$ at the beginning of year 2. There is an exact equivalence between receiving $I_2/(1 + i)$ in year 1 and receiving I_2 in year 2. We can say that the present value of I_2 is $I_2/(1 + i)$. To determine the present value of income received at the beginning of year n, divide income in year n by $1 + i$ raised to the power $n - 1$, or $I_n/(1 + i)^{n-1}$.

Column 3 of Table 16-1 shows the present value of income in each future year when an individual receives income at the *beginning* of the year. The present value of an income stream is equal to the sum of the present value of each year's income.

Table 16-1   PRESENT VALUE OF INCOME

YEAR (1)	INCOME (2)	PRESENT VALUE OF INCOME RECEIVED AT BEGINNING OF YEAR (3)
1	I_1	I_1
2	I_2	$\dfrac{I_2}{1 + i}$
3	I_3	$\dfrac{I_3}{(1 + i)^2}$
.	.	.
.	.	.
.	.	.
n	I_n	$\dfrac{I_n}{(1 + i)^{n-1}}$

Table 16-2   PRESENT VALUE BASED ON NUMBER OF PAYMENTS AND INTEREST RATE

INTEREST RATE (%)	5 PAYMENTS RECEIVED ($)	10 PAYMENTS RECEIVED ($)
3%	$94,342	$175,722
4	92,598	168,707
5	90,919	162,156
6	89,302	156,034

The present value of an income stream of $I_1, I_2, I_3, \ldots, I_n$ is

$$\text{Present value} = I_1 + \frac{I_2}{1 + i} + \frac{I_3}{(1 + i)^2} + \cdots + \frac{I_n}{(1 + i)^{n-1}} \quad \text{(16-1)}$$

where the interest rate is constant over time.

The formula for the present value of an income stream reduces to a concise and useful expression when the income stream is constant. In the special case where $I_1 = I_2 = I_3 = \cdots = I_n = I^\bullet$, the present value of the income stream[1] at the beginning of the year is

$$PV = \frac{1 - [1/(1 + i)^n]}{1 - [1/(1 + i)]}I^\bullet \quad \begin{array}{l}\text{(Present Value of} \\ \text{a Finite Constant Income Stream)}\end{array} \quad \text{(16-2)}$$

Table 16-2 shows the present value at different interest rates if you receive $20,000 at the beginning of each year for 5 years or for 10 years. If the interest rate is 5

---

[1] The present value of n equal annual payments of $I^\bullet$ is

$$PV = \text{Present value} = (1 + D + D^2 + \cdots + D^{n-1})I^\bullet$$

where $D = 1/(1 + i)$. Multiplying and dividing the expression for present value by $1 - D$ yields

$$PV = \text{Present value} = (1 - D)(1 + D + D^2 + \cdots + D^{n-1})\frac{I^\bullet}{1 - D}$$

$$= (1 - D + D - D^2 + D^2 + \cdots - D^n)\frac{I^\bullet}{1 - D}$$

Canceling successive terms results in

$$PV = \frac{1 - D^n}{1 - D}I^\bullet = \frac{1 - [1/(1 + i)^n]}{1 - [1/(1 + i)]}I^\bullet$$

Note that for an *infinite* constant income stream, $D^n = D^\infty$ is sufficiently small, so that the present value formula becomes

$$PV = \frac{I^\bullet}{1 - D} = (1 + i) I^\bullet/i$$

percent, the present value of income is $90,919 when there are 5 installments, and $162,156 if there are 10 installments. Notice that doubling the number of years comes nowhere near doubling the present value. The contribution to present value of income received far into the future is progressively lower because of the discounting effect. The larger the interest rate, the lower the present value, since any sum received immediately will increase more rapidly with a higher rate of interest. Here again, the higher the interest rate, the smaller the contribution of a more distant payment to present value.

APPLICATION **16-1**

Mustering Out of the Military

With the decline of the Soviet Union and the diminished intensity of the Cold War, the United States reduced the size of the armed forces drastically. The army planned for a 25 percent reduction in personnel starting in 1992 and recognized that it would have to offer financial incentives to reach this target.[2] For example, a staff sergeant leaving the Army with 13.5 years of service could choose between a lump sum payment of $34,000 or time payments of 27 annual checks of $5,600 each for a total of $151,200. If you ignore discounting, the 27 annual checks of $5,600 each far exceed the one-time payment of $34,000. However, this is not the right comparison to make because a dollar received in the future is worth less than a dollar received in the current year.

Assume that a staff sergeant decides to separate from the Army and must select one of the two options. He or she must calculate the present value of the income stream and determine if it is greater than $34,000. To get a sense of the magnitudes involved, let's find an interest rate that equates $34,000 to the present value of 27 annual checks of $5,600 each. Then the sergeant can decide if the interest rate that he or she can hope to earn is greater or less than this interest rate. If it is less, then the sergeant should select the 27 annual payments of $5,600 each because the present value of the series of payments exceeds $34,000.

Equation 16-2 can be used to calculate present values. The present value of 27 annual checks of $5,600 each at a 19 percent interest rate is $34,753, and for a 20 percent interest rate, $33,355. It appears that the sergeant would have to earn an interest rate of slightly more than 19 percent on savings before the lump sum payment would be the superior choice. This seems an unlikely eventuality for most individuals. In most cases the present value of 27 annual checks of $5,600 each is larger than $34,000. On the other hand, some individuals may have a high personal discount rate because of a severe liquidity constraint, and so they will accept the lump sum payment. (Incidentally, we have ignored any reductions in income because of taxes.)

[2] Based on David Evans, "Army Lures Volunteers to Retire," *Chicago Tribune*, January 10, 1992.

16-2   CONSUMPTION SPENDING OVER TIME

The present-value concept comes in handy when studying a consumer's intertemporal consumption decisions. In Chapters 2 through 4 the consumer maximized utility given the income and prices in a one-period model. The savings decision was ignored because there is no reason to save in a one-period model.

The limitations of the static model become apparent when we ask what determines how much a consumer saves or borrows. Answering this question requires a more sophisticated model of consumer behavior that explains savings and borrowing decisions over time.

Consider the following scenario that you may hope to experience sometime during your career. Your annual salary in year 1 is I_1. In January of year 1 you receive some great news during your annual job performance review. Your manager tells you that the company is very pleased with your job performance. She announces your promotion to her position in January of year 2 when she retires, at which time you will receive a 50 percent raise so I_2 will be $1.5I_1$.

You can look forward to a hefty salary increase. How will your salary increase in year 2 affect your consumption spending in year 1 and in year 2? If you mechanically applied the theory in Chapter 2 to this situation, you would predict that your consumption spending in year 1 will remain relatively low because your annual income remains low, but will soar in year 2 when your income increases by 50 percent. You will go from a relative pauper in year 1 to a prince or princess in year 2.

This prediction assumes that you are unable to borrow, an unlikely event in an economy awash in credit cards and personal loans. If you can borrow by promising to repay the loan when you earn the higher income, you can moderate the sharp swing in consumption spending and, depending on your preferences, may be able to increase your utility. Somehow, your future income should affect your current consumption spending.

The Intertemporal Budget Constraint

A building block in the theory of intertemporal consumer behavior is the **intertemporal budget constraint.** This concept shows how future consumption spending is related to current consumption spending. Let's demonstrate how to derive the intertemporal budget constraint. I_1 is the income of the consumer in the first year, and I_2 is the income in year 2. Given the income earned in the two years and an annual interest rate i, we can derive a relationship between consumption spending in year 2 and in year 1. Savings in year 1 equal income less spending on consumption, or $S_1 = I_1 - C_1$, where S_1 represents savings in year 1 and C_1 is spending on a composite good in year 1. The consumer saves if income is greater than consumption spending in year 1 and borrows if income is less than consumption spending in year 1.

Consumption spending in year 2 (C_2) is related to consumption spending in year 1 (C_1) through the equation

$$\begin{array}{c}\text{Consumption} \\ \text{in year 2}\end{array} = \begin{array}{c}\text{Income} \\ \text{in year 2}\end{array} + \begin{array}{c}\text{Savings} \\ \text{in year 1}\end{array} + \begin{array}{c}\text{Interest on savings} \\ \text{in year 1}\end{array}$$

$$C_2 = I_2 + (I_1 - C_1) + i(I_1 - C_1)$$

Rewriting this equation to show how C_2 is related to C_1 results in

$$C_2 = I_2 + (1 + i)(I_1 - C_1)$$

$$= [I_2 + (1 + i)I_1] - (1 + i)C_1 \qquad \text{(Intertemporal Budget Constraint)} \quad \textbf{(16-3)}$$

Equation 16-3 is the consumer's intertemporal budget constraint and shows how spending in year 2 relates to spending in year 1. If borrowing is not permitted, the budget constraint in equation 16-3 is valid only for $I_1 \geq C_1$. If the consumer does not save in year 1, so $I_1 = C_1$, consumption in year 2 must be I_2. Suppose the consumer saves $I_1 - C_1 > 0$ in year 1. Then, total consumption in year 2 exceeds I_2 by $(1 + i)(I_1 - C_1)$, or the savings in year 1 plus the interest earned on the savings in year 1.

> The intertemporal budget constraint shows how consumption spending in year 2 is related to consumption spending in year 1.

The intertemporal budget constraint is graphed in Figure 16-1. The vertical axis measures consumption spending, C_2, on a composite good in year 2, and the horizontal axis measures consumption spending, C_1, on a composite good in year 1. Given an income of I_1' in year 1 and I_2' in year 2 and the interest rate on savings, the intertemporal budget constraint is a straight line. The intercept on the vertical axis is $I_2' + (1 + i)I_1'$, or the consumer's maximum consumption spending in year 2 if nothing is spent on consumption in year 1. The slope of the intertemporal budget constraint is $-(1 + i)$. For every dollar increase in consumption in year 1, consumption in year 2 decreases by a dollar plus the forgone annual interest of i percent. Therefore, the opportunity cost of increasing consumption in year 1 by a dollar is a fall in consumption in year 2 by $1 + i$.

$$\frac{\Delta C_2}{\Delta C_1} = -(1 + i) \qquad \text{(Slope of Intertemporal Budget Constraint)} \qquad \textbf{(16-4)}$$

The intertemporal budget constraint is line $a'a$ in Figure 16-1a if the consumer cannot borrow and represents all affordable market baskets. Point a is the **endowment** point of the consumer. It shows that the income of this individual is I_1' in year 1 and I_2' in year 2. In Figure 16-1a the individual's income is lower in year 1 than in year 2 at point a. Consumption spending in year 1 cannot exceed I_1' because the individual cannot borrow. Although the future looks rosy, it is not possible to convert future prosperity into greater immediate consumption because the consumer cannot borrow.

Figure 16-1b shows that the affordable market baskets of the consumer expand to include the dashed segment ab when the consumer can borrow at an annual

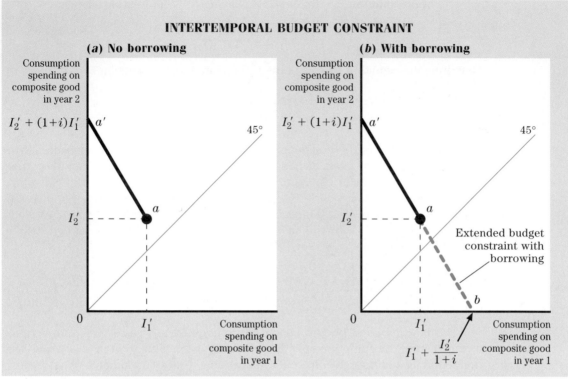

Figure 16-1   (*a*) The intertemporal budget constraint is line $a'a$ when the consumer cannot borrow. Consumption in year 1 cannot exceed I_1', income in year 1. Consumption in year 2 can increase to $I_2' + (1 + i)I_1'$. (*b*) The individual can borrow at an annual interest rate of i percent per year. Although income is lower in year 1 than in year 2, consumption in year 1 can exceed income in year 1 because the consumer can borrow. The intertemporal budget constraint is extended to include the segment ab.

interest rate of i. The intertemporal budget constraint now becomes the extended line $a'ab$. By borrowing against future income, the individual can spend more than I_1' on consumption in the first year.

By how much can consumption be increased in year 1 by borrowing against income in year 2? Hypothetically, let's assume the consumer is willing to use all the income in year 2 to pay off a loan assumed in year 1 to support consumption spending in year 1. In this case consumption in year 2 is zero. The maximum value of C_1 can be determined by setting C_2 equal to zero in the consumer's intertemporal budget constraint and solving equation 16-3 for C_1.

$$0 = [I_2' + (1 + i)I_1'] - (1 + i)C_1$$

$$C_1 = I_1' + \frac{I_2'}{1 + i} \qquad \text{(Maximum Spending on Consumption in Year 1)} \qquad \textbf{(16-5)}$$

The expression on the right-hand side of equation 16-5 is the present value of income in the two years. The consumer can spend at most $I'_1 + I'_2/(1 + i)$ in year 1 by borrowing $I'_2/(1 + i)$ from the lender in year 1 and paying I'_2 to the lender in year 2.

Intertemporal Preferences

The intertemporal budget constraint shows the consumer's affordable market baskets for the two years. To determine which one the consumer selects in each year, we must know the consumer's preferences over present and future consumption.

The intertemporal preference map of the consumer describes his or her intertemporal tradeoffs. Utility depends on consumption spending on a composite good in each year.

$$U = U(C_1, C_2) \qquad \text{(Intertemporal Utility Function)} \qquad \textbf{(16-6)}$$

Each indifference curve of the utility function shows the rate at which the consumer is willing to substitute future consumption for current consumption, keeping utility constant.

> The slope at a point on an indifference curve is defined as the **marginal rate of time preference** (MRTP).[3]

$$\text{MRTP} = \left.\frac{\Delta C_2}{\Delta C_1}\right|_{U=U_0} \qquad \text{(Marginal Rate of Time Preference)} \qquad \textbf{(16-7)}$$

Consumers' relative valuations between future and current consumption differ just as their indifference curves between goods differ. Some individuals are willing to sacrifice more than a dollar of future consumption for a dollar of current consumption, and others are willing to sacrifice less than a dollar of future consumption. The intertemporal utility functions of consumers differ because their time preferences between present and future consumption differ.

Figure 16-2 shows indifference curves for three consumers. Figure 16-2a illustrates an indifference curve of an impatient consumer. At any point on the thin 45-degree line spending on current consumption is equal to spending on future consumption. When future and current consumption spending are equal, this consumer remains indifferent by substituting more than a dollar of future consumption for a dollar less of current consumption. He values current consumption so much

---

[3] If we consider a tiny change of dC_1 in current consumption and a tiny change of dC_2 in future consumption such that utility is constant, then we must have

$$dU = 0 = \frac{\partial U}{\partial C_1} dC_1 + \frac{\partial U}{\partial C_2} dC_2$$

or

$$\text{MRTP} = \frac{dC_2}{dC_1} = -\frac{\partial U/\partial C_1}{\partial U/\partial C_2}$$

The marginal rate of time preference (MRTP) equals the negative of the ratio of the marginal utility of current consumption to the marginal utility of future consumption.

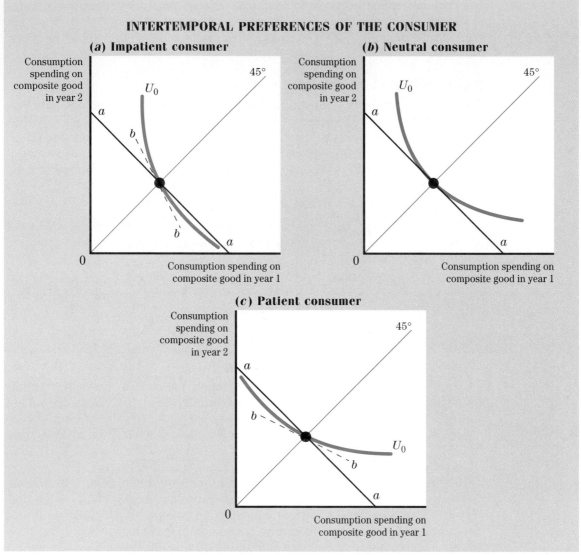

Figure 16-2 (*a*) Indifference curve of an impatient consumer. The slope of line *aa* equals −1. Line *bb* is tangent to the indifference curve when consumption in the 2 years is the same and has a slope that is less than −1. Therefore, the slope of the indifference curve is less than −1. This consumer will be indifferent to giving up a dollar of current consumption only if future consumption spending increases by more than a dollar. The indifference curve of the consumer in (*b*) has a slope equal to −1 when spending is the same in both years. The consumer in (*c*) remains indifferent to giving up a dollar in current spending if future consumption spending increases by less than a dollar.

that he must receive more than a dollar of future consumption in order to give up a dollar of current consumption and remain indifferent. For example, he might be indifferent between sacrificing a dollar of current consumption for $1.25 more in future consumption when current and future consumption are equal. The line *aa* has a slope of -1 and cuts through the indifference curve as it crosses the 45-degree line. The line *bb* is tangent to the indifference curve U_0 at the point where the indifference curve passes through the 45-degree line, and its slope is less than -1. The marginal rate of time preference of an impatient consumer is therefore numerically less than -1 (or greater than 1 in absolute value). In other words, the indifference curve is steeper than *aa* when C_1 and C_2 are equal.

In contrast, Figure 16-2*b* shows the indifference curve of a consumer who is neutral between current and future consumption spending. She has a marginal rate of time preference equal to -1 when current spending and future spending are equal and is indifferent between forgoing a dollar of current consumption for one more dollar of future consumption.

Finally, Figure 16-2*c* shows an indifference curve of a patient consumer who remains indifferent when sacrificing a dollar of current consumption for less than a dollar increase in future consumption. The marginal time preference is numerically greater than -1 when current and future consumption are the same (or less than 1 in absolute value).

Intertemporal Utility Maximization of the Consumer

The goal of a consumer is to maximize utility while satisfying the intertemporal budget constraint. To find a market basket of current and future consumption spending that maximizes utility, we superimpose the intertemporal budget constraint *cc'* on the intertemporal preference map in Figure 16-3. To maximize utility, the consumer equates the marginal rate of time preference to the slope of the intertemporal budget constraint.[4]

$$\text{MRTP} = -(1 + i) \qquad \text{(Condition for Maximizing Utility)} \qquad \textbf{(16-8)}$$

---

[4] The consumer maximizes

$$U = U(C_1, C_2)$$

subject to the intertemporal budget constraint

$$C_2 = I_2 + (1 + i)I_1 - (1 + i)C_1$$

After substituting for C_2 into the utility function, we have

$$U = U(C_1, I_2 + (1 + i)I_1 - (1 + i)C_1)$$

which depends only on C_1.

Maximizing U with respect to C_1 requires

$$\frac{\partial U}{\partial C_1} - \frac{\partial U}{\partial C_2}(1 + i) = 0$$

or

$$\text{MRTP} = -\frac{\partial U/\partial C_1}{\partial U/\partial C_2} = -(1 + i)$$

The left-hand side of the equality is the consumer's marginal rate of time preference (MRTP) which equals the negative of the ratio of the marginal utilities of current and future consumption. The right-hand side is the slope of the intertemporal budget constraint.

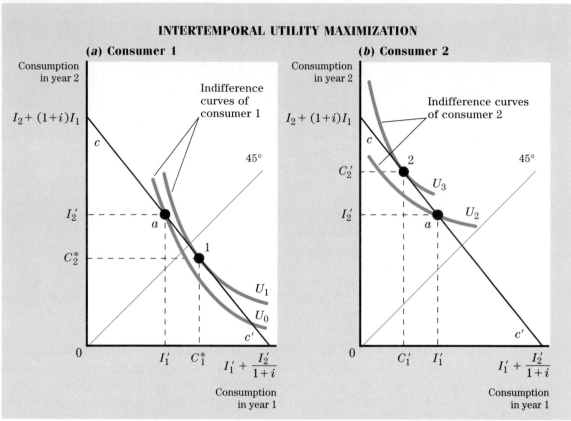

Figure 16-3   Point a in (a) and (b) shows that two consumers have the same income endowment. (a) Consumer 1 reaches indifference curve U_1 at point 1 by borrowing $C_1^* - I_1$ in year 1, spending C_1^* in year 1, and spending C_2^* in year 2. The marginal rate of time preference equals the slope of the intertemporal budget constraint at point 1. (b) Consumer 2 is more patient and saves $I_1' - C_1'$ in year 1 and reaches indifference curve U_3 at point 2.

Figure 16-3 shows the indifference curves of two consumers. The endowment point of both is at point a on cc'. For each consumer income is I_1' in year 1 and I_2' in year 2. While the two individuals have the same income endowment, they have different time preferences and their saving or borrowing behavior differs. The indifference curves U_0 and U_1 in Figure 16-3a are the indifference curves of consumer 1, an **impatient consumer.** When current and future consumption are equal, he remains indifferent by substituting more than a dollar of future consumption for one less dollar of current consumption. At point a his indifference curve is steeper than the intertemporal budget constraint. He is willing to give up more dollars of future consumption for one more dollar of current consumption than is required by the market. The indifference curves U_2 and U_3 in Figure 16-3b are those of consumer 2, a **patient consumer.** At point a the slope of the indifference curve is less steep than the slope of the intertemporal budget constraint.

In Figure 16-3a consumer 1 maximizes utility by moving from point a to point 1 where the slope of the intertemporal budget constraint equals the marginal rate of time preference. At point 1 the interest rate at which the consumer can trade future consumption for current consumption equals the rate at which he is willing to do so. In contrast, at point a he is willing to give up more future consumption for one more dollar of current consumption than is required by the intertemporal budget constraint. Therefore, his utility increases by increasing current consumption. Consumer 1 borrows $C_1^* - I_1'$ in year 1 and spends C_1^* in year 1 and C_2^* in year 2 on a composite good. He reaches the indifference curve U_1 by borrowing to increase consumption spending in year 1 and to reduce consumption spending in year 2. If he were prohibited from borrowing, he would be forced to remain at point a on indifference curve U_0, a lower indifference curve.

In Figure 16-3b consumer 2 maximizes utility at point 2. By saving $I_1' - C_1'$ in year 1, she is willing to forgo current consumption to increase future consumption to C_2'. Consumer 1, unlike consumer 2, does not want to postpone consumption. As you can see, consumer 1 is demanding loanable funds at the interest rate i, while consumer 2 is supplying loanable funds at the interest rate i. A consumer who maximizes utility at some point along the line segment ca saves in year 1, whereas a consumer who maximizes utility at some point along the line segment ac' borrows in year 1.

This comparison of the behavior of impatient and patient consumers shows that two consumers with the same income endowment make different consumption choices because they have different time preferences between current and future consumption. Impatient consumers tend to borrow and demand loanable funds, while patient consumers tend to save and indirectly lend funds. Both are better off by being allowed either to borrow or save as the case might be.

The Importance of Present Value of Income

The theory of **intertemporal utility maximization** contains a key implication that is easy to miss if you are not careful. Given the interest rate, spending on a composite good in year 1 and in year 2 is determined not by current income but by the present value of income. Consumer spending in either year does not depend on the particular values of I_1 and I_2 but on the present value of income, $I_1' + I_2'/(1 + i)$.

The theory of maximizing utility over time predicts that a change in the distribution of income between the first and second years that does not affect present value of income has no effect on consumption spending. To demonstrate this, suppose that you receive two job offers, one from a firm in industry A and another from a firm in industry B. The position in industry A pays a higher income than the position in industry B in year 1, but a lower income in year 2. Although the two jobs involve different salaries over time, the present value of income is the same. To illustrate, let's assume the interest rate on savings is 8 percent per year and the position in industry A pays $35,000 in year 1 and $38,000 in year 2.-

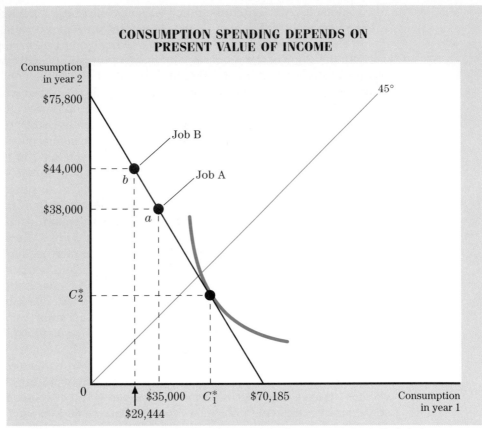

**CONSUMPTION SPENDING DEPENDS ON
PRESENT VALUE OF INCOME**

Figure 16-4   The consumer has a choice between job A and job B. Job A pays more in the first year than job B but less in the second year. The present values of the two jobs are the same and they are on the same intertemporal budget constraint. The theory of intertemporal consumption behavior says that the consumer will spend C_1^* in year 1 and C_2^* in year 2 no matter which job is selected.

The present value of future income is $35,000 + $38,000/(1 + 0.08) = $35,000 + $35,185 = $70,185. The position in industry B pays $29,444 in year 1 and $44,000 in year 2. The present value of future income is $29,444 + $44,000/(1 + 0.08) = $29,444 + $40,741 = $70,185, and so the present values of the incomes for the two positions are equal.

Will your consumption spending differ if you select one job instead of the other? The theory of intertemporal utility maximization says it should not. In the perfect foresight model point *a* in Figure 16-4 shows your income in the two years if you accept job A. Point *b* represents your income in the two years if you accept job B. Income in year 1 is lower in industry B but higher in year 2. The horizontal intercept of the intertemporal budget constraint equals the present value of income, or $70,185 at an 8 percent interest rate, whether you take job A or job B. The vertical intercept of the intertemporal budget constraint is $I_2 + I_1(1 + i) =$ \$75,800. Because the present value of future income is the same, the intertemporal budget constraint is the same no matter which of the two positions you accept, assuming that you can borrow at the interest rate i. Even if you select job B and earn only \$29,444 in year 1, you will go into debt and spend C_1^* on consumption in year 1 and C_2^* in year 2. Although you have less income in year 1, you maximize utility by spending C_1^* on consumption in year 1. You borrow more in year 1 when you accept job B, but your borrowing power is greater because you will have a higher income in year 2. You maximize utility by consuming C_1^* in year 1 whether you accept the position in industry A or industry B. In the perfect foresight model, no matter what is the starting point on the intertemporal budget constraint, the consumer spends C_1^* in the first year.

> When a consumer can borrow, the intertemporal theory of utility maximization says that the present value of income, and not the income in any one year, determines consumption spending in each year.

The theory of intertemporal utility maximization changes our predictions of consumer behavior. The intertemporal theory of consumption predicts that an individual with a short-term or transitory increase in earnings in the current year will increase consumption spending in year 1 by less than another individual who receives the same increase in the current year but whose income increase is permanent. The permanent increase raises the present value of income by more than the short-term increase. For an example of this situation consider two individuals who experience a salary increase in year 1. The first individual is a firefighter who extinguishes oil fires. After the 1991 Gulf War, he experienced a large short-term blip in earnings. Let's say for the sake of argument that his earnings doubled. The second individual is an executive whose salary doubles when she is promoted. Income doubles in year 1 for both, but the increased earnings of the executive continue into the second year as well, whereas the firefighter's income in year 2 drops back to what it would have been had the Gulf War not taken place. Assume that the earnings of the firefighter would have been $_fI_1$ in year 1 and $_fI_2$ in year 2 if the Gulf War had not occurred, and that the earnings of the executive would have been $_eI_1$ in year 1 and $_eI_2$ in year 2 if she had not been promoted. Because of the Gulf War and because of the executive's promotion, the present value of the earnings of the two individuals at the beginning of year 1 are $2_fI_1 + _fI_2/(1 + i)$ for the firefighter and $2_eI_1 + 2[_eI_2/(1 + i)]$ for the executive.

The present value of earnings of the executive doubles, while the present value of the earnings of the firefighter increases but does not double, and so the consumption behavior of these two individuals will differ. A simple one-period model predicts that both individuals will increase consumption in year 1 by approximately the same percentage because the current income of both doubles. The intertemporal theory predicts that the consumption spending of the executive will rise by a larger percentage in year 1 because her present value of future earnings increases by a larger percentage.

The Effect on Saving of an Increase in Current or Future Income

Given current income, a rise in an individual's future income shifts the intertemporal budget constraint outward. In Figure 16-5 a consumer with an income endowment of I_1' and I_2' would maximize utility by consuming C_1' in year 1, saving $I_1' - C_1'$ in year 1, and consuming C_2' in year 2. Suppose this individual learns at the beginning of year 1 that income in year 2 will be $I_2^{\bullet}$ rather than I_2', and so the endowment point shifts up vertically from point a to a' because income in year 2 is higher. How will this consumer's intertemporal behavior change now that the

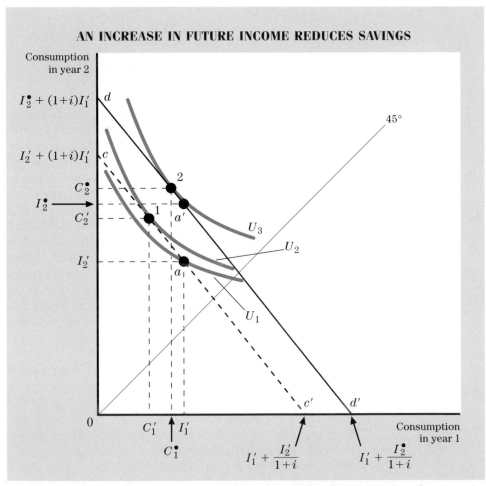

AN INCREASE IN FUTURE INCOME REDUCES SAVINGS

Figure 16-5   If C_1 and C_2 are normal goods, a higher income in year 2 causes the consumer to reduce savings and increase consumption spending in year 1 from C_1' to $C_1^{\bullet}$.

intertemporal budget constraint becomes dd' and the present value of income is now $I_1' + I_2^{\bullet}/(1 + i)$? The consumer maximizes utility at point 2 by increasing consumption spending from C_1' to $C_1^{\bullet}$ and by saving less in year 1. Assume that consumption is a normal good, so that an increase in the present value of income increases consumption in both years. Because future income is higher, this individual does not have to save as much in year 1 as before to increase consumption in year 2. Therefore, we conclude that an increase in future income prospects will reduce the share of current income saved. For example, an individual on a fast track may rationally save less and spend more lavishly in the current year compared to others who have the same current income but who do not have future prospects that are as bright.

Instead of examining the effect of an increase in future income on savings, let's consider the effect of an increase in current income on savings. When income in year 1 increases from I_1' to I_1'', so that the present value of income is the same as in the previous example where income in year 2 increased to $I_2^{\bullet}$, the consumer maximizes utility by moving to point 2 in Figure 16-6. While the intertemporal consumption behavior is the same because the present value of income is the same in the two circumstances, the consumer saves more in year 1 because of the increase in current income. A rise in current income raises savings, while a rise in future income reduces savings.

APPLICATION 16-2

Personal Bankruptcy

We can use the intertemporal model to explain why more and more Americans are filing for personal bankruptcy. Popular explanations rely on the easy credit made available by mass solicitations for credit cards. Economists are more inclined to put their finger on unanticipated decreases in income or increases in interest rates as the cause of the rise in personal bankruptcies.

A consumer with current income of I_1 and an anticipated income of I_2 in Figure 16-7 borrows $C_1 - I_1$ to increase consumption in year 1. The consumer's marginal rate of time preference equals $-(1 + i)$ at point a. The consumer expects to repay the loan in year 2 where $I_2 - C_2$ is enough to repay the loan with interest. This intertemporal allocation of consumption assumes income in year 2 will be I_2. Assume, however, that the worker is terminated because of downsizing and the next best job that the worker can find in year 2 has an income of only $I_2' < I_2$. If I_2' is less than $I_2 - C_2$, there is no way the consumer can repay the loan with interest. So, the consumer must file for bankruptcy. Even in a growing economy, some workers experience large negative income shocks because of technological changes that simultaneously create new industries and eliminate or reduce the size of others. The decision to borrow for the purchase of a new house or a car that appears justifiable based on anticipated income growth now appears extravagant in light of the lower actual income. Similarly, an unexpected increase in interest rates can cause more consumers to file for personal bankruptcy. If a consumer

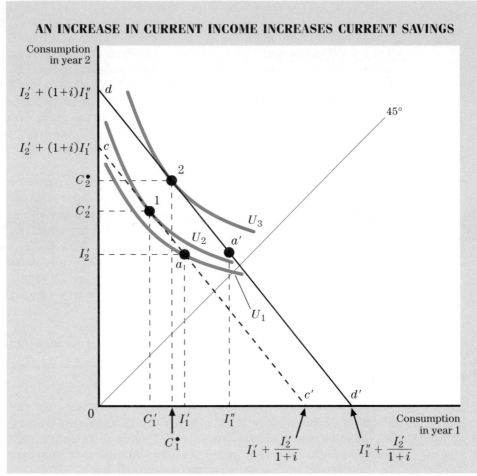

Figure 16-6 If C_1 and C_2 are normal goods, a higher income in year 1 increases savings and increases consumption spending in year 1 from C_1' to $C_1^\bullet$ and from C_2' to $C_2^\bullet$ in year 2.

selects an adjustable interest rate mortgage and interest rates rise unexpectedly, the consumer may have to declare bankruptcy.

Saving, Borrowing, and the Interest Rate

We can use our model of intertemporal consumption behavior to analyze how a change in the interest rate affects savings. Will a consumer reduce first period consumption and save more when the return on saving increases? Surprisingly, we cannot make an unambiguous prediction and the reason that we cannot is because the substitution and income effects of an interest rate change work in opposite

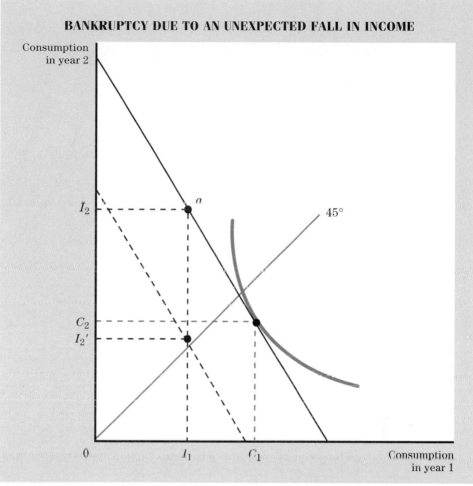

Figure 16-7   An unexpected decrease in income in year 2 from I_2 to I_2' causes the consumer to declare bankruptcy. Expecting an income of I_2, the consumer borrows C_1 − I_1 in year 1. Income in year 2 is only I_2' rather than I_2. The consumer will not pay off the loan with interest.

directions. As you recall from Chapter 3, the effect of a price change on the quantity demanded can be decomposed into a substitution effect and into an income effect. The substitution effect measures the change in the quantity demanded when the price of a good declines relative to other prices, holding utility constant. In the present context a change in the interest rate represents a change in the relative price of current versus future consumption. A higher interest rate makes current consumption relatively more expensive. The substitution effect induces the consumer to reduce first period consumption and save more. But a change in the interest rate also creates an income effect. A rise in the interest rate increases the

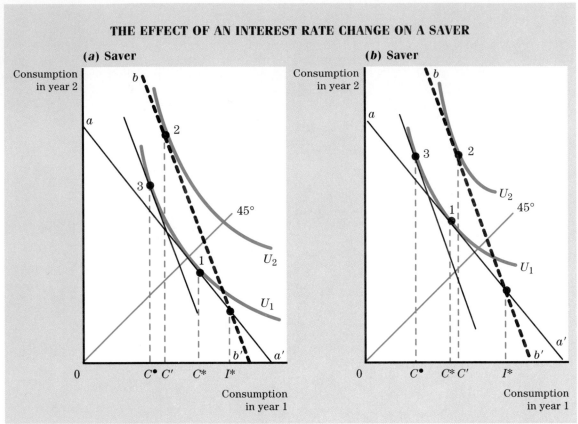

Figure 16-8 (*a*) A rise in the interest rate increases saving because the substitution effect of $C^\bullet - C^*$ is larger than the income effect of $C' - C^\bullet$. (*b*) A saver reduces total saving when the interest rate increases because the income effect of $C' - C^\bullet$ is larger than the substitution effect of $C^\bullet - C^*$.

wealth of a saver since the return to saving increases. As with our earlier discussion of the income effect in Chapter 3, here a rise in interest income increases current and future consumption, assuming consumption spending is a normal good. What will be the net effect on first period consumption and therefore on saving? We cannot say on theoretical grounds alone since the substitution effect works in the opposite direction from the income effect. Saving could either increase or decrease when the real interest rate increases.

The two possible outcomes are shown in Figure 16-8. In Figure 16-8*a* the substitution effect is larger than the income effect so the consumer saves more at a higher interest rate. To simplify Figure 16-8 as much as possible, we show only the levels of first period consumption and drop the first period subscript. Before the interest rate increases, the budget line is *aa'*. A consumer with income endowment I^* maximizes utility U_1 by spending C^* (point 1) on first period consumption and saves $I^* - C^*$. After the interest rate increases, the intertemporal budget constraint becomes bb' and the consumer maximizes utility on U_2 at point 2, and first period consumption spending decreases from C^* to C' so total saving increases from $(I^* - C^*)$ to $(I^* - C')$. This total change can be decomposed into a substitution and income effect. The substitution effect measures the reduction in first period consumption of $C^* - C^{\bullet}$ at point 3 where utility is held constant at U_1. The income effect is the increase in consumption spending of $C' - C^{\bullet}$. Because the substitution effect dominates, the consumer saves more at the higher interest rate.

However there is another possibility that is shown in Figure 16-8b. The substitution effect equals $C^* - C^{\bullet}$ but is now smaller than the income effect of $C' - C^{\bullet}$. Unlike the previous case, the consumer now saves less when the interest rate increases. There is a theoretical ambiguity of how saving responds to an interest rate change because it depends on the relative size of the substitution and income effects.

So far, our analysis has focused on a saver. A similar analysis can be applied to a borrower. Fortunately, the analysis of a borrower is simpler because the substitution and income effects act in the same direction. Just as a saver substitutes away from first period consumption when the interest rate increases, so does a borrower. However, unlike a saver who receives more income from a higher interest rate, a borrower must pay more in interest when the interest rate increases. So the income effect causes the borrower to reduce current and future consumption assuming consumption spending is a normal good. Figure 16-9 shows the two effects for a borrower. The substitution effect is $C^* - C^{\bullet}$ and the income effect is $C^{\bullet} - C'$. So, a rise in the interest rate causes the borrower to reduce the size of his or her loan.

The Equilibrium Interest Rate

As we've seen, the interest rate affects how much a consumer saves or borrows—and a change in the interest rate affects the amount he or she saves or borrows in year 1. Just what determines the interest rate that prevails in any year? This section answers this question by deriving the equilibrium interest rate from the demand for and supply of loanable funds.

Our first task is to derive the individual's **demand function for loanable funds.** Consumers who borrow in the first period are demanding loanable funds in year 1. The amount they demand depends on the interest rate. Let's consider a demander of loanable funds and derive the individual's demand function for these funds.

In Figure 16-10a income is I'_1 in year 1 and I'_2 in year 2 as represented by point e, and the intertemporal budget constraint is cc when the interest rate is i'. The consumer maximizes utility by borrowing $C'_1 - I'_1$, while spending C'_1 on consumption in year 1. In Figure 16-10b loanable funds demanded is $DL' = C'_1 - I'_1$ when the interest rate is i'. As the interest rate increases, the intertemporal budget constraint rotates around the endowment point e in Figure 16-10a and becomes line aa when the interest rate is i'' and then line bb when the interest rate increases to $i^{\bullet}$. Point e is on each of the intertemporal budget constraints as the interest rate

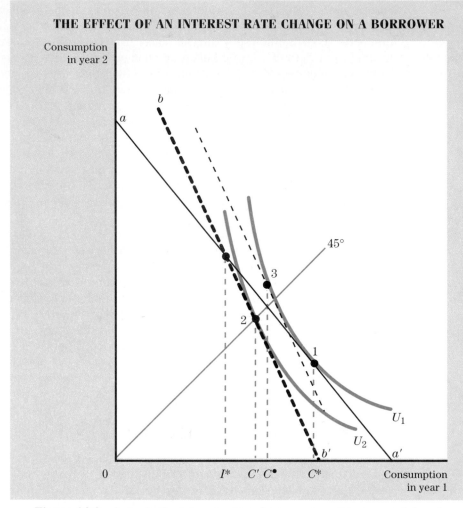

THE EFFECT OF AN INTEREST RATE CHANGE ON A BORROWER

Figure 16-9   A rise in the interest rate reduces consumption in year 1 for a borrower and reduces total amount borrowed. The substitution effect of $C^\bullet - C^*$ and the income effect of $C^\bullet - C'$ work in the same direction.

changes because the individual can always choose to consume all income in each year. Because the income and substitution effects work in the same direction, consumption spending on a composite good decreases to C_1'' when the interest rate is i'', and the amount borrowed decreases to $C_1'' - I_1'$. At an interest rate of i'', loanable funds demanded by the consumer decreases to $\text{DL}'' = C_1'' - I_1'$. When the interest rate increases to $i^\bullet$, this individual reduces consumption spending on the composite good in year 1 to $C_1^\bullet$ and the amount borrowed decreases to $C_1^\bullet - I_1'$. Figure 16-10*b* shows that loanable funds demanded is $\text{DL}^\bullet = C_1^\bullet - I_1'$ if the interest rate is $i^\bullet$. Connecting all the points on the demand function for loanable funds produces the consumer's demand function *dd* for loanable funds. As the interest

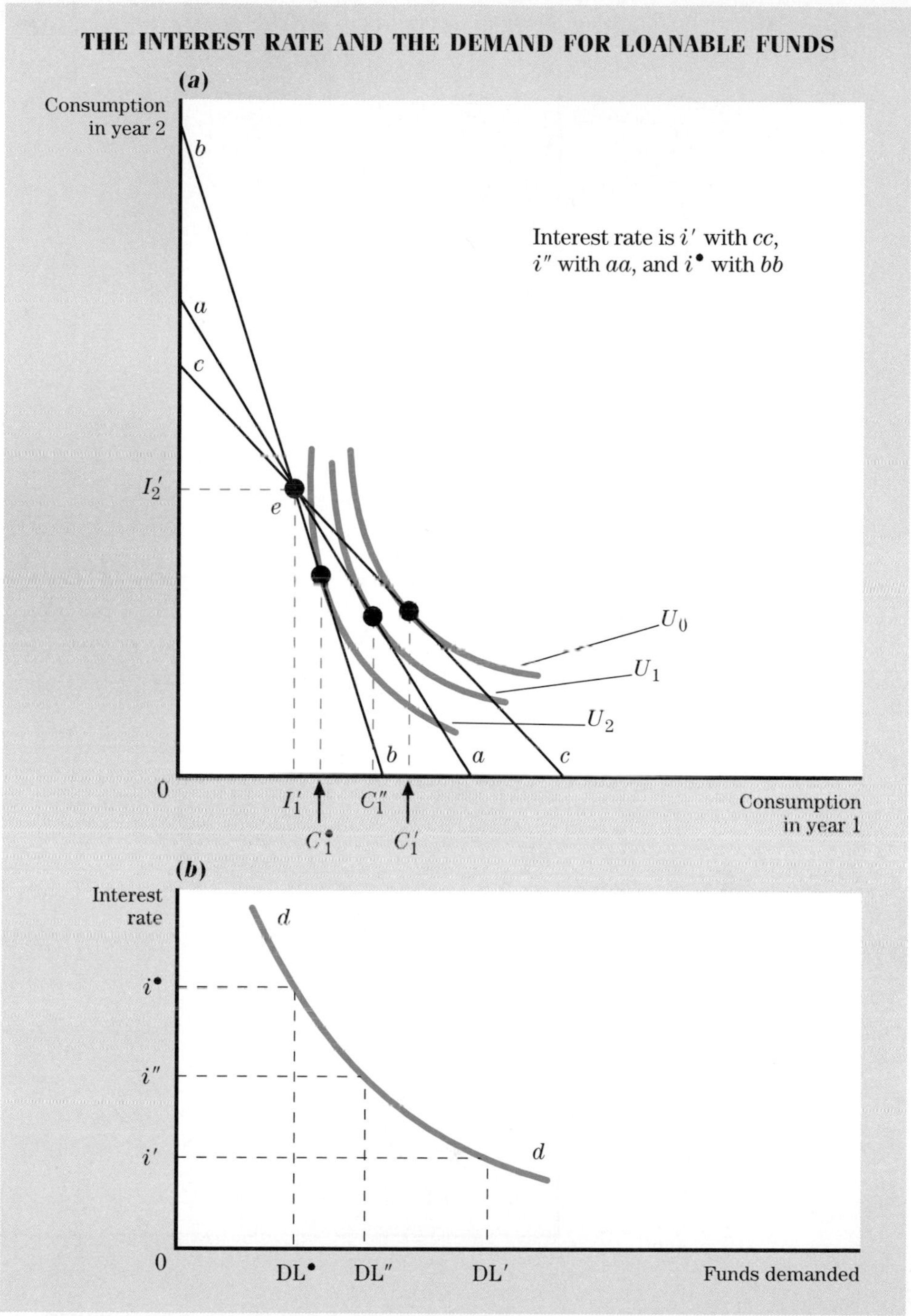

THE INTEREST RATE AND THE DEMAND FOR LOANABLE FUNDS

(a)

Interest rate is i' with cc,
i'' with aa, and $i^{\bullet}$ with bb

(b)

Figure 16-10 (a) Point e is the consumer's income endowment. The intertemporal budget constraint is cc when the interest rate is i'. The impatient consumer borrows $C_1' - I_1'$ in year 1. The interest rate increases to i''; the intertemporal budget rotates around endowment point e, becoming aa. The consumer reduces the loan to $C_1'' - I_1'$. When the interest rate increases to $i^{\bullet}$, the budget constraint is bb and the demand for loanable funds is $C_1^{\bullet} - I_1'$. (b) The individual's demand function for loanable funds.

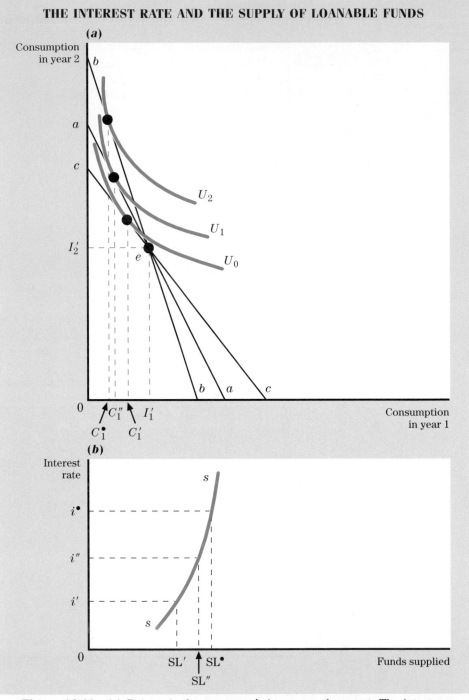

Figure 16-11 (*a*) Point e is the consumer's income endowment. The intertemporal budget constraint is cc when the interest rate is i'. This patient consumer saves $I_1' - C_1'$ in year 1. The interest rate increases to i'', and the intertemporal budget rotates around the endowment point e and becomes aa. The consumer increases savings to $I_1' - C_1''$. When the interest rate increases to $i^{\bullet}$, the supply of loanable funds is $I_1' - C_1^{\bullet}$. 1(*b*) The supply function of loanable funds.

rate increases, the demand for loanable funds decreases because the opportunity cost of borrowing increases. Other consumers will have different endowment points and tastes, and their demand functions for loanable funds will differ. It is a short step from an individual's demand function to the aggregate demand function for loanable funds derived by adding the individual demand functions horizontally. One caution should be mentioned. Although the impatient consumer is a demander of loanable funds over the interest rates investigated, even this individual can become a supplier of loanable funds if the interest rate becomes high enough and induces him to lend rather than borrow.

A consumer's **supply function of loanable funds** can be derived similarly. In Figure 16-11a the intertemporal budget constraint of a more patient consumer is cc when the interest rate is i', and the endowment point is point e. The consumer saves $I'_1 - C'_1$ and spends C'_1 on a composite good in year 1. Figure 16-11b shows that the amount of loanable funds supplied by this consumer is $SL' = I'_1 - C'_1$ when the interest rate is i'. As the interest rate increases, the intertemporal budget constraint rotates around point e in Figure 16-11a. At an interest rate of i'', the consumer saves $I'_1 - C''_1$. The supply of loanable funds increases to $SL'' = I'_1 - C''_1$. When the interest rate increases to $i^\bullet$, the supply of loanable funds increases to $SL^\bullet = I'_1 - C^\bullet_1$. Note that in deriving this particular individual's supply curve for loanable funds, we have assumed the substitution effect outweighs the income effect, leading to a rise in saving as the interest rate increases. Connecting all the points on the supply function produces the supply function of loanable funds of this more patient consumer. Other consumers with different endowment points and time preferences will have supply functions as well. Summing these supply functions horizontally produces the aggregate supply function of loanable funds.

The market equilibrium interest rate is the interest rate that equates the market demand to the market supply of loanable funds. In Figure 16-12 the equilibrium interest rate is i^* and the equilibrium volume of loans is L^*. This analysis has assumed that there is only one interest rate. In fact, there are many markets for loanable funds that depend on the duration of the loan and the risk characteristics of the borrower.

> The market equilibrium interest rate equates the quantity demanded to the quantity supplied of loanable funds.

The equilibrium interest rate and the total amount saved and borrowed will depend on the distribution of income among consumers in the economy and on differences in time preferences over current and future consumption.

The distribution of income frequently depends on the age distribution of individuals in an economy and is one determinant of the interest rate. The interest rate is higher in an economy with more relatively young individuals who have lower current earnings but higher future earnings. Because current income is low, these consumers borrow to finance spending on such items as durable goods and housing. The aggregate demand function for loanable funds shifts outward when there are more relatively young individuals in a population, and this causes the equilibrium interest rate to rise.

The supply of loanable funds is greater when there are more relatively old

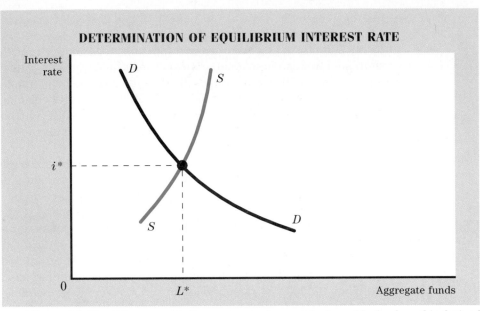

Figure 16-12   *DD* represents the aggregate demand for loanable funds and is derived by summing the individual demand functions horizontally. *SS* is the aggregate supply of loanable funds and is derived by summing the individual supply functions horizontally. The equilibrium interest rate *i** determines the equilibrium quantity of funds where funds demanded is equal to funds supplied.

individuals in the economy who have higher current earnings but face lower future earnings prospects as they age. These individuals prefer to save for the future when their earnings will be lower. When there are relatively more individuals of this type in the population, the aggregate supply function for loanable funds shifts outward and causes the equilibrium interest rate to fall. In summary, the age distribution of the population is an important determinant of the level of interest rates.

16-3 DEPLETION OF A NATURAL RESOURCE

The future affects current decisions on the supply side of the market also. Suppliers have to decide how much to supply in each period. If an automobile parts retailer has an inventory of parts, he or she must decide whether to sell them in the current month or in the next month or in both months. Similarly, Saudi Arabia has huge oil reserves and must decide when to sell them. Interest rates affect supplier decisions just as they influence decisions of consumers over time. To explain intertemporal decisions of suppliers, let's first examine the market for a nonrenewable resource— a resource that cannot be augmented, for example, a known stock of some mineral or energy source. Later, we investigate the case of a renewable resource.

A **nonrenewable resource** is a stock of units that cannot be augmented.

This section develops a theory that explains how the price of a nonrenewable resource changes as the stock of this resource is depleted. To develop the analysis, let's first look at the decisions of a single owner of a nonrenewable resource and derive optimal decision rules for such an individual. Then, we will look at the market for a nonrenewable resource where there are many individual owners and demanders and determine the market equilibrium prices over time as owners sell units of this resource.

When to Sell a Nonrenewable Resource

When is the best time for a single supplier of a nonrenewable resource—say, an oil producer—to sell the resource? This question can be answered by employing our favorite two-period model. Let's clearly specify the situation to be analyzed. An owner has a stock of b^* units of a nonrenewable resource at the beginning of year 1. The owner is a price taker and can sell each unit costlessly at a price of P_1 at the beginning of year 1 or at a price of P_2 at the beginning of year 2. The objective is to determine how many units to sell in year 1 and in year 2 so that the present value of the seller's stock, b^*, is maximized.

The amount sold in year 1 is b_1, and the amount sold in year 2 is b_2. Therefore,

$$b_1 + b_2 = b^* \qquad \text{(Quantity Constraint)} \tag{16-9}$$

Equation 16-9 simply says that the quantity sold in years 1 and 2 must equal the total initial stock.

You already know that a dollar next year is worth less than a dollar this year. The price of a unit sold at the beginning of year 2 is worth only $P_2/(1 + i)$ at the beginning of year 1 because of discounting. To determine when to sell the nonrenewable stock, the owner has to compare the per unit price, P_1, received at the beginning of year 1 with the discounted price, $P_2/(1 + i)$, if a unit is sold in year 2.

To maximize the present value of selling b^* units, the owner follows these decision rules:[5]

---

[5] We assume the goal of the owner is to select b_1 and b_2 so as to maximize present value of b^*:

$$PV = P_1 b_1 + \left(\frac{P_2}{1 + i} \right) b_2$$

subject to the constraint $\mathbf{b}_1 + \mathbf{b}_2 = \mathbf{b}^*$.
   After substituting $\mathbf{b}_2 = \mathbf{b}^* - \mathbf{b}_1$ *for* $\mathbf{b}_2$, *the problem requires the owner to select* $\mathbf{b}_1$ *to maximize present value.*

$$PV = P_1 b_1 + \left(\frac{P_2}{1 + i} \right)(b^* - b_1)$$

In this problem present value depends only on b_1. The first-order necessary condition for a maximum with respect to b_1 is

$$\frac{dPV}{db_1} = P_1 - \frac{P_2}{1 + i} = 0$$

   If $P_1 > P_2/(1 + i)$, the present value increases as owners sell more of the stock in the first year, $dPV/db_1 > 0$. For each unit sold, the owner receives P_1 that can be invested. The owner will have $P_1(1 + i)$ at the beginning of year 2, which is greater than P_2. Therefore, the owner maximizes present value by selling all the stock in year 1. If $P_1 < P_2/(1 + i)$, then the owner maximizes present value by holding all the stock in year 1 and selling all of it in year 2 since $dPV/db_1 < 0$.

1. Sell all units in year 1 if the price in year 1 is greater than the present value of the price at the beginning of year 2, $P_1 > P_2/(1 + i)$.

2. Sell units in either year or in both years if the price in year 1 equals the present value of the price at the beginning of year 2, $P_1 = P_2/(1 + i)$.

3. Sell all units in year 2 if the price in year 1 is less than the present value of the price at the beginning of year 2, $P_1 < P_2/(1 + i)$.

There is a more intuitive explanation of these conditions in terms of the **price appreciation of the resource** and the appreciation of a dollar. In essence, the owner of the resource decides when to sell by comparing P_2/P_1, the price appreciation of the resource, with $(1 + i)/1$, the appreciation because a dollar earns interest. If the price appreciation of the resource is greater than $1 + i$, then the optimal policy is to hold the stock for a year and sell it in year 2. If the price appreciation is less than $1 + i$, then the present value is maximized by selling the resource in year 1 and investing the proceeds to obtain the greater appreciation of a dollar. Therefore, the selling decision depends on the price appreciation of the resource versus the appreciation of a dollar.

For example, suppose that the price in year 1 is \$5.00 per unit and \$5.50 in year 2 and the interest rate is 6 percent. The price appreciation is \$5.50/\$5.00 = 1.10, while the appreciation of a dollar is only 1.06. So the owner should hold the stock for a year and then sell all of it at \$5.50 per unit in year 2.

> A single owner of a resource will sell a resource in year 2 if the price appreciation of the resource is greater than $1 + i$.

APPLICATION 16-3

Freeing Prices in Russia

On January 1, 1992, Russia entered a brave and uncertain world by freeing prices. In 1992 stores could sell at whatever price they desired except for certain exempt foods, medicines, and gasoline. For years, the former Soviet Union had kept prices artificially low and nowhere near the marginal cost of production for many goods. Some government economists predicted prices would double or triple for many consumer goods. Freeing prices was the first courageous step toward privatization and a market economy.

Suppose it is November 1991 and you own a small herd of cattle. Say you expect prices will be free to rise at the beginning of the new year and you think they will double. What should you do? If you are a present-value maximizer, you compare the current low controlled price with the present value of the future higher free price. If you expect prices to double, the choice will be an easy one for you to make. You will hold the cattle off the market until prices are higher. What are the consequences of announcing that prices will be free in the future? The immediate consequences have to be disastrous. The plan to free prices will drastically reduce the total supply of goods until prices rise, and before the freeing of prices the shortage of goods will become more severe.

While the rationale for allowing prices to rise is to increase supplies in the long run, the announcement to raise them in the future discourages suppliers from offering goods in the short run. This example also illustrates one of the many difficulties of gradual reform versus a rapid transition to a market economy.

Market Equilibrium Prices

Let's expand our sights from the optimal actions of a single price-taking owner to the behavior of the market as a whole in years 1 and 2. When examining the market as a whole, we cannot take the prices as given, as in analyzing the behavior of a single seller, but must determine the **equilibrium prices over time.** To determine these prices, assume that a downward sloping inverse demand function exists for the good in each year. Furthermore, assume that there are many owners of the nonrenewable resource, so that each is a price taker who maximizes the present value of the stock held.

Assuming each owner follows these decision rules, what will be the market-clearing equilibrium prices in years 1 and 2? How P_1 relates to P_2 in a market equilibrium can be determined through a process of elimination. Can there be a market equilibrium if $P_1 < P_2/(1 + i)$? The answer is clearly no. The present value of the price in year 2 exceeds the price in year 1. Every owner would sell in year 2. As more of the stock is supplied in year 2 and less in year 1, the price declines in year 2 and increases in year 1. Therefore, an equilibrium cannot exist if $P_1 < P_2/(1 + i)$. The same reasoning says that an equilibrium does not exist if $P_1 > P_2/(1 + i)$. Now all owners want to sell in year 1. If they all sell the stock in year 1, the price will fall in year 1 and rise in year 2. This pair cannot represent an equilibrium pair of prices either. Therefore, only one other alternative remains. An equilibrium pair of prices exists if

$$P_1 = \frac{P_2}{1 + i}$$

or

$$(1 + i)P_1 = P_2 \qquad \text{(Market Equilibrium Prices)} \qquad \text{(16-10)}$$

An intertemporal market equilibrium exists if the current price equals the present value of the future price.

This condition was first stated by Harold Hotelling, who predicted that the price increases by i percent a year for a nonrenewable resource as equation 16-10 indicates.[6] If the interest rate is 3 percent per year, the price of the nonrenewable

---

[6] Hotelling analyzed the problem of allocating a nonrenewable resource over n periods and reached the conclusion that the discounted price must be equal for all periods: Harold Hotelling, "The Economics of Exhaustible Resources," *Journal of Political Economy* 39 (April 1931), pp. 137–75.

resource will increase by 3 percent a year so as to induce enough owners to hold their stock for another year and then sell it in year 2.

We know the relationship between the prices in the two years if the market is in equilibrium. However, we still do not know what the price will be in year 1 or how much of the aggregate stock will be consumed in year 1 and in year 2. To find these values, assume that the total quantity of the nonrenewable resource is B^*. B_1 represents the total units sold in the market in year 1, and B_2 is the total quantity sold in the market in year 2, with $B_1 + B_2 = B^*$. To determine the price in each year, we must know the market demand functions in each year. Our investigation assumes that the demand function for the nonrenewable resource is the same in each year. However, our analysis is more general than that and applies when the demand functions differ in the two years.

Let the demand functions be

$$P_1 = D(B_1) \qquad P_2 = D(B_2) \qquad \text{(Market Demand Functions)} \qquad \textbf{(16-11)}$$

The same symbol, $D(\quad)$, for both periods signifies that the market demand functions are the *same* in each year.

Given this information, let's find the quantity sold in each year and the equilibrium price in each year. In Figure 16-13 the length of the horizontal axis is equal to B^*, the total stock of the nonrenewable resource. The vertical axis on the left side measures the price in year 1. Starting at the left-hand origin 0 and reading from left to right, we find the market demand function, $P_1 = D(B_1)$, in year 1. Now consider the vertical axis on the right-hand side. This axis shows the price in year 2. Starting at the origin $0'$ and moving from right to left, we find the market demand function $P_2 = D(B_2)$ in year 2. Because demand functions are the same, they are mirror images of each other.

Any point on the horizontal axis identifies an allocation of the total stock between the two periods. For example, if owners sell B_1' units in year 1 and B_2' units in year 2, the prices in the 2 years will be the same and will equal P'. You can immediately see why this allocation does not describe a market equilibrium. By selling in the first year, owners receive P'. They can invest this and have $(1 + i)P'$ in year 2 which is greater than P', the price that they would receive by selling in year 2. Equation 16-10 says that the price in year 1 must equal the discounted price in year 2 in a market equilibrium. This condition is not satisfied when owners sell the same quantity in both years and the prices are equal in the 2 years.

An allocation of the total stock of B^* where the price in year 1 equals the discounted price in year 2 can be found by constructing a **discounted price demand function** for year 2.[7] This function shows the present value of P_2 for each B_2. The discounted price, DP, is defined as $[1/(1 + i)]P_2$. Therefore, the discounted price demand function is

---

[7] For an extended analysis of intertemporal equilibrium, the reader should consult Paul A. Samuelson, "Intertemporal Price Equilibrium: A Prologue to the Theory of Speculation," in *The Collected Papers of Paul A. Samuelson*, vol. II, J. E. Stiglitz, ed. (Cambridge, Mass.: MIT Press, 1966), pp. 946–84.

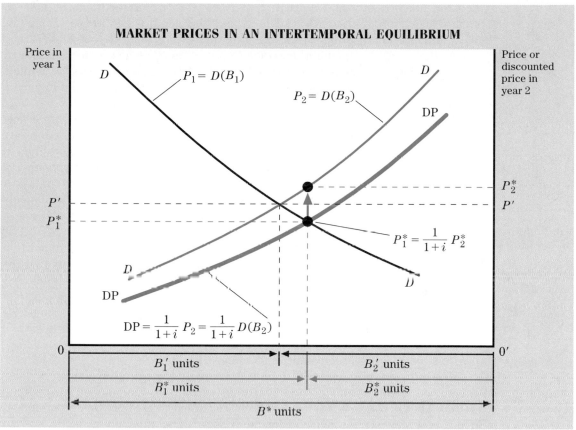

MARKET PRICES IN AN INTERTEMPORAL EQUILIBRIUM

Figure 16-13   The stock of a nonrenewable resource is allocated to the two years so that B_1^* is sold in year 1 and B_2^* is sold in year 2. The equilibrium market-clearing prices are P_1^* and P_2^*. $P_2^* = (1 + i)P_1^*$.

$$DP = \frac{1}{1 + i}P_2 = \frac{1}{1 + i}D(B_2) \qquad \text{(Discounted Price} \qquad \textbf{(16-12)} \\ \text{Demand Function)}$$

For each value of B_2, calculate $D(B_2)/(1 + i)$. Since $1/(1 + i)$ is less than 1, the discounted price demand function is below $P = D(B_2)$ for year 2. For example, if the interest rate is 10 percent, the discount factor is $1/1.10 = 0.9094$. For each B_2, find the discounted price by reducing P_2 to $0.9094P_2$. The *discounted price demand function* for year 2 is DP-DP in Figure 16-13 and lies below *DD* in year 2. The vertical distance between the *DD* and DP-DP demand functions increases as P_2 increases. This occurs because the discounted price is a constant fraction of P_2. In this illustration the discounted price is \$90.94 if $P_2 = \$100$, and \$9.094 when $P_2 = \$10$.

In equilibrium P_1^* must equal the discounted price in year 2. This condition is satisfied at the point where the demand function in year 1 intersects the discounted demand function in year 2 so that $P_1^* = P_2^*/(1 + i)$. In Figure 16-13 the market-clearing equilibrium price in year 1 is P_1^*, and the quantity sold in year 1 must be B_1^*. Therefore, the quantity of the nonrenewable stock sold in year 2 is B_2^*, and $B_1^* + B_2^* = B^*$. The equilibrium price in year 2 is P_2^*, which can be found by extending the point where DD for year 1 and DP-DP cross vertically to the demand function $P_2 = D(B_2^*)$. When owners sell B_1^* units in year 1 and B_2^* units in year 2, $P_2^* = (1 + i)P_1^*$.

One implication of the two-period model of a nonrenewable resource is that consumption of the resource decreases over time when the demand functions are the same in the two years. Because the price in the second year is higher than in the first year, the quantity consumed is lower in year 2 than in year 1. If the model were expanded to include n years, we could prove that price increases from year to year by a factor of $1 + i$ and consumption declines over time when the demand functions are the same in all years. Therefore, the depletion rate of the nonrenewable resource decreases over time.

This basic model of a nonrenewable resource points up a common fallacy that marks public policy discussions of natural resources. Many express fears that the world will run out of these resources. What better way of estimating the time when a resource will be depleted than by dividing total known reserves by current consumption? The ratio of total reserves to annual consumption is the number of years before the resource will be depleted. If the known total reserves of a natural resource are 100,000 units and current annual consumption is 10,000, this logic predicts that the resource will be depleted in 10 years.

The ratio of total reserves to annual consumption predicts the number of years before the resource runs out, and in terms of the two-year model, this ratio is B^*/B_1^*. What is wrong with this estimate? The glaring defect of this procedure is that it assumes that the demand for the resource is completely inelastic, so that consumption does not change when price rises. It fails to recognize the effect of a rising price on consumption. In Hotelling's analysis of intertemporal equilibrium, price rises over time and therefore the consumption of the resource decreases. Therefore, B^*/B_1^* underestimates the time when the nonrenewable resource will be depleted. Failure to recognize the effect of price on quantity demanded often leads to erroneous and pessimistic forecasts in public policy discussions of natural resources.

The Effect of the Interest Rate on Equilibrium Prices

In the analysis of intertemporal equilibrium prices the interest rate was taken as given. Let's consider how a change in the interest rate alters the behavior of owners of a nonrenewable resource. At higher interest rates, the opportunity cost of holding a resource increases, and so supply in year 1 will increase because suppliers want to convert the stock into dollars so they can earn the higher interest. To use the model to find the effect of a higher interest rate on prices and quantities consumed, we have to determine how the market-clearing prices change when the interest rate changes. Figure 16-14 shows that the discounted price demand function for year 2 shifts downward by still more than it did in Figure 16-13 and becomes

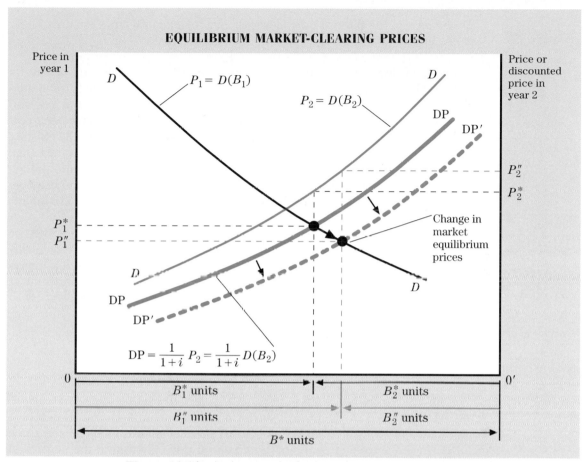

Figure 16-14   An increase in the interest rate increases the quantity sold in year 1 from B_1^* to B_1'' and decreases the quantity sold in year 2 from B_2^* to B_2''. The price in year 1 decreases to P_1'', and the price in year 2 increases to P_2''. A rise in the interest rate increases current consumption and decreases future consumption.

DP'-DP' because of the higher interest rate. The intersection of the new discounted price demand function and the demand function in year 1 occurs farther to the right. Therefore, owners sell more units of the nonrenewable resource in year 1 when the interest rate increases ($B_1'' > B_1^*$). A rise in the interest rate *decreases* the price in year 1 and *increases* the price in year 2, thereby increasing the percentage difference between the prices in years 1 and 2. Because an increase in the interest rate raises the opportunity cost of holding the resource, owners sell more of the total stock in the first year and invest the proceeds to earn a higher interest rate. The percentage increase in prices must be enough to induce some owners to hold their stocks and sell in year 2. This analysis shows that changes in the interest rate affect the level and the rate of price increase.

An increase in the interest rate causes the percentage difference between the prices in years 1 and 2 to increase.

How well does the Hotelling model describe the price behavior of natural resources? Is the assumption of a nonrenewable resource applicable to such minerals as nickel, lead, copper, and iron ore or such fuels as coal, natural gas, and crude oil? Strictly speaking, no. In virtually all of these cases there have been new discoveries of these resources that have created random additions to the existing stock of reserves. So, few natural resources would qualify as strictly nonrenewable. Nevertheless, the Hotelling model may yet produce reasonably accurate predictions if the additions to reserves are small in comparison with the total initial stock. For those natural resources where this is the case, the assumption of a nonrenewable stock is not far from the truth.

The Hotelling model can serve as a useful benchmark for determining whether a natural resource is nonrenewable. If the price behavior of the resource is consistent with the predictions of the theory, the resource can be considered a nonrenewable resource. If the price predictions of the model are wrong, then we must conclude that the theory of a nonrenewable resource is not applicable and try to understand what went wrong.

APPLICATION 16-4

The Historical Trend in Crude Oil Prices

While we could look at the price behavior of any number of natural resources—from aluminum to lead to nickel to coal to petroleum—we examine the price behavior in the petroleum market. The crude oil price is often in the news, and claims that there is only so much crude oil in the earth and that it will run out sometime in the future are commonplace. If this view is correct, the stock of crude oil is a nonrenewable resource, at least as a first approximation. The validity of this claim can be examined by determining if inflation-adjusted crude oil prices have increased by i percent per year over time. Robert Manthly has studied the long-term price trends for many minerals and fuels up to 1973.[8] Figure 16-15 extends his series and shows the inflation-adjusted price of crude oil from 1920 to 1987. What is striking about this graph is the absence of a rising price trend from 1920 to 1973. The per barrel price did rise after 1973 when OPEC increased prices, but the inflation-adjusted price declined throughout the 1980s. While there are short intervals of price increases and decreases, no long-term trend is discernible over the 53-year period from 1920 to 1973. Certainly, price has either declined or remained steady over long periods of time rather than increased. Manthly's study shows that the long-term real price for many minerals and fuels does not exhibit an upward trend.

---

[8] Robert S. Manthly, *Natural Resource Commodities—A Century of Statistics*, Resources for the Future (Baltimore: Johns Hopkins University Press, 1978).

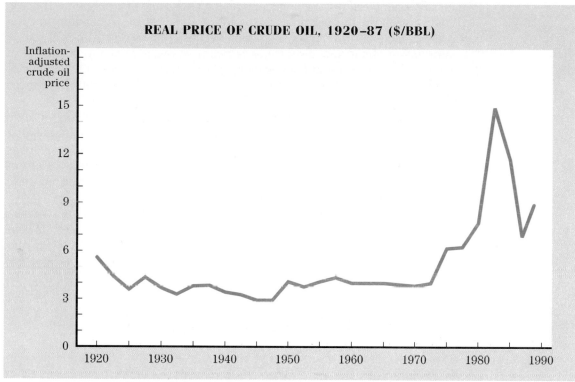

Figure 16-15   Real crude oil prices were steady from 1920 to 1973. [Robert S. Manthly, *Natural Resource Commodities—A Century of Statistics, Resources for the Future* (Baltimore: Johns Hopkins University Press, 1978); and U.S. Bureau of the Census, *Statistical Abstract of the United States* Washington, D.C.]

The nonrenewable resource theory predicts that real prices increase over time. In the case of petroleum the theory's predictions seem to go haywire. We must recognize and accept what history tells us. Price behavior from 1920 to 1973 indicates that the assumption of a fixed initial stock of crude oil is untenable.

A Renewable Resource

The behavior of crude oil prices appears to differ from the predictions of Hotelling's model of intertemporal equilibrium. What modification of the model might help explain why prices do not increase annually by $1 + i$? By modifying the model we might be able to explain the price movements and still retain some of its essential features.

The assumption of a fixed initial stock appears to be the most questionable. Let's modify this assumption and see how it helps to explain why price in year 2 can be equal to or less than $(1 + i)$ times price in year 1. Instead of assuming that

B^* units are available at the beginning of year 1, let's assume that only some fraction of B^* is available at the beginning of period 1 and that the remaining fraction becomes available only in the second period because of new discoveries in year 2. The information about new discoveries is public knowledge at the beginning of the first year. For example, at the beginning of year 1, discoveries of a known size are announced, but it takes a year before owners can sell any units from these new discoveries.

Admittedly, this scenario is rather extreme. The size of a discovery is often uncertain, and the actual size becomes known over time. Discoveries are similar to random events with considerable luck involved. We will not model discovery as a random variable because such an analysis requires a more extensive set of analytical tools. A simpler certainty formulation can be adopted that can still explain why prices are stable or fall over time.

Assume that the total quantity consumed during the 2 years is still B^*. Owners of the initial stock must still decide whether to sell their stocks in year 1 or in year 2, but owners of new discoveries cannot sell units from their discoveries in year 1. The new discoveries cannot increase consumption in year 1. This way of formulating the problem places more constraints on the solution. The original model assumed that the total stock, B^*, was available at the very beginning and that owners could sell all units in the first period if they decided to. In the renewable version of the theory the most that owners can sell in the first year is the stock available in year 1.

How large must the discoveries be in year 2 before the equilibrium price in period 2 is less than $(1 + i)P_1$? Figure 16-16 reproduces the demand functions in Figure 16-13. In Figure 16-13 $P_2^* = (1 + i)P_1^*$ when owners sell B_1^* units in year 1 and B_2^* units in year 2. If the discoveries are greater than B_2^*, so that the initial stock in year 1 is less than B_1^*, P_2 will be less than $(1 + i)P_1$. In Figure 16-16, when the initial stock in year 1 is B_1' and discoveries are equal to B_2' units, the equilibrium price is P_1' in year 1 and P_2' in year 2. The owners of B_1' have no incentive to hold the stock and sell it in year 2 since the price in year 2 is less than the price in year 1. While it is true that the price in year 1 exceeds the present value of the price in year 2, there is no way to sell more units in year 1 since only B_1' units are available. For a renewable resource, P_2 can be less than $(1 + i)P_1$.

$$P_2 \leq (1 + i)P_1 \qquad \text{(Intertemporal Price Condition with a Renewable Resource)} \qquad \textbf{(16-13)}$$

If, on the other hand, the new discoveries in year 2 are less than B_2^* and therefore the initial stock is greater than B_1^*, then the discounted price in year 2 would be greater than P_1 if owners sell all the initial stock in year 1. Consequently, owners will hold some of the initial stock off the market and sell the remainder in year 2. This raises the price in year 1 and lowers the price in year 2 until $P_2^* = (1 + i)P_1^*$. When the initial stock is B_1'', the quantity that owners carry over to year 2 is $B_1'' - B_1^*$ in an intertemporal equilibrium. Therefore, if future discoveries of a renewable resource are relatively small, prices will again increase by $1 + i$ each period. Figure 16-17 shows two possible price paths. The arrows indicate the direction of prices. When the initial stock B_1'' in Figure 16-16 is greater than B_1^*, the colored arrow slopes upward because price increases by $1 + i$ from

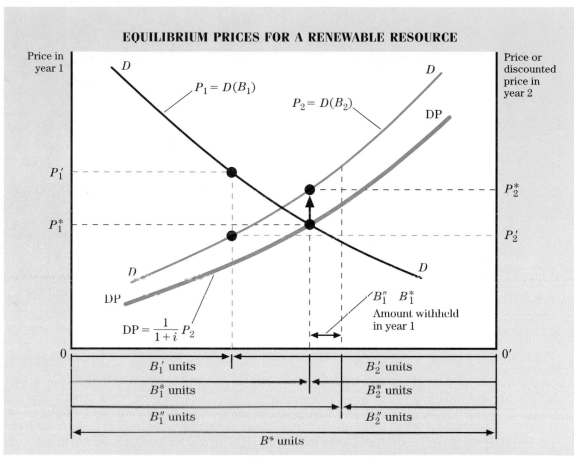

Figure 16-16 The initial stock of a renewable resource available in year 1 is B'_1. Discoveries in year 2 make B'_2 units available. The equilibrium market price in year 1 is P'_1. The equilibrium market-clearing price in year 2 is P'_2. The price in year 2 is less than $(1 + i)P'_1$. A long-term decline in real prices indicates that the assumption of a nonrenewable resource is untenable since additions to the stock cause the price to fall. If the initial stock is B''_1, the equilibrium prices in an intertemporal equilibrium equal $P^*_2 = (1 + i)P^*_1$. $B''_1 - B^*_1$ of the initial stock is sold in year 2.

year 1 to year 2 in an intertemporal equilibrium. When the initial stock is B'_1, less than B^*_1, the black arrow slopes downward because P'_2 is less than $(1 + i)P'_1$.[9]

The long-run stability in inflation-adjusted crude oil prices from 1920 to the early 1970s suggests that Hotelling's model of a nonrenewable resource does not explain the price behavior of crude oil. Crude oil prices have been stable, although the demand function has shifted outward over time. This price stability suggests that the fundamental assumption of a fixed initial reserve of crude oil is not valid.

[9] If the stock in year 1 is slightly less than B^*_1, price will increase, but by less than iP_1.

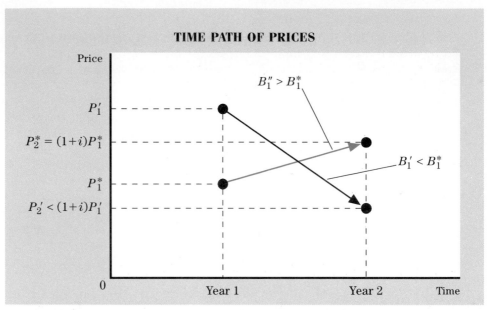

Figure 16-17   If the initial stock of a renewable resource is greater than B_1^*, then the equilibrium price in year 2 is $(1 + i)P_1^*$. If the initial stock is B_1', the price in year 2 is less than $(1 + i)P_1'$.

Rather, the long-run behavior of prices indicates that the available stock has increased over time through a combination of new discoveries and because of technological innovations in extracting more oil from known formations, thereby reducing the production costs of petroleum.

Since the formation of OPEC and throughout the 1970s and 1980s, natural resource economists have vigorously debated whether Hotelling's nonrenewable model might have greater current applicability than in the past. Some economists, policy makers, and conservationists claimed that there was a break in the data after the 1970s and that generous additions to reserves would no longer be forthcoming. They believed the future was more likely to be one of fixed supply and increasing real prices. In other words, the Hotelling model would be more applicable in the future than it had been in the past. The debate continues. However, the behavior of mineral and fuel prices in the 1980s indicates that inflation-adjusted prices have eased. It appears that more pessimistic predictions made during the dark days of the early 1970s have not been borne out.

SUMMARY

▪ The present value of future income is an amount received immediately that is equivalent to the income received in a future year.

▪ The intertemporal budget constraint shows how consumption spending in year 2 relates to consumption spending in year 1.

- The intertemporal utility function shows that the utility of a consumer depends on current and future spending on a composite good.
- A consumer maximizes utility when the marginal rate of time preference is equal to $-(1 + i)$, the decline in future consumption because of a dollar increase in current consumption.
- The intertemporal theory of consumption predicts that consumption spending in each year depends on the present value of income.
- If C_1 and C_2 are normal goods, a rise in future income with current income fixed reduces the amount saved by a consumer.
- If C_1 and C_2 are normal goods, a rise in current income with future income constant increases the amount saved by a consumer.

- The amount saved or borrowed in an economy depends on the interest rate.
- A saver may either increase or decrease saving when the interest rate increases.
- A borrower will reduce the size of the loan when the interest rate increases.
- The equilibrium interest rate equates the quantity demanded to the quantity supplied of loanable funds.
- In a two-period model of a nonrenewable resource the current price is equal to the present value of the future price. Equilibrium prices of a nonrenewable resource increase by i percent per year.
- The depletion of a nonrenewable resource occurs more rapidly at a higher interest rate.
- Equilibrium prices do not necessarily increase by i percent per year for a renewable resource.

KEY TERMS

present value of future income
endowment
intertemporal preferences
impatient consumer
intertemporal utility maximization
demand function for loanable funds
equilibrium interest rate
when to sell a nonrenewable resource
equilibrium prices over time

intertemporal budget constraint
marginal rate of time preference
patient consumer
saving and borrowing
supply function of loanable funds
nonrenewable resource
price appreciation of the resource
discounted price demand function
renewable resource

REVIEW QUESTIONS

1. If the interest rate is 6 percent, would you be indifferent between receiving $20,000 at the beginning of the year or $25,000 at the end of the year?
2. Rearrange equation 16-3 to show that the present value of consumption equals the present value of income.
3. What distinguishes a patient from an impatient consumer?
4. A neutral consumer has a marginal rate of

time preference equal to -1 when spending on a composite good is the same in each of 2 years. Will a neutral consumer spend more on a composite good in year 2 than in year 1 if the interest rate is positive?
5. Why does a higher interest rate cause a consumer to borrow less?
6. If an individual receives the same income in years 1 and 2, he will spend the same

amount on consumption in both periods if he cannot borrow. Explain why you agree or disagree with this statement.

7. If the price of a resource increases by 6 percent and you can borrow at 4 percent, would you sell the resource in year 1 or in year 2? Explain.

8. If demand is stable, the theory of a nonrenewable resource predicts that consumption in year 2 will be less than consumption in year 1. Explain why you agree or disagree with this statement.

9. Suppose the market demand function for a nonrenewable resource decreases over time. Explain why a decrease in demand can or cannot explain why the price is lower in year 2 than in year 1.

10. For a nonrenewable resource the equilibrium price in year 2 is $(1 + i)$ times the equilibrium price in year 1. For a renewable resource, the price in year 2 can equal or be less than $(1 + i)$ times the equilibrium price in year 1. Explain why you agree or disagree with these statements.

EXERCISES

1. In the past the government placed no restrictions on borrowing by individuals. A new government sweeps into power on a platform of prohibiting the payment of interest. If consumers are no longer able to borrow, explain why you would or would not expect them to respond in the following ways.
   a. Decrease savings in year 1.
   b. Decrease consumption spending in year 1.
   c. Decrease consumption spending in year 2.
   d. Increase savings in year 1.

2. Suppose the government announces a tax of 33 percent on income in year 2. Show how this tax policy changes a consumer's saving decision if there is no tax in year 1.

3. A higher interest rate will cause a borrower to borrow less and a saver to save more. Explain why you agree or disagree with this statement.

4. In Chicago, transit riders use tokens to ride local buses. Transit riders buy packs of 10 tokens at currency exchanges, banks, supermarkets, and so forth, located throughout the city. The vendors who sell tokens to the general public buy the 10-packs from the Chicago Transit Authority

(CTA). In November 1995 the CTA announced that a 10-pack that cost a rider $12.50 would rise in price to $13.50 on January 1, 1996, an 8 percent increase. Predict what happened to the availability of tokens between November and January.

5. The larger the outward shift in the demand function for a nonrenewable resource over time, the larger the rate of increase in the price of the resource over time. Explain why you agree or disagree with this statement.

6. How do the equilibrium prices of a nonrenewable resource in years 1 and 2 change if the initial stock of the resource is larger?

7. Suppose the quantity demanded in year 1 is twice the quantity demanded at each price in year 2. Show that the equilibrium price in year 2 is $(1 + i)P_1^*$ for a nonrenewable resource.

*8. Use a two period model to explain why you agree or disagree with the following statements.
   a. If the demand for a nonrenewable natural resource is decreasing over time, the price of the resource will decrease over time.
   b. If demand is increasing over time and

the price of a natural resource is stable over time, this indicates the resource is a renewable resource.

*9. If the equilibrium price in year 2 is less than $(1 + i)$ times the equilibrium price in year 1, an increase in the interest rate will have no effect on the equilibrium prices for a renewable resource. Explain why you agree or disagree with this statement.

10. If the government announces in year 1 that it will sell all of its reserves of crude oil in year 2, what effect will this have on prices in year 1 and in year 2?

■ C H A P T E R 17

WAGE DETERMINATION IN LABOR MARKETS

■ **17-1   The Derived Demand Function for Labor**

A Competitive Firm's Short-Run Demand Function for Labor

A Competitive Firm's Long-Run Demand Function for Labor

Application 17-1: Substitution and Scale Effects in the Airline Industry

The Short- and Long-Run Market Demand Functions for Labor

■ **17-2   The Supply Function of Labor**

The Work-Leisure Choice

The Income and Substitution Effects of a Wage Change

Application 17-2: A General Assistance Program and the Work-Leisure Choice

The Aggregate Supply Function of Labor and the Equilibrium Wage

The Effect of a Minimum Wage on the Employment of Workers

■ **17-3   Demand for Labor by a Price-Making Firm**

■ **17-4   Investment in Human Capital**

The Present Value of Earnings

The Equilibrium Earnings of a College Graduate

Application 17-3: Has the Wage Premium for a College Education Peaked?

■ **17-5   Training Employees**

General Training

Firm-Specific Training

Application 17-4: Turnover and Tenure in the United States and in Japan

■ **17-6   Compensation Based on Input or Output**

Application 17-5: Problems with the Use of Incentive Pay

■ **17-7   Using Wage Policy as an Incentive Mechanism**

Incentive Compensation and Mandatory Retirement

■ **Summary**

■ **Key Terms**

■ **Review Questions**

■ **Exercises**

Firms use factors of production such as labor and capital to produce products. To employ such factors of production, firms enter markets called factor markets and must pay the prices that the factors command. In this chapter we focus on how prices of factors of production are determined. An important factor market is the labor market. When we look at labor markets, we see an array of different wage rates and salaries. In any one year there are vast differences in worker earnings. What determines these earning differentials? There is common agreement that earnings are systematically related to the education and the experience of the worker. Historically, the average earnings of college graduates have exceeded the average earnings of high school graduates. Indeed, as of this writing, the percentage difference between the average earnings of a college-educated worker and the average earnings of a worker with only a high school education is near an all-time high in the United States. One issue we are interested in addressing is what determines the differential between the earnings of college-educated and high school–educated workers.

Firms demand labor services. How is the firm's demand function for labor derived and how is this demand function related to the price of the product that the firm sells and the productivity of its workers? The first part of the chapter demonstrates how an individual firm's demand function for labor and the market demand function for labor are derived. On the supply side of the factor market, we examine how individuals decide whether to participate in the work force and how much work time to supply. By working within this demand and supply framework, we are able to show how wage rates are determined in one important factor market, the market for labor.

17-1   THE DERIVED DEMAND FUNCTION FOR LABOR

To find a firm's demand function for labor, assume initially that the firm is a price taker in both the product and the factor markets. Therefore, it can sell each unit at a given price and employ workers at a given wage. Later we will consider a firm that is a monopolist in the product market but is still a price taker in the labor market, for example, a cable TV firm that has a local monopoly but competes with many other firms for technicians and executives in factor markets.

In this section we derive the short- and long-run demand functions for labor. Economists describe the demand functions for factors of production as **derived demand functions.** The demand function for each factor of production exists because there is a demand function for the product. Consequently, the demand function for every factor is derived from the market demand function for the product.

The analysis begins with the production function of a firm, which, you will recall, shows how the firm combines factors of production to produce output. In Chapter 5 we defined the production function of the firm as

$$q = f(L, K) \qquad \text{(Production Function)} \qquad \textbf{(17-1)}$$

where q is total quantity produced per period, L is labor input, and K is capital input. For example, in a clerical office, the output might be the number of pages

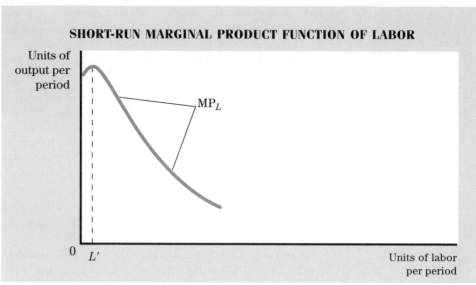

Figure 17-1   The marginal product of labor eventually declines as more workers are added to a fixed number of machines.

per month of word processing. The factors of production are the number of operators skilled at word processing (L) and the number of personal computers (K). The price of labor is w, and the price of capital is the rental value of capital, r.

A Competitive Firm's Short-Run Demand Function for Labor

In the short run we assume that the firm has a fixed quantity of capital, K_0, and the cost of the K_0 units of capital is a sunk cost. So, rK_0 is a sunk cost. Given K_0, the **marginal product** of labor is defined as

$$\text{MP}_L = \left.\frac{\Delta q}{\Delta L}\right|_{K=K_0} \qquad \text{(Marginal Product of Labor)} \qquad (17\text{-}2)$$

The marginal product of labor function shows the increase in output, Δq, when the number of workers increases by ΔL with the number of machines held constant. Figure 17-1 displays the marginal product of labor function with capital held constant. The increment in output relative to the increment in labor, $\Delta q/\Delta L$, is on the vertical axis, and the units of labor, L, are on the horizontal axis. In the figure the marginal product of labor increases initially, but adding still more labor to a fixed number of machines causes it to decline eventually so that the marginal product function slopes downward and to the right when the firm hires more than L' units.

The incremental revenue due to an increase in labor of ΔL is the **marginal revenue product** of labor (MRP_L):

$$\text{MRP}_L = \frac{\Delta R}{\Delta L} \quad \text{(Marginal Revenue Product)} \qquad \textbf{(17-3)}$$

$$= \frac{\Delta R}{\Delta q} \frac{\Delta q}{\Delta L}\bigg|_{K=K_0}$$

The marginal revenue product of labor equals the marginal revenue from selling the additional output times the marginal product from employing ΔL more units of labor.

> The marginal revenue product measures the additional revenue the firm receives when it sells the additional output produced with ΔL more workers.

Table 17-1 shows how the marginal revenue product is derived in a numerical example when the price is $20. For example, when the firm increases the number of workers from 1 to 2, total output in column 2 increases from 5 units to 9 units. The marginal product from adding the second worker is 4 units of output (column 3). Because the firm is a price taker, the price remains at $20 (column 4) although the firm is now selling 9 rather than 5 units and is receiving $180 rather than $100 in total revenue (column 5). The marginal revenue, $\Delta R/\Delta q$, from the sale of 4 additional units is $80/4 = $20 per unit (column 6). The marginal revenue product from adding the second worker is 4($20) = $80 (column 7).

When the firm is a competitor in the product market, marginal revenue equals price. When price is substituted for MR into equation 17-3, we have the marginal revenue product of a *price-taking firm*, which is called by convention the **value of the marginal product.**

$$\text{VMP}_L = P \frac{\Delta q}{\Delta L} \quad \text{(Value of the Marginal Product)} \qquad \textbf{(17-4)}$$

Table 17-1   DERIVING THE MARGINAL REVENUE PRODUCT OF LABOR FOR A PRICE-TAKING FIRM

NUMBER OF WORKERS, L (1)	TOTAL OUTPUT, q (2)	MARGINAL PRODUCT, $\Delta q/\Delta L$ (3)	PRICE, P ($) (4)	TOTAL REVENUE, R ($) (5)	MARGINAL REVENUE, $\Delta R/\Delta q$ ($) (6)	MARGINAL REVENUE PRODUCT, $\text{MRP}_L = (\Delta R/\Delta q)(\Delta q/\Delta L)$ ($) (7)
1	5	5	20	100	20	100
2	9	4	20	180	20	80
3	12	3	20	240	20	60
4	14	2	20	280	20	40

The value of the marginal product measures the increase in revenue due to an increase in the number of workers, or $\Delta R/\Delta L$, for a price-taking firm and equals price times the marginal product of labor.

> For a price-taking firm the value of the marginal product equals the price times the marginal product of labor.

To determine how many workers it should employ, the firm must compare the incremental revenue from employing another worker with the incremental cost of hiring another worker. Let's demonstrate this important proposition and show how the firm determines the number of workers.

The short-run profits of the firm are

$$\text{Profits} = \text{Revenue} - \text{Labor cost} - \text{Capital cost}$$

$$\pi = Pq - wL - rK_0 \qquad \text{(Short-Run Profits of Firm)} \qquad \textbf{(17-5)}$$

where r is the rental value of capital and rK_0 is a sunk cost. Substituting $f(L, K_0)$ for q yields an equation showing how the firm's short-run profit depends on the number of workers.

$$\pi = Pf(L, K_0) - wL - rK_0$$

Assume that the firm selects the number of workers, L, to maximize short-run profits. The value of the marginal product measures the increase in revenue a competitive firm receives by employing another worker. Equation 17-5 shows that the additional cost of another worker is w since the firm pays each worker w per period. Therefore, the firm increases the number of workers until the value of the marginal product equals the marginal cost of hiring another worker.[1]

$$\text{VMP}_L = w \qquad \begin{array}{l} \text{(Profit-Maximizing Employment Condition} \\ \text{for a Price-Taking Firm)} \end{array} \qquad \textbf{(17-6)}$$

Substituting $P\,(\Delta q/\Delta L)$ for VMP_L,

$$P\frac{\Delta q}{\Delta L} = w$$

> A price-taking firm increases the number of workers until the value of the marginal product equals the wage of the additional worker.

---

[1] In the short run the fixed factor is capital. The short-run profits of the firm are

$$\pi = Pf(L, K_0) - wL - rK_0$$

where rK_0 is a sunk cost. The company maximizes profits by increasing L until

$$\frac{d\pi}{dL} = P\frac{\partial f}{\partial q} - w = 0$$

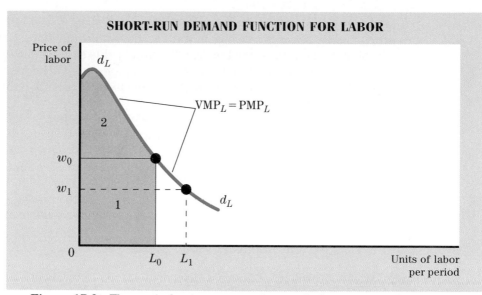

Figure 17-2   The vertical axis measures the marginal revenue product of labor, or price of labor. The firm's short-run demand function for labor is the value of the marginal product function. If the wage is w_0, the firm will demand L_0 units of labor to produce the profit-maximizing quantity in the short run. The value of the marginal product function represents the firm's demand for labor as long as revenues at least equal total labor cost.

In Figure 17-2 the wage is w_0 and so the firm demands L_0 units of labor in the short run, where $\text{VMP}_L = w_0$. This is one point on the firm's short-run demand function for labor. The firm maximizes profits if it employs L_0 workers when the wage is w_0, given the price of the product, the rental value of capital, and K_0. Area 1 shows the total labor cost of the firm, or $w_0 L_0$. The total revenue received by the firm when it employs L_0 workers is equal to the area under the value of the marginal product function up to L_0. Since area 1 is equal to total payments to labor, area 2 represents the total amount paid to all other factors of production plus any profits or losses. If the wage decreases to w_1, Figure 17-2 shows that quantity demanded increases to L_1 units of labor. This is another point where $\text{VMP}_L = w$ but where the wage is lower. Other points on the value of marginal product function are also points on the firm's short-run demand for labor function.

> The value of the marginal product function is a competitive firm's short-run demand function for labor.

Because the value of the marginal product of labor function slopes downward, the number of workers hired by the firm increases in the short run when the wage decreases.

A Competitive Firm's Long-Run Demand Function for Labor

The long-run effect of a change in wage on the employment of a factor differs from the short-run effect. In the long run the firm is able to substitute labor for capital when the wage declines and change its scale of output. The long-run effect of a change in the price of a factor must take account of the **substitution effect** and the **scale effect.**

To observe how these changes influence the firm's long-run demand function, consider how a single firm responds to a wage reduction assuming the price of the product is constant. Recall from Chapter 5 that when a firm produces a given quantity at minimum total cost, it is at some point on its **expansion path.** The expansion path identifies that combination of factors that produces each quantity at lowest cost. At each point on this path the slope of the firm's isocost line equals the slope of the isoquant as the firm uses the least-cost combination of factors to produce each rate of output.

When the firm is on its expansion path,

$$\text{MRTS}_{KL} = -\frac{w}{r} \qquad \text{(Condition for Minimum Cost)} \qquad \textbf{(17-7)}$$

MRTS_{KL} is the marginal rate of technical substitution between capital and labor—the slope of an isoquant—and the slope of the isocost line is $-w/r$. You may want to review Chapter 5 to see why a firm must satisfy equation 17-7 if it produces a given output at minimum total cost. Given the price of the product, there is one point on the firm's expansion path that coincides with its profit-maximizing quantity. In Figure 17-3a the firm maximizes profits by producing q_0 units where P_0 equals the long-run marginal cost. This profit-maximizing quantity can be used in Figure 17-3b to find the corresponding isoquant q_0 at point A. Point A shows that the lowest cost of producing q_0 units combines L_0 workers with K_0 machines. Given P_0 and r_0, we can say that this company's long-run demand for workers is L_0 when the wage is w_0. This is one point on the firm's long-run demand function for labor.

To produce q_0 at long-run minimum cost, the firm combines K_0 machines with L_0 workers. The value of the marginal product of labor given that the firm has K_0 machines is VMP_0 in Figure 17-4. Notice that the short-run demand function for labor, VMP_0, intersects the long-run demand for labor when the wage is w_0 and employment is L_0. Given that the firm has K_0 machines and the wage is w_0, the firm maximizes short-run profits by employing L_0 workers. In the long run, when the numbers of machines and workers are variable, the company maximizes profits by producing q_0 units with L_0 workers and K_0 machines. Therefore, we can say that the firm demands L_0 workers when the wage is w_0, given r_0 and P_0.

To grasp how a change in the wage changes the number of workers demanded by the firm in the long run, consider what happens to the quantity of labor demanded when the wage rate decreases from w_0 to w_1. First, the isocost lines in Figure 17-3b pivot around point A and become flatter because w decreases relative to r. Labor becomes cheaper relative to capital, and so the firm substitutes labor for capital to produce any given output at minimum cost.

In Figure 17-3b the firm's expansion path becomes bb because the wage falls.

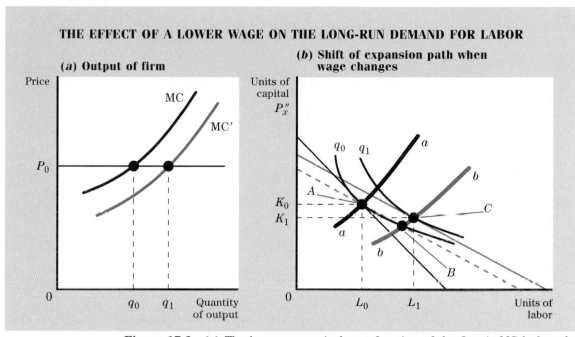

THE EFFECT OF A LOWER WAGE ON THE LONG-RUN DEMAND FOR LABOR

(a) Output of firm

(b) Shift of expansion path when wage changes

Figure 17-3 (*a*) The long-run marginal cost function of the firm is MC before the wage rate decreases from w_0 to w_1. The expansion path of the firm is *aa* in (*b*). At a price of P_0 the company produces q_0 at minimum total cost by combining L_0 units of labor with K_0 units of capital. When the wage is w_0, the firm demands L_0 units of labor. A fall in the wage rate shifts the marginal cost function to MC′, and the company expands output to q_1. (*b*) A fall in the wage rate makes labor less expensive relative to capital, and the isocost lines become flatter. Because of the lower wage, the firm's new expansion path becomes *bb*. It produces q_1 units by increasing the number of workers to L_1.

The long-run total and average cost functions of the firm shift downward. The quantity where long-run average cost reaches a minimum may either increase or decrease when the wage falls. In the more common case the minimum increases and the new long-run marginal cost function shifts down. This can be seen in Figure 17-3*a*, where the MC function shifts down and becomes the MC′ function and the firm's new profit-maximizing output becomes $q_1 > q_0$. In the long run the firm produces q_1 units at lowest total cost at point C in Figure 17-3*b*, where the slope of the new isocost line equals the slope of the isoquant for q_1. Therefore, the firm incurs the minimum cost of producing q_1 units by combining K_1 machines with L_1 workers when the wage rate falls to w_1. This is another point on the firm's long-run demand function for labor. Given P_0 and r_0, the company demands L_1 workers when the wage is w_1.

Figure 17-4 highlights two points on the firm's long-run demand function for labor when the wage is either w_0 or w_1. When the company has K_1 machines, the value of the marginal product function is VMP_1 and it intersects the long-run

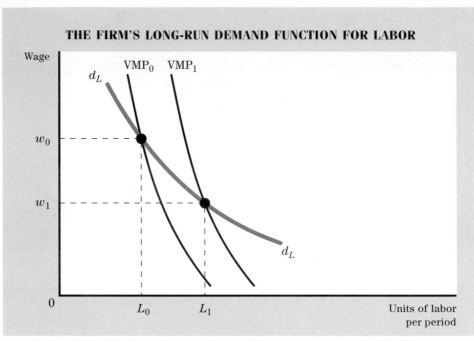

THE FIRM'S LONG-RUN DEMAND FUNCTION FOR LABOR

Figure 17-4   The firm's long-run demand function for labor is $d_L d_L$. If the company has K_0 machines, the value of the marginal product is VMP_0. If the firm has K_1 machines, the value of the marginal product is VMP_1. The long-run demand function for labor is more elastic than the short-run demand function.

demand for labor where the firm hires L_1 workers when the wage is w_1. The firm maximizes short-run profits by employing L_1 workers when the wage is w_1. So, the quantity of labor demanded by the firm is L_1 in the short run when the wage is w_1, a point on the *short-run* demand function for labor. This point is also on the firm's *long-run* demand function for labor because the company maximizes profits by producing q_1 units with L_1 workers and K_1 machines given the price of the product and factor prices.

The firm's long-run demand function for labor is the net result of two effects caused by the decline in the wage. The first is the substitution effect. For a given output, the firm substitutes more labor for less capital when the wage falls. In Figure 17-3*b* the substitution effect is the move from point *A* to point *B* along the isoquant representing q_0 (holding output constant). The second effect is the **scale effect.** A fall in the wage rate can (but need not) lower the long-run marginal cost of producing the product near q_0. When it does shift the long-run marginal cost function down in the vicinity of q_0, a wage cut increases the firm's profit-maximizing quantity. This is shown in Figure 17-3*a* where the profit-maximizing output increases to q_1 units. Since output increases, the scale effect is the move from point

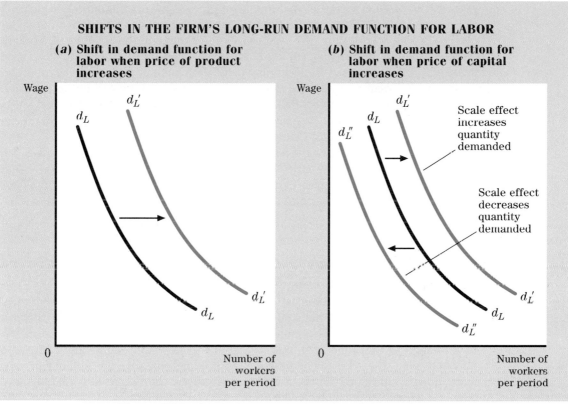

Figure 17-5 (*a*) An increase in the price of the product causes the firm's demand function for labor to shift outward. (*b*) The firm's demand function for labor can shift outward or inward when the price of capital increases.

B to point *C* in Figure 17-3*b*. The scale effect also increases the firm's long-run demand for labor.[2]

> The change in the quantity of labor demanded by a firm due to a wage change is equal to the sum of a substitution effect and a scale effect.

Now that we have derived the short- and long-run demand function for labor, we want to consider several factors that cause the long-run demand function for labor to shift. One determinant is the price of the product. An increase in the price of the product shifts the value of the marginal product to the right. In Figure 17-5*a* the company's demand function for labor shifts from $d_L d_L$ to $d'_L d'_L$ when the

[2] A more advanced analysis would show that the firm demands more units of labor at a lower wage even when the scale effect causes the firm to produce less output.

price of the product increases and the firm produces more units. Another factor is the price of capital. The firm substitutes labor for capital when the price of capital increases. The substitution effect measures the change in the number of workers employed when the price of capital changes, holding output constant. When the price of capital increases, the firm may produce a smaller or a larger output, and so the scale effect can either decrease or increase its long-run output and the number of workers employed. Figure 17-5b shows that the demand function shifts outward and becomes $d_L'd_L'$ because the scale effect increases output and, consequently, the quantity of labor demanded. The figure also shows the case where the demand function shifts inward and becomes $d_L''d_L''$ because the scale effect decreases output and the demand for labor by more than the substitution effect increases the quantity of labor demanded. Therefore, a rise in the price of capital can either shift the firm's long-run demand function for labor outward or inward depending on the size and sign of the scale effect.

APPLICATION **17-1**

Substitution and Scale Effects in the Airline Industry

Daniel Rich investigated the elasticity of demand for airline pilots in a statistical study of labor demand. In his study he used observations from individual airlines over the 1971–85 period.[3] He wanted to estimate the substitution and scale effects of a change in the wage of pilots. He estimated how the employment of pilots changed when the wage of pilots changed holding constant the number of seat miles flown, a measure of firm output (substitution effect), and how employment changed when output changed (the scale effect). By combining the two effects, he derived an estimate of the full price elasticity of demand for pilots. As for the substitution effect, he expected to find a negative elasticity since a fall in the wage of pilots should increase the demand for pilots. As for the scale effect, he expected to find that a fall in pilot compensation lowers the marginal cost of producing a seat mile and increases the number of seat miles that an airline produces. So, the scale effect should yield a negative elasticity as well.

What were Rich's major findings? First, his estimated substitution elasticity turned out to be $-.51$. A 1 percent wage decrease increases pilot employment by about a half of one percent holding constant seat miles. His econometric estimates indicate that the ratios of pilot employment to planes, to maintenance staff, or to other employees are not fixed but change as the wage of pilots changes. From Rich's estimate of the substitution effect, we can say that the quantity of pilots demanded increases when pilot wage decreases. Hence, the demand for pilots satisfies the law of demand.

However, the substitution effect underestimates the wage elasticity of the demand for pilots because it ignores the scale effect of a wage decrease. A fall in the wage increases the output of an airline and this scale effect increases the demand for pilots. Rich finds a scale effect of $-.07$ so that the total effect of a 1

[3] Daniel P. Rich, "On the Elasticity of Labor Demand," *Quarterly Review of Economics and Business* 30, no. 3 (1990), pp. 31–41.

percent wage decrease equals $-.58$, or an increase of nearly six-tenths of one percent in pilot employment. It is through studies like this that economists learn more about the quantitative magnitude of labor demand elasticity. The results of Rich's demand study indicate that the demand function for pilots slopes downward.

The Short- and Long-Run Market Demand Functions for Labor

Now let's move from the firm's demand function for labor to the industry's demand for labor. In the model, workers are employed in many industries, and so the aggregate demand for labor (of a given quality) is made up of the demand by companies operating in many industries.

Since each firm is a price taker, the price of the product does not change when the firm's output changes because of a wage change. While the firm has no effect on the price, the price of the product does change whenever a wage change causes the total industry output to change. Therefore, the long-run market demand function for labor by all firms in a competitive industry must take account of the effect on price of an increase in industry output when the wage rate falls.

Therefore, we cannot simply add up each firm's long-run demand function for labor to get the industry's long-run demand function for labor because the firm's demand function was derived by assuming that price is constant. While a change in the output of one firm does not affect price, the market price will change when *industry* output responds to the wage change. When the wage falls, the long-run average cost function of all existing firms and for potential entrants into an industry shifts downward. When the long-run industry supply function of the product shifts outward, the equilibrium price decreases and industry output increases. The industry scale effect increases the quantity of labor demanded by all firms in the industry in the long run. Therefore, each industry's long-run demand function for labor slopes downward—a wage decrease increases the total quantity of labor demanded.[4]

Similar logic applies to the short-run industry demand function for labor. A fall in the wage rate shifts the industry short-run supply function of the product down and causes the price to fall. The fixed number of firms in the industry will supply more units in the short run, and so the industry scale effect is positive. Because the firms demand more labor to produce more output, the short-run industry demand function for labor also slopes downward.

> The market demand function for labor slopes downward in both the short and long runs.

Our analysis of the demand side of the market for labor is now complete. We have derived the short- and the long-run market demand functions for labor for each industry. Now let's consider the supply side of the market.

---

[4] If other industries in the economy used this type of labor, the demand functions of the firms in these industries would have to be included in deriving the long-run demand for labor.

17-2   THE SUPPLY FUNCTION OF LABOR

The supply function of labor is based on the optimizing behavior of a consumer-worker. For a given wage, an individual must decide whether to participate in the labor force and, if so, how much time to devote to work. Starting with a utility-maximizing consumer-worker, we derive the supply function of a worker and then aggregate the supply functions of all workers to produce an aggregate supply function of labor.

The Work-Leisure Choice

Consider a one-period model and assume that each consumer has a utility function that depends on C, total *spending on a composite good*, and h, hours or *days of leisure*. The consumer's utility increases with an increase in either C or h, and the utility function is

$$U = U(C, h) \qquad \text{(Utility Function)} \qquad \textbf{(17-8)}$$

The individual's indifference curves in Figure 17-6 are negatively sloped because an increase in either C or h must coincide with a decrease in the other good for utility to remain constant.

The budget constraint of the individual requires total spending on goods to equal income. The wage per unit of time is w and a worker of a particular quality cannot affect his or her wage by working more or less. So, total income of the individual is $w(H - h)$, where H is total time available and can represent 24 hours per day or 365 days per year depending on what the model is to explain.

Total income $=$ Total spending (C)

Total spending $(C) =$ Wage rate [Total hours (H) $-$ Hours of leisure (h)]

$$C = w(H - h) \qquad \text{(Budget Constraint)} \qquad \textbf{(17-9)}$$

Because this is a one-period model, the consumer spends all income on consumption. To keep within the confines of the two-good model, assume that H represents the total time for work and leisure activities. The budget constraint of the consumer is line bc' in Figure 17-6. The consumer's opportunity cost of taking one more hour of leisure is a reduction of w in spending on consumer goods, and so the slope of the budget line equals $-w$. The consumer maximizes utility by selecting C_0 and h_0 at point A where the consumer's marginal rate of substitution between spending on goods and hours of leisure equals $-w$. By this method, we have derived one point on the worker's supply curve since this worker will supply $H - h_0$ hours of work when the wage is w_0. The inset shows that the consumer will not supply any hours of work when the wage rate is only w^* and the budget constraint is ac'. At this relatively low wage the worker consumes only leisure. w^* is said to be the worker's reservation wage.

If the wage rate increases to w_1, the budget constraint rotates around point c' on the horizontal axis and becomes cc'. Hours of leisure decrease to h_1 because the worker has the incentive to devote more time to work and less time to leisure, and so spending increases to C_1. If the wage rate increases to w_2, the budget

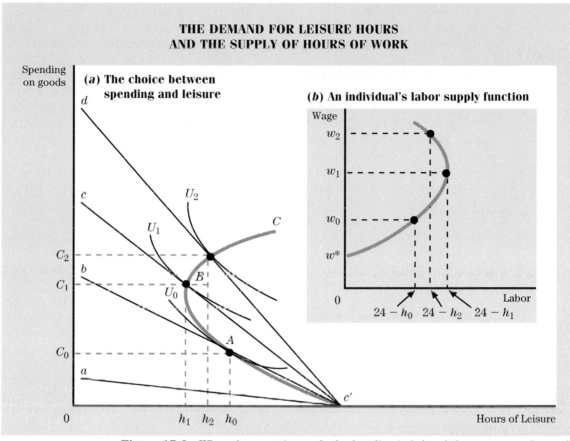

Figure 17-6   When the wage is w_0, the budget line is bc' and the consumer demands h_0 hours of leisure. When the wage increases to w_1, the budget line becomes cc' and the demand for leisure decreases to h_1 hours. At a still higher wage the budget line becomes dc' and the demand for leisure increases to h_2. The wage-leisure curve is the curve $c'ABC$ and shows how the wage affects leisure hours. The supply function of work hours is $24 - h$ and is shown in the inset.

constraint becomes dc' and hours of leisure increase to h_2. At the higher wage, the consumer's income is sufficiently high that he or she wants to consume more leisure.

The curve $c'ABC$ connects all points of tangency between the different budget lines and the corresponding indifference curves. From point c' to point B along the curve, wage increases decrease leisure and increase work. From point B to point C wage increases increase leisure and reduce hours of work. The graph in the inset shows that the individual works more hours when the wage increases from w_0 to w_1 and then works fewer hours when the wage increases to w_2.

The Income and Substitution Effects of a Wage Change

We can better understand the different responses of the individual to a wage increase by developing the income and substitution effects of a wage change. In Figure 17-7a an increase in wage decreases hours of leisure from h_0 to h_1. The total change in leisure caused by the change in wage is the sum of a substitution effect and an income effect. Recall from Chapter 3 that the substitution effect of a price change with utility held constant measured the change in the quantity demanded when the price of one good fell relative to that of another. In the same way the substitution effect of a wage change measures the change in hours of leisure when wage changes, holding utility constant. The substitution effect is the move from point 0 to point 2 in Figure 17-7a. Hours of leisure decrease from h_0 to h_2 because of the increase in wage. The income effect measures the change in hours of leisure demanded because of the increase in individual income. It is measured by a parallel shift in the budget line, in this case from dd to cc. As income increases, this individual's demand for leisure increases from h_2 to h_1 since leisure is a normal good. However, the substitution effect is larger than the income effect so a rise in wage has the net result of reducing the demand for leisure hours and increasing the hours of work supplied by the worker.

Figure 17-7b differs from Figure 17-7a because the income effect is larger than the substitution effect. Again, the substitution effect is the move from point 0 to point 2 where the demand for leisure decreases from h_0 to h_2 when wage increases. The income effect is the move from point 2 to point 1 and in this case increases the demand for leisure from h_2 to h_1. The income effect is larger than the substitution effect in this case. Consequently, a rise in the wage rate increases the demand for leisure and decreases the supply of hours of work. It can be concluded that a backward-bending supply function of labor will occur when the income effect outweighs the substitution effect.

> A worker supplies less labor at a higher wage if leisure is a normal good and the income effect outweighs the substitution effect.

As you can see from this analysis, the substitution effect and the income effect work at cross-purposes. The substitution effect encourages the worker to supply more hours of work at a higher wage. On the other hand the income effect of a higher wage increases the worker's demand for leisure hours. At a relatively low wage rate the substitution effect of a higher wage is likely to dominate the income effect, leading to a net increase in hours of work supplied, but at higher wage rates, the income effect is likely to dominate the substitution effect so that hours of work supplied decline. Over this range of wages, the supply curve of a worker is backward bending and should come as no surprise.

APPLICATION **17-2**

A General Assistance Program and the Work-Leisure Choice

Our model of the work-leisure choice can be used to evaluate the consequences of a public policy that guarantees all members of society a minimum income. In

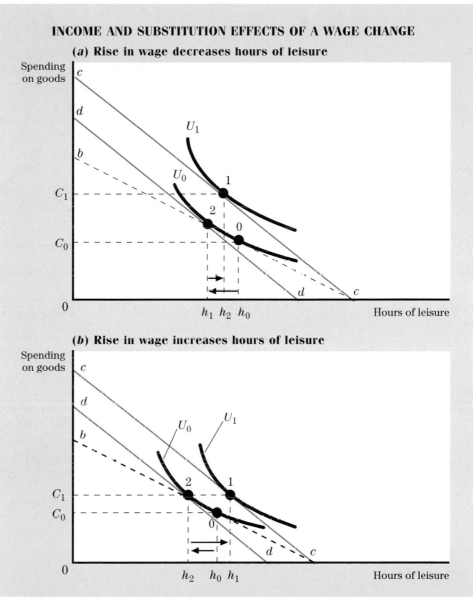

Figure 17-7   (*a*) As the wage increases, the demand for leisure falls from h_0 to h_1. The substitution effect is the move from point 0 to point 2 such that the demand for leisure decreases from h_0 to h_2. The utility of the individual is held constant at U_0 when the wage rate increases because the income of the individual is reduced. As a result, the new budget line *dd* is tangent to U_0 at point 2. The income effect is the move from point 2 to point 1. An increase in income increases the demand for leisure from h_2 to h_1. The substitution effect is larger than the income effect so the net result is that hours of leisure decrease. (*b*) The income effect outweighs the substitution effect, so the net result is that hours of leisure increase.

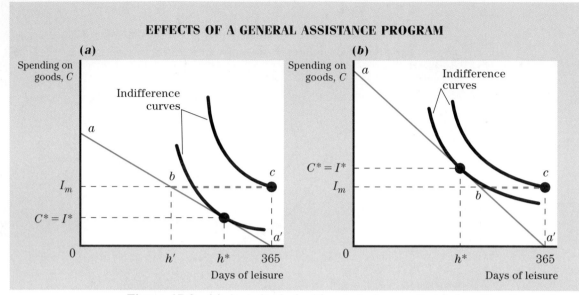

Figure 17-8   (*a*) An individual with private income that is less than the minimum income of I_m increases days of leisure from h^* to 365 and income from I^* to I_m. (*b*) An individual has a private income of I^* and h^* days of leisure before a general assistance program becomes available. When the general assistance program becomes available, this individual increases leisure from h^* to 365 days, preferring 365 days of leisure and an income of I_m to h^* days of leisure and I^* income.

many countries the general public has supported general assistance programs that establish a safety net for the less fortunate members of society by guaranteeing each individual a minimum income. Initially, it was thought that the primary effect of a general assistance program was simply to redistribute income but there is now a growing recognition of the disincentive effects of general assistance programs.

Let's look at the effect of a general assistance program on the work-leisure choice. In Figure 17-8*a* the individual's budget constraint is aa'. Given the wage rate of this individual, he chooses to consume h^* days of leisure a year and to spend C^* on a composite good. Now suppose that society deems this outcome unacceptable and introduces a general assistance program which guarantees an individual a minimum income of I_m per period. The first step in analyzing the economic effects of a general assistance program is to determine how it changes the budget constraint. The new budget constraint of the individual becomes abc since income cannot fall below I_m. If private income is less than I_m, he receives general assistance, and so the sum of private earnings plus public assistance equals I_m.

If the individual does not work at all, general assistance guarantees an annual income of I_m. What incentive does this individual have to work? If he earns a daily wage of w, each day of work results in a dollar-for-dollar decrease in public assistance. In essence there is 100 percent taxation of private income up to an annual income of I_m. You can imagine the disincentive effects of a general assistance program. At any point on the flat segment bc the individual is still receiving some general assistance. If he consumes less than h' days of leisure, his market income exceeds I_m and he is no longer eligible for general assistance.

What are some of the consequences of general assistance programs? First, there is a redistribution of income. However, the redistribution of income creates a disincentive effect because of the 100 percent tax on private earnings up to annual income of I_m. Figure 17-8a shows an individual moving to a higher indifference curve at point c by opting for general assistance and performing no work at all. The reward for not working is an increase in income *and* an increase in days of leisure from h^* to 365 days.

You might think that this analysis of the economic effects of a general assistance program is complete. However, those with incomes below I_m are not the only ones affected. In the long run a general assistance program can affect individuals with private incomes greater than I_m. Figure 17-8b shows an individual with higher earning power and a budget constraint of aa'. Without a general assistance program, she selects h' days of leisure and earns income of I^* that is greater than I_m. With the introduction of a general assistance program she reaches a higher indifference curve by opting for the combination of I_m and 365 days of leisure. So, this type of assistance also encourages some individuals with earnings greater than I_m to reduce their hours of work in order to qualify for the program.

The disincentive effects that the theory points out have become a matter of controversy in political debates in recent years. A growing recognition of the disincentive effects of general assistance programs has led to calls to modify these programs in ways that will reduce these effects.

The Aggregate Supply Function of Labor and the Equilibrium Wage

Individual supply functions are summed horizontally to derive the aggregate supply function of labor. Each point on the aggregate supply function is obtained by simply summing the labor supplied by all individuals at that wage. Figure 17-9 shows the different supply functions of hours worked for *selected* workers and a positively sloped aggregate supply function *SS*. In this instance the long-run supply of labor has a positive slope even though some but not all workers have backward-bending supply curves.

In a competitive labor market, the equilibrium wage occurs where the demand and the supply functions intersect. In Figure 17-10 quantity demanded equals quantity supplied when the wage is w^* (for a given quality of worker) and the total units of labor employed in the industry is L^* units. Total labor earnings are w^*L^*, and area 1 represents supplier "surplus." The supply function shows how much of a wage increase is required to increase the quantity of workers supplied. While every worker except the last one employed is willing to work at a lower wage, all workers receive w^*. For example, the first worker is willing to supply labor if the

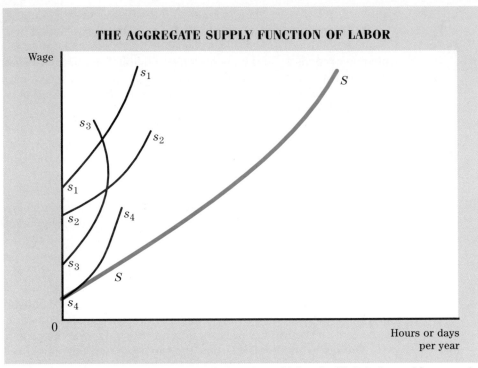

Figure 17-9   The aggregate supply function of labor is *SS*. It is formed by summing horizontally the individual supply functions of workers in many firms and industries. The supply functions of only four workers are shown here.

wage is only w_0. The difference between w^* and w_0 is the surplus the first worker receives. By adding up all these surplus areas, we arrive at area 1 which is supplier surplus. Area 2 is equal to total payments to other factors of production.

To retrace our steps, we began with the production function of the firm and derived the firm's and the market demand functions for labor in the short and long runs. By relying on utility maximization, we determined the individual's labor supply function and the aggregate supply function. Finally, we noted that the intersection of the aggregate demand and supply functions determines the equilibrium wage.

The Effect of a Minimum Wage on the Employment of Workers

Economists have been interested in the effect of a minimum wage on employment. The man-on-the-street view of minimum wage legislation is that it will increase the income of lower-income workers. We now know that this view is too simple because it erroneously equates a higher wage rate with a higher income. This would be true if the minimum wage had no employment effects. However, eco-

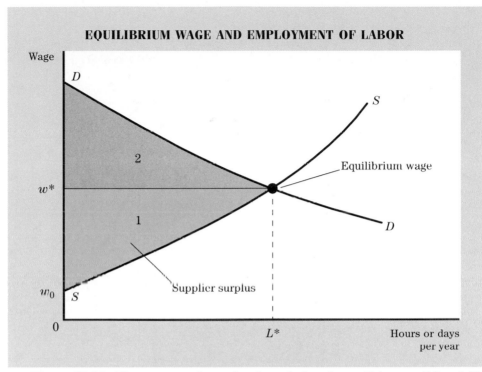

Figure 17-10   The aggregate demand and supply functions of labor are *DD* and *SS*. The aggregate demand function is formed by summing each industry's demand function horizontally. Equilibrium wage is w^*, and total employment is L^*.

nomic theory and empirical studies indicate minimum wage legislation has employment effects. In this section we examine the economic consequences of minimum wage legislation.

When the first minimum wage legislation in the United States was passed in 1938, it was applicable only to certain sectors and to larger firms in the economy. Over time the coverage of the legislation has expanded so that it now covers about 90 percent of private industry employees. Nevertheless, an "uncovered" sector has always existed in the United States. The presence of an uncovered sector means that some workers who can no longer get jobs in the covered sector when the minimum wage increases will find jobs in the uncovered sector. Consequently, some workers, who were employed in the covered sector, can no longer find employment there because of the higher wage and can find employment only in the uncovered sector. This means that the supply curve of workers in the uncovered sector shifts outward as some workers move from the covered sector to the uncovered sector, and find employment but at a lower wage. Figure 17-11 shows this adjustment to a rise in the minimum wage. Before a minimum wage is imposed, the demand and supply curves in what will become the covered sector after the

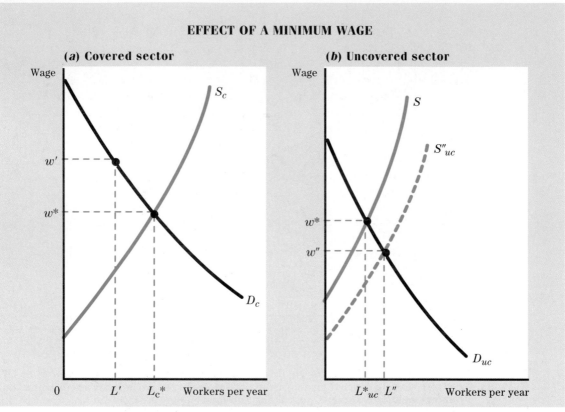

Figure 17-11   A minimum wage of w' decreases employment in the covered sector and increases employment in the uncovered sector by lowering the wage to w''.

minimum wage law is passed are D_c and S_c in Figure 17-11a. The equilibrium wage and employment in this sector are w^* and L^*.

In Figure 17-11b the demand and supply functions in what will become the uncovered sector are D_{uc} and S_{uc} before the passage of minimum wage legislation. The same wage must exist in both sectors before the minimum wage legislation is passed since workers in the two sectors are perfect substitutes for each other. After a minimum wage of w' is imposed, the wage increases in the covered sector and, consequently, the quantity of workers demanded in the covered sector decreases to L'. The minimum wage increases the cost of producing goods in the covered sector and prices in the covered sector rise relative to the prices of goods produced in the uncovered sector. Therefore, output and employment fall in the covered sector. Some of the workers who were previously employed in the covered sector will become unemployed or will move into the uncovered sector. This is shown in Figure 17-11b. As some workers move to the uncovered sector, the supply function in this sector shifts to S''. The wage in the uncovered sector falls to w''

and employment in the uncovered sector increases to L''. So, minimum wage legislation creates two markets for the same quality of labor and two wage rates.

Which groups of workers are most affected by minimum wage hikes? The results of most empirical studies point to teenagers, a larger fraction of whom are low-wage workers than is true for older and more experienced workers. Minority teenagers are especially affected by increases in minimum wage. While some workers benefit by being employed at w', others leave the work force permanently, become unemployed, or find employment in the lower-paying uncovered sector. As you can see, minimum wage legislation causes wage discrimination by creating two different wages for the same quality of labor. Some economists favor dealing with the problem of low-income workers by other means, for example, using income tax credits, rather than by direct intervention into the functioning of labor markets.

17-3   DEMAND FOR LABOR BY A PRICE-MAKING FIRM

While the firm's demand function for labor was derived assuming that the firm is a price taker, the analysis can be extended to include a price-making firm where marginal revenue is less than price. We substitute marginal revenue for price and calculate the marginal revenue product which is equal to the firm's *marginal revenue* times the marginal product of labor. Therefore, MRP_L is less than VMP_L for a price-making firm. For this type of firm the MRP_L automatically takes account of how the increased output produced by another worker affects price.

Table 17-2 displays a numerical example where the price decreases as the firm sells more units. It differs from Table 17-1 in two ways. First, the price decreases

Table 17-2   DERIVING THE MARGINAL REVENUE PRODUCT OF LABOR FOR A PRICE-MAKING FIRM

NUMBER OF WORKERS (1)	TOTAL OUTPUT, q (2)	MARGINAL PRODUCT, $\Delta q/\Delta L$ (3)	PRICE, P ($) (4)	TOTAL REVENUE, R ($) (5)	MARGINAL REVENUE, $\Delta R/\Delta q$ ($) (6)	MARGINAL REVENUE PRODUCT, $MRP_L = (\Delta R/\Delta q)(\Delta q/\Delta L)$ ($) (7)	MARGINAL COST OF FACTOR (w) ($) (8)
1	5	5	20	100	20.00	100	30
2	9	4	18	162	15.50	62	30
3	12	3	16	192	10.00	30	30
4	14	2	14	196	2.00	4	30

as the firm sells more units (column 4). Second, column 8 shows that the marginal cost of hiring another worker is $30 per day. The marginal revenue product can be determined by calculating the marginal revenue per unit increase in quantity. For example, when the firm hires the second worker, total output increases by four units (column 3). This causes the price to fall to $18, and so total revenue increases to $162. Therefore, the marginal revenue product of labor $\Delta R/\Delta L = \$62/1 = \$62$. Since the marginal cost of hiring another worker is $30 per worker, the marginal revenue product of labor exceeds w, and so the firm's profits increase. The company maximizes profits when it hires three workers where the marginal revenue product of labor is equal to the marginal cost of hiring another worker.

With a price-taking firm the marginal revenue product of the company becomes its demand function for labor whether it is operating in the short or in the long run. The only difference between the short- and long-run analysis is that the marginal product is calculated with units of capital that are fixed in the short run and variable in the long run. In either case the firm increases profits by expanding employment until the marginal revenue product of labor equals the marginal cost of labor.

17-4   INVESTMENT IN HUMAN CAPITAL

Until now, it has been assumed that each unit of labor is of a uniform quality and so all workers receive the same wage. Yet, we know that there are many wage rates and that workers are not all alike. Two important determinants of a worker's earnings are educational attainment and experience. Some workers enter the work force with considerable schooling—some with professional degrees—whereas others have only a high school degree or less.

What are the added benefits and costs that an individual receives from the additional schooling? Consider a high school graduate who must decide whether to enter the work force or to attend college. If she enters the work force immediately, annual earnings per year average I_h. If she attends college, she forgoes earning income for four years. This choice is reasonable if she expects to earn sufficiently more on average as a college graduate than as a high school graduate.

Figure 17-12 shows what the typical income streams will be if the individual has a high school degree or a college degree. The earning stream will be hh if she has a high school degree. If she attends college and enters the labor force after graduating from college, the income stream will be cc. In both instances earnings rise with experience, eventually level off, and subsequently decline. If the average earnings of a high school graduate would equal $20,000 per year over the first four years of work, the college student's opportunity cost, or the income forgone, is $80,000 if we ignore discounting and other payments and receipts such as tuition and summer earnings while in college.

The Present Value of Earnings

Because an individual forgoes income while attending college, a college education can be worthwhile only if the average annual earnings of the college graduate not

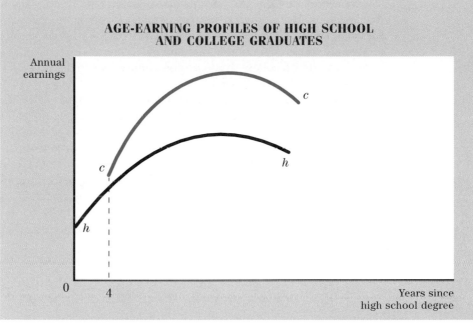

Figure 17-12 Typical age-earnings profiles of high school and college graduates. High school graduates earn income while college graduates are taking college courses. College graduates begin work four years later.

only exceed those of the high school graduate but exceed them by enough to make college the superior choice. To make two earning streams comparable, we must calculate the present value of each stream. Let the earnings of the high school graduate received at the end of year i be H_i and the earnings of a college graduate received at the end of year i be C_i. The present value of the earnings of the high school graduate is

$$PV_h = \frac{H_1}{(1 + i)^1} + \frac{H_2}{(1 + i)^2} + \frac{H_3}{(1 + i)^3} + \frac{H_4}{(1 + i)^4} + \frac{H_5}{(1 + i)^5}$$

$$+ \frac{H_6}{(1 + i)^6} + \frac{H_7}{(1 + i)^7} + \cdots + \frac{H_i}{(1 + i)^i}$$

The present value of the college graduate's income stream is

$$PV_c = \frac{C_5}{(1 + i)^5} + \frac{C_6}{(1 + i)^6} + \frac{C_7}{(1 + i)^7} + \cdots + \frac{C_i}{(1 + i)^i}$$

The college graduate forgoes income in years 1 to 4. Going to college is an investment, and in this case it is an investment in **human capital.** By forgoing income the college student hopes to increase future earning power by increasing her human capital.

By comparing the two earning streams, we can identify the main factors that encourage individuals to postpone earning income and to continue schooling. One factor is the interest rate. Given the two income streams, a higher interest rate makes a college education a less attractive choice because the higher *future* income earned by a college graduate contributes less to the present value of a college degree.

Why are college campuses populated with younger members of society? The later one begins a college education, the lower the present value of a college or postgraduate degree. The horizon over which the higher stream of income is earned shrinks as the age of the individual increases. A second reason an older individual is less likely to attend college is that the opportunity cost of an education is usually higher. Earnings increase with age as an individual gains experience. Therefore, the opportunity cost of attending college—the forgone earnings—is higher because the individual is more productive in the labor force. It is no accident that most people make investments in schooling when they are young and not at the end of their lifetime.

The Equilibrium Earnings of a College Graduate

This section compares the benefits of a college degree with those of a high school diploma and determines how much more valuable a college degree has been and is now. The decision to go to college depends on how much higher an individual's income will be with a college degree than with a high school diploma. Given his earnings with a high school diploma, what must a college graduate's minimum earnings be before he would consider going to college? To develop this analysis, we make a few assumptions.

1. The average annual earnings of high school graduates are I_h in each year, and the average annual earnings of college graduates are I_c in each year. We are simplifying the analysis by assuming that the annual income of each type of graduate is constant over time. Furthermore, we assume that each individual is paid at the end of the period.

2. Both types of graduates have infinite lives.

3. Tuition and part-time earnings are ignored.

4. The decision to attend college is based on present values.[5]

These assumptions simplify the analysis. In any real-world application they would be modified to take account of finite lifetimes or for different age-earning profiles of the two groups or for nonpecuniary benefits of a college education.

---

[5] For some individuals who value learning for learning's sake, our analysis would not be appropriate. Some students attend college to obtain a liberal education or to broaden their understanding. Others attend to have a broader set of job opportunities. They might be willing to attend college even if the present value of a college education is less than the present value of a high school education. They would instead be maximizing *utility*.

   Given these assumptions, the present value of the stream of income of the high school graduates is $PV_h = I_h/i$. The high school graduate receives an annual income of I_h at the end of the first year. The college graduate receives an annual income of I_c at the end of the fifth year. The present value of the stream of income for the college graduate is $PV_c = I_c/i(1 + i)^4$.

   Assuming the decision to pursue a college degree depends strictly on present-value considerations, the minimum annual earnings of the college graduate can be determined, given the earnings of the high school graduate, for the two present values to be equal. In other words, we can find the minimum earnings of a college graduate that will just compensate the individual for postponing income for the four years it takes to earn a degree—and it will provide a measure of the value of a college degree when we look at actual earnings data. If the earnings of a college graduate exceed the minimum required earnings, then the present value of a college degree exceeds the present value of a high school degree, and so the benefits of a college education are greater and more individuals will attend college.

   Given these assumptions, we can describe a long-run equilibrium in the market for a college education when the present values are equal. The present values of the two income flows are equal when

$$\frac{I_c}{i(1 + i)^4} = \frac{I_h}{i}$$

This equation can be solved for I_c/I_h by dividing both sides by I_h and then multiplying both sides by $i(1 + i)^4$. The ratio of a college graduate's earnings to the earnings of a high school graduate is

$$\frac{I_c}{I_h} = (1 + i)^4 \qquad \text{(Equilibrium in the Market for College Graduates)} \qquad \textbf{(17-10)}$$

   Figure 17-13 shows three possible values for the earnings of a college graduate while the earnings of a high school graduate are I_h. The present value of a college graduate's earnings exceeds the present value of a high school graduate's earnings, and so more high school graduates enroll in college if the earnings of college graduates are I_c'. If the earnings of a college graduate are I_c, the present value of a college graduate's earnings is equal to that of a high school graduate, and so fewer high school graduates enroll in college. If the earnings of a college graduate are only I_c'', the present value of a college graduate's earnings is less than that of a high school graduate, and so still fewer high school graduates will enter college.

   Table 17-3 shows the equilibrium ratio of earnings for selected interest rates. If the interest rate is 5 percent, then a college graduate must earn 22 percent more than a high school graduate to make the college education worth it, whereas if the interest rate is 10 percent, then the individual must earn 46 percent more annually. The higher i, the higher the annual earnings of college graduates must be relative to the annual earnings of high school graduates so that the present values of earnings are equal. These estimated ratios of annual earnings are suggestive. The particular numerical values will change somewhat when tuition costs, earnings from part-time work, and different age-earnings profiles are introduced.

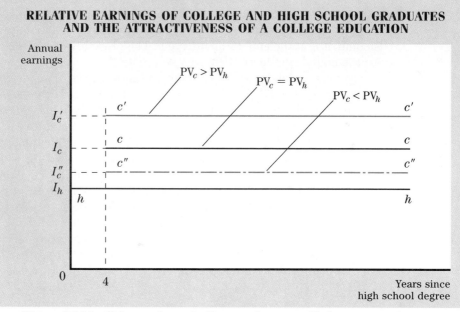

Figure 17-13   If the earnings of college graduates are I_c', the present value of a college graduate's earnings is greater than the present value of a high school graduate's earnings and more high school graduates enroll in college. If the earnings of college graduates are only I_c, fewer high school graduates enroll in college since the present value of a college graduate's earnings is the same as the present value of a high school graduate's earnings. If the annual earnings of a college graduate are only I_c'', still fewer high school graduates enroll in college.

Let's look at how actual annual earnings of college graduates compare to earnings of high school graduates. Table 17-4 compares the average earnings of full-time male workers with four years of college with the average earnings of full-time male workers who completed four years of high school from 1967 to 1989.

Table 17-3   EFFECT OF THE INTEREST RATE ON THE EQUILIBRIUM RATIO OF EARNINGS

ANNUAL INTEREST RATE (%)	EQUILIBRIUM RATIO OF EARNINGS OF COLLEGE GRADUATE TO EARNINGS OF HIGH SCHOOL GRADUATE
5.0%	1.22
7.5	1.34
10.0	1.46

Table 17-4   RELATIVE AVERAGE EARNINGS OF FULL-TIME WORKERS WITH HIGH SCHOOL AND COLLEGE DEGREES FROM 1967 TO 1989 (1984 DOLLARS)

YEAR (1)	AVERAGE EARNINGS OF MALES WITH 4 YEARS OF HIGH SCHOOL ($) (2)	AVERAGE EARNINGS OF MALES WITH 4 YEARS OF COLLEGE ($) (3)	RATIO OF EARNINGS, (3)/(2) (4)	IMPLIED VALUE OF i (5)
1967	$23,779	$35,586	1.50	10.7%
1970	25,562	37,062	1.45	9.7
1975	23,636	34,970	1.48	10.3
1980	25,247	32,483	1.29	6.6
1985	23,064	34,454	1.49	10.5
1989	21,937	34,445	1.57	11.9

Source: Current Population Reports, Series P-60, annual issues.

Columns 2 and 3 of Table 17-4 list the earnings of the two groups in 1984 dollars. Column 4 shows the ratio of the average earnings of college graduates and high school graduates. Using equation 17-10 and the actual ratio of earnings, we can derive an estimate of what value of i equates the present values. For each year we substitute the ratio in column 4 into equation 17-10 and solve for i. The derived estimate of i tells us what the interest rate must be in that year—given the ratio of earnings—that equates the present values. Column 5 shows the estimates of i.[6] The estimated interest rates vary from a low of only 6.6 percent in 1980 to a high of 11.9 percent in 1989. Therefore, if an individual could borrow and invest at an interest rate of more than 6.6 percent in 1980, a college education would not be as attractive an investment.

As Table 17-4 demonstrates, the actual ratio of earnings has fluctuated over time, and so the benefits of a college education have changed from decade to decade. The ratio of incomes was relatively high in the late 1960s, and college enrollments soared. By the late 1970s and early 1980s the ratio of incomes had fallen dramatically. The 1980s witnessed a complete reversal as the ratio increased. However, the rise in the ratio was due to a decline in the real income of high school graduates and not to an increase in the real income of college graduates. Researchers have attempted to understand the reasons for these fluctuations in the benefits of a college education. Currently, they are investigating the possible

[6] Since $I_c/I_h = (1 + i)^4$, both sides can be raised to the power $\frac{1}{4}$ to obtain

$$\left(\frac{I_c}{I_h}\right)^{1/4} = 1 + i$$

Therefore

$$i = \left(\frac{I_c}{I_h}\right)^{1/4} - 1$$

causes of the decline in the real earnings of high school graduates throughout the 1980s and are focusing on the effects of import competition in such industries as steel and autos and the introduction of computers in the workplace on the earnings of workers with different educational attainments.[7]

APPLICATION **17-3**

Has the Wage Premium for College Education Peaked?

The earnings premium of a college education increased throughout the 1980s. In 1980 the average earnings of a recent college graduate were about 40 percent larger than the average earnings of a recent high school graduate. The ratio soared throughout the 1980s so that by 1990 the college premium was nearly 80 percent, an all-time high. Throughout the 1980s, the demand curve for college graduates shifted outward. The supply of college graduates could not respond immediately. As the relative earnings of college graduates increased, more and more high school students began to look favorably on a college education. In response the percentage of high school graduates enrolled in college increased from 32 percent in 1980 to 41 percent in 1991. Slowly, the increased supply of college graduates began to have an impact. Since 1990, the earnings ratio has stabilized and has even begun to decline. Some economists believe the ratio will decline still more as more students earn college degrees and fewer are content with just a high school degree. They predict that the shift outward in the supply curve of college graduates will depress the average earnings of recent college graduates and the shift inward of the supply curve of high school graduates will increase the average earnings of recent high school graduates. Hence, some economists expect that the college premium will decline unless there is a demand shock that shifts the demand curve for college graduates outward once again.

17-5 TRAINING EMPLOYEES

Contrary to common opinion, education does not stop the moment the graduate clutches the diploma.[8] In many occupations worker skills improve with on-the-job training. Some firms may offer training to employees to improve their skills, such as teaching a worker how to repair a scanner or to operate a computer program. Other companies provide orientation programs for new workers to introduce them

[7] For an informative study, see Lawrence F. Katz and Kevin M. Murphy, "Changes in Relative Wages, 1963–1987: Supply and Demand Factors," Working Paper No. 3927, National Bureau of Economic Research, December 1991; John Bound and George Johnson, "Changes in the Structure of Wages in the 1980's: An Evaluation of Alternative Explanations," *American Economic Review* 82 (June 1992), pp. 371–92.

[8] The material in this section is based on Gary S. Becker, *Human Capital* (New York: National Bureau of Economic Research, 1964); Ronald G. Ehrenberg and Robert S. Smith, *Modern Labor Economics* (Glenview, Ill.: Scott, Foresman, 1982).

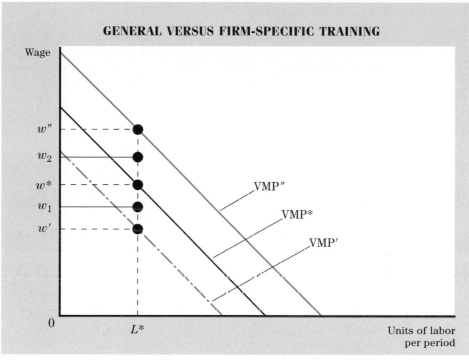

GENERAL VERSUS FIRM-SPECIFIC TRAINING

Figure 17-14   If a firm offers general training, the worker pays for the training. During the training period the worker receives w' because the marginal product of the employee is reduced. After completing the training, the worker receives w'' because the value of the marginal product increases no matter where the individual is employed. If the training is specific, the worker and the firm share the training cost. The pay of the employee during the training period is w_1. After the training period is completed, the firm pays w_2, a wage that is less than the value of the marginal product of the trained worker.

to company rules and practices. Often firms encourage employees to take courses such as accounting or business writing to improve their business skills. A company trains workers because it expects their marginal products to increase. From the workers' perspective, the training makes them more productive and increases their future wages. If both workers and employers benefit from training, you would think that no special problems arise when firms offer training programs. Unfortunately, this isn't always true. There are some special and interesting problems that occur when firms offer on-the-job training.

A two-period analysis can be used to examine these special problems where a firm offers training in the first period and the worker qualifies as a trained worker in the second period. If the worker does not receive on-the-job training, he or she receives a wage of w^* in both periods. In Figure 17-14 the firm hires L^* workers if the wage is w^*, and the value of the marginal product is VMP* in each period for workers without training.

General Training

First, let's consider a case where the training offered by the firm is general. When training increases the marginal product of workers in this *and* in other firms, we say the training is **general training.** If a worker enrolls in an introductory accounting course or learns welding techniques, the training is general. The marginal product of the worker increases whether he is employed by the firm that supplies the training or by another firm. What the worker learns is applicable in many companies.

> General training increases the worker's marginal product in many firms.

Let's consider what happens to the value of the marginal product of the worker during and after training. While he is receiving training, he is less productive because some time and effort are devoted to training and not to production. Consequently, the value of his marginal product during the first period declines to VMP′ in Figure 17-14. After the worker completes the training program, his marginal product shifts up to VMP″ in the second period.

Who pays for the training? If the firm continues to pay the worker w^* during the training period, it is paying for the training. The company is making an investment in the worker of $w^* - w'$ which is equal to the decrease in the worker's marginal product during the training period. The firm will incur this loss in the training period only if it expects to earn a surplus in the second period by paying the trained worker less than w'', the increased value of the marginal product of the trained worker in period 2, to recoup its loss in the first period. However, there is a hidden defect in this wage policy. If the firm pays less than w'' in period 2, the worker will resign and seek employment at some other firm because other firms in the labor market will pay w'' for a trained worker. The implication of this is that the firm will not pay for general training. Consequently, we conclude that the wage of the worker falls to w' during the training period because his marginal product is smaller. Then, the company will pay w'' for the services of the trained worker in the second period.

> A worker pays for general training that raises the value of his or her marginal product in other firms.

The experience of the armed forces is an example of an employer offering general training. For many years young recruits received training in the military and acquired skills that the private market valued highly. For example, before the voluntary army, the armed forces trained many pilots who subsequently were bid away by commercial airlines. Because military wages were below those in the private market, the military could not retain individuals with these valuable skills when the recruitment period expired. The training provided by the military performed a valuable educational service for certain industries and occupations. Because a recruit could receive w'' by leaving the military, the turnover of military personnel was relatively high.

The same issue arises when firms pay for courses that their employees take at universities and vocational schools. Many companies pay for some or all of the tuition of workers who earn MBA degrees. Since an MBA degree is a form of general training, you would expect that the worker and not the firm would pay for the training. Is this a contradiction of the theory? Most firms protect themselves with contracts requiring employees to remain with the firm for x years or to compensate the company for tuition if they leave prematurely. There are some firms that do not impose this restriction, and this behavior is puzzling. In another situation some companies pay tuition for employees to attend executive programs. Usually, the firm selects employees for such programs who have been with the company for many years and are likely to remain even after completing the program.

Firm-Specific Training

Let's go to the opposite extreme and assume that the training is **firm-specific training.** This means that the value of the marginal product increases in the second period only if the employee remains with the firm. Because the training is firm-specific, the worker would not be as productive if employed by another firm. Learning how to operate a firm-specific machine is an example of firm-specific training.

> Specific training increases the value of the marginal product of the worker only to the firm offering the training.

Who pays for firm-specific training? If the firm pays for the training by paying workers w^* during the training period and a worker leaves in period 2, the company suffers a loss. For example, suppose the firm pays w^* in the first period. Since the value of the marginal product of the worker decreases during the training period, the firm loses money by providing the training in the first period if she leaves in the second period.

Suppose the worker pays for the training. Then, she suffers a loss if the firm does not pay her the higher value of the marginal product in the second period. She has made the investment by taking a wage of w' during the training period since she would have received a higher wage of w^* without training. She wants a guarantee of being paid more than w^* in the second period. However, the firm can pay her just w^* although her marginal product increases to w''; because the training is firm-specific, she cannot earn more than w^* elsewhere.

When the firm offers specific training, both the worker and the employer must make a commitment to the employment relationship by sharing the cost of training. Suppose the firm pays w_1 in Figure 17-14 in the first period, which is greater than the value of the marginal product when $L = L^*$. The worker also loses because she receives less than w^*, but the firm pays for some of the training. In the second period the firm pays w_2, less than w'', and recoups its losses (after taking account of discounting which we ignore here) in the first period. The worker also recoups her first-period loss because the company pays more than w^* in the second period.

The worker and the firm share the cost of firm-specific training.

Because the firm pays more than w^* in the second period—what the worker could earn if employed by another firm—she has no incentive to leave the firm in the second period. Because w_2 is less than the value of her marginal product in the second period, the firm would be foolish to lay off the worker. In this solution both sides make an investment in the employment relationship. Neither has an incentive to terminate the relationship unless there is a significant unforeseen event. Therefore, the theory of firm-specific training predicts that the turnover of employees will be lower in firms that provide firm-specific training. In some large American and Japanese firms the turnover of employees is very low. In these cases it is likely that the training of workers is firm-specific. In contrast, the turnover of university professors is relatively high because little university-specific training occurs.

APPLICATION 17-4

Turnover and Tenure in the United States and in Japan

Japanese firms appear to invest more in training their workers than U.S. firms do. Moreover, available evidence suggests that the training is firm-specific. Researchers Masanori Hashimoto and John Raisian studied turnover rates in Japan and in the United States.[9] Table 17-5 shows the percentage of workers in different age-tenure

Table 17-5   PERCENT OF WORKERS STAYING WITH SAME FIRM BY AGE AND TENURE OF WORKER IN JAPAN AND IN THE UNITED STATES

AGE OF MALE WORKER IN JAPAN (1962) AND IN THE UNITED STATES (1963) (YRS)	TENURE CLASS WITH FIRM IN JAPAN (1962) AND IN THE UNITED STATES (1963) (YRS)	PERCENT STAYING WITH SAME FIRM AFTER 15 YEARS (1962–1977) IN JAPAN	PERCENT STAYING WITH SAME FIRM AFTER 15 YEARS (1963–1978) IN THE UNITED STATES
20–24	0–5	45.1%	13.0%
	5+	65.3	30.0
25–34	0–5	42.7	22.2
	5+	73.0	47.3
35–39	0–5	37.7	24.4
(35–44 for Japan)	5+	75.9	54.5

Source: This table is a condensed version of Table 1 in Masanori Hashimoto and John Raisian, "Employment Tenure and Earnings Profiles in Japan and the United States," *American Economic Review* 75 (September 1985).

[9] Masanori Hashimoto and John Raisian, "Employment Tenure and Earnings Profiles in Japan and the United States," *American Economic Review* 75 (September 1985), pp. 721–35. Copyright © 1985 by the American Economic Association.

classes that remain with the same employer for over 15 years in Japan and in the United States.

The results in Table 17-5 show considerably more stability in the employment relationship in Japan than in the United States. For example, 45 percent of Japanese workers who were between 20 and 24 years old and had anywhere from 0 to 5 years of tenure with their employer in 1962 remained with the same company after 15 years, while only 13 percent of American workers with the same initial characteristics did so. Long-term employment relationships are clearly more common in Japan than in the United States. These findings suggest that more firm-specific investment and training occur in Japan than the United States.

A different explanation for the different employment practices in the two countries emphasizes cultural differences between Japan and the United States. Could it be that large Japanese employers are more paternalistic than large U.S. employers are and could this explain the differences? Hashimoto and Raisian think not; they note that Japan had higher turnover rates before World War II and so it is unlikely that cultural factors are the primary reason for the lower turnover rate of Japanese workers.

17-6   COMPENSATION BASED ON INPUT OR OUTPUT

Compensation of an employee can depend on some measure of worker effort or on worker output. If an employee receives a straight salary or is paid by the hour, compensation depends on some measure of worker effort. The firm agrees to pay the employee a salary as long as he makes an effort to show up for work a certain number of days per month or hours per day.

Compensation based on output is piecework because the output of the worker determines his compensation. For example, firms often pay salespeople by commission and so compensation is a function of the dollar volume of sales each generates, or a farm worker's pay depends on the number of bushels harvested.

Whether compensation depends on output or effort is determined partly by which is less costly to measure. When the output of the worker is easier to measure, compensation will depend on worker output. When an employee shirks by not working conscientiously, he will bear the cost because compensation depends on output.

The theory of wage determination presented at the beginning of the chapter assumed that measurement problems are unimportant. If the cost of measuring output is negligible, the wage equals the value of the marginal product of labor in a competitive labor market. In practice, it is easier to measure output when a worker's marginal product is independent of the marginal product of other workers. In many job situations it is costly to base pay on output. Paying on the basis of piecework means that the firm must measure output, and measurement uses up resources. Defining just what is a unit of output is not always straightforward. For example, if the pay of an agricultural worker depends on pounds of fruit harvested, the worker will pay little attention to the quality of the fruit or pick only the larger fruit.

More often than not, the output of the individual worker is so costly to measure that compensation does not depend on worker output. This is especially true when output depends on team production or committee deliberations. Measuring the contribution of each member to a team is often difficult and costly. The number of yards gained by a running back in professional football depends on the performance of other members of the team, for example, the blocking ability of his teammates. In other situations output depends on a random factor like weather. A risk-averse worker may prefer compensation that depends on effort rather than output because compensation based on output is too variable. A drawback of compensation based on effort is that it encourages *shirking* by employees. Workers show up for the job and go through the motions but find ways of shirking some work.

APPLICATION **17-5**

Problems with the Use of Incentive Pay

Incentive pay (that is, pay based on an observable measure of output) for officers of large firms is common. Incentive pay for employees is less common but may be slowly increasing over time. The slow pace of acceptance of pay-for-performance indicates that it is more difficult to implement than it first appears.[10]

Firms are making greater efforts to introduce pay-for-performance, but this deceptively simple idea is often difficult to put into practice. In the early 1990s DuPont's attempt to introduce incentive pay was a resounding failure. The company introduced performance pay in its fiber business group and required employees to risk some of their pay for a higher return if fiber business profits increased. If profits increased, employees would earn more than they earned under the old compensation policy. If profits fell, they would earn less. Management was trying to encourage workers to find ways to reduce costs, but unfortunately the profit incentives created some unintended effects. One employee noted that her secretary would route her well out of her way on a business trip if it reduced the cost. Mailroom employees began to question her mailings, suggesting she should lower costs. The new compensation plan faced an acid test at DuPont when the profits of the business fell because of a slow-down in the industry. The employees revolted and wanted out of the new plan, which DuPont eliminated. Many employees appear to be risk-averse and to prefer steady to variable pay.

At Corning, Inc., a pay-for-performance plan was adopted and enabled workers to earn bonuses of 4 to 6 percent of pay for high performance. One manager implemented the new awards policy hoping to keep the awards confidential but was unable to do so. He noted the good news–bad news effect of giving a bonus. Employees are happy because they receive a bonus but are upset when they don't

---

[10] Based on Amanda Bennett, "Paying Workers to Meet Goals Spreads, but Gauging Performance Proves Tough," *The Wall Street Journal*, September 10, 1991.

receive the bonus they believe they deserve. Managers are often a major stumbling block to introducing pay-for-performance plans.

Pay-for-performance can create unintended incentives if firms using it fail to anticipate all the consequences. One company introduced a bonus plan hoping it would encourage its buyers to reduce the cost of the raw materials they purchased. The firm expected the bonus plan would induce the buyers to search more intensively for lower prices in the market and to negotiate lower prices. It failed to recognize that the plan would create a perverse incentive for buyers to purchase a lower-quality raw material and thereby lower costs. Later, the company incurred higher costs to repair the defective product that the firm sold to customers long after the firm had paid bonuses to the buyers.

17-7   USING WAGE POLICY AS AN INCENTIVE MECHANISM

Firms shape their wage policies over the years to solve the particular problems that they face. This section highlights one labor problem and describes how a firm can structure its wage policy to solve it.

Incentive Compensation and Mandatory Retirement

Compensating a worker at the end of the period or at the end of a job can be an effective mechanism for reducing shirking by workers. If workers are likely to remain with a firm for most of their lifetime, an age-pay profile where compensation is backloaded (largely paid at the end of the work period) discourages shirking and malfeasance.

Backloading pay can help explain the wage policies of some firms. It is a central idea in one explanation of why firms insist on mandatory retirement. In many large firms all employees must retire at a specific age, usually by their seventieth birthday. For many years, the firm would send you on your way with a retirement party or a wristwatch when your seventieth birthday arrived no matter how effectively you were performing. Why does a firm force all employees to retire at seventy no matter how productive a worker is? If the marginal product of the worker declines after a certain age, why doesn't the firm simply lower the wage of the employee instead of arbitrarily terminating the employment relationship? On the face of it, mandatory retirement appears to be a short-sighted, capricious policy.

Edward Lazear has advanced an interesting explanation for the use of mandatory retirement.[11] In his model the firm pays a wage w^* to an employee when the worker reaches seventy years of age, but once the worker reaches seventy, the firm is no longer willing to offer him a contract. What this implies is that the

---

[11] Edward P. Lazear, "Why Is There Mandatory Retirement?" *Journal of Political Economy* 87 (1979), pp. 1261–84.

worker's wage w^* exceeds his value of marginal product at age seventy, the year of mandatory retirement.

Why does the firm pay the employee more than his marginal product when he reaches seventy years of age? To explain this, Lazear introduces the notion of worker shirking. **Shirking** can take many forms. Perhaps, the worker slacks off or "borrows" tools from the factory or uses the fax machine for his private business. The firm would like to discourage such conduct.

It can reduce shirking by altering its wage policy. Workers are more productive and shirk less if the firm pays them less than their value of marginal product in the early stages of the employment relationship and more than their marginal product later in the employment relationship. This type of wage policy penalizes malfeasance and shirking. The firm fires a worker who steals from the company or does not put forth the expected effort if the violation is gross enough. Since the wage is initially less than the value of the marginal product, the worker suffers a loss if the firm discharges her for shirking because her wage is less than the wage she could earn in the next best job. Moreover, because she is fired, she loses the opportunity to earn more than her value of marginal product in the later stages of the employment relationship. She is unable to recoup the investment she made in the firm in the early years of the employment relationship when the wage is less than the value of the marginal product. Because of this incentive structure, the worker is less likely to shirk.

We can present the argument in more detail with the aid of a graph. In Figure 17-15 the wage is on the vertical axis and time with the firm is on the horizontal axis. The value of the marginal product of the worker is line bb. If there is no shirking problem, the worker's wage is equal to the value of the marginal product in each period. The line rr is the worker's reservation wage and measures the opportunity cost of working at the firm. It is shown to be rising over time, perhaps because the worker desires to spend more time in nonwork activities as she grows older. When the wage of the worker is less than the reservation wage, she retires voluntarily. Assuming the worker's wage equals the value of the marginal product, the worker will retire voluntarily at date T_m where rr intersects VMP. Before T_m, the wage of the worker exceeds her reservation wage, and so she continues to work. After T_m, the reservation wage is greater than the worker's wage ($=$VMP), and so she voluntarily retires. If the firm pays the value of the marginal product, it does not have to introduce a mandatory retirement policy. Each worker will retire voluntarily at T_m.

Now suppose shirking is a problem and the firm adopts the wage policy ww in Figure 17-15. To discourage shirking by workers, it pays less than the marginal product up to date T' and then pays more than the value of the marginal product. The firm selects ww so that the present value of the wage payments along ww equals the present value of the wage payments along bb where the wage equals the value of the marginal product. Therefore, a risk-neutral employee is indifferent between the two wage streams. With the pay scale ww the worker's wage is more than VMP at time T_m. This explains why the employee does not retire voluntarily at T_m.

Lazear assumes that wage policy ww induces more worker effort than the

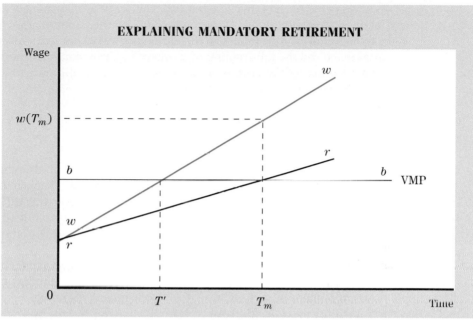

Figure 17-15   *ww* is the wage paid by the firm over time, and *bb* is the worker's value of the marginal product, VMP. The wage is less than the value of the marginal product until T', after which the worker is paid more than the VMP. If she were paid the value of the marginal product, she would retire at time T_m when the opportunity cost *rr* equals her wage. With the wage function *ww* the wage of the worker is $w(T_m)$ at T_m and exceeds the opportunity cost. She will not retire voluntarily, and the firm forces her to retire through a mandatory retirement policy.

constant wage policy along *bb* does. If so, the wage policy *ww* solves or at least reduces the incidence of shirking, but it creates another problem. Because the wage exceeds the opportunity cost of the worker's time at T_m, she will not retire voluntarily. Without a mandatory retirement program, she is eager to continue working. The firm must prevent this. Otherwise, the present value of the wage payments *ww* will exceed the present value of the value of marginal product of the worker over the whole work experience. Therefore, the firm adopts a mandatory retirement program and requires the worker to retire at age T_m to prevent this from happening.

In this model mandatory retirement is a derivative policy that springs from a wage policy designed to reduce shirking by employees. The wage policy *ww* is another illustration of backloading pay to foster the desired behavior by employees.

Recently, federal law has made it illegal for firms and nonprofit institutions to adopt mandatory retirement. A firm that has a wage policy such as *ww* will not be able to impose mandatory retirement. It will be interesting to see what changes in compensation policies emerge because of this change in federal law.

This chapter has investigated how the wage is determined in many different labor market situations. Our examination of the labor market has touched on explanations for differences in the earnings of workers with different educational attainment, on-the-job training of workers by firms and how the wage policy of a firm depends on the type of training, and using wage policy to create incentives that discourage employee shirking.

SUMMARY

- A competitive firm determines the quantity of labor to employ such that the value of the marginal product equals the worker's wage.
- In the long run the market demand function for labor is negatively sloped. Firms demand more units of labor at a lower wage.
- The supply function of labor of an individual is derived from utility maximization. An individual's supply of work function may have either a positive or a negative slope.
- A minimum wage creates two wage rates for the same quality of worker.

- The major cost of attending college is the forgone income. The decision to enter college depends on the difference between the earnings of a college graduate and a high school graduate and on the interest rate.
- The worker pays for general training, while the worker and the firm share the cost of firm-specific training.
- By paying a worker less than his or her value of marginal product initially, a firm can structure its wage policy to reduce shirking by workers.

KEY TERMS

derived demand functions
marginal product
value of the marginal product
scale effect
work-leisure choice
human capital
firm-specific training

marginal revenue product
substitution effect
expansion path
general training
shirking
mandatory retirement

REVIEW QUESTIONS

1. Why do economists describe the demand for labor as a derived demand?
2. How does the value of the marginal product differ from the marginal revenue product?
3. In a competitive industry a profit-maximizing firm tries to maximize output per worker. If it doesn't, it has no chance of surviving against firms that do. Explain why you agree or disagree with this statement.
4. What are the substitution and the scale effects for a single competitive firm?
5. If the price of capital increases, a firm will increase the demand for labor. Explain

why you agree or disagree with this statement.

6. If the price of capital increases, each firm will demand fewer units of capital, and so the firms in the industry will demand more units of labor. Explain why you agree or disagree with this statement.

7. Why is a firm's long-run demand function for labor more elastic than its short-run demand function for labor?

8. What is the industry scale effect?

9. Predict the effect of a decline in military spending on the wage of aeronautical engineers. Show the effect on a graph.

10. If an increase in income increases hours of leisure, a worker will supply less work when the wage increases. Explain why you agree or disagree with this statement.

EXERCISES

1. If a price-taking firm receives a higher price for a product, this will increase the firm's demand for labor and increase the wage rate of its workers. Explain why you agree or disagree with this statement.

2. Explain why an individual is either not affected or stops working completely after the introduction of a general assistance program.

3. If a general assistance program establishes a minimum income of $7,500, it will affect the work-leisure choice of only those individuals with incomes less than $7,500. Explain why you agree or disagree with this statement.

4. The current distribution of income in a country is shown in column 2 below:

Suppose a general assistance program is being considered with a maximum payment of $5,000. The predictions of two experts concerning the effect of the program on the size distribution of income are in columns 3 and 4. Select one of the two predicted distributions and explain why it better describes the program's effect. Explain why you did not select the alternative prediction.

5. With the aid of graphs show how days of leisure are affected if the current income tax of 28 percent of income increases to 40 percent on income above $120,000.

6. Why do most students enter college immediately after graduating from high school?

PER CAPITA INCOME ($) (1)	ACTUAL DISTRIBUTION OF INCOME (%) (2)	PREDICTED DISTRIBUTION BY EXPERT 1 (%) (3)	PREDICTED DISTRIBUTION BY EXPERT 2 (%) (4)
0–4,999	15	0	0
5,000–9,999	30	50	50
10,000–14,999	25	20	26
15,000–19,999	15	15	11
20,000–29,999	10	10	8
30,000–39,999	3	3	3
40,000+	2	2	2

*7. The average age of MBA students has increased over time. These students begin their studies after four to five years of work experience, whereas in the past MBA students entered school with fewer years of experience. Why do you think this change has occurred? Does your answer explain why the same change has not occurred to the same degree in law and medicine?

8. In recent years regulated taxi fares in New York city have not changed while the cost of living increased by 20 percent. Some critics have argued that taxi drivers earn only about $7 per hour after paying their costs of driving their cabs. If cab companies are allowed to raise taxi fares, the critics claim that the cab owners can then give the cab drivers a wage increase. Cab owners agree. Explain why you think that a higher taxi fare will or will not increase the hourly wage of cab drivers.

9. Assume a worker is risk-averse and prefers certain earnings of E. The company wants to introduce a pay-for-performance plan that ties the compensation of the employee to the profits of the company in hopes of reducing costs. Given the market that the firm operates in, a worker will either receive $0.8E$ with probability $.5$ or $1.2E$ with probability $.5$ under the new compensation plan. With the aid of graphs show what E the firm must pay the worker to accept the pay-for-performance plan if the employee maximizes expected utility. Use the expected utility hypothesis (see Chapter 3) to explain your answer.

10. One firm pays a worker based on output, and another pays a worker on the basis of input. Which firm is more likely to have a mandatory retirement policy? Explain why.

PART VII

MARKETS AND ECONOMIC EFFICIENCY

- **Chapter 18**
  Economic Efficiency
  and General Equilibrium
- **Chapter 19**
  Externalitics and
  Public Goods

ECONOMIC EFFICIENCY AND GENERAL EQUILIBRIUM

■ **18-1 General Equilibrium Analysis**

■ **18-2 Command and Control Policies of the Wizard**

■ **18-3 Economic Efficiency**

Pareto Efficiency in Exchange

The Contract Curve

A Competitive Product Market and Pareto Efficiency in Exchange

Application 18-1: Minimizing Information Requirements in Experimental Competitive Markets

Impediments to Pareto Efficiency

Application 18-2: Impediments to Trading Water Rights in California

Pareto Efficiency in Production

Competitive Factor Markets and Pareto Efficiency

Application 18-3: Reducing the Price of Capital by Subsidizing Small Businesses

Pareto Efficiency in Product Mix

Competitive Markets and Product Mix Efficiency

■ **18-4 Departures from Pareto Efficiency Caused by Monopoly**

■ **Summary**

■ **Key Terms**

■ **Review Questions**

■ **Exercises**

Our investigation of markets has largely focused on how individual markets work. The scope of this investigation has ranged from how a competitive price is determined by the interplay of demand and supply, to how a monopolist sets the price of a product, to how a small number of sellers affects price, to how a firm sets discriminatory prices. In each discussion, the impact of changes in one market on other markets was on the whole ignored. The analysis was clearly a **partial equilibrium** analysis. We assumed implicitly that the theoretical predictions of the partial equilibrium analysis are reasonably accurate even if a change in one market causes several rounds of repercussions in other markets in the economy. In earlier chapters we resisted any inclination to examine how a change in one market affects other markets. When we concluded that a monopolist sets marginal revenue equal to marginal cost and thereby raises the price of a good and produces less than a competitive industry would, we did not stop to ask what happens to the resources that leave the monopolized market and go to other markets because a monopolist produces less than a competitive industry does.

This chapter abandons the partial equilibrium approach for another which looks at many markets simultaneously. The reason for this change in emphasis is that we are interested in exploring the elusive but important topic of the economic efficiency of a whole economy, not of just a single market. This requires an investigation of more than one market at a time, indeed all markets in an economy, and is such an imposing task that a more measured investigation seems appropriate. Our investigation will be less venturesome by considering the simultaneous equilibrium in a simple economy with just two goods and two factors of production. Still, our investigation of multimarkets is broader than a partial equilibrium approach, and economists describe this type of analysis as **general equilibrium** analysis to contrast it with the partial equilibrium analysis discussed in earlier chapters.

The goals of this chapter are to define what economists mean by economic efficiency and to explain how competitively organized markets for goods and for factors of production can achieve economic efficiency. Chapter 19 will extend the analysis to cover more complicated but realistic situations where the behavior of one or several parties affects other parties, or where there are demands for public goods.

18-1 GENERAL EQUILIBRIUM ANALYSIS

A general equilibrium analysis examines the repercussions of a change that occurs in one market on prices and outputs in other markets. Because general equilibrium analysis is more difficult, we make a gentle transition from partial equilibrium to general equilibrium analysis by employing the familiar demand and supply model to study how several markets simultaneously adjust to equilibrium. Chapter 2 noted that the price of chicken declined by 75 percent from 1950 to 1990 and suggested this decline was due to new methods in raising chickens. Chapter 2 also showed how technological change shifted the supply function for chickens outward and lowered the equilibrium price. A general equilibrium analysis expands this approach and investigates the effect of this technological change not only on the market for chickens but on other markets as well. Figure 18-1*a* shows that the supply function for chicken shifts outward and the equilibrium price falls from P_c^* to P_c'. The fall in the price of chicken creates repercussions in other markets. Figure 18-1*b* shows that because chicken and beef are substitutes the demand function for beef shifts inward from $D_b D_b$ to $D_b' D_b'$ when the price of chicken falls to P_c' since $D_b D_b$ was derived assuming the price of chicken was P_c^*. The equilibrium price of beef falls from P_b^* to P_b' because of the shift in the demand function for beef. Figure 18-1*c* shows how the technological change in the chicken industry affects the demand and supply functions for steak sauce. The demand function for steak sauce shifts inward from $D_s D_s$ to $D_s' D_s'$ because beef and steak sauce are complements. Because the demand function for steak sauce shifts inward, the price of steak sauce falls to P_s'. This more general analysis has traced some of the effects of the technological change in the chicken industry. Not only is the chicken industry affected by the change, but repercussions are felt in the beef and the steak sauce industries as well.

You might think the analysis is complete by now. However, there are secondary repercussions. The fall in the price of beef causes the demand function for chicken to shift inward since the demand function for chicken assumes the price of beef is P_b^*. So the demand function for chicken in turn shifts to $D_c' D_c'$, and the price falls to P_c''. The fall in the price of chicken in turn shifts the position of the demand function for beef. There may be several rounds of adjustments before the demand and supply functions in these markets stabilize and all three reach a new equilibrium.

As you can imagine, general equilibrium analysis can become complicated with so many markets to keep track of. To simplify the analysis and yet retain a semblance of reality, throughout this chapter we will look at a simpler economy with two goods and two factors of production.

18-2   COMMAND AND CONTROL POLICIES OF THE WIZARD

We introduce the topic of economic efficiency in a general equilibrium setting with a parable about the Wizard of Zeoz.

Your spacecraft touches down on a newly discovered planet called Zeoz, and strange-looking inhabitants surround the ship. You become a prisoner and receive notice that you will be interviewed by the Wizard, the stern ruler of Zeoz. On the way to the Wizard's castle you learn that the Wizard rules with an iron but paternalistic hand; he has a reputation for being capricious, but he can be swayed by a logical argument.

You enter a magnificent room in the castle for your encounter with the Wizard. The Wizard strides in and says he will ask you one question. If you answer the question satisfactorily, you will become his lifelong adviser. If you answer it incorrectly, your life will end.

The Wizard begins by noting that there are two types of beings on Zeoz, an A type and a B type. Each year a large bureaucracy distributes stocks of nutrients X

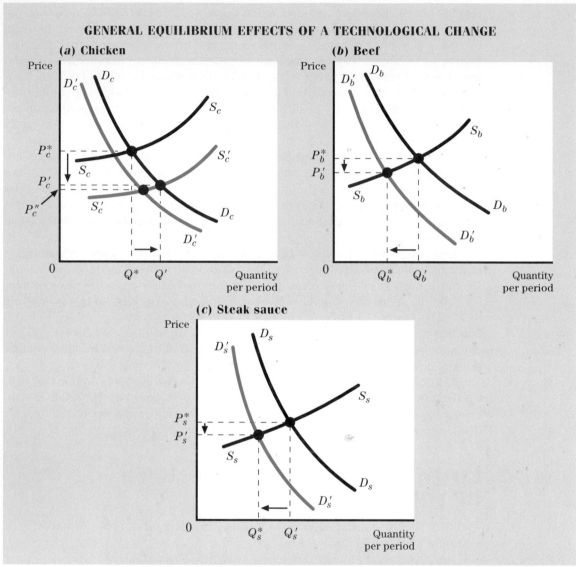

Figure 18-1 (*a*) A technological change shifts the supply curve for chicken downward and causes the price of chicken to fall. (*b*) The fall in the price of chicken causes the demand function for beef to shift inward and the price of beef declines to P_b' since beef and chicken are gross substitutes. (*c*) The demand for steak sauce shifts inward and the price of steak sauce falls to P_s' because beef and steak sauce are gross complements. Secondary repercussions cause the demand for chicken to shift from D_cD_c to $D_c'D_c'$.

and Y to each inhabitant. Somehow, the A types know how to manipulate the bureaucracy and manage to get more of the nutrients than the B types. Upset by this, the B types petition the Wizard to redistribute the nutrient stocks so that they receive more. Each year the Wizard spends valuable time redistributing the stocks, only to receive an earful of complaints from the A types.

Since the Wizard has to spend considerable time and effort redistributing the nutrients, he expects each B inhabitant to consume all the nutrients received. Executive decree 1074 imposes the death sentence on any inhabitant caught selling or buying nutrients.

In public the Wizard proclaims that his redistribution policy is the fairest, but in private he expresses some reservations. He does not know whether Zeoz is better off with or without the redistribution and hopes you will supply a scientific justification for the policy. This leads to the fateful question. The Wizards asks, "Is Zeoz better off after my redistribution of the nutrient stocks?" With your life hanging in the balance, you stall for time and ask for an hour to prepare an answer. Fortunately, you have brought along your copy of *Price Theory and Applications* and you quickly read the relevant sections of this chapter. After an hour you rejoin the Wizard who is awaiting your response.

You come directly to the point: "After consulting a state-of-the-art textbook from planet Earth, I cannot say whether you should or should not redistribute the nutrients." The Wizard jumps up from his chair and shouts, "What kind of adviser will you be if all you can say is that you cannot say?" The Wizard becomes extremely angry and is about to call the guards to lead you away. Anticipating this reaction, you quickly add, "But I do know how you can redistribute the nutrient stocks and increase the welfare of all inhabitants of Zeoz." Upon hearing this, the Wizard grows interested and asks you to expound your views. At this point you weave the following argument.

18-3   ECONOMIC EFFICIENCY

The Wizard wants to know whether his kingdom is better off with his redistribution policy. A similar question has baffled scholars and policy analysts for centuries because the Wizard's redistribution policy increases the utility of each B inhabitant but decreases the utility of each A inhabitant. As an economic adviser, you cannot say whether the redistribution makes Zeoz better or worse off because the modern theory of consumer behavior makes no allowance for interpersonal comparisons of utility. You have no objective way of determining if the kingdom is better off because you have no scientific basis for comparing the utilities of the different inhabitants. As an economic advisor, you do not want to take sides in the tradeoff between the As and the Bs and thus simply plan to present the conclusions that can be drawn without showing partiality toward either side.

To demonstrate your point in the simplest way, you argue as follows. Suppose a small economy consists of just one A and one B inhabitant. Each starts with a market basket of the two nutrients or, more generally, goods. Let's call them good X and good Y. Between them, the two inhabitants or consumers have a total of X'

CHANGING THE ENDOWMENTS OF TWO CONSUMERS

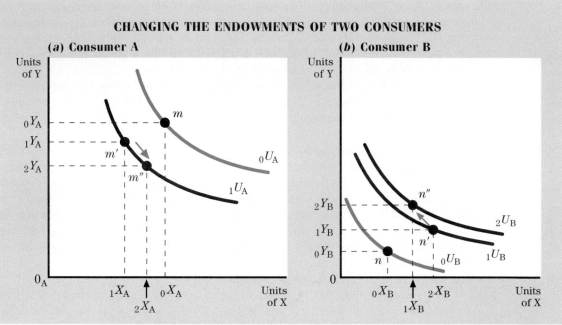

Figure 18-2   The initial endowment is at point m in (a) for inhabitant A and at point n in (b) for inhabitant B. After a redistribution of each consumer's endowment, consumer A moves from m to m', making A worse off, and consumer B moves from n to n', making B better off. Because interpersonal comparisons of utility cannot be made scientifically, you are unable to say whether the Wizard's redistribution increases the welfare of the inhabitants of Zeoz. On the other hand, the move from m' to m'' leaves A indifferent, and the reciprocal move from n' to n'' increases B's utility. Although the total endowment is still X' and Y', B would be better off given the utility of A if the trade were allowed.

units of good X and Y' units of good Y. A **consumer endowment** is an assigned market basket of goods that each inhabitant starts with. The Wizard assigns an initial endowment of $_0X_A$ units of X and $_0Y_A$ units of Y to consumer A and an initial endowment of $_0X_B$ units of X and $_0Y_B$ units of Y to consumer B. The sum of the endowments of each good adds up to the total units of the good available.

$$_0X_A + {}_0X_B = X'   \qquad   _0Y_A + {}_0Y_B = Y'   \qquad \text{(Goods Endowment Constraints)} \quad \textbf{(18-1)}$$

Figure 18-2a shows the indifference curves of consumer A, and the endowment of A is at point m. The indifference curves of consumer B are shown in Figure 18-2b where the endowment of B is at point n. Consumer A is more adept at manipulating the bureaucracy and has more of both goods than consumer B. Since the Wizard's redistribution policy moves consumer A from point m to point m', consumer A is now on $_1U_A$, a lower indifference curve, and is worse off. However, consumer B moves to point n' on $_1U_B$, a higher indifference curve, because of the redistribution policy and is better off. As an economic analyst, you have no objective way of comparing A's discomfort from a loss of both goods with B's satisfaction from receiving more of both goods. Therefore, you cannot determine whether the welfare of all the inhabitants (As and Bs) of Zeoz is higher or lower under the redistribution policy.

The Wizard mistakenly thinks all redistribution policies either make B better off and A worse off, or vice versa, and inevitably require interpersonal comparisons of utility. The first point that you hope to impress upon the Wizard is that some policies can improve the welfare of at least one inhabitant without harming the other inhabitants. Only a capricious ruler would *not* implement such policies.

There is a second but more delicate point that you think the Wizard should consider. It is clear to you that the Wizard's demonstrated penchant for command and control policies is an expensive luxury. Commands determine what goods the economy of Zeoz produces and how they are distributed to each consumer. Although the Wizard has more information about the economy than any other being on Zeoz, he does not have complete information. It is likely that there exists some redistribution that could increase the utility of one consumer without reducing the utility of the other. You hope to persuade the Wizard to rely more on competitive markets and less on command and control policies to achieve his goals.

Let's consider the first point. Is there a redistribution policy, other than the one selected by the Wizard, that allocates X' units of X and Y' units of Y so that at least one consumer's utility increases while the other's remains unchanged? The Wizard's command and control policy requires A to consume the market basket at point m' in Figure 18-2a, and B to consume the market basket at point n' in Figure 18-2b. How does the Wizard know that the mandated allocation is optimal? If the Wizard's allocation is in the best interest of the inhabitants, why must he issue a decree that requires A and B to consume the redistributed market baskets under a threat of death? By mandating consumption, the Wizard is coercing consumption and implicitly admitting that another allocation of goods could make one consumer better off without making the other one worse off.

By mandating consumption and preventing trade between A and B, the Wizard is preventing other voluntary redistributions that are superior to his redistribution. For example, suppose that consumer A is indifferent if she receives one more unit of X for one less unit of Y. Consumer B gives up one unit of X but receives one more unit of Y as compensation. Consumer A moves from point m' to point m'' on the same indifference curve, but consumer B moves from point n' to point n'' on a higher indifference curve and his utility increases. The inhabitants of Zeoz are clearly better off if they could make this trade. This is what you had in mind when you told the Wizard that you knew how to increase the welfare of his subjects.

Pareto Efficiency in Exchange

The proposed deviation from the Wizard's mandated market baskets shows that not all redistributions inevitably make one consumer better off at the expense of another. There are some redistributions of X and Y that can increase B's utility while holding A's utility constant. How can we find an allocation of goods X and Y to the two consumers that maximizes B's utility given A's utility?

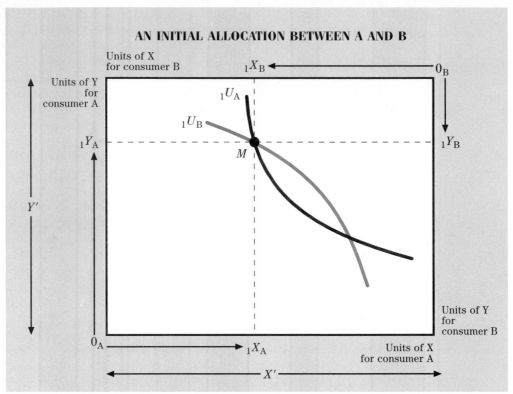

Figure 18-3   The initial distribution of X' units of X and Y' units of Y is at point M. Consumer A has $_1X_A$ units of X and $_1Y_A$ units of Y. With these market baskets the utility of A is $_1U_A$ and the utility of B is $_1U_B$.

An allocation of goods among consumers is **Pareto-efficient**[1] if any reassignment of the goods that holds the utility of one consumer constant reduces the utility of the other consumer.

How can the Wizard determine whether an allocation satisfies the criterion of Pareto efficiency? Figure 18-3 is an *Edgeworth box diagram.*[2] The dimensions of the box are X' by Y', the total endowment of the two goods. The horizontal axis measures X' units, and the vertical axis measures Y' units. The point 0_A is the origin for consumer A's indifference curves. Starting from 0_A, a movement from the southwest to the northeast increases A's utility since A has more of both goods. Point 0_B in the northeast corner is the origin for B's indifference curves. Starting

[1] Vilfredo Pareto derived the Pareto efficiency conditions at the beginning of the twentieth century.
[2] Named for Francis Edgeworth who appears to have been the first to introduce it.

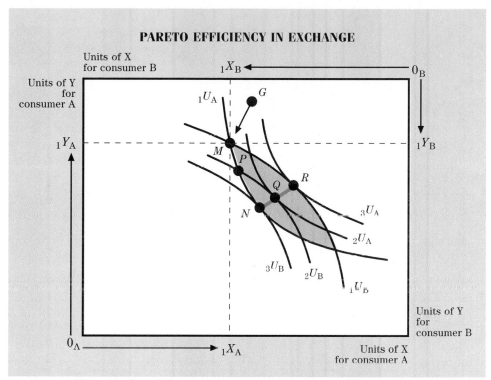

Figure 18-4   The initial distribution of resources is at point *M*. Any point in the shaded area increases the utility of A and B. Points along *NR* are Pareto-efficient allocations. Starting at any point on *NR*, a redistribution of resources will lower the utility of at least one inhabitant, holding the utility of the other constant.

from 0_B, a movement from the northeast to the southwest represents an increase in B's utility.

Any point in the box represents an allocation of the total endowment between the two consumers. For example, point *M* represents an allocation of X' and Y' units between A and B. Consumer A has an initial market basket consisting of $_1X_A$ units of X and $_1Y_A$ units of Y, and consumer B's market basket includes $_1X_B$ units of X and $_1Y_B$ units of Y. The sum of the endowments of X is X', and the sum of the endowments of Y is Y'. Given $_1X_A$ and $_1Y_A$, A is on indifference curve $_1U_A$ and, given $_1X_B$ and $_1Y_B$, B is on indifference curve $_1U_B$.

Is point *M* Pareto-efficient? Compare point *M* with the allocation at point *P* in Figure 18-4. Consumer A has more of X and less of Y at point *P* but is still on $_1U_A$, and so A's utility is the same. Consumer B has less X but more Y but is now on $_2U_B$, a higher indifference curve, and is therefore better off. The redistribution of the goods between points *M* and *P* increases B's utility, while A's utility is unchanged. Therefore, the allocation at point *M* is not Pareto-efficient. Now let's compare *P* with *N*, where A has still less Y but more X. Again, consumer A's utility is constant since A remains on $_1U_A$, but B's utility increases by moving to indifference curve $_3U_B$ and so the allocation at point P is not Pareto-efficient. Now consider point N. Any reallocation of the total stocks of goods that moves A and B away from point N along the indifference curve $_1U_A$ in either direction reduces B's utility. In other words, holding A's utility constant at $_1U_A$, any reassignment of the good away from N reduces the utility of B. Therefore, point N is Pareto-efficient in exchange.

What distinguishes point N from points M and P is that the indifference curves of A and B are *tangent* to each other at point N and *intersect* at points like M and P. Therefore, a Pareto-efficient allocation requires equal marginal rates of substitution between Y and X for the two consumers.

$$^A\mathrm{MRS}_{YX} = {}^B\mathrm{MRS}_{YX} \qquad \text{(Condition for Pareto Efficiency in Exchange)} \qquad \textbf{(18-2)}$$

Pareto efficiency in exchange requires that the marginal rates of substitution between the two goods be equal for all consumers.

Consumers A and B prefer any point in the shaded area of Figure 18-4 to point M because a redistribution of the total endowment that places both consumers at some point in the shaded area allows each to reach a higher indifference curve, thereby increasing the utility of both. Each consumer **gains from trade.** Among all the points in the shaded area, only those where the indifference curves are tangent to one another are Pareto-efficient in exchange. For example, point Q is Pareto-efficient because the indifference curves $_2U_A$ and $_2U_B$ are tangent to each other, and so point Q represents another Pareto-efficient allocation. The indifference curves are also tangent at point R, and so point R is still another Pareto-efficient allocation. Indeed, all points on the curve running from N to R represent Pareto-efficient allocations where the slopes of the indifference curves of A and B are equal.

The Wizard's redistribution policy moves A and B from point G to point M in Figure 18-4. Consumer A has less of both goods at point M and is worse off, while consumer B has more of both goods at point M than at point G. You cannot prove to the Wizard that the inhabitants of the kingdom are better off after he redistributes the goods. However, you can conclude that the Wizard's policy of mandating consumption at point M is not Pareto-efficient in exchange. Only those points along the curve from point N to point R are Pareto-efficient allocations, starting from point M. But the inhabitants of Zeoz cannot reach any of these points because of the Wizard's policy of prohibiting trade.

The Contract Curve

While the Wizard's redistribution policy at point M serves to demonstrate that other allocations of X and Y improve the welfare of the inhabitants of Zeoz, your argument has broader applicability. Whatever the initial distribution of the total endowments of X' and Y' between the two consumers, both can benefit by reaching a Pareto-efficient allocation. If the indifference curves are not tangent to one another

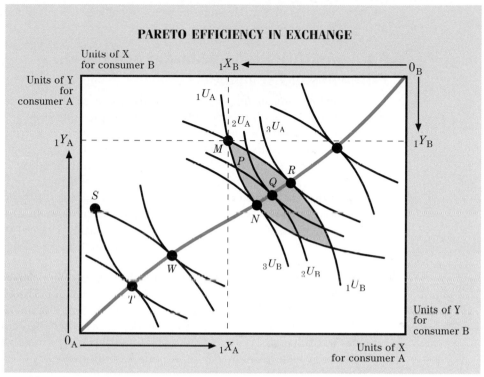

Figure 18-5   The curve running from 0_A to 0_B is formed by connecting all points of tangency between indifference curves and is called the contract curve. Any movement along the contract curve increases the utility of one consumer at the expense of the utility of the other consumer.

at the initial allocation, there is another allocation that can make one consumer better off given the utility of the other consumer.

For example, suppose the initial allocation is at point S in Figure 18-5. The curve running from T to W connects all points of tangency of the indifference curves. Therefore, all points along the curve from point T to point W are preferable to point S and are also Pareto-efficient points because the indifference curves of A and B are all tangent along this curve. The curve running from 0_A to 0_B is the **contract curve** and connects all points of tangency of the indifference curves of A and B. All points on the contract curve are Pareto-efficient in exchange.

> The contract curve connects all points of tangency for the indifference curves of the two consumers.

Moreover, once an allocation is on the contract curve and is therefore Pareto-efficient, you cannot say that a redistribution from one point to another on the contract curve is preferable since movements along this curve increase the utility of one consumer at the expense of the other.

A Competitive Product Market and Pareto Efficiency in Exchange

The Wizard recognizes the logic of your argument but raises a serious objection. He admits he knows little about the shapes of the indifference curves of either type of consumer. How can he ever know whether his redistribution makes the inhabitants' indifference curves tangent? He says the theory is elegant but irrelevant because he cannot see how to apply it, and his impatience shows again.

You expected the Wizard to ask this question and have prepared an answer. You agree that the Wizard cannot possibly know what the inhabitants' indifference curves look like. Fortunately, you tell the Wizard, he does not have to know the shapes of the indifference curves to reach the contract curve if only he is willing to lift the ban on trading and allow markets to function. In other words, he must relinquish his command and control policies. You bluntly tell the Wizard that competitive markets in nutrients X and Y will produce Pareto efficiency in exchange, while his command and control policies will not. The Wizard finds your claim intriguing but remains dubious. He has more information than anyone else about the economy, and even he does not know whether the economy is Pareto-efficient in exchange. How can trading by imperfectly informed but self-interested consumers magically produce a Pareto-efficient allocation?

You present this argument: When a market exists, inhabitants can trade so many units of Y for a unit of X. The relative price of Y for X indicates how many units of Y a consumer can exchange for a unit of X. For example, A and B can trade two units of Y for one unit of X if the price of X is $10 and the price of Y is $5, so that $-P_X/P_Y = -2$. Because there are many A consumers and many B consumers in Zeoz, not just two, each A or B is a price taker and can trade as much of each good as desired when the exchange rate is two units of Y for one unit of X.

Starting with the allocation at point M in Figure 18-6, A and B determine independently how many units of each good they will trade at each $-P_X/P_Y$. Each consumer maximizes utility subject to a budget constraint by trading Y for X or X for Y until the slope of his or her indifference curve equals the slope of the budget constraint.

Consumer A maximizes utility when

$$^A\mathrm{MRS}_{YX} = -\frac{P_X}{P_Y} \qquad \text{(Equilibrium for Consumer A)} \qquad \textbf{(18-3)}$$

where $^A\mathrm{MRS}_{YX}$ is the marginal rate of substitution between Y and X for consumer A. The slope of the budget constraint is $-P_X/P_Y$, and so each consumer receives $\Delta Y = (-P_X/P_Y)\,\Delta X$ units of Y in exchange for ΔX units of X. For example, if $-P_X/P_Y = -2$, then $\Delta Y = -2\,\Delta X$, and so consumer A can exchange two units of Y for one unit of X. Similarly, consumer B maximizes utility when

$$^B\mathrm{MRS}_{YX} = -\frac{P_X}{P_Y} \qquad \text{(Equilibrium for Consumer B)} \qquad \textbf{(18-4)}$$

COMPETITIVE EQUILIBRIUM AND PARETO EFFICIENCY IN EXCHANGE

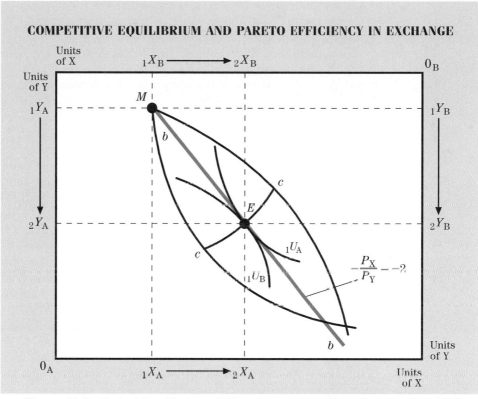

Figure 18-6   Budget line *bb* shows that each consumer can trade two units of Y for a unit of X. Consumer A is willing to supply $_1Y_A - {_2Y_A}$ units to the market and demands $_2X_A - {_1X_A}$ units of X. Consumer B demands $_2Y_B - {_1Y_B}$ units and is willing to supply $_1X_B - {_2X_B}$ units of X when two units of Y can be traded for a unit of X. The quantity supplied of Y equals the quantity demanded of Y, and the same is true of good X. Trade between competitive demanders and suppliers places consumers A and B on the contract curve at point *E*.

Therefore, in a competitive equilibrium we have

$$^A\text{MRS}_{YX} = -\frac{P_X}{P_Y} = {^B}\text{MRS}_{YX} \qquad \text{(Condition for Pareto Efficiency in Exchange)} \qquad \textbf{(18-5)}$$

Equation 18-5 says that the **marginal rates of substitution are equated** for the two consumers when each trades as many units as desired at the equilibrium price ratio.

The Wizard claims that he understands what the symbols mean, but you suspect that he does not grasp the significance of your proof. So, you decide to use a geometrical proof. In Figure 18-6 the initial allocation is at point *M*. The slope of budget line *bb* equals $-P_X/P_Y = -\$10/\$5 = -2$. So, A and B can trade two units of Y for one unit of X. Consumer A is willing to trade two units of Y for one unit of X along budget line bb until it is tangent to the indifference curve $_1U_A$ at point E. To reach point E, A is demanding $_2X_A - {_1}X_A$ more units of X and is supplying $_1Y_A - {_2}Y_A$ units of Y to the market when $-P_X/P_Y = -2$.

Consumer B is willing to supply $_1X_B - {_2}X_B$ more units of X for $_2Y_B - {_1}Y_B$ more units of Y when the exchange rate is -2. Because point E is on the contract curve, cc, the slope of consumer B's indifference curve is tangent not only to budget line bb but to A's indifference curve as well. The markets for X and for Y are in equilibrium because the quantity demanded of X by A equals the increased quantity supplied of X by B when the price of X is twice that of Y. Both A and B are better off by trading away from point M to point E because there are gains from trade.

This is a remarkable result even for a relatively simple two-person exchange economy. Each participant knows only his or her own utility function. Yet, trading by price-taking participants yields a result where the quantity demanded equals the quantity supplied in each of the two markets and both participants reach the contract curve by exchanging goods at a market-determined relative price ratio. Adam Smith's invisible hand guides demanders and suppliers to a point on the contract curve although each participant in the market has only a tiny piece of private information about the market—what quantity the individual will demand or supply at each price ratio. Neither A nor B knows anything about the utility of the other market participants or the quantities of X and Y held by them. Each takes the price ratio as given and trades with the sole objective of maximizing his or her own utility. Yet, a competitive market guides all inhabitants to the contract curve so that the marginal rates of substitution of all consumers in the economy are equal to each other and to the relative price ratio, and the economy achieves Pareto efficiency in exchange.

APPLICATION 18-1

Minimizing Information Requirements in Experimental Competitive Markets

Researchers have constructed markets in a laboratory setting to determine just how much information market participants must have before the market reaches a competitive equilibrium price. These experiments shed light on a proposition advanced by Friedrich Hayek that competitive markets economize on the acquisition of information by market participants.

In these experiments the researcher designates an individual as a demander or a supplier and assigns an individual demand function to each demander and a firm supply function to each supplier. For example, the researcher instructs a demander that the highest (reservation) price the demander will pay for the first unit of a hypothetical good is $15, for the second unit is $10, and so on. Each demander receives a monetary reward equal to the difference between the reservation price of the unit and the price the demander actually pays for the good. A demander maximizes her winnings from participating in the experiment by buying each unit at as low a price as possible.

If a participant is a supplier, the researcher gives each firm a supply function.

For example, the supplier offers one unit at $3, a second unit at $6, and so on. The monetary reward for a supplier is equal to the difference between the actual price received for the unit and the lower (reservation) price. Each supplier maximizes his winnings from participating in the experiment by selling each unit at as high a price as possible.

In a typical experiment, there are several demanders and several suppliers, with demanders trying to purchase the good at the lowest price possible and suppliers trying to sell it at the highest price possible. Market demand and supply functions are simply the horizontal sum of the individual demand and supply functions. Only the researcher knows what the aggregate demand and supply functions look like and the equilibrium competitive price. The individual demand and supply functions of the market participants are private information that only each participant knows.

The experiments create a *double-auction* trading process similar to that seen on the New York Stock Exchange. Each demander and supplier sits at a computer terminal. Each demander enters a bid price, the price that the consumer is willing to pay for a unit, and the bid price flashes on all the terminals. All participants can see if it is higher than an outstanding bid price. A supplier may enter an ask price, the price at which the individual is willing to supply a unit. If the ask price is less than an outstanding ask price, it replaces the existing ask price and appears on the screen. What each market participant knows is the highest bid and the lowest ask. A bid or an ask is binding until another bid or ask displaces it or a sale occurs. When that happens, the auction for that unit ends and the computer waits for a new pair of bid and ask prices.

Vernon Smith has summarized the results of about 200 experiments performed by different researchers and reports that they invariably indicate that the double-auction trading mechanism converges quickly to the competitive equilibrium price where quantity demanded equals quantity supplied, whether experienced or inexperienced subjects participate in the experiment.[3] This uniformity of results is especially true when individual demand and firm supply functions are stable. The experimental results indicate that convergence to the competitive price does occur, although each participant has only a tiny bit of information about the market and no information about other demanders and suppliers. The demanders or suppliers do not have to know what the market demand and supply functions look like for the market to reach the competitive equilibrium price. Not only does price settle to the equilibrium price, but it appears in a way that economizes on the amount of market information that each participant must possess.

Impediments to Pareto Efficiency

To reach the contract curve, traders must be free to trade in competitive markets. If hurdles are placed in the way, consumers will not reach the contract curve.

---

[3] Based on Vernon L. Smith, "Markets as Economizers of Information: Experimental Examination of the 'Hayek Hypothesis,' " *Economic Inquiry* XX (April 1982), pp. 165–79.

There are instances where legal restrictions prevent a competitive market from developing, and so voluntary trade is prevented. For example, during a recent drought in California many communities adopted water rationing. There was no provision for a household to sell part of its water allotment for money in a market. Another example concerns an owner of a historical building who cannot sell it to a developer who plans to tear it down and replace it. An owner of a kidney cannot sell it legally. In some of these cases the prohibition of voluntary transactions can be justified because the transaction might adversely affect other parties. In other cases the prohibition is an indirect way of redistributing income from one group to another group. In still others, trade is prohibited because the principle of consumer sovereignty is rejected.

APPLICATION **18-2**

Impediments to Trading Water Rights in California

Water is often treated differently from other goods.[4] In many states legal codes establish a hierarchical set of priorities for uses of water. Certain "higher" uses receive priority status over "lower" uses. This makes it costly to transfer water designed for higher priority uses to lower priority uses. These restrictions make the sale of water rights more costly and prevent the sale of water to the *user* with the highest valuation as opposed to the *use* with the highest priority. By limiting transfers of water from one use to another, differential prices for water exist. For example, water is cheap in California when used for farming but is very expensive when used by urban dwellers. Why should water be priced differently for different uses? If there were a competitive market for water in California, the price of water would be the same for all uses unless costs were different. Yet the purchase price paid can be over 100 times higher for urban use than for farm use.

Let's illustrate the water situation with an Edgeworth box diagram. Consider two individuals, one of whom is a farmer endowed with W_f acre-feet of water. The farmer's endowment is W_f and I_f where $S_f = I_f$ is spending on a composite good and is equal to the farmer's income. The other individual is an urban dweller who has little water, W_u, but spends more on a composite good $S_u = I_u$. The endowment of the urban resident is W_u and S_u. Figure 18-7 shows the Edgeworth box diagram for the two consumers. The dimensions of the box are $W_f + W_u$ by $S_f + S_u$.

Both consumers are at point M in Figure 18-7. Given the existing endowments, their utility functions intersect at point M. Therefore, there is room for trade. The city dweller is willing to trade income for water, and the rural inhabitant is willing to trade water for income. Both will be better off. Yet, this trade will not occur. Why? Because, the property rights to the land limit the transfer of water. The trading of water depends on the water laws of each state, and in California state laws have made it very difficult to sell water for other uses. There may be justifi-

---

[4] Based on Jack Hirschleifer, James C. De Haven, and Jerome W. Milliman, *Water Supply* (Chicago: University of Chicago Press, 1960), chap. 3.

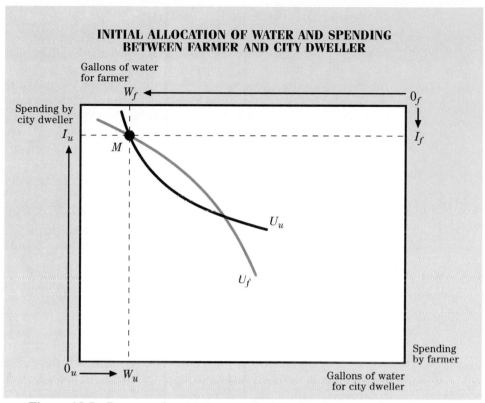

Figure 18-7   Because of restrictions on the transfer of water, urban consumers are unable to trade income for water. Therefore, Pareto efficiency in exchange is not reached.

cation at times for this prohibition, but often the restrictions reduce economic efficiency. Except where the sale of water causes parties apart from those involved in the transaction to suffer losses, economic efficiency would improve if the property rights to water were clear and owners of water were able to trade water just as they are able to enter into trades for workers, fertilizer, and tractors.

By now, the Wizard's understanding of and fascination with the role of competitive markets have grown immensely. With a functioning competitive market, the marginal rates of substitution are equal for all market participants at the equilibrium competitive price ratio, and so exchange is Pareto-efficient. Moreover, this equilibrium appears to minimize information requirements since it does not require every participant to know the utility functions and demand and supply functions of all the other market participants.

Pareto Efficiency in Production

Our Wizard of Zeoz fable does not end here. The Wizard correctly notes that the economy in Zeoz produces as well as exchanges goods. While he admits shortcomings in his command and control policies, he wants to know how markets can function to produce goods more efficiently than with the use of his policies.

You begin your explanation by specifying what resources are available in Zeoz to produce goods X and Y. The economy has factors of production of L' units of labor and K' units of capital. To produce the goods that the Wizard assigns to inhabitants, he must assign these factors of production to industry X and industry Y so that the required quantities of X and Y are produced. The production function of each good shows the quantity produced for any combination of labor and capital that the Wizard assigns to produce the good.

Suppose the Wizard assigns $_1L_X$ units of labor and $_1K_X$ units of capital to produce X and $_1L_Y$ and $_1K_Y$ units of labor and capital to produce Y. The total number of units of labor and capital assigned to produce X and Y must equal L' and K'.

$$_1L_X + {_1L_Y} = L'   _1K_X + {_1K_Y} = K'$$ (Factor Endowment Constraints) **(18-6)**

The Wizard's assignment of factors to products determines the quantities of X and Y that the economy produces. We illustrate the amounts of X and Y produced with this assignment of factors in a production version of the Edgeworth box diagram. In Figure 18-8 the dimensions of the Edgeworth production box are L' by K'. 0_X is the origin for the production function of good X. By proceeding from southwest to northeast, more units of labor and capital produce more units of X. The production function of Y starts with point 0_Y at the origin in the northeast corner. Proceeding from northeast to southwest represents an increase in the production of Y. Figure 18-8 shows several isoquants of the production function for X and of the production function for Y. The Wizard's initial allocation of factors is at point a, and so the economy of Zeoz produces X_0 units of X and Y_0 units of Y.

How should the Wizard assign factors to the two industries so that production is efficient? The natural procedure is to adopt a standard similar to the one for efficiency in exchange. Production is Pareto-efficient if any reallocation of factors of production reduces the output of one good given the output of the other good.

> An allocation of factors is Pareto-efficient if any reallocation of factors reduces the output of one good given the output of the other good.

Which points in Figure 18-8 satisfy this definition? Starting at point a, suppose the Wizard reassigns the factors so that the output of X remains constant and the movement is along the isoquant X_0 to point b and then to point c. The output of Y increases from Y_0 to Y_1 and then to Y_2, while the output of X is constant. Therefore, neither point a nor point b is Pareto-efficient in production because the output of Y is increasing for a given output of X. However, point c is Pareto-efficient. Given X_0, a movement away from point c in either direction lowers the output of Y.

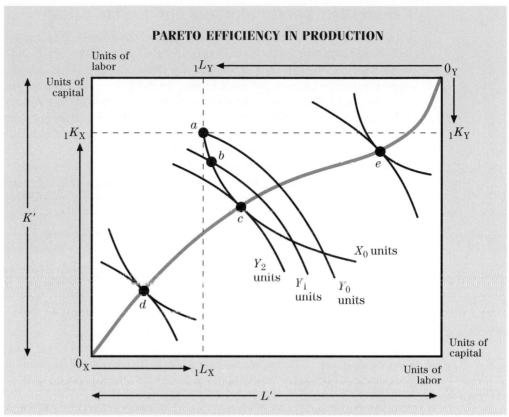

Figure 18-8   The initial allocation of factors is at point a. An allocation is Pareto-efficient if any reallocation of factors reduces the output of one good while holding the output of the other good constant. At point c, the slopes of the isoquants are equal and the allocation of factors is Pareto-efficient. The curve running from 0_X to 0_Y connects all points of tangency and is called the contract curve.

The slopes of the isoquants X_0 and Y_2 are equal at point c.

$$^X\text{MRTS}_{KL} = {}^Y\text{MRTS}_{KL} \quad \text{(Condition for Pareto Efficiency in Production)} \quad \textbf{(18-7)}$$

where $^X\text{MRTS}_{KL}$ is the marginal rate of technical substitution between capital and labor in the production of X and $^Y\text{MRTS}_{KL}$ has the corresponding interpretation in the production of Y. Therefore, Pareto efficiency in production requires the slopes of the isoquants to be equal. In Figure 18-8 all points of tangency between the isoquants are connected to derive the contract curve 0_X0_Y. For example, the slopes of the two isoquants are equal at points d and e.

> **Pareto efficiency in production** requires the marginal rate of technical substitution between labor and capital to be equal for the two products.

Competitive Factor Markets and Pareto Efficiency

If factor markets are competitive, each firm in the economy is a price taker in all factor markets and employs as many units of each factor as it desires at given factor prices. When prices of factors are determined so that quantity demanded equals quantity supplied for each factor, production is Pareto-efficient.

The proof of this proposition is similar to the proof that exchange is Pareto-efficient with competitive product markets. The slope of the isocost line facing each firm producing either X or Y equals $-w/r$, the factor price ratio. From Chapter 5 you know that a firm maximizes output given a total cost by equating the slope of the isoquant with the slope of the isocost line. Let's consider a single competitive firm supplying X. A firm produces X at minimum cost when the marginal rate of technical substitution between capital and labor equals the factor price ratio.

$$^X\text{MRTS}_{KL} = -\frac{w}{r} \qquad \text{(Minimum Cost Condition for X)} \qquad \textbf{(18-8)}$$

Similarly, a firm produces product Y at minimum cost when the marginal rate of technical substitution equals the factor price ratio.

$$^Y\text{MRTS}_{KL} = -\frac{w}{r} \qquad \text{(Minimum Cost Condition for Y)} \qquad \textbf{(18-9)}$$

Because all firms in the economy pay the same prices for the factors of production and each firm minimizes total costs, the slope of the isoquant of a firm producing X equals the slope of the isoquant of a firm producing Y.

$$^X\text{MRTS}_{KL} = -\frac{w}{r} = {}^Y\text{MRTS}_{KL} \qquad \begin{array}{l}\text{(Condition for Pareto Efficiency}\\ \text{in Production)}\end{array} \qquad \textbf{(18-10)}$$

In Figure 18-9 aa' is the isocost line faced by both firms. It shows the exchange rate of factors so that total production cost is constant. If the price of labor is \$36 per worker per period and the price of capital is \$12 per machine per period, the slope of the isocost line is -3 and each firm can purchase three units of capital by releasing one unit of labor and keep total cost constant. At point a the firm produces X_0 units at a total cost of \$36 times $_0L_X$ units of labor plus \$12 times $_0K_X$ units of capital. The isocost line aa' shows the rate of exchange between labor and capital. A firm producing good X can increase the output of X to X_1 by substituting labor for capital until it reaches point e. The firm wants to expand employment by $_1L_X - {}_0L_X$ more workers and reduce the number of machines by $_0K_X - {}_1K_X$ units of capital if the exchange rate between factors is -3. The firm producing Y increases the output of Y from Y_0 to Y_1 by substituting capital for labor. It is demanding $_1K_Y - {}_0K_Y$ more units of capital and employing $_0L_Y - {}_1L_Y$ fewer workers. The quantity demanded of labor by the firm producing X equals the quantity supplied of labor by the firm producing Y when the price of labor is three times the price of capital. In moving from point a to point e, each firm produces more units at the same total cost as at point a.

The curve 0_X0_Y is the contract curve for production and connects all points of tangency between the isoquants for X and for Y. The contract curve shows the

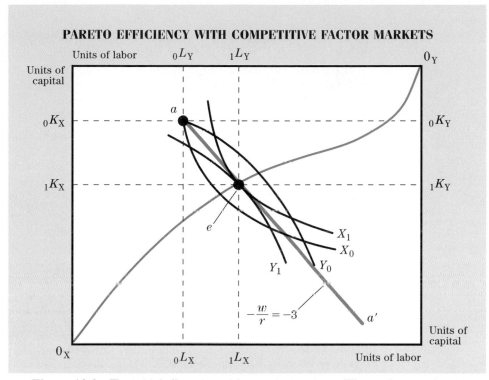

Figure 18-9   The initial allocation of factors is at point *a*. When a firm can hire three units of capital for one unit of labor, the firm producing X increases the output of X while holding total costs constant by moving to point *e*. The output of X increases from X_0 to X_1. The firm producing Y increases the output to Y_1 when moving to point *e*.

maximum quantity of Y that can be produced for each quantity of X. The **production possibility curve** in Figure 18-10 is another way of showing this. It indicates the maximum quantity of Y for each quantity of X and is derived from the contract curve in Figure 18-8. For example, point *c* in Figure 18-10 corresponds to point *c* in Figure 18-8. Given an output of X_0, the maximum output of Y is Y_2 units. Production is Pareto-efficient at any point on the production possibility curve. Any point inside the production possibility curve implies that production is not Pareto-efficient, and so the economy does not maximize the output of Y given the output of X. Note that point *a* is inside the production possibility curve in Figure 18-10. This point corresponds to point *a* in Figure 18-8 which is off the contract curve so that the economy produces only Y_0 units and X_0 units because of inefficient allocation of the factors of production.

The production possibility curve shows the opportunity cost of increasing the output of one good in terms of the other good. Starting at point *e* we can increase the output of Y by ΔY but only by decreasing the output of X by ΔX as we move along the production possibility curve in Figure 18-10. The opportunity cost of

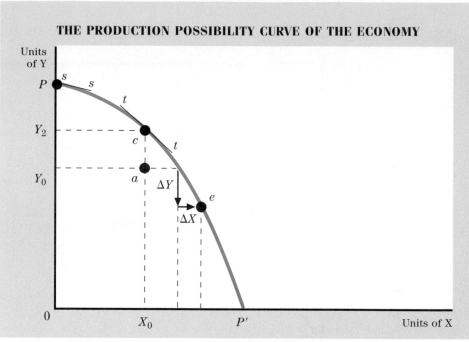

Figure 18-10   The production possibility curve shows the maximum amount of Y that can be produced for a given output of X. The production possibility curve is derived from the contract curve.

increasing Y by ΔY is ΔX. Factors released from producing X enter industry Y to produce more Y in such a way that production is always Pareto-efficient.

The slope of the production possibility curve is defined as the **marginal rate of transformation** between Y and X, or

$$\text{MRT}_{\text{YX}} = \frac{\Delta Y}{\Delta X} \qquad \text{(Marginal Rate of Transformation)} \qquad \textbf{(18-11)}$$

You may have noticed that the production possibility curve in Figure 18-10 bows outward. When the economy is producing only Y at point *P*, a unit decrease in the output of Y causes a relatively large increase in the production of X. Geometrically, this means that the production possibility curve is relatively flat at this point. The reason for this is that the marginal cost of producing the last unit of Y is relatively high when virtually all the factors in the economy are employed in industry Y. In contrast, the marginal cost of producing the first unit of X is relatively low. For example, at point *P* the marginal cost of producing the last unit of Y might be $20, whereas the marginal cost of producing the first unit of X is only $2. By producing one less unit of Y and transferring the costs saving of $20 to increase the output of X, the economy produces 10 more units of X. Therefore, the marginal rate of transformation is $\Delta Y/\Delta X = -MC_X/MC_Y = -\$2/\$20 = -1/10$. Line ss is tangent to the production possibility curve at point P and is virtually flat because a reduction of 1 unit of Y increases the output of X by 10 units.

$$MRT_{YX} = \frac{\Delta Y}{\Delta X} = -\frac{MC_X}{MC_Y} \qquad \begin{array}{l}\text{(Marginal Rate of Transformation}\\ \text{Equals the Negative of the Ratio} \quad \textbf{(18-12)}\\ \text{of Marginal Costs)}\end{array}$$

As the economy produces fewer units of Y and more units of X, the marginal cost of producing Y decreases and the marginal cost of producing X increases. At point c in Figure 18-10 the marginal cost of Y falls to \$10, while the marginal cost of producing X increases to \$10. When the economy produces one less unit of Y, it can produce only one more unit of X, and so the marginal rate of transformation is $-MC_X/MC_Y = -\$10/\$10 = -1$. The line tt has a slope of -1 and is tangent to the production possibility curve at point c. To summarize, the slope of the production possibility curve equals the negative of the relative marginal costs of producing X and Y.

APPLICATION 18-3

Reducing the Price of Capital by Subsidizing Small Businesses

Suppose that industry C has many small firms and industry D only has large firms. The many small firms in industry C successfully lobby Congress to give them a capital subsidy. Congress writes the law so that firms below a certain size receive a subsidized interest rate on purchases of machines. The firms in industry D are too large to qualify for the subsidy. What is the effect of this subsidy on one factor of production on Pareto efficiency in production?

Figure 18-11a shows an isoquant Q_C of a representative small firm in industry C. The isocost line is cc and reflects the subsidy in the purchase of capital. Figure 18-11b shows an isoquant Q_D of a representative large firm in industry D. The isocost function of the large firm is dd and is less steep than that of the small firm because the subsidy allows the small firm to purchase capital at a lower net price than the large firm can.

Both firms minimize the cost of producing any rate of output by equating the slope of the isoquant to the slope of the isocost line. The small firm minimizes the cost of producing Q_C by employing M_C machines and L_C workers at point C. The large firm produces Q_D by employing M_D machines and L_D workers at point D. Because the slopes of the isocost lines of the large and small firms differ, the slopes of the isoquants of these firms differ as well. Therefore, the marginal rates of technical substitution between the two types of firms differ and production is no longer Pareto-efficient. Subsidizing the use of a factor of production for a small firm and not a large firm creates a production distortion. For a given output of the small firm, the subsidy prevents the economy from maximizing the output of the large firm.

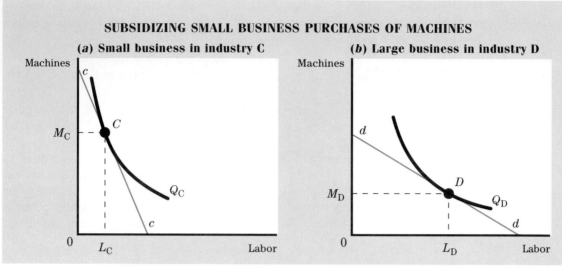

Figure 18-11 By giving small firms a subsidy for the purchase of machines, the economy is no longer Pareto-efficient in production.

Pareto Efficiency in Product Mix

You have patiently described the requirements for Pareto efficiency in exchange and in production to the Wizard. He is already thinking ahead and wonders how the quantities of X and Y produced are related to the quantities of X and Y demanded by consumers A and B. He asks, "It is all well and good that competitive markets can produce any combination of X and Y efficiently and that competitive markets will distribute what is produced so that exchange is Pareto-efficient, but what assurance do I have that competitive markets will produce the combination of X and Y that consumers demand?" To answer this important question, you need to demonstrate that competitive markets can align the production side of the market with the consumption side of the market by producing the product mix that maximizes the efficiency of the economy.

Pareto efficiency in product mix requires that the marginal rates of substitution between Y and X in exchange equal the marginal rate of transformation of the economy.

Pareto efficiency in product mix requires the marginal rates of substitution of consumers to equal the marginal rate of transformation.

$$^A MRS_{YX} = {}^B MRS_{YX} = MRT_{YX} \quad \text{(Condition for Pareto Efficiency in Product Mix)} \quad \text{(18-13)}$$

Equation 18-13 requires that the slope of the production possibility curve equal the slope of each consumer's indifference curve.

To show this, you ask the Wizard to consider a point on the production possibility curve where a small movement along the curve reduces the output of Y by one unit and increases the output of X by four units so that $MRT_{YX} = -\frac{1}{4}$. Suppose the economy's product mix is distributed to consumers so that exchange among consumers is Pareto-efficient and that each consumer is indifferent between substituting one less unit of Y for one unit of X ($^AMRS_{YX} = {}^BMRS_{YX} = -1$). By producing four more units of X and one less unit of Y, the economy can make at least one consumer better off while holding the utility of the other constant. In other words, one consumer is left undisturbed so that this consumer's utility is constant. Yet the economy produces four more units of X for one less unit of Y. The utility of the other consumer will increase if she receives four more units of X for one less unit of Y since she is indifferent with a one-to-one tradeoff. By changing the product mix, the utility of one consumer can be increased holding the utility of the other consumer constant. Therefore, the product mix of the economy is not Pareto-efficient because the marginal rates of substitution of consumers are *not* equal to the marginal rate of transformation of the economy. The economy is producing too little X and too much Y for it to be Pareto-efficient in product mix.

You ask the Wizard to consider the production possibility curve in Figure 18-12. At point a the economy is producing X' and Y' units efficiently. Given the production of X' and Y' units, let's say that consumer A has $_1Y_A$ of Y and $_1X_A$ units of X at point g, where point g is on the contract curve (not shown). Consumer B has the remaining units of goods X and Y. Because nn is tangent to the indifference curves of A and B at point g, there is Pareto efficiency in exchange.

Although there is Pareto efficiency in exchange (because the marginal rates of substitution are equal) and Pareto efficiency in production (because we are on and not inside the production possibility curve), we still do not have product mix efficiency. The slopes of the indifference curves at point g equal the slope of nn, but the slope of nn is not equal to the slope of dd on the production possibility curve at point a. If this economy produced more X and less Y, at least one consumer could be made better off given the utility of the other consumer.

If the economy is producing a Pareto-efficient product mix, the slopes of the indifference curves of consumers must equal the slope of the production possibility curve. Figure 18-13 shows an economy that is producing a Pareto-efficient product mix. In this figure line nn is tangent to the indifference curve $_1U_B$ and to $_1U_A$ at point h and has the same slope as line cc. The slope of cc equals the marginal rate of transformation of the production possibility curve at point a. Therefore, the marginal rates of substitution of A and B are equal, and both are equal to the marginal rate of transformation on the production possibility curve at point a.

Competitive Markets and Product Mix Efficiency

If all participants in each market are price takers, so all markets are competitive, the economy will produce a Pareto-efficient product mix. If both the product markets for X and for Y are competitive, then price equals marginal cost in each

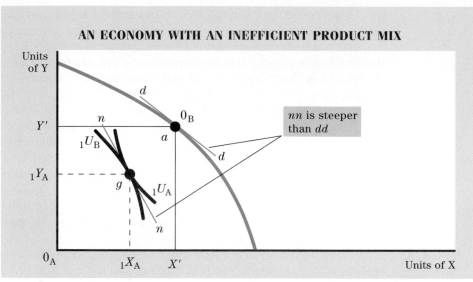

Figure 18-12   The product mix at point a is inefficient. The economy produces X' and Y' units efficiently at point a on the production possibility curve. If consumer A consumes $_1Y_A$ and $_1X_A$ units, then consumer B consumes the remainder of both goods. At point g the marginal rates of substitution for consumers A and B are equal. However, the marginal rates of substitution of consumers A and B do not equal the marginal rate of transformation at point a. The economy is producing too many units of Y and not enough units of X. By producing more X and less Y, the utility of one consumer increases while the utility of the other remains constant.

market, a hallmark condition for a competitive industry. If price equals marginal cost in each market, then the ratio of prices equals the ratio of marginal costs.

$$\frac{P_X}{P_Y} = \frac{MC_X}{MC_Y}$$

With competitive markets the ratio of prices conveys accurate information to consumers about the relative marginal costs of producing X and Y. We already know that each consumer maximizes utility by equating his or her marginal rate of substitution to $-P_X/P_Y$. Furthermore, we already know that $-MC_X/MC_Y$ equals the marginal rate of transformation. Therefore,

$$^A MRS_{YX} = {}^B MRS_{YX} =$$

$$-\frac{P_X}{P_Y} = -\frac{MC_X}{MC_Y} = MRT_{YX} \qquad \begin{array}{l}\text{(Condition for Pareto}\\ \text{Efficiency in Product Mix)}\end{array} \qquad \textbf{(18-14)}$$

When all markets are competitive, the marginal rate of substitution of each consumer in the economy is equal to the marginal rate of transformation, the requirement for Pareto efficiency in product mix.

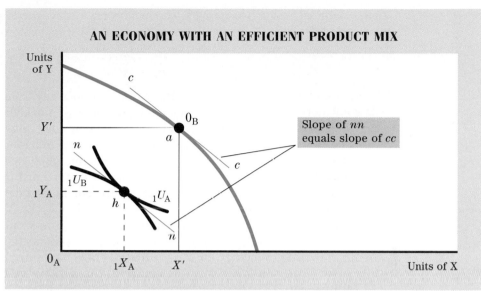

Figure 18-13   The economy provides an efficient product mix by producing X' and Y' units at point a on the production possibility curve. If A consumes $_1Y_A$ and $_1X_A$ units, then B consumes the remainder of both goods. At point h, the marginal rates of substitution of the two consumers are equal and equal the slope of nn. The marginal rates of substitution of each consumer equal the marginal rate of transformation at point a (the slope of cc) on the production possibility curve.

18-4   DEPARTURES FROM PARETO EFFICIENCY CAUSED BY MONOPOLY

Monopoly power is one impediment to achieving Pareto efficiency. You explain to the Wizard that total output is smaller under monopoly and in certain oligopoly models than under competition because $P > $ MC. To investigate the consequences of monopoly on resource allocation, you propose to the Wizard that he consider the following model.

In an economy with two goods, X and Y, the production of X is monopolized and Y is produced competitively. Price exceeds marginal cost in the monopolized market but equals marginal cost in industry Y. When a monopolist produces X,

$$\text{Price} > \text{Marginal revenue} = \text{Marginal cost}$$

$$\text{Price} > \text{Marginal cost}$$

Because the monopoly price exceeds the marginal cost in industry X, the price of X relative to the price of Y is greater than the marginal cost of producing X relative to the marginal cost of producing Y. The relative price of X is no longer an accurate measure of the relative marginal cost of producing X.

$$\frac{P_X}{P_Y} > \frac{MC_X}{MC_Y} \qquad \text{(18-15)}$$

In this situation consumers will sensibly substitute away from X and purchase relatively more units of Y because the monopoly price of X is higher relative to the price of Y than it would have been if X were supplied by competitive firms. Because every consumer faces the same higher price ratio, each purchases a market basket where the higher price ratio equals the consumer's marginal rate of substitution. Consequently, the marginal rates of substitution are still equal for all consumers in the economy. So the economy is Pareto-efficient in exchange even when a monopolist produces product X.

Although the producer of X is a monopolist in the product market, it can still be a price taker in factor markets. Consequently, all producers in the economy, whether they are producing Y or X, are price takers in factor markets and face the same factor price ratio. Therefore, the **marginal rates of technical substitution will still be equal** for firms in the two industries, and so production is Pareto-efficient.

Nevertheless, the economy is not hitting on all cylinders. The reason is that the product mix is no longer Pareto-efficient. Because price of X is higher under monopoly than under competition, the economy produces too little of X and too much of Y. We have

$$^{A}MRS_{YX} = {}^{B}MRS_{YX} = -\frac{P_X}{P_Y} < -\frac{MC_X}{MC_Y} = MRT_{YX} \qquad \begin{array}{c}\text{(Product Mix Is Not}\\ \text{Pareto-Efficient)}\end{array} \qquad \text{(18-16)}$$

where $^{A}MRS_{YX}$ is the marginal rate of substitution of consumer A and $^{B}MRS_{YX}$ is the marginal rate of substitution of consumer B. Therefore, the marginal rate of substitution of each consumer is less than the marginal rate of transformation.

$$^{A}MRS_{YX} = {}^{B}MRS_{YX} < MRT_{YX}$$

When a firm monopolizes the market for X, the marginal rates of substitution of consumers no longer equal the economy's marginal rate of transformation. For example, consumers might be indifferent between giving up one unit of Y for two units of X given P_X/P_Y, but the economy can produce four more units of X by producing one less unit of Y. The economy is producing too few units of X, the monopolized good, and too many units of Y, the competitive good. This means that the slope of each consumer's indifference curve is steeper than the slope of the production possibility curve when there is a monopoly in X given the mix of goods produced in the economy.

Figure 18-14 shows a situation where P_X/P_Y is greater than MC_X/MC_Y because a monopolist produces X. At point *e*, *mm* is tangent to the indifference curves of consumers A and B but is steeper than *bb*, the slope of the production possibility curve at point *a*. The marginal rates of substitution of the two consumers are equal, but they do not equal the marginal rate of transformation. A monopoly producer of X creates a distortion by causing resources that would produce more X to shift

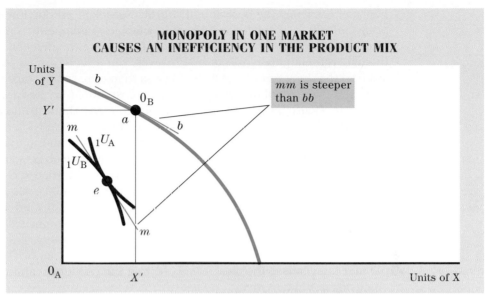

Figure 18-14   When a firm monopolizes the production of X, the economy produces Y' and X' units. Less of X is produced and more of Y because a monopolist produces X. At point e the slope of mm equals the marginal rate of substitution of consumers A and B. Line bb is tangent to the production possibility curve at point a. Line mm is steeper than line bb. Therefore, the product mix is not Pareto-efficient because the ratio of prices does not equal the ratio of marginal costs.

to the production of Y. Because the price ratio no longer mimics the relative marginal costs, there is a wedge between each consumer's marginal rate of substitution and the marginal rate of transformation of the economy, and so the product mix is no longer Pareto-efficient.

You have convinced the Wizard that the intellectual case against monopoly relies on the fact that a monopoly creates a **wedge between consumers' marginal rates of substitution and the marginal rate of transformation** and not on the idea that a monopolist earns profits. The objection to monopoly is still valid even if the profits of a monopolist are negligible, as they would be when the monopoly price equals the monopolist's average cost of production.

You point out to the Wizard that in the United States the Sherman Antitrust Act and other antimonopoly laws are designed to introduce more competition into a monopolized market so that the price approaches the competitive price. There is a consensus that such antimonopoly laws have prevented firms from adopting the more effective collusive devices, such as joint sales agencies, and thereby made some markets more competitive. Moreover, the antitrust laws have been used successfully to break up cartels and trusts. In markets where there is a natural monopoly because of increasing returns to scale, increasing the number of firms in the industry may increase competition among firms but will result in inefficient production. In these markets governments have regulated natural monopolies in hopes of obtaining the best of both worlds—efficient production and competitive prices. Ideally, a regulator would try to simulate a competitive market by setting price equal to long-run marginal cost, that is, where the demand curve intersects the long-run marginal cost curve. However, when there are increasing returns to scale so that long-run marginal cost is less than long-run average cost, setting the regulated price equal to long-run marginal cost would create losses for the regulated firm. Consequently, without a subsidy to cover the firm's losses, a regulator can at most lower price to long-run average cost.

Just as monopoly creates a wedge between price and marginal cost, so too will a per unit tax or subsidy on the price of a competitively produced good. These too create distortions by introducing a wedge between price and marginal cost of production. A per unit tax on X raises the price of X above the marginal cost of producing it (excluding the per unit tax). Here again, relative price is no longer an accurate signal of relative marginal cost of production. Imposing a per unit tax on the production of X raises the price of X, reduces the amount of X produced, shifts the demand function for Y outward, and increases the quantity of Y produced. A per unit tax changes the product mix so that the economy cannot achieve Pareto efficiency in product mix.

The Wizard leans back in his chair, impressed by your arguments, and decides to appoint you his lifelong adviser. The most important point that you hope the Wizard appreciates is that Pareto efficiency conditions can be achieved by relying on competitive product and factor markets. The Wizard can rely on the self-interest of consumers, producers, and factor suppliers, all of whom are price takers in competitive markets, to satisfy all Pareto efficiency conditions. Moreover, this is true even though individual agents, be they consumers, producers, or factor suppliers, have only tiny bits of information about the economy. The Wizard does not have to rely on command and control policies. The next chapter considers some important qualifications to these general conclusions.

SUMMARY

- Pareto efficiency in exchange requires that the marginal rates of substitution of all consumers be equal.
- If consumers can trade goods in competitive markets, they reach the contract curve and achieve Pareto efficiency in exchange.
- Pareto efficiency in production requires all marginal rates of technical substitution to be equal for all firms.
- If all firms face the same factor price ratio,

they reach the contract curve and achieve Pareto efficiency in production.
- Pareto efficiency in product mix requires the marginal rates of substitution of all consumers to equal the marginal rate of transformation.
- When all product and factor markets are competitive, an economy satisfies the Pareto efficiency conditions.

KEY TERMS

partial equilibrium
consumer endowment
Pareto-efficient

general equilibrium
equating marginal rates of substitution
gains from trade

Pareto efficiency in exchange
contract curve
Pareto efficiency in production
competitive factor markets and Pareto
    efficiency in production
production possibility curve
competitive product and factor markets and
    Pareto efficiency in product mix

competitive markets and Pareto efficiency
    in exchange
equating marginal rates of technical
    substitution
marginal rate of transformation
Pareto efficiency in product mix
wedge between consumers' marginal rates
    of substitution and the marginal rate of
    transformation

REVIEW QUESTIONS

1. What is a consumer's endowment?
2. Consumer A has all units of good X, and consumer B has all units of good Y. Show this position in an Edgeworth box diagram.
3. What is the required condition for Pareto efficiency in exchange?
4. When will two price-taking traders end up on the contract curve?
5. What is the required Pareto efficiency con-

dition if firms are to reach the contract curve in production?
6. What is the production possibility curve and how is it derived?
7. What does Pareto efficiency in product mix mean?
8. Does an economy produce a Pareto-efficient product mix when all markets are competitive?

EXERCISES

1. If there are gains from trade, what should be true of the marginal rates of substitution between Y and X for consumers A and B? If there are no gains from trade, how should the marginal rate of substitution between goods Y and X for consumer A be related to the marginal rate of substitution for consumer B?

2. Consumer A has an endowment of 20 units of good Y and 6 units of good X, while consumer B has an endowment of 12 units of Y and 30 units of X. Draw an Edgeworth box diagram and show the endowment point. Given this information, will A trade Y for X or X for Y if a competitive market opens? Explain.

3. Consumer A's endowment includes 6 units of Y and 1 unit of X. Consumer B's endowment includes 3 units of Y and 1 unit of X. If A and B trade, the equilibrium price ratio will be between -6 and -3. Explain why you do or do not agree with this statement.

4. Is there some justification for calling the contract curve in exchange a "conflict curve"?

5. If you were asked why owners of kidneys cannot sell their organs, what explanation would you give?

6. Use the Edgeworth box diagram in Figure 18-6 to show how the utility of consumers A and B changes when the government regulates the price of Y. Suppose the price of Y falls to $2 while the price of X is $10.

7. Suppose the assignment of labor and capital to the production of good X and good Y is not Pareto-efficient. Show what the wage-rental factor price ratio must be if the firm that produces X is minimizing cost and if the firm that produces Y is minimizing cost. Will the wage-rental factor price ratio be different for the two firms?

8. Suppose a technological change allows firms in industry X to produce more units of X for each combination of L and K.

Show how this technological change shifts the production possibility function of the economy.

9. If more immigrants enter the United States, how will this affect the production possibility curve?

10. What are the consequences of imposing a quota on U.S. wheat production on the relative price of wheat and the quantity of wheat produced? Use the production possibility curve to illustrate the consequences. Show how the price ratio facing consumers is related to the relative marginal costs of producing wheat and another good.

11. The social cost of monopoly occurs because the monopolist does not produce at the minimum point of its long-run average cost function. Explain why you agree or disagree with this statement and carefully describe the social objection to monopoly.

*12. Assume that a monopolist has a constant long-run average and marginal cost function. Suppose that a monopolist can engage in perfect price discrimination and therefore leaves no consumer surplus. With a graph show the output of a monopolist. Which Pareto efficiency conditions are satisfied?

CHAPTER 19

EXTERNALITIES AND PUBLIC GOODS

■ **19-1 External Effects and Pareto Efficiency**

Internalizing the Externality

Application 19-1: Internalizing an Externality in a Shopping Mall

Maximizing Social Surplus with a Per Unit Tax

The Coase Theorem

Application 19-2: Allowing the Coase Theorem to Work

Transaction Costs

Application 19-3: Neighborhoods for Sale

Application 19-4: View Wars and Defining Property Rights

Application 19-5: Saving the African Elephant

Taxation and Pareto Efficiency

■ **19-2 Public Goods and Pareto Efficiency**

The Optimal Quantity of a Public Good

Financing a Public Good

■ **Summary**

■ **Key Terms**

■ **Review Questions**

■ **Exercises**

In Chapter 18 we demonstrated that Pareto efficiency conditions are satisfied when all product and factor markets are competitive. When price exceeds marginal cost, as it does when a market is monopolized, an economy does not produce the socially optimal product mix and, therefore, one of the Pareto efficiency conditions is violated. In our derivation of the Pareto efficiency conditions in Chapter 18, we presumed that all product markets existed. However, as we have already showed in Chapter 14, some markets may not exist or some goods may not trade that would otherwise have traded had information been distributed symmetrically. So, asymmetric information is another reason why the Pareto efficiency conditions are not satisfied. In this chapter we investigate two other reasons why the Pareto efficiency conditions may not be satisfied: externalities (third-party effects) and public goods.

19-1 EXTERNAL EFFECTS AND PARETO EFFICIENCY

Until now, we have assumed that a decision by a consumer or by a firm has no external effects on other consumers or other firms. However, there are many situations where external or third-party effects are important. If I have asthma and the maître d' seats someone who smokes at a nearby table, I begin to cough and have difficulty breathing. The transaction between the smoker and the restaurant imposes a cost on me, the offended party. If a steel factory's emissions pollute the air, it adversely affects nearby residences or could raise the cost of production of a firm located nearby. If airplanes fly over my residence periodically, noise interrupts all conversation until the planes pass. If you get a flu vaccination, others benefit to whatever degree you are less likely to be a carrier of the flu. If my wonderful view of San Francisco Bay is blocked because my neighbor allows his trees to grow, I suffer a loss in utility. If my neighbor allows his trees to grow and extend over my fence so that my yard receives little sun and I am unable to plant a beautiful garden with attractive flowers and foliage, my utility decreases. If my neighbor keeps her dog inside the house at night, my utility increases because I do not hear her barking dog.

In all these cases a consumer or a firm receives an external benefit or suffers an external loss because of the behavior of another consumer or firm. We say there is a **negative externality** if third parties are worse off, or a **positive externality** if third parties benefit. In each case a consumer or a firm incurs costs and receives no compensation for the costs incurred or receives benefits and pays nothing for the benefits enjoyed. For example, no feasible mechanism may exist for airlines to pay homeowners for the discomfort caused by noise pollution or for the owners of steel factories to pay the nearby residents for their discomfort. Because it is too costly to monitor, there is no simple mechanism by which juveniles who purchase cans of spray paint and cover walls with graffiti may be required to compensate the owners of the walls. We want to examine the consequences of externalities on Pareto efficiency when markets for compensation do not exist and, later, when they do.

> An **externality** exists when a firm or individual benefits from or is harmed by the behavior of other firms or individuals.

The externality problem can be introduced by way of a numerical example. The Bright Paint Company produces paint and discharges wastewater into a river. Bright Paint sells its paint at the equilibrium competitive price of $14 a unit. Pure Water Company sells bottled water from the same river and is downstream from Bright Paint. Because of the lower water quality, Pure Water must incur additional costs to purify the water before bottling it.

Table 19-1 shows the marginal production cost of Bright Paint (column 1) and the *marginal external (damage) cost* incurred by Pure Water (column 2) for different quantities of paint produced by Bright Paint.

Since Bright Paint is a competitive firm, it sells each unit of paint for $14 and maximizes its profits by producing five units of paint where the price equals Bright Paint's marginal cost of production. Yet, the fifth unit imposes a *marginal cost on society* that is far greater than $14 because Pure Water Co. incurs a marginal damage (external) cost of $18. **Marginal social cost** (MSC) is in column 3 and equals marginal production cost (MC) plus **marginal damage cost** (MDC). The marginal social cost incurred by society when Bright Paint produces the fifth unit is not $14 but $32. From a societal perspective, Bright Paint is producing too much paint because it takes only its marginal production cost into account when it maximizes its profits by producing five units. The competitive price received by Bright Paint for the fifth unit sold is less than the marginal social cost imposed by producing it.

An environmentally concerned individual might demand that the polluting facility shut down to eliminate the external effect completely. Note that the optimal solution does not require Bright Paint to shut down completely but rather to determine production where price equals marginal *social* cost. Marginal social cost equals $14 when Bright Paint produces three, not five, units of paint. Completely eliminating Bright Paint's output would leave price above the marginal social cost of producing the first unit. The sum of consumer and producer surplus is maximized

Table 19-1   MARGINAL PRODUCTION COST, MARGINAL DAMAGE COST, AND SOCIAL COST

QUANTITY PRODUCED BY BRIGHT PAINT (UNITS)	MARGINAL PRODUCTION COST OF BRIGHT PAINT, MC ($) (1)	MARGINAL DAMAGE (EXTERNAL) COST INCURRED BY PURE WATER PER UNIT INCREASE IN OUTPUT, MDC ($) (2)	MARGINAL SOCIAL COST PER UNIT INCREASE IN OUTPUT, MSC = MC + MDC ($) (3)
1	5	2	7
2	6	4	10
3	7	7	14
4	10	11	21
5	14	18	32

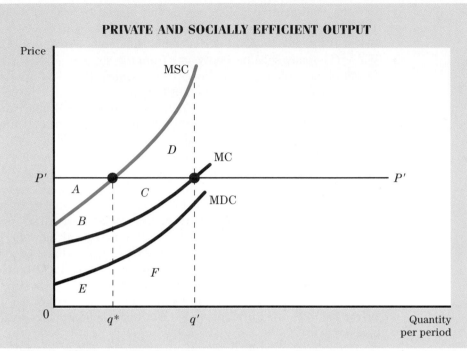

Figure 19-1   A competitive firm maximizes profits by producing q' units where $P' = \text{MC}$. MSC is the marginal social cost caused by the discharges of Bright Paint and MDC is the marginal damage cost incurred by Pure Water. If Bright Paint had to pay marginal damage cost, it would produce only q^* units. Because the firm incurs only its marginal cost, the output of Bright Paint is too large when there is a negative externality.

when Bright Paint produces three units, not zero units. Just because there are negative externalities, this does not imply that Bright Paint should stop the production of paint.

Now let's consider the externality problem somewhat more generally. In Figure 19-1 Bright Paint is a price taker and can sell each unit at P'. The firm's marginal cost function is MC. The marginal damage cost incurred by Pure Water is MDC. MSC is the marginal social cost function and equals the vertical sum of the private marginal production cost function of Bright Paint and the marginal damage cost function of Pure Water.

Bright Paint maximizes its profits when it produces q' units where $P' = \text{MC}$. Producer surplus is equal to the sum of areas A, B, and C in Figure 19-1. However, from a social point of view, producer surplus is smaller because Pure Water incurs marginal external costs. We can measure total damage costs incurred by Pure Water in either of two ways. It is equal to the area under the marginal damage cost function, $E + F$, or the area between MSC and MC, $B + C + D$.

Social surplus, S, is defined as the producer surplus of Bright Paint less the total external (damage) costs incurred by Pure Water.

$$S = \text{Producer surplus} - \text{Total external cost}$$

When Bright Paint produces q' units, producer surplus equals $A + B + C$. The total damage costs incurred by Pure Water are equal to $B + C + D$. Therefore, social surplus is

$$S = (A + B + C) - (B + C + D) = A - D$$

An omniscient central planner would maximize social surplus by setting Bright Paint's output at q^*, where $P' = \text{MSC}$, so that social surplus equals area A. In the absence of an all-knowing central planner, how can a market system, where agents are maximizing either utility or profit, induce Bright Paint to produce q^* and not q' units? Until a path-breaking article by Nobel Prize winner Ronald Coase appeared, most economists argued that a decentralized competitive price system could reach the social optimum by either costlessly internalizing the externality or by the government's assessing taxes on the firm creating the negative externality.[1] Let's consider the two possibilities in order.

Internalizing the Externality

In some but not all cases the externality problem can be dealt with by **internalizing the externality.** Paint manufacturing and the bottling of water are figuratively placed under one roof. Instead of assuming that Bright Paint and Pure Water are two separate companies, let's assume that they are simply two divisions of a diversified firm and that the cost functions for producing paint and bottled water are unchanged. The manager of the diversified firm must decide on the paint output of the Bright Paint division and on the number of bottles of water supplied by the Pure Water division so that the firm earns maximum profits. In this situation the manager knows that a unit increase in the output of the Bright Paint division costs the firm the marginal cost of paint plus the marginal damage cost incurred by the Pure Water division. The manager will take account of the marginal damage cost inflicted by the Bright Paint division on the Pure Water division when determining the output of the paint division.

> An externality is internalized when the decision maker bears the full cost or receives the full benefit of a decision.

The significance of this point is that the manager of a profit-maximizing firm will want the paint division to produce an output where $P' = \text{MSC}$. By internalizing the externality, the decision maker takes account of the external cost when determining the profit-maximizing output of paint and selects the socially correct output.

This is the desired solution if the manager of the firm can perform both functions without a loss in efficiency. Clearly, there are limits to this. Otherwise, one giant firm in the economy could internalize all externalities. A single firm does not produce all the goods where there are external effects because at some point the

[1] R. H. Coase, "The Problem of Social Cost," *Journal of Law and Economics* 3 (1960), pp. 1–44.

firm experiences diseconomies of scale or incurs higher costs because it produces diverse goods.

APPLICATION 19-1

Internalizing an Externality in a Shopping Mall

An interesting example of internalizing an externality is the modern shopping mall. Typically, a shopping mall has one or more anchor stores—well-known department stores—and a group of smaller specialty and other types of stores. Historically, the recognized name of a department store is the magnet that attracts customers to the shopping mall. The other stores want to be in the mall because they can take a free ride on the name of the department store and receive a positive externality since the department store name attracts shoppers to the mall and to the other stores. Therefore, these stores save on promotion expenses. A standard contractual arrangement is for the developer of a shopping plaza to give the anchor store a lower rental fee per square foot or to offer some other subsidy. In this case the marginal social cost is less than the marginal cost of operating a well-known department store.

How do we know that anchors increase the sales of other stores by increasing mall traffic? If so, anchors should pay lower rent per square foot relative to other mall stores. Table 19-2 presents relevant information and shows that department stores are compensated for the positive externality that they create by attracting customers to the mall and increasing the sales of other mall stores. Median per-square-foot rent paid in 1993 (column 1) and the ratio of median per-square-foot

Table 19-2   RENT AND RENT/SALES RATIO FOR SELECTED STORE GROUPS IN LARGE SHOPPING MALLS, 1993

STORE GROUP	MEDIAN PER-SQUARE-FOOT RENT PAID (1)	MEDIAN PER-SQUARE-FOOT RENT/MEDIAN PER-SQUARE-FOOT SALES (2)
Department stores	$ 1.95	0.015
Clothing and accessories	18.58	0.079
Shoes	22.00	0.085
Food service	32.41	0.095
Gift/specialty	22.00	0.088
Jewelry	42.00	0.076

Source: B. Peter Pashigian and Eric D. Gould, "Internalizing Agglomeration Economies: The Pricing of Space in Shopping Malls," George J. Stigler Center for the Study of the Economy and the State, Working Paper No. 115, August 1996.

rent paid to median per-square-foot sales in 1993 (column 2) are shown for stores in selected groups.

Column 1 shows just how much lower is the per-square-foot rent paid by anchors compared to other mall stores in other groups. Stores in the department store group pay $1.95 per square foot, or 90 percent less than the median per-square-foot rent paid by clothing stores of $18.58. Even after adjusting for the lower per-square-foot sales of department stores, column 2 shows that department stores pay substantially lower rent relative to their sales than do stores in other groups. Stores in the other groups pay between 7.6 and 9.5 percent of their sales in rent. Anchors stand out by paying only 1.5 percent of sales in rent. These results indicate that mall developers reward anchors for the positive externality that they create in increasing the sales of other mall stores. The shopping mall not only allows consumers to economize on shopping time but is a market organization that internalizes a positive externality.

Maximizing Social Surplus with a Per Unit Tax

The government could use its taxing power to maximize social surplus. By imposing a per unit tax on Bright Paint, it raises the marginal cost inclusive of the per unit tax and reduces Bright Paint's output. Bright Paint's marginal cost inclusive of the tax becomes MC + t, where t is the per unit tax. If Bright Paint is to produce the socially optimal output of q^*, the government must set the per unit tax so that the MC + t function intersects P' at q^*. Figure 19-2 shows the required per unit tax. The function MC + t goes through point a. Therefore, the optimal per unit tax equals the marginal damage cost caused by producing the q^*th unit.

In Table 19-1, the socially optimal output is three units, or where the competitive price of $14 equals the marginal social cost. At this output the marginal damage cost is $7. If the per unit tax is $7, Bright Paint will produce only three units, the socially optimal quantity.

Economists thought that the invisible hand of Adam Smith became truly invisible when there were externalities. In these situations some form of governmental intervention was required because the self-interest of Bright Paint would prevent the economy from reaching the social optimum. By judiciously using taxes or subsidies, many economists believed the government could guide a decentralized competitive price system to the socially optimal output when there are external effects. Later, we will see that a per unit tax is not always the ideal solution to the externality problem and, in some cases, can lead to an inferior solution.

The Coase Theorem

In 1960 Nobel Prize winner Ronald Coase published an influential article that suggested the traditional analysis was incomplete. In terms of our example, Coase would say that the fundamental difficulty is not that Bright Paint creates an externality but that no one owns the quality of water. Coase argued that Bright Paint will produce the socially correct output if (1) transaction costs are negligible and

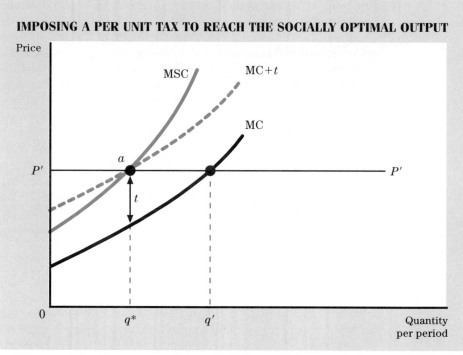

IMPOSING A PER UNIT TAX TO REACH THE SOCIALLY OPTIMAL OUTPUT

Figure 19-2   When a per unit tax of t is imposed, the marginal cost of Bright Paint shifts upward and becomes MC $+ t$. The optimum per unit tax equals the marginal damage cost when Bright Paint produces q^* units. The tax induces Bright Paint to produce the socially optimal output of q^* units.

(2) one or the other party has clearly defined property rights over water quality. Transaction costs refer to the cost of negotiating, verifying, and enforcing contracts. What was truly remarkable at the time was Coase's claim that the output produced by Bright Paint did not depend on which party possessed the property rights. Coase claimed that Bright Paint would produce the socially optimal output even though the law gave it the unrestricted right to pollute the river. He argued that private markets would solve the externality problem without the need for direct government intervention if transaction costs were negligible. This was a startling claim at the time because economists had so long believed that government intervention was absolutely essential to solve the externality problem. Equally astonishing was his second claim that the socially optimal output would emerge no matter which party owned the property rights.

     To expound on Coase's reasoning, we compare the solutions when Pure Water possesses the property rights in the river's water quality and then when Bright Paint has the right to pollute the river. Suppose the law gives Pure Water property rights in the water quality of the river. What does this mean? Pure Water can costlessly collect damages from Bright Paint if Bright Paint degrades the pristine water quality of the river by producing paint.

With the property rights assigned in this way, Bright Paint pays for the damages it causes. What options does Bright Paint have? It can:

- *Option 1.* Continue to produce paint *and* pay damages.

- *Option 2.* Clean the water before it is released so that the quality of water is not degraded.

- *Option 3.* Pay to have Pure Water invest in expensive filtering equipment to clean the discharges of Bright Paint or pay to have Pure Water relocate.

For the time being, let's set aside options 2 and 3 for later consideration and investigate only option 1. If Bright Paint pays the marginal damage cost to Pure Water for each unit produced, it will produce only q^* units where $P' = \text{MSC}$ because MSC becomes Bright Paint's marginal cost when the law assigns the property rights to Pure Water. For your convenience, Figure 19-3 reproduces the graph in Figure 19-1. The area between MSC and MC up to q^*, or area B in Figure 19-3, is equal to the total damage costs that Bright Paint pays to Pure Water.

Now consider the other extreme, that Bright Paint possesses the unencumbered right to degrade water quality. Bright Paint is creating the negative externality by producing paint, and yet Coase says society does not have to fear the conse-

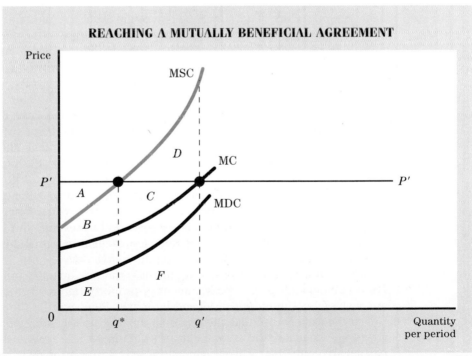

Figure 19-3 Pure Water can bribe Bright Paint to produce q^* units because Pure Water gains more (area C plus area D) than Bright Paint loses (area C) by reducing output from q' to q^* units.

quences even if Bright Paint possesses the right to pollute the river. Coase argues that the delegation of property rights to Bright Paint is inconsequential and will have no effect on water quality as long as transaction costs are negligible. To see this, put yourself in Pure Water's shoes. True, Pure Water can no longer collect damages. Even so, is it in the self-interest of Pure Water to allow Bright Paint to pollute the river? The answer is no. The management of Pure Water has an incentive to make the production of paint more expensive for Bright Paint, although Pure Water does not "own" the water quality.

If Pure Water could somehow persuade Bright Paint to reduce paint output from q' *to* q^*, by how much would Bright Paint be worse off and by how much would Pure Water be better off? Bright Paint is worse off because its producer surplus decreases by area C in Figure 19-3. Pure Water is better off because marginal damage costs incurred by it decrease by area C *plus* area D. Therefore, the loss by Bright Paint is less than the gain by Pure Water. Clearly, a mutually beneficial deal is possible. Suppose Pure Water offers to pay Bright Paint area C plus some fraction of area D if Bright Paint reduces output to q^*. Bright Paint and Pure Water will both be better off by striking a deal whereby they share the proceeds of area D. Of course, it is assumed that both parties will not be so stubborn while bargaining over area D that no deal is possible. This is what we mean when we say there is no transaction cost.

In the extreme case, Pure Water could pay Bright Paint all of area D to produce q^* rather than q' and would not be worse off. How might Pure Water structure the deal? Suppose Pure Water agrees to pay Bright Paint the marginal damage cost for each unit *not* produced by Bright Paint. How does this offer affect the marginal incentives of Bright Paint? For each unit produced, the marginal costs of Bright Paint are equal to MC *plus* the opportunity cost of not receiving a check from Pure Water for marginal damage cost of that unit. Therefore, MSC becomes Bright Paint's relevant marginal cost of producing another unit of paint. Bright Paint will produce only q^* units where $P' =$ MSC. In this extreme case Pure Water pays $C + D$ to Bright Paint. For example, consider Bright Paint's alternatives as it decides whether to reduce output from five units to four units and then from four units to three units in Table 19-1. If it reduces output from five units to four units, Bright Paint loses $14 from the lost sale but receives a check for $18 from Pure Water and does not incur the marginal production cost of $14. On balance it pays Bright Paint not to produce the fifth unit. Similarly, when Bright Paint reduces output from four units to three units, it loses $14 in revenue but receives a check worth $11 from Pure Water and it does not incur a marginal cost of $10. Bright Paint is clearly better off not producing the fourth unit.

The central point of Coase's argument is that the quantity produced by Bright Paint is independent of the assignment of property rights when transaction costs are negligible. The output produced by Bright Paint will be the same. While the Coase theorem shows that the real solution will be the same no matter how the rights are assigned, the assignment of rights is no idle matter as far as the two parties are concerned. The assignment of rights affects the distribution of income. When Pure Water has the right to degrade the water, the payments are from Bright Paint to Pure Water. On the other hand when the rights are assigned to Bright

Table 19-3   THE EFFECTS OF THE ASSIGNMENT OF PROPERTY RIGHTS

| | Assignment of Property Rights to: | | |
VARIABLE	NO ONE (1)	BRIGHT PAINT (2)	PURE WATER (3)
Output	q'	q^*	q^*
Value of damages	$B + C + D$	B	B
Payment by Pure Water	0	Between C and $C + D$	—
Payment by Bright Paint	0	—	B

Paint, the payments are from Pure Water to Bright Paint. Not surprisingly, in situations where externalities are important, the different parties often turn to the political process to obtain a more favorable rights assignment.

Table 19-3 summarizes the solutions under different property right assignments. In column 1 no one owns property rights, and so Bright Paint produces q' units and total damages are equal to $B + C + D$. In column 2 Bright Paint owns the property rights and produces only q^*. Payments by Pure Water are somewhere between C and $C + D$ depending on the bargaining strengths or negotiating capabilities of the two parties. The monetary value of the damages is area B. In column 3 Pure Water owns the property right to clean water. Bright Paint produces q^* and pays Pure Water area B for the damages sustained.

APPLICATION 19-2

Allowing the Coase Theorem to Work[2]

Conservation groups are making life harder for the Forest Service and the Forest Service is making life harder for conservation groups. In 1996, the Forest Service decided to cut down a stand of trees that had sustained fire damage in the Okanogan National Forest in the state of Washington. The Forest Service asked for bids for a salvage timber sale covering 275 acres.

In all previous salvage sales only timber companies had submitted bids. This sale was different. Because Congress had passed a law in 1995 that barred administrative appeals and court challenges to stop the sale of fire-damaged trees, conservation groups decided to use their resources to bid for the use of the land rather than to mount court challenges. For the first time, a conservation group, the Northwest Ecosystem Alliance, outbid two logging companies. The Alliance became the first winning bidder in a Forest Service auction ever to have *no intention* of cutting

[2] This discussion is based on Linda E. Platts, "Environmental Group Bids on Salvage Sale," *PERC Reports* 14 (March 1996), pp. 6–7.

the trees. Members of the Alliance wanted to preserve the habitat and believed that clearing 275 acres of live and dead trees would seriously injure wildlife and the ecosystem.

Learning of Alliance's intent, the Forest Service rejected the winning bid, claiming the Alliance had no intention of fulfilling the terms of the contract, and awarded the contract to the second-highest bidder. In so doing the Forest Service argued that it had accepted the highest bid from a qualified bidder and that it had not accepted a lower bid.

This case raises some interesting and difficult public policy issues. The Forest Service decided the damage to the ecosystem would be minimal and ordered a salvage sale only after it had conducted its environmental review. But in reality, neither the Forest Service nor the conservation groups had enough information to know whether cutting was or was not the best use of the land. By using the bidding process, the Forest Service could discover which was the highest-value use. The higher bid by the conservation group raises some doubt that cutting the trees was the best use of the land. If resources are to go to the highest-value use, then allowing conservation groups to bid provides information to the Forest Service about what is the highest-value use. By preventing the environmental groups from bidding, the Forest Service prevented these groups from participating in the market process and encouraged them instead to devote their resources to lobbying Congress or to initiating legal challenges.

The Forest Service would be on a more secure footing if it could demonstrate that not cutting the trees would increase the potential for fire or insect damage outside the 275 acres. If this type of externality were deemed important, there would be less justification for relying on the bidding process to determine the highest-value use since the bids by the conservationists and the timber firms would not reflect the net social benefit of the different uses of the land.

Transaction Costs

Our discussion of the externality problem has been somewhat artificial because it sweeps aside the cost of negotiating and enforcing agreements among the parties. The magnitude of **transaction costs** will vary from one situation to another and presumably will increase as the number of parties who must agree increases. Anyone who has worked in small and large groups recognizes that the cost of negotiating an agreement increases with the number of members in the group.

Negotiation costs can be considerable even when only a few parties are involved. Let's consider a developer that would like to renew an area by buying out several dilapidated properties in the middle of a city block and replacing them with a large apartment complex. The developer must negotiate with a small number of independent owners. The total value of the city block will be higher with the development than without it. The question is: What price can each property in the development command? If you own one of the properties in the middle of the block, you may be in a particularly envious position. The development cannot proceed unless you agree. You are willing to be bought out but at the highest feasible price. Your best strategy may be to wait until the developer acquires the other properties. Then, you can hold out for a higher price. Without your property it will be difficult but not impossible for the development to proceed. The cost of negotiating the deal can be considerable for the developer, and the *hold-up problem* is a potential stumbling block in the deal.

Let's see how the assignment of property rights makes a difference when transaction costs are large by returning to our initial example. Instead of assuming Pure Water is the only downstream firm, let's assume there are other downstream firms. Perhaps there is a soft drink manufacturer, a beer manufacturer, and several food processors located downstream. Now, the production of paint harms all users but in varying degrees. If Bright Paint owns property rights in water quality, the other firms must get together and haggle over how much to pay Bright Paint Co. and determine the contribution of each downstream firm. The negotiations among the downstream firms can be lengthy and frustrating because of legitimate differences of opinion about the size of the damage costs and strategic bargaining among the parties. There is apt to be a free rider problem. Each downstream firm wants the others to incur the negotiating costs.

We assume the transaction costs of getting together and agreeing are higher for the downstream firms. Recall that if the downstream firms own the property rights to the river water quality, Bright Paint has three options. Let's reconsider options 2 and 3, repeated here:

- *Option 2.* Clean the water before it is released so the quality of water is not degraded.

- *Option 3.* Pay to have Pure Water and others invest in expensive filtering equipment to clean the discharges of Bright Paint or pay to have Pure Water and other firms relocate.

Which of the two options will the parties adopt? Let's assume that it is cheaper for Bright Paint to clean the water before discharging it into the river than for each of the downstream firms to clean the water separately. In Figure 19-4 MSC is the marginal social cost function described earlier when options 2 and 3 did not exist and where q^* is the initial optimal quantity. MSC_1 is the marginal clean-up cost of Bright Paint (option 2) and is less than MSC_2, the marginal cost of a clean-up by all the downstream firms at each rate of output (option 3). Therefore, the lower-cost solution is for Bright Paint to clean the water before discharging it into the river.

If transaction costs are higher for the downstream firms, then the assignment of property rights does affect the quantity of paint produced by Bright Paint. Suppose Bright Paint has the property rights. Consider the extreme case in which the potential transaction costs for the downstream firms are so large that they do not even attempt to get together. Then, Bright Paint produces q' units because it owns the rights to water quality.

On the other hand, Bright Paint will produce q_2 units, the socially efficient output given the different clean-up costs, if the downstream plants have property rights to clean water. The low-cost solution has Bright Paint cleaning the waste-

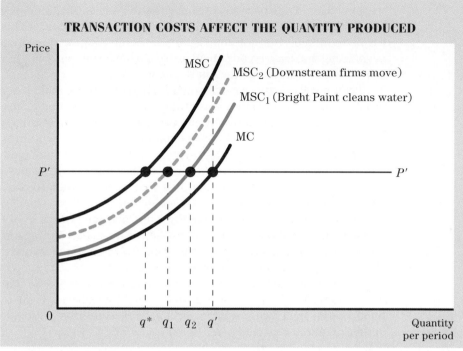

TRANSACTION COSTS AFFECT THE QUANTITY PRODUCED

Figure 19-4   The marginal social cost is MSC_1 if Bright Paint cleans the water before discharge into the river. The marginal social cost is MSC_2 if the downstream firms move farther downstream or elsewhere. The lower-cost solution is for Bright Paint to clean the water and to produce q_2 units of paint. If the property rights are given to Bright Paint and transaction costs are sufficiently high for the downstream firms, then Bright Paint will produce q' units. Transaction costs affect the quantity of paint produced.

water before discharge into the river rather than paying damages to each downstream firm.

This example shows why the initial assignment of property rights is critical when transaction costs are significant. When Bright Paint owns the property rights, the high transaction costs prevent the downstream firms from meeting and bribing Bright Paint to clean the water, the efficient solution. If the downstream firms own the property rights, then Bright Paint produces the socially optimal output. An improper assignment of property rights leads to a higher marginal social cost and to a socially inferior solution.

APPLICATION 19-3

Neighborhoods for Sale

Living next to a refinery can be a trying experience. The odors are hardly pleasant, and the health consequences are unknown. Refineries and nearby residences are becoming increasingly strange bedfellows.

In Port Arthur, Texas, one oil company, Fina Inc., has agreed to buy out a neighborhood so that the residents can leave.[3] Fina's Port Arthur refinery is at the forefront of technology, and so it is not as if the refinery is emitting sulfur dioxide on a daily basis. Nevertheless, the patience of nearby residents is wearing thin with each confrontation between their representatives and the refinery. Residents are demanding plant inspections whenever they detect real or imagined odors, confronting company executives, petitioning the city council, and persuading state regulators to threaten to close the refinery after neighbors reported leaks of sulfur dioxide and hydrogen sulfide, two dangerous gases.

What Fina decided to do, after publicly stating it would not, is to create a buffer zone, a greenbelt. Fina plans to purchase the 211 residences in the immediate area. It could cost over $10 million, but after the purchase no one will be left to protest pollution.

In this case the property rights are somewhat fuzzy. However, the residents appear to have effectively organized so that regulators listen to them with sympathetic ears. In this uncomfortable situation Fina Inc. has the option of closing down, introducing still more expensive controls to prevent additional leaks, or buying out the neighborhood. It appears that Fina Inc. is convinced that the low-cost solution is to buy out the neighborhood.

If Fina Inc. possesses the property right to pollute, it is unlikely that the residents will be capable of organizing and bargaining at low cost to buy out the refinery. Although some of them have demonstrated remarkable skill in organizing and bringing considerable political pressure on Fina, it is likely that the transaction costs of negotiating an agreement among 211 independent parties would be extremely high. Therefore, the efficient solution may well be for the property rights to be assigned to the residences in the neighborhood and for Fina to buy out the neighborhood rather than close the refinery or reduce the probability of a leak by introducing more costly equipment.

APPLICATION **19-4**

View Wars and Defining Property Rights

Along the Pacific coast, neighbors are going to war over who owns the property rights to a view.[4] Some neighbors have even taken the law into their own hands and damaged or poisoned their neighbors' trees.

Here are some illustrations of view wars. A neighbor asked Catherine Armstrong if he could cut her tree so that he would have a better view of the Olympic Mountains. She ignored him. A few months later Armstrong heard a chain saw and

[3] Based on Caleb Solomon, "How a Neighborhood Talked Fina Refinery into Buying It Out," *The Wall Street Journal*, December 10, 1991.
[4] Based on Kathleen A. Hughes, "Neighbors Seeking to Better Their Lot Are Often up a Tree," *The Wall Street Journal*, April 15, 1992.

when she rushed out of the house she saw a tree trimmer in her fifty-year-old fir cutting away. When she asked the trimmer what he was doing, he said the owner of the property had given permission to cut down the tree. Armstrong made it abundantly clear that she was the owner and that she had given no such permission and ordered the trimmer off the property immediately.

In another case the Arnolds had a beautiful view of the cliffs, ocean, and Catalina Island. Over time two eucalyptus trees on the McNabb property grew taller and taller until they interfered with the Arnolds' view. The Arnolds asked the McNabbs to trim the trees, but the McNabbs refused to do so. The Arnolds then tried unsuccessfully to cut the trees. The McNabbs then obtained an injunction prohibiting the Arnolds from cutting the trees. Later the town of Rolling Hills passed a view law and the McNabbs reluctantly trimmed their trees.

Some towns and cities are passing view laws, which can reduce negotiation costs. In such cases, the cost of negotiating agreements is likely to be high so that the assignment of property rights is likely to make a difference.

Take the McNabb case. Before passage of the view law, the McNabbs valued their trees more than the Arnolds valued their view. We infer this because the Arnolds did not pay the McNabbs enough to have the McNabbs trim the trees voluntarily. The view law passed the property rights from the McNabbs to the Arnolds. If transaction costs were low, the Coasian solution would have the McNabbs agree to pay the Arnolds to waive their right to the view. Both would be better off after the payment. Yet, this did not happen. The McNabbs reluctantly trimmed their trees. Here, we can infer that the transaction costs of negotiating between hostile neighbors were great and so the solution changed from no tree trimming to tree trimming when the view law reassigned the property rights.

The externality problem becomes increasingly intractable when the ownership of the rights is unclear. When property rights are fuzzy, the cost of negotiating a bargain increases substantially because no one knows what is to be transacted. If no one owns the rights, everyone owns the rights. So, a transaction with one party does not transfer the rights since others can claim that they own the rights. Without clearly defined property rights it is next to impossible to reach the low-cost solution.

APPLICATION 19-5

Saving the African Elephant

The tusks and hide of an elephant are very valuable. In recent years an average tusk has been valued at $2,000 and the hide could be worth this much or more. Because they are so valuable, profit-maximizing poachers have been killing African elephants at an alarming rate. The elephant population in Central and East Africa dropped from 1,044,050 to 429,520 between 1979 and 1989. Because of this slaughter, some have called for a total worldwide ban on the ivory trade.

What are the possible causes of the predicament of the African elephant? We can learn much from a study by researchers Randy Simmons and Urs Kreuter on the different policies of African governments.[5] In Kenya the government is dedicated to ending the trading of ivory and for more than a decade has banned the hunting of elephants. Yet, Kenya's elephant population has fallen from 65,000 in 1979 and 19,000 in 1989. Clearly, declaring a ban on hunting has failed to establish property rights over the elephants so poaching continues.

On the other hand, the government of Zimbabwe discovered the best way to protect the elephant was to give the villagers property rights to the elephants. In Zimbabwe the selling of ivory is legal but controlled and ivory is readily available in shops. Zimbabwe's elephant population increased from 30,000 to 43,000 between 1979 and 1989. Why are the trends in elephant population so different in the two countries? In Zimbabwe elephants are culled from the herds and the proceeds from the sale of tusks and hides are returned to the game parks and used in part to prevent poaching. Even more important, native villages have earned more than $5 million by selling elephant hunting rights on their common lands to safari operators.

When the peasants do not own the property rights to the animals, they have an incentive to kill elephants and other wild animals because wild animals compete for the use of the land. Elephants and other wild animals destroy crops, kill domestic animals, and drink valuable water. In Zimbabwe poachers are shot on sight. The government spends over $500 per square mile protecting the wildlife on state-owned land and sells the rights to hunting and photographing for handsome prices. On communal lands peasants have the right to hunt a certain number of elephants per year and they often sell these rights to safari operators. The villagers have a property right to the elephants and therefore they protect them. In one case villagers near a national park gave up some land in return for hunting permits that the village sells to safari operators. The village used the proceeds to improve community facilities and distributed some of the proceeds to the villagers.

The different policies of African governments illustrate the consequences of establishing property rights to a common resource that would otherwise not be owned by anyone. Where property rights did not exist, the size of the elephant herds decreased; because the government did not create any property rights, poachers had every incentive to kill elephants since they did not own the future property rights to the resource. In Zimbabwe the government established a property rights system that created funds to protect the elephants and provided incentives for villagers to protect the elephants.

Taxation and Pareto Efficiency

Now that you know that the assignment or defining of property rights can affect the equilibrium outcome when transaction costs are large, let's examine a potential pitfall from using per unit taxes to solve the externality problem. Suppose that

---

[5] Based on Randy T. Simmons and Urs P. Kreuter, "Herd Mentality, Banning Ivory Sales Is No Way to Save the Elephant," *Policy Review*, Fall 1989, pp. 46–49.

society adopts the principle that a per unit tax is assessed on the party causing the externality. What are the possible repercussions of this taxation principle?

While this proposal sounds attractive, it has several drawbacks. The first point to note is that it is not always easy to determine who is responsible for the externality. Suppose that Bright Paint began production first, perhaps on a small scale, and expanded output later. In the meantime Pure Water and others established facilities downstream. Who is the damaged party? Is Bright Paint the damaged party after Pure Water and the others established their facilities downstream? In the example of the Fina refinery the company originally built the refinery on an isolated parcel of land. Later, individuals built suburban residences nearby. Who is the damaged party? There is a reciprocal nature to damages in most cases. Consequently, it is often difficult to identify the damaged party.

The second point is more important. A per unit tax can prevent the low-cost solution from being implemented. Let's return to the earlier example but now assume that the *higher* cost solution occurs when Bright Paint cleans the water before discharge. In Figure 19-5 MSC_1 is the relevant marginal cost if Bright Paint introduces the filtering equipment and cleans the water before discharge. MSC_2 is the social marginal cost if the downstream firms move farther downstream or elsewhere, and so the lower-cost solution is for the downstream firms to move. What are the consequences if the local government assesses a tax so that Bright Paint must pay a per unit tax t equal to the marginal damage cost at the former social optimum because the government does not consider option 2 or 3? In Figure 19-5 the per unit tax t is equal to the difference between MSC and MC when Bright Paint produces q^* units.

Look at the problem that Bright Paint faces. If it continues production and pays the tax, its marginal cost becomes MSC and it will produce q^* units. However, it prefers the lower-cost solution of cleaning the water before discharge to paying the tax. Therefore, it voluntarily incurs the filter and other costs and produces q_1 units where $P' = MSC_1$. An even lower-cost solution, however, is for the downstream firms to move elsewhere and for Bright Paint to pay for the relocation costs. If the downstream firms move, Bright Paint would equate P' to MSC_2 and produce q_2 units, the socially desirable quantity based on the *lowest* possible MSC. However, Bright Paint will not adopt this solution because it would still have to pay a per unit tax since the tax is assessed on discharges of dirty water. In this case imposing a per unit tax on the firm discharging degraded water prevents the lower-cost relocation solution from being adopted.

19-2   PUBLIC GOODS AND PARETO EFFICIENCY

Throughout this book we have considered *private* goods, goods that are *rival* in consumption so that consumption by one person prevents consumption by anyone else. With a private good the owner of the good can also exclude use of the good by others. You can prevent me from using your jeans. Private goods are rival in consumption and are also *excludable*. There are other goods, called **public goods,** whose consumption by one consumer does not prevent their consumption by another consumer. Consequently, public goods are nonrival in consumption. It is

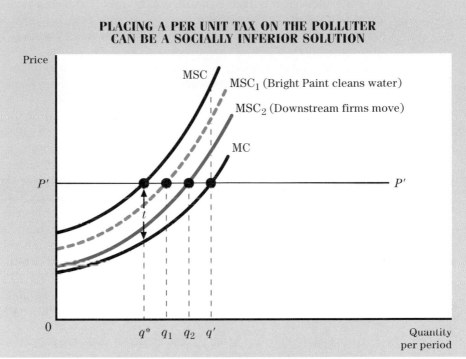

**PLACING A PER UNIT TAX ON THE POLLUTER
CAN BE A SOCIALLY INFERIOR SOLUTION**

Figure 19-5   The marginal social cost is MSC_1 if Bright Paint cleans the water before discharge into the river. The social marginal cost is MSC_2 if the downstream firms move farther downstream or elsewhere. The lower-cost solution is for the downstream firms to move. If a per unit tax is imposed on Bright Paint for any damages, it will clean the dirty water before discharge and produce q_1 units, a socially inferior solution. Applying the principle that the firm that causes the problem should pay a per unit tax will not always result in the lower-cost solution being adopted. The lower-cost solution is not to tax Bright Paint but for Bright Paint to pay for relocation costs (and other costs) of the downstream firms.

these special features of public goods that create an impediment to achieving Pareto efficiency.

Let's consider some examples. If you purchase a new car or new shoes, no other individual can drive your new car or wear your shoes simultaneously. When you receive utility from wearing your shoes, someone else does not receive more utility simultaneously. Now consider the classic example of a public good, national defense. Suppose the citizens of a country build a sophisticated national defense system with elaborate radar and missile defenses. Such a defense system has two features. The services are nonrivalrous and nonexcludable. The fact that I receive benefits from national defense does not preclude other citizens from receiving the same benefits. All citizens consume the benefits of the system simultaneously. Therefore, the services are **nonrivalrous.** Second, the services are **nonexcludable** because the defense against an incoming missile benefits one and all. To take another example, all farmers in an area benefit from a cloud-seeding program. Cloud-seeding is a public good for the farmers because it is nonrivalrous and nonexcludable.

> The services of a public good are nonrivalrous and nonexcludable.

Some goods are nonrivalrous but are excludable. A television signal has some characteristics of a public good. My consumption does not preclude others from receiving the signal. Yet, cable systems are able to exclude those who do not pay for their service. Here, the service is nonrivalrous but excludable.

Many but not all the goods supplied by governments have the characteristics of a public good. Governments provide police and fire protection, public gardens, programs for mosquito elimination, tuberculosis screening and treatment, and other public health services. These programs are typically nonrivalrous at least to some degree. If I receive police protection, so does my neighbor. A mosquito prevention program simultaneously benefits many inhabitants. Consumption is nonrivalrous and nonexcludable. Because of this nonexcludability property, there is an inescapable free rider problem in the delivery of public goods. Each prefers that someone else pay for a pure public good while everyone experiences the benefits from it.

Our discussion of a public good assumes that the good is nonrivalrous and nonexcludable. These features require a modification of the condition for Pareto efficiency in product mix. Let's assume that consumers A and B have separate demand functions for Y, a private good supplied by a competitive market, and for X, a pure public good. Because X is a pure public good, a unit decrease in X decreases the utility of both consumers since X is nonrivalrous. For example, suppose that the economy can produce five more units of Y by producing one less unit of the public good, and so MRT $= -5$. Assume that consumer A remains indifferent by consuming one more unit of Y for one less unit of X and that consumer B remains indifferent by consuming two more units of Y for one less unit of X. Collectively, consumers A and B require just three more units of Y for one less unit of X for each to be indifferent. However, the economy can produce five more units of Y by producing one less unit of the public good. Therefore, we can say that the utility of at least one consumer will increase if the economy produces one less unit of the public good. Therefore, the product mix is not Pareto-efficient. For a public good, Pareto efficiency in product mix requires

$$\Sigma MRS = MRT \qquad \text{(Pareto Efficiency in Product Mix with a Public Good)} \quad \textbf{(19-1)}$$

With a public good the marginal rates of substitution are summed for all consumers in the economy because consumption is nonrivalrous and this sum is equated to the marginal rate of transformation.

The Optimal Quantity of a Public Good

The special characteristics of a public good raise two questions: What is the optimal quantity of a pure public good, and how will the public good be financed? To

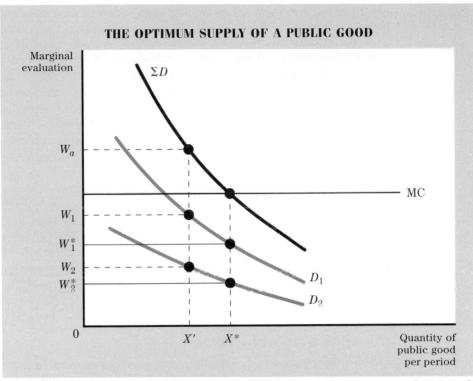

THE OPTIMUM SUPPLY OF A PUBLIC GOOD

Figure 19-6 The vertical summation of the marginal willingness-to-pay functions for consumers 1 and 2 (D_1 and D_2) determines the community's inverse demand function for different amounts of a public good. The optimal provision of a public good is X^* where the community's demand function intersects the marginal cost of providing the public good.

answer the first question, we must derive the demand function for a public good. What is the willingness to pay of members of society for each quantity of the public good? Then, we must consider the marginal cost function of providing the public good. Chapter 3 derived the marginal value function of each consumer for different quantities of a good. These functions are the individual demand functions of consumers and have negative slopes reflecting the decreasing amounts a consumer is willing to pay for additional units of a good. Each consumer has a marginal value function for a public good that shows how much he or she is willing to pay for successive units of a public good. Because consumer tastes and incomes differ, so too will the positions of their marginal value functions. Figure 19-6 shows the inverse demand functions of consumer 1 (D_1) and of consumer 2 (D_2) and shows that consumer 1 is willing to pay a higher price for each quantity of the public good than consumer 2 is.

If this were just an ordinary private good, the kind of good discussed in Chapters 2 and 3, we would simply sum the demand functions horizontally to derive the market demand function. In the case of a pure public good we have to proceed more cautiously because consumption of a public good is nonrivalrous.

To derive a function that shows the total valuation for different quantities of the public good, we must find the total value that consumers are willing to pay for another unit of the public good. Because each demander consumes the same quantity of the good simultaneously, the inverse demand functions of both consumers must be summed vertically for each quantity of the public good to find out what society is willing to pay for different quantities. The summation is vertical because both individuals can consume the public good simultaneously. Figure 19-6 shows the vertical sum for ΣD. For example, let's consider the quantity X' in Figure 19-6. Consumer 1 will pay W_1 and consumer 2 will pay W_2 for the X'th unit. The maximum amount that both consumers are willing to pay for the X'th unit is W_a on the function labeled ΣD. The ΣD function shows the maximum amount that both consumers will pay for each quantity of the public good.

In Figure 19-6 the marginal cost of supplying the public good is MC. The optimal quantity of the public good is X^* units where ΣD intersects the marginal cost function. The sum of consumer and producer surplus is maximized if the quantity of the public good is X^* units. Consumer 1 is willing to pay W_1^*, and consumer 2 is willing to pay W_2^*, so that $W_1^* + W_2^* = \text{MC}$.

Financing a Public Good

While it is comparatively easy to find the optimal quantity of the public good once the demand for and the marginal cost of providing a public good are known, it is less clear how to finance a public good. Consider a city that is thinking of providing a public park. How large should the park be? To determine the optimum size of the park, the city needs to know the marginal value function of all potential users. To find the demand function for the park, the local government could simply ask each resident how much each would be willing to pay for parks of different sizes. The trouble with this approach is that everyone has an incentive to underestimate the value of the park and in this way hope to free-ride on the contributions of others. If individuals expect that the amount they will have to contribute to finance the park depends on their stated valuation of the benefits, then each will understate the benefits. Sometimes municipalities conduct elaborate surveys to estimate the value of a public good to potential consumers. If consumers believe that the results of the survey will not affect the contributions of each one, it may be possible to obtain truthful answers. There still remains the basic question of whether most consumers can even give an accurate answer about frequency and type of use of a pure public good except based on experience. Therefore, the accuracy of estimates based on survey techniques is an open question.

Could we turn over the responsibility of providing a pure public good to the private market? The inability to exclude demanders makes it difficult, if not impossible, for private firms to provide the optimum quantity of a pure public good. Each demander avoids paying while hoping others will contribute to the provision of a public good. The free rider problem is a serious one for a pure public good, and this is probably the most important reason why governments supply these goods.

If a competitive market existed to supply a public good, each firm would have to find a way of requiring payment by consumers. Each firm or firms in the market would have to charge different prices to consumers for the same quantity of the public good. Consumer 1 would be required to pay a higher price than consumer 2 because of the different marginal valuations. If one firm incurs the cost of finding out what each one should pay, another competitive firm could copy the pricing policy and not incur the cost of finding out. So, a free rider problem of another form would appear. If a single firm receives a license to supply the public good and has information about the marginal value functions, it will have to be regulated or it will practice third-degree price discrimination and charge different prices. The main defect in this solution is that a price-discriminating monopolist would raise prices and equate aggregate marginal revenue to marginal cost and produce less than the socially optimal quantity of the public good. We are assuming the monopolist cannot engage in first-degree price discrimination.

Because of these difficulties, public goods are likely to be undersupplied compared to private goods when produced in competitive markets.[6] A private market is unlikely to provide the optimal scale of a pure public good. It is for this reason that governments supply public goods and often use general tax receipts to finance such projects. When the government finances the public good out of general tax funds, the revelation problem may be less severe because the revelation of the marginal willingness to pay is unrelated to the financing of the public good. Consequently, the government may be the preferred supplier since it can secure more accurate information about the willingness to pay than a private firm can.

SUMMARY

- Departures from Pareto efficiency can occur if significant third-party (external) effects exist and if the market supplies public goods.
- Private markets can resolve the externality problem when transaction costs are negligible and property rights exist.
- Firms will produce the optimal social output independent of the assignment of property rights if transaction costs are negligible. When transaction costs are significant, a market system may not produce the socially preferred output.
- Pure public goods are nonrivalrous and nonexcludable. Private markets are unlikely to provide the optimal quantity of a pure public good.

KEY TERMS

externality
positive and negative externalities
marginal social cost
internalizing an externality
transaction cost
public good

marginal damage cost
social surplus
Coase theorem
defining property rights
Pareto efficiency with a public good
nonrivalrous and nonexcludable

[6] For an extensive discussion of the role of government in supplying public goods, the reader is referred to Joseph E. Stiglitz, *Economics of the Public Sector* (New York: W.W. Norton, 1988).

REVIEW QUESTIONS

1. List some impediments to Pareto efficiency. Explain how each one affects the Pareto efficiency conditions.
2. Draw a diagram showing when it is Pareto-efficient for Bright Paint not to produce any output. What is the lowest per unit tax that will induce Bright Paint not to produce any output?
3. A familiar saying is, "Everyone's property is no one's property." What does this mean?
4. At the Graduate School of Business a joint student-faculty committee works on a wide range of problems and recommends the adoption of policies that affect all MBAs. How would you describe the policy of the GSB? Is it a private or a public good? What problems might appear if it is a public good?
5. In the accompanying figure there are four consumer demand functions for good X. Draw a graph and indicate what the market demand function is if X is (*a*) a private good or (*b*) a public good.
6. Is the temperature in a house a private or a public good? Explain your answer.
7. Since everyone benefits from national defense, every member of a country should pay the same amount to finance national defense. Do you agree or disagree with this statement? Answer this question assuming the willingness to pay of each consumer is known.
8. Show the optimal quantity of a pure public good when marginal cost increases with the quantity produced.
9. Every citizen should pay some amount to maintain a program of flu vaccination. Every citizen should pay some amount to keep the Public Broadcasting System operating. Do you agree or disagree with these statements?

EXERCISES

1. When there is a positive externality on Firm A, the marginal cost function of firm A shifts downward when the output of firm B increases. What is the appropriate per unit subsidy to offer firm B when there is a positive externality?
2. This question applies to Table 19-1. Suppose that Bright Paint has an unencumbered

right to pollute when producing up to five units of paint. What is the maximum amount Pure Water is willing to pay Bright Paint if Bright Paint produces the socially optimal output?

3. This question applies to Table 19-1. Suppose that Pure Water is willing to pay Bright Paint $7 for each unit not produced by Bright Paint. What output will Bright Paint produce?

4. Propose a market experiment that would tell you whether transaction costs are small or large. (*Hint:* Think of the consequences of assigning property rights.)

5. Suppose the marginal social cost, MSC_1, is less if Bright Paint cleans the water before discharge than if the downstream firms move farther downstream. Under this condition is it at all necessary to impose a per unit tax to reach the social optimum output for Bright Paint?

*6. Victoria's Secret and Borders Bookstore moved into a prime location on the Magnificent Mile, a fashionable shopping area in Chicago. Unlike other stores, both stores have erected large signs, and Victoria's Secret's lingerie displays in its windows have upset the other tenants on the Magnificent Mile. Tenants complain that the commercial signs are too "tacky" and that Victoria's Secret displays are too "pink." One nearby offended tenant is FAO Schwarz, a seller of children's toys. Some tenants on the Magnificent Mile want Victoria's Secret and Borders to reduce the size of their signs and Victoria's Secret to tone down its displays.

One analyst of the retail scene suggests that the opposition of the other tenants is just sour grapes. "The opposition by the other tenants is unjustified. If the signs harmed the sales of other stores more than they benefited Victoria's Secret and Borders, the other stores would have outbid both companies and bought up the leases and prevented both stores from opening stores. Consequently, the market solution is pro-consumer and efficient."

a. Does the fact that Victoria's Secret and Borders Bookstore outbid the other stores indicate that the harm to the sales of other stores is less than the benefit of the location to Victoria's Secret and Borders? Explain.

b. Suppose the property rights were assigned to the other stores and transaction costs were negligible so that Victoria's Secret and Borders have to pay the other stores for any harm these stores suffer from the "tacky" signs. Explain why the size of the signs and the displays would or would not be different if the other stores owned the property rights.

7. The demand curves for national defense by three consumers are shown in the table below:

a. Derive the aggregate willingness-to-pay schedule for airplane squadrons.

b. What is the optimal quantity of national defense?

8. Give some examples of public goods that are excludable.

NUMBER OF AIRPLANE SQUADRONS	CONSUMER 1	CONSUMER 2	CONSUMER 3	MARGINAL COST OF A SQUADRON
1	$100	$400	$250	$250
2	90	300	200	350
3	80	200	150	430
4	70	150	100	600
5	60	100	50	800

SUGGESTED ANSWERS TO SELECTED EXERCISES AND PROBLEM SETS

Chapter 1

1. Knowing the position of the demand function tells you nothing about the incidence of a shortage. To determine whether a shortage exists, you would have to know the position of the supply function and the market price.

3. **a.** Let the initial price be P_1. The price after the increase is $P_2 = 1.75P_1$. Q_1 is initial quantity demanded, and Q_2 is quantity demanded after price increases. Total revenue is $R_1 = P_1Q_1$ before price increases, and $R_2 = 1.52R_1$. Substituting $R_2 = P_2Q_2$ and $R_1 = P_1Q_1$ into $R_2 = 1.52R_1$ yields

$$\frac{Q_2}{Q_1} = 1.52\frac{P_1}{P_2} = \frac{1.52}{1.75} = 0.869$$

Therefore, quantity decreased by 13.1 percent.

b. The expression for the price elasticity is

$$E_P = \frac{\Delta Q}{\Delta P}\frac{P_1 + P_2}{Q_1 + Q_2}$$

Substituting the respective expressions, we have

$$E_P = \frac{0.869Q_1 - Q_1}{1.75P_1 - P_1}\frac{P_1 + 1.75P_1}{Q_1 + 0.869Q_1}$$

$$= \frac{-0.131Q_1}{0.75P_1}\frac{2.75P_1}{1.869Q_1} = -0.257$$

Therefore, demand is price-inelastic since E_P is between -1 and zero. Revenue is higher at the higher price.

4. This statement does not distinguish between a movement along a supply function and a shift in the supply function. Imposing a tax on the product shifts the supply function inward. For any Q, suppliers are now willing to supply the same quantity only if the price is higher by the per unit tax. The supply function becomes $S'S'$ after the tax is levied. Because the supply function shifts inward and to the left, the equilibrium price increases to P_2 and the equilibrium quantity decreases to Q_2. See the accompanying figure.

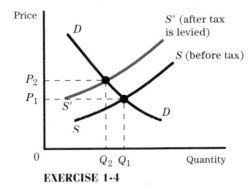

EXERCISE 1-4

6. If the supply curve of *imported* steel is horizontal, i.e., perfectly elastic, the other steel producers will not benefit because the strike will not change the price. Before the strike, the equilibrium price is P^* and the equilibrium quantity is Q_T as shown in Exercise 1-6. The combined domestic and import supply curve is the dashed line *abc*. The domestic industry supplies Q_{dns} units and imports account for $Q_T - Q_{dns}$. Because of the strike, the domestic supply curve shifts to the left and becomes *de*. Nevertheless, the combined supply curve intersects the demand function at P^* and domestic producers supply Q_{ds}. Therefore, the price remains at P^*. Domestic output falls to Q_{ds}, but this output reduction is matched by an increase in foreign supply. To test your understanding of this model, predict what will happen after a strike if the foreign supply curve has a positive slope.

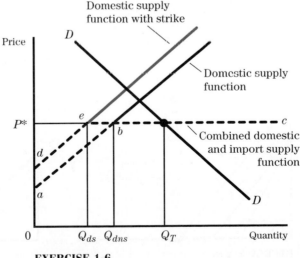

EXERCISE 1-6

Chapter 2

1. A fall in the price of beef relative to the price of fish makes the budget line flatter. You consume just a few more pounds of beef and more pounds of fish. See the accompanying figure.

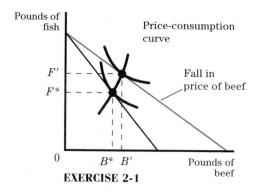

EXERCISE 2-1

2.   a. To calculate the price elasticity, the price of X must change while income and other prices are constant. Income and the price of Y are constant between 1988 and 1989, while the price of X decreases from \$110 to \$90. Arc price elasticity is $E_P = -(10/20)(200/190) = -0.53$, and so demand is price-inelastic.

   b. If all prices and income are constant, a quantity change would have to be due to a taste change. Prices and income are constant in 1987 and 1990, but quantity demanded of X increases from 80 to 100 units.

   c. Consider the years 1988 and 1989. The price of X decreases, but the price of Y and income are constant. You can determine what happens to quantity demanded of Y.

   d. There is no year where the price of Y changes and the price of X, income, and the consumer's tastes all remain constant.

3. The demand for X will be zero if $-P_X/P_Y < \text{MRS}$ when $X = 0$. The consumer purchases only Y. It becomes positive when the price of X falls. The inequality is reversed when the consumer purchases only X. The budget constraint then becomes $P_X X = I$, and so the demand function is $X = I/P_X$. The demand function for X is shown in the accompanying figure.

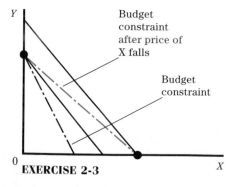

EXERCISE 2-3

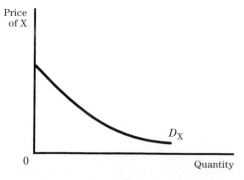

6. The slope of the budget constraint equals -5 in Exercise 2-5. The consumer's marginal rate of substitution equals the market's marginal rate of substitution when the consumer buys 3 containers of detergent. Therefore, the consumer's marginal rate of substitution must equal -5.

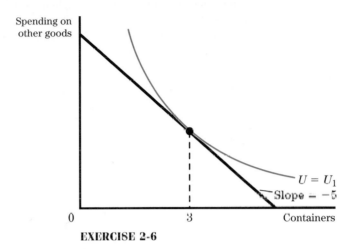

EXERCISE 2-6

8. **a.** The two goods in the utility function are spending on other goods (S) and days of leisure (L). The budget constraint is $S = D(365 - L)$, where D is the daily wage. As days of leisure increase to 365, income and spending on other goods decrease. The budget constraint of the consumer is line aa in the accompanying figure. In the initial equilibrium the consumer works 210 days and has 155 days of leisure.

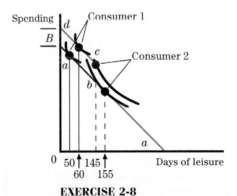

EXERCISE 2-8

b. Under the bonus system the worker qualifies for the bonus if workdays equal or exceed 220 days, and so leisure equals 145 or fewer days. The budget constraint becomes *abcd* with the bonus system.

c. Without the bonus, consumer 1 is a workaholic and consumes only 50 days of leisure. With the bonus, days of leisure increase to 60. So a flat bonus increases leisure. For consumer

2 days of leisure decrease from 155 to 145. The bonus system has both incentive and disincentive work effects.

d. In the two situations, days of leisure change in opposite directions, and so you cannot predict that the average days of work will rise to 220.

11. The utility function of a family depends on spending on other goods (S) and spending on education (E). Assume that all families in each district are alike but that families differ across districts. If a family spends over $100 for education, the district receives a lump sum of $50 per child.

a. Currently, each family spends $500 per child on education. The budget constraint of the family is *abcd* and becomes *abefg* under lump sum grant 1. Given spending on other goods, the family can now spend $50 more on education because of the state grant. See the accompanying figure.

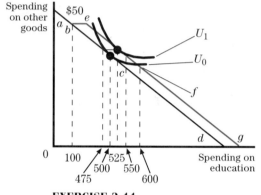

EXERCISE 2-11

b. Under lump sum grant 1 the family cuts back on private spending on education to $475, and so total spending increases to $525 with the state grant. Therefore, a lump sum subsidy induces the family to spend more on other goods. Consequently, total spending on education does not rise by $50. Draw the indifference curves for a family in a different district that is currently spending less than $100 per child and show how the subsidy will either not affect family spending or increase family spending to $150. In this case total spending on education will increase by more than $50. Therefore, you cannot tell whether spending per child will increase on average by $50 because of the state subsidy.

Using a similar analysis, you should be able to analyze the effects of lump sum grant 2 and answer Exercise 11*c*.

Chapter 3

3. The first experiment indicates that X is a superior good. Therefore, the consumer's demand function should slope downward to the right. Yet, the second experiment indicates that the consumer's demand function has a positive slope. Therefore, the model of consumer behavior cannot explain this behavior.

6. The equation for the slope of a consumer's demand function is

$$\frac{\Delta X}{\Delta P} = \frac{\Delta X}{\Delta P}\bigg|_{U=c} - X\frac{\Delta X}{\Delta I}$$

Since the slope of the demand function is -1.2, $X = 3$, and $\Delta X / \Delta I = 5$, this implies that $\Delta X / \Delta P|_{U=c}$ is 13.8. This is impossible because the substitution effect is always negative.

8. If the substitution effect of the two consumers is the same, the income effect is larger for the wealthy consumer and the wealthier individual's demand function is more elastic.

13. A consumer with this utility function has a *marginal* utility function of $dU/dW = (.5)100(W)^{-.5} > 0$. The *slope* of the *marginal utility function* is $d^2U/dW^2 = (.5)(-.5)100(W)^{-1.5} < 0$. Therefore this individual is risk-averse.

    a. If the consumer enters occupation 1 or 2, expected wealth equals

$$EW_1 = (.6)(133,300) + (.4)(50,000) = \$99,980$$

$$EW_2 = (.5)(180,000) + (.5)(20,000) = \$100,000$$

Since expected wealth is larger, the individual would enter occupation 2.

    b. The expected utility from entering occupations 1 or 2 is

$$EU_1 = (.6)100(133,000)^{.5} + (.4)100(50,000)^{.5} = 30,850.44 \text{ utils}$$

$$EU_2 = (.5)100(180,000)^{.5} + (.5)100(20,000)^{.5} = 28,284.27 \text{ utils}$$

The consumer would select occupation 1 if the consumer is maximizing expected utility.

    c. This individual is willing to forgo the extra $20 in expected income to obtain less variability in wealth outcomes. Hence, this individual is risk averse. If the utility function is $100(W)^{1.5}$, you should show that this individual is a risk taker and would select occupation 2.

Chapter 4

2. The cost of buying the services in the market equals 2,900. The do-it-yourself cost equals $w92 + \$550$. If your wage rate exceeds $25.54 per hour, it pays for you to use a professional.

3. The slope of the full price budget constraint equals

$$-\frac{P_X + wt_X}{P_Y + wt_Y}$$

Assume that $P_Y = 0$ for leisure and $t_Y = 1$, and so the full price budget constraint becomes

$$Y = \frac{wT + V}{w} - \frac{P_X + wt_X}{w}X$$

Then, t_Y/P_Y is larger for leisure than for good X. A rise in w increases the full price of leisure by more than the full price of X. So, the full price budget constraint becomes flatter as it shifts outward and the consumer substitutes toward good X.

4. Solving the time constraint for T_w gives

$$T_w = T - C_X - t_X X - t_Y Y$$

Substituting T_w into the budget constraint and collecting terms yields

$$Y = \frac{wT + V - wC_X}{P_Y + wt_Y} - \frac{P_X + wt_X}{P_Y + wt_Y}X$$

when $X > 0$. If $X = 0$, then the consumer can purchase

$$Y = \frac{wT + V}{P_Y + wt_Y}$$

units of Y because she does not incur C_X unless she purchases X. If the consumer buys only X, she can purchase only

$$X = \frac{wT + V - wC_X}{P_X + wt_X}$$

units of X. The number of units of X is equal to full income less the cost of traveling to the store, C_X, divided by the full price of X. The slope of the budget constraint still equals the ratio of the two full prices. The accompanying figure shows the full price budget constraint.

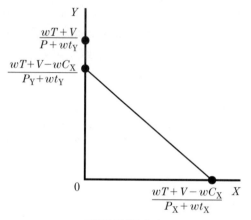

EXERCISE 4-4

10. Because the cost of time of shoppers has increased by relatively more for females, manufacturers are introducing more branded goods that help consumers economize on shopping time. If information supplied by manufacturers through branding is a substitute for information obtained from salespeople, then consumers will demand less information at stores and will purchase from discount and other stores that offer brand names but less service and avoid higher-service department stores.

Chapter 5

2. To determine which factor increases and which decreases, calculate the ratio of the marginal physical product to the price of a factor. For factor A we have 40/$20 = 2 units per dollar, and for factor B we have 60/$300 = 0.2 units per dollar. The last dollar spent on factor A produces more output. Therefore, the firm should hire more units of factor A and fewer units of factor B.

3. Two expansion paths cannot cross. Let the expansion path be ee when the wage is w and let the other expansion path be $e'e'$ when the wage is w'. Because of the difference in wage rates, the slopes of the two isocost functions differ. When the two expansion paths cross, the slope of the isoquant is the same; however, the slopes of the two isocost functions are different at that point. Therefore, the expansion paths of a firm that minimize the cost of producing each rate of output will not cross. See the accompanying figure.

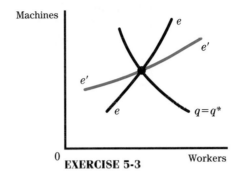

EXERCISE 5-3

4.　a. The relative price of labor to capital is lower in Malaysia than in the United States. Therefore, Malaysian producers will use relatively more labor to capital to produce 20,000 bedsheets as is shown in Exercise 5-4a.

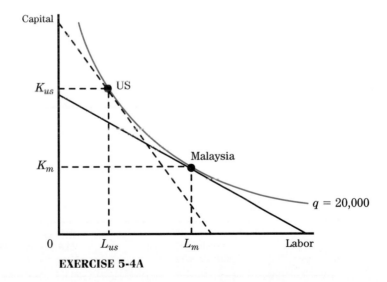

EXERCISE 5-4A

b. The expansion paths of the two countries will differ because the relative factor prices differ. Exercise 5-4b shows that as Malaysia produces more bedsheets, it always uses more labor relative to capital.

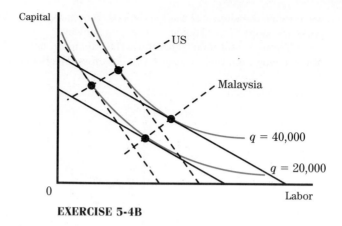

EXERCISE 5-4B

9. Given the prices of the two factors, the isocost line for a given total expenditure is *aa'* in the accompanying figure. The firm has 100 computers and 30 workers. When the company receives a subsidy of 10 percent for every extra computer that it purchases, the isocost line becomes steeper since the rental price of a computer falls relative to labor. The firm's isocost line becomes *abc*.

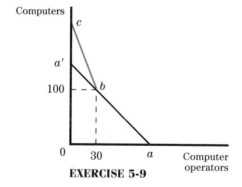

EXERCISE 5-9

Chapter 6

2. a. The completed table is:

$q_1 + q_2 = 9$	AVERAGE COST OF PLANT	SUM OF VARIABLE COST, $V_1 + V_2$	SUM OF TOTAL COST, $C_1 + C_2$
$q_1 = 4, q_2 = 5$	$AC_1 = 90, AC_2 = 15$	86	436
$q_1 = 3, q_2 = 6$	$AC_1 = 112, AC_2 = 16$	81	431
$q_1 = 2, q_2 = 7$	$AC_1 = 158, AC_2 = 20$	105	455

b. The sum of the averages is $AC_1 + AC_2$. Minimizing total cost requires that

$$q_1AC_1(q_1) + q_2AC_2(q_2) = F_1 + V_1(q_1) + F_2 + V_2(q_2)$$

be minimized.

3. The firm wants to minimize total cost subject to the condition that $q_1 + q_2 = 25$. A necessary condition is that the marginal costs of the two plants are equal. Solve for $q_2 = 25 - q_1$ and substitute into the equality of marginal costs to get

$$50 + 5q_1 = 25 + 5(25 - q_1) \text{ or } 100 = 10q_1$$

Therefore, $q_1 = 10$ units and $q_2 = 25$ units.

6. There are two ways to satisfy the order. One way is to produce q_1 units in September and incur an inventory cost of h per unit. If one more unit is produced in September, the total marginal cost is $\Delta C(q_1)/\Delta q_1 + h$. Another way to satisfy the order is to produce q_2 units in October. If one more unit is produced in October, the marginal cost is $\Delta C(q_2)/\Delta q_2$. Minimizing total cost requires the marginal cost of production in September plus h to equal the marginal cost of production in October, or

$$\frac{\Delta C(q_1)}{\Delta q_1} + h = \frac{\Delta C(q_2)}{\Delta q_2}$$

The quantities to be produced in September and in October can be determined from the accompanying graph.

c. Since the cost function is the same for both months, equality of marginal production costs would require the same amount to be produced only if $h = 0$.

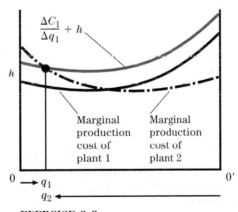

EXERCISE 6-6

d. An increase in h reduces the quantity produced in September and increases the quantity produced in October. The increase in h increases the total marginal cost of producing another unit in September but does not affect the total marginal cost of producing another unit in October.

8. First, short-run marginal cost does not go through the minimum point of the short-run average cost function. Second, average cost does not become infinite as q approaches zero. Finally, average variable cost does not reach a minimum at the quantity where the straight line from the origin is tangent to the variable cost function.

Chapter 7

1. The price elasticity of demand of a firm depends on its market share, the supply elasticity of other firms, and the price elasticity of market demand. In the short run other firms will increase the quantity supplied when the price increases, but not as much as in the long run when they can adjust all factors of production. The elasticity of supply measures the percentage increase in the quantity supplied for a given percentage increase in price. This means that the elasticity of supply of the other firms is larger in the long run than in the short run. As consumers learn of alternative sources of supply, the price elasticity of market demand becomes more elastic in the long run. Both factors will make the firm's demand function more elastic in the long run than in the short run.

5. Average variable cost reaches a minimum of $4 when the firm is producing 3 units. Therefore, the firm will close down if the price is less than $3, which occurs in years 4 and 6.

8. Since the smallest plant is closed first, its minimum average variable cost must be higher than the minimum average cost of the other four plants that close later. Later, when price increases, this price-taking firm behaves irrationally by opening the plant with the highest minimum average variable cost first. It is more profitable to open the other plants before it opens the smallest plant.

9. While the farmer has incurred costs to raise the young calves, these costs are sunk. The farmer must look forward and decide if the price that will be received for the calves in the future exceeds the average variable cost incurred while fattening the calves. If the expected price is less than minimum average variable cost, the farmer will decide to shoot the young calves. This behavior is consistent with profit maximization if the price is less than minimum average variable cost.

Chapter 7 Problem Set:
Should Your Company Honor a Contract?

1. Your three options are fulfill the original contract, don't fulfill the original contract or sign the new contract, and fulfull the new contract. The loss incurred from fulfilling the original contract is

$$L_1 = (P'' - b)q_c - F - T \quad \text{where } b > P''$$

2. If the firm does not fulfill either contract, its loss is

$$L_2 = -F - (P' - P'')q_c$$

The second term represents the penalty assessed because the original customer pays P' in the marketplace.

3. If the firm fulfills the new contract, the loss is

$$L_3 = -F - T + (P^* - b)q_c - (P' - P'')q_c$$

4. You will fulfill the new contract if the losses are smaller, or

$$L_3 > L_2$$

$$-F - T + (P^* - b)q_c - (P' - P'')q_c > -F - (P' - P'')q_c$$

$$-T - (P^* - b)q_c > 0$$

If you decide not to fulfill the original contract, then you should select option 3 if the franchise tax is less than the difference between total revenue and total variable cost. T and $(P^* - b)q_c$ are under your control and are determined by your decision. F, P', and P'' do not affect this decision, and F is a bygone. The penalty is incurred under option 2 or 3, and so it cannot affect the decision. If $L_3 > L_2$, then you will need to decide whether it is better to fulfill the original or the new contract.

5. You will fulfill the original contract if

$$L_1 > L_3$$

$$(P'' - b)q_c - F - T > -F - T + (P^* - b)q_c - (P' - P'')q_c$$

$$P' > P^*$$

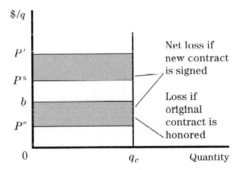

CHAPTER 7: PROBLEM SET

This condition will be satisfied because $P' > P^*$. See the accompanying figure. The firm will fulfill the original contract. Notice that F, T, and b have no bearing on this decision. F is a bygone, and you must pay T whether you fulfill the old or the new contract. Likewise, bq_c is irrelevant because you will incur these costs whether you fulfill the new or the old contract.

Chapter 8

4.   a. Since the supply of citrus produced abroad is perfectly elastic at $5, then the equilibrium price will be $5 if the domestic industry cannot supply the quantity demanded at a

price of $5. The quantity demanded at a price of $5 equals $20,000 - 250(5) = 18,750$ units. The quantity supplied by the domestic industry at a price of $5 equals $5,000 + 200(5) = 6,000$ units. Therefore, imports will account for the difference between the quantity demanded and the quantity supplied, or $18,750 - 6,000 = 12,750$ units.

   b. If the quota on imports equals 5,000 units, the equilibrium price must be higher than $5. The total supply curve (domestic and imports) becomes $10,000 + 200P$ for $P > \$5$. The equilibrium price is determined where the quantity demanded equals the quantity supplied:

$$20,000 - 250P = 10,000 + 200P \quad \text{or} \quad 10,000 = 450P$$

Therefore, $P = \$22.22$.

   c. Consumer surplus *decreases* by the area *abcdef* because the price rises from $5 to $22.22. However, producer surplus *increases* by area *abdef*. Therefore net surplus decreases by area *bcd*.

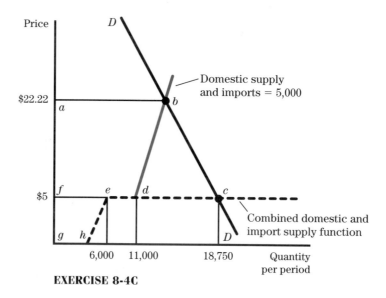

EXERCISE 8-4C

5. A special type of land is required for the production of cranberries. Therefore, this industry is an increasing-cost industry where a higher price for a barrel of cranberries will attract less efficient producers into the market. When demand function shifts outward because of the growing use of cranberries in juice drinks, the price of cranberries increases and the total quantity of cranberries increases. The higher price increases the rent received by the owners of the scarce factor, the land to grow cranberries.

14. There are two sources of supply in this problem, the domestic industry and the foreign source. Because there are external diseconomies of scale, the supply function of the domestic suppliers has a positive slope. Foreign suppliers are willing to provide an indefinite quantity at the price of P_w. The supply function of domestic and foreign producers is the heavy colored line in the accompanying figure. The equilibrium price is determined by the world price of P_w. At this price the domestic industry supplies Q_D and the difference between quantity demanded and Q_D is equal to imports, Q_I. See the accompanying figure.

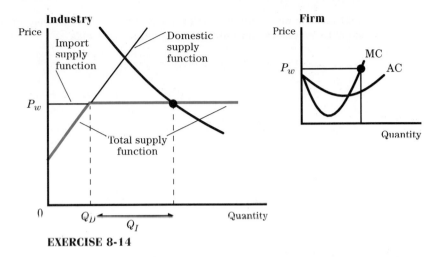

EXERCISE 8-14

15. **a.** The quantity of imports is reduced by 20 percent. No longer is the supply of imports perfectly elastic at the world price. Only 80 percent of the previous level of imports can enter the domestic economy, and once this occurs the only way to increase the quantity

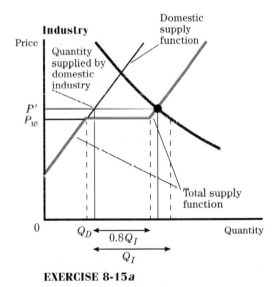

EXERCISE 8-15a

supplied is for the domestic industry to supply more. However, the domestic industry will supply more only if the price increases. The new total industry supply function is the heavy line in the accompanying figure. Because the equilibrium price increases from P_w to P', the quantity supplied by the domestic industry increases. Imposing an import constraint raises domestic prices, increases the earnings of the scarce factor of supply, and harms consumers.

b. The price elasticity of demand is -1, and the quantity is to be reduced by 20 percent. Let Q be the original quantity and P be the original price. Then, the new quantity will be

$0.8Q$ and the new price will be $(1 + t)P$, where t is to be determined. Substituting these expressions into the formula for the arc elasticity yields

$$-1 = \frac{Q - 0.8Q}{P - (1 + t)P} \frac{P + (1 + t)P}{Q + 0.8Q}$$

$$= \frac{0.2Q}{-tP} \frac{(2 + t)P}{1.8Q} = \frac{0.2(2 + t)}{-1.8t}$$

Solving for t yields $t = 0.25$. The import duty must increase price by 25 percent for the total quantity consumed to decrease by 20 percent. See the accompanying figure.

    c. Because the total quantity consumed decreases by 20 percent and the domestic price increases by 25 percent, the quantity supplied by the domestic industry increases. Therefore, the total quantity imported must decrease by more than 20 percent.

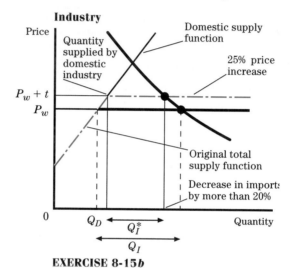

EXERCISE 8-15*b*

Chapter 9

2. Because the marginal cost function shifts upward, the new equilibrium will occur at a higher value for marginal revenue, a movement along the marginal revenue function at the new quantity, where $MR = MC$. The increase in the value of marginal revenue implies that the firm is producing a smaller quantity, and this must mean that the profits of the monopolist decline because total revenue declines and the total cost of producing the smaller quantity is higher than before.

7. Currently, the competitive price is P_c. The marginal cost of production of the new firm is lower and is $0.8P_c$ because of the invention. The question asks: What is the smallest value of the price elasticity of demand at the monopoly price at which the monopolist can set the price so that $MR = MC$?

    If the monopoly price of the new firm is greater than P_c, it cannot sell any units at this price. On the other hand, the profit-maximizing monopoly price can be either equal to or less than P_c if the market demand function is sufficiently elastic. Marginal cost is $0.8P_c$, and marginal revenue is

$$MR = P\left(1 + \frac{1}{E}\right)$$

To find the required price elasticity where the monopoly price just equals P_c, we must have

$$MR = MC \qquad MC = 0.8P_c$$

$$MR = P_c\left(1 + \frac{1}{E_P}\right) \qquad P_c\left(1 + \frac{1}{E_P}\right) = 0.8P_c$$

Solve this equation for E_P to get $E_P = -5$. So, if the price elasticity is -5, marginal revenue is $0.8P_c$. The profit-maximizing monopoly price is 20 percent greater than the marginal cost of the monopolist. If the price elasticity is less than -5, say, -10, then the profit-maximizing price will be less than P_c and no competitive firm will produce at this price. See the accompanying figure.

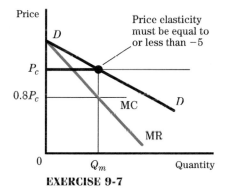

EXERCISE 9-7

8. If there are many firms in the domestic industry instead of just one, placing an import quota on the foreign firms will not affect the market price. While the shape of the supply function of the foreign firms changes when the quota is imposed, the demand function and the modified supply function still intersect at the competitive equilibrium price of P_I, and so the price does not change. The cost functions of a representative firm are shown in panel a in the accompanying figure. The supply function of the domestic and foreign suppliers is S_LabS_L before the quota is imposed. After the quota is imposed, the supply function of domestic and foreign producers becomes S_Labc. At P_I foreign suppliers will supply their quota equal to the distance ab. With a quota only domestic suppliers are able to supply

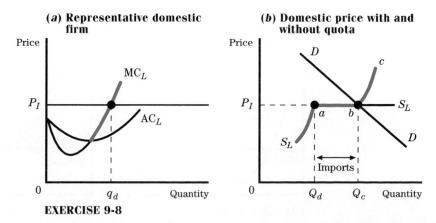

EXERCISE 9-8

more units at prices above P_I. The equilibrium price remains at P_I after the government imposes the quota because there are many price-taking domestic firms in the market.

When the domestic industry is competitive, the price will not change when the quota is imposed. If the price in an industry increases when a quota is imposed, this indicates that the domestic firms have monopoly power.

9. **a.** The regulated price is determined where the marginal cost function of the monopolist intersects the demand function. When the regulated price is determined in this manner, the firm's demand function becomes horizontal to the market demand function at the regulated price and then is the market demand function at lower prices. See the accompanying figure. When the regulated price is R^*, the demand function facing the regulated firm is the horizontal line at R^*. The firm will equate R^* to marginal cost and produce Q^*. Area 1 is equal to the firm's profits—the difference between R^*Q^* and the area under the marginal cost function. If there is competitive bidding for the right to become a monopolist, the winner of the auction will pay a sum equal to area 1.

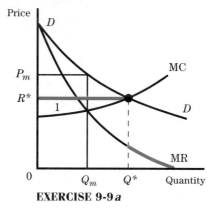

EXERCISE 9-9 *a*

b. If the demand function intersects the marginal cost function when marginal cost is greater than average cost, the firm will earn profits and will be willing to bid a positive amount. If the demand function intersects the marginal cost function where marginal cost is less than average cost, the firm will incur losses and therefore will not be willing to bid anything. If the firm bids a positive amount, it implies that average cost is increasing. If it does not bid anything, average cost is decreasing. If it bids a positive amount, marginal cost is increasing. If it does not bid, marginal cost may be either decreasing or increasing, but it is less than average cost. See the accompanying figure.

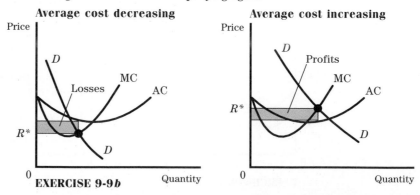

EXERCISE 9-9 *b*

Chapter 10

2. **a.** If the firms have different cost functions, then an arbitrary 15 percent output reduction will not minimize the cost of producing whatever output the cartel decides to produce.

b. The quotas should be determined so that marginal cost is equalized across firms.

c. To reach a consensus among the members when side payments are not possible, the cartel may simply take the easiest way out and assign a 15 percent output reduction to all firms.

4. With Bertrand competition a tiny price cut increases the firm's market share from 50 to 100 percent. Suppose that two Bertrand competitors try to cooperate. How might they credibly commit to cooperation? Each could build a plant with a rigid capacity equal to 50 percent of the market at the monopoly price. By building a plant with a rigid capacity, each Bertrand competitor is signaling the opponent that it will not be able to expand output. Therefore, a price cut will be self-defeating.

7. False. Clearly, two firms sharing the market represent an oligopoly. If a hundred firms of the same size are in the market, then each accounts for only 1 percent of the market and the industry behaves like a competitive industry.

15. A Bertrand rival with an infinite horizon can threaten to cut price to marginal cost if any firm undercuts the cooperative agreement. This capability to harm a rival discourages price cutting by each Bertrand competitor. On the other hand, in a single period problem, no firm can adopt a punishment strategy and can harm a rival. Consequently, price will fall to marginal cost.

Chapter 11

1. A firm cannot live a quiet life if the capital market operates at a low transaction cost. Then, a management that does not maximize profits is subject to a takeover. If impediments are placed in the way so that the capital market cannot replace an inefficient management, then a protected management can deviate from wealth maximization.

4. During a recession the demand for the firm's product declines and the profit function shifts downward. The profit constraint may no longer be binding, and the firm becomes subject to the discipline of the capital market. See the accompanying figure.

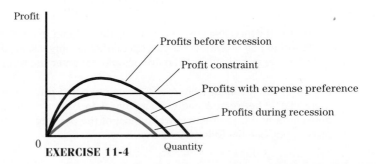

EXERCISE 11-4

6. When the regulator commits to a fixed price, the firm will earn profits by being efficient in production. Therefore, the firm's management will have a greater incentive to be cost-efficient. Any increase in profits will not be taken away by the regulator through a lower regulated price. The danger is that the regulator's commitment may not be binding if the firm's profits rise by too much.

Chapter 12

3. A price-discriminating monopolist will never sell in a market where demand is price-inelastic because marginal revenue [$MR = P(1 + 1/E)$] is negative when $0 > E_P > -1$.

4. **a.** If marginal cost is decreasing and the firm expands into the foreign market, the price in the domestic market decreases. The horizontal summation of the marginal revenue functions intersects the marginal cost function where marginal cost of producing the last unit is lower. See the accompanying figure. The summation of the marginal revenue functions intersects the downward-sloping marginal cost curve when the firm produces Q^* units. The firm allocates Q^* to the two markets so that marginal revenue in the markets is equal. When the firm enters the foreign market, it should reduce price in the domestic market if marginal cost is decreasing.

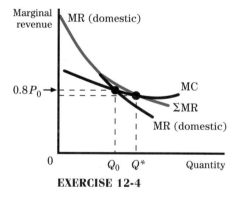

EXERCISE 12-4

b. If the price elasticity of demand is -10, marginal revenue of the last unit sold in the domestic market is

$$MR = P_0\left(1 + \frac{1}{-10}\right) = 0.9P_0$$

Therefore, the marginal cost of producing the last unit in the domestic market is $0.9P_0$. Since the first unit can be sold in the foreign market as only $0.85P_0$, the first unit sold abroad will *not* cover its marginal cost. The firm should not enter the foreign market.

5. **a.** While the flight from A to C costs more, the price could be lower if the demand is more elastic between A and C than from A to B. For example, suppose most passengers between A and C are tourists while most of the passengers between A and B are business passengers. See the following figures.

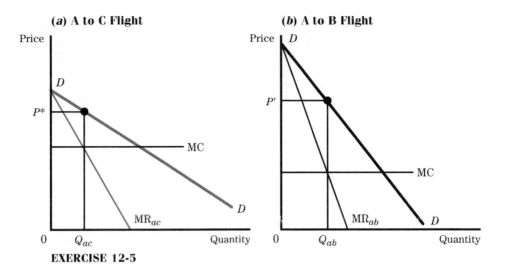

(a) A to C Flight

(b) A to B Flight

EXERCISE 12-5

b. The airline may have more difficulty separating the business flyer from the tourist customer by combining flights. What may happen is that a passenger flying from A to B will buy the cheaper A to C ticket and simply get off the plane at B. The airline must be able to prevent this type of arbitrage behavior or it will lose more business customers to the low-price segment of the market.

12. a. *Policy 1:* The per unit fee equals marginal cost of $c + d$. The entrance fee is equal to area A, and total profits equal A.

Policy 2: Because there is no per unit charge, the consumer determines the number of rides where the demand function intersects the horizontal axis. The entrance fee collects all the consumer surplus or $A + B + C + D + E + F$. The cost of providing the rides equals $D + E + F + G$. Therefore, profits equal $A + B + C - G$.

b. Profits under policy 2 will be greater if $B + C > G$.

c. Suppose that you could limit the number of rides to the quantity where the demand function intersects the marginal cost function c. Then, the entrance fee would be $A + B + C + D + E$ and profits would be $A + B + C$.

14. a. Over a two-day period profits from the old price policy are $2A$. Under the new price policy profits are $A + B + C$ since the consumer purchases the requirements for a two-day period and shops every other day. Profits from the new price policy will be greater if $B + C > A$.

b. Suppose that you raise the entrance fee to $2(A + B + C)$ and allow consumers to purchase as many units as desired whenever they buy. Then, your profits over a two-day period are $2(A + B + C)$.

Chapter 13

5. Proposal 1 makes the retail margin large enough so that the costs of providing the product and pre- and postservices are covered. However, it does not solve the free rider problem. There is nothing in proposal 1 that encourages an individual dealer to supply the special service. The dealer's profits are higher if the service is not provided.

Will proposal 1 encourage the dealer to provide postsale service? Notice that the consumer pays up front for the lessons. The problem here is that there is a short-run profit gain from not delivering the lessons or from delivering lesser-quality lessons. There is an incentive to cheat by promising more than the firm will deliver.

With proposal 2 RPM is designed to solve the free rider problem when a dealer provides presale services. Does RPM solve the problem of postsale services? There is no guarantee that the dealer will provide these services since short-run profits are higher when there is cheating on the lessons.

6. **a.** Under policy 1, if the firm adopts RPM, first-time buyers will receive the information. Under policy 2 there is a danger that first-time buyers will free-ride by acquiring information from a dealer who sells under RPM but purchase at the other type of dealer. Unless this can be controlled, dealers operating under RPM will suffer losses.

    b. Under policy 1 a dealer has a greater incentive to sell to experienced buyers who require less information. So the dealer will earn profits on sales to experienced buyers. Under policy 2 dealers selling under RPM will earn a normal return if the free rider problem is solved and will suffer losses if it is not. Dealers selling to experienced buyers will earn a normal rate of return.

7. **a.** If you allow customers to listen before purchase, you may be creating a free rider problem. If most of your customers are high cost-of-time consumers, then it is unlikely that they will listen and then go elsewhere to purchase. If, on the other hand, most of your customers are teenagers with a lower cost of time, then this is more likely to be a serious problem. Also, you need to know what happens to used CDs. Will manufacturers accept them in return, or can you sell them at a discount?

    b. By limiting the selection to classical CDs, the assistant manager recognizes that most buyers of classical CDs are older, high cost-of-time customers who are less likely to shop elsewhere after they hear a CD.

Chapter 14

5. When an insurance company offers a health plan to firms with employment above a minimum size, they usually offer substantial discounts. All workers for that employer are required to join the health plan, or they find the health plan rates sufficiently attractive to join. Thus, the insurance company is more likely to get an unbiased sample of workers. On the other hand, by offering a voluntary insurance policy to a trade association group, the insurance company is more likely to find that those who accept the policy are an adverse selection of all members of the group.

8. If consumers know the quantity produced by a firm, they can tell if the firm is acting honestly by the amount it produces. A firm could still cheat by producing the profit-maximizing quantity supplied by a firm delivering high-quality output. While profits of a cheater are not as large as they would be if it could produce the quantity that maximizes its profits, they exceed the profits earned when acting honestly.

9. If the number of retailers is limited, the price of the product and franchisee profit will increase until the price premium is large enough so that the present value of honest behavior is equal to the present value of cheating. Therefore, you should limit the number of franchises so that the price premium deters cheating.

Chapter 14 Problem Set:
Integration and Opportunistic Behavior

1. If X acts opportunistically and raises price by P percent, it will earn profits for one period and then be terminated. The present value of profits is

$$\text{PV}_1 = \left[\left(1 + \frac{P}{100}\right)A - A\right]q_c \frac{1}{1 + i} = \frac{PAq_c}{(1 + i)100}$$

2. If Y offers a price premium of k percent, the present value of profits earned by X is

$$\text{PV}_2 = \left[\left(1 + \frac{k}{100}\right)A - A\right]q_c \frac{1}{i} = \frac{kAq_c}{i(100)}$$

X will act not opportunistically if $\text{PV}_1 \leq \text{PV}_2$. This implies that

$$\frac{PAq_c}{1 + i} \leq \frac{kAq_c}{i} \qquad P\frac{i}{1 + i} \leq k$$

3. Given the price premium, the price that Y offers X is

$$\left(1 + \frac{k}{100}\right)A = \left(1 + \frac{P}{100}\frac{i}{1 + i}\right)A$$

If r or P is sufficiently large, it will pay Y to produce the part although it is a less efficient producer because the required price premium exceeds the cost inefficiency factor. Y will purchase the part rather than produce it if

$$\left(1 + \frac{P}{100}\frac{i}{1 + i}\right)A < \left(1 + \frac{I}{100}\right)A$$

or

$$\frac{I}{P} \geq \frac{i}{1 + i} \qquad \text{or} \qquad i \leq \frac{I/P}{1 - I/P}$$

assuming $I < P$. If $I > P$, it will always pay Y to purchase the part.

Chapter 15

3. Under a two-price policy, the expression for expected revenue is

$$\text{ER}(P_i, P_m) = P_i[1 - F(P_i)] + P_m[F(P_i) - F(P_m)]$$

Substituting the expressions for the probabilities gives

$$\text{ER}(P_i, P_m) = P_i\left(1 - \frac{P_i}{\$450}\right) + P_m\left(\frac{P_i}{\$450} - \frac{P_m}{\$450}\right)$$

$$= P_i\frac{\$450 - P_i}{\$450} + P_m\frac{P_i - P_m}{\$450}$$

Given P_i, the optimal markdown price is derived from

$$\frac{\Delta \text{ER}}{\Delta P_m} = \frac{P_i - P_m}{\$450} - \frac{P_m}{\$450} = 0$$

So we have derived the 50 percent decision rule, $P_m = P_i/2$. Substituting this decision rule into the expected revenue equation yields

$$\text{ER}(P_i, P_m) = P_i\left(\frac{\$450 - P_i}{\$450}\right) + \frac{P_i}{2}\left(\frac{P_i}{\$450} - \frac{P_i/2}{\$450}\right)$$

$$\text{ER}(P_i) = P_i\left(\frac{\$450 - P_i}{\$450}\right) + \frac{1}{\$450}\frac{P_i}{2}\frac{P_i}{2}$$

Expected revenue is maximized when P_i satisfies

$$\frac{\Delta \text{ER}}{\Delta P_i} = \frac{1}{\$450}(\$450 - P_i - P_i + P_i/2) = 0$$

Therefore,

$$P_i = \tfrac{2}{3}(\$450) = \$300 \qquad \text{and} \qquad P_m = \$150$$

The firm will charge these prices and sell five colors at $300 and five more colors at $150. Expected revenue is

$$\text{ER} = \$300\frac{150}{450} + \frac{1}{450}\left(\frac{300}{2}\right)^2$$

$$= \$100 + \$50 = \$150$$

5. The compensation policy of the firm penalizes a buyer who purchases a fashion line because the probability of not selling all the dresses is higher when there is greater uncertainty. The store buyer will have an incentive to select lines where the price distribution has a smaller variance, and the percentage of dresses sold will be higher.

6. This policy is better suited for goods where there is less uncertainty about the prices that consumers will pay. It should be applied to the sale of paint or hammers rather than to fashion merchandise. Therefore, a store that adopts this policy will offer less fashionable clothing.

10. For tract housing there are many sales and thus more information about market prices so that the dispersion in prices that buyers are willing to pay is much smaller. On the other hand, a mansion is often a unique and higher priced property. There are few or no other comparable mansions around to allow a prospective buyer to infer the market price, and the market for mansions is likely to be thinner. Thus, there is more uncertainty about a mansion's market price, and the number of potential buyers is smaller. Consequently, a seller that puts a mansion on the market will not know if the mansion is not selling because her offer price is too high or because not enough buyers have seen the house. Before the seller is willing to lower the offer price, the seller will want to wait until enough potential buyers have rejected the house before concluding that the offer price is too high.

Chapter 16

2. If a tax of 33 percent of income in year 2 is announced at the beginning of year 1, the consumer's intertemporal budget constraint becomes $C_2 = 0.67I_2 + (1 + i)I_1 - (1 + i)C_1$. Therefore, the intertemporal budget constraint shifts from dd' to cc'. If consumption in years 1 and 2 consists of normal goods, consumption in both years will decrease and savings in year 1 will increase. In the accompanying figure consumption spending in year 1 decreases from $C_1^\bullet$ to C_1', and so savings increase to $I_1 - C_1^\bullet$. Consumption spending in year 2 decreases from $C_2^\bullet$ to C_2'.

5. An increase in demand for the nonrenewable resource in year 2 shifts the discounted demand function for period 2 from DP to DP'. See the accompanying figure. This means less of the resource is sold in period 1 and more is sold in period 2. Since less of the resource is sold in period 1, the price in period 1 rises from P_1 to P_1' and the price in period 2 increases from $(1 + i)P_1$ to $(1 + i)P_1'$. Although prices rise in both years, the rate of increase is still $1 + i$.

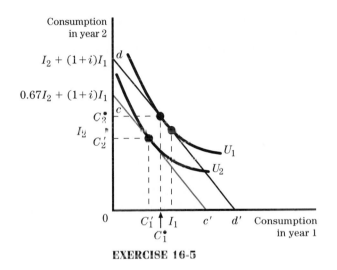

EXERCISE 16-5

9. If P_2 is less than $(1 + i)P_1$, the supply of a renewable resource is augmented in period 2. An increase in i causes the discounted demand function in the second period to shift downward. Since the discounted price is less in the second period than before, the price in the second period will be the same and the price in the first period will be unaffected.

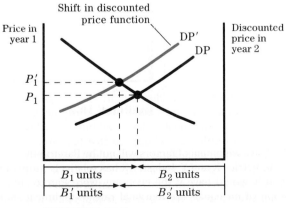

EXERCISE 16-9

4. To determine if transaction costs are large or small, you must determine whether the assignment of property rights affects the outcome. If transaction costs are small, the outcome should be independent of the assignment of property rights. If transaction costs are large, the assignment should make a difference.

6.   **a.** This is not a valid conclusion. The transaction costs of organizing the other stores may have been so large that they could not organize to bid for the leases. It appears that the real solution will differ depending on who has the property rights.

　　b. If transaction costs are negligible, Victoria's Secret and Borders will post smaller signs because larger signs create greater damage in the form of lower sales by the other stores. These damages would have to be paid by Victoria's Secret and Borders Bookstore.

Accounting costs, 219n
Adams, William J., 474n
Adjustment of an industry to shift in market demand, 289
Adverse selection, 519
  and asymmetric information, 520–532
Affordable market baskets, 58–62
  and budget constraint, 145–152
  and changes in nonwage income/wage rate, 154–156
  intertemporal budget constraint, 589–591
  intertemporal preferences, 591–593
  time constraint on, 143–145
  using full price budget constraint to find, 147–148
African elephants, 714–715
Age groupings, 453
Aggregate supply function of labor, 641–642
Agriculture, 489–490
Airline industry
  fuel prices, 303–305
  scale effect, 634–635
  substitution effect, 634–635
Akerlof, George A., 520n
Alchian, Armen A., 429n
Alcoa, 328
Allensby, Greg M., 73n
Allis-Chalmers, case, 394–398
Allshouse, Jane E., 77
Aluminum producers, 207–208
Alumni contributors, 89–92
Anchor stores, 704–705
Antitrust Division of the Justice Department, 362–363
Antitrust laws, 362, 695–696
  and cartels, 370–371
  price-fixing case, 394–398
  and Toys "R" Us, 510
Apple Computer, 499, 504
  restrictions on dealers, 493
Arbitrage
  control by leasing, 479–480
  prevented in price discrimination, 467–469
Arc cross-price elasticity of demand, 81
Arc income elasticity of demand, 99
Arc price elasticity of demand, 30–34
Arc price elasticity of supply, 37
Area under the marginal cost function, 226–228
Armed forces, 587
Armstrong, Catherine, 713–714
Asgrow Seed, 490
Assignment of property rights, 706–709, 711
Asymmetric information; see also Information

and adverse selection, 520–532
  consequences of, 518–520
  equilibrium prices and quantities, 522–526
  lemons model, 521–532
  market equilibria with, 525–526
  missing markets with, 528
  modeling competitive behavior under, 536–540
  and moral hazard, 532–534
  and nonsalvageable investments, 546–548
  overcoming, 528–529
  and potential for cheating, 534–540
  unknown price premium, 548
  in used car sales, 521–529
Athletic footwear, 100
Auction market, 390–391
  preventing collusion, 393–394
Audi, 208
Automobile industry
  aluminum versus steel use, 207–208
  payoff matrix, 403–404
Automobile insurance, 510
Average cost (function)
  and cost-reducing innovation, 300–302
  determined by prices, 299
  and marginal cost, 224–226
Average production function of labor, 177–181
Average revenue, 563
Average variable cost function, 267

Backloading pay, 659
Bacon, Nathaniel T., 376n
Banana wars, 315–318
Bank loans, 519–520
Bankruptcy, 599–600
Barnett, Paul M., 490n
Barret, Paul, 493n
Barriers to entry
  ice cream distribution, 511–512
  posed by monopolists, 328–329
  and sequential games, 406–409
  through licensing, 307–310
Baseball free-agency, 530–531
Becker, Gary S., 22n, 143, 342, 652n
Below-market price, 156–157
Ben & Jerry's Homemade, Inc., 511–512
Bennett, Amanda, 658n
Bertrand, Joseph, 384n
Bertrand model
  and collusion, 396–397
  lessons from, 388
  prices and number of rivals, 388–391
Bethlehem Steel, 246
Bishop, R. L., 299n, 347n
Blackstone, E. A., 479n

Board of directors
  ex post settling up costs, 424–425
  as internal monitor, 422–425, 438
Boeing 707, 303–305
Boeing 747, 304–305
Bond, Eric, 531–532
Bonyhard, Peter, 489
Borrowing
  demand function for loanable funds, 603–608
  interest rate, 600–603
Bound, John, 652n
Bowen, Brian, 454
Bradley, Michael, 440
Brand extension strategy, 401–402
Brand loyalty
  and relative frequency of purchase, 73–75
  of women shoppers, 166
Brands/Brand names
  as asset, 547
  early or late entry, 402–403
  protection of, 490–491
Break-even analysis, 265–266
Bresnehan, Timothy F., 389
Brokers, 237–238
Bubble concept, 236–237
Budget constraint; see also Full price budget constraint; Intertemporal budget constraint
  affordable market baskets, 58–62
  definition, 58–59
  and income effect, 96–99
  and maximal utility, 64–65
  shifts in, 62–64
  and time constraint, 145
Bundling, 471–474
Bureau of Labor Statistics, 162
Burrough, Bryan, 423n
Buyers/sellers, and adverse selection, 520–521

Cable franchise, 351–355
California earthquake insurance, 132–134
California water rights problem, 682–683
Capital costs, 267
Capital goods
  leasing versus selling, 479–480
  two-part tariff for pricing, 477–479
Capital loss, 547–548
Capital market
  as external monitor, 417–422
  free rider problem, 419–422
  tender offer, 419–422
Capital subsidies, 689–690; see also Subsidies
Carlton, Dennis, 446n
Cartel behavior, 368–371

Cartels, 368
  caviar, 382–383
  duopoly models, 376–388
  orange producers, 371
  and resale price maintenance, 507
Catalog industry, 166
Caviar, 382–383
CEOs (chief executive officers)
  expense preference, 423
  influence with board, 424–425
  performance and pay, 436–437
  in principal-agent relationship, 425
Certainty, market equilibrium prices under, 575–576
Chandler, Alfred D., Jr., 246
Cheating
  and collusion, 395–396
  versus honesty, 543–544
  incentives for, 372–376
  potential for monopolists, 534–536
  price premium incentive for, 542
Chevrolet, 471–473
Chevron gas stations, 156–157
Chicago Bulls, 180–181
Chief executive officers; *see* CEOs
Christian Dior, 117
Christiansen, Richard, 358n
Chrysler Corporation, 173
Cigarette industry, 340–342
Coase, Ronald H., 173, 355–357, 703, 705–708
Coase theorem, 705–710
Cobb-Douglas production function, 187–188
Coca-Cola Company, 219, 401
Cold War, 587
Cole, Robert J., 133
College graduates
  equilibrium earnings, 648–652
  wage premium, 652
Collusion
  case, 394–398
  and cheating, 395–396
  cost of detecting price cutting, 397–398
  facilitating and preventing, 391–398
  preventing, 393–394
  product and industry characteristics, 396–397
Command and control policies
  nature of, 669–671
  problems with, 673
Compensated price elasticity of demand, 115n
Compensation; *see also* Wage policies
  based on output or input, 657–659
  and education, 646–652
  ex post settling up costs, 424–425
  and firm's performance, 437–438
  incentive effects, 659–662
  incentive pay, 658–659
  with profit constraint, 432
Competition
  behavior under asymmetric information, 536–540
  Bertrand model, 384–388
  Cournot model, 376–384, 414–415
  meeting, 391–393
  to be monopolists, 351–355

  nonprice, 502
  prices and number of rivals, 388–391
  among suppliers, 387–388
Competitive bidding, 354–355, 394
  and cheating, 395–396
Competitive equilibrium price, 680–681
Competitive factor markets, Pareto efficiency in production, 686–689
Competitive firms
  break-even analysis, 265–266
  definition, 256
  in Eastern Europe/Russia, 260
  effect of per unit tax, 311–315
  equating price to marginal cost, 270
  exhaustion of all internal economies of scale, 272
  long-run demand function for labor, 630–635
  long-run marginal cost function, 272
  long-run supply firms, 269–273
  marginal revenue, 258–259
  need to maximize profits, 261–262
  price elasticity of demand, 259–260
  price-taking assumption, 256–259
  profit-maximizing behavior, 265–266
  short-run costs, 265–266
  short-run demand function for labor, 626–629
  short-run marginal cost function, 263
  short-run supply curve, 264
  short-run supply function, 261–269
  shutdown price, 264
  supply elasticity, 260
  total revenue, 258
Competitive industries
  and nonsalvageable investments, 546–548
  price premium, 540–541
  supplying high quality products, 540–549
  typical, 279
Competitive markets
  product mix efficiency, 691–693
  for public goods, 721
  quality produced in, 540
Competitive product market
  minimizing information requirements, 680–681
  Pareto efficient exchange, 678–680
Complements; *see also* Substitutes
  in consumer behavior model, 78–81
  and price changes, 9
Complete information, 673
  equilibrium prices/quantities, 521–522
Completeness, 48–49
Composite goods, 70–71
Concentrated share ownership, 422
Concentration ratio, 371–372
Conservation groups, 709–710
Consistency, 49
Constant-cost industry
  assumptions, 280–281
  compared to increasing-cost industry, 291, 293
  and increase in market demand, 289
  long-run industry equilibrium, 282–283
  long-run industry supply function, 281–282
  price determination, 279–283

Constant returns to scale, 185–187
Consumer behavior model; *see also* Intertemporal theory of consumer behavior
  and affordable market baskets, 143–152
  applying, 81–84
  brand loyalty, 73–75
  and budget constraint, 58–64
  building, 48–49
  changes in nonwage income, 154–156
  changes in wage rate, 154–156
  choosing a market basket, 153
  with composite goods, 70–71
  consumer demand function, 94–118
  consumer preferences, 49–57
  consumer surplus, 94, 118–123
  and consumption decision, 64–69
  cost of women's time, 163–166
  decision making with uncertainty, 123–124
  finding lowest full price, 157–163
  full price budget constraint, 145–152
  and market demand function, 71–78
  price-time tradeoff, 143–166
  revised, 152–157
  substitutes and complements, 78–81
Consumer demand function, 94–118
  combining income/substitution effects, 101–105
  deriving marginal values, 139–141
  effect of each determinant, 117–118
  effect of price change, 105–107
  income effect, 96–99
  income elasticity of demand, 99–101
  size of income/substitution effects, 115–117
  slope of demand function, 113–115
  and subsidized day care, 107–110
  substitution effect, 96, 101
Consumer endowment, 672–673
Consumer groups
  characteristics and types, 453–454
  in third-degree price discrimination, 452–454
Consumer preferences, 49–50
  indifference curves, 50–58
  indifference map, 55–56
  and marginal rate of substitution, 52–55
Consumers
  and adverse selection, 520–521
  assumptions about, 48–49
  and asymmetric information, 518–520
  budget constraint, 145–152
  with complete information, 521–522
  demand function, 71–73
  and demand function for loanable funds, 603–608
  effects of changes in nonwage income/wage rate, 154–156
  endowment point, 589
  and expected income hypothesis, 124–125
  and free rider problem in retailing, 505
  gains from trade, 676
  indifference curves and efficiency, 672–680
  marginal rate of substitution, 679
  marginal rate of time preference, 591
  marginal value, 139–141

meat versus poultry purchases, 75–78
minimizing information requirements,
  680–681
personal bankruptcy, 599–600
and risk, 128–130
self-selected, 450
supply function of loanable funds, 607–
  608
time constraint on, 143–145
utility function, 56–57
utility of income function, 125–126
willingness-to-pay values, 471–473, 719
and work/leisure choice, 636–637, 638–
  641
Consumer surplus, 94, 118–123, 310
  and bundling, 471–474
  and deadweight loss, 123
  effect of monopoly, 361
  effect of per unit tax, 318–321
  and evaluating government policies,
    122–123
  and first-degree price discrimination,
    448–449
  and marginal value, 119–120
  and price controls, 321
  and price discrimination, 446
  and revenue enhancement, 447
  and two-part tariffs, 474–480
  use of concept, 120–123
Consumer tastes, 559–565
Consumption
  time constraint on, 143–145
  time/cost elements, 143
Consumption decision, 64–69
  maximizing utility, 65–67
  specialization, 67–68
Consumption spending over time, 588–608
  effect on saving of increased income,
    598–603
  intertemporal budget constraint, 588–
    591
  intertemporal preferences, 591–593
  intertemporal utility maximization, 593–
    597
  and present value of income, 595–597
Contract curve, 676–678
Convenience, price of, 162–163
Cookenboo, Leslie, 188–189, 199–200
Cooperative behavior
  and incentive to cheat, 372–376
  oligopoly, 371–376
Cooperative solution, 373
Copyright laws, 491–492
Corning, Inc., 658–659
Corporate control, 435–441
  effectiveness of external monitors, 438
  effectiveness of internal monitors, 436–
    438
  and stock performance, 439–441
Cost-benefit reasoning, 234
Cost functions
  identifying relevant costs, 228–238
  long-run average cost function, 238–247
  short-run average cost function, 238–239
  types of, 221
Cost minimization, 228–233
Cost of detecting price cutting, 397–398
Cost-reducing innovation, 299–307
  at Boeing, 303–305

and evolution of industries, 305–307
by monopolists, 347–351
Costs; *see also* Production costs
  accountants' treatment, 219*n*
  long- and short-run, 219–220
  types of, 218–219
Cotton prices, 22–24
Cournot, Augustin, 376*n*
Cournot model, 376–384
  compared to Bertrand model, 384
  effect of rivals on output/prices, 414–
    415
  lessons from, 388
  with *n* competitors, 383–384
  prices and number of rivals, 388–391
Cournot-Nash equilibrium, 381
Cowan, Alison Leigh, 434*n*
Credible commitment, 408–409
Credit market, 519–520
Crude oil prices, 616–617
Cummins Engine Company, 434–435
Cumulative distribution of prices, 565
Czech Republic, 342–343

Day care subsidies, 107–110
Deacon, Robert T., 156–157
Deadweight loss, 123, 320
  of monopoly, 360–362
Decision making under uncertainty, 123–
  124
Decision rules for selling nonrenewable
  resources, 609–611
Decreasing returns to scale, 185–187
Defining property rights, 712–713
De Haven, James C., 682*n*
Del Monte, 116
Demand; *see also* Demand function; Market demand function
  arc cross-price elasticity, 81
  excess of, 14–15
  long-run equilibrium and increase in,
    283–291
  and price for timber, 7–8
  price-inelastic, 29
  unitary elasticity, 29
  for water, 110–113
Demand and supply
  everyday meaning, 15–16
  meaning of, 5
Demand and supply model, 4
  and changes in equilibrium, 17–26
  cotton prices, 22–24
  and input prices, 24–26
  market demand function, 5–10
  market equilibrium, 13–17
  market supply function, 10–13
  price elasticities, 27–38
  price elasticity of supply, 36–38
  problems with analysis, 17
  and shortages/surpluses, 19–22
Demand function, 564–565
  of Bertrand competitor, 385
  and consumer behavior model, 71–78
  of consumers, 94–118
  of Cournot competition, 378
  discounted price, 612–614
  individual, 75
  inverse, 562–563

in monopolistic competition, 409–410
of monopolists, 329–331
movement along, 6–7
for nonrenewable resources, 612–614
of price-taking firms, 256–257
for public goods, 719–720
shifts in, 8–10, 17–26
slope of, 113–115
in third-degree price discrimination, 455
Demand function for labor
  airline industry, 634–635
  long-run, 635
  by price-making firms, 645–646
  short-run, 626–629, 635
Demand function for loanable funds, 603–
  608
Demand shifts, and monopolists, 347, 348
Department of Agriculture, 76–77
Deregulation, profit constraint, 432–433
Derived demand function
  for factors of production, 625–626
  for labor, 625–626
Diet Coke, 401
Differences in managerial ability; *see* Man-
  agerial ability
Differentiated products, 409–410
Diminishing marginal rate of substitution,
  54–55
Diminishing marginal rate of technical
  substitution, 185
Diminishing returns, 180
Discounted price demand function, 612–
  614
Discounting, 553, 585
Diseconomies of scale, 242–244
Disincentive effects of general assistance
  programs, 641
Disneyland, 474
Dixit, Avinish, 398*n*
Dominant strategy, 398–403
  in free rider problem, 501
  for only one firm, 400–403
Double-auction trading process, 681
Downing, Paul, 184*n*
DRAM chips, 209–210
Duopoly
  Bertrand model, 384–388
  Cournot model, 376–384
  Nash equilibrium, 380–382
  punishment strategy, 405–406
Du Pont, 328, 392, 658

Early entry, 402–403
Earmarked subsidies, 82–84
Earnings; *see* Compensation; Wage policies
Earthquake insurance, 130–134
Eastern Europe, 260
Economic efficiency, 671–693
  in competitive product market, 678–680
  contract curve, 676–678
  impediments caused by monopoly, 693–
    696
  impediments to Pareto efficient
    exchange, 681–683
  minimizing information requirements,
    680–681
  Pareto efficiency in production, 684–693

Economic efficiency (*continued*):
  Pareto efficient exchange, 673–676, 678–680
Economic models, 4
Economic rent, 293–295
Economies of scale, 242–244
  at Standard Oil, 244–245
Economist, 468
Economizing information, 680–681
Edgeworth, Francis, 674*n*
Edgeworth box diagram, 674–675, 682–683
Education
  and earnings, 625
  and lifetime earnings, 646–652
Educational information, 499–500
Effect of product durability on monopoly pricing, 355–358
Ehrenberg, Ronald G., 652*n*
Elasticities, 81
Elasticity of demand for airline pilots, 634–635
Electrical manufacturers, collusion case study, 394–398
Elephant poachers, 714–715
Emissions control, 183–184
Emission standards, 234–237
Empire Blue Cross/Blue Shield, 518–519
Employees
  incentive effects of compensation, 659–662
  incentive pay, 658–659
  wage determination, 657–659
Employee shirking, 660–661
Employee training, 652–657
  firm-specific, 655–656
  general, 654–655
  and worker turnover, 656–657
Employee turnover, 656–657
Employment effects of minimum wage, 642–645
Endowment point, 589
Engel curve, 97–99
Environmental Protection Agency, 234
Environmental regulation, 234–237
Equating price to marginal cost, 270
Equilibrium with asymmetric information, 525–526
Equilibrium earnings of college graduates, 648–652
Equilibrium interest rate, 603–608
Equilibrium price, 13–15
  with asymmetric information, 522–526
  with complete information, 521–522
  effect of interest rate, 614–616
  impact of demand shifts, 17–26
  of inputs, 24–26
  and price controls, 21–22, 321
  for renewable resources, 617–620
  and short-run industry supply function, 283–286
Equilibrium price over time, 611–614
Equilibrium quantities, 14
  with asymmetric information, 522–526
  with complete information, 521–522
Equilibrium wage, 641–642
Erector sets, 509
Ethyl Corporation, 392
European markets, 462–467
European Union, 491
  banana import quotas, 315–318

Evans, David, 587*n*
Excess demand, 14–15, 22
Excess supply, 14
Excludable goods, 716
Exclusive distribution
  ice cream, 511–512
  of toys, 509–510
Executive pay; *see also* CEOs; Compensation
  ex post settling up costs, 424–425
  and performance of firm, 436–438
  with profit constraint, 432
Exhaustion of all internal economies of scale, 272
Expansion path, 196–197, 630–631
Expected income hypothesis, 124–125
Expected revenue
  formula, 569
  initial and markdown prices, 568–572
  from single-price policy, 566–567
  from two-price policy, 572
Expected utility, 127–128
  and risk, 128–130
Expected utility hypothesis, 125–128
  and earthquake insurance, 132–134
Expense preference, 423
  ex post settling up costs, 424–425
  manager as partial owner, 427–428
  manager as sole owner, 426–427
  under profit constraint, 429–433
  and unregulated firms, 434–435
Explicit costs, 218
Ex post settling up costs, 424–425
Externalities
  Coase theorem, 705–710
  defining property rights, 712–713
  internalizing, 703–705
  marginal damage cost, 701–702
  marginal social cost, 701–702
  maximizing social surplus, 705
  Pareto efficiency, 700–706
  positive and negative, 700
  social surplus, 702–703
  taxation and Pareto efficiency, 715–716
  and transaction costs, 706–708, 710–715
External monitors
  definition, 417
  effectiveness of, 438
  increased role of, 435
  product and capital markets, 417–422
External pecuniary diseconomies of scale, 291–293

Facilitating practices, 392–393
Factor endowment constraint, 684
Factor prices, 191–193
  changes in, 204–206
  external pecuniary diseconomies of scale, 291–293
  and increased output, 291–293
  scale effect, 632–634
  substitution effect, 630–632
Factors of production; *see also* Fixed factors
  array of wage policies, 625
  definition, 172
  derived demand functions, 625–626
  explicit costs, 218

isocost line, 192–193
isoquant, 182
long- and short-run changes, 174–175
marginal rate of technical substitution, 694
and marginal rate of technical substitution, 184–185
substitution among, 182–184
Fama, Eugene, 424*n*
Fantasia video, 358
Farm policies, 123
Fashion apparel, 560–565
Federal Pacific, 395
Federal Trade Commission, 392, 510
Fina, Inc., refinery, 713
Finley Hospital, Dubuque, 362
Fire insurance, and moral hazard, 532–534
Firms; *see also* Competitive firms; Cartels; Monopolists
  Bertrand model of duopoly, 384–388
  cartel behavior, 368–371
  changing factors of production, 174–175
  cheating *versus* honesty, 543–544
  compensation and performance, 437–438
  in constant-cost industry, 279–283
  cooperative behavior and incentive to cheat, 372–376
  cooperative solution, 373
  cost functions, 218–247
  cost-reducing innovations, 299–307
  Cournot model of duopoly, 376–384
  credible commitment, 408–409
  derived demand function for labor, 625–626
  differences in managerial ability, 295–297
  differentiated products, 409–410
  dominant strategy, 398–403
  economic rent/producer surplus, 293–295
  effect of change in management, 418–419
  effect of rivals on output/prices, 414–415
  employee training, 652–657
  evidence about takeovers, 438–439
  expansion into European markets, 462–467
  expansion path, 196–197, 630–631
  expense preference, 423
  expense preference under profit constraint, 429–433
  ex post settling up costs, 424–425
  external monitors on, 417–422
  facilitating and preventing collusion, 391–398
  forces constraining managers, 417
  game theory, 398
  identifying relevant costs, 228–238
  and increased market demand, 283–291
  increasing-cost industry, 291–299
  internal monitors, 422–425
  isocost function, 191–193
  learning by doing, 208–211
  long-run production function, 182–191
  market for corporate control, 435–441
  minimizing production costs, 193–196
  models of noncooperative behavior, 376–388

monopolistic competition, 0
nonsalvageable investments, 546–548
number and market share of, 280
number of, 242–244
oligopoly, 371–376
operation of, 172
ownership structure, 425–429
prices and number of rivals, 388–391
principal-agent relationship, 425–429
production function, 172–174
pure monopoly model, 328–329
raising cost for new entrants, 307–310
regulated, 429–433
repeated games, 404–406
repeated interaction, 406
self-enforcing agreement, 373
sequential games, 406–409
short-run cost function, 220–238
short-run production function, 175–181
strategic interaction among, 368
supplying high quality products, 540–549
total cost function, 196–207
unregulated, 434–435
wage policy as incentive mechanism,
    659–662
Firm-specific training, 655–656
First class mail, 34–35, 330
First-degree price discrimination, 448–449
Fisher, Lawrence M., 310n
Fixed cost fallacy, 234
Fixed costs, 220–221
Fixed factors, 174–175, 219–221
Fixed fee/per unit price
    for different customers, 476–477
    for identical customers, 474–476
Ford Motor Company, 468
Forest Service, 709–710
Franchises, 351–355
Free agency sports market, 530–531
Free entry into retailing, 494–497
Free-rider problem
    in agriculture, 489–490
    and capital market, 419–422
    and copyright laws, 491–492
    dominant strategy, 501
    and exclusive distribution, 509–512
    in intellectual property, 490–491
    in labor market, 488–489
    between manufacturers, 510–512
    in markets, 488–492
    origin of, 488
    for public goods, 718, 721
    and quality certification, 507–510
    in retailing, 505
    and retail price competition, 492–498
    and shareholders, 421–432
    and special service theory, 499–507
    without minimum suggested retail price,
        505–507
Freudenheim, Milt, 518n
Full income, 145–147
Full price budget constraint
    deriving, 145–147
    to find affordable market basket, 147–
        148
    shifts in, 148–152
Full prices, 146–147
    dependence on market price, 158–162
    lowest, 157–163
    minimizing, 160–161

Gains from trade, 676
    banana wars, 315–318
Game, 398
Games
    repeated, 405–406
    sequential games, 406–409
Game theory
    definition, 398
    dominant strategy, 398–403
    Nash equilibria, 403–404
    and noncooperative strategies, 398–409
    Prisoner's dilemma, 372–376
    repeated games, 405–406
    sequential games, 406–409
Game tree, 407–408
General assistance programs, 638–641
General Electric, case, 394–398
General equilibrium analysis, 668–669
General Foods, 490
General Motors, 173, 499, 504
    restriction on dealer sales, 492–493
General training, 654–655
Gerlin, Andrea, 22n
Giffen good, 105
Giordano's Pizzeria, 409–410
Giorgio Armani, 117
Goods; *see also* Public goods
    complements, 9
    demand for water, 110–113
    Giffen good, 105
    inferior, 99
    normal, 97–98
    substitutes, 8
Goodsbee, Austan, 305n
Goodwill, 219n
Gort, Michael, 305, 307
Gould, Eric D., 704n
Government
    creation of monopolies, 351–353
    grants of franchises, 351–355
    marketing orders, 371
    patent policy, 329
Government grants, 82–84
Government policy/regulation
    and consumer surplus concept, 122–123
    and supply function, 13
Green Giant, 116
Grether, David, 392
Griffin, James, 342
Grossman, Michael, 342
Grossman, Sanford, 420–422
Group health insurance, 518–519
Gruley, Bryan, 362n, 509n
Guyon, Janet, 342n

Haagen-Dazs, 511–512
Hahn, Robert W., 236
Hanke, Steve H., 113
Hanson PLC, 435
Harrington, Joseph E., Jr., 355n
Hart, Oliver, 420–422
Hasbro, 510
Hashimoto, Masanori, 656–657
Hayek, Friedrich, 680
Health insurance, 518–519
Health maintenance organizations, 362
Helyar, John, 423n
Hendricks, Kenneth, 393–394
High-price policy, 560–561

High prices, 286–289
High quality products
    versus low quality products, 537–540
    means of supplying, 540–549
    with price premium, 541–542
Hirschleifer, Jack, 682n
Holderness, Clifford G., 437–438
Hold-up problem, 711
Home sales, 237–238
Honesty, 543–544
Horizontal industry supply function, 280,
    281–282
Hospital mergers, 362–363
Hostile takeovers, 435
Hotelling, Harold, 611, 614, 617, 619–620
Household expenditures, 100
Hughes, Kathleen, W., 713n
Human capital
    employee training, 652–657
    investment in, 646–652
    present value of earnings, 646–648
Hurricane Andrew, 289–290
Hybrid supply function, 523, 524

IBM, 479–480, 489, 499, 504, 506
    restrictions on dealers, 493
Impatient consumer, 590, 592, 594
Import competition, 432–433
Import quotas; *see* Quotas (trade)
Incentive compensation and mandatory re-
    tirement, 659–662
Incentive effects of wage policy, 659–662
Incentive pay, 658–659
Incentive to cheat, 372–376
Income
    effect on saving, 598–603
    and full price budget constraint, 145–
        146, 148–152
    and marginal utility, 125–126
    shifts in budget constraint, 82–84
    utility of income function, 125–128
Income-consumption curve, 98
Income effect
    combined with substitution effect, 101–
        105
    definition, 96
    and demand for water, 110–113
    measuring, 95–99
    size of, 116–117
    and slope of demand curve, 113–115
    and subsidized day care, 107–110
    of wage change, 638
    and work/leisure choice, 636–637, 638–
        641
Income elasticity of demand, 99–101
Income groupings, 453
Income redistribution, 641
Increasing-cost industry
    costs and managerial ability, 295–297
    economic rent/producer surplus, 293–
        295
    price determination, 291–299
Increasing returns to scale, 185–187
Independence Day, 409
Indianapolis 500, 210–211
Indifference curves
    diminishing marginal rate of substitu-
        tion, 54–55
    and economic efficiency, 672–680

Indifference curves (*continued*):
  with full price budget constraint, 153
  impatient consumer, 590, 594–595
  and marginal rate of substitution, 52–55
  and market baskets, 50–58
  and maximal utility, 65–67
  neutral consumer, 590
  patient consumer, 590, 595
  and perfect complements, 52
  and perfect substitutes, 51–52
  properties of, 57–58
  utility numbers, 56–57
Indifference map, 55–56
Individual demand functions, 75
Industrial Equity, 435
Industries
  characteristics and collusion, 396–397
  concentration ratio, 371–372
  demand function for labor, 635
  evolution of, 305–307
  with few firms, 243–244
  with many firms, 243
  monopolistically competitive, 409–411
  raising cost for new entrants, 307–310
Industry concentration ratio, 280
Industry equilibrium, 278
  long-run requirements, 278–279
  short-run requirements, 279
Industry output; *see* Output
Inferior goods, 97–99
Information; *see also* Asymmetric informa-
    tion
  complete, 673
  economizing, 680–681
  minimizing requirements, 680–681
Information groupings, 454
Initial price, 568–572
Inputs; *see also* Factors of production
  compensation based on, 657–659
  prices, 24–26
Insurance, 130–134
  and moral hazard, 532–534
Intellectual property, 490–492
Interest rate
  and demand for loanable funds, 603–608
  effect of change in, 604
  effect on equilibrium price, 614–616
  and saving/borrowing, 600–603
  and supply function of loanable funds,
    607–608
Interest rate equilibrium, 603–608
Interfax, 382
Internal diseconomies of scale, 242–244
Internal economies of scale, 242–244
  exhaustion of, 272
  at Standard Oil, 244–245
Internalizing externalities, 703–705
Internal monitors
  board of directors, 422–425, 438
  concentrated share ownership, 422
  definition, 417
  effectiveness of, 436–438
  on management, 422–425
International trade; *see* Gains from trade
Internet, 491
Intertemporal budget constraint, 588–591
Intertemporal equilibrium price
  effect of interest rate, 614–616
  nonrenewable resources, 611–614
  of renewable resources, 617–620

Intertemporal preferences, 591–593
Intertemporal theory of consumer behav-
    ior, 584, 588–608
  and demand function for loanable funds,
    603–608
  effect of income on saving, 598–603
  and equilibrium interest rate, 603–608
  intertemporal budget constraint, 588–
    591
  intertemporal preferences, 591–593
  intertemporal utility maximization, 593–
    597
  marginal rate of time preference, 591–
    593
  and personal bankruptcy, 599–600
  present value of income, 584–587, 595–
    597
  saving, borrowing, and interest rates,
    600–603
Intertemporal theory of supplier behavior
  with nonrenewable resources, 608–611
  with renewable resources, 617–620
Intertemporal utility function, 591
Intertemporal utility maximization, 593–
    597
  and present value of income, 595–597
Inverse demand function, $30n$, 330, 562–
    563
Inverse wholesale demand function, 496–
    497
Invisible hand, 680, 705
Irwin, Douglas A., 209–210
Isocost function, 191–193
Isocost line, 192–193
  slope of, 195
Isoquant, 182
  and marginal rate of technical substitu-
    tion, 184–185
  of pipeline production function, 189
  of production function, 186
  and returns to scale, 185–187
  slope of, 195
ITE, 395
Ivory trade, 614–715

Jacobs, Sanford L., $511n$
Japan
  car makers, 346
  employee turnover, 656–657
Jensen, Michael C., $426n$, 436–437
Jet fuel prices, 303–305
Johnson, George, $652n$
Johnson, Robert, $434n$
Jordan, Michael, 180–181
Joskow, Paul L., 437
Justice Department Antitrust Division,
    362–363

Kaplan, Steven, 418
Katz, Lawrence F., $652n$
Kaufmann, Patrick J., 544
Kenya, 715
Kessel, Reuben, $429n$, 452
Keuter, Urs P., 715
Key money, 26
Kim, E. Han, 440
King, Ralph Y., Jr., $371n$
Klein, Ben, 536

Klein-Leffler model of price premium, 536–
    537, 548–549
Klenow, Peter J., 209–210
Klepper, Steven, 305, 307
Known-reserves fallacy, 614
Koosh balls, 509
Kreps, David M., $521n$
Kreuger, Alan B., 545–456
Krosszner, Randall S., 437–438

Labor/Labor market
  array of wages and salaries, 625
  derived demand function, 625–626
  effect of minimum wage, 642–645
  free rider problem, 488–489
  investment in human capital, 646–652
  long-run demand function, 626–629,
    630–635, 635
  marginal product of, 196
  price of, 196
  price premium, 545–546
  short-run demand function, 635
  supply function, 636–645
Lafontaine, Francine, 544
Lagrange multiplier, $195n$
Landes, William M., $490n$
Late entry, 402–403
Latin America, 315–318
Law of demand
  definition, 6–7
  example, 7–8
Law of diminishing returns, 180
Lazear, Edward P., $568n$, 659–660
Learning by doing
  at Indianapolis 500, 210–211
  production function, 208–211
  in semiconductor industry, 209–210
Leasing versus selling, 479–480
Leffler, Keith, 536
Lehn, Kenneth, 530–531
Lemons model
  general treatment of, 526–528
  for used cars, 521–529
  used pickup trucks, 531–532
Levin, D., $493n$
Licensing, 307–310
Lichtenberg, Frank K., 419
Linear demand function, $31n$
Liquor licenses, 310
Load factor, 131–132
Lobbying, 24–26
Long-run average and marginal cost func-
    tions, 240–242
Long-run average cost function, 198–199
  with continuum of plant sizes, 240–242
  derived from short-run average cost
    function, 238–242
  with limited choice of plants, 238–239
  of retailers, 495–496
  at Standard Oil, 244–246
  steel industry, 246–246
Long-run cost function, 242–244
Long-run costs, 219–220
Long-run demand function for labor, 630–
    635, 635
Long-run equilibrium
  adjustments from one to another, 347
  consumer surplus in, 319
  producer surplus in, 319

Long-run equilibrium price and quantity, 282
Long-run factors of production, 174–175
Long-run industry equilibrium
    in constant-cost industry, 282–283
    and increase in demand, 283–291
    and managerial ability differences, 297–299
    price determination, 279–283
    requirements, 278–279
Long-run industry supply function
    in constant-cost industry, 281–282
    in increasing-cost industry, 291
    and licensing, 307–310
    and managerial ability differences, 296–297
Long-run marginal cost function, 272
Long-run price elasticity of demand, 342
Long-run production function, 182–191
    and marginal product, 190–191
    marginal rate of technical substitution, 184–185
    and marginal rate of technical substitution, 190–191
    returns to scale, 185–187
    substitution among factors, 182–184
Long-run supply function, 269–273
Long-run total cost function, 196–198
    and changes in factor prices, 204–206
    and long-run average cost function, 198–200
    shifts in, 204–208
    and technological change, 206–208
Lowest full price, 157–163
Low-price policy, 560–561
Low quality products versus high quality products, 537–540

MacAvoy, Paul, 342
Macy's, 508
Male/female time/cost differences, 163–164
Management
    effect of change in, 418–419
    external monitors on, 417–422
    forces constraining, 417
    internal monitors, 422–425
    and market for corporate control, 435–441
    in principal-agent relationship, 425–429
    with profit constraint, 429–433
    of unregulated firms, 434–435
Management buyouts, 418–419
Managerial ability
    and costs, 295–297
    differences in, 291
    and long-run industry equilibrium, 297–299
Managerial change, 246
Mandatory retirement, 659–662
Manne, Henry G., 418n
Manthly, Robert S., 616–617
Manufacturers
    behavior and special service theory, 503–504
    desire for lower retail prices, 493–498
    and exclusive distribution, 509–512
    free entry of retailers, 494–496
    free rider problem, 510–512
    interest in retail prices, 492–494

inverse wholesale demand function, 496–497
    profit maximization by, 497–498
    quality certification, 507–510
    resale price maintenance, 502–503
    and special service theory in retailing, 499–502
    and Toys "R" Us, 509–510
Marginal cost, 218
    and average cost, 224–226
    cost minimizing solution, 230–231
    definition, 221
    of emissions control, 234–237
    equalized at all plants, 231
    markup over, 340
    prices equal to, 575
Marginal cost function
    area under, 226–228
    and long-run average cost function, 240–242
Marginal damage cost, 701–702
Marginal production function of labor, 177–181
    and marginal rate of technical substitution, 190–191
Marginal product of labor, 106, 626–260
    and firm-specific training, 655–656
Marginal rate of substitution, 52–55, 153, 679
    market versus personal, 66
    wedge between marginal rate of transformation and, 695
Marginal rate of technical substitution, 184–185, 694
    between labor and capital, 630
    and marginal product of labor, 190–191
Marginal rate of time preference, 591
Marginal rate of transformation, 688–689
    wedge between marginal rate of substitution and, 695
Marginal revenue
    of competitive firms, 259–260
    definition, 256
    equal on third-degree price discrimination, 456–457
    of wholesale demand function, 497n
Marginal revenue equals long-run marginal cost, 338
Marginal revenue function of monopolists, 332–337
Marginal revenue product of labor, 626–269
    in price-making firms, 645–646
Marginal social cost, 701–702
Marginal utility, 57n
    and income changes, 125–126
Marginal value, 119–120
    deriving, 139–141
Markdown pricing
    growth of, 557–559
    to maximize revenue, 568–572
    by merchandise groups, 574–575
    using theory to understand, 573–577
Market baskets; *see also* Affordable market baskets
    and assumptions about consumers, 48–49
    and budget constraint, 58–62
    choosing, 153
    comparisons of, 50

with composite goods, 70–71
    definition, 48
    indifference curves, 50–58
    indifference map, 55–56
    and marginal rate of substitution, 52–55
    and maximal utility, 65–67
    specialization of consumption, 67–68
Market demand
    adjustment of industry to shift in, 289
    after Hurricane Andrew, 289–290
    and long-run equilibrium and increase in, 283–291
    and role of profits, 289
Market demand function, 5–10, 106
    and consumer behavior model, 71–78
    for first class mail, 330
    and individual demand functions, 75
    of monopolists, 329–331
    shifts in, 17–26
Market equilibrium, 13–17
    with asymmetric information, 525–526
    impact of changes in, 17–26
Market equilibrium interest rate, 603–607
Market equilibrium prices
    under certainty and uncertainty, 575–576
    for nonrenewable resources, 611–614
Market for corporate control, 435–441
Marketing orders, 371
Market price, 13
    dependence of full price on, 158–162
    and full price, 146–147
    purchases below, 156–157
Market restrictions, 310–311
Markets
    with asymmetric information, 518
    auction markets, 390–391
    capital, 417–422
    cartel behavior, 368–371
    command and control policies, 669–671
    economic efficiency, 671–693
    economizing information, 680–681
    facilitating and preventing collusion, 391–398
    free rider problem, 488–492
    general equilibrium analysis, 668–669
    for lemons, 539–532
    monopolistic competition, 409–411
    non-price-taking firms, 368
    oligopoly, 371–376
    Pareto efficiency in production, 684–693
    partial equilibrium analysis, 668
    product, 417–422
    supply side, 608
    for used cars, 520–529
    used pickup trucks, 531–532
Market share
    case, 394–398
    of competitive firms, 259
    of leading firms, 280
    in oligopoly, 371–372
    Philip Morris, 343
Market supply function, 10–13
    shifts in, 17–26
Markup over marginal cost, 340
Marquez, Jaime R., 342
Marshall Field's, 508
Marvel, Howard, 507
Mattel, 510
Mattus, Reuben, 511

Maximal utility, 65–67
Maximizing total surplus, 310
Mayer, Jane, 382*n*
MBA degree, 655
McCafferty, Stephen, 507
McCarthy, Scott, 22*n*
McDonald's, 173
  price premium, 544–545
McGee, John S., 244
McGinley, Laurie, 362*n*
Mean-preserving spread, 572
Meat versus poultry purchases, 75–78
Meckling, William H., 426*n*
Medium-price policy, 560–561
Meeting competition, 391–393
Mercedes Benz, 172
Merchandise groups, markdowns by, 574–575
Mercy Health Center, Dubuque, 362
Mergers
  effect on stock performance, 439–440
  of hospitals, 362–363
  and technological change, 246
Metallica, 22
Microsoft, 488
Microsoft Excel, 471
Microsoft Word, 471
Milgrom, Paul, 173*n*
Miller, J. Irwin, 435
Miller, Michael W., 489
Milliman, Jerome W., 682*n*
Minimills, 246–247
Minimizing cost of producing a given output, 193–196
Minimizing full price, 160–161
Minimizing information requirements, 680–681
Minimum income, and work/leisure choice, 638–641
Minimum prices, 321
Minimum suggested retail price, 505–507
Minimum total cost, 231
Minimum wage, 642–645
Models, 4
Modified production function, 208
Monopolistic competition, 409–411
Monopolists; *see also* Price discrimination
  actions to reassure buyers, 357–358
  cigarette industry, 340–342
  competing to be, 351–355
  cost-reducing innovations, 347–351
  Czech Republic, 342–343
  demand function, 329–331
  departures from Pareto efficiency caused by, 693–696
  inverse demand function, 330
  limitation of sales, 358
  marginal revenue function, 332–337
  oil industry, 340–342
  output decision, 338
  potential for cheating, 534–536
  price discrimination by, 447–448
  as price makers, 328–333
  as price takers, 362
  pure model of monopoly, 328–329
  short- and long-run adjustments, 347
  social objections to, 360–363
  taxation of, 358–360
  total revenue function, 332–337

two-part tariff, 474–480
  using quotas to create, 344–346
  wedge created by, 695
Monopoly pricing
  effect of per unit tax, 358–360
  effect of product durability, 355–358
  social costs, 360–362
  theory of, 337–346
Montreal Canadiens, 22
Moral hazard, 532–534
Movement along a demand function, 6–7
Movements along supply function, 11
Murphy, Kevin J., 342, 436–437, 652*n*
My Fair Lady, 22

Naelbuff, Barry, 398*n*
Nalco Chemical Company, 392
Nash, John, 380
Nash equilibrium, 380–382
  auto industry, 403–404
  in prices, 385–386, 388
  in quantities, 381
National Collegiate Athletic Association, 329
National Steel, 246
National Timber Service, 390
Natural gas prices, 26
Natural monopolies, 243–244, 695–696
Natural resources
  known-reserves fallacy, 614
  nonrenewable, 608–617
  oil reserves, 15–16
  renewable, 617–620
Negative externality, 700
Negotiation costs, 710–711
Neiman-Marcus, 508
Nesbett, Richard, 234
Neutral consumer, 590
New York City taxi licenses, 309–310
New York Stock Exchange, 328, 436
Nissan Motor Company, 435
Noncooperative behavior/strategies
  Bertrand model, 384–388
  Cournot model, 376–384
  and game theory, 398–409
Nonexcludable goods/services, 717–718
Nonnegative profits in long run, 270
Nonprice competition, 502
Nonrenewable resources
  crude oil prices, 616–617
  definition, 608
  demand function, 612–614
  discounted price demand function, 612–614
  effect of interest rate on prices, 614–616
  equilibrium price over time, 611–614
  oil reserves, 15–16
  price appreciation, 610
  when to sell, 609–611
Nonrival in consumption, 716–717
Nonrivalrous goods/services, 717–718
Nonsalvageable investments, 546–548
Nonsatiation, 49
Nonwage income
  effect of changes in, 154–156
  and full price budget constraint, 148–152

Normal goods, 97–99
Northwest Ecosystem Alliance, 709–710

Oi, Walter, 477
Oil industry, 340–342
Oil price increases, 36
Oil reserves, 15–16
Oil tankers, 267–269
Okanogan National Forest, 709–710
Oligopoly
  and incentive to cheat, 372–376
  prices and output with, 371–376
  propensity to cheat, 374–376
O'Neil, June, 165
Operating costs, 267
Operations, and change in management, 418–419
Opportunity cost, 218, 219
  in production possibility curve, 687–689
Opportunity cost of time, 146, 154–156
  and finding lowest full price, 157–163
Orange growers cartel, 371
Organization of Petroleum Exporting Countries, 616
  price increases, 620
Otten, Stan L., 234*n*
Output
  in cartels, 368–371
  compensation based on, 657–659
  decision of monopolists, 338
  from different factors of production, 174
  by duopoly, 376–388
  effect of number of rivals, 414–415
  and factor prices, 291–293
  isocost function, 191–193
  from long-run production function, 182–191
  to maximize long-run profits, 270
  minimizing total cost of production, 193–196
  Nash equilibrium, 380–382, 381
  with oligopoly, 371–376
  profit-maximizing quantity, 630
  propensity to cheat, 374–376
  restricted by marketing orders, 371
  returns to scale, 185–187
  and self-enforcing agreement, 373–374
  and shifts in long-run total cost function, 204–208
  from short-run production function, 175–181
  and state of technology, 172–173
  and third-degree price discrimination, 460–462
Ownership structure, 425–429

Pareto, Vilfredo, 674*n*
Pareto efficiency
  in exchange, 673–676
    in competitive product market, 678–680
    contract curve, 676–678
    impediments to, 681–683
  in externalities, 700–706
  externalities and taxation, 715–716
  impediments caused by monopoly, 693–696
  in production, 684–693

competitive factor markets, 686–689
in product mix, 690–693
and public goods, 716–721
Partial equilibrium analysis, 668
Pashigian, B. Peter, 454, 559, 568n, 575, 704n
Patent policy, 329
Patient consumer, 590, 592, 595
Pay-for-performance, 658–659
Payoff matrix
auto industry, 403–404
and brand extension, 402
and dominant strategy, 401
for shareholders, 420–421
Pereira, Joseph, 509n
Perfect complements, 52
Perfect price discrimination; *see* First-degree price discrimination
Perfect substitutes, 51–52
Perloff, Jeffrey M., 446n
Perry Ellis, 117
Persian Gulf crisis, 267–268
Personal bankruptcy, 599–600
Per unit tax
effect on competitive firms, 311–312
effect on consumer surplus, 318–321
effect on monopoly, 358–360
effect on producer surplus, 318–321
long-run effects, 312–315
to maximize social surplus, 705
to solve externalities problem, 715–716
Phase-of-the-moon pricing, 395
Philip Morris, 343
Philips, Louis, 446n
Pipeline, 199–200
Pipeline production function, 188–190
Plant sizes
continuum of, 240–242
limited choice, 238–239
Plant Variety Protection Act, 490
Platts, Linda E., 709n
Playmobile, 509
Plott, Charles R., 392
Point elasticity of demand, 29–30
Point income elasticity of demand, 99n
Point price elasticity of supply, 37
Pollution, 712–713
Pooling equilibrium, 526
Port Arthur, Texas, 713
Porter, Robert, 393–394
Positive externality, 700
Posner, Richard A., 490n
PPG Industries, 392
Premium, 130–132
Present value of an income stream, 585–587
and education, 648–652
Present value of a profit stream, 535, 553–555
Present value of future income, 585–587
Present value of income, 595–597
Price appreciation, 610
Price ceilings, 24–26
Price changes
and complements, 9
and consumer demand function, 94–99
effect on quantity demanded, 105–107
and income effect, 96–99
and market supply function, 10–13

and quantity demanded, 27
and substitutes, 8
Price chiseling
cost of detecting, 397–398
short-term gains, 405–406
Price controls, 21–22, 321
Price cutting
cost of detecting, 397–398
punishment strategy, 405–406
Price determination
in constant-cost industry, 279–283
in increasing-cost industry, 291–299
Price discrimination
in apparel sales, 557
and bundling, 471–474
comparison of second- and third degree, 469–471
and expansion into European markets, 462–467
first-degree, 448–449
revenue and profit from, 447–448
revenue enhancement by, 446–448
second-degree, 449–452
senior citizen discounts, 460
third-degree, 451, 452–471, 575–576
two-part tariff, 474–480
Price elasticity of demand, 27–29
arc elasticity, 30–34
college students, 458–459
compensated, 115n
of competitive firms, 259–260
determinants, 35–36
effect of per unit tax, 312–314
estimating, 42–43
for first class mail, 34–35
long-run, 342
and marginal revenue, 336
and markup over marginal cost, 340
for oil/cigarettes, 340–342
point elasticity, 29–30
in Russia/Eastern Europe, 260
and third-degree price discrimination, 457–460
Price elasticity of market demand function, 259–260
Price elasticity of supply, 36–38
effect of per unit tax, 313–315
Price fixing, case, 394–398
Price-inelastic demand, 29
Price information, 398
Price-making firms
demand for labor, 645–646
monopolists, 328–333
Price of a factor; *see* Factor prices
Price of labor, 196
Price policy; Pricing strategy
Price premium, 540–541
delivering high quality with, 541–542
incentive for cheating, 542
Klein-Leffler model, 536–537, 548–549
in labor markets, 545–546
at McDonald's, 544–545
unknown, 548
Prices
after deregulation, 432–433
and aggregate quantity demanded, 6
airline jet fuel, 303–305
in auction markets, 390–391
average cost determined by, 200

below-market, 156–157
changes in probability distribution, 572–573
and consumer surplus, 118–123
of cotton, 22–24
cumulative distribution, 565
and demand for timber, 7–8
and economic rent, 293–295
effect of number of rivals, 414–415
equal to marginal cost, 575
facilitating practices, 392–393
full price, 145–152
impact of demand shifts, 17–26
and marginal value, 119–120
at market equilibrium, 13–17, 575–576
and marketing orders, 371
Nash equilibrium, 385–386, 388
and number of rivals, 388–391
under oligopoly, 371–376
probability distribution, 562–563, 572–573
and quantity demanded, 527
reasons for differences in, 446n
reservation price, 394
retail prices, 492–498
retail tires, 389–390
in Russia, 610–611
seasonal variations, 575–576
as signal, 4
social cost of monopoly, 360–362
Price support policies, 123
Price takers, 256
cartel behavior, 368–371
monopolists as, 362
Price-taking assumption, 256–259
Price-taking firms, 256
marginal revenue product, 627–628
Price-time tradeoff, 143–166
Price-to-marginal cost ratio, 341
Pricing strategies
and bundling, 471–474
disparities, 557
by duopoly, 376–388
of fashion apparel, 560–565
growth of markdowns, 558–559
high-price policy, 560–561
initial and markdown prices, 568–572
low-price policy, 560–561
for market entry, 68–69
markup over marginal cost, 340
medium-price policy, 560–561
meeting competition, 391–393
minimum suggested retail price, 505–507
by monopolists, 337–346
phase of the moon, 395
and price strategy, 457–460
punishment strategy, 405–406
resale price maintenance, 502–503
selection of, 565–576
senior citizen discounts, 460
sequential game, 406–409
single-price policy, 560–561, 566–567
sing- versus two-price policies, 568–572
in third-degree price discrimination, 455
tit-for-tat pricing, 406
with two-part tariff, 474–480
two-price policy, 561, 567–568, 570
uncertainty about tastes, 559–565
understanding markdowns, 573–577

Prince Manufacturing, 493, 499, 504, 506
Principal-agent relationship, 425–429
Prisoner's dilemma, 372–376
Private goods, 716–717
Probability, 125
Probability distribution of prices, 562, 563
  changes in, 572–573
Producer surplus, 293–295, 310
  effect of monopoly, 361
  effect of per unit tax, 318–321
Product characteristics
  and collusion, 396–397
  differentiated products, 409–410
Product durability, 355–358
Production, Pareto efficiency, 684–693
Production costs
  changes in factor prices, 204–206
  cost-reducing innovation, 299–307
  deriving long-run average cost function,
    238–247
  fixed, 220–221
  identifying relevant costs, 228–238
  and learning by doing, 208–211
  long- and short-run, 219–220
  long-run average, 198–200
  long-run total, 196–199
  and managerial ability, 295–297
  minimizing, 193–196
  oil tankers, 267–269
  and price differences, 446n
  with profit constraint, 430
  relevant, 228–238
  short-run, 265–266
  short-run cost functions, 220–238
  short-run total cost function, 200–203
  spillover effects, 210
  sunk costs, 220
  and supply function, 12
  types of, 218–219
Production function, 172–174, 625–626
  Cobb-Douglas, 187–188
  isoquants, 186
  and learning by doing, 208–211
  long-run, 182–191
  pipeline, 188–190
  short-run, 175–181
Production possibility curve, 687–689
Production scheduling, 228–233
Product market, 417–422
Product mix, 690–693
Products
  and bundling, 471–474
  exclusive distribution, 509–510
  high- versus low-quality, 537–540
  quality certification, 507–510
Profit constraint
  and deregulation, 432–433
  expense preference under, 429–433
  import competition, 432–433
Profit maximization, 256
  competitive firm's need for, 261–262
  cooperative solution, 373
  and cost-reducing innovation, 347–348
  dominant strategy, 398–403
  by duopoly, 376–388
  long-run, 270
  by manufacturers, 497–498
  output decision, 338
  output for, 262

propensity to cheat, 374–376
  self-enforcing agreement, 373
  theory of monopoly pricing, 337–346
  and third-degree price discrimination,
    460–462
  validity of, 417
Profit-maximizing behavior, 265–266
Profit-maximizing employment condition,
  628–629
Profit-maximizing quantity, 630
Profit payoff matrix, 384
Profits
  after deregulation, 432–433
  and bundling, 473–474
  of competitive firm in long run, 269–270
  in duopoly, 376–388
  economic rent, 293–295
  effect of per unit tax, 311–312
  in monopolistic competition, 409–411
  nonnegative, 270
  and nonsalvageable investments, 547
  and price premium, 540–542
  and resource allocation, 289
  role of, 289
Profit stream; *see* Present value, 535, 553–
  555
Promising/delivering high or low quality
  products, 537–540
Propensity to cheat, 374–376
Property rights
  in African elephants, 714–715
  assignment of, 706–709, 711
  Coase theorem, 705–710
  defining, 712–713
  to a view, 713–714
Public goods
  competitive markets, 718, 721
  definition, 716–717
  financing, 720–721
  nonrivalrous and nonexcludable, 717–
    718
  optimal quantity of, 718–720
  and Pareto efficiency, 716–721
Punishment strategy, 405–406
Pure monopoly model, 328–329
Putnam, Judith Jones, 77

Quality certification, 507–510
Quantity demanded
  and arc price elasticity, 30–34
  effect of price change, 105–107
  and market equilibrium, 13–17
  and point elasticity of demand, 29–30
  and price, 527
  and price changes, 6–7, 27
  and price elasticity of demand, 27–29
  and shifts in demand function, 8–10
Quantity supplied
  and market equilibrium, 13–17
  and price elasticity, 36–38
Quotas (production)
  in cartels, 370
  orange growers, 371
Quotas (trade), 315–318
  used to create monopolists, 344–346

Racket Doctor, 493
Raisian, John, 656–657
Ratio of full prices, 150–151

Reaction function, of Cournot rivals, 377–
  380
Reagan administration, 346, 440
Real estate agents/brokers, 237–238
Regulated firms, 429–433
Regulation
  bubble concept, 236–237
  environmental, 234–237
Reiss, Peter C., 389
Relative frequency of purchase, 73–75
Relevant costs, 228–238
Renault, 468
Renewable resources, 617–620
Rent control, 22, 26, 321
Repeated interaction, 406
Reputation, 529
Resale price maintenance, 502–503
  limits on, 505–507
  objection to, 507
  and quality certification, 507–510
Reservation price, 394
Resource allocation, 289
Retailers
  allowing for entry, 494–496
  educational information, 499–500
  growth of markdowns, 558–559
  long-run average cost function, 495–496
  premium ice cream, 510–512
  price policy selection, 565–573
  quality certification, 507–510
  reason for free rider problem, 505
  seasonal price variations, 557–558
  special service theory, 499–502
  toy stores, 509–510
  uncertainty about tastes, 559–565
Retail price competition, 494–498
Retail prices
  free rider problem, 492–494
  manufacturer's desire to lower, 493–498
Retail tire prices, 389–390
Returns to scale, 185–187
  and Cobb-Douglas production function,
    187–188
  and long-run average cost function, 198–
    200
  and substitution, 188–190
Revenue changes under marginal revenue
  function, 334–337
Revenue enhancement
  and consumer surplus, 447
  goal of price discrimination, 446–448
Revenue maximization, 568–572
Rich, Daniel P., 634
Risk
  attitudes toward, 128–130
  and insurance, 130–134
Risk-averse consumers, 128–130, 131
Risk-neutral consumers, 128–130, 131
Risk-taking consumers, 128–130, 131
Rival in consumption, 716–717
RJR Nabisco, 423
Roberts, John, 173n
Rockefeller, John D., 244, 246
Role of profits, 289; *see also* Profits
Rose, Nancy L., 437
Rosenberg, Nathan, 7
Rossi, Peter E., 73n
Russia, 260, 382–383, 610–611
Ryan, Nancy, 147n

Samuelson, Paul A., 612n
San Francisco earthquake of 1989, 132–133
Sanka, 490
Saving, 600–603
Scale effect
  in airline industry, 634–635
  and factor prices, 630, 632–634
Schacht, Henry, 434
Seagate Technology, Inc., 489
Seasonal price variation, 557–558, 575–576
Second-degree price discrimination, 449–452
  compared to third-degree discrimination, 469–471
Securities and Exchange Commission, 440
Self-enforcing agreement, 373
  Nash equilibrium, 380–382
Semiconductor industry, 209–210
Senior citizen discounts, 460
Sequential games, 406–409
Setting prices based of elasticity of demand, 458
Shapiro, Eben, 147n
Shareholders, 417–418
  concentrated ownership, 422
  free-rider problem, 421–422
  limited power of, 420–422
  in principal-agent relationship, 425–429
Sheehan, Dennis P., 437–438
Sherman Antitrust Act, 362, 695
Shifts in budget constraint, 62–64
Shifts in demand function, 8–10, 17–26
Shifts in full price budget constraint, 148–152
Shifts in supply function, 12–13
Shifts in the long-run cost function, 204–208
Shirking, 660–661
Shleifer, Andrei, 422n, 438–439, 440
Shopping malls, 704–705
Shortages, 19–22
Short-run average cost function, 221–223
  long-run average cost function derived from, 238–239
Short-run cost function, 220–238
  area under the marginal cost function, 226–228
  graphing, 221–224
  identifying relevant costs/problems, 228–238
  marginal/average costs, 224–226
Short-run costs, 219–220, 265–266
Short-run demand function for labor, 626–629, 635
Short-run factors of production, 174–175
Short-run industry equilibrium requirements, 279
Short-run industry supply function, 283–286
Short-run marginal cost, 224n
Short-run marginal cost function, 223, 263
Short-run marginal production function, 626
Short-run production function, 175–181
Short-run profits, 262
Short-run supply function
  of competitive firms, 261–269
  oil tankers, 268

Short-run total cost function, 200–203, 221
Shutdown price, 264
Siegal, Donald, 419
Simmons, Randy T., 715
Single-price policy, 560–561
  expected revenue from, 566–567
  versus two-price policy, 568–572
Slope of demand curve, 102–107, 113–115
  Slutsky equation, 114
Slope of the isocost line, 195
Slope of the isoquant, 195
Slutsky equation, 114
Small business subsidies, 689–690
Smith, Adam, 680, 705
Smith, Robert S., 652n
Smith, Vernon L., 681
Social costs of monopoly, 360–363
Social surplus, 702–703
  per unit tax to maximize, 705
Software pirating, 488
Solomon, Caleb, 713n
Sonstelie, Jon, 156–157
Source-by-source regulation, 234–236
Soviet Union, 382–383, 587
Specialization of consumption, 67–68
Special service, 499
Special service theory
  characteristics, 499–502
  to explain manufacturer behavior, 503–504
  resale price maintenance, 502–503
  role of assumptions, 504–505
Spillover effects, 210
Standard Oil Company, 244–246
State of technology, 172–173
  and production methods, 182–184
Steel producers, 207–208, 246–247
Stigler, George J., 397
Stiglitz, Joseph E., 612n, 721n
Stillman, Richard P., 78
Stock performance, 439–440
Strategic interaction, 368
Subsidies
  day care, 107–110
  earmarked versus unrestricted, 82–84
  for small business, 689–690
Substitutes
  in consumer behavior model, 78–81
  and monopolists, 328
  and price changes, 8
Substitution
  among factors of production, 182–184
  and returns to scale, 188–190
Substitution effect, 96
  in airline industry, 634–635
  combined with income effect, 101–105
  and demand for water, 110–113
  and factor prices, 630–632
  measuring, 101
  size of, 116–117
  and slope of demand curve, 113–115
  and subsidized day care, 107–110
  and wage change, 638
Sullivan, Mary W., 403
Sultan, Ralph G., 395n, 396
Sunk costs, 220
Sunkist Growers Inc., 371
Suppliers
  competition among, 387–388

preventing collusion among, 393–394
of renewable resources, 617–620
selling nonrenewable resources, 609–611
time horizon, 608–620
Supply; *see also* Demand and supply; Market supply function
  excess of, 14
  and shortages/surpluses, 19–22
Supply elasticity of other competitive firms, 260
Supply function
  definition, 10
  movements along, 11
  shifts in, 12–13, 17–26
Supply function of labor
  basis of, 636
  effect of minimum wage, 642–645
  effect of wage change, 638
  and work/leisure choice, 636–637, 638–641
Supply function of loanable funds, 607–608
Supply-side markets, 608
Surpluses, 19–22
Sutherland, Robert G., 435
Switch over to a new technology, 299
Synergistic gains, 439–441
Synergy, 439–441

Tabak SA, 343
Takeovers, 420–422, 435
  effect on stock performance, 439–440
  evidence about, 438–439
  synergistic gains from, 439–441
Tastes, 49
Taxation; *see also* Per unit tax
  effect on total surplus, 310–321
  of monopolists, 358–360
  and Pareto efficiency, 715–716
Taxicab licensing, 307, 309–310
Technological change; *see also* State of technology
  and cost reducing innovation, 299
  general equilibrium effects, 668–669, 670
  and long-run total cost function, 206–208
  and mergers, 246
  monopolists' adoption of, 347–351
  steel industry, 246–247
  and supply function, 12–13
  switch to new technology, 299
Telser, Lester, 499
Tender offer
  free rider problem, 419–422
  government regulation, 440
Testing, 529
Theory of monopoly pricing, 337–346
Third-degree price discrimination, 451, 452–471
  compared to second-degree discrimination, 469–471
  and expansion into European markets, 462–467
  methods of grouping consumers, 452–454
  optimal pricing policy, 454–457
  optimum output and price, 460–462
  preventing arbitrage, 467–469

Third-degree price discrimination (*continued*):
  price elasticity/price strategy, 457–460
  and seasonal price variation, 576
Thomas the Tank Engine, 509
Thunderbird, 471–473
Timber resources, 7–8
Time
  cost for women, 163–166
  limits of, 144–145
Time allocation, 143–144
Time constraint, 143–145
  and finding lowest full price, 157–163
  opportunity cost of time, 146, 154–156
  and opportunity cost of time, 146
Time groupings, 453
Time horizon, 594
  of consumers, 588–608
  of suppliers, 608–620
Time preference, 591–593
Time-price combinations, 158–163
Tire prices, 389–390
Tit-for-tat pricing, 406
Total cost function
  deriving, 202
  long-run, 196–198
  short-run, 200–203
Total production function of labor, 175–181
Total product of labor, 176–181
Total quantity demanded, 6
Total quantity supplied, 10
Total revenue
  of competitive firms, 258
  equals or exceeds total variable cost, 263
Total revenue function of monopolists, 332–337
Total short-run profits, 262
Total surplus, 315–318
Toys "R" Us, 509–510
Toy stores, 509–510
Trademarks, 490–491
Trade restrictions
  effect on total surplus, 310–321
  European Union banana quotas, 315–318
  and monopolists, 344–346
Trade secrets, 489
Training programs, 652–657
Transaction costs
  and assigning property rights, 706–708, 710–715
  defining property rights, 712–715
Transitivity, 49

Two-part tariffs
  definition, 474
  for different types of customers, 476–477
  for identical customers, 474–476
  to price capital goods, 477–479
Two-price policy, 561, 567–568
  example, 570
  expected revenue, 572
  versus single-price policy, 568–572

Uncertainty
  and decision making, 123–124
  and expected income hypothesis, 124–125
  expected utility hypothesis, 125–128
  and insurance, 130–134
  price policy selection, 565–576
  risk aversion/risk-taking, 128–130
Uncertainty theory
  and consumer tastes, 559–565
  market equilibrium prices, 575–576
  seasonal variation in prices, 557–558
  single- versus two-price policy, 568–572
  to understand markdown pricing, 573–577
  when to apply, 576–577
Unitary elasticity, 29
United Nations, 491
United States, employee turnover, 656–657
United States Steel, 246
United States Supreme Court, 505
Unregulated firms, 434–435
Unrestricted subsidies, 82–84
Upjohn Company, 490
Used car market, 520–529
Used pickup trucks, 531–532
Utility function, 56–57
  and risk, 128–130
  and work/leisure choice, 636–637, 638–641
Utility maximization, 65–67
  with full price budget constraint, 153
  intertemporal, 593–597
Utility numbers, 56–57
Utility of income function, 125–128
Utils, 57

Valentine's Day, 19
Value of the marginal product, 627–629
Variable costs, 221
Variable factors of production, 174–175, 221

Vernon, John M., 355n
Viscusi, V. Kip, 355n
Vishny, Robert W., 422n, 438–439, 440
Voluntary export restraints, 346

Wage policies
  array of, 625
  backloading pay, 659
  based on input or output, 657–659
  and employee shirking, 660–661
  as incentive mechanism, 659–662
  substitution effect and wage changes, 638
Wage premium of college graduate, 652
Wage rate
  diversity of, 646
  effect of changes in, 154–156
  and full price budget constraint, 148–152
  male/female differences, 163–166
  present value of earnings, 646–648
Walgreens, 147
Wal-Mart, 13, 509
Walt Disney Company, 358
Warehouse clubs, 509–510
Warranties, 529
Water rights trading, 682–683
Wedge between consumer's marginal rate of substitution and marginal rate of transformation, 695
Weiman, Mark R., 78
Weiss, Leonard, 390
Westinghouse Electric Company, case, 394–398
Wholesale demand function, 497n
Wholesale price, 496–497
Williams Amendment, 422, 440
Williamson, Oliver E, 547n
Willingness-to-pay values, 471–473
  for public goods, 719
Wolack, Frank, 34
Women
  brand loyalty, 166
  rise in earnings, 164–166
  rising cost of time, 163–166
  in workplace, 163
Work, time allocation, 144–145
Work/leisure choice, 636–637, 638–641

Xerox Corporation, 479–480
Yellen, Janet L., 474n
Zenith, 506
Zimbabwe, 715

LIST OF APPLICATIONS

1-1 The Rising Price of Wood and the Demand for Wood

1-2 Demand and Supply on Valentine's Day

1-3 Cotton Is King Again, but How Long the Reign?

1-4 Should Your Company Support a Lobbying Effort to Reduce the Price of an Input?

1-5 The Price Elasticity of Demand for First Class Mail

2-1 Pricing to Break into an Established Market

2-2 Measuring Brand Loyalty by Relative Frequency of Purchase

2-3 Why Are Americans Eating More Poultry and Less Red Meat?

2-4 Earmarked versus General-Purpose Grants

3-1 Subsidizing Day Care

3-2 How Different Is Water?

3-3 Why is Earthquake Insurance a Slow Seller in California?

4-1 Walgreens Offers Convenience

4-2 Which Consumers Purchase Gasoline at Below the Market Price?

4-3 How Much More Will Some Consumers Pay to Save Time?

5-1 Distinguishing between Marginal and Average Productivity

5-2 Substitution and Returns to Scale for a Pipeline Production Function

5-3 The Long-Run Average Cost Function of a Pipeline

5-4 Substituting Aluminum for Steel in Autos

5-5 Learning-by-Doing in the Semiconductor Industry

5-6 Learning-by-Doing at the Indianapolis 500

6-1 How to Schedule Production between a New Plant and an Old Plant

6-2 Why "Never Give Up" Is Not Always the Best Advice

6-3 Inefficient or Efficient Environmental Regulation

6-4 Why Are Fewer Sellers of Used Homes Using Brokers?

6-5 The Emergence of the Standard Oil Company

6-6 Size of Firm and Technological Change in the Steel Industry

7-1 The Price Elasticity of Demand of Firms in Eastern Europe and Russia

7-2 Short-Run Costs, Break-Even Analysis, and Profit-Maximizing Behavior

7-3 When to Lay Up an Oil Tanker

8-1 Helping the Victims of Hurricane Andrew

8-2 Higher Jet Fuel Price Downs the Boeing 707

8-3 Regularities in the Evolution of Industries

8-4 The Value of a License

8-5 Raising Profits by Working with Regulators

9-1 Are Firms in the Cigarette and Oil Industries Monopolists?

9-2 Privatizing a Near Monopoly in the Czech Republic

9-3 Using a Quota to Create a Partial Monopolist

9-4 Alternative Methods of Selling a Monopoly